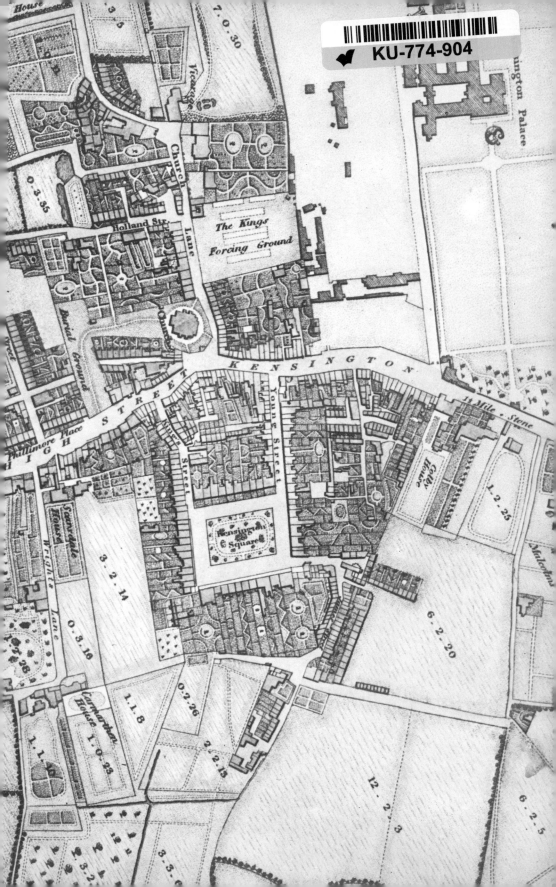

House

7 . 0 . 30

Vicarage

ington Palace

Church Lane

Holland Str.

0 - 3 - 35

The Kings
Forcing Ground

Burial Ground

KENSINGTON

1¼ Mile · Stone

H I G H     S T R E E T

Phillimore Place

Young Street

Colby House

1 . 2 . 25

Scarsdale House

Wrights Lane

Nigel Street

3 - 2 - 14

Kensington
Square

6 - 2 - 20

0 - 3 - 16

Malcolm

28

0 - 2 - 26

1 . 1 . 8

6 . 2 . 5

Carnarvon
House

1 . 0 . 23

2 . 2 . 15

12 . 2 . 3

1 . 1 . 40

6 · 2 · 3

3 · 2

3 . 3 . 0

# THE NAPOLEONISTS

# The Napoleonists

## A Study in Political Disaffection
## 1760–1960

### E. TANGYE LEAN

LONDON

*Oxford University Press*

NEW YORK · TORONTO

1970

*Oxford University Press, Ely House, London W.1*

GLASGOW  NEW YORK  TORONTO  MELBOURNE  WELLINGTON
CAPE TOWN  SALISBURY  IBADAN  NAIROBI  DAR ES SALAAM  LUSAKA  ADDIS ABABA
BOMBAY  CALCUTTA  MADRAS  KARACHI  LAHORE  DACCA
KUALA LUMPUR  SINGAPORE  HONG KONG  TOKYO


SBN 19 215184 3

Printed in Great Britain by
Richard Clay (The Chaucer Press) Ltd
Bungay, Suffolk

*For Sara Tangye Lean*

# Contents

*Preface*   xi

I Napoleon at the Gate
1 The Last Invasion   2
2 The Napoleonist and the Loyalist   12
3 Italian Volunteers   27

II The English Napoleonists
1 Motives for Exile   36
2 The Tenth Muse   45
3 A Clue to Byron   70
4 Whitbread and Caroline   90

III The Napoleonist Centre 125

IV The Napoleonist Syndrome 201

V Moderns 287

Postscript   368

*Note on Sources*   371

*Index*   379

# List of Illustrations

## Colour plates

|  |  | facing page |
|---|---|---|
| I | The Whig Opposition in the Commons, 1793, by Hickel | 34 |
| II | Samuel Whitbread, by Opie | 106 |
|  | *Courtesy of Samuel Whitbread, Esq.* | |
| III | Elizabeth Inchbald, by Lawrence | 210 |
|  | *Courtesy of H. M. Adams, Esq.* | |
| IV | The third Lord Holland, by Fabre | 210 |
| V | The future Lady Holland, by Romney | 250 |

## Black and white plates

*following page* 26

1 Charles James Fox in boyhood, by Zoffany
   *Courtesy of Sidney F. Sabin*
2 *Renard Stating His Accounts:* caricature of the first Lord Holland
3 *Billy in the Devil's Claws:* cartoon by Gillray
4 *French-Telegraph making Signals in the Dark:* cartoon by Gillray
5 Surrender of the French invasion force near Fishguard, 1797
6 Agostino Aglio
7 Ugo Foscolo
   *Courtesy of Lord Crawford*
8 William à Beckett
9 John Gregory
10 The first Lord Kensington, by House
11 *Very near Kensington:* caricature of the second Lord Kensington

*following page* 170

12 *A Swarm of English Bees Hiving in the Imperial Carriage!!:* engraving by Cruikshank
13 *Whitbread's Intire:* cartoon by Sayers
14 Whitbread's house at Southill Park, Bedfordshire
15 Princess Caroline, by Lawrence
16 The Duke of Sussex, by Head
17 *Introduction of Citizen Volpone & his Suite, at Paris:* cartoon by Gillray
18 *Sketch for a Prime Minister:* cartoon of Lord and Lady Holland

19   Napoleon, by Canova
20   Capel Lofft
21   The *Bellerophon* with Napoleon on board, by Chalon

*following page* 266
22   Thomas Holcroft and William Godwin, sketched by Lawrence
       *Courtesy of Dr. Kenneth Garlick*
23   Lord Byron, by Phillips
24   Leigh Hunt, by Haydon
25   William Hazlitt: self-portrait
26   John Thelwall, by Hazlitt

*following page* 346
27   *Unrecorded History:* cartoon from *Punch*, 1899
28   Napoleon on the *Bellerophon*, by Orchardson
29   Lloyd George with Hitler and von Ribbentrop
30   Lloyd George as a circus-master: Low's cartoon on an ash-tray
       *Courtesy of Giles Playfair, Esq.*
31   *Labour M.P.'s Unwanted Title: Manchester Guardian*, 22 September 1928
32   *The Other Test Match:* cartoon by Low
33   Kingsley Martin with a boa constrictor
34   Kim Philby with a fox cub
       *Courtesy of Patrick Seale, Esq.*

Illustrations in text

|   |   | *page* |
|---|---|---|
| A | Plan of Holland House in 1822 | 25 |
| B | Lord Holland's draft translation of an inscription for Canova's bust of Napoleon | 127 |
| C | Passport issued to Lord Holland and his party in 1800 | 133 |
| D | Passport issued to Lord Holland and his party in 1815 | 157 |

Endpaper map
Kensington in 1822, by Thomas Starling

ACKNOWLEDGEMENTS. In addition to those individuals acknowledged above, thanks are due to the following for permission to reproduce the illustrations indicated: Trustees of the British Museum, 2, 3,

6, 8, 9, 11, 12, 13, 18, 20, A, B, C, D; National Portrait Gallery, I, IV, 15, 16, 23, 24, 26; Tate Gallery, 28; Carmarthen Museum, Abadam Collection, 5; Shire Hall, Haverfordwest, 10; National Maritime Museum, Greenwich Hospital Collection, 21; Maidstone Museums and Art Gallery, 25; Paul Popper, Ltd., 29; *The Guardian*, 31; Trustees of David Low and the London *Evening Standard*, 32; Kensington Library, endpaper map. Nos. 4 and 17 are in the possession of the author; No. 14 is from a photograph by the author.

# *Preface*

English admirers of Napoleon during the Napoleonic wars have left a very complete account of themselves, but they have not been compared as a group. They had intriguing resemblances of character but across a gulf of social and intellectual difference. Some were held to be traitors and others statesmen who had served their country. This book only took shape when I had traced their individual origins in the eighteenth century and looked at them together. I then noticed a situation recurring in closely similar terms which seemed to throw light on all of them. Eleven or twelve had dealt with the situation in the same way, and their admiration of Napoleon became intelligible as a response to it. Among their other resemblances, were some which had predisposed them to make that response and others which arose in the process of making it. There was in fact a Napoleonist syndrome, which went some way to explain the psychology of defection.

The material in the twentieth century was barren by comparison, and I did not venture into it with any enthusiasm. The modern admirers of dictators again included patriots and defectors, but they were more reticent about themselves, and so far from forming a group, they were politically at daggers drawn and the advocates of conflicting systems. But stray points of similarity, which would have seemed meaningless before, now struck me as forcibly as they would a detective who had worked out the description of a wanted man. I had to look again for the original motive in circumstances which were apparently quite different.

England has been seen from the mainland of Europe as '*le pays le plus trahi du monde*'. Froissart held this view in the Hundred Years War, and it gained ground in the sixteenth century when English Catholics began to depend on continental support. The French Revolution gave new life to it with the arrival of Tom Paine and the English radicals, and in spite of the reaction against the Revolution and its heirs, English visitors poured in on Napoleon until he came to believe in a Bonapartist faction, whose support became his main hope of relief. Continental scholars have continued to take the view. Professor Jules Dechamps, a dedicated admirer of Napoleon, has been tireless in insisting on his English support and believes that an accommodation between Britain and Napoleon was only frustrated by the ruling oligarchy.[1] Eggert, Holzhausen, von Treitschke, have taken more seriously than English critics the enthusiasm felt by Byron for Napoleon.

England on the whole has refused to accept these aspersions. Little of the continental work has been translated into English. While it suited the Government of the day to exaggerate Napoleon's hold on the opposition, no one took it seriously after his death. English historians acknowledge the influence of the English Jacobins until Pitt suppressed them, but they have denied any serious support for Napoleon. The word 'Napoleonist' has died out. According to the *Oxford English Dictionary* a Napoleonist was 'an adherent of Napoleon or the Napoleonic dynasty'; but the word has been superseded by the more rigorous 'Bonapartist', 'an adherent of the government and dynasty of the Bonapartes in France'.

There were few if any Bonapartists in England in the sense of adherents to a Bonaparte dynasty, and it was justifiable to ignore them. But there were certainly Napoleonists, in the looser sense used in this book, and the word seemed to me necessary to uncover the problem which remained when Bonapartism had been disposed of.[2]

Throughout the Napoleonic wars a small but significant minority of Napoleonists was centred mainly on London. Their admiration for Napoleon normally stopped short of treason and was connected with their demand for peace and emancipation. In the Commons they were led by Fox until his death in 1806, and by Samuel Whitbread until he committed suicide at Waterloo. In the Lords their most faithful exponent was Lord Holland. Outside Parliament, Byron, Godwin, Hazlitt, Hobhouse, and Leigh Hunt were among Napoleon's erratic but determined champions.

To denounce these people as traitors was a part of the Government's technique for disposing of demands for peace and reform. There were spies in the country—on an average thirty Frenchmen a year were deported throughout the twenty years of war—but more traitors were discovered by the English among themselves than since the time of the Spanish Armada. The cartoon shops were gay with tricolours in the hats of well-known Englishmen who had instructions from Bonaparte sticking out of their pockets.

[1] See particularly *'L'Opposition Parlementaire en Grande-Bretagne au temps de Napoléon'*, in the *Revue de l'Institut Napoléon*, No. 59 (April 1956). I have owed much to the work of Professor Dechamps without being converted to his belief in the implications of British support for Napoleon.

[2] The words 'Napoleon' and 'Napoleonists' were often preferred by sympathizers in England to 'Bonaparte' and 'Bonapartist', which were used by adversaries to emphasize his Italian origins. 'The Napoleonists have been marked with every principle of forbearance,' wrote John Cam Hobhouse from Paris in 1815; but John Croker, in the same year, found Abbeville garrisoned by 'savage Bonapartists'. *'Je l'entends appelé M. Buonaparte par des gens qui le haïssent,'* says Stendhal.

Rumours were invented to undermine the popularity of individual radicals, and suspicion flourished spontaneously in an atmosphere where opposition, which was widespread, was denounced as disloyal.

I have started by taking one of the rumours as literally as possible. A story sprang up four years before Waterloo that a barracks or cantonment for French forces of occupation was being built by an agent of Napoleon at the western entrance to London. The people who moved on to the scene once the rumour had started gave continuing life and substance to it. Holland House and Kensington Palace on the other side of the road were both centres of opposition which had their own hierarchies, rivalries, and hangers-on. The area made up a kind of Napoleonist centre where the motives for supporting Napoleon can be seen in concentration.

Whilst the release of the Holland House papers to the British Museum has provided fresh detail on the Napoleonists, the material for a study has always been available in their published works, and in Hansard, and the newspapers. I have avoided as far as possible holding up the reader by quoting references as they arose; the sources are covered in a Note on page 371.

I have been helped in finding my way through the material by many people who would be unlikely to share my conclusions and have no part in any surviving inaccuracies. They have included Mr. John Young, of Haverfordwest, on the origins of Lord Kensington; the late Sir Lewis Namier and Lord Hinchingbroke on his politics; and M. Jacques Delarue, of the French Ministry of Security, on the origins of Changeur. Sir Paul Reilly and Sir John Summerson gave me invaluable help on Regency London, Professor E. R. Vincent and Professor G. Calogero on Foscolo, Mr. Croft Murray on Aglio, Mrs. Joan Thornton and the late Mr. Jim Thornton on Hazlitt and Byron, and Mr. Roger Fulford on Samuel Whitbread.

I have owed much to Mr. Noel Sharp, the former Director of Printed Books in the British Museum, and to Mr. T. C. Skeat of the Manuscripts Department, who gave me access to the Holland House Papers while the task of arranging them was in progress. I am also grateful to Mrs. Darsie Gillie and Commandant Lachouque for guidance in the Bibliothèque Nationale and the French National Archives; to the late Lord Ilchester for introducing me to the complexities of the Holland House Papers; to Mrs. St. George Saunders for information about the Royal Navy; and to Dr. Stephen Pasmore for his expertise in all matters related to Kensington.

I owe thanks to Mr. B. G. Owens, Keeper of Manuscripts and Records in the National Library of Wales; to the patient supervisors of the Public Record Office, the Middlesex County Records, and the Literary Department of Somerset House; to the Managers of Brooks's Club for access to the Betting Books; to the Secretary of the Naval and Military Bible Society;

the Librarian of Friends' House; the Vicar of Kensington for access to parish registers; and to the Librarians of the Public Libraries of Bury St. Edmunds and Haverfordwest. I was sustained by Mr. C. G. Boxall, in the Kensington Library, among the records of the Frenchman's building site and the minute books of the turnpike.

The stimulus for the summary of findings in Part IV, 'The Napoleonist Syndrome', came from Sir Isaiah Berlin's remarkable Mellon Lectures, 'Some Aspects of Romanticism'.

In research for Part V, on the modern Napoleonists, I have owed much to the encouragement of Mr. Philip Toynbee; and to Mr. W. M. Rogers for translating *Richard Lloyd*, the Welsh biography of Lloyd George's foster-father.

The book would not have survived without the generous help of Miss Catharine Carver, whose severity as a critic is equalled by her determination as a publisher.

*April* 1970                                                                      E.T.L.

# I. NAPOLEON AT THE GATE

# 1. The Last Invasion

*An army of principles will penetrate where an army of soldiers cannot.*

Tom Paine to the French Directory, 1797

The last landing on the mainland of Britain was made by the French Directory in 1797, several months before Napoleon was given charge of the invasion forces. As a military event it was negligible because of the assumption that there would be enough volunteers to make support from France unnecessary.

The original plan was to penetrate three areas of disaffection at the same time. Fifteen thousand men were to land in Ireland while smaller forces made their way through Wales and the industrial areas around Manchester. When insurrection was general and the Government had lost the power to counter-attack, a further landing would be made to set up a republic.

Only the Welsh expedition, which was the smallest, actually made the landing, and it did so two months after the others had failed. The fact that the invasion took place at all can only be explained by the contradictory ideas which went into it.

In command of the plan as a whole was General Hoche, who took advice from Wolf Tone, the founder of the society of United Irishmen and an intimate of Tom Paine. Hoche had acquired a hatred of England in suppressing the royalist revolt in La Vendée and the landing in Quiberon Bay. Wolf Tone was committed to the liberation of Ireland. They both wanted to punish England, to do, in Wolfe Tone's phrase, 'the greatest possible mischief', and were ready to use convicts and émigrés for the purpose.

But the thinking behind the invasion was based on the brotherhood of man. The most influential Englishman in France was Tom Paine, who had been in Paris for five years since escaping from London on the eve of arrest for treason as the author of *The Rights of Man*. He was imprisoned under the Terror but restored to favour by the Directory. His influence was reinforced immediately before the attempt in Wales by the example of Italy, where volunteers joined Napoleon in large numbers against their Austrian masters. Paine foresaw the day when England, 'like Italy [would] become a sister republic'.

The Directory was more concerned with plunder than the rights of man, but they had discovered that Napoleon could live off the territory he had invaded while extorting enough in taxes to balance the French budget. Undeterred by the failure of Hoche to land in Ireland, they transferred him without dishonour to the Rhine and ordered the Welsh landing to go ahead.

The commander was an American, William Tate, from South Carolina, who was probably of Irish descent. He had been an artillery lieutenant in the War of Independence and was embittered by the loss of his family in an Indian rising promoted by the English. He was awarded $1,100 and 300 acres of land by the Federal government, but his activities on behalf of the French grew too extreme for Washington and he had to seek refuge in France, where he became a French citizen. He was already in his late sixties, a rather wooden figure and a disciplinarian, who was nevertheless full of adventurous ideas.

Tate had detailed instructions to land either near Bristol or in Wales, form the volunteers into companies and march up through the full length of Wales to Chester, and then destroy Liverpool. Liverpool was the centre of the slave trade, 'the Sodom and Gomorrah of brutality', in a phrase later used by Paine in America.

Technical obstacles were covered. If bridges were destroyed Tate was to improvise others with ropes; 'if trees can be found on the bank long enough to reach across, they are still better than ropes; in which case you will fell several of them.' Advice on how to bring in the disaffected went into less detail. He was to hunt down peers and clergymen. To the poor he was not simply to inveigh against the Government but to hand out drink and cash. He was to remember always that he had become a Frenchman and brilliance was expected of him.

The landing was made from a small squadron off the headland of Pencaer in Pembrokeshire, on the southern tip of Wales, in the evening of 22 February 1797. It consisted of a thousand French convicts and a hundred émigrés captured by Hoche at Quiberon. Tate's second in command, known as Jacques Lebrun, was another former émigré. In addition he had three Irish officers, one of whom had been in America.

Two local Welshmen acted as guides, one of whom was taken by force from a sloop which was then scuttled. The other, James Bowen, had come with the expedition from Brest. He had been a servant in a farmhouse on

B

the headland of Pencaer before being transported for theft, and Tate made the farmhouse his headquarters. The advance party met no resistance and planted the tricolour at a point 500 feet high which dominated the area. The squadron which had put Tate ashore sailed back to France at a signal from him that the landing was complete.

An invasion committee was set up by the English militia twelve miles to the south, in Haverfordwest, and officers were sent the same night to discover what had happened at the fort in Fishguard Bay within three miles of the landing. One of them was a Captain Edwardes, son of Lord Kensington, who lived near Haverfordwest. They got to the fort about midnight to find the French had been greeted with a salute. When Knox, the colonel in charge, had realized they were invaders, he hesitated to attack because he had only 150 men against over a thousand coming ashore. The militia officers urged him to make at least a show of resistance while they rode back for support.

At midday next morning reinforcements set off from Haverfordwest under the command of Lord Cawdor, with Captain Edwardes as one of his aides. They had four hundred men and two nine-pounders—together with the men from the fort about half as many as the French. Their guns lagged behind and as darkness began to fall Cawdor shared the view of Knox at the fort that discretion was the better part of valour. He decided to postpone the attack until the following morning; but meanwhile things had been going so badly with the French that no attack was needed.

Tate seems to have ordered his ex-convicts to bring in carts, food, and as much drink as possible for the advance, while the officers were posted around the tricolour as a kind of reception committee. A smuggler had just been wrecked on the headland and every hut and farm happened to have its cask of wine. Instead of bringing them to Tate's headquarters the convicts got drunk on the spot and looted indiscriminately. Several were then clubbed or otherwise disposed of by the Welsh. Tate ordered the execution of one of his men who tried to recruit a farmer by stripping him of his watch and cash. His order was disobeyed.

Meanwhile no one came in to the reception committee. Most people on the headland had already made off with as much of their own property as they could take. An officer wandered inland waving a tricolour but without effect. A Congregationalist was lured to Tate's headquarters, where he accepted that 'they had come to fraternize', and later repeated it to his friends, but that was the nearest approach to a recruit, and it came after Tate had decided to surrender.

In a night and a day Tate had seen that his own men were hopelessly undisciplined and no effective support could be expected from the Welsh. He believed he was outnumbered. When he sent his second in command into Fishguard to negotiate, Cawdor was sensible enough to say he was getting reinforcements every hour and would only accept unconditional surrender. Tate so far forgot his initiative as a Frenchman as to allow his men to be chivvied out by Captain Edwardes to surrender on Goodwick Sands. On the journey across England they were nearly lynched.

In London news of the invasion was a severe shock and there was a run on the banks. In his relief on hearing of the surrender George III sent a message of 'particular thanks' to those who had taken part. Meetings were held up and down the country to celebrate but were followed almost at once by a reaction. How had a landing been allowed to take place, and why on the southern tip of Wales?

The leader of the opposition, Charles James Fox, had just resisted an increase of the militia on the ground that invasion was unlikely and the motive for more troops was to divert the country's attention from the demand for liberty at home. Among Welshmen and particularly Welsh Dissenters, the demand for reform was loud. The peasants lived in huts about five feet high under roofs of oat straw. In the big houses a manservant like James Bowen, who had been sentenced to transportation, was paid twopence halfpenny a day. The best-known Welshman of the period had been Dr. Richard Price, a dissenting minister who was an admirer of Tom Paine and *The Rights of Man*. Price had advocated the American cause so strongly that he was invited by Congress to become a citizen. He died after glorifying the opening stages of the French Revolution but left many political converts.

The investigations undertaken by the Government were pressed against any Welsh Nonconformist who had come in touch with the invaders. The Duke of Rutland, who toured the landing area, found it full of Anabaptists, 'and the meeting houses swarm'. When a farmer who had piloted Lebrun to Cawdor was found to be a churchman, the case against him was dropped, but the Congregationalist who had talked with the invaders, a Baptist, and a Methodist were put on trial. The French prisoners were bribed to invent evidence against these men but withdrew most of it before the trial, so that all three were acquitted and the stigma of disloyalty left hanging in the air.

As the Government picked on Dissenters, so the Welsh found their own culprit. A few miles from the farmhouse which Tate made his headquarters was another owned by a yeoman farmer whose family had lived in Wales for centuries. His name was Batine. A rumour grew up locally that he was a French General Batine who was responsible for bringing in the French. The English thus blamed disloyalty in Wales and the Welsh passed on the blame by inventing a French agent. It was a pattern which was to repeat itself in the main centre of disaffection, which was London.

*

Napoleon was given charge of the invasion forces on 2 October 1797. By then the Directory were more sober about the prospects and expected him to be cut down to size. But the Italian campaign had given Napoleon reason to think he could do better than Hoche. Little as he admired the radical idealism of Paine, he found support in *The Rights of Man*, which had sold nearly a quarter of a million copies in England. Both its success and its argument suggested that the invasion plan had failed because of its own shortcomings and not because the English were more loyal to their masters than the Italians. Napoleon went to call on Paine and told him he slept with the book under his pillow.

The author of *The Rights of Man* had been born at Thetford, in Norfolk, the son of a disastrous marriage between a Quaker father and a mother who was loyal to the Church of England. He grew up with his father's belief in the divinity in man and his mother's authority to revolt against the moral discipline of his father. After a dismal career in England in his father's trade of stay-making, as a schoolmaster, excise-man, and inventor, he emigrated to America in 1774 on the advice of Franklin, and in the next two years probably did more than anyone to persuade the colonists that their interest lay in throwing off the control of George III. As well as being a revolutionary, he was an inventor of bridges, insisting on the virtues of the single span which reached from bank to bank without intervening support. When he returned to Europe after the War of Independence to promote his technical ideas, he pined for America and wrote that 'my heart and myself are 2,000 miles apart'. He visited Paris soon after the fall of the Bastille and Lafayette handed him its key to present to Washington as a symbol that 'the principles of America' had brought about the fall of the great prison.

The crucial argument of *The Rights of Man*, which Paine wrote on his return to England in reply to Burke's attack on the French Revolution, was that the English had as much interest as the Americans in disowning George III. The mistake of the English Revolution of 1688 had been to replace the Stuarts with another line of kings. The Americans, he believed, had changed the course of history by proving they could rule themselves. Until the Declaration of Independence a tide of influence had flowed from Europe to America, imposing European patterns of society on the colonists. Thereafter it was Europe which would copy America.

Napoleon's experience in Italy had convinced him that there were two conditions needed to win. The first was a spectacular entry, like the crossing of the Alps and the battle in which he led the way across the bridge of Lodi under the fire of the Austrians. It was only then that a second stage might develop. After Lodi the people of Milan had come out to greet him as a hero. Volunteers joined the ranks in such numbers that he became largely independent of the communications back to France. The question was whether the English would do the same.

Paine's belief in the subversive power of ideas had not been shaken by the failure of Hoche and Tate. He reassured Napoleon that there were lasting grounds for the alienation of the majority. He had already submitted his plan for a further invasion which would include himself as an agitator in Norfolk and would cross under cover of darkness with heavier support.

To Napoleon the Channel now became a problem like the Alps. Once across in force, the descent into Italy would be repeated. After the first battle, the Hanoverian oligarchy would be unable to prevent the flow of recruits. On St. Helena he reminded O'Meara that the Austrians had laughed at him when he began to enlist Italians, but their sense of release had inspired Italians to fight like Frenchmen. He would have landed at Chatham. 'Four days would have brought me to London.' It had taken him four days from Lodi to Milan. He would have come 'as a liberator, a second William III, but more disinterested and generous than he'.

Paine differed sharply. The point of *The Rights of Man* was that the English could not be liberated by a second William III. They had been disabused of the idea of kings in any guise. If Napoleon came in as a conqueror he would be defeated as a conqueror. Paine wrote to Jefferson that 'the intention of the expedition was to give the people of England an opportunity of forming a government for themselves and thereby bringing about peace.'

Napoleon doubled the size of Paine's expedition. He would need two hundred thousand men and to these he later added an escort of ships of the line while the English fleet was decoyed into the Atlantic. He pressed Paine to encourage the Military Council, who were doubtful of success. 'He will tell you,' he said, when they went in front of it together, 'that the whole English nation, except the royal family and the Hanoverians who have been created peers of the realm and absorb the largest part of the landed property, are ardently burning for fraternization.'

Paine refused to support the role Napoleon gave to the French army. 'I think the people are very disaffected,' he said, 'but I am sorry to add that if the expedition should escape the fleet, I think the army would be cut to pieces. The only way to *kill* England is to annihilate her commerce.'

The invasion plan of 1798 was abandoned when the nights lengthened, and Napoleon could see no hope of getting across a big enough force to gain his initial victory. He wrote to the Directory on 23 February that the moment had passed, 'perhaps for ever'. In the future it seemed to him unlikely that the army would be able to free itself from other fronts to concentrate on the Channel in enough strength. 'We should therefore give up any real attempt to invade England and content ourselves with the appearance of it. . . .' The appearance was important. It had the tactical advantage of keeping British troops at home, and it seemed to Napoleon the obvious way of heightening the respect of his sympathizers in England.

Meanwhile he had no further use for Paine, who went back to Washington in the Peace of Amiens. Although Jefferson had him to stay in the White House, he found himself so persecuted by a new American orthodoxy that he revised his view of life under Napoleon. 'I know Bonaparte,' he said. 'I have served under his government, and he allows as much freedom as I wish or anybody ought to have.'

Napoleon's chance to invade came six years after the Welsh landing when the Peace of Amiens had broken down. Not only was England alone in the field, so that he could concentrate his forces, but he had seen at first hand more convincing evidence of British sympathy than Paine had given the Directory.

The truce had been popular in England, and especially in London. When the preliminaries were signed at the end of 1801 there was a general illumination; the windows of prominent people who did not light up were broken and the carriage of the French envoy was dragged down Pall Mall by the crowd. In fourteen months more visitors crossed the Channel to Paris than had done in any year before. Opposition figures were prominent, especially Fox and his friends, but there were also sightseers, holiday-makers, and people satisfying their curiosity. If it was hard to be sure of the extent of their admiration for Napoleon, the right-wing press in London was not in doubt. 'None bow so low as the British,' said the *True Briton*.

On the renewal of war in May 1803, Napoleon began to put his own ideas into practice. In May there were to be a few hundred invasion craft; in July over a thousand; in August over two thousand. Paine's faith in ideological conversion disappeared. The propagandists became a small corps of 'guide-interpreters' whose main qualification was to be under thirty-five, to have lived in England, and to be able to translate. In 1804, as the moment for action approached, Napoleon abandoned the idea of slipping across at night and gave orders for the ships of the line to escort the invasion barges. He continued to plan a direct attack on London and the invasion camps stretched out opposite the Thames estuary from Boulogne to Flushing.

The threat was defeated by Pitt in 1805 with a new European coalition which diverted Napoleon's Army of England to the battlefields of Ulm and Austerlitz. In spite of Trafalgar, which followed the first and gave the assurance that the French army could never cross the Channel if it came back, Napoleon kept up a show of preparations for another six years. They reached a secondary peak in 1811 to pin down as many British troops as possible in the island while he collected his own for the attack on Russia.

It was easy, perhaps inevitable, for patriotic Englishmen to link the preparations in the Channel with the growth of radicalism in London. The death of Fox in office after the failure of his own negotiations with Napoleon did not put an end to the demand for peace. To Whitbread, his successor in the Commons, and to Holland in the Lords, it seemed that the process of blockade and counter-blockade could only end in the defeat of Britain by exhaustion. Rising prices and stoppages of work through lack of raw materials gave popular support to this view, which found its steadiest expression in the success of a new radical newspaper, *The Examiner*.

Leigh Hunt and two brothers, one of whom was a printer, founded the *Examiner* as a weekly review in 1808. They were the sons of an eccentric preacher, whose adventures in America and England, in pulpits, meeting houses, and a debtors' prison, seemed to have made them immune to established opinion. Leigh Hunt was so scrupulous of his independence that he refused to take advertisements or have contact with organized political groups, however sympathetic. He wanted radical reform at home and peace with Napoleon. He was critical of Napoleon, but admired him for the virtues which were lacking in George III and his allies.

There was a sting and clarity in the *Examiner*'s attack which was strengthened by the best prose writers from Lamb to Hazlitt, and occasionally by poems from Byron. Circulation rose almost at once towards 3,000 copies, which was more than half the daily circulation of *The Times*. The Government prosecuted the paper four times in its first four years. Early in 1811, in the first case to come to trial, the Attorney-General denounced Leigh Hunt as a Bonapartist who was preparing the way for invasion. The charge had been made before against Fox and Whitbread, but not by the Attorney-General or so widely by the press against Whigs and Radicals in general. Lord Holland, Fox's nephew and political heir, was cartooned as entering No. 10 Downing Street with Napoleon under his wife's cloak.

The stimulus for these attacks did not only come from the new outburst of activity in the invasion ports; the Tory Government in 1810 had seen its position undermined by the final onset of the King's madness. For fifty years George III had proved the staunch enemy in turn of the American Revolution, the French Revolution, and Napoleon. The Prince of Wales had sided as reliably with Fox, and made no secret of his intention to send for the Whigs on his accession and reverse his father's policy. When the preparations for the Regency began at the end of 1810, it seemed likely that Lord Holland would be Prime Minister within a year.

In January 1811 a Frenchman called Changeur began building a square with accommodation for a thousand people below Holland House at the gate outside London where the Great West Road came into Kensington. He had no entitlement from Lord Kensington, the owner of the land, until the end of May, when two lodges like blockhouses went up to protect the site against intruders.

Among loyal passers-by who noticed what was going on were the poet Coleridge, on his way to the offices of the right-wing evening paper, *The Courier*, and a rate-collector, Mr. Davis, who entered in his notebook that a hundred houses had sprung out of the earth in what had once been called 'West Town'. On 3 June, a road surveyor made a report to the trustees of the turnpike that the Frenchman was a Colonel Charmilly, who had been denounced in the House of Lords as an agent of Napoleon.

A formidable committee was convened, including the chairman of the turnpike, Mr. John Gregory, the Lord Lieutenant of Middlesex, and the captain of the local Volunteer Infantry, who was responsible for repelling attempts at invasion. The Frenchman was ordered to present himself on 8 June at the White Horse public house on the turnpike opposite his buildings.

He turned up at eleven o'clock, a self-possessed man of just over thirty, who defended himself in bad English. He may have protested that his name, Changeur, had only three letters in common with Charmilly; he was Louis Léon Changeur, a victim of the Revolution, who had built several houses in the development of the Duke of Bedford's estate above Covent Garden and was now trying to make his fortune by giving the middle classes a setting worthy of them where land was cheap. He listed his own demands, which included four new roads giving access to his buildings, and permission to put up a set of ornate lamp-posts by his lodges.

When the committee had relaxed, they decided that Changeur should be allowed to get on with his project. Gregory, the turnpike master, even became his ally and did his best to defend him when he was denounced by others. But the rumour had gained hold and was fed by the course of the war.

Changeur's main financial support had come from a French shopkeeper in Bond Street, Philippe Lebrun.[1] In 1812, when Napoleon abandoned the invasion ports to turn on Russia, Lebrun suddenly refused to make further advances and Changeur had him declared bankrupt. A group of Lebrun's creditors then denounced Changeur to Eldon, the Lord Chancellor, as an undesirable alien who was 'liable to be sent out of the kingdom'.

At an investigation at the Guildhall in February 1812, Lord Eldon, a high Tory, found that Changeur had been wrongfully imprisoned in the Fleet for six months in the year before Trafalgar, but otherwise had nothing against him, and he acquitted him with costs against the petitioners. His only reservation was to grant a stay of execution on the ground that some of Lebrun's

---

[1] Philippe Lebrun had no connection with Jacques Lebrun, Tate's second in command, who had been the Baron de Rochemure.

executors were in America where they were inaccessible because the War of 1812 had broken out.

The delay was fatal to Changeur, who could not finish his houses. Wages and prices were rising steeply in the economic war and timber supplies from Scandinavia were interrupted. He went to desperate lengths by borrowing money at 100 per cent interest and evading building regulations without submitting his plans. When the Surveyor of Middlesex discovered that he was interfering with the road, Changeur pleaded an agreement with John Gregory, but a demolition party was sent out to destroy his encroachments and he was declared bankrupt on 2 November 1812. The date happened to coincide with the retreat from Moscow.

A few tenants had already arrived—they included a Mr. Foveaux and a Mrs. Bourgeois—but the houses around them remained unfinished until several years after the war, when the square was organized as a community by its residents. The rumour that it had been planned for Napoleon's forces of occupation grew stronger. Leigh Hunt gave it a new lease of life when he went to live there later in the century, by painting a whimsical picture of the veterans finding cheap lodging and rest after victory in what the builder must have intended as 'a French arcadia . . . a little Palais Royal, in an English suburb'. It was understandable, he thought, that French imaginations should have run a little wild; he did not see how an Englishman could have invented the rumour. Hunt was by then in need of a pension from Queen Victoria and managed to forget his own part in the affair. There was, in fact, much the same reason for loyal passers-by to find an agent of Napoleon at the Kensington Gate in 1811 as there had been for the Welsh to discover a French general on the headland of Pencaer.

# 2. *The Napoleonist and the Loyalist*

*All our misfortunes were owing to the misconduct and fatal*
*obstinacy of the King's servants ... they were equally mis-*
*trusted and despised.*

Charles James Fox, May 1781

When William III arrived from Holland in the English Revolution of 1688, he looked for a palace on new ground which would be free from the abso-lutist reputation of the Stuarts. There happened to be two sites in the remote suburb of Kensington, Nottingham House on its east side, and Holland House, the grander of the two, on the west. He may have rejected Holland House because of the name (which was taken, in fact, from a district of Lincolnshire) or because the first Earl of Holland was a Royalist who had been executed by Parliament. It was the house on the London side which was enlarged to become Kensington Palace, and William was succeeded there by Anne, George I, and George II. Their courts spread out around them.[1]

When George III came to the throne with the intention of recovering its lost powers, he made his own symbolic move by leaving the scene of Whig control for Windsor and Kew. His disappearance was perhaps the only thing that could have preserved the Whig character of the place. The half-empty palace became the refuge of members of the royal family who were dis-graced or out of favour. In the houses of the old court suburb their retainers sympathized with their desire for vindication and revenge.

The ownership of Holland House itself was the subject of a long-standing feud between the families of Lord Holland, which had drifted into opposi-tion, and Lord Kensington, a loyal servant of the Crown. The titles of Lord Kensington and Earl of Holland had originally been granted to Henry Rich, second son of the Earl of Warwick, early in the seventeenth century after he had married the daughter of the man who built Holland House, but the

---

[1] Kensington formed part of the county of Middlesex until late in the nineteenth century, but the palace itself was in an enclave of the giant parish of Westminster.

titles died out a century later for lack of male heirs, and Holland House passed without them to a Welsh family called Edwards. Lady Elizabeth Rich, daughter of the second Earl of Holland, had married a Francis Edwards in the decline of the family fortunes when she was penniless. Edwards had been a ship's purser, earning £60 a year, before becoming mayor of Haverfordwest, and their children were not brought up in the expectation of a great future. Lady Elizabeth added a second 'e' to their name to give them what distinction she could, but when Holland House came to them in 1721 with the manors of Earls Court and Kensington, the effect was at first paralysing. Francis Edwards (who refused to change the spelling of his own name) entered Parliament and leased a house in London for his wife, but she was already an invalid. Within four years they both died and Holland House passed on to their eldest son, Edward Henry Edwardes.

The boy was then sixteen and never managed to face London at all. He built his own little court, Johnston Hall, a few miles outside Haverfordwest, where he hunted, gambled, and drank. He took out a first mortgage for £9,000 on Holland House when he was eighteen, another for £6,000 when he was twenty, and then minor ones until they totalled £17,000. By his middle twenties he was seriously ill from drink and the pressure of his creditors. He had an elaborate will drawn up, leaving the great house to his brother and his brother's heirs and making a final bid for fame for himself. In the church of St. Mary's in Haverfordwest, a memorial had gone up to a Welshman from a rival family, Sir John Philipps, who had helped to rebuild London after the great fire. The little group of columns and cherubs had the distinction of Wren and drew attention to the space on the other side of the chancel. Edward Henry willed that a still further mortgage of a thousand pounds should be raised for a memorial to himself, 'that is to say six hundred pounds for a Monument and four hundred pounds for my funeral expenses.' He then died, and it was probably his brother William who persuaded his executors not to act on the ground that there was nothing left to mortgage.

The tradition of Pembrokeshire and Haverfordwest, its county town, had been of loyalty to the throne ever since it was colonized as an English outpost beyond the rebellious mass of Wales. A club called the Sea Serjeants, to which the Edwardes family belonged, drank to the King across the water for half a century after the Revolution, until loyalty to the Stuarts turned gradually into loyalty to the Hanoverians. There was already a touch of George III about William Edwardes. He had the same nose jutting out from the structure of his head, and eyes which tended to stare with the same concentration. His likeness to the King grew as he devoted himself to regaining the lost titles.

He spent the first year after his brother's death in Haverfordwest, where he became mayor like his father and married a cousin. He then went to London and let Holland House to Lord Bruce, Earl of Ailesbury. The Earl, a godson of Charles II, was impoverished by his Stuart connections and hardly paid enough rent to cover the mortgage interest. Edwardes resorted to felling his trees and digging gravel from the pits near his manor house at Earls Court. The gravel was highly profitable because the last section of the Great West Road from Kensington into London had been turned into a turnpike with a toll gate below Holland House, and repairs were continuous. In 1747, the year he met Henry Fox, he entered Parliament for Haverfordwest.

Fox was the rising star of the Whigs and the most obvious successor to Walpole and Pelham at the right hand of George II. He had married a great-granddaughter of Charles II, Lady Caroline Lennox, who was having children and wanted Holland House with its Stuart background as their home. When Lord Bruce died in 1747, Fox asked Edwardes for the lease. Edwardes had no reservation in giving it until he saw Fox settle down as if he owned the place. The farms and surrounding land had been let by Edwardes to a dozen different tenants, but Fox now insisted on taking the leases himself as they fell in. In ten years he added a churchyard, an orchard, several farms, and the public house on the turnpike where in 1811 one of Changeur's trials was to take place.

Under his brother's will, Edwardes only held Holland House for his lifetime; it was to pass to his children, but in twenty years of marriage he had had none, and Fox was establishing a claim which might be hard for a political dependant to resist. When Mrs. Edwardes died in the year George III came to the throne, Edwardes made the best answer he could by marrying a second wife, Elisabeth Warren, who was thirty years his junior.

Fox had enough to preoccupy him at the time in his own prospects. As Paymaster-General in the Seven Years War, he earned widespread contempt by manipulating the funds which kept a great army and navy in action. In a corrupt age only Pitt had scorned such an opportunity, and Fox was in most ways the opposite of Pitt. He held on to the post for nearly ten years at a salary of £3,000, while making half a million from his own investments. Cartoons showed him as a fox with a goose in his mouth, or as a procuress sitting on a cash box. Holland House shared in the odium and was turned into a burrow of ravenous cubs.

The war was popular, and as long as it lasted George III could not assert himself against the rival groups of Whigs. How far he was responsible for forcing Pitt and Newcastle out of office is in doubt, but he certainly chose Fox to organize a majority in the Commons for a peace treaty which seemed to public opinion a betrayal of the Whig victories in the war. Using offices and titles as bribes, and the removal of offices and sinecures as punishment, Fox destroyed the Whig majority and forced through the peace.

A second wave of hatred broke on him. To Hogarth he was a gardener laying cut plants at the feet of the King; to others the King's master, riding him as a donkey or advising him from behind the throne. George was not sorry to see him take the blame. Instead of giving him the earldom at which he had hinted, he revived the title of Holland as a barony and grudgingly allowed him to keep the Pay Office. Embittered and insulted, Fox turned back to the warmth of his family in Holland House and came to Edwardes with a demand for the freehold.

Edwardes must have felt at least as bitter. He had followed Fox into the Court Party, and seen him pick up one of the titles which belonged to Holland House for the thriving family which occupied it. He was now fifty-five and his new marriage had proved as barren as the first. Still hoping for reward, he agreed to sell the freehold of the house with the territory Fox had added for £17,000—the total of his brother's mortgages on the house. First in an undertaking of 1767, and then in an Act of Parliament of the following year, the claim of Edwardes's descendants was 'barred and extinguished'.

But the new Lord Holland was no longer in a position to reward him. Hated by the Whigs he had helped to break, denounced by the City of London as 'the public defaulter of unaccounted millions', he spent his few remaining years in complaining that he had not got the earldom he had been promised. He died shortly before his eldest son, Stephen, and the house passed on to a grandson, Henry, the third Lord Holland of the Napoleonic wars. In the meantime it was Charles James Fox, his favourite and only other surviving son, who had taken his place in the Commons and offered Edwardes the last hope of repayment for his compliance.

In his father's lifetime, Charles James Fox acted as his somewhat erratic representative in the Court Party. Returned for the rotten borough of Mid-hurst at the age of nineteen, he quickly made his mark in debate and was twice a junior minister under Lord North. He denied the right of the big Middlesex electorate to return John Wilkes, and was so reckless in provoking public opinion that he was thrown in the gutter by the mob. It was only an incalculable streak in him which gave George III the impression that he was not to be trusted.

As a father and husband, Henry Fox had been as loving as he was ruthless to his colleagues in politics. He indulged the whims of his children as readily as his wife in her passion for Holland House. 'Young people,' he said, 'are *always* right and old people in the wrong.' If young Charles was disappointed that a wall had been blown up in building operations when he was not there to see, it was rebuilt for demolition when he was. At seven he was allowed to choose his own school. Because he had learnt French before he could walk, he chose a French school, run by a Huguenot, which he attended before going to Eton. His French was so fluent that only Napoleon found fault with it for traces of the *ancien régime*. He showed signs of genius in the breadth and speed of his intelligence, but he grew up a dandy, a gambler, and an enthusiastic actor in amateur theatricals. The gambling became so serious that it made Henry Fox regret having introduced him to it as a schoolboy. Charles was capable of losing £11,000 in a night at Brooks's, and drained off nearly half the father's ill-gotten fortune. According to Lady Holland, the losses were mainly responsible for his death.

If the behaviour of Charles in his father's lifetime was disturbing to Edwardes, it must have seemed more so after his death. When the conflict with the American colonies broke out in Massachusetts Charles simply crossed the floor and joined Pitt and Burke in opposition. The minorities in which they voted were at first small, but by the end of 1775 amounted to over a third of the Commons. Fox denounced the war as a bloodthirsty act of oppression, and accused Lord North and the Court Party of 'servile acquiescence'. He put a deep enthusiasm into his attack: the American people were 'of the same original' and their cause was the same as Hampden's.

The King's supporters had little to say. Gibbon, who attended as regularly as Edwardes, admitted he 'at no time found either the courage or capacity to speak'. Edwardes never spoke at all. There were times after Fox had argued for hours when no one replied. He accused North of 'impudent and shameless silence'. 'I am clear,' he wrote, 'the *opinion* of the majority of the House is now with us. I cannot help flattering myself that opinions will in the long run have their influence on votes.'

When Congress passed the Declaration of Independence, Edwardes had been voting for the King for fifteen years and was rewarded with the title of Lord Kensington. He said afterwards that he 'demurred some time about taking up the title', not because he felt any doubts about having earned it, but because it was an aristocratic fiction known as an Irish peerage, which gave him no privileges in England beyond the name. He was left, intentionally, in the Commons, to vote on in the hope of an English peerage.

A year later when Burgoyne surrendered to the Americans at Saratoga, and France soon afterwards entered the war, the discontent of the country began to have its effect. In the spring of 1780 a motion against 'the increased, dangerous and alarming influence of the Crown' was carried by twenty votes, and the Court Party at last showed up as a minority, with Lord Kensington among them.

When North went to the country, Fox exchanged his rotten borough of thirteen voters for the growing constituency of Westminster where there were over ten thousand. Westminster returned two representatives and North had two candidates. One of them, Admiral Rodney, was away at sea, and the other, Lord Lincoln, the previous member, had represented the King's interests instead of his constituency's. The Treasury put down £8,000 to be spent on bribes, while Fox trusted to an election committee in intimate touch with the new voters.

Covent Garden, where he spoke every day, was the centre of a traditional court borough and had been the first square to be laid out in London. Planned on the lines of a palace by Inigo Jones, under the influence of Charles I, it was lined by piazzas and closed by the façade of the local church of St. Paul's. There were dukes and earls in the seventeenth century who put up with the narrow houses which composed it because of the optical illusion that they had brought their mansions to town, but in the eighteenth century hotels and cafés began to encroach on them. In the crowded streets round about, an ever-growing number of retailers and craftsmen had qualified for the vote and took over the square at election time. While Fox's committee combed the streets with lists of voters, the interloper spoke in an urgent, intimate, voluble style as 'the Man of the People'. The question, he said, was 'whether you will choose a representative for yourselves, or whether an implicit dependant of Lord North shall be forced on you'.

To this new kind of appeal, which included lifts to the poll and endearments from Whig ladies, the electors responded with a new sense of their dignity. The previous member came bottom of the poll, and Fox, who was near the top, was chaired by a procession which reached its climax outside St. James's Palace. With only one short interval, he represented Westminster for the rest of his life. His campaign colours became the buff and blue of Washington's volunteers.

In the election at Haverfordwest, Lord Kensington was not challenged at all, under a long-standing arrangement with Sir John Philipps, who had his support for the county seat of Pembrokeshire in return for keeping clear of the town. Despite this easy victory, Kensington suffered almost as much as George III from the growing unpopularity of the war and was often ill; but there were complaints if he missed a division, and in 1782 he dragged himself into the last stand for the King. After the surrender of Cornwallis at Yorktown, he voted against a motion of censure, which was lost by only ten votes, then against another which was lost by nine. Before there could be still another, North reported to the King that it was 'totally impossible for the present ministry to conduct His Majesty's business any longer'.

The defeat of North meant the end of the King's personal rule and the triumph of Fox. It was particularly ugly for Kensington because he could not change sides. He voted on in the Commons for the King whether sane or mad until he was ninety, and gained no other title than Father of the House.

Kensington's frustration was increased by the fact that ten years after he had sold Holland House a son was born. The boy, also called William, discovered what had happened at some point in his childhood, and grew up with two ogres to contend with: Fox, who had betrayed his country, and his father who had betrayed his interests to Fox, There was much in his father he admired. His loyalty to the throne, his devotion to the status of his family, his prowess in the hunting field, were all things the son tried to imitate, but he would not accept the sale of Holland House or any other restraint on himself which seemed a deprivation. Robert Adair, a Napoleonist who was a friend of Fox, wrote in 1797 to the third Lord Holland warning him that young William Edwardes would lay claim to the house as soon as Lord Kensington died. He was then twenty-two.

As a boy he had almost as close a resemblance to the Prince Regent as his father had to George III. In an early portrait in the style of Lawrence, his hair tumbles around a heavy, rather formless face which seems confident of nothing but caresses from life. He remained an only child, cherished the more by his mother because of the thirty years which separated her from her husband.

Lady Kensington would not allow William to go away to school, and the main attempt to influence him was made by the Methodist Sunday School. The family had been converted to Methodism by John Wesley himself in the repeated visits he paid to Haverfordwest. But William rebelled against the Sunday School, as he rebelled against the authority of his father. His hobby became cock-fighting, where he caught the fever around the pit as the bets mounted and the feathers flew. He had a precocious passion for girls, and escaped from the watchful eye of his mother to roam the country in pursuit. A tall, commanding figure, he met little resistance.

He was twenty and a captain in the militia when Tate's landing party appeared on the Pencaer headland in 1797. That evening he was preoccupied by a neighbour's daughter, Dorothy Thomas, but on hearing the news he had no doubt what to do. His leading part in the defeat earned him the King's thanks and immunity from the suspicions which pursued the Dissenters. He even joined in the hunt for disloyalty and signed a letter which threw suspicion on Knox, the colonel in charge of the Fishguard fort.

He was now a hero in Haverfordwest, and married Dorothy Thomas in the year of the invasion, probably against his father's will. They married a second time in St. James's, Westminster, in 1802. Meanwhile she bore him two sons, the first called Edward Henry after the uncle who had left him Holland House, and the second after his father and himself.

When his father died in 1801 he raised a mortgage of £12,000 on Earls Court, and put up for Brooks's Club. Although he entered the Commons as a Whig in the following year, Brooks's was enemy territory because it was dominated by Fox and Lord Holland. Its political reputation had been

FACING PAGE
Charles James Fox in boyhood, by Zoffany.

In *Renard Stating His Accounts* (FACING PAGE), Henry Fox, having become owner of Holland House and Lord Holland, is caricatured as the corrupt Paymaster-General, whose son exhorts him to 'take care of' his cubs.

Gillray's cartoons represented Charles James Fox as a traitor from the end of the American war. In *Billy in the Devil's Claws* (RIGHT), 1797, he made Fox a devil in a French *bonnet rouge*, foisting on Pitt his own responsibility for the landing in Wales. In 1795 he drew Fox as a *French-Telegraph making Signals in the Dark* (BELOW), directing the French fleet to London.

A contemporary painting in the Carmarthenshire Museum shows the surrender of the French invasion forces under Colonel Tate, on the Goodwick

Sands, near Fishguard, on 24 February 1797. William Edwardes, later the second Lord Kensington, was a captain in the opposing English militia.

Agostino Aglio, bankrupt painter and sometime Napoleonist, who settled in England, thought of himself as a Roman and signed his name 'Aelius', a patrician. But his crest (BELOW) revealed that *aglio*, in Italian, can mean garlic.

A·AGLIO

In Italy in his youth the neo-classical poet, Ugo Foscolo (LEFT, by J. B. Wicar), had tried to convert Napoleon to the lost ideals of the revolution; as a refugee in London he concentrated on converting his talents into cash. 'He was not a good man,' wrote Hobhouse, 'but he had great genius.'

Edwardes Square, in Kensington, built by a Frenchman rumoured to be an agent of Napoleon, became a refuge for foreigners and those of radical sympathies. But William à Beckett (LEFT, in an engraving by Harland), the municipal reformer who drew up its constitution, had been a captain in the Royal Westminster Volunteers, one of the groups formed to resist Napoleon.

John Gregory, Justice of the Peace and master of the Kensington turnpike, which ran past the square, was himself the son of a toll-collector and had been treasurer of the Whig Club in Fox's time. His political enthusiasm declined as his turnpike empire grew; the £30,000 he left at his death may have come from investing the tolls.

A Welsh family, the Kensingtons, once owners of Holland House, gave the name to Edwardes Square. Unlike some of the square's inhabitants, they were ardent monarchists. William Edwardes, the first Lord Kensington (RIGHT, ABOVE, painted by William House of Bath after gaining his peerage), in a lifetime of voting for George III came to resemble him. His son William, who succeeded to the title, in boyhood resembled the Prince Regent. But by late middle age (when he was caricatured, RIGHT, BELOW, by Jones), the second Lord Kensington —'Og, King of Bashan', Creevey called him—had come to look like one of the lesser Welsh mountains.

Very near Kensington.

made in the American war when Fox was gambling there and turned it into a centre of resistance to George III. The Prince of Wales joined to outrage the King and see more of Fox. Burke, Gibbon, and Windham had been members, but when Fox shifted his loyalty from the American to the French Revolution, their places were taken by Lord Holland and his friends.

The invitation to Kensington must have come from Fox or Lord Holland in the hope of disarming him. He was proposed by a close friend of Fox, Lord Thanet, who had just spent a year in the Tower for trying to organize the escape of an Irish Republican. His seconder was Lord Sefton, another intimate of Fox and a believer in Napoleon until after Waterloo. In a club where blackballs were common, Kensington's election went through in April 1802 without a hitch.

For a new member, he did not look as deferential as Holland House may have hoped. Creevey, the Club gossip, called him Og, King of Bashan, 'the last of the giants', whose territory had been occupied by the Israelites. Thanks to his height and a quite unusual appetite, he already looked like one of the lesser Welsh mountains. The Prince of Wales's tailor had reached new levels of skill in dealing with similar problems, but Og was more careless of himself than the Prince. A cartoon of him in middle age shows his great cutaway coat straining back from its buttons as if he had been stuffing game in his tail pockets. He spoke with a Welsh accent, carried a stick, and looked out on the world from under drooping eyelids.

Lord Thanet was attached to another club whose members were still more closely identified with Fox. After his victory during the American war as the Man of the People, Fox had compromised his reputation by an alliance with Lord North to outwit the manoeuvres of George III against himself. The King replied in 1784 by dissolving Parliament and throwing him to the electors. In Westminster the poll lasted forty days. The Treasury grant for bribes rose to £9,000 and would have succeeded in keeping Fox out if the election committee had not used all its skill. 'Desert him,' said one of the leaflets, 'and you sink into the same servility and contempt again. Support him and you support yourselves.' On the fortieth day only two people could be found to be brought to the poll and both voted for Fox. Although the Whigs took a severe beating in the rest of the country, he was back.

The election committee decided to extend its work by forming the Whig Club of England. John Bellamy, the founder, was a middle-aged silk mercer, and the treasurer was John Gregory, the son of a toll-collector, who later gained control of the Kensington turnpike.

The meetings took the form of eight dinners a year, at which the faith of the club was pronounced in toasts that circulated through the country like jokes or epigrams. They were not very provocative in the eighties, when any Whig could drink to 'the Friends of the People' or 'the cause for which Hampden bled on the scaffold'. Until 1789, and even a year or two later, the most loyal of Whigs could toast 'the Friends of Freedom' or even 'the principles of the Revolution'. But Tom Paine and the French Revolution changed the meaning of words. In the Terror 'the Friends of the People' seemed to justify what was happening in Paris. 'May the Rights of one Revolution prevent the necessity of another' threatened George III with the guillotine. A Tory parodist only dotted the i's of the scandal by suggesting 'The Glorious French Revolution of 1789' and 'His Excellency Thomas Paine and *The Rights of Man*.'

It took two years for the club to be torn apart. The French declaration of war in 1793 led to the defection of those who valued their careers, because Fox would not give up his demand for radical reform.

Bellamy had always worked by conciliation. He was an animal-lover who left instructions in his will that his horses should be destroyed a month after his death. He treated the club and its distinguished members rather like his horses, as a team which would respond to humane guidance; but forty members left led by the Duke of Portland and William Windham who took office under Pitt. The opening dinner of the 1794 session was to have been organized by Bellamy and Gregory but was never held. Gillray was publishing cartoons of the club in French republican bonnets carrying bludgeons marked 'Whig Club'; Fox himself was a blue-bearded traitor who beckoned in the French fleet. In September Bellamy was taken ill. He died ten days before the anniversary, and Gregory became the driving force in his place.

At the dinner in May 1794, Fox drank to 'a speedy peace on honourable terms between the King of Great Britain and the French Republic', which became a standard toast. He was convinced, and said repeatedly, that the war would run the same course as the American war, but although Robespierre had been guillotined and the Directory ruled in his place, it was easy for the Government to reply that there was no one with whom peace could be negotiated. The Whig Club itself had no alternative but to go on drinking to Washington. As Napoleon began to emerge, he became at once the Washington of France. He was a moderate man, Fox wrote in 1797, who would in no circumstances seize power within the state by force. When he did so, in the *coup* of Brumaire, Fox told Lord Holland that the state needed a new organization 'and General Bonaparte reframed it as military men are apt to, by taking all the power into his own hands'. Washington, too, had been a general.

When the risk of invasion was at its height, Fox never proposed to join or support it. He lacked the patriotic reflex of Captain Edwardes in going out to attack Tate's landing party, and was caricatured as leading it in, but he was clear when the party pressed him to declare himself: no promises should be made in advance, but when invasion came they should exert themselves 'to the utmost against the French' and he would offer his services to the King. It was when the war entered a period of stalemate with Napoleon evidently landlocked after the Battle of the Nile, that his enthusiasm got out of hand.

The peace negotiations were conducted by the Addington ministry on the fall of Pitt, and they happened to coincide with the twenty-first anniversary of Fox's victory in Westminster. Covent Garden was illuminated and the single word REJOICE, surrounded by olive branches, shone out above the piazzas. At the club dinner Fox acclaimed Napoleon as the victor, to whom peace was more glorious than to George III, and he recalled that England in the past had not been ashamed to get rid of one king and elect another.

Although Og had consented to join Brooks's, he refused to join the Whig Club, and in the Commons he accepted the leadership of William Windham, the most violent of Fox's critics.

Windham had been Secretary at War under Pitt, and forced a division against the peace treaty as a device for extending Napoleon's power in Europe. His minority, including Og, numbered only twenty and were nicknamed the Bloodhounds. Fox, on the other hand, said he had never voted for anything with more pleasure; if the treaty was unfavourable to England, the fault was Pitt's for having persisted so long in his attempt to intervene against the will of a people. He then went to Paris, where he could not avoid having talks with Napoleon.

As the French expansions began to prove Windham's case, Fox returned to London to argue that they were not aimed against England and in any event could not be undone. Og made his maiden speech a fortnight after the renewal of war in 1803. The ambition of Napoleon and the excuses of Fox may have reminded him of the seizure of Holland House through the connivance of his father. He could not agree, he said, that Pitt and his ministers had put the country in its present danger. Their administration had been 'high and honourable', whereas Addington had been submissive in accepting the treaty and deceitful in concealing its breaches, which had included 'the sequestration of property'.

In Brooks's he bet fifty guineas against twenty-five 'that Mr Pitt is a Cabinet Minister before Mr Fox'. The Betting Book was standard reading in the club and Fox and Lord Holland knew what to expect.

Og won his bet in March 1804 when the Government was forced to resign, but he still had reason for caution. Pitt was obviously a sick man and pressure was growing to form a coalition of All the Talents which would include Fox and might even extend to himself. When Pitt died in little more than a year, Lord Grenville did in fact form the only Whig ministry to hold power in half a century. It included Fox as Foreign Secretary, Lord Holland as Lord Privy Seal, and Windham once more as Secretary at War. The last, who did not forget Og's support in the Peace of Amiens, lobbied Grenville for him. He was made a Lord of the Admiralty at £1,000 a year and bet fifty guineas in Brooks's that the Government would stay in office for five years. The Talents lasted a year, during which Fox opened negotiations with Napoleon, slowly gave them up as hopeless, and died.

When Og and Lord Holland left office together in the spring of 1807, Holland was able to console himself by giving the Prince of Wales dinner at Holland House and setting off with his family for a tour of England and Scotland. Og, who was not invited to dinner and had never been in the house, stayed behind in London with a bitterness which needed no further restraint. He called on the Whig barrister, Sir Samuel Romilly, who had been Solicitor-General in the Talents, and put the Holland House Act of 1768 in front of him. At the same time he wrote a formal note to Holland naming Romilly as his lawyer.

The Hollands were bowling into Scotland when the letter caught up with them. It was nine years since they had had Adair's warning, and they had come to believe that the blow might never fall. According to Lord Holland, it fell most heavily on his wife. She was as strongly attached to the house as his grandmother, Lady Caroline, had been, not as a Stuart but by the insecurity of her background. Born in Jamaica of American descent, she had been brought to England on the eve of the American War of Independence and in the impressionable years of her childhood found herself by no means taken for granted. She married a baronet but involved herself in scandal by leaving him after a few years for Lord Holland. The great house was in a sense her last stronghold, She saw herself, says Holland, 'turned out homeless and houseless, immediately'.

Lord Holland did what he could to reassure her. He had confidence in the skill of his grandfather and the solidity of the Act. He countered Og's retention of Romilly by going to Lord Erskine, who had been presented to Napoleon with the Hollands in the Peace of Amiens and had been Lord Chancellor in the Talents. He found him preoccupied by a paper he was writing on the value of rooks to agriculture and the folly of shooting them. When Erskine gave his mind to Holland's problem he scored an early success by removing Romilly from the scene with the argument that it was improper for Whig advocates to engage in civil war. He capped this by retaining Sir Arthur Pigott, the Whig Attorney-General.

The case lasted fifteen years. Og had to face not only heavy costs and a relay of legal talent, but a growing risk that the Prince would bring in Holland at the head of a Whig ministry. The defence of his powers as

Regent, when the moment came, fell on Lord Holland and Lord Lansdowne. Although Og believed Holland would gain power, he refused to relinquish his claim to the house. When the Tory diarist Plumer Ward stopped him in the street in January 1811 to ask about the Foxites in Brooks's, he spoke of them as Jacobins, in 'a tone of great enmity'. In February, when the Prince took the Regent's oath in front of the Privy Council, a bust of Fox stood beside him.

In the Commons Og made the strongest speech of his career. Napoleon and the Prince seemed to him natural opponents between whom peace was impossible. The Prince had not only the love of his people 'but also the admiration of all Europe'. To limit his power to create peers was a form of treason; the proposal to do so at the first onset of the King's madness in 1788—a measure for which the first Lord Kensington had voted—had been the greatest of Pitt's errors and should be expunged from the Journal of the House.

By the autumn of 1811 it was clear that the Prince Regent meant to drop the Whigs and rely on the Tories to win the war. Instead of rewarding Lord Kensington with the English peerage his father had claimed, he gave him a minor sinecure as Steward of the Manor of Fishguard. In the election of the following year, the Whigs suffered heavy losses and for the first time a challenger appeared in Haverfordwest. He was a descendant of the original Sir John Philipps. Og defeated him, but it was a stiff fight and he did not stand again.

As the Regency settled down, he could see that his suburb was more firmly in the hands of his Jacobin enemies than before. The Hollands surrounded themselves increasingly with poets and artists who were not less damaging for being above the day-to-day battle. Opposition in its most strident form simply moved to Kensington Palace, where Whitbread revenged himself on the Prince by making a heroine of his deserted wife, Princess Caroline. Demonstrations of a new kind streamed out of London. They began with a traditional address of loyalty from the City, but soon took a revolutionary shape. Supporters came together who had no previous identity in politics—women, workers representing particular trades, people from remote localities (which included Haverfordwest), even young people 'of the metropolis'.

There was a third centre of power in Kensington which might have attracted Og if it had not been largely in the hands of the Whig Club. The connection had started with Bellamy, who had a house in Kensington and was a trustee of the turnpike. After the American war Gregory tried to join him on the turnpike board, but was voted down because of his background. In 1789 he stood again. This time the meeting was attended by five members of the Whig Club and he was elected.

Gregory soon surprised the board by successful economies which he was able to make from his knowledge of the road. In the French war, when the Whig Club reached the height of its notoriety, he was rewarded with a grudging vote of thanks. His chance came in the Peace of Amiens, when he succeeded in taking the chair. He then brought in another half-dozen members of the Whig Club, joined the office of treasurer to the chair, and held both for life. The trustees from the Whig Club included Henry Holland, the architect who had built Carlton House for the Prince of Wales, William Whitehead who had been dismissed as a Yeoman of the Guard for his support of Fox, Goding, a permanent steward of the club, and William Donaldson, a solicitor.

In the next ten years the income from the turnpike tolls rose from £8,000 a year to nearly £15,000, while Gregory imposed ruthless economies. At Hyde Park Corner he blacked out a third of the lights and along the road every other one. He reduced wages after Trafalgar by a shilling, to twelve shillings a week, but had to restore them 'in consequence of the necessaries of life being so expensive'. He increased the standing debt to £10,000 while holding £4,000 unaccounted for and 'disposable'. He became the public defaulter of unaccounted thousands and prepared the way for the liquidation of the turnpike by William Cobbett after the war.

As Gregory rose in his empire so his enthusiasm for the Whig Club declined. In the Peace of Amiens, he persuaded Fox to reduce the number of dinners, which 'had been so frequent and the expense so rising'. A year after Fox's death, when Holland and Whitbread presided instead, he resigned. His interests, which had been canalized into the club, became 'multitudinous', in the phrase of an obituary in the *Gentleman's Magazine*. Besides being chairman and treasurer of the turnpike, he was a Commissioner of Taxes, and a Justice of the Peace. In all these capacities he was a dictator, 'respected more than beloved and unquestionably dreaded more than respected'. He died of heart failure at the Kensington Gate in December 1813, and the £30,000 he left must have come mainly from the tolls.

Og did not become a trustee until the end of Gregory's life, though he had increasing need of money for the cost of the struggle for Holland House and for his substitute comforts. In the West End he put himself down for Carlton House Terrace which John Nash was building for would-be neighbours of the Prince Regent. In Wales he found an Elizabethan mansion in Carmarthen Bay which was not unlike Holland House but had the advantage of a cockpit in front and a hinterland of farmsteads offering a wide variety of mistresses. His sons went to Eton instead of a Sunday School and he already had a number of illegitimate children, two of whom were christened Fitz-Edwardes. The scandals of Carmarthen Bay did much to injure

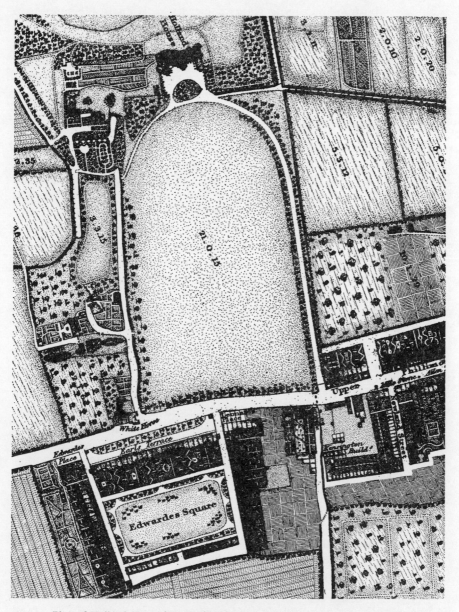

Plan of Holland House in 1822 by Thomas Starling, showing the turnpike
gate and Edwardes Square.

him in the election of 1812 in Haverfordwest, and he found a similar mansion in easier reach of London.

Og had found a form of speculation which was denounced by Lord Erskine as the most damaging form of cruelty to animals. He bought up cavalry horses rejected by the Army as unfit and sold them to contractors for use on the roads before final sale to the slaughterer. The price paid by the contractor depended on the length of time his purchase could be exploited. Og threw up the business before Waterloo, not because of misgivings about the fate of his victims, but as a 'very unprofitable speculation'. He had come to depend more and more on his solicitor Foulkes, to make money out of his mortgaged estates.

The first trustee nominated by Gregory when he became chairman of the turnpike had been Evan Foulkes, then solicitor of Bellamy, later of Lord Kensington. Foulkes was already a rich man from property dealings in London and the north of England, and had a close view of builders and building experiments from his offices in Covent Garden. He served on a control board with Samuel Pepys Cockerell, an architect who had discovered that by extending the idea of Covent Garden he could fulfil a huge demand which was drawing people out of London. Cockerell insisted on 'features of attraction', open spaces, gardens in squares and crescents, to be shared by houses worth £25 a year and others worth five times as much. In the fields of Bloomsbury to the north of Covent Garden a new middle-class world sprang up which became the main architectural development of the war. Louis Léon Changeur had survived after coming out of the Fleet by building a small group of houses in this area under Cockerell's influence. They faced the gardens of the British Museum and backed on a rather cramped courtyard. Foulkes offered him a field of eleven acres at the Kensington Gate with a view into Holland House and an ample pleasure ground at the back.

No doubt Og took into account the pain he would cause the Hollands. The houses went up in the middle of their view, first the lodges at the corners of Earls Terrace, the main line on the turnpike, with wings on either side beyond it, leaving room for nearly forty houses in front, and fifty smaller ones in a square behind. When building stopped midway at Changeur's bankruptcy, the scene of chaos was advertised for sale as 'Edwardes-square'.

The Hollands built up their front wall and Lady Holland interrupted dinner to denounce Regency building. 'I could not catch any more of Lord Holland's story,' wrote Byron's friend Hobhouse, 'as Lady Holland kept me in play with talk of the exceeding melancholy, as she called it, of English houses. She disliked the uniformity of our habitations, and liked a shop and a palace ranged alternately.' She hated Og's development as an attack on her distinction, without thinking that she might be strong enough to prevail.

# 3. Italian Volunteers

*Who would not have Bonaparte as law-giver, captain and*
*perpetual chief?*
Foscolo: *Address to Bonaparte,* 1802

Among the first arrivals in the square were people who were attracted by
Holland House for more pressing reasons than its atmosphere of distinguished opposition. The Hollands were known for their patronage, especially of Italians.

Aglio, a bankrupt painter, and Foscolo, a neo-classical poet, came out to
the half-built terraces in the hope of recovering their fortunes. They came
independently and had no obvious resemblance, but they had both greeted
Napoleon as the liberator of their country.

Aglio was twenty and Foscolo nineteen when Napoleon forced the western passage of the Alps, and they saw him at once as the man who would
free them from the long domination of the Austrians, the Spaniards, and the
Church. Both young men had a vivid sense of the past. They were dazzled
by the striking power of the French, but more still by the Italian-speaking
revolutionary at their head who promised to give them back a dignity they
had lost.

Agostino Aglio believed himself to be a Roman and sometimes signed
himself Aelius. The Latin name was patrician, whereas *aglio* in Italian meant
his father or garlic. He was the son of a lawyer in Cremona and grew up
under the cathedral without accepting its authority, but he was known to be
docile and no one was more surprised than the Barnabite monks who educated him when he joined the French army on his way to take up a scholarship in Pavia. His journey happened to pass a few miles south of Lodi at the
moment when Napoleon crossed the bridge under Austrian fire, and he

followed into Milan like a pin drawn by a magnet. In the general rejoicing Aglio heard Napoleon's announcement of the advance on Rome—'to restore the Capitol, to replace the statues of the heroes who rendered it illustrious, to rouse the Roman people'—and he joined the Italian Legion as a Roman reborn. Outnumbered five to one by Papal troops at Faenza, the French drove straight through and did not allow them to deploy their strength again.

The advance had its trials. Aglio marched fifteen miles a day and heard Napoleon's threat to shoot any Italian who took horses; but at Tolentino, after a fortnight's campaign, the Pope capitulated. 'We shall have everything of beauty in Italy,' Napoleon assured the Directory, 'except for a small number of things in Turin and Naples.'

It was perhaps the theft of the statues he had come to restore which made Aglio realize once and for all that Napoleon was a conqueror like others. He went down with a fever, crept back to his parents in Cremona and then on to Rome, where he apprenticed himself to the landscape painter Campovecchio of Mantua. When a sightseeing architect, William Wilkins, offered to take him back with him to England, he accepted.

His sense of subjection followed him to Cambridge. Resenting his work as an anonymous illustrator of handbooks, he escaped to London, exhibited at the Academy, was let down by patrons and went bankrupt. Within a year he rented a house in Changeur's square with space for two gardens where he could put up a studio. 'I could never resolve to live like a workman,' he said, 'nor live in a garret.'

Aglio had black side-whiskers which reached under his chin as if holding in position his carefully trained head of hair. He was a pioneer in the new process of lithography and ran off innumerable pictures of Napoleon's battles. His neighbours might have disapproved of him if he had not been able to help them in bringing order into the wasteland in their centre. He gave them an idea for their pleasure ground which was a little too grandiose, with paths winding to and fro as if in a park —'there being,' as Leigh Hunt objected, 'no inequalities of ground to render the winding natural.' At the same time he was commissioned to paint a series of frescoes which gave him the chance of his life.

In 1790 a Catholic Relief Act had allowed mass to be celebrated in public n certain circumstances, and a few Catholic churches began to appear during the war. A Milanese architect, Comolli, was commissioned to build the first in the City to have some of the magnificence of a cathedral. It was St. Mary's, known as Moorfield Chapel. To Aglio went the main contract for frescoes, which included an elliptical surface, the full width of the choir, above and behind the altar. For this he worked out a Crucifixion with two hundred figures which was to be his masterpiece.

He was not a great artist. Landscape, with its lesser demands, was his happiest medium, and his preparations were slow and a little nervous. The Church pressed him to hurry, and when St. Mary's opened in 1819, he was criticized for incorrect drawing. At once he felt himself back in the shadow of the cathedral in Cremona. He had been a victim, he said, of 'reverent gentlemen', who gave him a hundred days to finish 'without any regard to the grave and delicate nature of the work entrusted to me'.

This time he had no chance to march against the Pope, but he strode down the turnpike in July 1820 to have his son christened in the Protestant church. It may even have been his whole family, because the child was entered as John William Emily.

In the square his plans for the pleasure ground were accepted and he found himself appointed a trustee in the Act of Parliament which set the place in order. The Duke of Bedford, a friend of the Hollands, commissioned him to paint landscapes. A Mr. Bullock, who mounted exhibitions in Piccadilly, commissioned him to lithograph scenes from Napoleon's campaigns. He lithographed the Prince Regent as George IV in his Garter robes and painted the Princess Victoria. But his acceptance in England came from his ability to supply a demand which went beyond royal and Napoleonic pageantry.

The ambition of the middle classes had turned into a kind of interior imperialism. In 1820 a Bond Street firm published a thousand designs by Aglio under the title *Architectural Ornaments from the Antique*. They reduced the range of classical ornament to a simplicity which could be handled by mass production, with friezes and capitals for the parlour and a confusion of griffins and votary symbols to add to its furniture. If the result seems to us remote from Rome, there is perhaps still a trace of Napoleon in the wreaths of laurel and myrtle whose ribbons fly out like battle standards.

A more rigid character than Aglio, whose loyalty to Napoleon had lasted ten years before he rejected him, Ugo Foscolo took a room in the square in September 1817. From the moment he appeared in a flamboyant version of Regency dress crowned by his own fiery red hair he refused to merge into his surroundings. By the time he left a year later he had been involved in enough scandals with Hobhouse, Byron, and Lady Caroline Lamb, to leave his mark for a generation. He had been born on the Ionian island of Zante and felt behind him the genius and broken dignity of Greece. His father was a Venetian by descent, a ship's surgeon who died without money before the boy was able to support his mother. In his youth in Venice, Foscolo became a republican agitator and acclaimed Napoleon as the liberator.

> The Hero appears—the brave fall in behind him—
> Vaunting on his brow,
> Blood-written, the name REPUBLICAN.

But Napoleon simply handed the fallen city to the Austrians in return for concessions elsewhere. In his disenchantment Foscolo wrote *The Letters of Ortis*, an Italian counterpart of Goethe's *Werther*, but with a hero whose suicide is from political disillusion.

The book had a success which gave Foscolo the new and more fantastic ambition of converting Napoleon through his poetry. He fortified himself by translating the *Iliad* and resurrecting the national heroes of the past to proclaim, in *Carme sui sepolcri*, the ideals for which they had fought. He moved about Italy addressing eulogy and advice in about equal parts to Napoleon, while proving his good faith by joining the army. After taking part in the siege of Genoa he was posted to Calais in the Army of England.

When, five years later, he gave the inaugural lecture in the chair of eloquence in Pavia on the political responsibilities of literature, Napoleon replied by abolishing the chairs of eloquence throughout Italy. When the Austrians returned to Milan in the Hundred Days, Foscolo tried to organize resistance, failed, and fled through Switzerland to London.

Holland House opened its doors to him at once, as if his brilliance and courage atoned for his poverty and negligible birth. One set of guests after another left the dinner table with the feeling that they had been closer to Napoleon than before. 'We are all engoué with him,' Holland told Samuel Rogers, though he noticed that he seemed to handle his table-knife like a stiletto.

At first Foscolo lived in Soho, staying the night if he came out to Holland House to dinner and spending a week at a time there to consult the strong Italian sections of the library. Holland discreetly advanced money and pressed him to get on with a masterpiece which would establish his fame beyond doubt; but Foscolo was unsure of himself as a refugee and tried to reinforce the status he had been granted on arrival by more solid means than his wavering inspiration. He bought clothes, plate for his table, gifts for his new friends. A year after his arrival he moved into one of the new houses on their doorstep.

At that moment the Hollands were in Paris, where they were trying to discover the truth about St. Helena and the persecution of Bonapartists in France. They gave him dinner on their return in November, but he was the only guest of distinction and had to listen to Lady Holland's American mother, Lady Affleck,[1] and their own first-hand news of France. There was no longer any point in staying the night, but on his way across the turnpike he was not sure whether by moving to the square he had joined them or been shut out. On Christmas Day, a month later, he was asked back. There were other guests, but they turned out to be old family friends, and when he said good-bye to those who were staying the night, he knew he had lost ground.

---

[1] After the death of her first husband, Mrs. Vassall married Sir Gilbert Affleck in 1796.

If the Hollands had had enough of him, he was sure their more eminent guests had not.

In love he had always had a taste for the spectacular, and among the Whig ladies who offered their sympathy was Caroline Lamb. Her pursuit of Byron had made her the most talked-of woman in London. She met Foscolo, as she had Byron, at Holland House, and he seemed to her to have much in common with Byron—a major talent which might go to waste, pride and an elusive weakness to which there must be a key. She invited him to Melbourne House to read his poems to her. 'What I listened to this evening made me long to hear the rest,' she wrote; her carriage, which had nothing to do, was at his disposal.

In the long run, Caroline Lamb's carriage was a lesser event in the square than the appearance of Hobhouse. He came out on horseback in the spring for his first visit. 'I am to begin life at forty,' Foscolo told him. 'I am nothing.' The Hollands were kind to him but 'knew nothing of real distress'. They were too well off. His mood was a shock to Hobhouse who had intended a collaboration which was to be political and literary. It was now clear that money must pass.

Hobhouse was the son of a leading Unitarian; he admired eccentricity in his friends but also a quality of independence and strength. Lacking in creative powers of his own, he kept voluminous diaries in which he recorded the doings of the great as if to make good his own deficiencies. At Cambridge he began a lasting friendship with Byron and persuaded him to join the local Whig Club which he founded. In the Hundred Days he went to Paris to get as close to Napoleon as possible. At the presentation of the eagles in the Champ de Mai he broke down in tears. 'I saw nothing but Napoleon—the single individual to destroy whom the earth was rising in arms from the Tanais to the Thames.' He came back to England after Waterloo, published his impressions under the title *Letters from Paris*, and sent a copy to St. Helena inscribed '*Imperatori Napoleon*'. It was impounded by the Governor, Sir Hudson Lowe, as an infringement of the rule forbidding the use of the title of Emperor, but another copy got through which was annotated by Napoleon and obsessed his entourage for days.

When Hobhouse returned from France he was no longer a Whig. He believed that England was going through a period of disaster which was due to her aggression, and he was about to stand for Westminster as a Radical when he met Foscolo. He had two ideas for collaboration, which were the result of a visit to Byron in Venice. The first was to be a treatise on revolution in Italy, for which Byron had given him the appetite without much substance, whereas the Italian had a lifetime of experience to offer. Hobhouse began to pay Foscolo at once, and he produced a thousand pages '*de matériaux*' in a year.

The second idea was intended to be purely literary. As *Childe Harold* came out in instalments, making a sensation canto by canto, the English reader knew he was missing references which might put more order into this wild new vision. Byron agreed that Hobhouse should annotate the poem in a volume of *Illustrations*, but although he had industry, Hobhouse distrusted himself when it came to explaining the Italian literary scene and appealed to Foscolo as the ideal ghost. They agreed on secrecy but little else. Foscolo gave himself about a hundred and fifty pages and set off at what was for him a smart pace. But it was not fast enough for Hobhouse. Murray, his publisher, was pressing, and he soon realized that Foscolo was endangering the proportions of the book.

The Italian had seen his chance to give an estimate of his time which would be studied for centuries. His own position, as a landmark within it, called for skill in its treatment and as much restraint as he could muster. He was ready to criticize himself as much as others, but while he pointed to central weaknesses in their work, it was only *Ortis* which he criticized in his own. The reputation of *Ortis* was secure but it was on the periphery of his work, and he advanced his poetry, which had been neglected, to immortality. 'His knowledge of Greek,' he wrote, 'is far superior to that of many of the most distinguished of his fellow countrymen.' By leaving out some of his closest rivals, like the Romantic Di Breme, he was even more provocative.

It says much for Foscolo's bravado that in the rows which were always breaking out with Hobhouse, he eventually threatened to claim his authorship. By then the threat amounted to blackmail, because they were quarrelling about money.

When the *Illustrations* were published with the Fourth Canto in 1818, a perceptive reader was able to guess their secret. The essay on Italian literature so outshone the rest that it could only be by the most articulate Italian in England. Di Breme sent 'a long and bitter letter' to Byron and soon afterwards one to Hobhouse. Byron, who liked to cause spasms of discomfort in Hobhouse, reserved all his praise of the book for Foscolo. 'The essay is perfect,' he wrote, 'and not exceeded by Johnson's Poets. . . .'

Propped up by his collaborator, Hobhouse managed to hit back in the Italian press at Di Breme and the rest of the wounded. 'Row him, I say,' wrote Byron, in delight, 'he gives you devilish bitter words and I long to see you have him by the ears, that I do. . . .' Soon he was able to report that Di Breme was ill and Vincenzo Monti 'frantic'.

Foscolo's relations with Holland House cooled further. Months passed and he was not asked again. He began referring to Holland as '*un esprit faible*' and to Lady Holland as a dictator. He was advised to see Sir Edward

Horne, a specialist in venereal diseases. The Hollands had begun to suspect he was suffering from syphilis.

The last prospects of help from Hobhouse ended some years later when Foscolo proposed marriage to one of his half-sisters—'he, being some 46 years of age,' wrote Hobhouse, 'to say nothing of his diabolical ugliness, and she not 23, besides being one of the prettiest girls in England.'

He died in 1827 at Chiswick when he was fifty. Hobhouse, who was by then certain about his disease, wrote to Lady Holland that he meant to write a memoir. 'Of course, I shall, as the first Md. de Stael said, give only a bust of him—as it would be a sorry picture if I followed him lower down than the chin. He was not a good man, but he had a great genius.'

The Whig Opposition in the Commons in 1793: detail
from a painting by Karl Anton Hickel. The central
figures on the front bench, left to right, are: Thomas
Erskine, with finger to his jaw; Samuel Whitbread, with
hand on knee; Fox clasping a stick; Sheridan, turning
to speak to Charles Grey.

# II. THE ENGLISH
# NAPOLEONISTS

# 1. Motives for Exile

*Quand on n'a pas son compte dans un monde,*
*on le trouve dans un autre.*

Voltaire: *Candide*

In the decade after Changeur left his square, a score of families with foreign names came to live in it.[1] The most conspicuous was probably Franz Hunnermann, who went in and out in uniform. He had been brought from Hanover by the Duke of Sussex to give his entourage in Kensington Palace as feudal an appearance as his father's at Windsor. The Jäger, as he was called by Sussex, shared the Duke's radical views but had his children respectably baptized in the parish church and called himself a gentleman of the household. Many of the other foreigners had an English background. The Cazalets were Huguenots, Rebecca Bourgeois a widow from St. Pancras, who had not converted her Huguenot name to Burgess; Michael Foveaux was a clerk in the War Office. They were hardly more remarkable than their Anglo-Saxon neighbours, but the shop-keepers and parish clerk found their names impossible to master—the War Office clerk became Michel Fonfoux, and de Franca, a wine-dealer, was promoted Joseph des Français, in much the same way as Changeur became the French agent Charmilly.

It took nearly a decade from Changeur's bankruptcy for the square to be fully occupied. In 1813 the unfinished houses were advertised repeatedly in *The Times* as 'a valuable and highly improvable leasehold property consisting of 34 well-built houses, partly finished and the remainder in carcase; presenting an opportunity to builders rarely to be met with'. But the builders did not take the opportunity; the sale was twice postponed, and the houses

[1] As well as Aglio and Foscolo, they included à Beckett, Bazalgette, Bourgeois, Madame Canat, Cazalet, Champain, de Franca, Delahante, Eichbaum, Fourdronier, Foveaux, Hunnermann, Lemprière, Monge, Provart, Weiner, Valpy, and Vommont. Several of the English also had foreign wives.

went up slowly in twos and threes until the square was finally tidied up by an Act of Parliament in 1819. It was not so much as if an army had moved into the square as a straggle of refugees. But the majority were not foreign at all, and their motives for coming were essentially English.

One of Changeur's last hopes in 1812 was a property dealer called Daniel Sutton who had spent his life as a carpet manufacturer in Wilton. Wilton was a pocket borough, controlled from Wilton House by the family of the Earl of Pembroke, a vice-chamberlain of George III's household, and although Sutton was a director of the largest firm in a national industry, he had none of the Earl's status in the town. At fifty Sutton sold his share of the business, took an office in Southampton Street, off Covent Garden, and began to buy up property in several parts of London. He bought ten of Changeur's houses before the bankruptcy, and during the retreat from Moscow moved into Earls Terrace at the point where it collapsed into foundations opposite Holland House. In the next decade he bought up almost half the square.

Sutton was a rich man and had no need to live in the wilderness himself. He had always had ambitions which went beyond his business. On his seal, which was massive, the monogram D.S. was draped in a pattern of laurel which might have come from one of his carpets but was surmounted by a crown. He suffered from heart attacks and brought with him a retinue of servants, whom he rewarded with bequests in proportion to their care of him. At his new address he was surrounded by a novel assortment of humanity as well as the debris of building. He devised ways of protecting himself. After Waterloo he moved to the west end of the terrace, where he built a corridor from his steps to the lodge and a passage through the gardens of his tenants to a coach-house with its own access to the turnpike.

In a neighbouring house he established his son, known as Daniel Sutton the Younger, who became a Justice of the Peace for Middlesex. Further down the row was his lawyer, William à Beckett, to whom he gave the task of drawing up a constitution for the square.

À Beckett spent much of his time in proving his descent from Thomas à Becket of Canterbury, but he had less resemblance to the saint than the king who martyred him. He was an administrator and reformer, who sent his sons to Westminster, a school with strong Whig traditions, but he had a streak of callousness which made him seem to a grandson 'a terrible old gentleman, as proud as Lucifer'. He already had four children when he came to the square, and a fifth was on the way, but his wife's pregnancy coincided with his admiration for one of his new neighbours, Jane Shaw, a young widow. When Mrs. à Beckett died in childbirth, he christened the child Jane and married Mrs. Shaw a few months later.

The problem of drawing up a constitution for the square was the unusual range of incomes in it. The rents varied from £130 a year for one of the big houses on the turnpike to £30 in the terraces behind. When the head of a household on the front terrace died, his estate averaged more than £30,000, but in the smaller houses the average was £3,000, and a high proportion of the occupants left no will. To add to the confusion a line of coach-houses backed by stables ran across the bottom of the square, where ostlers and coachmen lived side by side with their horses, a group of labourers, and a chimney sweep and his boy.

The most valued possession à Beckett brought with him was his portrait as captain of the Royal Westminster Volunteers, with the initials R.W.V. on his breastplate. The Volunteers were a body of amateurs he had reorganized to resist Napoleon, and his experience may have influenced him in drafting the Act of 1819. To represent the gradation of houses, he picked twelve trustees from the front terraces, ten from the more numerous houses behind, and none from the coach-houses. Sutton the Younger, as a Justice of the Peace, was formally entitled to judge offences under the Act. He and his father were named trustees for life, whether or not they left the square or sold their property in it.

The trustees were to levy a rate on the inhabitants which gave them independence from the parish of Kensington. They were to have armed watchmen to arrest intruders and enforce their by-laws. The roads were to be made up and lighted, the lodges completed, and the rubbish dump in the centre turned into a pleasure ground. No one from the outside world was to be admitted to the pleasure ground without the permission of five trustees, and a majority could exclude a rate-payer himself 'on any fair and reasonable ground'.

Lord Kensington, who was excluded automatically with the coachmen, was not consulted about the measures until they became law. He was then offered £25 a year for the pleasure ground by à Beckett, and accepted not long before he settled his claim to Holland House.

The fact was that Og had found another Elizabethan mansion in Norfolk, called Heydon Hall, which offered none of the resistance which the Hollands still succeeded in putting up to him. He needed a fortune to run Heydon Hall, according to Creevey—who attended his first 'state dinner' there in 1823—but Og had a perfectly good plan for making the fortune by diverting the westward goods traffic of London into a canal owned by himself. The Kensington Canal was to by-pass Kensington by running north from the Thames to a basin on the Great West Road outside the turnpike gate. The capital he needed was £10,000, and Lord Holland offered £4,000 in return for abandoning his claim. The abdication was sealed in July 1823 at a dinner in Holland House, to which Og made a point of bringing his son and heir, Edward Henry Edwardes, who might otherwise have shared his sense of deprivation.[1]

The Kensington Canal turned out to cost four times as much as the estimate. A loyalist to the end, Og opened it with appropriate ceremony on the birthday of George IV in 1828. Leaving the Thames at the head of a flotilla of barges, he sailed up to the turnpike, where they were greeted by a band playing 'God Save the King'. Unfortunately he had overlooked a plan for a railway out of London to the west, and when it opened seven years later, he was ruined. In the meantime he lost an eye, perhaps in a duel, and he put on so much weight that his friend Lord Sefton, who had proposed him for Brooks's, bet 100 guineas that no horse in his stables could carry him from London to Oxford. It was not from kindness to animals that Og abandoned the attempt. He died 'of age and infirmity' in 1852 in a house by his insolvent canal. He was still a commoner in England, and it was a grandson who at last gained the English barony by serving Queen Victoria for five years as Comptroller of her household.

If the Act which established Edwardes Square was draconian, it had to deal with more dangerous characters on its borders than Lord Kensington, and there were other, less calculable risks within. Some of the residents were indifferent to life in the capital and came out for air, but more were disqualified—by youth, or old age or poverty, by religion, or birth, or by various kinds of failure, which ranged from bankruptcy to lack of acceptable talent. As attractive as the seclusion of the square was the neighbourhood of Holland House and Kensington Palace with their aura of opposition. There were Catholics in the square and Nonconformists of all the main sects. Those who recorded their political views were advanced Whigs or Radicals.

Schools were founded in the square while it was still half derelict—the first a year after Waterloo in Earls Terrace, and the second in a pair of houses bordering the fields. There were soon half a dozen. Their make-up in the middle of the century suggests they were for children without parents to look after them. Some were orphans. At Miss Charlotte Orme's establishment on the west side five of the pupils belonged to Civil Servants or merchants in India, two were born at the Cape of Good Hope, and only three in London. On the opposite side, in a school which had existed continuously since 1817, there were Philip and Gertrude Kempthorne, who were born on St. Helena, and two boys from separate families in India.

The young, who had a habit of revenging themselves on the pleasure ground for their exile, were a greater threat to good order than the old, and the old were more numerous. As many as a third of the residents buried

[1] Edward Henry Edwardes died in 1831 in Wales, perhaps from deprivation after all. He left less than £50 and was succeeded as heir by his younger brother, another William.

in the parish churchyard in the first quarter of the century were over seventy.

There was a trustee, William Snow, who believed that a message for posterity could be extracted from the gravestones of people who left no other mark. He had been a glazier, whose business took him to widely scattered churches, but his findings, in *Sepulchral Gleanings*, suggest that stones can say no more than the lives they commemorate. We know that Ann Jeffreys, who died on the west side when she was seventy, left £100 to her sister who had lived with her for thirty years since they left the Strand, and that old Mary Rein, who shared a house with her 'much respected friend Nancy Caley', left her all the £450 she had. But their only message to posterity was that it is better to withdraw in good company from a world in which they no longer had a place.

The reign of the Suttons, which lasted sixty years, had little need of the severity allowed by the Act. They held court in a close group of neighbours, who gave them support in the law, finance, and even the arts. They entertained Henry Westmacott, a mason who cut the bases for statues sculpted by his brother, Sir Richard, who dined with the Hollands. They had the services of Richard Brown, an architect who lost the competition for designing Regent's Park and rebuilt Lord Holland's lodge instead. They intermarried with the family of the Reverend Richard Valpy, which flourished on the terrace longer than their own. Valpy was a schoolmaster and a famous preacher, but he was also a Whig, and the establishment blocked his appointment as a bishop because of his alleged Jacobinism. He turned to the classics, which he purged of impurity from the fifth century B.C. to his own, and they sold so well on both sides of the Atlantic that he outwitted the establishment by leaving £70,000.[1]

By the end of the Napoleonic wars there were more Dissenting chapels in London than churches of the establishment. The best-known of several chapels in Kensington was 'the Church of Christ Assembling in Hornton Street', built in the first year of the war within a stone's throw of the parish church. It had a classical façade with a ventilator in the pediment and plain windows, which were not broken by the mob as others had been. Founded by servants from the palace, the congregation had access to George III through his favourite coachman, who remained in his service at Windsor and left tracts on his seat. The King proved impervious to the claim that Christ was the sole head of the Church, but gave the chapel a certain im-

---

[1] Valpy was the same age as Thomas Bowdler but preceded him as an expurgator. In his editions of Shakespeare he kept to the original only so far as was 'consistent with grammatical correctness and moral delicacy'. His *King John* was produced at Covent Garden in 1803 without the first act on grounds of decency, and his *Merchant of Venice* was produced in private without the last act to prevent an anti-climax.

munity. After his death they chose as their pastor an uncompromising young Welshman, Robert Vaughan, who had shown courage in challenging the Church in Worcester.

Vaughan moved into the square with his family although it was half a mile from his chapel by the church. He had grown up when the Five Mile Act still forbade Dissenting ministers to enter cities. The Act was repealed when he was training for the ministry, but he still liked to keep his distance. At twenty-four, he had ridden into Worcester with the prayer 'Now, God help me,' and he disliked working in the shadow of the cathedral. He had a belief that the countryside closed the minds of its inhabitants but that townsmen were shrewd and open-minded from their association with others. He told his new neighbours they were 'a noble people' but needed goodness and the education of which they were deprived. He gave them what he could of both. He was eloquent and handsome, 'with a lordly bearing' and compelling eyes. When he quoted Greek to them, they looked at one another and found to their surprise that visitors were joining them from London.

Vaughan had three heroes, Wyclif, Cromwell, and Napoleon. His admiration was based on their power to break through their limitations and transform those of their time. Cromwell and Napoleon seemed to him equally ahead of their contemporaries, but he put Wyclif above them because Wyclif came from nowhere and inspired the Reformation, which was still transforming the world. He was 'the Proto-Reformer'.

Vaughan's personal problem was that he was an historian who had had to educate himself from the age of twelve, when he bought Raleigh's *History of the World*. He believed that history had been written by conformists who overlooked the role of Dissent and slighted history written by Dissenters. His solution was to become a 'laborious minister' with the double task of leading his own flock into direct contact with God while at the same time he opened the eyes of his countrymen to the unnoticed role which Dissent had played in their history.

The first memory of Vaughan's eldest son, who was two when they came to the square, was the scratching of his father's pen. He was writing a life of Wyclif, which meant research in the libraries of London and long journeys by stage-coach to consult manuscripts which he believed had been ignored. He spent three years on the book. It was greeted by Nonconformists as a major work and gained him the chair of history in London University. He went on to write another score of volumes on the history of Dissent. They won him regard in spite of a tendency to attack other sects than his own; but his dedication to hard labour left no room for the play of intuitive insight or humour.

Vaughan moved out of the square to a bigger house after his first success, but he carried on his ministry in the chapel for a total of eighteen years. In the intervals of academic work, he baptized the children of upholsterers, clerks, hairdressers, printers, and a new generation of palace servants. Their eulogy, when he left, melted his pride, but they suppressed a complaint that he preached to them as if he had already gained them admission to the universities. He went on to become the national spokesman of the Congregationalists, and found his heroes in politics.[1]

There were other kinds of nonconformity in the square. William Hasledine Pepys, who called himself a Philosophical Instrument Maker, came out from London for reasons not unlike those that brought Sutton from Wilton. Pepys was the son of a cutler in the City, who sometimes made surgical instruments to order. The business prospered, but William had the hope of breaking out of it as a scientist. He began to make apparatus for a rich Quaker chemist, William Allen, and their experiments gained them election to the Royal Society. They had access to the Duke of Sussex, who became the Society's president through his interest in chemistry.

Pepys moved out to the square a year after Waterloo to have space for his experiments. Allen was closely involved with Kensington Palace, where he was trying to salvage the Duke of Kent from his debts and drive the Duke of Sussex deeper into heresy.[2] From the palace Allen came on to Pepys in the square. They worked together on diamonds—burning as many as seven at a time in a furnace—and on guinea-pigs, which Pepys induced to breathe a mixture of hydrogen and oxygen for an hour without ill effects. They proved that the carbonic acid going out of the lungs is almost equal in volume to the oxygen going in.

As time passed Pepys turned to botany and the breathing of plants. He worked chiefly on vines and fig trees, and it may have been the difficulty of growing them that made him move from house to house in all directions. With his bell jars and gasometers and pipes, he achieved his own kind of notoriety. He was generally believed to be a Quaker, but this was probably because of his association with Allen, who was known to be a pacifist and an opponent of capital punishment. The only Quaker in the square was Raphael West, the son of the great patriotic painter, Benjamin West, and Raphael did not live up to either of his names.

[1] Vaughan was head of the Congregational Union when Kossuth led the Hungarian revolution of 1848 against the Habsburgs. When the revolution collapsed because of Kossuth's intolerance to other national minorities, Vaughan gave the exile his warmest reception in England. 'I did not imagine,' wrote Walter Savage Landor, 'that any Englishman, now living, could exert such a force of eloquence.' (*Imaginary Conversations*, V. 480.)

[2] Allen had limited success with these projects, but the nation owed it to him that Queen Victoria was born in England. When the Prince Regent had finally declined to pay the Duke of Kent's debts (amounting to a quarter of a million), he went to the Continent for four years, where he married the Princess of Leiningen. It was Allen who found the money for him to return to Kensington Palace in 1819 for the confinement.

There was one community which was brought together by its background. Naval officers on half-pay took a liking to the square, though they hoped it would prove to be a port of embarkation. The turnpike may have attracted them because it led out to Portsmouth and Plymouth. At various times in the decade after Waterloo there were more than a dozen lieutenants, commanders, and captains. Most had been retired on half-pay in 1815 or early in 1816 and found that Sutton could accommodate them at half the rent they would have had to pay in the centre.

At the top of the naval hierarchy was Captain Henry Pitfield Sturt, who sailed his frigate the *Phaeton* to St. Helena after Napoleon's death and had a nephew based on the island during Napoleon's exile. Sturt was perhaps chosen as a trustee because of his success in getting commissions which took him away from the square and his duties there, but he was in a minority of one in his good fortune. At the bottom of the hierarchy was Thomas Evans, an old seaman who made weekly trips from Greenwich Hospital to visit his married brother, Jeremiah. Thomas had been an engraver, and his wrist was broken on the *Minotaur* at the end of the war, leaving him with no chance of a new profession. Jeremiah Evans gave him five shillings a week pocket money, and when Jeremiah died, his widow raised it to six shillings.

Next in rank was Sampson Coysgarne, a former purser of Nelson's flagship, the *Foudroyant*, who lived on the west terrace with a married daughter and her husband on a pension of a pound a week. He had saved a little from his pickings, and the memory of his ship, with her 80 guns and 1,000 men, remained more vivid to him than life in the suburb. He was a widower and made a will five years after Waterloo, leaving a little hoard of jewellery—a gold watch, rings, seals, and sleeve-buttons—to his children and grandchildren. He wrote the name of the *Foudroyant* at the beginning of the will, like a title to salvation, and died a few months later.

Joseph William Bazalgette, who lived a few doors above Coysgarne, had more strictly religious hopes. He was the son of a French planter from the West Indies who was naturalized at the beginning of the Terror. With his foreign name and accent, and a limp like Long John Silver's, he aroused curiosity.

Bazalgette had grown up in London with the knowledge that his French origin was a stigma. He joined the Navy when he was fifteen and fought with dogged courage in intercepting supplies to the French armies in Spain. At night, when he was boarding a vessel in the port of Ondarroa, he was hit at point-blank range in the thigh. His men took him back with their prize, but when the surgeons had worked on him at sea and in hospital at Gosport, he was lame for life. He went back to raiding on the Italian coastline, where the biggest of his successes was to capture the French batteries at Genoa and turn them on the city. He was given his own command in 1814, but the Admiralty warned him there could be nothing further. His pension was £150, to which £50 was added 'in consideration of his wounds'.

Bazalgette was still in his early thirties and had been converted to evangelical Christianity, perhaps after he was wounded. The experience was an overwhelming one which reduced the horrors of the war and his own lameness to minor proportions. Since he had become 'infinitely a debtor', it seemed to him that he must devote the rest of his life to the salvation of his fellows.

For a while he moved uncertainly about the outskirts of London, boarding incoming ships from a craft called the Seaman's Floating Church and distributing Bibles. He married, settled down in the square, and had children, but his ambition was to see a Bible in the hands of 'every man whose business is on the great waters'. He became secretary of the Naval and Military Bible Society and limped off regularly to their offices near Piccadilly. He sometimes spoke in public, but preferred to buttonhole people individually for subscriptions. He approached relatives, service-men, clergymen, and neighbours. To those who defended themselves with the argument that he might weaken the fighting spirit of the Navy, he replied that religion could only strengthen it. When he saw the first frigate weigh anchor with a Bible for every man on board, he felt she was sailing into an era which might convert the world.

There were poorer and less confident ex-officers than Bazalgette. Commander Pedlar, at the top of the west side of the square, won a medal from the Turks at Aboukir Bay but had nothing of the sort from the British because medals were given exclusively to the Army. As a cabin boy he had been captured by the French off Falmouth, was exchanged a year later and was already a lieutenant on the *Foudroyant* when Sampson Coysgarne was reading the Articles of War to the ship's company. He fought in a score of engagements and captured three vessels from the Potomac in the American War of 1812. Like Bazalgette, he was appointed a commander in the last few months of the war against Napoleon. He had no wounds to justify an increase of pension, but an unshakeable belief that he would sail again from Portsmouth. For a decade he sent applications to the Admiralty, and died at forty, leaving a widow, and a son in Holy Orders.

The Navy were admired by their neighbours, who saw them as guardians of the national liberty over a longer period than the Army. The ex-officers and widows responded by keeping their dignity; they did little services for one another, exchanged servants and houses, witnessed one another's signatures, and heard their complaints in private. The Government, they believed, had neglected them. There had been too few honours and too little pay, and the memory of Trafalgar seemed to have been forgotten at Waterloo.

# 2. *The Tenth Muse*

*There are few things so mortifying to a proud spirit as to
suffer by immediate comparison—men can hardly bear it,
but to women the punishment is intolerable.*
Mrs. Inchbald: *A Simple Story*

Among the Londoners who came out to live opposite Holland House
during Napoleon's exile on St. Helena was a Catholic widow who was at
the end of her career as an actress and writer. Mrs. Elizabeth Inchbald at
sixty-three had been doing her own housework in rooms high up on the
north side of Hyde Park when she decided on the move to a boarding-house
in Earls Terrace in September 1816. 'Such a horror I have of packing my
trunks and furniture,' she wrote to a friend, 'of seeing new faces, and hearing *new* voices, with *old* observations, that I never leave one lodging house
for another without wishing myself in *jail*.' But she needed company. She
had a habit of keeping her papers and accounts as well as a hoard of guineas
in a basket, and her trunks were so big that a landlady on the south side of
the park refused to let her in; it was a Catholic friend in Kensington who
got her into the unfinished terrace and helped with her things. Mrs. Inchbald found herself with four other ladies, two of whom were older than
herself, and one a daughter of former stage friends. When the boarding-
house went bankrupt at the end of 1817 they moved on in a compact body
to the east wing of the terrace.

In March 1818 William Hazlitt gave the last of a famous series of lectures
on English poetry at the Surrey Institution. His subject was 'The Living
Poets', but he began surprisingly with a tribute to women novelists. 'I am
a great admirer of the female writers of the present day; they appear to
me like so many modern Muses.' The audience waited for his next words
and for a moment must have failed to take them in. 'I could be in love with

45

Mrs. Inchbald,' he said, and he repeated the compliment when he gave the lectures in the Crown and Anchor two months later, and again when he published them in the same year. In *A View of the English Stage*, which appeared at the same time, he included a notice of a play by Mrs. Inchbald, *Lovers' Vows*, which had been revived after Waterloo. 'More tears', he wrote, 'were shed on this one occasion, than there would be at the representation of Hamlet, Othello, Lear and Macbeth, for the whole season.'[1]

Although Mrs. Inchbald was a Catholic and Hazlitt the son of a Unitarian minister, who brought him up with strong anti-Catholic prejudices, there was an affinity between them which did much to account for Hazlitt's sudden burst of praise. Mrs. Inchbald and he had not only been enthusiastic admirers of Napoleon since his early victories but they remained loyal to him in defeat and exile. Byron, who was a fellow admirer, turned on Napoleon at his abdication, and Hazlitt attacked Byron for the lapse in the lecture in which he crowned Mrs. Inchbald.

Hazlitt had not confessed in public before to his love of Mrs. Inchbald, but it had grown in him ever since reading her novel, *A Simple Story*, when he was first seriously in love in Manchester with an auburn-haired girl. The book became part of his dreams. 'I recollect walking out to escape from one of the tenderest parts, in order to return to it with double relish. An old crazy hand-organ was playing "Robin Adair", a summer shower dropped manna on my head, and slaked my feverish thirst for happiness.' When the girl had faded from his memory, Mrs. Inchbald, who also had auburn hair, remained, 'like Venus writing books'.

She had grown up in circumstances which seemed as unpromising as those of her old age. The eighth child of Mr. George Simpson, a small farmer in Suffolk, she was from birth one of the Catholic minority which was still in decline after two centuries of penalization. There remained a handful of land-owning Catholics around Bury St. Edmund's, and Mr. Simpson was a tenant of Sir Thomas Gage of Coldham Hall, which stood above the village of Stanningfield. The Simpsons' farm lay close to the parish church, but on Sundays the family walked off up the hill in the opposite direction for mass in the chapel of the Hall. The priest attached to the Gages was their neighbour across the fields. He was one of a few hundred left in the country and his authority was still evident when, at the end of her life in Kensington, Mrs. Inchbald destroyed her Memoirs on the advice of a Dr. Poynter, whose doctorate came from the Catholic college at Douai.

Mr. Simpson died when Elizabeth was eight. She had been devoted to him, and thereafter 'longed to see the world'. She was an exceptionally

---

[1] *Lovers' Vows*, originally produced in 1798, was adapted by Mrs. Inchbald from *The Child of Love* by A. von Kotzebue. She knew no German, and worked from a French translation, introducing new characters.

beautiful child, but she developed a stammer. She fought it with determination. She had a 'bag with words', in which she stored the phrases which
gave her most difficulty and worked on them until they were manageable.
Excluded from school, the Simpson children were encouraged to take part
in family play readings, partly as a game and partly as a form of education.
Elizabeth found that speaking on the stage, 'a raised and artificial thing',
gave her time to control herself. She was jealous of her elder sister Deborah,
who became her mother's lieutenant and stand-by on the death of Mr.
Simpson. Deborah seemed to her 'prettier than me', but not when they were
acting together.[1] When Elizabeth was seventeen and her brother George
became an actor, she decided to make her own escape to the stage. The
manager of the theatre at Norwich treated her with a slightly ironical
respect, and she wrote him desperate letters signed 'Mr. Royal', which was
perhaps his nickname for her. In 1771, when she was eighteen, she ran away
to London.

According to the contemporary playwright, James Boaden, who saw her
and had access to her papers, she was 'in truth now a figure that could not
be seen without some degree of astonishment for its loveliness—tall,
slender, straight, of the purest complexion, and most beautiful features; her
hair of a gold auburn, her eyes full at once of spirit and sweetness; a combination of delicacy that checked presumption, and interest that captivated
the fancy.' But only one woman on the English stage, Mrs. Centlivre, had
managed to fulfil the range of Miss Simpson's ambitions, and Mrs. Centlivre
had not had a stammer.

Elizabeth Simpson at once made a further difficulty for herself. She had
three sisters in London when she got down from the coach in the City, but
she was determined to make her own way without their help. She was
accosted, pursued by would-be friends and villains, enticed—at least in her
imagination—by a procuress. She moved on to a coaching inn on Holborn
Bridge, read and learnt parts by herself when too frightened to go out, and
after ten days of the nightmare, took refuge with her sister Ann Hunt.

Elizabeth's only contact with the stage was through actors, and James
Dodd, of Drury Lane, gave her an agreement. He had just lost his wife, and
a few days after making the agreement, Elizabeth found herself 'terrified
and vexed beyond measure at his behaviour', and threw a basin of hot water
over him. Dodd cancelled his undertaking, and although she called on him
four times, would not renew it.

[1] 'My sister Deborah is prettier than me' survives from Mrs. Inchbald's papers because
of criticism of her grammar. Her nickname for Deborah in childhood was 'Orah'—'Orah
ill and recovers,' she noted in a summary of life in Stanningfield. In a letter to William
Godwin she wrote, 'Orah prettier than I.' '*Ora pro nobis*', which resounded through her
childhood, may have helped to convince her of her subordination.

Meanwhile she was taking advice from Joseph Inchbald, a moderately successful provincial actor, who had met her a year previously and then proposed marriage. She had not been very kind to Inchbald. When he wrote to her after making his proposal, she 'wondered', as she said in her reply, 'what new correspondent I had got; for so many things of consequence had occurred since I saw the hand, it had really slipt my remembrance.' Inchbald was a fellow Catholic and like Elizabeth a not very strict one. He was almost exactly twice her age and had two illegitimate children, but the shock of loneliness in London made her aware of his honest and fatherly devotion. Six weeks after leaving the farm in Suffolk she was married to him by a priest in her sister's house and on the following day the marriage was legalized in a Protestant church.

Inchbald was due to join his company in Bristol and in two months' time had her playing Cordelia to his Lear. She survived with credit. On their return to London they took coach to Bury St. Edmund's and drove on triumphantly in a post-chaise to the farm.

The next four years in the provinces put their hopes to the test. Mrs. Inchbald proved a draw in leading roles. She played Desdemona to her husband's Othello, Juliet to his Capulet, Aspasia to his Tamerlane. Sometimes on tour they were adopted by local Catholics, and she found constant admirers in the company as well as its audiences, but most of their engagements were in Scotland, and they became increasingly exiles from London. They developed subsidiary ambitions. Mrs. Inchbald had a strong interest in foreign countries, and when her sister Deborah went to France, she began to learn French. Her husband had talent as a miniaturist but not more than as an actor. They spent the first six months of 1776 acting in Edinburgh, where the bigotry of the Kirk had prevented the existence of a theatre until the middle of the century. Anti-Catholic violence was common, and on 12 June part of the audience in the Theatre Royal demonstrated against Mr. Inchbald. When he appeared again three days later there was a riot. They decided to go to France. It meant giving up the stage and relying on their second talents, but Mrs. Inchbald believed they were emigrating for good.

They sailed from Shields at the mouth of the Tyne less than three weeks after the riot and landed at St. Valéry-sur-Somme. From the coast they took a vessel up river to Abbeville, where there was an Ursuline convent and several other convents and monasteries. She made a note of 'convent expences'. They were used to discretion in Catholics and the sober but nondescript dress of English priests. They found themselves with pride among priests and nuns going openly about their business. Mrs. Inchbald claimed afterwards to have visited every one of the convents on their first day and then attended mass and a sermon in the great church of St. Vulfran next morning.

In Paris, where they were when news came of the Declaration of Independence, sympathies were running strongly in favour of the Americans. But the Inchbalds, as English Catholics, were received everywhere with affection and honour. An abbé and a Carmelite Friar Jerningham adopted them and kept up their spirits as they searched the city for openings. They made more progress with the sights and Mrs. Inchbald's study of French history than with finding employment. Mr. Inchbald's miniatures had an amateur look by the side of their French counterparts, and the theatre was a strange new world to his wife. She had made it a rule never to accept money from her relatives, but before acknowledging failure in Paris, she took the extreme step of writing to her mother for a loan. When a refusal arrived, they set off for the coast, crossed the Channel in a storm, and arrived back in England after an absence of less than three months.

If France had rejected them, it soon had an explosive influence on their lives. On landing they were reduced to eating turnips in the fields near Brighton, but in October got parts in the company in Liverpool, and there met Mrs. Siddons, who had not yet become famous. In January, Mrs. Siddons introduced them to her brother, John Philip Kemble, who at twenty already had some of the dignity of a senator. He had taken his doctorate at the end of four years in Douai, which was the largest of the continental colleges for English Catholics and conferred a prestige that was said to leave its students 'not proper Englishmen'.[1] On his return to England, Kemble defied his father, who wished to make him a priest, by insisting on becoming an actor. He was three years younger than Mrs. Inchbald, with as easy a mastery of Greek and Latin as of French. They were natural companions in age and ambition.

In February 1777, a month after meeting Kemble, she began to write *A Simple Story*, the first English novel about a Catholic priest, which was to take her fourteen years to publish. In it she subordinates the English qualities of character and local colour to the interplay of character and desire as a psychological problem. Its inspiration is French.

For six months the Kembles, sister and brother, and the Inchbalds acted together on tour, studied together, and spent their leisure together. Between Manchester and York, when they were not near a chapel, Mrs. Inchbald and her husband read the mass to Kemble in French. In April, when French volunteers under Lafayette landed in America, they took country lodgings on Kersal Moor, and while Mr. Inchbald painted, his wife read and studied history with Kemble; all four played children's games, blindman's buff and puss in the corner, on the moor. Kemble began to write

[1] Joseph Berington, himself a Catholic priest, who uses this phrase in *The State and Behaviour of English Catholics* (1780), adds: 'They must contract something of the manners, and something, I fear, of the principles of those countries which give them so hospitable a retreat.'

a play and called Mrs. Inchbald 'the Tenth Muse'. At the end of June, Mrs. Siddons left for Liverpool and the Inchbalds for Canterbury. Mrs. Inchbald now had more leading roles than her husband, and they were able to give a helping hand to Thomas Holcroft, the son of a shoemaker, who was struggling out of the chorus and walking-on parts.

Although Mrs. Inchbald was in a strict sense faithful to her husband, they had always had passionate quarrels in spite of his restraint. He flirted with other women, but she told him the details of unimportant approaches to her. In the year they met Kemble, Inchbald once failed to come to dinner when she was ready because he was copying a drawing of Garrick. She tore up his sketch. They quarrelled about money, and she threatened to go back to the farm in Stanningfield, where they eventually spent three weeks. She wrote to Friar Jerningham in Paris asking, hypothetically, whether someone could be admitted to the sacraments who submitted their reason but confessed 'to strong doubts of revealed religion'. The Friar answered with reserve. When Inchbald and she went back to York, he became violently jealous of Davis, a humble actor who was devoted to her and dressed her hair with unusual skill.

The year 1778 opened badly for Kemble. In February war broke out against France. Kemble finished his play, *Belisarius*, but in May it was rejected by the manager of Covent Garden. In June he sent the news to Mrs. Inchbald. 'Write a little in French,' he urged her, 'but at all events write often.' Actors had to accept that they were on the edge of society, liable to be pushed altogether outside it, but in Liverpool the audience rioted in front of him and insulted Mrs. Siddons for no better reason than that they had never appeared in a command performance. But in Hull, on the next to last day of 1778, *Belisarius* was put on. Mrs. Inchbald appeared in it and spoke the epilogue.

In June of the following year, when Mr. Inchbald was acting in Leeds with his wife, he had a sudden seizure and died. She was distracted with 'grief, horror and almost despair'. The company gave her a benefit performance and Kemble wrote an epigraph for Inchbald —he was *'pater optimus, maritus fidelis'*—but although Kemble was assiduous as a comforter, he showed less sign than before of becoming her lover. He was not so preoccupied with his own ambitions that he could not see the independence of hers. She summarized a chapter of her Memoirs, 'Kemble no lover—determine on London', and in York she accepted an offer from Covent Garden.

London in September 1780 was not reassuring to her. She was an admirer of Fox, and she arrived at the height of the Westminster election in which he was relying for victory on opposition to George III and the American war. A subsidiary issue threatened to defeat him. Two months before the election a Scottish anti-Papist, Lord George Gordon, had organized riots in protest against the first Catholic Relief Act. The cry 'No Popery!' proved so infectious among Londoners that Catholics were terrorized and pillaged for a week, and the mobs were only dispersed by cavalry. Fox was known for his support of Catholic emancipation. Faced by ten thousand Westminster electors, he was now asked whether he would pledge himself to work for the repeal of the 'popish Bill' giving the Catholics relief—and the questioner made it clear that his vote depended on the answer. Fox replied simply, 'I will not.' After his victory a recount was demanded; it was still awaited when Mrs. Inchbald came on for the first time at Covent Garden on 3 October 1780.

It was her stammer which gave her most anxiety. The play was Fletcher's *Philaster*, in which she had the part of the young man Bellario. Bellario has no big speeches, and male dress, says Boaden, 'suited Mrs. Inchbald exactly, who looked the fond and faithful youth with a loveliness that could not but interest.' She controlled her stammer, though she discovered later that she was denounced for it to the manager. The applause was normal, and back in her lodgings she only remained anxious about the critics. Davis, whom she had allowed to take a room in the same house, brought her up the newspapers in the morning, and she hurried through them. She was criticized for too much deliberation in her speech. She had behaved strangely about her hair, keeping her page's cap *on* when she was presented to the Princess and all through the play until it was taken off, but she had passed as a decorative addition to the company, if not a star. In the months following she appeared as the Queen in *Richard III*, Cordelia in *Lear*, and Cleopatra in Dryden's *All for Love*. For three years her stammer was almost unnoticeable.

The cries of 'No Popery' did not break the surface again, but in London she described herself in her diary as 'unhappy' or 'mostly unhappy'. She could see that she would never be completely at ease on the stage in spite of her success, and her strains in private were great. There were many suitors. She was particularly vulnerable to doctors, whether of divinity or medicine. In Aberdeen a Dr. Brodie had cured her of a fever and swollen face, and although he was superseded by a Dr. Aikin in Edinburgh, who cured her of a cold, Brodie came to stay with them in York before her husband's death. He was moving his practice to London, and she used him as a literary agent when she had finished the first version of *A Simple Story*. Dr. Brodie had to report his failure to find a publisher, and when she began acting at Covent Garden, a Dr. Grey was glad to attend her without fees. Once when Dr. Brodie came to her door, he was refused admittance; he burst into the dining-room, and 'on hearing this,' says Boaden, 'she rose, and with great indignation turned him out.'

E

She was surrounded now by people who had no intention of marrying her. The Marquess of Carmarthen sometimes called and took her to a masquerade in a man's costume. She was pursued by Sir Charles Bunbury, the Foxite member of Parliament for Suffolk, who thought the Americans were 'invincible'. When a rich colonel proposed marriage and a settlement which would have made her comfortable for life, her liking for Bunbury made her refuse him. But whether the intentions of her admirers were honourable, or dishonourable, as they more often were, she had now a technique of transforming over-excited admirers into friends whom she kept.

She earned not much more at Covent Garden than in the provinces, and she lived with the utmost economy. When she had quarrelled with her husband about money, it had been over the amount she could afford to send her relatives. She paid the rent of one of her sisters, gave presents to the others and to an aunt, and made loans to actors and to Inchbald's sons, most of whom failed to repay her. The faithful Davis, who had his meals with her on most days, had refused to accept payment for making her up, but when she had been three years at Covent Garden, he was forced by some disaster to give her a bill for £44, which she cheerfully paid. Among other achievements, Davis had sent her on at Covent Garden at the end of the American war without a wig and with no powder on her hair. She won the first notable success in a new fashion, but it did not put an end to her depression.

A year previously Mrs. Siddons had made her first appearance at Drury Lane. There was a freedom and intensity in her acting which Mrs. Inchbald could never hope to achieve, and in a few months she was established as an actress of genius. Kemble followed his sister out of the shadows with a controversial but almost equally successful appearance as Hamlet. A new theatrical reign had started which was to last a generation, and with or without powder in her hair, Mrs. Inchbald 'was now become no more than a waxen taper in the solar blaze'.

In the summer of 1783, Mrs. Inchbald had a sudden idea of emigrating to India, where Tippoo Sahib had just inflicted a humiliating defeat on the British and declared himself Sultan of Mysore. Her only visible motive was that she had performed well in *The Indian Queen*, a play which ran for no more than a few nights. But she had deeper reasons for an interest in Tippoo Sahib, who had emerged from the ruins of the Mogul empire as a kind of Mohammedan Bonaparte. In the final stages of the American war a large French force had reached Mysore by sea to support resistance to the British; there was a French diplomatic mission, and Catholic missionaries were making converts. Mrs. Inchbald consulted Sir Charles Bunbury on whatever practical ideas she had of going out. He was critical of British policy in India and a supporter of Fox's India Bill, but gave her no encouragement. The plan, says Boaden, 'fell to the ground'.

In the autumn her mother, who had been ill, died on the farm in Suffolk before Mrs. Inchbald could get away to see her. She had to content herself with a visit to the grave. She helped to keep a sister on the farm, and had been irritated by her mother's continuing preference for Deborah, now a barmaid in London, who wrote to Mrs. Inchbald that the old lady was being ill treated.[1] Mrs. Inchbald wrote back to Deborah in some impatience that her mother might be suffering from a touch of persecution mania. 'I don't say it *is* thus; but I would wish it were, rather than suppose there was such a monster in our family as an undutiful child to a sick mother.'

In the gloom which had settled on her since the triumph of the Kembles, she refused to see visitors or go out, and tried to concentrate more on her writing. A single idea stood out as the basis of a comedy. The newspapers at the beginning of 1784 were reporting the plans of the French balloonist, Jean Pierre Blanchard, who made a successful ascent from Paris at the beginning of March, landed without disaster at Sèvres, and promised to fly out of London and land in France. Mrs. Inchbald took as her theme a balloon ascent from Hyde Park Corner, with a doctor as pilot and a shoemaker and his wife, Fanny, as passengers. After a month they come down in the seraglio of the Grand Mogul, where Fanny protects her virtue by claiming to be a nun. The tyrant threatens them with all the terrors he has learnt from Europe: boiling oil, chains and torture implements. When despair is at its height, the Mogul pardons them on the ground that European methods have so shocked him that he is determined to introduce a humane regime.

*The Mogul Tale* was at once accepted by the manager of the Haymarket theatre, the elder Colman, and after skilful revision opened on 6 July 1784 with Mrs. Inchbald as the First Lady of the Seraglio. The curtain duly rose on the Mogul's gardens, where the ladies of the harem believed themselves to be watching the descent of the gods. When the balloonists came on, Fanny said to her husband, 'I am sure it is near a month since we left Hyde Park Corner.' At this, the First Lady was to echo uncomprehendingly, 'Hyde Park Corner!' so that Fanny could continue, 'Yes, just by the turnpike going to Knightsbridge.' But at this moment of moments in her career, the First Lady was quite unable to speak. She turned white and the play stopped. In a sepulchral voice she blurted out, 'H-h-hyde Pa-park C-c-corner!'

There was loud laughter and applause. Although the confusion was clearly English, it was forgivable in a Lady of the Seraglio, and Mrs. Inchbald, who had a tendency to giggle on stage, joined hectically in the laughter,

[1] In her Memoirs Mrs. Inchbald referred to 'Mother's Letter to Orah' at this time.

so that the mood of the audience was confirmed. 'I played in *The Mogul Tale*, my own farce,' she wrote when she got back to her lodgings. 'It went off with the greatest applause.' *The Mogul Tale* became the success of the season.

In the following year Colman took another comedy, *I'll Tell You What*, 'a pretty, light, summer piece', which had a command performance and was seen by the Prince of Wales. In the next twenty years Mrs. Inchbald had something produced almost every year at the Haymarket or Covent Garden, but she did not challenge the Kembles on their home ground of Drury Lane. She kept in touch with them but declined an invitation to act at Drury Lane at several times her salary.

France was now the main source of comedies on the English stage, and more than half Mrs. Inchbald's plays were translations or adaptations from the French. She worked for success, contriving situations and characters for immediate effect, but occasionally throwing off something of more lasting value. *Everyone Has His Fault*, which was perhaps the best of her own work, pricked the complacency and pretensions of the ruling class, but it appeared a week before the French Republic declared war on England, and in the *True Briton* she was denounced for Jacobinism.

The number of her admirers began to increase when she became a playwright, and there was soon a slight change in their character. She had useful criticism from Francis Twiss, the compiler, who married the sister of Mrs. Siddons. In 1787 Kemble himself married the widow of an actor. The colonel who proposed to Mrs. Inchbald after her husband's death returned to the attack, but was defeated by her interest in Dr. Gisborne, physician in ordinary to the King, who hesitated to come to the point. The standing of her doctor friends had noticeably risen. Dr. Wolcot, better known as Peter Pindar, wrote a poem 'To Eliza', beginning,

> Eliza, when with private art
>  You seem to shun, and yet pursue,
>  You act a false, a soul-less part,
>  Unworthy love, unworthy you.

Dr. Gisborne, who 'talked seriously of *marrying*—but not ME', received what he called 'a severe and pointed speech', and was supplanted by Dr. Richard Warren. Dr. Warren was already married and had been for five years physician to the Prince of Wales. Mrs. Inchbald records her habit of walking up and down Sackville Street, where he lived, to see whether there were lights in his apartment. When his portrait by Gainsborough was reproduced as a print in 1792, she bought a copy and hung it above her work table as if it had been of a saint.

She worked hard. 'That woman, Inchbald, has solemnly devoted herself to virtue and a garret,' said Harris, the manager of Covent Garden, whose office was half a mile away from Sackville Street. Three years after the success of *The Mogul Tale*, she was able to give up acting altogether. It was as a writer that she had met the challenge of the Kembles, and she gradually realized that she must concentrate on her novels and memoirs as lasting achievements. She first finished a version of her Memoirs in 1786, and they remained an obsession for the next thirty years. On Dr. Brodie's failure to find a publisher for *A Simple Story* in 1779, she had dropped work on it, in all probability because of the Gordon Riots which followed almost at once and seemed to threaten an unsympathetic reception to a novel with a Catholic hero. But demands for the repeal of the first Catholic Relief Act died away, and in 1790 a second Act allowed mass to be celebrated in public provided the chapel where it was held was registered with the magistrates and the doors left unlocked. It seemed possible that her novel might even be welcomed for throwing the doors open. When *A Simple Story* was published in 1791, it was an immediate success, and soon went into a second edition. She received £400 for it and almost as much for *Everyone Has His Fault*, which came on at the Haymarket in 1793.

She had taken rooms in Leicester Square from a landlord, Mr. Shakespear, to whom she lent money, and she made distributions as usual to almost all her needy relatives. For several years she had been investing in Government stock, and she limited her gifts to amounts which would enable her to give again. She made notes of her serious reading and circulated them to her sisters so that they should have the benefit of her work without the effort. In 1793 she found a job for her sister Dolly as a lady's companion and gave her money when she deserted it, but when Deborah called at Leicester Square, 'in a coach', she turned her away at the door. Eighteen months later Deborah died in extreme poverty, and Mrs. Inchbald only reached her in time to call a priest and do what she could at the end. Her misery afterwards was as great as at the death of her husband. 'Orah dies' formed the climax of her Memoirs.

Mrs. Inchbald's reputation was now at its zenith. The admirers who had hitherto besieged her, from 'Ireland, Scotland, and the provincial towns of England', were joined by discriminating critics and people in authority. She was given an Aeolian harp by Mrs. Dobson, the translator of Petrarch's memoirs, and Mrs. Dobson introduced her to the King's physician, Dr. Phillips. Sir Thomas Gage, who regularly saw her on his visits to London from Stanningfield, invited her for the first time to stay at Coldham Hall. A rival beauty complained to Mrs. Shelley that when 'Mrs. Inchbald came into a room and sat in a chair in the middle of it as was her wont, every man gathered round it, and it was vain for any other woman to attempt to gain attention.'

But she retained her simplicity, and from the outbreak of the French Revolution, she singled out the radicals from those who surrounded her for her brightest smiles. Holcroft, the shoemaker's son, had come to her door at intervals since they acted together at Canterbury. He had published a successful novel, several plays and translations, and gained first-hand experience of Paris as a newspaper correspondent. On the fall of the Bastille, says Hazlitt, he was 'among the foremost and most ardent of those who indulged their imagination'; he believed that gratitude to benefactors would be forgotten, 'not from a selfish, hateful spirit, or hardened insensibility to kind offices; but because all men would be equally ready to promote one another's welfare.' In 1789 he gave valuable help to Mrs. Inchbald in revising *A Simple Story*, and his influence is more strongly marked in *Nature and Art*, which appeared seven years later. But from the start their work was violently interrupted. In August 1789 she 'received a very passionate and supplicating letter from Mr. Holcroft,' and a few days later 'another letter, with my own back'. He demanded the withdrawal of two of her plays on the ground that one was frivolous and the other damaging to the radical cause. In the first year of the war she inspired 'a very fierce flame' in him and he 'wrongfully reproached her for her behaviour'. She broke off relations in 1794 shortly before he was arrested for treason. At the risk of compromising herself, she then took a coach with her publisher and visited him in Newgate prison.

With Hardy and the other accused members of the Corresponding Society, Holcroft was acquitted, thanks largely to the defence of Thomas Erskine and a powerfully argued letter by Godwin in the *Morning Chronicle*. Holcroft died in the course of the war, but Godwin lived on to pursue Mrs. Inchbald in Changeur's square in spite of rebuffs during nearly twenty years.

William Godwin, like Hazlitt, was the son of a Unitarian minister, and was himself to have become one, but changed his faith to politics after two attempts in the ministry. He was an admirer of Fox and much under the influence of the French philosophers, but it was the surge of optimism produced by the Revolution which enabled him to write his masterpiece, *Political Justice*, putting the case for the application of reason to political institutions. For a time he was the most courted writer in England, but he would not modify his views as the course of the Revolution exposed his failure to allow for the strength of unreason, and his reputation faded under attack. He met Mrs. Inchbald during his rise to fame, when he read *A Simple Story* for her publisher. The book so impressed him that he wrote to her, and she accepted many of his corrections to her style. As her lover he had to tread much the same path as his friend Holcroft, but he did so with more self-reliance. He called her in private 'a piquante mixture between a lady and a milkmaid'. Amelia Alderson, afterwards Mrs. Opie, who was a member of Mrs. Inchbald's circle, found Godwin in 1794 'with his hair bien poudré, and in a pair of new, sharp-toed, red morocco slippers, not to mention his green coat and crimson under-waistcoat'. Amelia was on the look-out for a husband and incurred Mrs. Inchbald's jealousy. 'Mrs. Inchbald says, the report of the world is that Mr. Holcroft is in love with her, *she* with Mr. Godwin, Mr. Godwin with *me*, and I am in love with Mr. Holcroft.' But in 1797 Godwin extricated himself from the circle by marrying Mary Wollstonecraft, the author of *A Vindication of the Rights of Women*.

Mrs. Inchbald was aware of being as deprived as a woman as she was as a Catholic—she once made an unseemly complaint against not having the vote. She recognized that Mary Wollstonecraft had outdone the example of her own career by fighting directly for women's rights. She therefore took sharp measures against Godwin. On hearing of his marriage she cancelled his name from a box reservation at Covent Garden and told him 'When you next marry, I will act differently.' But the next event was Mary Wollstonecraft's death in childbirth, and when Godwin wrote to her two years later asking to be allowed back, she replied that 'with the most sincere sympathy in all you have suffered, with the most perfect forgiveness of all you have said to me, there must nevertheless be an end to our acquaintance *for ever*.'

The influence of Holcroft and Godwin on Mrs. Inchbald was lasting. At the outbreak of the Revolution she was a practising Catholic, and she heard with dismay of the persecution of the Church. She wrote a play, *The Massacre*, against the Parisian excesses, and only withdrew it when Godwin added his pressure to Holcroft's. She sometimes went ardently to confession, but in 1791 she attended a Quaker meeting, and later attended Protestant services and consulted a Protestant minister about her loss of faith. She began a translation of Rousseau's *Confessions*, and after the acquittal of the Radical John Thelwall on a charge of treason, she read his *Natural and Constitutional Rights of Britons to Universal Suffrage*.

Her second novel, *Nature and Art*, which appeared in 1796, tries to convert the reader to a revolutionary view of society. The father of the hero, Henry Norwynne, emigrates to the island of Zocotra after failing to prove his talents in England, and Henry, who is brought up in natural surroundings, is only introduced to England at the age of thirteen. He stays with his uncle, a Dean of the Church, and his questions expose civilization as a sham. The Dean's wife goes about town 'much less for the pleasure of *seeing* than for that of being *seen*'. She 'forgot everything she heard others say, from the minute attention she paid to everything she said herself'. The conflict between nature and art is summed up in Henry's attitude to a wig, which he is taught to respect as a distinction. 'Having been told, that every morning, on first seeing his uncle, he was to make a respectful bow, and coming into the dean's dressing room just as he was out of bed, his wig lying on the table, Henry appeared at a loss which of the two he should bow to—at last gave the preference to his uncle; but afterwards bowed reverently to the wig.' Artifice is thus the enemy of nature, and simplicity the only true crown.

Until Napoleon's Concordat of 1801 settled relations with the papacy, Mrs. Inchbald was unable to admit her confused sympathies for the French cause, and her private life did not entirely bear out her confidence in the virtues of nature. Davis, the hairdresser, had been in disgrace since the beginning of the Revolution for revealing secrets of her make-up. She 'forbad him her house FOR EVER', but three years later lent him £10 at the request of an intermediary, and hearing he was ill in 1797, sent him a bottle of wine and a guinea. In the same year Dr. Warren, the Prince of Wales's physician, died, but thanks to Mrs. Dobson, she was already being attended by the King's surgeon, Dr. Phillips. When she broke a tooth at the age of forty-six, she went to the Prince of Wales's dentist, Chevalier Ruspini, and was 'much hurt, that Ruspini would do so little.' A few months later she sat a second time for Thomas Lawrence, who had been introduced to her in 1794 by Godwin.

She liked to live in rooms which were high up, with a view over the surrounding streets or an open space. At Mr. Shakespear's in Leicester Square, where she spent ten years, she had the first floor for working and sleeping, and received important guests on the ground floor. As she grew older she became less accessible in spite of continuing success with the plays. When Mr. Shakespear came into money and sold the lease of the house, the new landlord and his wife produced a baby son, whom Mrs. Inchbald called 'Pretty' and more or less adopted as her own. Lacking help in her rooms, she employed her sister Dolly as a servant, but Dolly found it 'too much' and left, preferring 'an idle dependance to an attempt to balance obligation'. Mrs. Inchbald sent her £5 and did the drudgery herself until she could get another servant to enable her to go out. The Kembles took her to a masquerade dressed as a bluestocking, and she was introduced to the Castlereaghs, the Abercorns and the Countess of Cork, but in the theatre she declined invitations to sit with such people in their boxes and chose the pit. She was twice invited to meet the Prince of Wales, and twice refused.

As well as living more to herself, she was now much more serious about her devotions, and at the end of the Peace of Amiens, moved out of Leicester Square to a Catholic sisterhood running a school in Turnham Green. She found the pupils under firm control. 'There are but twenty; and my poor little boy in Leicester Square made much more noise in one hour than they all together do in a month.' Within a few weeks she adopted one of the staff, a Miss Meade, who worked in the school 'under the most harsh and insulting treatment'. At the same time she fell foul of the school's director, Mrs. Wyatt.

On the renewal of the war Mrs. Inchbald showed her first sign of welcoming the success of Napoleon. It was a consolation, she told Mrs. Phillips, that ' "if Buonaparte should come and *conquer,*" I may then, without reproach, stand with a barrow of oranges and lemons in Leicester Square, and once more have the joy to call that place my HOME.' Her only visits to London, except when she called on 'Pretty', were to see new rooms, and eventually—leaving Mrs. Wyatt 'for *ever*', but the unhappy Miss Meade with money for a fire—she moved to the first floor above a milliner's shop in the Strand with a view across the river to the Surrey hills. There, with Lady Bunbury and her sister Dolly, she watched Nelson's funeral procession passing up the Thames to Whitehall.

Her success at Covent Garden was not quite over. In the year of Trafalgar, Kemble appeared in her new play, *To Marry or Not to Marry*. Godwin sent a warm tribute, signing himself '*votre ancien ami*', and there was a command performance; but it had been her only work in the five years before it came on and she was aware of a creeping sterility in her. She had been offered £1,000 for her memoirs, and wrote an addition while she was in the Strand. She had agreed with Longmans to choose and write introductory 'Remarks' to a selection of plays in ten volumes to be called *The British Theatre*. For a woman to write criticism was an innovation and she had the greatest difficulty with the Remarks in spite of her own experience in many of the plays. She writes with little grace or perception, treating the views of Queen Elizabeth on a level with those of Johnson. In 1808, when she reprinted *The Jealous Wife*, by the elder Colman, who had accepted and revised *The Mogul Tale*, she commented that after writing it, 'Mr. Colman's talents for dramatic writing failed; or, at least, his ardour abated.' The younger Colman came to his father's defence at once with an attack on 'an ingenious lady, who was originally encouraged, and brought forward, as an authoress, by *that very man*.' Mrs. Inchbald replied with apparent spirit, but finally lost any confidence she had had in herself as a critic. When her *British Theatre* proved a marked success, she was asked to make a selection of farces, and she refused to preface them with any comment at all.

In the preface to *A Simple Story*, Mrs. Inchbald had confessed to 'the utmost detestation to the fatigue of inventing', and she now found that her fatigue amounted to a kind of paralysis. In April 1801, she had been struck in the face 'by a cask' while making her way among rioters demonstrating in support of the Radical Sir Francis Burdett, and she was inclined to date her creative failure from that moment. But there was another and steadily increasing threat to her own reputation as a novelist in the emergence of Maria Edgeworth, who was sixteen years younger than herself and had no apparent limit to her powers. Miss Edgeworth published *Castle Rackrent* in 1800, *Belinda* and *Moral Tales* in 1801, *Irish Bulls* in 1802, *The Modern Griselda* and *Popular Tales* in 1804, and *Leonora* in 1806. She was praised by the critics for an ease of style and a steadiness of vision which matched her regularity. Mrs. Inchbald, according to Boaden, 'persisted in many ineffectual attempts' to write a further novel after the blow in her face, but at last 'submitted'. Her submission was 'unwilling', but she must have recognized that she could no more compete with Miss Edgeworth than she could have done with Mrs. Siddons at the time when she planned to emigrate to India.

For the Kembles indeed Mrs. Inchbald now had some sympathy. A boy actor, Master Betty, had become the craze of London. He deposed the Kembles from their throne and appeared in her own play. She hated 'all *prodigies*' and was particularly disgusted by this one, but she heard critics in Covent Garden solemnly compare him with Garrick. 'All that is said for him is in a *loud* voice, and all against him in a *low* one,' and she seemed to be watching the end of her own era. In 1806 she did not visit the theatre at all.

Her other sisters were in failing health. Her favourite, Dolly, was so often ill in 1808 that Mrs. Inchbald grew irritated, especially when Dolly's landlady suggested that she was not sending enough money. She replied to the landlady with details of the last £100 she had sent and to Dolly with advice on her diet.

Take chocolate for breakfast. If you be faint, wine and toasted bread between breakfast and dinner; *and thus vary your dinner each day*:—Sunday, a joint of meat; Monday, two lean mutton chops boiled but not stewed, with an onion, a turnip, and a carrot; Tuesday, a beef-steak, preferably beef roasted; Wednesday, a broiled mutton chop; Thursday, a veal cutlet; Friday [for religious reasons], stewed oysters or eggs; Saturday, nice boiled beef from the cook's shop, a rabbit, or anything more novel you can think of.

Eat, whenever you have an appetite, but never eat too heartily, especially off different things . . . but go to bed satisfied, or you will not sleep.

Dolly rallied under this intensive treatment, and Mrs. Inchbald was able to take her for an airing in a coach in June 1809, only to hear that she died almost at once after their return.

Meanwhile she sometimes thought of the invasion, which had first struck her as a possibility at Mrs. Wyatt's school in 1803. The floor above her lodgings in the Strand was rented by a Mr. Hood, who was so ardent a Napoleonist that he used to break in on her 'two or three times a day' to give her details of Jena and Austerlitz. She relied on Mr. Hood to tell her more news than she could find in her newspaper, and when Mrs. Phillips invited her to escape from London for a week with herself and the King's surgeon in the country, she refused. 'I regret the calamity which has fallen on Germany,' she wrote back, 'but it has reconciled my little hovel to me. A dungeon would hardly seem lonely with so sublime a subject for meditation.' She would only accept her invitation 'when the war is over'.

In 1807, when Napoleon closed the ports of Europe to British ships, she was convinced by the son-in-law of Thomas Erskine, who had been Lord Chancellor, that she should 'make a small purchase of *land* and not trust all my money in the funds'. She asked Mrs. Phillips to keep her eyes open in Norfolk. 'I do not care how small a farm I am mistress of provided it will only keep me a cow, a sheep, a pig, and a donkey, in case of invasion or other equally perilous event to the Bank of England.' She had no real intention of leaving London, and looked around on its borders for a farm near Edgware. As the blockade began to take effect, she refused to sympathize with the losses of English merchants—'they have always pleaded for the war, gloried in it; and let them now partake of its pains, as they did of its former pleasures'. When her own interests began to suffer in 1809 after the battle of Wagram, she made light of it. 'I feel such interest in the war in Germany,' she told Mrs. Phillips, 'that it almost repays me for the two shillings in every pound which was stopped at the Bank out of my dividend last Thursday. The triumph of Napoleon will perhaps avenge me!' Once she admitted to a little thrill of delight at the expectation of England's defeat. 'It is probable that, only through bitter adversity, we shall ever ascend to prosperity, and the interesting manner in which the adversity is likely to come is highly gratifying to my romantic sense of chivalry.'

For a moment in 1809, when Drury Lane Theatre burnt down five months after Covent Garden, it seemed as if the invasion had come. Mrs. Inchbald did not see the first of these fires, but she woke up just before midnight when Drury Lane was alight and the flames blowing down towards the Strand. At first she watched from a window in a north room.

I love sublime and terrific sights, but this was so terrible I ran from it; and in my own room was astonished by a prospect more beautiful, more brilliantly and calmly celestial, than ever met my eye. No appearance of fire from my window except the light of its beams; and this was so powerful, that the river, the houses on its banks, the Surrey hills beyond, every boat upon the water, every spire of a church, Somerset House and its terrace on the side,—all looked like one enchanted spot, such as a poet paints, in colours more bright than nature ever displayed in this foggy island.

It was almost as if an avenging angel had set fire to the world which had been hers.

When her sister Dolly died in 1809, leaving her with only one other sister, Ann Hunt, Mrs. Inchbald realized that she was herself getting old. Holcroft died in the same year, and she sent money to his wife and children. Sir Thomas Gage had been dead for ten years. She wrote to Mrs. Phillips that when she looked in the glass, only one thing prevented her from 'screaming with horror'. Her beauty had seemed to her more gratifying 'than any *other* gifts in the world', and she survived by means of 'APATHY'. But she clenched her teeth on the word; apathy was 'the substitute for patience', a necessity of old age. 'I had thirty-five years of perpetual crowd and bustle. I have now had five of almost continual loneliness and quiet;—extremes justified only by necessity.'

She had forgiven her young friend Amelia Alderson for her interest in Godwin as soon as she married the painter, John Opie, in 1798, and the two women continued to meet regularly. Amelia was an auburn-haired replica of herself, nearly twenty years younger, less successful, childless, but with her own literary and stage ambitions, and the same interest in Napoleon. In Paris in the Peace of Amiens Mrs. Opie had seen the great man face to face and so close that she 'shook with excitement'. Mrs. Inchbald tried to extract an avowal of her unreserved admiration, but Mrs. Opie could not rid herself of a suspicion that Napoleon was the enemy of liberty, 'a sort of Dictator', who had turned his back on the revolutionary example set by Washington. In 1809 Mrs. Inchbald grew indignant with her for finding proof in Napoleon's seizure of Spain and declaration of war on the Spanish people. She lectured Mrs. Opie as if she had been her sister Dolly. She had 'no doubt,' she wrote on 7 December, that many Spaniards 'of the first importance' invited Napoleon to take over the government.

That he did so by artifice, I can only excuse, upon the supposition that he meant thus to spare the people all that calamity, which open violence must now draw upon them. No doubt his reign would have been a blessing to them, would they at first have submitted. But now the avenger is the character he must take, and we shall have to lament another nation, added to the number of those, on whom we have forced him to draw the sword.

In the summer of 1810 she moved away from the wreckage above the Strand to rooms on the top floor of St. George's Terrace overlooking Hyde Park from the north. She now did most of her own housework in order to increase her payments to Mrs. Hunt. She could have put her capital into an annuity which would have saved her from such economies, but she was already conscious of a rising generation of nephews and nieces who needed her help. The view across the park was splendid. 'I *now* see two of the most sublime sights, every fine day that this world can bestow, and I see them both from my window—the rising and the setting sun.'

On the border of the park she was disturbed by the firing of the guns to mark the stages of Wellington's progress through Spain on the heels of Masséna. The guns, she said in the spring of 1811, fired for 'pretended' victories. On 6 April before the battle of Fuentes d'Onoro, a visitor told her that Masséna had already been beaten, and she was sunk in gloom, but next day she was 'glad to find the guns fired yesterday for little boast'. As the light of the fire which destroyed Drury Lane seemed to her 'celestial', so she felt an almost religious appreciation of Napoleon's communiqués; they were 'miracles of composition' which had 'wisdom' and the 'plain grandeur of truth'. 'Our great enemy,' she told Mrs. Opie, 'is less wicked than most heroes and politicians have been; at the same time a vast deal wiser than them all.'

The defeats of 1812 and 1813 could not be laughed off, but she thought they would be made good. The year 1813, says Boaden, was 'all but devoted to her religious duties.' She went to the Spanish and Portuguese chapels, and when her confessor became seriously ill, put herself under the direction of Dr. Gandolphy, a Jesuit educated at Liége, who was giving dangerously provocative sermons in the Spanish chapel 'in defence of the ancient faith'. She brought her sister to live next door so that she could supervise her health. She went out little, but met Miss Edgeworth and once Mme. de Staël. 'I admired Madame de Staël much,' she told Mrs. Phillips; 'she talked to me the whole time; so did Miss Edgeworth. . . . These authoresses suppose me dead, and seem to pay a tribute to my memory.'

The abdication of Napoleon in April 1814 was 'so little expected' by Mrs. Inchbald, that she was literally sunken and dejected as at some public calamity.

The rejoicings of her country were bitter to her; and from her windows, she could not well avoid seeing, on the 12th of June, the Sovereigns of Russia and Prussia, with their suites, enjoying the Sunday ride of Hyde Park, and a very absurd review of troops there on the 20th. . . . Under the iron scraping of the cavalry, and the dust from the sand, every blade of grass seemed as if burnt up.

In another two months she was severely ill, and the King's surgeon, Dr. Phillips, visited her. He found her unexpectedly resilient, and she was soon able to take Mrs. Phillips to see the portrait of Napoleon by David and Lefebvre on exhibition in Leicester Square. It is perhaps the only time an exhibition of a single portrait has kept open for six months at an entrance fee of a shilling. It was advertised in October 1814 as 'a magnificent painting of Buonaparte taken in Paris by his special permission, on his return from Moscow'. He stood upright on the imperial throne as if no defeat had occurred. Some of the visitors, like Crabb Robinson, came away with a sense of guilt, but Boaden credits Mrs. Inchbald with the kind of veneration she had felt for her print of Dr. Warren: *'Tacito venerantur murmura Numen.'* Hazlitt, who went in a less religious mood, thought it best 'when each part is seen through a magnifying glass'.

In March 1815, when Napoleon landed from Elba at the beginning of the

Hundred Days, Mrs. Inchbald was fully restored. 'The newspapers must afford you great amusement just now,' wrote Miss Edgeworth's brother, but she had come to believe that 'the Bank must break in good earnest'; she paid 'every debt I owe in the world', and for the first time destroyed 'a vast heap of papers'. Her misery after Waterloo was confused with her alarm for her sister, Ann Hunt, who became ill in her turn and died in the severe cold of February 1816. Mrs. Inchbald 'cried with cold' many times that winter, and reflected that she was the only survivor of the Stanningfield family. She was now in need of support.

There was a sense in which she was glad to move into the terrace opposite the Hollands. 'I am now,' she wrote to Mrs. Opie, 'once again living something like a lady opposite Holland House, Kensington, where I hope you will call and see me. . . .' She invited Mrs. Phillips 'when I have been settled a few days—*not before*: it's No. 4, Earl's Terrace, opposite Holland House.' But her object was not to gain admission to the Holland House circle so much as to re-establish her own. In February 1816 she refused an invitation from the poet, Samuel Rogers, to meet Byron in his box at Drury Lane; it had been her rule never to sit in the boxes where she was introduced to the aristocracy, but to watch the performance from the pit, where she was sometimes recognized by the audience.

In the boarding-house she was greeted by Miss Whitfield, whose parents had been with her in the company at Covent Garden. Miss Whitfield gave her a feeling of youth, because it was her brother with whom, at the age of thirty-five, Mrs. Inchbald had once gone around Covent Garden ringing at the doors of the houses and running away before they were opened. Miss Whitfield introduced her as a writer of eminence to a widow, Mrs. Henley, who was in her eighties, and two elderly maiden ladies, Miss Williams and Miss Whitingdale. The company may not have accepted all that was said on Mrs. Inchbald's behalf until it was confirmed by the repeated acclamation of Hazlitt, but they began to succumb almost at once to her charm, which showed itself in all kinds of minor acts of solicitude.

From Mrs. Inchbald's point of view there were immediate rewards to be had from the human problems which now pressed themselves on her. Her companions suffered from 'swoln legs, nervous head-aches, or slow fevers, brought on by loss of appetite, violent thirst, broken sleep and other dog-day complaints.' She was used to prescribing for such things in her sisters, and was in a strong position to overcome the resistance of strangers by quoting her medical connections. She still insisted on paying fees at the fashionable level to Dr. Phillips of Pall Mall, and when John Taylor, the son of her oculist, was in financial difficulties in 1818, she sent him £50 by means which were unlikely to be attributed to her. Davis, who had first done her hair forty years previously, called for the last time, gave her his best thanks, and died in May 1817. She sent money to a niece and the niece's son, to the younger of her husband's illegitimate sons, and to a nephew, George Huggins, who had asked her for a lump sum of £400 on the success of *Everyone Has His Fault*.

Meanwhile there were visitors who conferred a different kind of honour on her. Kemble had long since recovered from the setback of Master Betty and was still apparently at the height of his powers when he decided to retire from the stage at the age of sixty. Talma, who was Napoleon's favourite actor, came across from Paris to attend his farewell performance as Coriolanus before an enraptured audience on 23 June 1817, and four days later Lord Holland took the chair at a banquet in Kemble's honour. Kemble and his wife twice came out to dinner at Holland House[1] before these proceedings and twice called on Mrs. Inchbald to persuade her to attend. When she proved adamant, Kemble brought out Talma and presented him to her.

The great French actor reciprocated Napoleon's admiration. After Waterloo he had gone to him at Malmaison and offered him his savings, and when Kemble presented him to Mrs. Inchbald he had round his neck the Emperor's medallion bearing the inscription '*tibi semper fidelis*'. Talma did not go on with the Kembles to Holland House, perhaps because Lord Holland had warned him that the scandal of his going there would reduce his chances of bringing back his patron from St. Helena.

William Godwin had left his card on Mrs. Inchbald on the north side of Hyde Park, but she had not acknowledged it. She had begun to forget his marriage but was then unable to forgive his politics, which had an irritating resemblance to those of Mrs. Opie. Godwin had not proved an apostate, like Coleridge or Wordsworth, nor was he unaccountable, like Byron. As late as 1801, after the Italian campaigns and the destruction of the Holy Roman Empire, he had supported Napoleon as 'an auspicious and beneficent genius'. But when Godwin was convinced that Napoleon had become an aggressor, he withdrew his support. He had logic, though not Mrs. Inchbald, on his side. He held it as fundamental that no state had the right to interfere in the internal affairs of another. The original war against the French Republic had seemed to him an extreme violation of this principle, and he believed it must fail because the French had been given an irresistible motive for defending themselves. But when Allied aggression had been repulsed and the war became a series of Napoleonic victories, Godwin acknowledged that 'the goodness of the cause changed sides'. The subjugation of Austria, Prussia, Poland, and Spain seemed to him so many crimes against

On 15 December 1816 and 11 May 1817.

liberty, and he was positively delighted by the Abdication, which spread dismay among most Napoleonists.

Then in 1815 he found himself against all probability back in line with Mrs. Inchbald, and returned to the fray with two important letters to the *Morning Chronicle*. Napoleon's escape from Elba left him unmoved. He thought it justified by the Allied intention to remove him to St. Helena; Napoleon had 'a right to anticipate that removal'. He had been welcomed by the people of France; the entry into Paris had been 'triumphant'. And Godwin was finally confirmed in his pro-French position by the Allied announcement from Vienna in March 1815 that Napoleon, like the Republic in 1793, had 'placed himself without the pale of civil and social relations'. This act of excommunication seemed to Godwin intolerable because it denied a people the fundamental right to choose their own government. Napoleon was now under popular control, ruling by sufferance. War would produce 'a tremendous reaction' of the kind that had left the French in possession of the field at Valmy. 'In a question like this,' he concluded, 'I feel that we cannot succeed and indeed I frankly confess I do not even wish we should succeed.'

Godwin's letters of 1815 share the political position of Whitbread and the authentic defeatism of Mrs. Inchbald. He was entering his sixties, and felt an overwhelming disaster was about to fall on the world. Britain seemed to him at the end of her economic resources. On the eve of Waterloo, he thought the war would 'not improbably last longer than I shall'.

He had in fact another twenty years to live, and although his daughter, Harriet Shelley, described him as growing 'old and unimpassioned', he recaptured in this last phase some of the enthusiasm of his youth. Lord Holland had come to his assistance by collecting and himself providing capital for the publication of his school primers, which were to correct the course of society. These were written under the name of Baldwin. 'I believed it necessary to substitute a feigned name,' Godwin wrote to Holland in 1806, 'on account of the clerical and Antijacobinical prejudices which are afloat against me.' In spite of this precaution, in 1813 he was charged in a state paper with teaching pernicious ideas to the young. In his *History of England*, published two years after Trafalgar, he had written as if France had won the war. 'The French Revolution produced one very extraordinary man, Napoleon Bonaparte, as the English civil war against Charles I produced Oliver Cromwell.' In the *History of Greece*, Marathon emerges as the crucial battle; 'the question was now to be tried whether a set of plain and frugal men, the citizens, as we would call them, of a few insignificant republics,' should check the King of Persia who lived in 'the wantonness and effeminacy of splendour'.

Godwin visited Mrs. Inchbald in both her lodging-houses in the square in 1816 and 1817, and the memory of these visits was warm enough to make him remind her of them when she next barred his entry. They were, he wrote to her, 'one reason of my confidence'.

The two of them had much to discuss in the year after Waterloo. They had not only to wring their hands at the treatment of Napoleon and the tide of reaction submerging Europe; she had again been working on her Memoirs and brought the four unwieldy volumes out to show him from the box where she kept them locked up. Once Godwin brought Constable, who had more professional experience publishing than himself, and they took the book away with them. In an interim report Godwin wrote that

Mr Constable has flown with the eagerness of a lover to the perusal of your MS. . . . I never saw a man so fascinated. I believe, the instant I leave the apartment at any time, he takes up the book and kisses it. He says he never saw a MS. so beautiful; you best know whether, in saying so, he alludes to the elegance of the penmanship, or the charms of the narrative.[1] Mr Constable is a widower, of an amorous complexion, and I am not sure that he has not been guilty of the indelicacy of having endeavoured to prevail on the book to come to bed to him.

While she waited for the verdict on her Memoirs, Mrs. Inchbald had flattering letters from Miss Edgeworth. Their correspondence had begun almost ten years before, when Miss Edgeworth had made the disarming confession that *A Simple Story* seemed to her a great book. 'I never read *any* novel,' she wrote, 'I except *none*—that affected me so strongly, or that so completely possessed me with the belief in the real existence of the people it represents.' With the same humility she invited Mrs. Inchbald to criticize her own novels, sending them one by one as they appeared. Miss Edgeworth was probably unaware that the mere appearance of the books was a reproach to Mrs. Inchbald's 'apathy', and she had to accept pointed criticism in reply. But Miss Edgeworth was modest, and in ten years only protested once.

Miss Edgeworth's novel, *Vivian*, deals with the destruction of a young man on the premature death of his father by the training given him by his mother, Lady Mary Vivian, who sends her son out into the world 'over-educated, over-instructed, over-dosed', so that he is unable to think for himself. To Miss Edgeworth's astonishment, her critic suggested that Lady Vivian had been right, and her son was to blame for his own weakness. 'I do not know what you mean by saying that every sensible mother is like Lady Mary Vivian,' she wrote to Mrs. Inchbald, in September 1812. 'You are requested to explain.'

If Mrs. Inchbald made any further justification of Lady Vivian, it did not deter Miss Edgeworth from sending her new novels *Harrington* and *Ormond* to Mrs. Inchbald in her boarding house in 1817. They lay, each more

---

[1] Mrs. Inchbald's handwriting was bad.

F

reproachful than the last, beside *The Court of Queen Elizabeth*, by Miss Aikin, which was Mrs. Inchbald's preferred reading in 1818.

By 1819 it must have been clear to Mrs. Inchbald that her position was not very different from Napoleon's on St. Helena. The *new* faces with *old* observations which surrounded her in the boarding-house had never acquired the reality of those she had loved. Her friends were dead or disappearing, and she lacked even the wish to attract others. The family on which she had depended as much as they had on her, was cut off. Her Memoirs had bound her to the past, but in 1818 she suddenly demanded them back from Constable, and destroyed them. A note in her handwriting reads,

Query—'What I should wish *done* at the point of death?'
Dr. P.   'Do it NOW.'   4 volumes destroyed.

'Dr. P.' was no longer the King's doctor, but Dr. Poynter, a radical divine, who had been educated like Kemble at Douai. He must have put it to her that the damage done by her Memoirs would not be confined to her own reputation.

In April 1819 she put herself back in the hands of the Catholics by moving to Kensington House, a retreat which had its own chapel and eminent priests. She still sometimes went out. On Sundays she preferred to go to mass in a chapel in Holland Street, and she saw the disturbances in the street during the attempt to depose Queen Caroline before the coronation of the Regent. It was only her sense of tact as a Catholic which restrained her from signing one of the petitions of loyalty to Queen Caroline which were circulating in the suburb.

At sixty-six she was often unwell. She refused to see Robert Inchbald when he tried to force his way to her with demands for money, and he had to be thrown out, but she saw Kemble to say good-bye at the end of 1820, when he left for Rome and his retirement in Switzerland. Mrs. Opie followed the example of Miss Edgeworth by sending her books, and seemed equally unaware of the irritation she caused. 'By the bye,' Mrs. Inchbald wrote to Mrs. Opie at the end of 1820, 'your books are lying on the table of our drawing room most days, and I hear great praise of them; and yet I do not feel the slightest curiosity to read them.' There were a hundred, she complained, by Sir Walter Scott. 'Besides, I have so many reflections concerning a *future* world . . . and there are on this awful subject, so many books still unread, that I think every moment lost, which impedes my gaining information from holy and learned authors.' Mrs. Opie was becoming a Quaker and in no position to help her.

She herself was about to emigrate for the last time. Her occasional fasts had always been hard to distinguish from her attempts to keep down her weight as her anxiety mounted at the loss of her figure. Boaden suggests that she brought serious complications on herself by tight-lacing.

She died on 1 August 1821, a few weeks after the news of Napoleon's death reached London. Godwin entered the event as tenderly as his standards allowed by writing into his diary the single letter E. To Hazlitt he dwelt 'with peculiar delight' on the days he had passed with her.

# 3. A Clue to Byron

*The Young Lord is a fine sharp boy. . . .*
John Hanson to James Farquhar, M.P.

I

When Byron left the country in 1816 on a wave of conservative hostility, his solicitor, Hanson, who had tried with Lord Holland to save Byron's marriage, gave up his establishment in Bloomsbury and came out to the west side of Changeur's square, where most of the houses were still empty shells. He installed himself soon after Byron reached Venice and continued to run his practice from Chancery Lane. A year later he brought his family and divided them up between one of the finished houses in Earls Terrace and the more modest house he had first taken in the square behind it. As time passed the gaps in the terraces slowly filled, and in 1820, when the space next to Hanson's original house was occupied by a Bond Street tailor, he and his family moved out. One of his sons, Newton, returned to the square as an old man in the middle of the century.

To some extent, no doubt, it was the Byron scandal which brought Hanson out into the wilds. He was a conspicuous figure with his carriage and four, but below Holland House the air was still congenial enough for him to be received with honour. He was already known in the district, having bought Dr. Hunter's famous house at Earls Court. For several years he had been a trustee of the turnpike, and was prominent among the trustees of the square appointed in 1819. In the meantime he drove off in the autumn of 1818 to visit Byron in Venice for the final sale of Newstead Abbey. He was appointed executor with Hobhouse in Byron's last will, and returned to the square after making his client very angry as well as frightened of what was to come.

Hanson, indeed, had a bigger scandal to hide than Byron's, though it was still developing more or less in seclusion. The main reason why he came to the square was probably that he was better placed to deal with it there than in Bloomsbury. When the facts finally came out, in 1823, Byron was beyond caring, and it was his executor Hobhouse who found himself in association with the most notorious lawyer in the country. 'By appointment to meet *Hanson*,' he then noted in his diary, with a slight over-emphasis which was characteristic of him. 'The Hanson,' he added.

John Hanson had first been recommended to Mrs. Byron by a Mr. James Farquhar, M.P. for Aberdeenshire, as the ideal family solicitor, and his influence made itself felt before the birth of her son. At her lying-in, the midwife and nurse were both nominees of Mrs. Hanson, and thereafter the couple were involved at the turning-points of Byron's life. At six, when he unexpectedly became heir-presumptive to the title, Hanson was given legal charge of his interests. When he was ten, it was Hanson and his wife who welcomed him as Lord Byron to Newstead Abbey. Hanson persuaded Lord Carlisle to accept the formality of guardianship and entered Byron at Harrow with his own sons, Hargreaves and Charles.

In the drama of Byron's life as it has survived, Hanson has only a walk-on part. Such politics as he had were those of a right-wing Whig. His patron was Lord Grenville, who led the brief coalition of All the Talents. Although Hanson claimed the role of a stepfather, Byron treated him like an old retainer, to be confided in at need and consulted on the law but rebuked as a servant. Byron himself did not see him as a person in his own right.

Of his real father Byron had a distinct picture before he was four when Captain Byron left him and his mother. 'I was not so young when my father died', he told Medwin, 'but that I perfectly remember him.' He had the glamour of a captain in the Guards and the elegance of the French military academy in which he was trained, but he was known as Mad Jack. He twice married for money and ruined both his wives. The second heiress, Byron's mother, found his cynicism irresistible. Even when he had reduced her to poverty, she welcomed his visits and yielded up some of the last resources she needed for herself and the child. When he finally deserted her for adventures in Paris, where he died, she held her child closer and alternately spoilt him and blamed him for being like his father. He was 'a little dog of a Byron', 'a Byron all over'. She was descended from the Stuarts at a further remove than Fox's mother, and impressed it on Byron as yet another reproach to his father, who was only descended from a line of rogue barons. But her Stuart ancestry did not prevent her from being a Whig. She admired the French Revolution and accepted the deposition of Louis XVI.

While Byron loved his mother, and maintained at her death 'she was without a *vice*', he was loyal to his father and imitated him by removing himself as far away from her as possible. 'The instant I hear of her arrival', he wrote from Trinity College to Hanson, 'I quit Cambridge, though Rustication or Expulsion be the consequence. . . .' And to his half-sister, Augusta, when he was at Harrow, he declared that he was 'in great hope' that the Hansons would take him for the Christmas vacation. 'I shall do all I can to avoid a visit to my mother wherever she is. . . .' He found her unbearably dictatorial.

The anxiety to disengage himself from his mother did not mean that Byron felt he belonged to Hanson. 'Home have I none,' he wrote to the solicitor when he was twenty, 'and if there was a possibility of getting out of the country, I would gladly avail myself of it.' To the man who had done what he could to give him a second home, this was a cold statement. Hanson had taken his charge seriously from the beginning. He had plenty of other irons in the fire, as Solicitor of the Stamp Office (to which he was appointed by Lord Grenville), as Secretary to the Chief Justice in Eyre, and eventually Solicitor to the Royal Military College. Yet he saw to all the important influences in the Byron household, and got rid of the Calvinist maid, Mrs. Gray, as soon as he found that she drank in ale-houses and left the eleven-year-old boy outside.

When Byron was four, the local doctor in Aberdeenshire had consulted the eminent Dr. John Hunter of Earls Court about his foot. Dr. Hunter lived opposite Lord Kensington's manor house and Hanson bought the doctor's house in 1797, four years after the doctor's death. Hunter was an anatomist with a passion for observing and dissecting every kind of zoological oddity. The remains of the dens and pits in which he kept his animals were visible until late in the nineteenth century, and Byron may have seen the place complete with its inhabitants during his early treatment. He spent many holidays there after Hanson bought the house, and no doubt regretted that the unimaginative solicitor failed to populate the cages as in the past. Byron's love of menageries and the least tameable of pets may date from this time. He had a lifelong feud with Hanson about the need to keep animals.

The holidays were as gay and carefree as they could be in the circumstances, though scenes of violence were never far under the surface. Mrs. Hanson had eight children, and Byron was on close terms with the elder brothers, Hargreaves and Charles, and according to Lord Lovelace, on too close terms with the eldest daughter, Mary Anne.

Mrs. Hanson was a kindly person who tried always to interpret the escapades of her difficult charge in the best possible sense. When the weak-minded Earl of Portsmouth was staying with them on the eve of his first marriage, he aggressively tweaked Byron's ear. It was not much of an assault, but Byron picked up a conch shell which happened to be within reach, flung it at his head, and smashed a pane of glass behind him. In the uproar which followed, Mrs. Hanson tried to restore order by saying that Byron had not meant it for the Earl. 'But I *did* mean it!' Byron retorted. 'I will teach a fool of an earl to pinch another noble's ear.'

If Mrs. Hanson was gentle, her husband provided something more than the hardness necessary to secure the family's standard of living. Byron maintained that Hanson could not be moved by anything outside 'the statute or record'. But it was not usually Byron who felt the impact, though he was treated sternly over pocket-money and other matters where his own views might have been expected to carry weight. Three people, for instance, were concerned in his choice of university: Hanson, Lord Carlisle, and Byron himself. 'Mr H. recommends Cambridge,' he reported to Augusta, 'Lord Carlisle allows me to chuse for myself, and I must own I prefer Oxford.' It was thus two to one against Hanson. Some months before actually going up to Cambridge, Byron repeated, 'I prefer Oxford but I am not violently bent upon it, and whichever is determined on will have my concurrence.' He had had to concur with Hanson's minority of one. Nearly twenty years later, in Italy, he wrote, 'I wished to go to Oxford and not to Cambridge.'

One of the drawbacks about Newstead Abbey, when it came to Byron with his title, was the number of old retainers who had been allowed by his eccentric uncle to keep on their tenancies at modest rents. For reasons of prestige Byron would not at first allow Hanson to sell the place, although the attorney wanted to—'I suspect', Byron wrote to Hobhouse, 'because some of his clients want to purchase it.' The solicitor saw that the logical alternative was to throw out the retainers, which he did. The rents, Byron noted, not ungratefully, were then 'raised beyond what I could have done, because I should not have liked to turn out the old (though stupid) tenants, and all that has been affected.'

Hanson's letters evicting the tenants extended over nearly a decade, from the time Byron left Newstead to its sale in 1817. The evictions took place in two waves, the first as Byron was preparing for the Grand Tour which resulted in *Childe Harold*, and the second as his marriage was breaking up and he was planning his own exile. Notices to quit 'the property which you now rent under the Right Honble. Gordon Lord Byron' were served on Whitehead, who had built his own house, and on 'Bell's woman', who pleaded that her husband's death on the estate gave her 'a right to continue on the farm to bring the children up'. Her goods at auction consisted of three cart-horses, ten cows, and two pigs. Mr. Mealey, Hanson's agent, who watched the sale, noticed that her son bought very little: the clover and hay, a cart and wagon-rope, and a cow crib.

Byron's mother extended the carnage by telling Hanson she wished 'some plan could be hit upon to lessen the expense of the live animals'. When she took up residence at Newstead soon afterwards, Mr. Mealey was able to report progress in decimating the menagerie. 'Mrs Byron has interred 5 doggs, the Bear is dead'—which left only the wolf unaccounted for. Among the human tenants, bailiffs and sheriff's officers were constant visitors. As late as 1815 Hanson distributed letters which read: 'Lord Byron is very much surprised to learn from Mr Mealey that you object to pay your rent as desired. I am therefore directed by his lordship to say that you will immediately comply with the direction that has been given you, otherwise you will be put to trouble.' The recalcitrants like Whitehead, who had several small children, argued that they had improved the property. Another of them, Whiteman, had the bailiffs in three times. Another, Walker, sold up his stock, paid Hanson £185, and left for Derbyshire with four horses, two wagons, and his furniture. The Sheriff's officer took possession of Whiteman's farm. Byron came of age when Hanson's policy was first put into effect and he could of course have intervened at any time during the years of fame to save his tenants.

As an instrument for extracting what the world could be made to yield, Hanson was clearly valuable, but as a father he was as cynical and intent on pillaging women as Captain Byron. Proof of this came with the marriage in 1814 of Mary Anne, his eldest daughter.

The middle-aged Lord Portsmouth, who had nearly fallen victim to Byron's marksmanship in Earls Court, outlived his first wife and in 1814 was a technically eligible widower. His estates produced between £17,000 and £18,000 a year, but his wealth, which was in trust, was offset by his deterioration into imbecility. Even by Regency standards his habits were extreme. He rode to his wife's funeral beside the coachman and tried to whip the undertaker. He ate, said a butler, 'not like other people, but voraciously and drank as if he would swallow glass and all.' He helped to drive cattle to the slaughter-house and dispatched them with an axe, shouting, 'That serves them right, ambitious toads!'

The Earl had one redeeming feature: he could be cowed. A threat 'to tell Mr. Hanson' was as potent as a whip. He had thus been kept more or less within bounds by a male nurse, his wife, and the exertions of four trustees, among whom Hanson was dominant. As soon as the Countess was buried, Hanson instructed the male nurse to bring the Earl up to London. With the help of his sister, but not his wife, he bullied and coaxed his daughter, Mary Anne, who was twenty-five years younger than Portsmouth, into the idea of marrying him. When, after a week, she yielded, Hanson arranged for the wedding to take place immediately, on 7 March 1814, by licence, in Bloomsbury Chapel, and got Byron to agree to give her away. He had prepared the way with Byron, but omitted to inform his fellow trustees of his plans.

After the wedding the Earl made a new will. His fortune went to Mary Anne, except for £2,000 to Hanson himself; Mary Anne became sole executor.

Byron had noticed little at the ceremony but the speed at which the Earl made his responses—'as if he had got the whole by heart', he recorded in his diary, 'and if anything, was rather before the priest.' He found himself giggling compulsively at the exhortation and joined their left hands by mistake, so that he had to undo the tangle. It did not escape him that Mrs. Hanson, the mother, was crying bitterly, but he reassured himself that women often reacted in that way.

In an affidavit he soon had to draft in defence of Hanson, he insisted that everything had been normal. He had walked to the chapel with the Earl, whose behaviour was calm. If he had thought him insane, he would have advised Hanson not to permit the marriage. The Earl 'seemed particularly attentive to the priest, and gave the responses audibly and very distinctly'.

Meanwhile Byron had given a different account to Hobhouse, with whom he spent the evening after the wedding. Hanson, according to this version, had intervened to prevent Portsmouth from marrying at the wish of his brother, Lord Grantley, also a trustee.[1] Byron impressed on Hobhouse the advantages of the arrangement to Mary Anne.

It took a decade for the consequences to become public and they then occupied a page of *The Times* every day for nearly three weeks. But the immediate comments were restrained. Jane Austen, who had been a neighbour of Lord Portsmouth in Hampshire, saw the announcement in the papers. 'What cruel weather this is!' she wrote to her sister; 'and here is Lord Portsmouth married to Miss Hanson.' A fortnight later, Mrs. Hanson suddenly died. She had suffered 'of a typhus fever', according to the *Gentleman's Magazine*, but her youngest son, Newton, wrote afterwards that it was from grief.

'From personal experience,' said Byron, some time before these events, 'I can vouch that my Attorneo is by no means the tenderest of men. . . .' But the question which should now have forced itself on him was whether he was not one of the most unscrupulous. Such ideas when they were pressed on Byron by Hobhouse, who wanted an investigation of Hanson's legal charges, had a way of irritating him. That Hanson had always been with him seemed reason enough that he should remain. 'You should have advised me before', he wrote from Venice, when Kinnaird, his banker, sent him a warning some years after Mary Anne's marriage, '—because though I generally suspect a man of being a rascal, I do not set him down as an actual felon (even though an attorney) without some overt indications, or at least previous hints. . . .'

But was this true, and had there been no overt indications or hints of

---

[1] There were still other accounts, of which perhaps the ugliest was from a physician of the Bethlem Hospital, who was told by Portsmouth that Hanson would only consent to a second marriage if it was to his daughter.

Hanson's character? When pressed for his view at the time of the marriage, Byron gave it with reservation. 'I have known him as a child,' he declared, as if that were in some sense enough, but added that 'as to his integrity, or ability, I cannot speak.' And without further investigation into his integrity, he went on to show that he could in fact speak of his ability, which was great. Byron could have got rid of him at any point, but fifteen years passed after he reached his majority, and he never did. The solicitor stood at his cradle and rode with Hobhouse in the first carriage at his funeral.

Byron's letters to Hanson are among his most pathetic. They are often wavering and slight, as if uncertain of the personality he is addressing. At first he seems to be making shy conversation, with little portmanteau jokes about experiences they had shared. At Earls Court and Hanson's country house in Berkshire, they went shooting together when Byron was a boy. 'I am glad you approve of my Gun . . . ,' he wrote from Harrow. 'I hope your Campaigns against the Partridges and the rest of the feathered tribe have been attended to with no serious accidents.' Three years later, when Hanson was ill, after a violent dispute about money, he wrote from Cambridge to Mrs. Hanson. 'Though the Governor and I have lately not been on the *best* of *Terms*, yet I should be extremely sorry to learn that he was in *danger*, and I trust he and I will live to have many more squabbles. . . .' And in another three years, from Constantinople, he could not resist telling Hanson, who was little interested in such things, how he had 'visited the plains of Troy and swam from Sestos to Abydos in the Dardanelles, any of your classical men (Hargreaves or Charles) will explain the meaning of the last performance and the old story connected with it. . . .' And he was hurt that Hanson failed to reply. There must be news of his affairs, but when he was abroad Hanson did not write to him for fifteen months at a time. 'I do conceive and declare', Byron wrote to his mother, 'that Mr Hanson has acted negligently and culpably in not appraising me of his proceedings; I will also add uncivilly.' One may be forgiven for guessing it was the incivility that drew blood. Hanson had evicted the Newstead tenants, married off Mary Anne to a cretin, and himself retreated to the outer suburbs, but Byron remained to him 'Ever yours truly and affectionately'.

There was of course another side to their relations. It was also as if, from the start, Byron knew it was no use writing to Hanson about partridges or how he had swum the Hellespont. If he was only interested in 'the Statute or record', such information would not register, whether or not he followed up the classical allusions; and Byron seems to have written, on the rare occasions when he tried, with the cramping knowledge that it was unwanted.

He had two sets of terms for Hanson, affectionate ones, like 'the Governor', 'Mr H.', and 'Spooney' (or 'Old Spooney', to distinguish him from

Charles Hanson, who was 'Young Spooney'); but at the same time he was a 'rogue', a 'queer fish', a 'mountebank', 'a damned tortoise', a 'monster', and 'an attorneo'. Byron used the last word like Dr. Johnson, who 'would not speak ill of any man behind his back, but believed the man was an attorney'. In writing he almost always addressed Hanson with Dr. Johnson's 'Sir'. Though he expressed regret to Mrs. Hanson about 'the Governor's illness', he wrote to the patient himself on a similar occasion: 'Dear Sir—Your illness is more than unfortunate—at least to me.'

Byron hoped when he was at Cambridge 'to take my New Year's dinner with you *en famille*'; but he almost assaulted Hanson for failing to borrow money on his behalf. He denounced him as untrustworthy and dilatory and said he would be damned before he took his advice; but a month or so later when there was a problem about his interests on which he was consulting Kinnaird, who was supposedly more reliable, he ended by advising Kinnaird to 'ask Spooney'. It was, he told his friends, 'a great disadvantage to me to have such a solicitor. However, he was made so when I was ten years old and I have no help for it.' The fact was that he was just not prepared to dismiss him.

With Hanson's main sins and villainies, so far as we know them, Byron kept in step, and he was an accomplice in the eyes of the evicted tenants of Newstead and the increasingly miserable Lady Portsmouth. When Hanson challenged the Solicitor-General of the Prince of Wales to a duel for calling him a rascal in the aftermath of the Portsmouth marriage, it was Byron who settled the affair and we would not be surprised to have seen him fight the duel. Hanson cast him as his main witness for the defence, and morally he became so. 'I saw no appearance of entrapment or compulsion,' he protested, '. . . it was no bad bargain for either party.' In many ways, and although Byron could dissolve into kindness at a touch, he became as insensitive to personal suffering as Hanson and his father.

Before we look at the Napoleonist tendencies in Byron, we have to notice the policy Hanson adopted towards him in the period after the Portsmouth marriage. It was a development of the influence he had tried to bring to bear on him since the age of six and took account of what was to be gained from the unexpected prospect of a peerage. Byron was the heir to a great tradition, Hanson insisted, and must honour it in the normal way. At twenty-one he would enter the House of Lords, 'the walls you were born to sit within', where his talents would secure him a dominant position. But it was important to keep this goal in view and not to waste himself on frivolous pursuits. Politics, although the most important vocation, had its own blind alleys, one of which had been taken by Fox, 'your admired luminary', who preferred the company of his mistress in the country to the business of Westminster.

Since Hanson's aim was to achieve profit in his own currency from his association with Byron, the respectability of the latter's career became doubly important after Mary Anne's marriage. It was only Byron's affidavit which dissuaded Lord Eldon as Chancellor from accepting a petition soon afterwards for a trial for annulment. There was no reason why the petitioners, who included Portsmouth's brother, should not return to the attack. Much of the evidence on which they relied could be smothered—by the dismissal of servants and denials by his family—but Hanson's only positive defence was the name of Byron. It was that which had to be kept intact.

Hanson's troubles grew with the difficulty of putting a decent appearance on the proceedings in his daughter's house, where violence and madness ran riot. No sooner had he made some kind of preliminary settlement than Byron himself—at the time of Napoleon's break-up—began to show signs of emotional upheaval which threatened his reputation. Hanson did his utmost to prevent the rift between Byron and Annabella. He advised against a separation, did what he could to prevent him leaving the country, and then —when the disaster of his exile had taken place—went as far as Venice to persuade him to come back. With his champion absent and discredited he must have known it was only a question of time before Nemesis overtook him.

A bad moment had come on 6 January 1816, when Lady Byron called on him at his home with a medical journal[1] containing an account of hydrocephalus which described the symptoms she believed she had seen in Byron since their marriage. She had marked them in the margin.

The first stage of the disease needed a suspicious eye to diagnose. There are alternations between languor and activity, the eyes become dull, with 'a dark coloured line' under them, 'the appetite is capricious, the stomach distended, there is occasional thirst'. Headaches then come on; the stomach distends; lethargy grows. Treatment should consist of calomel, rhubarb, jalap or scammony, or opium as a sedative.

The second stage was due to infection of the lateral ventricles of the brain:

... for a few minutes there will be perfect silence and quietism, with a fixed steady stare of the eyes . . . when a sudden start will take place with a loud screaming and quick tossing of the arms over the head, frequent moaning, deep sighing . . . convulsions frequently take place . . . palsy supervenes, either partially or

---

[1] Hanson (and Hobhouse afterwards) called this publication the *Medical Journal*. It was probably the *Edinburgh Medical Journal* for October 1815, which has an account of hydrocephalus in two dramatic stages from which the quotations are taken. The article had probably been given Lady Byron by her Scottish doctor, Matthew Baillie, whom she had sent to examine Byron for his suicidal tendencies.

generally, and death, most commonly in one convulsive struggle, closes the painful scene.

The convulsions could only be staved off by mercury administered internally and externally, bleeding, forcible restraint.

Hanson felt in need of restraint himself when he had read the article. He had seen Byron's tantrums since childhood. He was himself a hypochondriac who knew all too well the rush of imagination from the first flicker of a symptom to a major illness. 'The symptoms', Lady Byron wrote later, 'correspond only too well not only with those in the *first*, but also the *second* stage of the Disease. . . . Not a moment must be lost.'

Hanson could not have been more angry. She was suggesting madness and the strait-jacket, which was at least as damaging to him as to Byron. He had to persuade her to go back to Kirkby in Leicestershire, where her imagination was less likely to do damage. He could account more simply for her fears, he said. For many years Byron had carried opium with him. He sometimes searched his bedroom before going to bed. He kept loaded pistols within reach, and at one time even a rope ladder because of the risk of fire. But he had not seen a trace of madness. Irritable and violent Byron might be, and the more so in his present state of financial worry, but it would pass. As to forcible restraint—and here he allowed a concession to his anger—what exactly was it Lady Byron feared? Was she perhaps frightened?

'Oh, no,' she replied. 'Not in the least; my eye can always put down his.' If she was afraid, it was simply of the violence he might do himself; she was afraid 'that Lord Byron might make an attempt on his own life'. He had told her that his grandfather had shot himself. Many years afterwards she wrote to Tom Moore that Byron's 'nearest relatives and personal attendant' had warned her of the possibility of suicide.

Hanson managed to scout these ideas so effectively that Annabella left 'more satisfied than when she entered his house'. She also promised to come back from the country 'at a minute's notice' if the malady (as she continued to call it) required her presence in London. Hanson, as a matter of policy, never revealed this visit to Byron, but shortly afterwards he took to his bed.

If Byron had been able to absorb some of Hanson's self-control when emotionally involved in a situation, he would have been better armed for the conflict with his wife and his half-sister. But it was not this he had learnt so much as the ability to pursue his advantage in spite of the emotions of other people. His advantage was not, of course, calculated in the crude terms of Hanson's conception of self-interest or in the political values of Napoleon —it was some Calvinist pursuit of his own fate. He had seen his foster-mother, Mrs. Hanson, sacrificed to her husband's interests and in a thousand small ways he had met such arrogance when the emotions of the family stood between Hanson and his advantage. Calculation of this kind must have been particularly impressive to Byron because of the strength of his attachments to people and his generosity towards them which regularly showed itself before he turned his back. There were thus always ghosts in his bedroom and fires creeping up the staircase—summoned by the ruthlessness he had to mobilize if he was to get his way. 'He inflicted misery', said Lady Byron, 'but I felt that he suffered more than he inflicted.'

It is difficult to accept someone throughout life as the manager of your affairs without taking more from him than the profits. Much of Byron's stamina in desertion and exploitation came from the man who played his father's role at home. He was probably the only English Napoleonist who could have said quite simply, as Lady Blessington reported, 'that what he most likes in his [Napoleon's] character is his want of sympathy.' For what it was worth—and perhaps it was invaluable—Byron owed that taste to Hanson's example.

But there was another reason further back which made Hanson seem to Byron a living confirmation of what a father was. His own father, whom he loved and missed, had deserted him in childhood without thought for his mother or himself and gone abroad. 'In separation', he believed, 'the one who goes away suffers less than the one who stays behind.' That men became unduly important to Byron after that key desertion, we may guess from the evidence of his overt homosexuality in adult life. The loss of his father was as important in his psychology as his maimed foot, which itself may have seemed to him some kind of terrible confirmation of loss. By these standards the ability to resist the appeals of an individual in despair was part of the climate of his mind.

The original desertion by his father took on more than life-size proportions. He wrote an astonishing number of poems on the subject, sometimes in grief, but more often in admiring appraisal of the deserter's technique. The theme changed its shape slightly, into one of exile, and became an investigation of what happened to the adventurer when he went away overseas, whether as Childe Harold or Don Juan. 'I am like Adam, the first convict sentenced to transportation,' he wrote from Falmouth in 1809, on the eve of his journey to the Mediterranean with Hobhouse, when no one has suggested that he was forced into exile. The theme acquired grandeur, as abdication, which conferred integrity and even salvation if it was an act of will performed spontaneously by a statesman like Washington. It changed again into suicide, which could bring shame or glory, according to the circumstances, and which Lady Byron told Hanson she dreaded in Byron more than anything else. When Napoleon was brought to Plymouth some months before his wife's call on Hanson, Byron told Hobhouse he sometimes thought there was no alternative but to commit suicide like Whit-bread.

To the men who stayed at his side, above all to Hanson, Byron developed the contradictory attitude we have seen, committed and attached, but vituperative and rejecting. After all, he might have argued, it was not he who had chosen Hanson as a substitute for a father. (It was his mother, and with the same intuition which marked her choice of husband.) But since Hanson was there, insensitive, grasping, dishonourable as he might be, Byron meant to have him to keep. No doubt the contrast between what he needed and what he actually had in Hanson favoured the wild ambivalence of Byron's relations with him—the reliance and the distrust, the advances and snubs, the endearments and insults, the love and hatred. These contradictions are at the centre of all his relations with men, and we find them at the extreme in his attitude to Napoleon.

## 2

It is clear from his journal, in an entry written some time later, that Byron was already holding his breath when he was eight years old and Napoleon crossed the bridge of Lodi under the fire of the Austrians. He was ten when Napoleon fought the battle of the Pyramids, fifteen and at Harrow when he had to defend a bust of his hero 'against the rascally time-servers' because the Peace of Amiens had broken up. As an infant Napoleonist Byron was already distinguished by his readiness to assault the great man as often as he praised him. Seeing a bully called Bob Speer pass by on one occasion, he shouted at him:

> 'Bold Robert Speer was Bony's bad precursor,
> Bob was a bloody dog, but Bonaparte's a worser.'

Byron said that he quarrelled with Napoleon 'as a lover does with the trifling faults of his mistress, from excessive liking'. Hazlitt alleged that he supported him in victory and deserted him in defeat, and certainly he was ready to forgive him time after time when he proved that he was not a liberal, a republican, or even an acceptable human being.

In the retreat from Moscow and for some time afterwards, Byron still hoped for victories for Napoleon while intermittently cursing him. He backed him, he declared, 'against the field', wished him success 'against all countries but this'. But from the defeat of Leipzig onwards he could never wholly forgive him for his growing weakness, and least of all for his tendency to desert his armies. Washington, he said, was greater because he renounced power at the right moment. 'Methinks Sylla did better; for he revenged and resigned in the height of his sway. . . .' And he lists others who did better: Diocletian, Amurath, Charles the Fifth, Dionysius, and Tiberius, who withdrew to Capri.

The cries of rage are impressive because they are the protests of a lover. It is as if he had known all along that Napoleon was an unheroic hero, a kind of villain, and his dismay is at the confirmation. He calls him at this stage his *Pa-god*—he came back to London in April 1814 to find 'my poor little pagod pushed off his pedestal'. He did not stir from his rooms for three days after the Abdication, and on the third wrote the 'Ode to Napoleon', a denunciation of his failure to commit suicide. He only forgave him on the return from Elba, but was thrown into a greater agony by Waterloo.

During the two years of classic Napoleonic disaster, Byron was so unstable as to be fair game for every kind of speculation. It was the period culminating in his flight to Venice, when he involved himself in his two really disastrous relationships—with Augusta, his half-sister, and with his wife Annabella Milbanke, who left him after scarcely a year of marriage, telling Hanson he was mad.[1] Often we get an impression that he was mimicking Napoleon in adversity.

Shortly after Waterloo a carriage taken from Napoleon by the Prussians at Jemappes was put on show in Piccadilly by the same Mr. Bullock whom we have met as the employer of Agostino Aglio. More than ten thousand visitors a month came to see it. They were caricatured by Rowlandson and Cruikshank, sprawling in the seat of their fallen enemy, sitting on the coachman's box, gaping in amazement and occasionally in grief at his bits and pieces of clothing and furniture. How often Byron was among them we do not know, but while he was still living with his wife a few yards away in Piccadilly Terrace he gave orders to Charles Baxter, a famous coachmaker in Long Acre, to reproduce the carriage.

It was an astonishing commission. The result was 'huge', said one of Byron's friends,

---

[1] The turns and eddies of these events are so complex that no biographer can follow them convincingly, but even the most conservative admit that Napoleon's catastrophe 'did something to darken the colour of his private mood', and Professor Wilson Knight sees it as the central cause.

but not unlike the latest English travelling chariot. Standing rather high, the front was made with strong outworks to prevent the driver seeing inside while giving his passenger a clear view. It was painted dark blue with a gold border and the imperial arms on the doors. Inside, drawers and compartments were fitted for every conceivable utensil of a Napoleonic campaign, and these were to be replaced in Byron's version by a bed, a library, a plate-chest and every apparatus for dining.

The order was among the most extravagant gestures in Byron's life because he had just bought a handsome new carriage for his married state. He was in debt, facing a growing clamour from his creditors, and although the cost is uncertain, Augusta reported to Hanson about the time it was delivered that her brother had to leave town, 'having received a bill from his coachmaker for £2,000 and his affairs being in such a state that if Lady B. came back, he should have nowhere to receive her.' No doubt the £2,000 included the other carriage he had just bought with his wife, but this was not the kind of figure that Hanson could let pass without reflections on the need to dispose of more of Byron's estates.

It has been suggested[1] that the carriage formed part of a direct political purpose whose details and outline are lost but can be assumed to have been aimed at the liberation of France from the restored Bourbons. There can be no doubt that Byron was seeing himself increasingly as the liberator. He had already thought of going to Holland 'to be in at the Revolution' and to 'listen to the shout of a free Dutchman'. In Italy he would shortly give help to the liberals and revolutionaries in ways which were to make the interest Hobhouse took in such matters academic. Afterwards he was to die working for the liberation of Greece. There is nothing unplausible in finding revolutionary intentions in the visit he planned with Hobhouse to France. In fact the Bourbon administration was suspicious enough to refuse him a passport.

Among the few surviving documents which point almost unmistakably to such a scheme, is a letter from Lady Byron to Augusta. It refers to the promotion by a certain 'H' of a 'foreign scheme', and to a sure way of defeating it, 'which appears likely to be effectual against any practices of H's, viz. that if requisite my father and Captain B should wait upon him, and state as their joint opinion that it would be a measure most injurious to B, after which H dare not promote it for his own character's sake.'

But who was the 'H' at the centre of the plan? It may have been Hanson,[2] but the aura of foreign adventure does not point to a man who only took risks when they promised advantage. A more likely candidate would seem to be Hobhouse, who was showing a passionate interest in revolutions on the Continent.

[1] By Professor Wilson Knight, in *Lord Byron's Marriage* (1957), pp. 266–71.
[2] As suggested by Lord Ernle in his edition of Byron's letters.

G

That a political scheme of some kind existed is easier to believe than that the carriage formed part of it. The Napoleonic replica seems like one of those clues in a detective story which we may discount as too obvious. Certainly its appearance on the roads of France would have announced the return of the Emperor, but there would have been no greeting of the kind which bore Napoleon to Paris on the return from Elba. A political realist would not have thought of such a plan, and least of all Hanson. He seems to have contented himself with impressing on Hobhouse that the carriage might be seized by the bailiffs as one of Byron's assets, and at Dover Hobhouse saw to it that priority was given to having it 'well packed up' and put aboard.

The possession of such a carriage is more likely to have grown in Byron's own mind than to have been a tactical device thought up by either Hanson or Hobhouse. Indeed we can almost see the idea taking hold of him. In January 1814, a year after Napoleon's retreat from Moscow, he wrote to Hanson from the countryside about a projected journey of his own, that 'Buonaparte's Moscow retreat was much easier'. The imperial carriages were becoming more and more publicized in the campaigns which took the Emperor across the Continent from one defeat to another, and finally into exile on Elba. After Waterloo, one of the most remarkable incidents of the crossing in the *Bellerophon* was Napoleon's attempt to get transport for six carriages and forty-five horses, for which the British Admiral actually issued a passport.

It would be absurd to suggest that Byron set about seriously imitating Napoleon's genius in action. There is very little that is Napoleonic in his involved proceedings with the Carbonari in Italy and the liberation movement in Missolonghi; the elements of speed and decision, for instance, are entirely absent. It is his own sense of identification with his hero which is important.

There was no need for Byron to go into exile six months after Napoleon reached St. Helena. He was better able than most to stand up to abuse, particularly when it was politically inspired. 'There was not the slightest necessity even in appearance for his going abroad,' according to Hobhouse. Hanson, who knew the financial position and the risks of Byron's dispute with his wife, wanted him to stay. But his own farewells (which he regularly elevated into a central theme of love) were already confused with four anonymous farewells which he wrote on behalf of Napoleon to the French nation.

> All I ask is to divide
> Every peril he must brave;
> Sharing by the hero's side
> His fall, his exile and his grave.

His destination, Venice, he called his 'greenest island', and it remained always very much his St. Helena, which visitors could only reach, he was at pains to point out, by leaving their carriages at Mestri. His own he prized too highly to leave; he brought it with him by sea.

The best-known of Napoleon's encounters on the *Bellerophon* had been with his future physician, O'Meara. Forming part of his suite, though recruited at the last moment, was his own physician, a young M. Maingaud, who was seasick all the way across and admitted that he had no wish to follow his master 'to the tropics'. Foreseeing this desertion, Napoleon got into conversation from the first day with the ship's surgeon, Barry O'Meara, who was able to respond in Italian and proved only too happy, when the time came, to accept the dramatic invitation to go with him to St. Helena. It was not long before he became Napoleon's most publicized disciple in the English press and gained, according to Byron in 'The Age of Bronze', 'the world's applause' for his devotion.

If ever it had been going to enter Byron's head to have his own personal physician, there could not have been a less convenient moment than at his own exile. He had no money for such follies. His health was admittedly not good at this moment. His foot was much as it had always been, but there was nothing that could be done to improve it. Nevertheless it fell to his publisher, John Murray, and to Hanson, who was feeling ill himself, to engage a Dr. Polidori to go with Byron into exile, just as O'Meara had gone with Napoleon.

The course of the appointment is well known thanks to Polidori's incongruity with Byron, Shelley, and everyone else who came in touch with the party. What has not been explained is why Byron tolerated him. He listened to Polidori's fantastic verses without laughing, although patience of this kind was foreign to him. He submitted to his assumption of equality and he did all this and more with a readiness which has impressed some with unsuspected depths of humanity in him. A more likely explanation is that he wished to preserve his Napoleonic cast for as many weeks as he could stand it. Before they reached Venice Byron sent Polidori back to Murray. 'I had no use for him and his temper and habits were not good,' he wrote to his sister.

Their actual route was as much linked with Napoleon as if Byron had gained the passport for that tour of the 'vestiges' which he had planned to make with Hobhouse. To the big naval installations at Antwerp, to the field of Waterloo, to Venice, his 'greenest island', he went as reverently as a bereaved son. There was the less tangible, more intimate magic of the monogram formed of the initials N.B. which he claimed as his own after signing the marriage contract with the Noel family. According to Leigh Hunt, Byron used the monogram because 'Bonaparte and I are the only public persons whose initials are the same.' He continued to use it even after Napoleon's death.

In the eleventh canto of *Don Juan* Byron sees himself settling down as the Napoleon of poetry, with *Don Juan*, *Marino Faliero*, and *Cain* as stages in his decline in public opinion. He had been reckoned

> a considerable time,
> The grand Napoleon of the realms of rhyme.
> But Juan was my Moscow, and Faliero
> My Leipsic, and my Mont Saint Jean seems Cain. . .

His stay in Venice had no more obvious term to it than Napoleon's on St. Helena. In his second year he took a three-year lease of the Palazzo Mocenigo, and this gave him room to house fourteen servants, a growing menagerie, the Napoleonic carriage, and the prospect of receiving his illegitimate daughter from the Shelleys.

News of this kind was profoundly disturbing to Hanson back in London, and for more compelling reasons than Byron's moral welfare. His flight from the country and his adventures in Venice were becoming a formidable danger to the Portsmouth marriage. Lord Portsmouth's relations were continuing to amass evidence of the measures which the Hansons were using on their victim and it became less and less likely that Lord Eldon would stay his hand because of Byron.

Hanson saw that much was to be gained if he could get him back to a reasonably normal life in England, and he had grounds for suspecting that Lady Byron was not opposed to a reconciliation. Mustering, therefore, the legal excuses to hand—the final sale of Newstead, Byron's will, his own charges which stood at £12,000—he proposed to come out to visit him. He took his son Newton, and tried to settle for Geneva as a compromise meeting point. 'What!' Byron protested, when he heard that Hanson would like him to come out from Venice to meet them. 'Am I to be made the Polichinelle of an attorneo at thirty years of age? He may be damned.' Byron insisted that they come all the way to Venice.

Newton Hanson, in his impressions of their arrival on the Grand Canal, gives one of the famous descriptions of the Palazzo Mocenigo.

. . . The Basement contained his lordship's carriages, two or three kinds of dogs, birds, monkeys, a fox, a wolf, in different cages, and, as his lordship passed to his gondola, he used to stop and amuse himself with watching their antics, or would feed them himself occasionally. We proceeded up a flight of marble staircases, through a lofty billiard-room, and then through a bedroom, to an apartment to the door of which his lordship advanced and cordially greeted my father. At their meeting I could not help observing a nervous sensitiveness in his lordship, which produced a silence for some minutes. It was broken by his lordship observing

'Well, Hanson! I never thought you would have ventured so far. I rather expected you would have sent Charles.' There were tears in his eyes.

Charles, the eldest son, had been left behind to supervise affairs at home, and it was Hanson alone who now set about the task of coaxing Byron back to England. Byron made no comment on his first approaches, but on the third day news came of the suicide of Romilly, the Whig lawyer, who had lost his wife. 'How strange it is', said Byron pointedly, 'that one man will die for the loss of his partner, while another would die if they were compelled to live together!' It was the end of Hanson's mission. He knew his client too well to doubt the consequences of a return to England.

The exile remained true to form in two important ways during this visit. He was being showered with warnings from England about Hanson's character. 'I wish you would *speak out*,' he had written to Murray, 'at least to *me*, and tell me what you allude to by your odd way of mentioning him. . . . The devil take everybody: I never get any person to be explicit . . . you all talk in the style of Caroline Lamb's novels.' In completing the sale of Newstead he had accepted Hanson's proposals and nominated him, with Hobhouse, as his executor. Further warnings came as the Hansons were on their way back to Kensington. 'Till this moment I did not suspect *falsification* or *substitution*,' he replied, 'but now I do because you say so; though, like all advice, it comes somewhat of the latest. . . .'

The Hansons, for their part, noticed that Byron's figure had itself become Napoleonic. It was perhaps their main topic of conversation to his friends on their return. 'Lord Byron could not have been more than 30, but he looked 40,' wrote Newton Hanson. 'His face had become pale, bloated and sallow. He had grown very fat, his shoulders broad and round, and the knuckles of his hands were lost in fat.'

It was now unlikely that Hanson could fend off the day of judgement much longer. Along the turnpike at Acton, where he had settled Mary Anne and her husband, things were going badly in a horrific ménage. The Hansons were 'in full possession of their victim', the prosecution said later. It was as if Lord Portsmouth's madness infected them, so that they used their fists and whips on him, as he would have done on them. A year after the marriage Mary Anne became the mistress of a Mr. William Alder, who looked at first like a 'shabby tradesman' but soon acquired a fashionable air. He had been employed on the turnpike since 1814, and may have owed the appointment to Hanson as a member of the board. He was introduced to Acton as a new trustee of the Earl's, and was to be seen walking arm in arm with the Countess on the green. After a miscarriage, she gave birth to an heir.

The Earl still had his pleasures. He drove the cook out of the kitchen with a bunch of stinging nettles and forced the servants to drink jalap, mustard, pepper, and nutmeg—a prescription like Lady Byron's for her husband. The Hanson daughters, Harriet, Laura, Bridget, and to a lesser extent Eliza, who remained permanently at Acton, turned into Valkyries. 'I have seen Miss Laura throw dirt and water at Lord Portsmouth,' said the under-butler. She used to spit in his face, and once, when he hit back at Miss Bridget, he was thrashed on his bed by Mary Anne and the butler. A few months after Hanson's return from Venice, the Earl managed to get to a local magistrate, Sir Richard Birnie, and asked for a warrant against his wife for flogging him.

If Hanson failed to stop them there was a sense in which he kept his head. Short of living with his daughter, he tried to keep the bedlam under control and out of sight. What was certain was his own link with a still illustrious client, his brilliant sale of Newstead Abbey, his visit to the Palazzo Mocenigo. The trustees of the square and the turnpike were glad to have such a man as one of them; his distinction added lustre to the parish register in 1818 when he benignly witnessed the wedding of the clerk of the square, à Beckett, a fellow lawyer and Whig.

But Hanson had seen the danger lights. It could not be long before the Chancellor acceded to a new petition for a Commission of Lunacy to investigate the evidence accumulated by the Earl's brother. In 1821 Hanson ordered the establishment to leave Acton and himself gave up his outpost in the square, which was now all too inhabited. They went as far as Edinburgh to shake off the scandal, but the case came on at the beginning of 1823 in front of a jury which heard over a hundred witnesses.

A chambermaid, who reported on the Alder relationship, said 'Lady Portsmouth seldom spoke. Her general appearance was very low—quite dejected.' Hanson himself came rarely. Portsmouth, said an under-butler, 'was sometimes at the door at Fairlawn when her ladyship got into her carriage to go to London. He used to seem anxious for her return.' But a written 'judgment' on the Hansons by the Earl was submitted in evidence which condemned his wife and her brother Newton to transportation to Botany Bay, Alder to be hanged on Acton Green, and Hanson 'to give up all his money on my behalf'.

The weakness of the defence was that no one could be found to give evidence of the Earl's sanity. They did what they could with the name of Byron, but the response was disappointing. Did the jury believe, they asked, 'that a man like Lord Byron would have witnessed the marriage if he had supposed it was a mere sacrifice on the altar of ambition and selfishness?' The jury seemed uncertain whether they could believe it or not. To those who had read the first cantos of *Don Juan* there were less unlikely propositions.

Byron was now in Genoa and about to sail for Greece, where he proposed to die in the struggle for liberation. He heard the verdict from Hobhouse. The Earl was found to have been insane; the marriage was later annulled, Mary Anne's child by Alder declared illegitimate, and costs awarded against her. According to Creevey the costs were over £40,000.

'You see', Hobhouse wrote immediately after the trial, 'what a mess Hanson has made of the Portsmouth business. The jury returned unanimously on Friday last a verdict of *lunacy since 1809* ... [the Portsmouths' wedding had been in 1814]. You recollect what a pretty smock-faced girl Laura Hanson was in our time, who looked as if butter would not melt in her mouth? Well, it turns out that she used to beat and whip and spit upon this poor creature, and joined in all the cruelties against him. . . .'

Byron replied defensively, ironically, but not as if he had ever had any confidence in the family which had brought him up. He had, he said, accepted what Hanson told him about the marriage. That was all he had to go on. 'It was no affair of mine to interfere in, and I thought that if Lord P. got a plain, quiet, housekeeping wife—*young*, too, instead of that tough morsel prepared by his brother, it was no bad bargain for either party. . . . I could have no interest of my own, for I never performed with the Miss Hansons, nor whipped Lord P. . . .'

It was perhaps as well in the circumstances that Byron could not be called as a witness. He was preparing supplies for the liberation of Greece and set sail at the end of the year with a war chest of 200,000 piastres—twice as much, he noted in his journal, as Napoleon had for the liberation of Italy.

He died on 19 April 1824, at the age of thirty-six. On 26 January 1824, when a surgeon, James Forrester, R.N., called on him at Missolonghi, he noticed that his hair had turned 'light auburn'; the auburn which had always been half hidden in it had been joined by white.[1]

---

[1] Forrester's impressions are reprinted in Doris Langley Moore, *The Late Lord Byron* (1961).

# 4. *Whitbread and Caroline*

*At no time has he been treated with the consideration
due to the situation he occupies and the
achievements which he has performed.*
Whitbread on peace negotiations
with Napoleon, 29 February 1808

## I

Kensington was twice at the centre of a great wave of disturbance which involved the whole country, first in the five years the Prince Regent's wife, Caroline, spent in the palace as princess and mother of the heir-apparent, and again after the war when she lived in Hammersmith as the uncrowned Queen.

She was a niece of George III, and had grown up in the North German court of Brunswick which was at once strict in its etiquette and relaxed in its tolerance of the infidelities of her father, the Duke Charles William Ferdinand. She spoke a mixture of French and English which sounded like German. She was kindly, brave, disorganized, and almost wholly without taste. Lord Holland, who had motives for avoiding her, claimed to believe she was mad. Her marriage to the Prince, who was already married to Mrs. Fitzherbert, only took place as a result of financial pressure by the King, and it broke up on the birth of their child, Princess Charlotte. Caroline then retired to Blackheath where her love affairs and attachment to orphans caused rumours that she had at least one illegitimate child. She was the mistress of Canning and of Perceval before he was Prime Minister. To investigate the rumours George III agreed to the setting up under the Talents of a commission known as the Delicate Investigation. Caroline was rebuked, but acquitted of the main charges, and the King gave her and her daughter a suite in Kensington Palace.

The limelight soon shone on the palace as it had not done for half a century. The air of radicalism it had already as the residence of the Dukes of Sussex and Kent caused no great stir. It was traditional in the House of

Hanover for the sons to resist the politics of their father. George III found he had nurtured a breed of Whigs almost indistinguishable in their virulence from Fox; his sons took to reaction only when they knew him to be past finding consolation in it, and Sussex, if not Kent, was irreconcilable.[1]

Sussex grew up during his father's unpopularity in the American War. He was punished as a child of six for wearing the Whig colours in an election. He suffered from asthma and skin diseases which are the classic examples of anxiety transformed into physical symptoms. In spite of his robust appearance, the doctors sent him out of the country on the ground that the English climate might prove fatal. But there were other risks in exile. In Rome, when he was twenty, he married beneath him, and much of his long life was taken up with the consequences. Because of his illness and his position as the sixth son with almost no chance of the succession, he was better placed to think for himself than his brothers were. He brought back to Kensington his library—which was strong in Bibles, chemistry, and the manuscripts of Italian operas—a collection of musical boxes, and the belief that reason could solve most human problems.

The Duke of Kent did not make the palace his home in the same sense. He used it as an office, where he received callers and did his business, but for his comfort he relied on a house further up the turnpike at Knightsbridge, where he kept a French-Canadian mistress, Madame St. Laurent. Kent's career had filled him with bitterness against the rest of the royal family. As Commander-in-Chief in Gibraltar and Canada, he had proved a disastrous failure because of his obsession with detail. At the age of thirty-five he had been retired, and he put it down to the malevolence of his brothers. His Whig and Radical views were little more than an expression of this hostility. He made provocative statements about them, ran a private information service inside Government departments, supported the Catholics and worked tirelessly for charities, while believing that charity was not enough 'to remedy the evil of a depressed working class'.

The Dukes had been consulted about the arrival of Caroline, and could see no objection to being involved in her feud with their brother, but they can hardly have foreseen its extent. The effects were at first mainly physical. *The Times*, in October 1807, announced that the palace was 'undergoing a thorough repair, nearly the whole of the interior has been pulled down'. It took a year for the Treasury to authorize expenditure of £23,000 on refitting, and in January 1810 a pipe burst on its way to Caroline's chapel, leaving the Duke without water and the chapel, according to *The Times*, 'wholly disfigured'.

When she moved in, Caroline found the palace cold and referred to it as 'this convent'. Her routine to enliven it included a family dinner on

[1] The exception was the Duke of Cumberland, who was a Tory all his life.

Saturdays, visits to the threatre, supper parties and a large dinner on Sundays with outside guests and a concert. She herself had a passable voice. At first the concerts were given by two professionals, Pucitti and Tramezani, who could be heard by Sussex in his library; but they were displaced by a tenor called Sapio who became Caroline's lover and brought in a whole family of singers to practise as an opera company in rehearsal. On weekdays she modelled herself on the living arrangements of the Duke of Kent. She kept on her house at Blackheath and rented a 'small cottage' to the north of Kensington Palace, in Bayswater, finding herself less constrained there than Marie Antoinette in the Petit Trianon. According to the unsympathetic account of her lady-in-waiting, who became Lady Bury, 'she received a set of persons wholly unfit to be admitted to her society. . . . All the follies, though not the elegance and splendour of Trianon were aped in the rural retreat of Bayswater.' Caroline was at pains to spread her contacts among the ordinary householders, who liked her as much as she liked them.

In the palace she set about organizing her own court, a 'rival court', as Lord Holland called it. From the beginning the guests shared an antipathy to the Prince and the Tories. Sir Francis Burdett, the Radical Member for Westminster, was a foundation member, and Lord Henry Fitzgerald added connections with the aristocracy. There were two poets, Thomas Campbell who was financed by Lady Holland, and Samuel Rogers, a regular defector from Holland House. Rogers soon introduced Byron and Lady Oxford, at that time his mistress, who became Caroline's closest confidante. Vain attempts were made to recruit the Hollands. Lady Charlotte Lindsay, one of the Princess's ladies-in-waiting, met Lord Holland on an autumn ride and tried to rush him into a dinner. When Caroline followed up with a written invitation, he declined, 'being called upon to transact some indispensable business tomorrow evening which admits of no delay.'

Byron went more often to the palace than to Holland House. He had some real affinity with Caroline's defiant pursuit of her pleasures and re-mained loyal to her, after his fashion, even in Ravenna. Caroline wrote very much as she spoke, and found him 'all couleur de rose last evening, and very pleasant; he sat beside me at supper, and we were very merry; he is quite anoder man when he is wid people he like, and who like him. . . .' Lady Bury, who was in attendance, noticed with distaste that Sir William Drummond was trying to convert Caroline's daughter to his belief that the Scriptures were astronomical allegories.

A new and more political atmosphere settled on the palace after the mad-ness of George III cleared the field for the Prince to take action. Step by step, after becoming Regent, he put restrictions on Caroline's contact with her daughter. The Whigs hesitated to take sides while they still saw a pros-pect of office, and they were compromised by having themselves set up the

Delicate Investigation in 1806. But when it was clear that the Prince had abandoned them, several began to support the Princess: Brougham, who hoped on becoming Foreign Secretary to renew negotiations with Napoleon, and Samuel Whitbread, who felt a sense of personal outrage at the Prince's behaviour to her.

Apart from political revenge it was hard to see what motive Whitbread had. He was as neat as Caroline was slovenly. He had eager blue eyes looking out from an honest, open face under a crown of auburn hair. Earl Spencer said that he 'alone, of the chiefs of the opposition, had an eminent capacity for business'. The others thought him 'arrogant and imperious' but admitted that he gave himself to the cause of economic and political reform as no one else did. He wanted a minimum wage for agricultural workers, national education, reform of prisons and lunatic asylums, and the abolition of flogging. While he fought for the outcasts, he assaulted the leaders of the ruling oligarchy for seizing public money and ignoring the interests of the nation by prolonging the war.

He was the son of the best-known brewer in the country, whose services in Parliament to George III had been rewarded with a patronizing visit to his brewery. Brought up under a rigorous Nonconformist discipline, which taught him that virtue brought something more than its own reward, Whitbread found himself treated by the Whig aristocrats very much as his father had been by the King. He replied by insisting on the pure doctrine of reform and peace with Napoleon at any price. The Whigs closed ranks against him, and his main occupation at the time he met Caroline was the rebuilding of Drury Lane Theatre, which had been burnt down in 1809.

Caroline, who knew about Drury Lane, thought he must be the architect. She soon found she had acquired a dominating manager. Whitbread deplored her parties, her cottage in Bayswater, her fits of laughter, and got his wife, Lady Elizabeth, to raise the line of Caroline's bodice.

When Princess Charlotte was removed to Windsor, Caroline drove up to the castle and insisted on seeing her, but got only a bleak interview with the Queen. Whitbread and Brougham advised her to demand either the removal of the restrictions or a fresh trial, but they warned her first 'to review her past life' and to hold her hand if there was anything that would incriminate her—'for even if it had passed at the centre of the earth, she must calculate upon its being proven'. Whitbread thought she might draw back, but she did not hesitate. The letter he drafted for her went first to the Prince Regent, and when it was rejected, to the Speaker of the House of Commons.

Debates followed which stirred the country and began to draw out its frustrated radicalism. 'Public expectation probably never rose so high,' commented Hansard. Lord Grey referred to the dispute as 'the war between Carlton House and Kensington'. The press was at first against Caroline, but

Leigh Hunt's *Examiner* took the lead in supporting her, and its circulation flourished.

Although he had a different background from Whitbread, Leigh Hunt had similar motives for championing the downtrodden. A month after he went to prison for calling the Prince Regent 'a libertine over head and ears in disgrace', Hunt's libel was sharpened and popularized by Whitbread, who compared Caroline to Anne Boleyn and the Prince Regent to 'a brutal tyrant', Henry VIII, who 'wished to get rid of the Consort of whom he was tired'. He asked the Commons to accept Anne Boleyn's plea that she should either be proved guilty or declared innocent.

Letters from the public began to flow into the palace in great numbers. Demonstrations followed, and Cobbett in the *Political Register* announced that the City of London would present an address. In a heated debate in Guildhall, the Lord Mayor showed himself reluctant to play his part, but on 12 April 1813 a hundred carriages formed up from Guildhall to Cheapside, and an 'immense assembly' cheered them on the way to Kensington. Outside the palace a Bow Street officer had already had to call in troops to clear the lawn between the railings and the palace walls, but when the procession arrived, the crowd overpowered the troops and police and broke open the gates. The reluctant Lord Mayor was booed, but the Aldermen were cheered and especially Alderman Wood as the strongest advocate of the address. They were followed by the mace-bearer, the sword of state, the sheriffs, and 150 liverymen in their gowns. It took half an hour for them to get out of their carriages in the yard and into the grand dining-room.

Caroline received them in front of a large looking-glass. Her ladies-in-waiting, Lady Bury, Lady Anne Hamilton, and Charlotte Lindsay, stood on her right, the vice-chamberlain, St. Leger, on her left. She listened graciously as the Town Clerk read the address. In the hearts of the citizens of London, he said, those sentiments with which they had hailed her arrival had never changed; they had difficulty in expressing their indignation at the conspiracy which had been carried on against her. She read an answer in the style of Whitbread as simply as she could, touching on the safeguards for the individual under the Constitution and ending with the hope that their kindness to her might be remembered by posterity.[1]

The grand dining-room looked out on Kensington Gardens and many thousands were able to catch a glimpse of the proceedings. Caroline came out and curtseyed from the palace doors and then went up to the first floor

---

[1] Caroline's hope was not fulfilled: the demonstrations at Kensington Palace were excluded from local histories in deference to George IV. Her residence there does not figure in the current guide-book or the display rooms, so that it is difficult to guess where her court was held. Similarly Hobhouse, when he became Lord Broughton, cut all references in his diary to this period when he was a visitor to the palace.

balcony, where she was received with cheers which rolled across to Hyde Park.

It was noted by Lady Bury that Whitbread did not like 'that the Princess should make all the play herself'. He liked her to stick to his over-weighted drafts, and if she tried to simplify them or add point, reminded her, accurately enough, that 'it was to him, to the weight of his politics she should owe whatever advantage she may reap from the present contest'.

His day came at a City Livery dinner in the London Tavern soon after the address. Five hundred liverymen then drank to the toast 'Mr. Whitbread, and may his manly eloquence be always exerted in the cause of freedom and oppressed innocence.' The correspondent of the *Statesman* assessed the applause as little short of that for Caroline and much greater than that for the Prince Regent.

In the weeks that followed, one deputation after another made its way to Kensington. The biggest were from Westminster and Middlesex, and both had an openly radical tone which linked Caroline's wrongs with an unreformed Parliament. The Freeholders of Middlesex hoped it would be impressed on her daughter, when she became Queen, 'that at a period when the borough-mongering factions, the detested oligarchy of Great Britain, united in one impenetrable phalanx against the cause of her royal mother, the people, the abused people of England, did justice to her innocence and virtue'. Caroline's reply acknowledged that she was being addressed by 'the great and most populous county of Middlesex'. She had the Sheriff and the two Representatives, George Byng and William Mellish, to lunch in the grand dining-room.

At the end of April the *Statesman* published a letter from Alderman Wood inviting 'all the few corporations and counties in which independence yet prevails' to imitate the example of the City. There were responses from as far away as Sheffield, the ports of Bristol and Rochester, and the county of Pembrokeshire. In Caroline's entourage it was impossible to resist a feeling that her popularity might win her the throne. Even Lady Bury noted in her diary that she had 'long had a foresight of some great interior revolution in these kingdoms'.

But Caroline was not good at standing a strain. There were rumours that the Prince Regent would close down the palace as a centre of Jacobinism. Napoleon was suffering defeat after defeat, and there was a new confidence in the Government. In July 1813, the Prince ordered Princess Charlotte to take up residence with him in Carlton House, Brougham advised her to accede, and after fluttering desperately from house to house, Charlotte moved in with her father. As the months passed she began to give him evidence on life in Kensington Palace.

Caroline started a diary in which she described her friends and enemies as she saw them, and they were not very clearly distinguishable. She made wax figures of the Prince Regent, stuck them with pins and threw them on the fire. In January 1814 she added horns to one of them. When Napoleon abdicated in the spring, Whitbread and Brougham had to warn her against the temptation to leave the country, which would be misunderstood as another abdication. In August she disappeared across the Channel in the frigate *Jason*, which was readily lent her by the Prince Regent.

The father wrote, manfully expressing his devotion, his approval of her flight, and 'zeal for her re-establishment in all the rights of the empire over which she is one day to reign'. His defence of Caroline, on which he had spent three years, was the biggest of his campaigns on behalf of an outcast and had behind it little or none of Brougham's tactical calculation but the deepest expression of his character. Few facts are known about his childhood except for Earl Spencer's statement that 'coercion and spartan discipline' were features of it. He was an only son, whose mother died a few weeks after his birth. His father, who represented Bedford in the Commons, managed to win the exquisitely beautiful Lady Mary Cornwallis as his second wife, but before she could bring her influence to bear on the family, she, too, died in childbirth. Whitbread did not try a third time; in his will he left instructions that he was to be 'interred in the same vault as the bodies of my two wives'. There are signs, but no proof, that some of the coercion and discipline of the boy's education was applied to them.

The father tried a dangerous experiment with his son's education. On the one hand he spent all he could by sending him to Eton, Oxford, Cambridge, and the northern capitals of Europe as a hardy variant of the Grand Tour. On the other, he impressed on him the importance of the brewery as an undertaking blessed by God which made an ever-increasing profit in reward for industry. As the boy's horizon widened, so his father tried to hold him to the brewery as if it were a nonconformist sect. 'There never was the like before,' he told him, when his education was complete. The son remained loyal to the brewery as an inescapable part of his background which was confused with the love and hatred he felt for his father. But at Eton he became a friend of Charles Grey, the son of Earl Grey, and in 1789, when he was twenty-five, he married his friend's sister, Elizabeth. By marriage as well as education, he had joined the great world.

His father resisted the marriage. Charles Grey belonged to the circle of Fox, and although they were not yet denounced as Jacobins, the elder Whitbread had voted steadily against them in the American war. In Bedford, he had to deal with a thousand voters. At the election of 1790, he abandoned the campaign at the last moment, 'and my son', he told John Howard, 'took it up with violence and has carried it....' The elder Whitbread had to change his constituency and was returned two years later for the Sussex borough of Steyning, where there were only a hundred voters. Thereafter, until his death in 1796, he watched his son grow in prominence as the right-wing Whigs crossed the floor and left the younger Whitbread on the front bench beside Fox. He joined Fox in the demand that a minister should be sent to Paris to avert war, and then, after the execution of Louis XVI and the declaration of war, that peace overtures should be made. He strongly supported Dissenters. 'The law', he said, 'exists for the protection of all, as well of those who dissented from, as of those who were attached to the establishment.' At the end of 1793, the Whig Club drank for the first time to 'Mr. Whitbread and the Independent Electors of Bedford'.

For a moment the caricaturists hesitated like marksmen surprised by a bird in their sights. The first, in 1794, could only think of Whitbread's bright red hair, and drew him as Redhead advancing against the powers of evil, but in 1795 James Sayers thought of showing him simply as a beer barrel.[1] His honest face, the slightly naïve lift of his eyebrows, his Etonian ease, his commanding presence, do not exist. He is 'Whitbread's Intire' and nothing else except for a few words, 'Liberty', 'Reform', 'Equality', frothing up from the bung-hole; his colleagues hide their faces, hold their heads and run. It was the first of more than a hundred cartoons in which the beer became so inseparable from him that it was only necessary to draw a porter pot or a drayman to represent him.

Trade was no barrier to a career in Parliament, but beer was in a class by itself. At the time the elder Whitbread went into business, a century of un-taxed spirits had brought misery to a large section of the population. An Act of 1751, which imposed a tax on spirits, raised the demand for beer and advertised its association with a contented working class. It was only a minority of reformers, like Priestley and some other Nonconformists, who thought of it as an evil. To the governing class, who stuck to their claret, it seemed the best way of keeping the workers from more dangerous addictions. They laughed at Whitbread's fortune and the visit to his brewery by the King. There was no resentment in the laughter and only a touch of snobbery.

But the young Whitbread did not find it easy to deal with laughter or to distinguish between good and bad humour. At Eton, he laboured with fervour at Latin verses and acquired a certain facility. It was only when he wrote them in English that something inflexible and essentially humourless showed up. He went from Eton to Oxford, but moved on again to Cambridge

---

[1] 'These caricatures have next to no merit as works of art, but were so powerful and direct in their purpose that Fox is said to have declared that Sayers' caricatures did him more harm than all the attacks made on him in Parliament or the Press.' (Article on James Sayers, *Dictionary of National Biography*.)

almost as soon as he got there. In the fit of persecution mania which ended his life he suddenly believed that Cambridge, where his sons were by then in residence, was equally unhealthy, and transferred them to Edinburgh. When he won Charles Grey's sister, he was marrying into an aristocratic family which did not laugh at him. His father was probably right to resist it.

Whitbread proved himself invaluable to the Whigs. No one else, except Fox, had his ability in mastering a case or his courage in pressing it in the face of entrenched privilege. He was particularly formidable in hunting out corruption, and his impeachment of Lord Melville, the treasurer of the Navy, in 1805 set the pattern for attacks on other highly placed officials, including the Duke of York, as Commander-in-Chief.

When the Whigs came to power in 1806, it seemed certain that he would be rewarded with office. But the Whig aristocrats hesitated. It was not only that Whitbread proved himself difficult in personal relations. They had to face the certainty that the jokes about the brewery would follow him into the Cabinet. The cartoonists had not relented. Although the impeachment of Melville had been popular, another twenty cartoons about beer appeared after it. The Duchess of Gordon, after one of Whitbread's masterly speeches, said he had taught his dray-horse to caper. Sydney Smith called him 'the fermentator'.

In the end Grey had the invidious task of telling him that he would have to give up the brewery before he was offered any important office. Whitbread indignantly refused. A cartoon which appeared in June 1806 may have sealed his refusal. He is quoted as saying:

> 'I'll e'en get a place—if not I'll retire
> From envious courtiers and Whitbread's Intire.'

When the Talents fell in 1807, Gillray drew George III as a farmer driving his pigs down a cliff into the sea. Whitbread is no more than a submerged barrel from which a pair of trotters project. The leadership of the party in the Commons was then thrown open by the elevation of Grey to the Lords on the death of his father, Earl Grey; but Grenville and the Hollands would not even consider Whitbread for the succession. When they chose Ponsonby, a nonentity related to Lady Grey, he knew that he had been declared unacceptable for life.

He had been married to Grey's sister for twenty years, and the link between the families was strengthened by the marriage of Grey's brother to one of his own sisters, but his relationship with Grey never recovered. If he had been less able than the Whig aristocracy, he might have been able to accept the slight. But he knew he was their superior. He had a grasp of his subject and an almost Napoleonic self-reliance which put him in a different class. He dictated to two secretaries at once and mastered the political complexities of five different countries in a speech.

When he was excluded from office, he first mentioned the 'sneers' which he was later to hear all around him in the weeks before his death. When he was passed over for the leadership of the Opposition as well, he began to show symptoms of illness and came under the care of Sir Henry Halford, a specialist in hydrocephalus. He suffered from depressions, lethargy, and a tendency to put on weight. But at this stage he was still far from collapsing into persecution mania. His field of expression was politics and he saw every hope of vindication in it. There was even a touch of sour grapes in his attitude to rejection. 'My object is certainly fair Fame,' he wrote to Creevey. 'Neither Place nor Power I hope.'

The strength of his response is shown by a revolution in the number of his speeches. Until the Whigs took office in 1806, and except during the impeachment of Lord Melville, he had made fewer than a dozen a year. He spoke less than Grey and immeasurably less than Fox. But in 1807, after his exclusion from the Cabinet, he made over fifty speeches, the following year over sixty, and so on progressively until 1812, when he made nearly a hundred and fifty. He spoke more than anyone in Parliament. It was torrential. 'She interrupted Whitbread,' said Byron, in an attempt to illustrate the iron will of Madame de Staël.

In what he said there was a sharp increase in his support for Napoleon. 'Contradiction', said Lord Ossory, 'made him become a vehement advocate of Bonaparte.' Napoleon, Whitbread argued, was a figure who had been wronged; he had been 'aggrandized', blown up, forced into his aggressive attitude by the refusal of the legitimate sovereigns to accept him. He warned the House there was no chance of destroying Napoleon or even curtailing his power, except (which he prayed God to prevent) by assassination. 'As to the French Emperor,' he said in July 1807, when he had been excluded from office in the Talents, 'I would here take leave to observe upon the idle and childish way in which many persons are pleased to indulge when speaking of that person. . . . It is by deeds of energy we shall maintain ourselves.' The following year, when he was excluded from the leadership, he said that Ministers who were reluctant to negotiate with Napoleon should be forced to do so with a proper degree of consideration for his extraordinary talents. 'You made it necessary for him to fight these battles. You combined the world against him. . . . It is the contest between the wind and the sun.' By their hostility, the powers had raised Napoleon up. Only by negotiation would they disarm him.

Whitbread's tactics with Ponsonby, the nominal leader of the party, were to ignore what he said and go over the same ground with greater ability. 'Only Ulysses can bend the bow of Ulysses,' he said in 1808, of Napoleon.

H

In home affairs, he exasperated the party leadership by perpetuating Fox's most extreme demands for reform of the whole system of government. At the Whig Club in 1808, he said the principles embodied in the toasts were 'immutable'. In 1809 he gave a toast to 'immediate reform'. In the Commons he carried further his campaign against outstanding figures of the aristocracy. His most prominent enemies were the Duke of York, whom he charged with corruption as Commander-in-Chief, and Wellington, the main general in the field.

The Duke of York was accused of rigging Army appointments and promotions under the influence of a former mistress, Mrs. Mary Anne Clarke, who had taken bribes from officers. In his indictment of the Duke, which lasted several hours, Whitbread dealt with him not simply as an individual or even as Commander-in-Chief, but as the symbol of corruption which seemed to him to dominate the country at the top and cripple its working by the appointment of people on other grounds than merit. The Duke was the head, he said, 'of a dark and dangerous cabal'. The struggle against privilege was a contest between the living and the dead. Napoleon was by comparison a negligible enemy.

The Duke of York was acquitted, but had to resign. Whitbread did not make the same charges against Wellington, but believed him responsible for the slow progress of the campaign in Spain and that he was over-praised by the Government. In 1809 he said he differed from the majority in the House, 'both with respect to the merits and services of Lord Wellington'. Wellington let him know that he had taken offence.

Besides attacking the leaders of the war, Whitbread took up the cause of outcasts, debtors, slaves, castaways, refugees, and enemies of the Court. Both in his attack on the Duke of York and his defence of Caroline, he came near to achieving his ambition of 'fair Fame' because he had something in common with the country. When there was a conflict between his loyalty to the oppressed and his identification with Napoleon—as there was in Napoleon's seizure of Spain—Whitbread sided with the people, and denounced 'the violence, the injustice and ambition of the Emperor of the French', in much the same terms as he normally denounced his enemies in England.

Sir Samuel Romilly, with the insight of someone who himself had suicidal tendencies, noticed a peculiarity in Whitbread which was significant but went unremarked by everyone except himself, because it was so much at odds with his surface manner. 'I am', he said, 'easily rebuked.' Romilly saw in him a compulsion at certain times to throw up his case, 'to give credit and to bestow praise on his political enemies to which they were in no respect entitled.' For a time he seemed to hand his weapons to his opponents with their point towards himself. Such a moment came at Napoleon's abdication and again at Waterloo.

In the defeats of November 1813 which preceded the Abdication a cartoon appeared showing Whitbread drowning in his own prophecies. Under a scroll *'Tis Madness to Oppose the Destinies*, his head emerges from one of his casks with the froth of his predictions about to suffocate him. Among others are *Futile British Assistance, Childish Imbecility, Emperor of Austria firmly attached to Boney.* John Bull, standing beside the cask, says, 'I say, Mr Brewer, I hope you have got enough of prophesying for your Friend—if you can't make a better brewing than that, I would advise you to leave off business.'

A reversal was already forming in Whitbread. At the Artists' Benevolent Society a few days before the Abdication, the painter, Farington, was astonished to hear him praise Wellington for restoring to their countries the works of art Napoleon had seized and denounce him as 'the usurper of France'. In the summer an address from the Commons to the Prince Regent was proposed congratulating him on 'the restoration of so many ancient and legitimate authorities on the continent', and praising the country for its unrelenting opposition to Napoleon. Whitbread, who admitted that he had opposed the war from the start, began his speech, as if talking to himself. He asked whether he could 'tamely submit to it as a fact', that all which had been 'said or thought, and still thought', was founded 'in error'. The supporters of the war, they were now given to understand, were 'infallible'.

But he did submit. He paid compliments to Castlereagh for his 'undaunted' stand in negotiations with Napoleon, and put his trust in him for the settlement of Europe. No man, Whitbread said, rejoiced more in the restoration of the Bourbons than he did. The peace treaty met with his entire satisfaction. The negotiations with Napoleon at Châtillon had, he was sure, only been broken off because of the moderation of Alexander and 'the folly, madness or what else of Bonaparte himself'. Five coalitions had 'erected Napoleon into the colossus of Europe', but his madness had 'unmade him and restored the Bourbon dynasty'. He twice called Napoleon mad and later said he had abdicated in a temporary fit of madness.

His symptoms had increased. Creevey, in 1812, noticed that his figure was becoming colossal. 'I was struck beyond measure just now at the prodigious gills and collops in his neck.'[1] He was small in build, and although he starved himself like Byron, he was approaching twenty stone.

One of the trustees of Drury Lane who had contact with Whitbread in 1814 said there was 'something very odd about him. . . '; he observed 'an appearance of somnolency in Sam'. In a man who always got up at six to

---

[1] Mr. Roger Fulford, in his biography, quotes a letter from Whitbread to Mrs. Creevey of eighteen months later in which he warns her not to be surprised to 'find me doubled in size'.

begin work, this was a development of the lethargy which had first appeared in 1808.

Whitbread's closing speeches before the summer recess of 1814 showed that he was already regretting his confidence in Castlereagh's intentions in Europe. Then, in October, he had an ugly quarrel with his wife. It was about the limits of her garden, and seemed quite inexplicable to her.

Whitbread had enclosed Southill Park, his estate in Bedfordshire, from common land at the end of the eighteenth century, and it was still not fully converted at the time of his suicide. He showed no sign of guilt about the enclosure because of the direct increase in cultivation it had brought about. But he was less indulgent to Lady Elizabeth, who had the territorial complacency of the Greys of Fallodon. She was a passionate gardener, and beyond the limits of her garden was a large tree and a beehive seat which she coveted as decorative features. With a touch of selfishness, 'being pleased with what I saw looking so pretty', she asked him to extend the boundary by enclosing the patch of ground on which they stood. She was astonished to see him almost incoherent with anger. Looking back afterwards, she could only explain it as the first sign of madness.

In the territorial scramble which was going on as a prelude to the Congress of Vienna, two main issues had begun to obsess Whitbread, apart from his general sense of outrage that the traditional rulers should be able to dispose of countries without the consent of the people. The first was that the Austrian Empire was annexing some of the states set up by Napoleon, and the other was the problem of Saxony. The King of Saxony, Frederick the Just, had been a progressive ruler, who improved the education of his countrymen, founded hospitals, and revolutionized agriculture. He had proved himself Napoleon's firmest friend in Europe. He refused to join the league against France in 1792, and after the defeat of Prussia at Jena, had fought in alliance with Napoleon, remaining loyal to the bitter end, when he was taken prisoner by the Allies. It was now rumoured, said Whitbread in the Commons, immediately after the quarrel with his wife, that because he was 'the last who adhered to Bonaparte', Frederick was 'marked out for vengeance'. Saxony was to be partitioned and a large part of its territory awarded to Prussia. But this, Whitbread said, would be 'as unprincipled a partition as any the world ever saw'. Saxony was known as 'the Garden of Germany—not only in a physical, but in a moral sense'—it was 'the garden of the human mind'.

To the Commons, who listened to his interventions on Saxony for six months after that first speech, Whitbread seemed as overwrought as he had to Lady Elizabeth and her family at Fallodon. 'The gentleman's questions, their number, and his mode of proposing them' were 'without parallel in the history of Parliament', said Castlereagh.

The fate of Saxony was a major issue on which the Government had to shift its ground, not least because of Whitbread's pressure, but his interest had a personal bearing which is unmistakable. H. G. Bennet wrote to Creevey that Whitbread was 'all for Boney'. He identified himself with Frederick the Just, not only because he was a progressive reformer, but because he had stood by Napoleon to the end. 'Bonaparte', he said, was 'in possession of his person'. For this Frederick was to be rejected by the dynasts who took credit for having escaped from their alliance with Napoleon as soon as they could.

Vienna was detested by Whitbread as the seat of the Austrian family into which Napoleon had married. It stood to Napoleon as Fallodon did to him. He did not blame the Emperor for marrying Marie-Louise, but he pointed bitterly to her failure to go with him to Elba, accused the imperial family of restraining her by force and of withholding the money due to Napoleon for her and their son. 'What a case', he said, in March 1815, 'can Bonaparte make out for those who have thus broken faith with him.' His name for them at this stage was 'the unholy Congress of Vienna'. They became 'the league of extermination against Bonaparte'. The name Vienna is repeated more often than any other, not excluding Napoleon's, in his speeches; it stands for the final triumph of the Bourbons and his own extinction.

Although he had doubled his speaking after his exclusion from the Talents, Whitbread actually doubled it again when he saw the Allies were going to combine against Napoleon's return. In the Hundred Days he made well over a hundred speeches. Many were no more than interventions which contradicted ministerial speakers and justified himself in the face of derision. He dealt with other subjects, notably the Alien Act, the Property Tax, and the situation of debtors who could not pay their sureties. But far the greater part of this burst of energy, which has no equal in volume in the history of the Commons, aimed at establishing the folly of the war, its injustice and predictable failure.

When Napoleon landed in France and Castlereagh almost at once returned from Vienna, Whitbread suspected that a decision had been taken by the Allies. In the following week he demanded a statement. In a speech of about three hours, on 20 March, he warned Castlereagh that Napoleon would be restored as a giant if the Congress adopted the attitude which had originally created him. He repeated Virgil's warning, 'Learn Justice, and do not despise the Gods.'

When the Declaration of Vienna was finally tabled he could hardly believe his eyes when he came to the sentence: 'As an enemy and disturber of the tranquillity of the world, he [Napoleon] has rendered himself liable to public vengeance.' If the House approved the Declaration, Whitbread said, it would be committing itself to a war of aggression. If words meant anything, it 'designated an individual for assassination'. Did the powers at Vienna mean that Bonaparte's head was 'on the block'? Impatient at the violence of these challenges, Castlereagh reminded him that it was less than a year since he had expressed his complete trust in him. Presumably it was because at the time of the Abdication his position had been unassailable. He warned Whitbread he had chosen a course which with due regard for his honour he 'ought to quit'.

But with Napoleon installed in Paris as a constitutional ruler and a vast plan of conscription bringing him new armies, Whitbread could not believe that the outcome of the war had been decided. He was jubilant. Napoleon was already showing the superiority of his intellect over the club of the dynasts by calmly accepting the Treaty of Paris and proposing peace to the world. Whitbread made a dozen points in the time he had formerly taken to make one; he laughed at the value of Castlereagh's calculations and intelligence system and rejoiced in his discomfiture.

The Declaration of Vienna absorbed him throughout as the key document which must be destroyed. The Duke of Wellington's name at the head of the British signatories seemed to him perhaps the most provocative thing about it. Not all the brilliance of Wellington's achievements, he said on 7 April, would be enough 'to drag him out of the abyss of shame' into which he had 'plunged himself'. He and the Lords Cathcart, Clancarty, and Stewart, who had also signed, deserved to be impeached. On whose authority, he asked on the 19th, had Wellington signed the Declaration? It had nothing to do with him—his trial had 'not yet begun': he had not yet 'had his day'. The league of extermination would never achieve its aim.

Castlereagh reminded Whitbread that he had made these prophecies of defeat at the hands of 'the great man', as he called Bonaparte, throughout the war. Whitbread interrupted to say that he had only called him a great man by comparison with the littleness of his opponents. He in turn was interrupted by cries of 'Spoke! Spoke!' Seven weeks before Waterloo, on 28 April, he moved formally against the war. Napoleon, according to the Declaration of Vienna, had forfeited 'his last and only claim to existence'. But the signatories had shown egotistic vanity. The war would last twenty years, and the chance of success became 'weaker every day, while the chance of Napoleon every day grows stronger.' The minority who voted for his motion was twenty-two and included Sir Samuel Romilly, the Hon. W. Lyttleton, and Ponsonby himself.

In May Whitbread spoke less than in the first sixty of the Hundred Days. A cartoon by Cruikshank was published on 10 May, called 'Treachery—Treachery—Treachery!!!', showing him as a barrel surrounded by enemy agents, who use it as a post-box for secret communications Castlereagh had accused him of receiving from the Continent. An officer labelled *Agent from Buonaparte* holds a bag. An American *Agent from Madison* holds documents. An *Agent from Fouché* posts a letter *To our esteemed Friends in England*. In the background stands the avenging figure of John Bull with a stick. He recalls Mr. Fox, who 'did escape', and adds, 'Alack!! 'twere better if justice were administered!!!!'

If Whitbread spoke rather less, he showed he had not changed his mind. Three weeks before Waterloo he voted against the motion to grant subsidies to the Allies. He thought their prospects were as hopeless as ever; even if Napoleon was destroyed, even if the Allies reached Paris, France would still not accept domination by the Bourbons. The object of subsidies was to enable the confederates to make 'a great, a sudden and a decisive effort'. But why was this sudden effort to be so long postponed? Two months had already passed since the return of Bonaparte. The subsidies would have to continue for as long as the war lasted, and how long that would be, no one could say. We were engaged on 'an insane project'—yes, 'insane' he would call it, 'especially as to the calculations upon its speedy conclusion'. It was impossible for anyone, for Castlereagh himself, to look for the end of the war within a year.

Only seventeen members now voted for him. In March, Whitbread had accused General Whittingham of entering Spain 'with tyranny on one side of his banner and perfidy on the other' to install a regime more ferocious than that of Robespierre. There had been a scene in the lobby when a member objected to the heat of his attack, and both were called back and rebuked by the Speaker. Now the Speaker intervened in his violent exchanges with Plumer Ward, the Clerk of the Ordnance, who had to defend the Army estimates on behalf of the Duke of York. The Duke had been reinstated as Commander-in-Chief two years after his acquittal on the charge of corruption, and Whitbread did not let any opportunity slip of suggesting inefficiency and waste of public funds. The armies were moving up to Waterloo, and Plumer Ward, in justifying an item of expenditure, had the misfortune to call Napoleon 'the ablest captain in the world', a description Whitbread himself might have used.

He exulted. This, he said, was an acknowledgement he had 'by no means expected in the present month' from a Government spokesman. At least the Clerk of Ordnance should have included Wellington with Napoleon, 'and so make out two first captains in the world'.

Plumer Ward counter-attacked until the Speaker had to ask him to withdraw, which he did with fairly good grace, disclaiming 'any wish to treat the gentleman with disrespect'. Whitbread rose. 'There is a word omitted', he said, 'which situated as I am before the committee, ought to have been

particularly used. The honourable Gentleman speaks of me as "the gentleman", not "the honourable Gentleman".'

Ten days later, when the battle was in progress, Whitbread took his place
on the platform at a meeting of the British and Foreign Bible Society. As he
sat in front of the rows of upturned faces, an intolerable pain came on in his
face and head. He told a friend it 'almost drove him out of his senses'. He
said 'charges' were being made against him, 'as well by the public voice as
by communications.' The charges seemed to centre on the finances of
Drury Lane Theatre, and when his friends tried to pin them down, he sent
for his secretary to explain, but they evaporated in front of them, so that
Whitbread had to accept that he was wrong. In spite of an immense feeling
of lethargy, he could not sleep.

Rumours of a decisive victory were coming in from Brussels which were
confirmed on 22 June by a Stop Press announcement from the Secretary of
War on the main page of *The Times*. At ten o'clock that morning the guns
fired at the Tower and in the Park. Crowds outside York House cheered the
Duke of York until he came out to join the celebrations of the household
brigades in St. James's Park. In the Commons Castlereagh read a message
from the Prince Regent. It reported an important and glorious victory over
the French Army 'under the immediate command of Bonaparte'.

The day before, Whitbread had drafted a final codicil to his will. Although his assets were over half a million pounds, he was more and more
preoccupied by debts. When he signed his will on 22 June, he had paid off
another three creditors, including his son-in-law and his bank. He wrote on
the back: 'Codicil to my will dated June 22, 1815', and he put a single exclamation mark after the date—which was two or three less than Gillray or
Cruikshank would have done.

In the Commons he made seven more speeches. They were short, slow,
and all but two concerned with Waterloo. He had difficulty in coming into
the Commons because of a swelling which had developed in his ankles.
When he sat down, a heavy sense of fatigue shut him from the laughter and
applause which he knew would come.

On the 23rd, Castlereagh proposed a vote of £200,000 to Wellington for
the completion of his mansion. For about an hour he described the course
of the battle, dwelling with emphasis on the role of the Prussians and the
continuing doubt of the outcome, then reached a climax. The House was
completely silent as if the doubt were once more a reality. On the battlefield,
said Castlereagh, the British commander had found himself 'immediately
opposed' to the man who had been 'called "the Greatest Captain of the
Age".' He had to stop. The tension had broken and shouts of applause
filled the House.

FACING PAGE
Samuel Whitbread by John Opie.

Members looked at Whitbread. One wrote to Creevey that he had 'lost all his spirits and could not speak'. Another noticed that 'his countenance often retired without apparent cause'. When he got up, he agreed with Castlereagh that Wellington was now 'distinguished above all other commanders of the earth'. It had indeed been 'a wonderful victory'.

The grant of £200,000 for Wellington's mansion was of particular importance to Whitbread. He had spent £120,000 from the profits of the brewery on his own house at Southill Park. The profits made him more uneasy than they did his father, who had shown him every year as a young man the balance of the trading account. Whitbread had a habit of intervening whenever a grant of money for a mansion was voted, and had found time in the Hundred Days to attack the extravagance of Nelson's family. At the Abdication, in May 1814, one of the clearest signs of his abasement was his proposal that the grant of £50,000 to Wellington for 'a splendid mansion' was not enough and should be increased to £100,000 at least. He now supported the grant of £200,000, which raised the status of Wellington's mansion above his own. What he could not accept, he said, was that the loss of life in the battle of Waterloo had been necessary at all. The war was one 'into which this country had neither occasion or right to enter.'

A twenty-one-year-old member for Devon, Sir Thomas Acland, who had graduated from Christ Church a year previously, got up at the end of the debate. He proposed that the superiority of Wellington over Napoleon as a commander in the field should be formally recorded in the motion and thus become embodied in Apsley House. Whitbread rose again. His fatigue had increased and confused what he said, but the meaning was clear. It was unnecessary to agree with Sir Thomas Acland's proposal. Wellington and Bonaparte had met in direct conflict.

That night the illuminations started and the glow in the sky could be seen from the windows of Whitbread's town house in Dover Street. Ackermanns had a great transparency of Wellington with a sabre galloping at a doomed figure, its arms flung wide in despair.

It was a Thursday, and Whitbread spent the week-end trying to work. But he could only think of the French retreat and their disorder as they reached Paris. If the Allied armies found it undefended, he foresaw 'horrors' in their final triumph.

His political future was now as much at stake as Napoleon's, and when he despaired of it, his misery seemed to fragment into accusations. The relief of clearing his debts on the 22nd did not last. He could pay no dividend to the people he had persuaded to subscribe to the rebuilding of Drury Lane. A stage carpenter had not been paid, and he sent round his personal cheque. In the mornings the papers were in full pursuit of Napoleon. There was a daily lampoon in verse in the *Morning Post*. *The Times* reported that he had been put to death at La Rochelle. A new rush of cartoons had started which were full of the joy of the chase.

On three days in the following week, Whitbread went back to the Commons. There was a debate on the Duke of Cumberland's marriage grant, which would once have roused his scorn, but now left him unmoved. On the Wednesday he simply voted in the minority who opposed it, with Romilly and Lord Ossulston. On the same day, there was a debate on new war credits, and he gave them his vote because of 'the splendour of our recent success', although there had been 'no change whatever' in his view of the injustice of the war. Wellington, he said, must prevent the horrors which might be committed if Paris was reached.

On Thursday, there was a second debate on the Duke of Cumberland's marriage, but Whitbread still gave the main weight of his speech to Waterloo. The Duke of York now had his admiration as well as Wellington; but he was sorry to see an order of the day in which Wellington had used 'epithets' against Napoleon. Had not the outcome been in doubt, on his own admission? Would it not have been more becoming in a great conqueror to have spared such language? There were murmurs of dissent.

News of Napoleon's abdication reached London in the middle of the week. 'My political life is ended', he had declared. But in the cartoon shops in the Haymarket and Piccadilly there was not even a parody of imperial grandeur any more. Napoleon is a dwarf with his hands tied behind his back, beaten and kicked by the victorious giants, Wellington and Blücher. He flees with a devil over his head to a capital which is already burning. His body hangs upside down with two devils upright beside him and a notice dangling from his neck, *Decree for Abolishing the Slave Trade*.

Whitbread was now sleeping for only half an hour at night. He continued to complain of violent headaches, and at some stage was cupped, as one of the first remedies prescribed for hydrocephalus. On Sunday, 2 July, Brougham wrote to Grey: 'If you see Whitbread, or Lady Elizabeth, do for God's sake, insist upon them immediately going away.' He said he was very seriously alarmed about Whitbread, and that he refused to see any medical man. But almost everyone had been trying to get him away. His friend and partner, Wilshire, had been brought up from the country by the family 'to rouse and restore him' because he would not go to him. He told Wilshire: 'My public life is extinct.' He said it repeatedly, in his own language as well as Napoleon's. He was 'an outcast from society'.

Lady Elizabeth got him to go with her to the Vauxhall pleasure gardens, but so far from it being a relief, he thought a group of footmen were jeering at him. 'They are hissing me,' he said to his wife. 'I am become an object of universal abhorrence.'

One friend did get him away. This was Launcelot Holland, the son of Henry Holland, the architect who had built Southill Park. He was much younger than Whitbread, who had known him ever since work on the building began twenty years previously. He was now a magistrate at Epsom and was able to give his evidence clearly at the inquest on 6 July. He had been unable, he said, to keep Whitbread with him for two full days. His friend did not sleep at night and seemed to be in a stupor in the day. He insisted on going back to London because 'a vast deal of public business remained to be done, and though he was incapable of performing it, he would struggle on at it, and do the best he could.' Holland added that in his own view, 'for the last fortnight [from 22 June] I have not thought him competent to go through the business he was accustomed to.' On the second morning at Epsom, he had found Whitbread lying naked on his bed and thumping his chest. He said to Holland: 'The devils are after me.'

Whitbread was able to hide his extremity from people who knew him less well than Holland. The swelling in his feet and ankles had spread. On the Opposition front bench he bent forward sometimes and nodded his head. But two days before his suicide, he made a last speech that was more or less coherent, and one day before, he took a committee meeting at Drury Lane. Holland came up to London and kept by his side.

On Monday, 3 July, from the House of Commons, he wrote his last letter to his wife as if she had deserted him as completely as Marie-Louise had Napoleon.

On Tuesday, 4 July, an obscure Tory, Sir J. Majoribanks, proposed on his own initiative a vote of thanks to the Duke of York as Commander-in-Chief of the Armed Forces. The Duke had been back in office for four years since Whitbread's accusation that he had promoted officers who had bribed his mistress. He had not known of their bribes at the time and had justified himself on his return to office by his conscientious work. Majoribanks used this opportunity to rebuke Whitbread more directly than Castlereagh had in the debate on Wellington. His vote of thanks covered the Duke's services 'during a period of twenty years', so that it included the period when Whitbread had denounced him as a greater menace to the country than Napoleon. Majoribanks dwelt on his honour and impartiality in choosing the right people for promotion. The suggestion that he was a threat of any kind to the country was scouted by his overwhelming achievement in preparing for Waterloo.

Majoribanks must have been irritated by the supine figure of Whitbread on the front bench opposite him. When blow after blow had brought no reaction, he used a hatchet. 'All I regret', he said, 'is that the motion has not been made by the Right Honourable Gentleman opposite'—he added

'Right' to recall Whitbread's protest to the Speaker a few weeks previously —'in the pretty and modest manner' in which he usually brought forward 'similar propositions.'

There was a shout of laughter, which died almost at once. Whitbread still did not move. Western, a member of the Whig Club, known as 'Squire Western', got up behind him and tried to block the motion by semi-constitutional arguments. He was fallen upon by Wellesley-Pole, the brother of Wellington, who had been at Eton with Whitbread and was a year older. Wellesley-Pole said that 'the strict impartiality of the Duke's administration' had been responsible for the efficiency of the Army and its glorious achievement. His brother himself had told him so. He thundered at Western for his unpatriotic attempt to block the motion and warned the Opposition of the risk they ran of acting with disloyalty.

Whitbread got up to make his last speech. At the end of the previous week he had paid his tribute to the Duke of York, saying he had 'placed the Army in such a state of efficiency as to achieve the most brilliant exploits'. Now, for a moment, it was as if he had regained his old defiance. An informant of Creevey's noticed that he spoke 'more in his usual style than of late'. He began by saying that the House should not be called on to thank the head of the Armed Forces any more than any other departmental head who had contributed to the victory. 'I sincerely regret that the brother of the Duke of Wellington has thought fit to take so high and loud a tone, as if any difference of opinion was little less than an act of ingratitude.' If a grant of money was proposed—and it had been hinted at—he would reserve his position. 'However,' he said, and the fight seemed to die in him, 'laying all this aside—laying aside different topics' which had been 'mixed up with the present question—wishing the honourable Gentleman had not now brought forward his motion ... still', looking to the compliments which had been paid to the Duke of York—compliments the result 'not of partiality, but of conviction'—he conceived the House 'ought to agree the resolution'.

His two enemies, the Duke of York and Wellington, had beaten him as completely as they had Napoleon. There remained only the thin chance of a regrouping outside Paris and the view taken of him by English public opinion. Whitbread had always been sensitive to public opinion, and his reputation had always seemed at stake among all men. When the Whigs rejected him, his need to stand well with the people had increased. Since the news of Waterloo, it had become an obsession. He wrote a note to his sister asking her to find out what Sam Reynolds, his amanuensis, thought of him. He watched the servants, the passers-by, the members of the British and Foreign Bible Society, the footmen. The cartoons would now catch up with him. At any moment he could expect to see himself drowning in a barrel of blood, which might be Napoleon's or simply fall drop by drop from his own false prophecies.

His last speech, in support of the vote of thanks to the Duke of York, was on Tuesday. On Wednesday, 5 July, it was known that Paris had capitulated. *The Times* carried a proclamation by Louis XVIII that he would re-establish the constitution, reward the good, and punish the guilty.

On Wednesday, Whitbread went to a meeting at Drury Lane instead of the Commons. He came back to Dover Street with the faithful Launcelot Holland, who had grown up with Southill Park. When they reached Piccadilly, he began muttering again about the scoffing and the jeers. He added— and this was new—'The populace will pull down my house.'

In the morning, Weir, his butler, used to shave him. On Thursday morning he heard him saying he was well; but the door of his room was locked. In the 'justice room' at Southill, he used to work in his dressing-gown from eight-thirty in the morning. He dressed on Thursday in Dover Street in a yellow striped morning gown, trousers to match, and a cotton shirt unbuttoned at the collar. He then sat down in front of the mirror and studied his throat as if it required the ability and strength of a major speech. He used the razor to make a great incision from the side and had time for its counterpart from the other before he fell. At the inquest a witness said, 'perhaps no act of self-destruction was so complete.'

Three months earlier, at the beginning of the Hundred Days, Whitbread had said in the Commons that people were 'generally favourable to the dead'. He was speaking jocularly, about the death of the Property Tax. 'Like all deceased personages,' he said, its vices had 'vanished from memory', and only its virtues remained. The Whig aristocrats, who had spent the past six or seven years grumbling about Whitbread's violence and conceit, were the first to be converted. They were aghast, and realized at once that more was at stake than his own reputation. Their carriages began to block Dover Street, which was impassable for three days. The *Morning Post*, which was to prove the least unreliable of the papers, noticed among other callers, the Earl and Countess Grey, Lord Grenville, Lord Lauderdale, the Duke of Bedford, Lord Molton, Lord Hamilton, Tierney, and Francis Horner.

The first aim laid down by Grey, who had become the guardian of Whitbread's children, was to conceal the fact of his suicide. The press were told he had died of apoplexy after complaining (in the words of *The Times*) 'of an oppressive fullness in his head'. But the doctors had already set the law in motion, and on the evening of his death a formal inquest was held in the house, with Wilshire, Launcelot Holland, and Weir, the butler, as chief witnesses. An attempt was made by Grey to refuse to admit journalists, but failed. Pressure was then put on the editors, but was resisted by the *Morning*

*Post* which reported next morning that the jury had returned a unanimous verdict of suicide while insane. It added that Whitbread was the real leader of the Whigs. The *Courier* said that doctors had tried to prevent him from taking 'so active a part' in the Commons.

With the first line of defence hopelessly breached, the Opposition leaders faced the risk that Napoleon's defeat would be generally accepted as the reason for Whitbread's suicide, with what would be fatal consequences for the party. They decided to emphasize the role of Drury Lane in his affairs and to omit all reference to his position in the Commons. The Government and its supporting newspapers had no wish to make an issue of it. Even the *Morning Post* atoned for its daring with a corrective in 'The Fashionable World'.

The subject which pressed most heavily upon the mind of the much-lamented Mr Whitbread was the state of the Drury Lane Theatre, in which he took an interest beyond all precedent. He exerted himself to the utmost to produce the last dividend, in the hope that the profits of the present season would cover everything; but the prospect being somewhat clouded, his disappointment was so great as to fall heavily upon his heart, and distress his mind to such a degree as to have been the principal cause of the melancholy catastrophe now so deeply and extensively deplored.

Those who had been closest to Whitbread united in support of the theory. When tributes were paid in the Commons, the barbed references and sarcasms were swept away as if they had never been thrown across the floor. Wilberforce was at pains to emphasize that Whitbread's virtues were peculiarly English, and he was praised on all sides for his integrity and sympathy with the oppressed. His expressed belief that death turns criticism into praise has not often been borne out so dramatically.

The doctors had their own theory. On Saturday, 8 July, his head was dissected by Sir Henry Halford, who found that 'the ventricles of the brain contained more fluid than usual by one third part at least'. Halford attended George III. When he was consulted some months later by Byron's family, he contributed to the view that Byron was also suffering from hydrocephalus.

The funeral procession moved out of Dover Street in the early hours of Monday, 10 July. Through the darkness which had followed the illuminations, five mourning coaches made their way behind the hearse up to Oxford Street and into the Edgware Road towards Bedfordshire, where he was buried in the family church at Cardington.

The belief that Whitbread killed himself not because of Drury Lane but because of Waterloo, was hinted at and even said plainly by those who shared his admiration for Napoleon. Lord Holland said he killed himself because his 'appetite for applause' was so great that he could not stand the prospect of it ending. When Napoleon was brought to Plymouth, Byron told Hobhouse he felt 'nothing was left but to follow Whitbread's example'. He told Medwin soon after Napoleon died that 'no event in ancient times ever struck me as more noble and dramatic than the death of Demosthenes.' Demosthenes committed suicide rather than submit to the Macedonians when they occupied Athens and secured a sentence of death on him. Byron compared only one of his contemporaries to him, and that was Whitbread— an insult to the oratory of both but the supreme compliment to Whitbread.

Hazlitt, as usual, was direct. 'His enthusiasm ran away with his judgement', he says, in *Parliamentary Eloquence*, 'and was not *backed* by equal powers of reasoning and imagination. He was a sanguine, high-spirited man, but not a man of genius or a deep thinker; and his fortitude failed him, when the last fatal blow was given to himself and his party.' The fatal blow can only have been Waterloo.

It was perhaps easier for Hazlitt than for Whitbread to show fortitude at the defeat of Napoleon, though it was not a word used by those who saw Hazlitt's collapse at the time. Whitbread had committed himself day after day to the issue of the campaign as no one has ever committed himself to the result of a battle. It was not a chance misjudgement but the logical out-come of his life. He did not complain of his isolation at Eton, or Oxford, or Cambridge, when he found there was something unacceptable about the source of his money. But he fell in love with the family which did accept him, and his insistence on marrying Lady Elizabeth against his father's opposition suggests the strength of his need. When it turned out that the aristocrats did not accept him after all but were in league to keep him out of office and the leadership, he was back where he had come from—the brewery.

He was not only educated for leadership. He had the strength and ability to succeed with the public where he had failed with the ruling class. When he thought Napoleon invincible, he was judging him by his own will to succeed.

Whitbread survived the first Abdication with his prospects seriously battered. When Napoleon returned, he had one more chance. The Declar-ation of Vienna seemed to him to deprive Napoleon of 'his last and only claim to existence'. There was really nothing left for him, either. If Napo-leon was crushed, his hope of vindication in the country was gone.

We must call Whitbread's obsession with what footmen and passers-by were thinking, by its medical name of paranoia. But he knew the revulsion of feeling which death can bring about. A week after the funeral, Wilber-force told the painter Farington quite firmly that Whitbread's 'understand-ing was not gone'.

## 2

Caroline was shocked by the news of Whitbread's suicide and expressed surprise that his religion had not been strong enough to prevent it. Freed from his restraints and careless of the Prince's spies around her on the Continent, she had been giving herself up to her pleasures. Lady Bury caught up with her in Geneva in the autumn of 1814, at a party given by Napoleon's wife, Marie-Louise, when she appeared in a topless dress. 'What was my horror when I beheld the poor Princess enter, dressed *en Vénus*, or rather not dressed further than the waist.' She waltzed obstinately through the night and made Lady Bury fear that she would 'lose herself entirely' when she reached the south. She very nearly did, but not in the sense Lady Bury expected.

On her way through Italy, on 23 October, she met the Hollands between Bologna and Florence, and spent an hour with them. It was an important hour. For the only time in their lives, the Hollands both recorded pleasant things about her. In Geneva, she had discussed Napoleon with Marie-Louise, who was torn between his demands to come to him on Elba and the insistence of her family that she should leave him. What Caroline and the Hollands had in common was a determination themselves to go to Elba.

Although Caroline was often denounced as a Jacobin by her enemies in England, they had not foreseen that her ostracism by the Court might actually throw her into the arms of the enemy. Her interest in Napoleon had begun to form in London when she denounced 'this vile country' to Lady Bury and stung that lady into suggesting she might prefer life in Brunswick. She had found an admiration for Napoleon in almost all her regular visitors —in Byron, Hobhouse, Burdett, Brougham, and Whitbread. If this was the tendency of her advisers, how much more justification had she herself who was actually confused in the Regent's mind with Napoleon, as his greatest enemy.

In October or November 1814, says Napoleon's valet, Marchand, Caroline wrote to Napoleon proposing a formal visit to Elba.[1] 'The Princess of Wales,' writes Marchand, 'had just sent a message to His Majesty proposing to come to the island of Elba. The Emperor, in the middle of public works and reconstruction, was unable to receive her appropriately, and asked her

---

[1] The statement was only published in *Mémoires de Marchand*, ed. Jean Bourguignon (Paris, 1952), and can be trusted even though Marchand is the sole source. The biographers who were allowed access to Caroline's papers were writing in her defence, and would have been tempted to ignore such a major indiscretion. Napoleon himself, who was greatly preoccupied with England's attitude to his return to France, was much too discreet to allow such a visit or leave evidence of her intention.

to defer the little visit. The Princess had seen the Empress Marie-Louise at Berne, during her journey in Switzerland. . . .'

Caroline left the Hollands in a more enthusiastic mood about Napoleon than before. She was making for Naples, which was the chief centre of communication with him, but she paused in Rome to pay her respects to Lucien Bonaparte, the most impressive of his brothers. In a letter to his sister on 10 November, Holland reported that the Princess made the call on Lucien so precipitately and showed 'so marked a preference for his society' that it was much talked of in that gossiping and ceremonious country.

In Naples the main link with Napoleon was Caroline Bonaparte, the wife of Murat, who was trying to prove himself acceptable to England. 'The Princess of Wales is gone there,' Holland reported, 'which will embarrass him [Murat] not a little. As an English Princess he must wish to overwhelm her with attentions, but if they please the English, will they not estrange the Prince Regent?' Caroline solved the problem for Murat by establishing herself in a villa at Portici, six miles outside the capital, and herself making the advances.

The son of an innkeeper, Murat had been Napoleon's greatest cavalry general, the 'golden eagle' of Marengo and Jena, who remained a product of the Revolution after Napoleon had given him the throne. Caroline was dazzled by his looks, his uniforms, and his court. '*La décence*', she wrote, '*est poussée à un point que même Whitbread et Lady Elizabeth en seraient édifiés.*' In her villa she had a bust of him which she crowned with a wreath. On his arrival at a party in his honour, a transparency was lit up with the legend '*À Joachim le Grand*'.

Caroline remained at Naples until Napoleon's return from Elba at the end of February 1815. As he made his way to Paris, she went to Rome, probably to contact Lucien again, and then on to Elba, which she reached about the time Napoleon was carried into the Tuileries. The rooms in his house still seemed to be occupied by him and she went over them hungrily, taking away a book from the library and one of his billiard cues.

She entered into negotiations with Lucien Bonaparte to rent one of his houses, and by 1817 was settled in his villa at Frascati. As the English fell away from her entourage, she had been converting it into a parody of a Napoleonic court, in which she alternately played the role of Emperor and Imperial Consort. In Milan she had appointed Bartolomeo Pergami as her courier. She called him 'Napoleon's Courier', and he had in fact served in the *état-major* in some capacity in the campaigns which followed the retreat from Moscow. 'Being puffed up with low anecdotes by Pergami,' wrote Lady Brownlow, 'she imagined that she was a staunch admirer of the great hero of this epoch, and nothing but Napoleon and his fame occupied her thoughts.'

I

Pergami became in turn equerry, chamberlain, and lover. She showered him with titles. In Jerusalem she persuaded the Capuchin Friars to found an order of St. Caroline with the motto *Honi soit qui mal y pense*. Pergami was installed as Grand Master and wore the motto round his neck. She wrote to Lucien Bonaparte asking for '*quelque marque d'attention pour lui*'. He became a Knight of the Grand Order of Malta and Baron of Sicily. His family was enthroned around her, on the model of Napoleon's. Louis Pergami directed her household, Vallotti Pergami kept her purse, the Countess Oldi, Bartolomeo's sister, became a lady of honour, and his daughter Victorine travelled in her suite. His mother she called 'Madame Livia', after Madame Mère. She got into such confusion about the honours that it was enough, she used to say, 'to die for laugh'.

At the beginning of 1820 George III died and Caroline became Queen of England.

The effect of her elevation was contradictory. On the one hand popular support flared up to an extent that confirmed her intention to return to England for the Coronation. On the other hand she found every kind of obstacle put in her way across Europe by the British Government, 'as if it were in time of war', she wrote. In Italy the authorities were briefed to deny her the honours of a sovereign. She was warned that Louis XVIII would make any journey through Paris undignified. When the revised liturgy of the Church of England was published she found that her name was excluded; the country was to pray only for George IV. On leaving Kensington in 1814 she had twice been assured that she could come back when she wished. She now found she would not be admitted to any palace.

On the way back from Italy she was met by her supporters: first, at Montbéliard near Besançon, by Alderman Wood and the ever-faithful Lady Anne Hamilton, and then a few miles from Calais by Brougham, with an emissary of the Government. The object of Alderman Wood and Lady Anne Hamilton was to encourage her; that of Brougham and the Government to send her back. The offer was a life pension of £50,000 in return for abandoning the title of Queen of England. If she declined, parliamentary proceedings would be started against her when she landed.

Brougham had been out of Parliament for three years after prophesying economic defeat at the hands of Napoleon. His reaction to Waterloo was grim but not suicidal. It seemed to be a defeat for all the causes to which he was committed and he had a period of serious emotional disturbance in which he retired to the country, was unable to write, and studied the cell formation of beehives instead. He recovered, and on returning to the Commons in 1816, saw hope for the radical forces of the country in the long run. Without much confidence in Caroline's chances after her adventures on the Continent, he succeeded to Whitbread's role as her champion.

He now suggested that better terms could be won and that Caroline might be able to retain the title in return for an undertaking to remain on the Continent. But she distrusted him and would not compromise. 'If my head is on Temple Bar,' she said, 'it will be his doing.' She landed at Dover on 5 June 1820, with Alderman Wood. A royal salute was fired by the garrison and her journey to London was a celebration.

There had been important changes in Kensington. Sussex was still in the palace, with more books and musical-boxes, but the Duke of Kent had died mysteriously at the beginning of the year after catching cold. In the background was the break-up of his affair with Madame St. Laurent. Three years after Caroline left the country, her daughter, Charlotte, who had married Prince Leopold Saxe-Coburg, had died in childbirth. The succession to the throne was endangered since none of the remaining sons of George III had provided an heir. Kent, in a crisis of conscience, jettisoned Madame St. Laurent, and married the German Princess of Leiningen. They were at her father's court when she became pregnant; Kent borrowed enough money to return so that the child might be born in England. Princess Victoria was born in the palace with Charlotte's former prospects. Madame St. Laurent took the veil, and remained an unknown figure to the future Queen.

Caroline at once sent Alderman Wood to pay her respects to the Duchess of Kent and her child. The atmosphere in the palace was now dominated by Sussex, who had no wish for a return of Caroline's musical soirées in spite of his sympathy with her politics. 'I can remember crawling on a yellow carpet', wrote Victoria, 'and being told that if I cried and was naughty my "Uncle Sussex" would hear me and punish me, for which reason I always screamed when I saw him.' The new and silent regime was to last nearly twenty years, until Victoria moved into Buckingham Palace.

Caroline, meanwhile, having stayed in turn with Alderman Wood and Lady Anne Hamilton, was reduced to taking Brandenburg House at Hammersmith, two miles down the turnpike beyond Kensington Palace. The Coronation, which had been fixed for 1 August, was postponed. A Bill was introduced into the House of Lords to deprive her of the title of Queen and dissolve her marriage with the King; the evidence, supported by Government witnesses, covered her indiscretions over the past six years. All peers were summoned to attend on pain of fines. The Duke of Sussex was excused after pleading the closeness of his relationship, but the Duke of York, who made a similar appeal, was persuaded to attend. No pressure was put on expatriates, and particularly not on Lord Byron in Ravenna. 'I think the Queen will win,' he wrote to Murray. 'I wish she may.'

The England to which Caroline returned was more revolutionary than the one she had left before Waterloo. 'We shall see, if we live, a Jacobin Revolution more bloody than that of France,' Grey wrote to Holland when he heard she was coming. With the lifting of the Napoleonic threat, the people found it less acceptable that they should be governed by an unrepresentative Parliament interested in retaining wartime prices on food by means of the Corn Laws and in denying the majority the political rights which would have enabled them to secure a reasonable share of the national income. A few months before Caroline's return a crowd of 80,000, meeting in St. Peter's Fields, Manchester, to demand reform, was dispersed at the cost of a dozen lives. Peterloo, as it became known, was then formally endorsed by the Six Acts, among which was one forbidding mass meetings in the open attended by people from a wide area.

The arrival of Caroline fitted the situation dramatically. Her appeal was a general one, which attracted everyone who felt in some sense excluded from the community. Beginning among the middle classes of London and the North, who were permanently outvoted in Parliament, support for her spread to more varied groups which had not hitherto been recognized as frustrated communities—they included adolescents, women, skilled craftsmen and workers, groups linked by no bond but the neighbourhood in which they lived.

Under the direction of Cobbett, who became the most active of her advisers, the demonstrations for Caroline dwarfed Peterloo in size, but avoided violence till the very end. Cobbett resisted compromise. He had himself always been a publicist of the most defiant kind, in the United States backing Britain and its establishment, in London choosing the Peace of Amiens as the time to demand war. Now his main anxiety was to strengthen Caroline against the temporizing policy of Brougham and to defeat a move by Wilberforce to put her under the protection of the Commons. 'Protection' was to be granted if she would accept the two conditions insisted on by her husband: no palace as a base of operations, and continued exclusion from the prayers of the country. Cobbett saw that her power as a symbol of rebellion was at stake.

The addresses presented to Caroline at first had the familiar sources of the past, in Middlesex, Westminster, and the industrial North. A combined meeting of the Middlesex and Westminster electors at the beginning of August was larger, according to Burdett, than any he could remember. Whitbread's second son, Samuel Charles Whitbread, who now represented Middlesex in the Commons, received a warning that so big a meeting so soon after the death of George III might be looked on as a treasonable attempt to tyrannize over the new King. Less able than his father, he was equally firm, and replied that the object of such a charge could only be to tyrannize over the Queen, 'who has too much courage and fortitude to be cowed.'

She received the deputation on 14 August, immediately before the crucial stage of proceedings in the Lords, which began with the second reading of the Bill. In her reply she showed understanding of her audience and an improvement in her style, both owing to Cobbett. When abroad, she had not forgotten them, she said. 'The improved spirit of the age, which is seen in the intellectual advancement of man through all the gradations of the social scheme, is particularly visible in this metropolitan county. Here the dissemination of knowledge is found to have the most salutary effects. . . . Here liberty finds its most impenetrable shield; and tyranny has to contend with its most devoted foe.'

For the hearing of the witnesses in Parliament Caroline had rooms in St. James's Square and became a temporary neighbour of Castlereagh, whose house was kept shuttered to protect it from her supporters. Protection was given to a group of Italians who were brought over via Dover to give evidence of her relations with Pergami. She herself went to the hearings with Lady Anne Hamilton and her chamberlains. Her spirits were raised by a report in the *Morning Chronicle* that Byron had returned, but it was a rumour; he had simply said that Italian evidence could be bought.

The first two witnesses, Majocchi and Louise Demont, showed they had taken Government money and perjured themselves. Three Italians who followed were also discredited. Brougham opened the case for Caroline with an appeal to the interest of the Lords as a credible court of justice. The witnesses he called were solid, Lady Charlotte Lindsay and other members of her suite proving as steady and disinterested as the Italians were mercurial and corrupt.

In Brooks's the betting was that the Bill would be withdrawn. S. C. Whitbread, in the Commons, said that the proceedings were so odious that Ministers themselves must be anxious to be rid of them. He estimated that the Government had spent a million pounds on the case and moved for itemized accounts. 'The nation has seen with joy', said *The Times* on 12 October, 'that all the witnesses against the Queen have been destroyed.'

The new tone of *The Times* was an admission of the widening extent of public indignation. As Caroline left Hammersmith to attend the trial she had received a deputation from 'the inhabitants', few of whom could call themselves freeholders or pretended to qualify for the vote. She replied with sympathy, as if they were as important as any other section of the community and more closely related to her as neighbours. The idea of local demonstrations exploded all over the country with outbursts as far away as St. Ives.

The climax of the trial was reached at the end of the evidence, when some

forty addresses were presented to Caroline in one day. The first, from Kensington, was delivered by S. C. Whitbread. *The Times*, now out to counteract
charges of republican violence, reported that the procession 'consisted of 42
carriages and chiefly filled with ladies of the first respectability'. They were
dressed in white and wore Caroline's medal on their necklaces. Whitbread
recalled her time in the palace, 'when we had abundant proofs of Your
Majesty's goodness of heart, charitable disposition and rectitude of conduct.' She replied that she had 'not forgotten and shall not readily forget'
that part of her life. 'The inhabitants of this parish were then more closely
united with me by the charities of neighbourhood; and those charities I
never suffer any change of place or any lapse of time, to efface. . . .'

As the deputations followed one after another, the first-comers were
reluctant to leave, and *The Times* estimated there were never less than ten
thousand in the grounds of Brandenburg House. At times the turnpike was
impassable; there were so many pedestrians that 'the metropolis seemed
almost to have emptied itself'. Brandenburg House was on the riverside and
over five thousand boats blocked the Thames when the lightermen and
watermen held their procession. Ordinary trades began to emerge most
prominently, mechanics and brass-founders, glass-blowers and printers;
but there were also groups cutting across trades and classes—'The Youths
of the Metropolis', and 'the Ladies and other inhabitants of the Metropolis'
led by Hobhouse. The *Courier*, the main newspaper opposed to Caroline,
quoted *The Times* as saying she had been 'cheered, addressed, congratulated
in a way that no sovereign ever was from the foundations of the monarchy'.
Could it be, asked the *Courier*, that carpenters and bricklayers would be
allowed to influence Parliament?

The Duke of Sussex was now being greeted on the turnpike with shouts
of 'The Queen and Sussex for ever!' He attended a Fox dinner and sang
louder than anyone else (for the size of his voice was in proportion to his
body):

> Fall, tyrants, fall, fall, fall,
> These are the days of Liberty!
> Fall, Tyrants, Fall!

His popularity rose to such a level that the Tories began to wonder if a
revolution would put him on the throne.

It was clear that the Bill would never pass the Commons. Brougham excelled himself in his peroration and the majority at the third reading fell to
nine. The Prime Minister had to announce that proceedings would be postponed. To the country it was an acquittal.

There was a general illumination, but with natural exceptions which
included Carlton House, the Duke of Wellington's mansion, and the office

of the *Courier*. 'The whole line of road from Hyde Park Corner to Hammersmith was splendidly illuminated,' according to *The Times*. 'We particularly remarked the house of Mr Wilberforce and Lady Elizabeth Whitbread, which was illuminated in all parts with equal taste and simplicity.' Cobbett's daughter, Anne, describes how her father hired a coach in Kensington 'and the spectacle was fine beyond anything you can imagine. All the ships in the river lighted to the mastheads, processions marching with bands of music carrying busts of the Queen with the crown on her head covered with laurel, playing *God Save the Queen* and bearing torches; altogether the sight was such as to overcome one, at the same time as it was most particularly gratifying to *us*.' Leigh Hunt, in the *Examiner*, claimed that London was still more brilliantly illuminated a week later, especially 'in the most obscure and most quiet streets—in lanes, alleys and courts', where candles burnt in the windows.

At the end of November, when Caroline drove to St. Paul's for a service of thanksgiving, against the wishes of the Church, *The Times* believed that the crowds were bigger than any in history. She was met at Temple Bar by the Lord Mayor and Sheriffs, and arrived at St. Paul's closely followed by Hobhouse in court dress and Sir Robert Wilson, who had organized the escape of one of Napoleon's aides from France. Immense cheers greeted each of them.

One of Caroline's chamberlains, the Hon. Keppel Craven, demanded from the Government without further delay, 'a palace and an establishment suitable to Her Majesty's rank in the country'. Lord Liverpool returned a blank refusal, and it was difficult for Caroline to know what to do next. Addresses continued to arrive at Brandenburg House, but they had an air of anticlimax and tended to come from the hard core of her supporters.

At the end of the year a second address came from Kensington, which shows up her local support in detail. The roll of signatures was about thirty feet long with the names and addresses of 900 from the area. The rich and the eminent on the whole did not sign. There was no one from Holland House and only one or two servants from the palace. The most densely represented areas were the High Street and the new square. The signatures were led by William à Beckett and included five other trustees. Daniel Sutton and Daniel Sutton the Younger, together with their immediate neighbours, were the richest. Other trustees included Aglio, who was commissioned to keep an eye on the progress of the pleasure ground. The Navy on half-pay abstained. The names were mostly grouped in families. There was Emma Aglio, who could just write, Aglio's wife Letitia, and his grown-up son Augustine. À Beckett's new wife signed, his fourteen-year-old son William, another son Thomas, who was in his second year at Westminster, and his eldest daughter. A Caroline Brothers signed twice, perhaps from pride in her christian name.[1] The servants in the Sutton family wrote their names with some difficulty on a separate sheet.

On the High Street there were the proprietors of the Star and Garter and Cobbett's public house the Bunch of Grapes. (Cobbett's seventeen-year-old son, James, signed in Brompton, but for some reason not Cobbett himself.) Besides the butcher, the baker, and Humblestone, the bootmaker, there was William Judson, who had made keys to the square for the rate-payers; John Wells, the pawnbroker by the palace, who attended Vaughan's Church of Christ; George Benson, builder, and Robert Lamb, the square's favourite undertaker. Many of these people with the lowest social status felt they were asserting themselves for the first time and made the gesture with solemnity.

But without the vote, what was to be done to secure Caroline's victory? In December S. C. Whitbread wrote to Lord Holland urging him to convene a mass meeting of the freeholders of Middlesex to demand the inclusion of her name in the liturgy, but Holland declined. In January 1821 a motion to the same effect was lost in the Commons. She declared she would accept no pension from the state for as long as she was excluded from the liturgy, and at Brooks's a group of members met under Lord Sefton and Lord Thanet to launch a public subscription scheme. The support never materialized.

She took advice by turns from Cobbett, Brougham, and Alderman Wood; when the latter advised her not to accept the pension at all, to the dismay of Cobbett and Brougham she accepted it. She was warned in April that there would be no place for her at the Regent's Coronation in July. She replied that she would attend as she was entitled to under constitutional law. But on Coronation Day she was refused entry first at one door of Westminster Abbey and then another.

That night Caroline was unwell. She drank a thick mixture of opium and magnesia, and although it seemed to make her worse, she recovered sufficiently to attend a performance of *Richard III* at Drury Lane ten days later. She fainted during the play and died a week later. The news of Napoleon's death had arrived, and when the Prince Regent heard that 'his greatest enemy' was dead, he assumed it was Caroline.

One of her last wishes had been that her body should be sent back to

---

[1] From the moment of Caroline's first arrival, more than a decade before, her name had been used increasingly at baptisms in the parish church. With rare exceptions (who included à Beckett and Hunnermann) the parents who called their children Caroline were shopkeepers or workers; they included two grocers, a hatmaker and a shoemaker, a barman and a porter at the Adam and Eve, a wheelwright, and nearly a dozen workers, who included a sweep. At the Church of Christ Vaughan christened three Carolines, born to a carrier, a turner, and a schoolmaster.

Brunswick. To avoid rioting, the Cabinet tried to divert the funeral procession from Hammersmith to the north of London, but in Kensington the crowd barricaded the road at St. Mary's where it was to turn north. Rain began to fall at dawn. The crowds stood patiently until about nine when the first carriages came into sight. When they reached the church they were stopped by police who tried to re-open the escape route. But by then the crowd had torn up the road surface to make doubly sure that the hearse should keep to the turnpike.

To Cobbett, just off the High Street, it seemed that some uncanny power had brought the hearse to a stop outside his own house. There was 'something so very singular, so affecting, so imperious over the mind, that it was impossible not to yield to its powers.' He was in tears. At eleven, the Cabinet's orders had to give way to the will of the crowd, 'and a shout, such as I never heard before, proclaimed the victory even of the dead corpse of this gallant queen.'

But had it been a victory? The radicals of Kensington had had their way with the procession, but as the backs of the carriages disappeared to meet new adventures on their way to the City, it was plain to everyone that the emotion that had gripped the place for so long might disintegrate for lack of a surviving cause. William à Beckett sold his lease, handed over his role in the square to a Mr. Cocksedge, and returned to the parish of St. James's from which he had come. He has not survived in the public memory as well as his sons over whom he tyrannized, but he was more representative of his time. He now found a better outlet than Caroline for the indignation he always felt at arbitrary privilege. Under a seventeenth-century Act, the parishioners of St. James's had a vestry (appointed by the neighbouring parish of St. Martin-in-the-Fields) which was in no way answerable to them. It did not take à Beckett long, in his new mood, to discover that the rates were being misappropriated. He demanded democratic reform: the parishioners themselves should select a committee, as they had done in the square he had just taught to administer itself. Moreover the qualification for voting should be the same £30 in the West End as at the turnpike gate, which meant that power would go to the least fashionable.

But à Beckett found himself in a different political atmosphere in St. James's. Mr. Gurney, a friend of Burke, told him he was 'not disposed to reform old systems', and it was fortunate for him that his Member of Parliament was now John Cam Hobhouse, who gave strong support for his 'election principle'. When à Beckett drafted a Bill for Hobhouse in 1829, it was held up by the passage of general legislation. The Reform Bill came first, but in its wake municipal reform quickly followed, and St. James's got its representative institutions like the rest of the country.

# III. THE NAPOLEONIST CENTRE

*He is not dead, he breathes the air*
*In lands beyond the deep!*
*Some distant sea-girt island, where*
*Harsh men the hero keep.*

I

In the second week of August 1815, as the *Northumberland* left England for
St. Helena with Napoleon on board, a heavy package arrived at Holland
House with a bust of the ex-Emperor by Canova. Lady Holland wrote to
thank the sculptor for 'a perpetual souvenir of the Hero'. She had commissioned the bust during Napoleon's first exile on Elba, and its arrival seemed
to her an omen of a second return.

The preparations for the erection of the bronze masterpiece lasted until
1818. It then appeared in the grounds on a column nearly seven feet high
inscribed with the opening lines of the prophecy by Athene that Odysseus
'will not be exiled much longer from his own dear country, not even if he is
kept in irons.' He will escape from the island where he is held captive, she
promises, and return home to Ithaca. 'Rely on Odysseus to get free; he
always finds a way.' A note in Lord Holland's handwriting suggests that
great care went into the inscription and the delay in putting it up may have
been due to exchanges with St. Helena.

The association of Holland House with Napoleon had become so much
stronger by the time the bust was on show that the publicity surrounding it
did not worry Lord Holland. Within a year of Waterloo, he had protested
against the principle and manner of keeping Napoleon prisoner. He shared
his roof with Napoleon's aide-de-camp, Flahaut, and kept open table for
the Bonapartist emigration. But all this was only the climax of a process
which began half a century before, when Fox chose to go to the Huguenot's
school at Wandsworth, and the family, while nursing the anti-Bourbon
tradition of the Whigs, had acquired French tastes.

Although Charles James Fox lived in Holland House before his politics
had crystallized, his French sympathies were linked with it in the public
mind. The cartoonists found the home of his father an appropriate background for the son. It was right that 'the public defaulter of unaccounted
millions' should be succeeded by a Jacobin. The house had passed, as we
have seen, through Henry Fox's elder son, Stephen, to Henry, the grandson,
who became the third Lord Holland when he was a year old. It was he,
more than anyone else, who gave the place its reputation during the Napoleonic period. His birth was a financial disaster for Fox, but he doted on the
boy. At Eton Henry seemed to him 'quite a miracle', and although the compliment was undeserved, Fox's admiration was returned with equal enthusiasm and more cause. The new Lord Holland became his uncle's disciple.

*Vendredi 25. Juillet. 1817*

He is not dead - he breathes the air
In lands beyond the deep
Some distant seagirt Islands, where
Harsh men their victim keep

the hero
the chieftain
their captive

Lord Holland's draft translation from the *Odyssey* (i. 196–9) for the base of
Canova's bust. The suggested variants for 'their victim' are in his handwriting,
but not the date in French. The phrase 'their victim' could not in fact be
extracted from the original (*dios Odysseus*) and Holland can only have used it in
deference to the campaign of protest which Napoleon had launched against his
victimization. The date of 25 July 1817 may mean that Napoleon himself
saw the draft; on St. Helena on that day Marshal Bertrand noted in his secret
diary that his wife had three callers: Napoleon himself, and two officers from
the *Conqueror*, which carried messages to him from Lady Holland through
Madame Bertrand. The decision seems to have gone in favour of heroism.
The lines are printed on the facing page in the form authorized for publication
in Thomas Faulkner's *History of the Antiquities of Kensington* (1820). On the
pillar itself the inscription went up in Greek.

He started off in this role by paying a long visit in 1791 to revolutionary
Paris, where he wrote verses in praise of liberty and dined with Fox's friend,
Lafayette. He also began an acquaintance with Talleyrand which he was to
renew at every possible opportunity during the war. Holland loved to travel,
but did so at his peril. Mild of temperament, gay and well-mannered, the
young Sal Volatile, as he became known, was the object of determined
female attentions from Copenhagen to Naples. In particular he was unable
to resist the young wife of an ageing English baronet, Sir Godfrey Webster.

Lady Elizabeth Webster, the future Lady Holland, had been born in
Jamaica in 1771, the only daughter of Richard Vassall, a rich sugar-planta-
tion owner whose family came from Massachusetts. Elizabeth's one complaint against her father was that he idolized her American mother 'and

was completely subjected to her dominion'. Mrs. Vassall made no use of her powers to educate her daughter; from 'fondness and inactivity' she allowed Elizabeth to run free among the slaves of the plantation, who inevitably spoiled her further. The child had splendid looks and a head of rich auburn hair. When the family emigrated to England before the American Revolution, Elizabeth had to face children of her own age who had mastered the rules of grammar and elementary subjects of which she was ignorant. She was a colonial, and her only assets were her beauty and her father's wealth.

In her sixteenth year Elizabeth Vassall appeared in a masque in London which was attended by the Prince of Wales. The Prince left early, but a minor poet, Richard Paul Jodrell, commemorated her performance as the mythical Clytie in love with the sun god Apollo.

> Imperial Nymph! ill-suited is thy name
> To speak the wonders of that radiant frame:
> Where'er thy sov'reign form on earth is seen,
> All eyes are Vassals; thou alone, a Queen.

A few months later in 1786 she married Sir Godfrey Webster, who may have commissioned the epigram by Jodrell as well as the portrait of her as Clytie by George Romney.[1] But Elizabeth's marriage to the baronet did not flourish. He was nearly twenty-three years her senior. She bore him two boys and a girl, but in the Sussex countryside where they lived she felt more shut in than on the plantation in Jamaica. Sir Godfrey was a stay-at-home, gloomy, incalculable, and a gambler. The young Lady Webster was as queenly as her mother. She differed from her husband in wanting travel and society, and in 1794, when she met Lord Holland in Naples, she was still only twenty-three.

Holland was then twenty-one. His patience and good humour were as obvious as his good spirits. He had a steadiness which allowed him to give way to a stronger will without entirely abdicating his own or leaving the other unaffected by it. As their enjoyment of each other grew, Holland discovered, in Florence, that he was committed to Lady Webster.

The divorce involved parliamentary proceedings and Sir Godfrey won damages which crippled Lord Holland. But Richard Vassall had died, leaving his daughter an income which she put at £10,000 a year. Holland added

---

[1] Although, in later life, Lady Holland put the portrait by Romney first among the many that were painted of her, it seems to have been left with the artist. In 1796, when Sir Godfrey Webster opened divorce proceedings against his wife, a rumour reached him that Lord Holland 'was considering the purchase of a picture of Lady Webster, if Sir Godfrey did not want it. It had for nine years been hanging in Romney's studio. Sir Godfrey promptly sent one of his relations to say that he would call Holland out for the insult.' (Lord Ilchester, *The Home of the Hollands*.) When the portrait finally passed to the Hollands, it was not hung at Holland House, but at their country house at Ampthill, Bedfordshire, which was sold at Lady Holland's wish soon after her husband's death in 1840.

Vassall to his name and his wife ordered a coach with her arms on the doors in spite of a statement from the College of Arms that she was entitled to none. Their son Charles was born before they could get married in July 1797, and Sir Godfrey shot himself three years later after heavy gambling losses.

The scandal of these events was more than enough to secure their ostracism by the court of George III, who were not sorry to impose it. The Hollands retained their friends and gained new ones, but it was noticeable that ladies who valued their position at Court kept away. Nor were they invited out. They had founded a club which had to make its way by the sheer brilliance of its members.

Lady Holland was not afraid of the challenge. Already in Florence she had shown a talent for arranging dinner parties to which people of literary or political distinction were glad to come. In 1799, soon after they settled in Holland House, she began a series of Dinner Books, which record the growth of her kingdom. The appearance of an individual at one of her dinners had little bearing on her likes and dislikes, but registered the extent of her influence. Among the guests were relatives, like Holland's sister, Caroline Fox, and her aunt, Miss Vernon, who came to live together at Little Holland House and could be relied on to fill vacant places. The Whig aristocrats loyal to Fox were the most regular attenders, bringing their wives and discussing policy as freely with Lady Holland as with her husband. Occasionally the King's sons came—the Prince of Wales, the Duke of York, and more often the Duke of Sussex. There were wits, and most notably Madame de Coigny, who had shone so brightly on the eve of the Revolution that Marie Antoinette called her the Queen of Paris. There were pretenders to the Whig leadership, including Whitbread, because he was married to Earl Grey's sister, and more tentatively there were philosophers, scientists, doctors, and writers.

A condition of entry was that Lady Holland should be granted something more than the courtesies normally due to a hostess. Her guests were expected to be deferential in inverse ratio to their status. Their wives had also to be reasonably correct. Byron's desertion of his wife in 1816 was deplored almost as much as Lady Caroline Lamb's infidelities. Caroline, Princess of Wales, was never asked.

Lord Holland, who contributed less to the strategy of the dinners than to their conviviality, had made his maiden speech in the Lords at the beginning of 1798, soon after Fox had ordered the Whigs to secede from the engagement which had become hopeless. Fox cheerfully allowed his nephew to be the exception. His liking for him had not grown less with the years and he recognized his need of a platform.

In the Lords Holland specialized from the start in the privilege known as the Protest, which might be entered in the journal by a dissentient without making a speech. He protested first against supplies for the war, then against the suspension of habeas corpus, and thirdly against the act of union with Ireland. In 1800 he argued against the rejection of the first peace over-tures from the French. He was not indifferent, he said, at the sight of one man—'and that one man one of the first military geniuses of the world'—in the possession of 'greater power than any man ever possessed in Europe since the days of Charlemagne'; but the way to meet the situation was not to ransack the dictionaries for terms of reproach, but to accept peace with honour.

There was a risk, not yet very great, that the combination of Holland's views and his friendships in France might involve him in the same charges of disloyalty that had been made against Fox since the early stages of the American war. Holland had grown up in cosmopolitan surroundings. Though without Fox's stamina as a rebel, he had the aristocrat's assump-tion of belonging to an international society. When he planned a trip to Germany and France with Lady Holland at the end of 1800, as a relief from the strains they had survived together, he was aware that a law had been passed two years previously which belonged to a new period of sovereign nationalism. 'There was then in force a severe and absurd statute against traitorous correspondence,' he wrote in his *Foreign Reminiscences*. It imposed the death penalty for anyone going to French territory without a permit or corresponding with officials of the French government. Holland decided to ignore the risk, and the journey soon took on the political and social colour of his later career.

The family crossed from Yarmouth to Cuxhaven at the end of June, taking with them Lord Duncannon, a leading Whig, Dr. Drew, a physician, the Reverend Matthew Marsh, a tutor from Christ Church, Oxford, and six servants. In Hamburg they called on General Dumouriez, an old friend who had driven the Allies back from Valmy before joining the emigration in Germany, and found him unspoilt by his triumphs or by his disgrace. They reached Berlin at the beginning of August and at once got into contact with the British Minister, Lord Carysfort, to arrange their access to France.

Lady Holland, who had not yet learnt the reserve appropriate to her situation, left her card on the Minister's wife. It was not returned. When Carysfort invited Holland to dinner, he felt he had to decline, but he did not abandon his business. He asked Carysfort to get agreement from Lord Grenville at the Foreign Office to their journey into France. He admitted his intention of visiting Talleyrand in Paris.

Carysfort had just married Lord Grenville's sister, and the connection had got him the post in Berlin. He was cautious. He was ready to approach Grenville, but suggested that Holland might be open to 'injurious surmises' and himself to censure if Holland insisted on seeing Talleyrand. When

Holland pressed him to get ahead meanwhile with an application to Paris, he made the excuse that it would have to go through the Prussian Minister in Berlin, who was away. 'I do not know how I could at this moment promote your Lordship's wishes,' he wrote, 'even if I thought myself at liberty, being here as an agent for the King's Government.'

The Hollands did not remain idle. Lady Holland took to her bed with a fever and sore throat after the rebuff from Lady Carysfort, but recovered sufficiently to go out. She met the King and Queen of Prussia, who were more gracious. Holland applied direct to General Beurnonville, the French envoy attached to the King of Prussia, for a permit to enter France.

The Hollands made visits to Potsdam, Weimar, and Dresden, met Klopstock, but not Goethe, and talked politics everywhere they went. It was clear that the French Revolution had had an overwhelming influence. 'A confederacy of princes for the purpose of interference in the affairs of a powerful and spirited nation has not and never will succeed,' Holland wrote from Berlin, and in Dresden he added that Britain was blamed for the continuation of the war. 'Nothing can be lower than our character throughout Europe for everything but riches and resources.'

In Berlin on 3 September, he was handed the Republic's passport with a most courteous note from the envoy explaining that it was left blank because of the unknown size of his party, but would be exchanged for a completed one at Cassel. In the interval a French *émigré* newspaper, *Le Publiciste*, had got wind of Holland's intentions and made play with them. Lord Carysfort wrote that he should now 'be more fully of opinion with me than you were that it was prudent not to write to Mr de Talleyrand'. A week later Carysfort had Grenville's reply. It was not entirely discouraging as far as Grenville himself was concerned, though he assumed that Holland had no intention of leaving at once for France, and it was clear that Portland, the Prime Minister, was likely to be less liberal. Carysfort took the risk of authorizing Holland to leave, but urged him to go straight through France to Calais and avoid contact with anyone of note. Holland prepared the way as best he could for their entry at Dover by asking his former guardian, the Earl of Upper Ossory, to press for passports. They were in an anxious mood when they left; Lady Holland, according to her husband, had 'an apprehension of a pain in her eyes', and their younger son Stephen was sickening.

When they reached Cassel before the French border at Coblenz, they were surprised to be handed a letter from Napoleon's aide-de-camp, Lavalette. It was written in such flattering terms that they did not forget it fifteen years later when Lavalette was sentenced to death after Waterloo. The completed passport was ready for them, he said. '*Le Gouvernement Français désire que vous regardez cet acte comme une marque de sa confiance et de son estime.*'

K

Lavalette's courtesy infected the French Minister at Cassel, and when Lady Holland pressed him about rumours of marauding deserters inside French territory, he offered authority for an escort. It was not only that Holland was to receive 'all the attention that his personal character and his public character entitle him to. The wife of Lord Holland has mentioned her uneasiness about the journey to the Minister attached to this court, and he instructs me to write to you with the object of providing everything that will contribute to the lady's security.' The Minister asked that his letter be used only if the worst of Lady Holland's fears were realized—'*mais alors ne balançez pas.*'

Spurred on by the fears of Lady Holland and the advice of Lord Carysfort, the party moved into France at the gallop. They reached Coblenz on 29 September, Aix-la-Chapelle two days later, and Brussels on 5 October, calling on the Prefects at all three. Lady Holland was in no state to notice much apart from the quality of the inns and the good looks of the Republican generals, which she put down to their promotion from the ranks. Lord Holland, when he got out of the coach, found people ready to talk, and he drew his own conclusions:

They were reasonably content with Napoleon's government, to which, without any enthusiastic attachment, they all (conquered countries and France) give the credit of good intentions and mild administration. What they most long for, both in the towns, the country and the armies, is peace, and were they to think that Buonaparte wished to continue the war, their confidence in him would be gone. As long as they believe, and we give them too much reason to believe, that it is the English that wish war, they will support and assist him.

The towns, except for Calais, seemed to them gloomier than before the war; the roads were neglected, but the posts were well served and the food cheap. Churches and convents everywhere were in ruins. Once they saw a monk wearing a revolutionary cockade and Lady Holland recovered enough spirit to laugh.

At Calais, the Channel seemed wider than they had expected. It was rough, and the only vessel which was likely to get them across did not sail for several days. The Reverend Marsh, who had had enough of the expedition, heard of a sloop sailing in the early hours of the 12th, and decided to leave by it, with a promise to clear the way for the Hollands at Dover. When he got aboard he found the sloop was no more than twenty-five tons; there were 'thirty people and a great deal of poultry'. The crossing was ugly and lasted thirty hours. As they fought their way towards the distant line of cliffs, Marsh was aware that they were likely to miss the tide which would allow them to anchor in the Downs between Deal and the Goodwin Sands. 'The French sailors are deplorable,' he wrote afterwards to Holland. 'They seem to do everything *en badinant*. It was a matter of joke when anything

The passport issued to Lord Holland and his party for their journey in 1800
through France to Calais.

broke or failed.' They made the Downs with half an hour to spare, and when the English pilot came aboard he told Marsh they were lucky not to have been thrown back into the North Sea to 'be blowed away'.

On land Marsh's reception was hostile. He had no passport and could only describe Lavalette's compromising welcome to France. His writing case was examined minutely by a customs officer who seized his shorthand journal, 'as pregnant with all mischief', and a copy of a letter to Bühl from Potsdam—'both which', he wrote, 'are now in the Alien Office for the inspection of the curious.' He was taken from the Customs House to the Ship Inn and a bailiff put on guard.

Holland had told Marsh of his efforts to get passports; the Earl of Upper Ossory had written to Grenville and sent word to the Prime Minister 'to explain it all'. But the passports had not come. Marsh sent anxious inquiries to Whitehall, and the passports then arrived with orders that Holland and his party might proceed to London 'without molestation'. From Marsh's window on the harbour he could now see their vessel tossing on a sea which had subsided a little. He left a note warning Holland that 'the Customs House people will plague you much', and took the coach to London and Oxford. In his rooms in Christ Church he collapsed with rheumatism, 'for the first time in my life'. The Dean's welcome had been warm enough, but Marsh heard 'from the best authority that I am to be summoned before the Privy Council along with Lord Duncannon for coming through France without a passport.' His letters were being intercepted.

The Hollands came ashore on 18 October to the same welcome. 'I find the Duke of Portland had in a manner refused my Uncle Ossory's application,' Holland wrote to his sister. Although Marsh had taken the edge off their reception, they limped into the Ship as invalids, Holland with toothache, his wife with the pain back in her eyes, young Charles Fox with a cough, and Stephen seriously ill. Back in London Sheridan told Holland that he had 'incurred hanging' and a pardon of some kind would be needed. He had to apply for a licence for the journey he had already made.

The hubbub died down. One of his friends offered to go to the Tower with him, but the scandal remained within limits mainly because of the approach of peace. Holland was overwhelmed with inquiries about France, as if, he said, he was Mungo Park on his return from Africa. Marsh spent a month applying mustard and flannel to his pains, and began to feel better when the Alien Office sent back his journal. Lady Holland lost her son Stephen that month, but she too slowly recovered and gave birth to another, Henry Edward, eighteen months later. He was her sixth child.

The next phase of Holland's dealings with France was published and caricatured, originally in the interest of the extreme Right who sought a renewal of the war when the uneasy Peace of Amiens proved to be working to England's disadvantage. The Hollands kept to the conventions and were less obvious targets than Fox, who brought with him from his secession at Chertsey an indifference to political gossip which outdid his own standards. He was intent on finishing his biography of James II, and could think of little but the royal memoirs which had been deposited in the Scotch College in Paris. The pressure to see them had been mounting in him as the war dragged on, so that his need to go to France seemed self-evident; but the public knew only that he had acclaimed the peace as a victory for Napoleon at the most notorious of all the Whig Club dinners. To Cobbett, who had not yet been converted to Radicalism, it seemed incredible that the journey Fox made in 1802 had not been planned for secret discussions. He could have sent a clerk for the research. Even to Coleridge, who knew that 'no man can examine MSS for another with reference to historical inquiries', the visit was an act of political betrayal which implied a readiness to bargain away English interests.

Fox could hardly have avoided seeing Napoleon after crossing the Channel, so that the scene was set, if he thought about it in political terms, for one of the major indiscretions of his life. To add the ideal base of gossip, he let it be known that he had been married for five years to his mistress, Mrs. Elizabeth Armistead. The maiden name of Mrs. Armistead is unknown, but she had been the mistress of the Duke of Dorset, Lord Derby, and the Prince of Wales. She had been as beautiful as Mrs. Fitzherbert, whom she resembled, and she had managed to save Fox's happiness as his political failure grew more marked. The fact of their marriage had been kept even from the Hollands, and Fox only revealed it now because he needed to make their visit to Paris together respectable. The French police entered Mrs. Fox's age as sixty-three.

The Hollands set off for France early in July 1802, and it is clear from Lord Holland's correspondence that they tried to be presented to Napoleon as soon as they got to Paris. The British Ambassador, Andrew Merry, had only just arrived. His reaction to their urgency was similar to that of Carysfort in Berlin. The question of presenting Lady Holland could not be decided overnight. Invitations for the next levee had already been sent 'to all the persons who were expected to assist at it'. On 18 July, Merry wrote that no one could be presented without going through the proper channels and there was no time to use them; nor could he get them tickets for a parade they wanted to see.

In the end the Hollands were presented with Robert Adair and Thomas Erskine, who had defended Tom Paine against the charge of treason. But this was not until September, by which time the delay had leaked to the British press. Lady Holland and Mrs. Fox were appraised as rivals for social disqualification. Were the circumstances of Lady Holland's divorce more scandalous or less, than the early life of Mrs. Fox? Lady Holland 'was at Madame Récamier's party a few days ago,' said the *True Briton*. If she had been admitted, why not Mrs. Fox?' Who could present either of them to Bonaparte? The wife of the British Ambassador?

Holland himself was presented in August when Napoleon received the deputation conferring on him the consulship for life. He spoke, Holland said, 'very civilly, but very little'.

When Fox arrived on the scene, he irritated Lady Holland by his obsession with research. He could see now that he had walked into a political trap. He had been received with military honours at Calais and all the towns on the route. When he went to the theatre the audience stood and cheered. At times he had nearly the whole front page of the *Moniteur*. To ask to be presented to Napoleon was to strengthen Napoleon's position in France as First Consul but to damage his own in England. He hesitated, but was under pressure from his wife, who was probably under pressure from Lady Holland. Nor had he much choice.

When Merry presented Fox, Napoleon offered the kind of formal compliments which the Englishman was not good at returning. A week later he dined with the First Consul. 'Near 200 people. Very magnif.' he noted in a style which might have disarmed his critics.

At the dinner Napoleon made a set speech in which he suggested that the world should be divided into two nations, one Eastern and one Western, which should be held in position by force, though it was not clear which should dominate the other. In a long tête-à-tête afterwards, Fox irritated him by insisting that big standing armies were a threat to liberty. Napoleon attacked Windham and the Right as well as the press. He was surprised to find that Fox defended them with spirit. '*Il me combattait avec chaleur en son mauvais français,*' Napoleon said afterwards with distaste.

The British press kept up its vigilance. Merry, who was relieved as Ambassador by Lord Whitworth at the end of the year, complained that there were as many as five thousand English in Paris at a time and the amount of consular work prevented him from getting on with diplomacy. There were peers and Members of Parliament of all parties, as well as private individuals. The *Moniteur* of 7 October included among those received in audience, Captain Maitland, *officier aux grades*. (Fortunately for Maitland the presentation had been forgotten twelve years later when he was under attack for receiving Napoleon with too much honour on board the *Bellerophon*.)

The Duke of Bedford was there, Lord Kinnaird, and the Bessboroughs. Hazlitt came in his early role of painter, Benjamin West and his son Raphael stayed in the rue Froid Manteau; Holcroft, Kemble, who made a friend of

Talma; Mrs. Opie also came, and Samuel Rogers and Allen, the Holland House librarian, and Sir Samuel Romilly. But it was Fox and the Hollands who were singled out for attack. Nothing much was to be made from the presentation of the Hollands apart from the fact that it took place, but there were enough hints of the exchanges with Fox to provide the basis of a major campaign.

It was led by Cobbett in his *Political Register* and developed to its extreme by Coleridge in two brilliant letters to the *Morning Post*. Both writers agreed that the motive of the expedition had been to gain Napoleon's support for Fox to take over power from Addington as Prime Minister. Such a *coup* might be achieved without force, according to Cobbett, because Napoleon, 'who had been able to impose such a peace on the country, would be able to impose a Minister on the King. . . .' Fox and Napoleon were simply awaiting the accession of the Prince of Wales, according to the *True Briton*, when Fox would be asked to form a Government. Coleridge had been an admirer of the Revolution and of Fox for defending it, but he felt a profound betrayal had taken place when Fox accepted a militarist as trustee of the Revolutionary ideals.

To have hoped too boldly of human nature, Coleridge argued, was a fault which all good men had an interest in forgiving. Nor did he reject, as Cobbett did, Fox's motive for the visit; but he thought it plain now that the British Government was going to be attacked by Fox 'at every moment and criminated in every measure', whereas the French were 'as regularly defended'. Fox, he said, had shut his eyes to the tyranny Napoleon had established over forty million subjects. By rejoicing over the peace at the Whig Club, he had openly transferred his allegiance to the French. There was a reason and a motive. His exclusion from the Court of St. James's had been a tragic misfortune, which did not reflect on him; but he had sought by his 'emigration' to recoup himself by gaining the favour of Napoleon. Holland and the others in Paris were 'a group of degenerate Englishmen' whose names would be forgotten because the name they had earned was that of 'Buonaparte's courtiers'. Fox himself deserved the title of Lord Chamberlain Designate for Foreign Affairs.

The letters from Coleridge had important results. They were a factor in Napoleon's determination to make use of the peace as no more than a truce before openly renewing the war; they were also a warning to Fox, as lesser attacks were not.

Fox had two other sobering experiences, the second of which was to prove fatal. On his return to England in November the climate of opinion prevented a return of the complacency he had built up in retirement at Chertsey. He talked wildly enough to surprise Creevey and wrote that between George III and Napoleon, Bonaparte was 'the fittest person to be master'; but his speech on the renewal of war in March avoided extravagant praise of Napoleon and fastened on the weaker points of British policy as the cause—in his view the only cause—of continued war. Within two years, in 1806, the death of Pitt gave Fox control of that policy. His appointment as Foreign Secretary and Leader of the House of Commons put the initiative in his hands.

It was at the moment which should have seen the fulfilment of his career, that Fox began to have doubts about his health. At first there were promising omens. A French madman, who planned to assassinate Napoleon, went to him for help and Fox exposed him. Talleyrand, with whom he began to negotiate, was sympathetic and apparently co-operative; but their talks, from a simple starting point, lost direction and ran into minor bargaining which had no end. Soon Fox came to the conclusion that his great opponent was shuffling and insincere; he was playing, he told Holland, 'a false game'. The cartoonists began to draw Fox as John Bull.

He hurried through Parliament the first stages of the Bill for the abolition of the slave trade, but symptoms of dropsy had begun to appear, a disease which had killed his elder brother. He had to give up the Foreign Office. He tried to get back to the country where his wife had always restored him in calamity. He was not strong enough and died on the way.

The Hollands had left Paris for Spain in September 1802 soon after Lady Holland's presentation to Napoleon. They carried with them the memory of his rather flat courtesies, his powerful little presence and winning voice. They had dined repeatedly with Talleyrand, cemented their friendship with Lafayette, and left caretakers of their interest. But they had missed the scandal caused in England by their visit. On the road to the Spanish frontier they were charmed by the attentions of every official they met.

They spent over two years in Spain, scarcely conscious of the new war. Holland was strongly attracted by Spanish literature and began work on a biography of Lope de Vega. Lady Holland found acquaintances of distinction among the Spaniards and the diplomatic corps in Madrid. In Barcelona she began collecting Spanish clothes and in Aranjuez thought of bringing back '*une brodeuse française*' who was not afraid of the voyage. A year after they left Paris they were told to their surprise that Talleyrand was unwilling to give them passports back through France. The new phase of the war had a grimmer quality and a heightened nationalism. When they sailed for England in the summer of 1805, it was through the complex preliminaries of Trafalgar. 'A *return* to this country always damps my Spirits,' Lady Holland noted in her journal.

The next few years were of crucial importance to the Whigs; they were in power, if only for the moment, and when they fell, there was the prospect

of lasting power under the Prince Regent. Although Holland was a favourite candidate both for Foreign Secretary and later for Prime Minister, he
gave the impression of a certain detachment from the rivalry which surrounded the appointments. His life of Lope de Vega appeared soon after
their return and was a success. He edited Fox's unfinished *Life of James II*,
which appeared two years later. He undertook a *Life of Fox*, which was left
in confusion for Lord John Russell to complete. He held office for some
months as Lord Privy Seal with a seat in the Cabinet, and he negotiated a
temporary settlement with the Americans in the dispute over naval rights in
the Atlantic. But he had no experience of dealing with Napoleon. In 1808
he announced his intention of going back to Spain, by then resisting the
French occupation. Brougham and other members of the party tried to
dissuade him because of his importance in the Lords. He promised to be
away no more than four or five months, but he was determined to go.

When he applied to Canning at the Foreign Office for a passport, he was
astonished to get an admonitory reply. He could not forward the passport,
Canning wrote on 8 October 1808, 'without adding a few words, which I
hope you will not consider as in the smallest degree *personally* unkind to
you . . . but I do feel it a duty to say to you, that I rely upon your candour
and fairness that in any communications which you may have . . . with the
persons in authority in Spain, you will carefully make it to be understood
that any opinions which you may give are purely your own and in no degree
sanctioned by the British Government.' Because of Holland's rank and
public reputation, it would in any event be necessary for the Foreign
Office 'to take precautions for preventing a misapprehension of that nature'.

On reading this at Falmouth, Holland sat down and wrote an eight-page
reply. In justice to himself, he said, he had always made it clear that he had
'no sort of connexion with the present administration'; but he expected the
protection of H.M.G., not its disparagement, and he would be grateful to
know what the Foreign Secretary proposed saying to the Spaniards. Holland
never forgave Canning for the admonition.

The Hollands took with them to Spain the Duke of Bedford's son, Lord
John Russell, John Allen, their librarian, as his tutor, four men-servants
and two maids. They stayed nearly a year and found themselves popular
with the Spaniards. At Badajoz, according to Lady Holland, ' a vast crowd
was assembled in and about the town to greet our arrival, and we got out of
the carriage amidst innumerable *vivas*.'

On their return, they were met by rumours that the Regency was impending, and of their own traitorous role as agents of Napoleon. Holland
was severely critical of the French seizure of Spain but continued to want
peace. In spite of Napoleon's tyranny, he said he joined in 'none of the
vulgar calumnies against the great ruler of the French nation', whom he

considered as 'the greatest statesman and the ablest general of ancient or modern times'. He was as grudging as Whitbread in his acceptance of Wellington's victories. When a vote of thanks on Talavera was proposed, Holland demanded an additional vote of thanks to an officer who had been omitted. The officer was Sir Robert Wilson, who was to prove the Scarlet Pimpernel of the Napoleonists after Waterloo. As a major in the Hussars he had been in Paris with the Hollands in 1802.

Holland was reluctant to abandon his belief in the Prince Regent's good intentions to the Whigs. In 1811 when the Prince declared it expedient to continue the administration for the present, Holland wrote to his sister that he had 'not the slightest doubt of his sincerity to us'. In June he dined with the Regent at Earl Grey's. But expediency proved to be a lasting attraction, and Holland began to suffer increasingly from gout, which the Right made more painful by a political diagnosis. In May 1812, when Perceval was assassinated, it was Lord Liverpool who was appointed in his place. The Prince Regent had changed sides. In June Lady Holland was delivered of her eighth child, which only lived a few hours.

But Holland House had tenacity. Although there were notes of Lady Holland's illnesses in the Dinner Books, the table had been extended. Spaniards came often, and among them the Duke of Infantado, one of the guerrilla generals. Lord John Russell, no longer in subjection to Allen, came as an adult. Captain Maitland, R.N., soon to take charge of the *Bellerophon*, was also a guest.

As the Premiership faded from sight, the Whig chiefs tended to yield their places at Lady Holland's table to poets and novelists. 'Our guests are foreigners, fashionables and courtiers,' Holland wrote to his aunt in 1813. Byron was added to Sheridan and Madame de Staël to Caroline Lamb. The reopening of Drury Lane proved a stimulus to conversation because Whitbread, as its owner, thrust the choice of the opening address on Holland; he rejected Whitbread's own address and commissioned one from Byron.

Caroline Lamb, soon to be expelled from the circle, gives a sketch of Holland House in her novel *Glenarvon*. Her heroine, Calanthia, drives out to visit the Princess of Madagascar, who has a resemblance to the former Miss Vassall of Jamaica. With her husband, the Nabob, she lives in an old-fashioned Gothic building, Barbary House, three miles down the turnpike. 'She spoke of her own country with contempt; and even in her dress, which was magnificent, attempted to prove the superiority of every other over it.' No patron of the fallen, she surrounds herself with men of talent who wear chains and collars round their necks. Those who bend the lowest are the best received. The great Nabob does something to redeem the atmosphere because he is good, kind, and clever, and 'would sacrifice much for a peaceful life'.

Lady Holland was aghast when she read the description and complained to Creevey that it was a travesty but an identifiable one. 'The outlines of few of the characters are portraits, but the *amplissage* and traits are exact.' Creevey sympathized, but ever after called her Madagascar.

It was true that the succession of dinners showed up Lady Holland's ambitions, which tended to grow with the failure of her husband's. But they were also a recompense for not being invited out, a denial of her isolation, and she writes once after the Abdication in 1814, 'I dined alone!' and next day 'again alone!!!' The dinners were a sort of front to their lives. They asked no one who was poor or undistinguished to dinner, but they saw and helped such people at other times of the day without putting chains on them.

Holland's speeches in the Lords are a better guide to his political principles than the names in the Dinner Books. He had been presenting petitions on behalf of debtors ever since his return from Spain, and his hatred of their indefinite imprisonment did much to secure the Act of 1812 which put a limit to their torture. He was good to individuals who were financially incompetent, like his tutor, Dr. Langford, and to a prisoner in Newgate who thanked him for his 'very kind interference on my behalf'. It was not the universal tendency of the Whigs. Lord Stanhope told Holland in 1798 that his sympathy for the French Republic forbade him 'to have the smallest connection with any of the emigrants', and he was sure Holland would not blame him. Holland, by contrast, was thanked by '*les prêtres français demeurant à* Kensington' for his generosity. In 1810 he protested at the Government's failure to exchange prisoners of war. In 1811, because of his 'generous and compassionate spirit', he received a petition from the crew of *La Baleine*, who had been prisoners for nearly eight years. The rumour of his generosity reached a Mr. Henry Whitehead, 'born to a respectable competency but which has been fatally intercepted', who asked that £50 should be sent to him as a loan to the Paddington Post Office, where he would call for it.

The Hollands tried to discriminate among beggars and to remain constant when they had begun to help. William Godwin was not the kind of genius who attracted them, but Lord Holland was patience itself in responding to his appeals for bigger and bigger investments in his publishing scheme. 'Your kindness', Godwin wrote in 1811, 'has laid the foundation of that little civic establishment which has since supported me.' Lady Holland made a less distinguished choice in the poet Thomas Campbell, but she stood by him even when he turned down a job she had imagined he would like. She sent money to people no longer identifiable, and when two girls were thrown out of a gig on the turnpike, she hurried them up to tea, if not to dinner.

She interested herself in dress as determinedly as in politics and with a similar reliance on France. Madame de Coigny had returned to Paris in the Peace of Amiens and readily did errands for her in the city of which she had been Queen. Mr. J. B. Church, an intermediary, arrived from her in 1810, with an account for £225, for a consignment of dresses. He was going back in two or three weeks, he wrote Lord Holland, and could send more if she wanted. Meanwhile he had called on Talleyrand, who received him with the greatest kindness and 'made many inquiries about you and Lady Holland and charged me to tell you that your friends in Paris, of which you have a great many, were very desirous of peace, that they might have the pleasure of seeing you again.' A few days later, on 5 September, Lady Holland had a letter from William Pinkerton on the same subject. Holland had got to know Pinkerton well when he was Lord Privy Seal; he had been one of the two United States commissioners with whom he had negotiated in the naval rights dispute. But Lady Holland managed to use him rather as she did Mr. Church and Madame de Coigny. He warned her in 1810 that it would be difficult to extricate her packets from the Customs; 'they are menaced with confiscation, but I believe the threat will not be executed.'

The brilliance of Holland House survived the eclipse of Lord Holland's hope of the Premiership, but the Hollands now had to face the decline of Napoleon. In public they put a brave face on it.

By the summer of 1813 it could be argued that Napoleon had recovered from the retreat from Moscow. He had been able, said Holland in the Lords, 'to call forth all the resources of France' by impressing on the French people that their national safety was endangered. If fair and moderate terms of peace had been offered he would have accepted them.

As he stuck in public to Napoleon's invincibility, so Holland refused to admit to himself the possibility of defeat. But at Dresden and Leipzig, at the end of October, it began to come very close. 'Bonaparte seems to have left Dresden with the hope of striking a blow,' he wrote to his sister, 'and our poor newspapers call it a retreat, an escape, a flight and what not.' (At Jena, when the boot was on the other foot, he had written to her, 'The Prussians badly defeated, routed, beat, destroyed, annihilated, than history or imagination can give one an idea of.') The blow which followed turned out to be Leipzig, and the news reached Holland House on the night of 3 November. It was entered in the Dinner Books as a guest. 'Lord Morpeth, Mr Tierney. . . . News arrived of the defeat of Bonaparte at Leipzig.' It was a political dinner, without the resources of Madame de Staël or the Spaniards to save it. The Dinner Books fall into disarray for two months as if a gale was blowing through the house. In February 1814 Hobhouse called to find 'Lady Holland on a sofa, Lord Holland writing notes and talking—in the gout.' At the Abdication in April, Creevey singled them out as hardest hit of all, 'in perfect despair'. Meanwhile, on the turnpike, Holland noticed that 'the Prince rides by here and looks well.'

There is a resemblance between Byron and Holland at this stage. Their distaste for the traditional rulers spreads to Bonaparte when he is on the run, but it has a vigour and punch which the Bourbons and Hanoverians escape. Holland's style is sometimes Byronic, as if a betrayal of some personal kind had taken place. And in a sense it had, because the English peace offers were approved of by Holland as reasonable. 'Bonaparte acts neither grandly not handsomely!' he wrote. 'He tries to make peace and yet, in making war, cants, whirls and truckles in a manner quite inconsistent with the part he has hitherto acted.' Spelling out disillusion to his sister, he found the language of Napoleon's proclamations disgusting.

He always prefers the cant and nonsense of a regular sovereign to the language which would become the military chief of a free nation. I feel like Madame de Staël—it is difficult to know what to wish. I hate and distrust Bonaparte more than ever, and yet I am not sure, if he were to fall, that the 'legitimate' sovereign would not be restored, and that in my mind is the last of misfortunes—bad for France, for liberty and for mankind and in a narrower view bad for England.

The cold weather, he added, had brought back his gout. It was in his elbows now as well as his legs.

Peace, in fact, found the Hollands greatly in need of a restorative, so that they planned a trip of more than a year, to begin in Paris and blossom in the Italian scenery of their courtship. 'If I were you,' wrote Sydney Smith, 'I would not stir from Holland House for two years, and then as many jolts and frights as you please, which at present you are not equal to.' But Lady Holland knew better about her sources of strength and illness, and was keen to be gone. In the middle of July she had to dinner J. N. Fazakerley, a Whig admirer of Napoleon, who had a house on Elba and was in close contact with his great neighbour. 'He was a man of accuracy and veracity,' according to Lord Holland, and that was important to their plans. They left at the end of July 1814 and had more jolts and frights than in all the rest of their journeys together.

They had always tried to absorb the shocks of travel by making up a self-contained party, which at times included a cook, a confectioner, a tutor, and a physician. Caroline Lamb suggested its size as it moved in and out was enough to account for the invasion rumours which surrounded Holland House. There were fifteen in the carriages this time: Lord and Lady Holland, their sons, Charles and Henry, Mr. Shuttleworth, the factotum, two girls, four maids, and four 'English men'. At Dover they found the wind was fair and Lady Holland decided to set out by the night tide, so that they were across in four and a half hours, with the carriages reassembled in the morning.

In Paris they felt they might never have been away. Madame de Coigny was there to greet them with practical advice about the fashion houses and a shoemaker she had found who was deaf but unique under guidance. Lady Jersey was already sitting for her portrait by Gérard, who was under-employed since the Abdication. Talleyrand gave them dinner with so much warmth that Holland looked for a motive and could see none. 'He received me, and yet more emphatically Lady Holland,' he wrote to his sister, 'with a *franchise* and cordiality, even a kindness, which I hardly thought were in his character.' (Caroline Fox wrote back that her wise old aunt saw a motive: 'She says that in the changes and chances of political life he may again find it necessary to seek an asylum here, and then will it be no advantage to have the hospitable doors of Holland House thrown open to him . . . ?')

In many ways it struck Holland that there was more liberty now than under Napoleon. Talleyrand introduced them to Flahaut, his illegitimate son, who had fought at Leipzig and shown astonishing calm and resource-fulness in the retreat. They noticed Flahaut was taking no steps to ingrati-ate himself with the Bourbons but lived more or less openly with Queen Hortense in a maelstrom of Bonapartist intrigue. Benjamin Constant, whom they had to dinner, was emerging as the main opponent of dictatorship and omitted to bow as low as he might have done to Lady Holland. They started a friendship with Gallois, a liberal who retained a furtive admiration for Napoleon from the time of the Peace of Amiens when he had acted as his private secretary. Finally, they met Lord Ebrington, who was on his way to Elba to see Napoleon for himself—a plan nursed in secret by Lady Holland as well.

They left Paris at the end of August and stopped at Fontainebleau to see, in Lady Holland's words, 'the fatal room where the great Napoleon was compelled to sign the act of abdication'. She noticed the locks and fittings which he had restored after they had been stripped by 'the fury of the Revo-lutionary mob'. She looked out of the window as he must have done and watched for a moment a fountain playing by a statue of Diana.

They went through Geneva, where they dined with Sismondi, spent a few days in Milan, and reached Florence on 23 October. On the last stage, after Bologna, they had their meeting with Princess Caroline. In Florence Holland signed her book, but 'avoided as far as I could, and hitherto with success, being invited to her parties'.

All the time a sense of Napoleon's presence was growing on them. Elba was within a hundred miles and when they looked back on their journey from Kensington, Holland reflected that the war had left France 'less ex-hausted than any country in Europe'. In Florence it seemed to him that 'Bonaparte's party is less strong here than elsewhere, but throughout the North and East of Italy it is so formidable that could he appear with the slightest force, I have no doubt that he would soon have an army stronger than that with which he defended the interior of France.' Joachim Murat, King of Naples, seemed to Holland the man most likely to bring him back, but the hatred between them had been 'inveterate' since Murat had gone in with the Allies, and the political risks of landing at Naples might be formidable.

Florence was more important than Naples as an open channel of communication with Elba. Colonel Neil Campbell, the British Commissioner on Elba, was regularly in and out of the city, and the new British Minister to the court of Tuscany, Lord Burghersh, had arrived. The Hollands settled down for nearly three weeks at Sneidorff's, 'a large inn upon the Arno, cold and noisy although it is the best establishment in Europe'. On the first day they went to see a statue by Canova whose composition Lady Holland disliked 'and execution not much better'. Thereafter her Florentine diary was left blank.

The London newspapers had arrived at that point, and in the *Courier* of 19 October was news of the greatest importance both to Lady Holland and Napoleon. For some time there had been rumours that Napoleon would be removed from Elba to an isolation which was more secure. It was announced that a schooner service was being established to St. Helena. The Duc de Berry, son of Louis XVIII, undertook a special mission to London to discuss the dangers of Elba. All this would have been enough to put Napoleon on his guard and make him begin preparations for an escape, but the *Courier* of the 19th went further.

... The Congress of Vienna will finally determine the future residence of Napoleon Buonaparte. At Paris it is believed to be quite certain, that Buonaparte will be removed after the Congress; the Duke of Berry, it is said, obtained this on his last visit to England, and it seems absolutely necessary for the future security of the repose of Europe; several places, it is said, have been proposed for his residence, among others the Island of St Lucie.

Lady Holland's list of dinner engagements in Florence culminates with Colonel Neil Campbell. As the chief Allied representative on Elba he was singularly vulnerable. He was deaf in one ear from an old wound given him by a Cossack. He was sorry for himself and, at forty, much preoccupied with his success with women. He laid it down as an axiom in his journal that in spite of his duties on Elba and at 'the sacrifice of my own feelings', he would travel about Italy for intelligence purposes, 'occasionally going to Leghorn, Florence and the baths of Lucca for my health's account.' In Florence he was known to have a mistress.

Lady Holland courted 'O'Neal Campbell' with the ardour she had once shown Lord Holland in Florence, and she gained her different objective as easily. She happened to be able to find guests who were politically interesting; Lady Westmoreland, wife of the Lord Privy Seal, Mrs. Wyndham, wife of a diplomat, 'Poodle' Byng, a clerk in the Foreign Office, and William Rose, clerk of committees in the Lords. Among them she put Mary Fabre, daughter of the portraitist who twenty years earlier had painted Holland as a Frenchman; Lawrence Macdonald, a sculptor, and his wife, who were in love with Italy; Fabroni, a director of museums. It may be that Mary Fabre or Mrs. Wyndham was of special interest to Campbell. Whatever the reason, Lady Holland felt strong enough in a week to press for her favour. Could he, she asked, send Napoleon a consignment of newspapers?

Campbell had no precedent to follow. He was not in the habit of making difficulties about contact with Napoleon, who was not technically a prisoner or an outlaw; he had no book of rules of the kind which Hudson Lowe was to know by heart on St. Helena. He was perhaps a little unperceptive, as if his deafness were more than a physical defect. At their dinners he astonished Lord Holland by his underestimation of Napoleon. 'I heard him myself declare that his [Napoleon's] talents did not seem to him superior to those which would be required in a *sous-préfet*.' Campbell agreed to send Lady Holland's papers at once, and even accepted a note from her to go with them.

Lady Holland was now anxious to leave for Rome, to get as close to Napoleon's brothers as possible before making her visit to Elba. They were to have Louis Bonaparte's house and to meet his formidable brother Lucien. Holland, whose gout was threatening again, would have preferred to stay in Florence because the Bedfords were converging on them from Leghorn. But it was enough that 'Lady H is eager for Rome.'

The Duke of Bedford and his twenty-one-year-old son, Lord John Russell, were in fact in the Lazaretto in Leghorn, where they had been put for forty days' quarantine on disembarking from Lisbon. The Bedfords liked to travel in even greater comfort than the Hollands. They suffered less at sea than Lady Holland, and preferred to make their longer journeys with the Navy, but they had passed through a severe epidemic at Gibraltar. Thunderous protests to the local Grand Duke reduced their quarantine by half, but the Duke had time to gain a quite novel sense of the comforts of life. In Rome, he told Lady Holland, 'you will be able to get us a good comfortable clean house in a warm situation and with a southern aspect.' On 21 November he wrote to Lady Holland that Fazakerley had visited them.

Whig traditions were as strong in the Bedfords as the Hollands. At Woburn Abbey they were building a Temple of Liberty, unfinished at the death of the fifth Duke, but soon to house a bust of Charles James Fox, 'the most distinguished champion of civil and religious liberty that ever adorned any age or country.'[1] A main object of their journey was to find and commission ornaments for the Temple.

[1] In the words of the sixth Duke.

The Duke's first wife, Georgiana, daughter of Viscount Torrington, had died leaving him three children; he then married another Georgiana, daughter of the Duke of Gordon, who had given him another five. They were on the whole a united family. Georgiana, the Duchess, wrote verses for the Carrara pedestal of Fox's bust; Georgiana, the four-year-old daughter, was to sit for a statue by Thorwaldsen in Rome, and the central group of the Graces was to be commissioned from Canova. The Bedfords formed a larger party than the Hollands. Lord John Russell, the youngest son of the first marriage, was showing independence; he had already been elected to the Commons for Tavistock, and was more or less forced to come abroad by his father. There was also the youngest son of the second marriage, Charles James Fox, born six months after the death of his namesake. In addition there was Edward, aged nine, Wriothesley, ten, and Louisa Jane, three, apart from the two surviving Georgianas, mother and daughter. With two cooks and half a dozen servants, they made twenty, not counting an English cow to provide milk for the children.

In the Lazaretto the Duke developed anxieties about bandits on the road to Florence. He himself was resourceful and in Spain had fought off a Frenchman who had claimed him as his prisoner; but he wrote to ask Lady Holland, a specialist in such matters, whether they should split into groups on the road. In the end they lumbered out of Leghorn in as compact a body as they could manage. They reached Florence on 8 December, and found letters from the Hollands who were by then firmly established in Rome. 'I long to see you all,' wrote the Duke.

The Bedfords inherited the Hollands' social round in Florence and heard with interest of Lady Holland's plan to visit Elba in the spring. Their interest grew on the return of Lord Ebrington from his interview, and Lord John Russell, after listening to him, took his chance to steal a march on Lady Holland. 'John leaves us to make a visit to Buonaparte at Elba and rejoins us at Rome,' the Duke wrote, a little sheepishly. 'I reserve myself to go with *you* in the spring. Lord Ebrington has just come from him, and everything I hear of this most extraordinary man, increases my desire to see him. Rely upon it, he will again be numbered on the great scene of history, and if France is contracted within the blessings of the Bourbons, Italy will look to some leader of energy, wisdom and courage to snatch her future destinies.'

Campbell now began to feel that the visits to Napoleon were becoming untidy. According to Lord John Russell, he urged him to wait till the spring when the weather would be better and the entire party could go. 'But I determined to go then.' Russell left Florence with Campbell and an English friend, Whitmore, on 17 December 1814. The Duke wrote to Lord Holland: 'John is gone this morning to Elba to pay a visit to Buonaparte and will very likely be at Rome before us, as he is to go to Civitavecchia in the *Partridge* sloop of war. Pray tell Lady Holland that Lord Burghersh says he has brought nothing for her.' Lady Holland received an enigmatic present from Napoleon of specimens of iron ore from his mines on the island, but it is not clear how they reached her. At this moment he may have thought it more discreet to avoid open contact through Campbell or Lord Burghersh and preferred to use Louis Bonaparte or his sister, Pauline Borghese, on one of her frequent trips between Elba and Naples.

Meanwhile, the Hollands were dividing their time in Rome between the study of Napoleon and antiquity. A week after their arrival they saw Canova, who combined both attractions; and by then archaeology had increased Holland's gout. 'Though I have been hardly twenty four hours in Rome,' he wrote to his sister on 21 November, 'I have visited the Colosseum, Forum, Trajan's pillar, Temple, etc. etc. much improved since I saw them by the removal of the ground in which the lower part of them has been buried.' He knew nothing of politics because, 'though there are four ex-Kings here, I have not yet seen any on whose intelligence I can depend.' He was by now very slightly in mourning for Napoleon. 'The military character of his government and the prodigious extent of his power were the chief evils,' he wrote on his last day in Florence, and these defects had vanished.

In Rome Lady Holland found a letter from Fazakerley who had had an interview with Napoleon. Immediately after seeing him he had written to Lady Holland from his near-by house, but the letter had gone astray. Fazakerley had then gone to Leghorn, where he saw Lord John Russell and the Bedfords in the Lazaretto. He had gone on to Florence only to find she had left for Rome. He wrote in evident confusion.

When they moved into Louis Bonaparte's mansion on the Corso, it was almost as if the Hollands had been co-opted into the family. Louis Bonaparte had abdicated from the throne of Holland in 1810 and lived in Rome as the Comte de St. Leu. He and his wife, Queen Hortense, had separated, but only two years before, and she had borne him an heir who was to become the Emperor Louis Napoleon.

They found St. Leu's rooms dirty and the noise of the traffic a contrast to Holland House. There was also a certain subordination in belonging to the family. When Lord Ebrington came on from Florence, he told them that Napoleon remained scornful of his brothers: it was they who had had the pleasures of royalty, and he the responsibility. Napoleon had laid waste, in their interview, much of the past, including Talleyrand, the greatest of rascals, *'un homme capable de tout'*. It was Murat who survived better than anyone else in Napoleon's talk, and in spite of his apostasy as King of Naples. *'D'ailleurs un bel homme, grand, bien mis, et avec beau-*

*coup de soin—quelquefois un peu fantasquement. Enfin un magnifique Lazarone.'*

Holland could see that Napoleon had managed to change Ebrington's outlook since they met in Paris. He 'acquits him of most and palliates him in the rest,' he summed up, with a touch of impatience.

The Bedfords reached Rome two days before Christmas and soon afterwards Lord John Russell came in from Civitavecchia. 'Pray', the Duke had written to Lord Holland,

have the goodness to order the house to be ready ... with good fires, etc. and I must beg you to let one of your servants order in all the *necessaries* of life such as fuel, provisions, wine for the servants, etc. etc. and pray take some means to provide us with dinner on the day of our arrival as my cooks will not be able to reach Rome much before us. I shall want stabling for two saddle-horses and standing for 4 carriages, and I must beg of you to get me an intelligent *laquais de place* who knows Rome perfectly, and a *beau coche* for the Duchess, that is, a good *carosse de ville*.

He was, said the Duke, so used to Holland's good nature that he was apt 'to rely upon it as a matter of course. Pray desire my banker too to stow my baggage in the house and to get my letters from the Post Office.'

Holland did as he was bid and had dinner ready on their arrival. But when Lord John Russell came from Elba, they dined alone.

The Hollands' relationship with him had been an intimate one ever since they had taken him with them to Spain for a year with Allen as his tutor. They could see at once that something important had happened on Elba since Ebrington's visit. To Ebrington the great man had given his views on the past and its characters with a detachment which suggested no immediate intention to escape. Russell he had pounced on and shaken as if he came with messages and secret information which for some reason he was withholding. Lady Holland's newspapers had arrived.

Russell's interview was on 24 December, and his first impression of Napoleon had been that he was extraordinarily short, which was 'partly owing to his being very fat; his hands and legs being quite swollen and unwieldy'. After the interview he made notes on Christmas Day, but they were sketchy and failed to account for the bewildering atmosphere. He thought Napoleon's rain of questions might be due to 'a habit which he has acquired during fifteen years of superior command'.

Lady Holland had no chance to warn Russell in advance about the papers, and although it was at once clear to him on Elba that she had sent something of the greatest importance, he failed to see that Napoleon had taken it as a warning on which he himself was expected to elaborate. Pressed for Holland's views about French opinion and the loyalty of the Army, Russell encouraged Napoleon to think he had been with the Hollands in Florence, which was untrue and inflamed Napoleon's expectations the more.

The first person Russell had seen on the island was General Bertrand, who asked him directly what was the meaning of the paragraph in the *Courier*. He replied that he knew nothing about it. He was surprised by Bertrand's excitement.[1] In the evening, when Napoleon had had a chance to hear Bertrand's impression of the visitor, he talked to him standing up for an hour and a half. What struck Russell most was a cunning look in his eyes, though he was affable and smiled a great deal. What he said seemed to imply an acute uneasiness,

a suspicion that something serious was about to happen to him, and he seemed to have a desire to entrap me into giving information which I was neither able nor willing to afford. With this in view, as I supposed, he asked me a number of questions of little interest to him—such as whether I was in the House of Commons or the House of Lords, whether my father had kept up much state as Lord-Lieutenant of Ireland. . . . These questions he would intersperse with eager enquiries respecting the state of France; and when I replied that I had not come through France, but by sea from Portugal, he would not let me off, but asked what Lord Holland, whom I had seen in Florence, thought of French opinion, '*L'armée est-elle contente?*'.

They talked about banditry on the roads, and how Napoleon had stamped it out in France. 'He seemed alarmed regarding his own safety, asking me more than once, whether our Minister at Florence [Lord Burghersh] was a man to be trusted; whether fearing that he might be carried off by force, or wishing to obtain some assurance of safety and protection from Lord Burghersh, the British Minister, I cannot tell. I told him that Lord Burghersh had been attached as a military officer, to one of the allied armies which had invaded France, but of this he seemed to know nothing.' As Lord Burghersh was still in Florence and had sent a message to Lady Holland in the Duke of Bedford's letter of 17 December, Napoleon's bewilderment is not surprising; he must have seen by now that Russell was no emissary and was perhaps not very well informed. He praised Lord Ebrington as '*un homme fort instruit*'. He pressed Russell on what was happening in Vienna, but he could only say he did not know.

'It was evident', Russell summed up, 'that the paragraph in the *Courier*, which had been mentioned to me by General Bertrand, had been shown to Napoleon, and had produced a great impression on him. He seemed to me to be meditating some enterprise, and yet very doubtful whether he should undertake it.' When Napoleon landed in France two months later, on 1 March, Russell was not surprised; and he, like Ebrington, had been half won. On 5 June he was protesting in the Commons that the war was

[1] We depend for the full account on Russell's memory half a century later when he wrote 'with only glimmering recollections'; and he admits that in the interval he failed to look up the *Courier* to see exactly what it had contained. The urgency and direction of Napoleon's cross-questioning thus remained bewildering to him.

'impolitic, unjust and iniquitous'. At the opening of the first session after the war Russell and Ebrington both voted against the Prince Regent's speech from the throne rejoicing in England's victory.

Colonel Campbell's first interview with Napoleon after delivering Lady Holland's newspapers was on 14 January, about a fortnight after he had read them. He noted in his journal that Napoleon 'spoke of the statements which had appeared in some of the newspapers respecting his removal to St Helena and St Lucia, in a way which showed his belief in them, said he would not consent to being transported from Elba, but would resist the attempt by force to the last. *"Avant cela il faut faire une brèche dans mes forti-fications".'* And according to Campbell, he added, '*Nous verrons.*'

Holland, when he heard of the escape, could see that the warning sent by his wife had precipitated it. Napoleon had information of discontent in the French Army and he was exasperated at the failure of the Allies to pay him his revenue under the Treaty of Abdication, an omission which was be-ginning to cause defections among his unpaid troops on Elba.[1] But as the Hollands listened to Russell in Rome at the end of December, they could not tell how far his impression was to be trusted, nor, if it was, where Napoleon might try to land. The sympathetic account he had given Ebring-ton of Murat suggested that Naples was as likely as France.

They now had various Frenchmen to dinner, who included (in Lady Holland's spelling) 'M. Crotod', 'Chatteleux', 'Dormesson', 'Fontenaye', and the French Ambassador.[2] On 27 January Holland wrote to his sister that he thought 'all are grown more persuaded than they were that it is not quite so gay to get rid of Buonaparte.' And he added, in the words Napoleon had used to Campbell, '*Nous verrons.*' On 1 February, he wrote that they were thinking of an excursion to Naples. Their tenure of the house on the Corso had run only two-thirds of its time.

Meanwhile Lady Holland plunged into Roman society. They were seeing a good deal of Lucien Bonaparte, Prince of Canino, the eldest brother, who had just been ennobled by the Pope. Firmer than the rest of the family, more authoritarian than Napoleon himself, Lucien had played a decisive part in

[1] Holland bases himself on Napoleon's justification in the *Mémorial de Ste. Hélène*: 'Napoleon was living on the island of Elba on the strength of the treaties: he learns that the Congress of Vienna proposes to deport him outside Europe; none of the articles of the Fontainebleau Treaty had been observed; the newspapers informed him of public opinion in France; his course was set' (II. 264). Queen Hortense says in her *Memoirs*: 'Several weeks passed without any newspapers being delivered. Then all which had been delayed came at the same time. The Emperor devoured them and suddenly resolved to leave the island' (II. 167).

[2] According to Lord Holland, the exchanges between Lady Holland and Napoleon continued while she was in Rome, but there is no sign of them in her surviving papers.

the *coup* of 18 Brumaire, which put an end to the Republic. Holland managed to forgive his undemocratic aims on the grounds that there would have been no liberty at all and little happiness for France without him. When the Prince gave a ball at the end of January, Holland was too feverish to attend, but Lady Holland went with Georgiana, Duchess of Bedford. In February his fever kept him away from the Carnival, but in the middle of the month he was able to leave for Naples. They drove through the Pontine Marshes on the Appian Way and reached Terracina; on the last stage of the journey, Holland was sent ahead to arrange about the house they had taken. Until it could be got ready, at the end of February, they stayed a few days in the Hotel Gran Bretagna on the sea-front.

Again they had a round of engagements and amateur archaeology. King Joachim Murat and his Queen, Caroline Bonaparte, had adopted a policy of warm friendship to the English, which was recommended to them in forceful terms by Napoleon from Elba. The King 'is indiscriminate in his politeness', Lady Holland noted in her journal, 'and there are many unfit people to be so noticed.' She was glad to have the Duke of Bedford for company. He had not wanted to go to Naples at all, according to Russell, 'on account of the large quantity of English who will be like so much dust on the streets.' The Princess of Wales was still at Portici, near Herculaneum, but the English members of her suite were deserting in boredom. The Hollands retailed to London the story that she had crowned a bust of Joachim with a wreath. They delayed calling on her, though they found time for an expedition to Pompeii and were dazzled by Murat's investment of 24,000 ducats a year in the site. Lady Holland and the Duke came back together to the opera, where they saw the King and his sons 'in a very splendid attire and all splendid about them'. The Hollands found Fazakerley in Naples and had him to dinner. Colonel Campbell turned up on his travels again and he also dined.

On 1 March Napoleon landed in France near Antibes. That evening the Hollands went to a ball given by the Princess of Wales at Portici and found the King and Queen of Naples, their fellow guests, already 'very civil'. Two days later they gave a ball. 'Went to the King and Queen,' Lady Holland noted, 'invited to their private society and concert after my presentation. She is very graceful and clever, made me sit by her the whole evening and conversed freely on various topics, her brother, etc.' Napoleon, in the *Mémorial de Ste. Hélène*, admits that he had warned Murat of his impending escape, and the Queen certainly knew of it. She was the youngest of the Bonaparte family and Napoleon showed a rather patronizing trust in her in spite of *une ambition désordonnée*. The guests came away without knowing that the Hundred Days had begun.

The Hollands went to the opera again on Saturday, 4 March, but Lady

Holland caught cold, and had to stay at home on Sunday. They had planned a long excursion to Paestum and postponed it till Tuesday.

They heard of Napoleon's escape on Monday, 6 March, four days before the news reached England. '*Le Congrès est dissous*,' he is supposed to have said, as he set foot on shore. For a moment, as at others in his life, Holland must have looked at his wife with something like awe in his eyes. Russell had not exaggerated. As he watched her mounting emotion, Holland could see she was identifying her future with Napoleon's. He resisted her excitement, raising fears, objections, his own lingering distaste for a tyrant; he found himself trying to stop her as if he had been in Metternich's place or Castlereagh's.

One of Holland's keenest pleasures in Naples had been to receive a newspaper cutting about himself from his sister. It was from Leigh Hunt's *Examiner* of 30 October, and did something to reduce the sense of guilt he felt at his absence from the Lords. 'He is ever at his post', said Leigh Hunt, 'to watch the progress of every measure, and if he cannot defeat the march of a bad project, he can at least lift up a protesting voice, which shall prevent the succession of others equally bad.'

When he got away from his wife on 6 March, Holland wrote back to his sister, but found himself disoriented by their argument.

Here's a job, Buonaparte escaped from his gaol! Where is he going? What are his chances of success? Whatever the result, I think it a misfortune. If he fails, he must be sacrificed, and who can contemplate the extinction of such genius and activity with thorough indifference? If he succeeds, we must have twenty years more war. Joachim has taken so violent a fancy to me that I think he must have read my character in *The Examiner*. His dress is somewhat coxcombical, *même un peu fantasque*, as Buonaparte said, and his countenance announces more good humour than sense. . . .

We are preparing an excursion to Paestum, but the escape of her *hero* has set Lady Holland's spirits in such a flurry and agitation that I suppose she will not be calm and sedate enough to enjoy the improving gravity of Doric architecture.

It was a misjudgement of his wife's resources. They duly set off to Paestum on 7 March. Her notes, like her spelling and her artistic criticism, were a little thick-fingered, but she did not fail to record them, although she had been to the site once before on her first visit to Italy. She found the Temple of Ceres 'almost a burlesque of Doric, the columns are so tapered at the top and bulge out so enormously at the base—the Temple of Neptune is much grander and better proportioned.' But she was impressed.

They drove back through Salerno to Naples and stayed a few days with Lord Clare and the Bedfords, who were determined to return to England by sea. Murat was declaring his admiration for Napoleon and they noticed he was moving his troops. The Hollands left Naples on 15 March and reached

Terracina again, half-way back to Rome. There were letters waiting for them with a report that Napoleon had been captured at Grasse. Lady Holland was so depressed that she could not sleep. Holland wrote to his sister that he distrusted the man, 'but yet I hope they won't catch him, nor do I think they will.' Under the last few words he added: 'MUM!'

Next day the news was that Napoleon had reached Lyons, and one of their Spanish friends, de Cabarrus, appeared on the scene with a 'similar account of Paris, certain of Napoleon's success'. Behind them in Naples Murat decided that the moment had come to free Italy from the Austrians, under his own leadership. Against the wishes of Napoleon, who saw that such a movement would encourage the Allies to reunite against him, Murat struck north at the Papal Territories before advancing on Florence. Holland told his sister that the war might alter his direction but would not quicken his pace. He would be 'north of the Alps before the end of June and snug in Holland House before the opening of Parliament next year'. The eruption in Naples jostled them a bit—'it will, I think, quicken our pace to the Alps' —but they went on with their sightseeing in Rome and attended a *Miserere* in the Sistine Chapel, while the Pope, Kings, and Cardinals fled to Verona.

The English, too, were hurrying off, and their disorder fortified the Hollands' complacency. They visited the Capitol, went out to Tivoli, and at Frascati saw Lucien's villa, La Rusinella, which would soon be occupied by Caroline, Princess of Wales. The weather was delicious. On 30 March, when they got back to dinner from the Villa d'Este, they heard that Napoleon had entered Paris. '*Vive l'Empereur*', wrote Lady Holland.

The Bedfords were still waiting for a passage in Naples among stranded Englishmen and bandits who were marauding in the streets. Caroline left in a British cruiser, and the Duke began to recover his affection for England. But it occurred to Lord John Russell in Naples and at about the same time to Lady Holland in Rome that a journey through France would be of exceptional interest. Both tried to get passports, Lady Holland by applying to Louis Bonaparte, while Russell set off to Genoa in the hope of getting one there.

The Hollands were now ready to go. The weather still held, but thirty days had passed since Napoleon's return, and there was an unreality about the great blue skies which made them want to find their feet in their own world. They left on 4 April with news that the entry into Paris was confirmed: Napoleon had been carried into the Tuileries and was making democratic speeches as the representative of the people. As they changed horses by Lake Bolsena next day, Lady Holland found a newspaper in a café 'and had the gratification of reading the triumph of Napoleon which I had only heard verbally.' Between Radicofani and Siena she noted that a courier from Louis Bonaparte had caught up with them on his way to the Emperor; he gave Holland a letter 'in which Louis very kindly tells him he has applied to the Emperor for passports to enable us to go through France and by way of Calais on account of my health.' They reached Florence, where there was fighting on the outskirts between Austrians and Neapolitans. They heard from Russell, who was ahead of them at Bologna, that the Neapolitans had beaten 12,000 Austrians outside Modena. On their entry, 'the people immediately illuminated and huzzaed for the independence of Italy.'

Holland wrote to his sister that she would hear of 'dreadful events, bella, horrida, bella, in Italy, but we and I believe that all English travellers are safe from our reputed enemies though put to some little inconvenience.' He was for the Neapolitans and increasingly for the Bonapartists in France. There were letters from Bedford, one to Lady Holland saying 'I cannot agree with you in wishing any success to this man'; but as the papers reached Italy from England showing the determination of the Congress of Vienna, both Bedford and Holland found themselves in support of Whitbread in the Commons. 'I shall certainly raise my voice against engaging in war with Napoleon,' Bedford conceded in his second letter. But he was stuck with his carriages in Naples and could not get a passage for more than fifty days.

The Hollands moved out of Florence, leaving the Neapolitans 'baffled and beaten by the Austrians' and went through Modena, which the Neapolitans had evacuated, and Verona, which they never reached, towards the Austrian Alps. Sometimes they found newspapers, but they had to struggle among 'regiments of Huzzars and Croats, stragglers, ammunition waggons, artillery'. In Verona they found the Pope and other exiles from Rome, and were disgusted by their complacency. A taste for the sights still flickered in them. 'At Vicenza', wrote Holland, 'we visited Palladio's buildings which are nearly as much specimens of fallen grandeur as the royal exiles at Verona.' They had to contend with strange seizures in their son, Henry, which began in Padua at the end of April and soon slowed them down to half a day's travel in the day. 'As to news,' Holland wrote, 'we are in utter darkness.' He had seen a report that the Congress had outlawed Napoleon and were preparing to invade France. 'Surely', he wrote, 'we do not mean to adopt the spirit of the mad declaration of Vienna?' But they dawdled in Venice very much as they had in Rome; it even took two hours in a boat to get back to the mainland.

It was June by the time they came down the passes into Germany, and by then Holland had done his political thinking. Without much information on the state of opinion in France, he was satisfied that the expulsion of the Bourbons must be sustained. Napoleon had chosen Constant, whom the Hollands knew as the most dedicated of liberals, to draw up a Constitution, the *Acte Additionel*. His Foreign Minister, the Duke of Vicenza, had written to Castlereagh that Napoleon owed his restoration 'entirely to the love of the French people; he has no other wish than to repay such affections no longer by the trophies of vain ambition,' but by securing peaceful relations with Britain. 'I am all for peace and go all lengths thereupon,' Holland wrote from Munich. 'I return to England with a much better opinion of Napoleon than I had, probably from having seen more of his successors and those who pretend to be his rivals.' He wrote as forcefully to Grey; but his pronouncements from the Alps sounded rather hollow at home where the Whigs were having to improvise as the Government moved into war. He would hardly be in time to record his dissent by a vote or a speech, his sister protested; his absence was deplorable; it left the case entirely to 'troublesome members' like Whitbread and Tierney. And Grey, reproached by Holland for not pressing his views harder, complained that 'I never so much wanted some advice and assistance'; to align themselves fully with Whitbread would be to alienate Grenville, which Grey was seeking above all things to avoid. At least, he warned Holland, do not come back through France.

They firmly intended to go through France and were moving north-west from Munich towards their old entry point on the Rhine at Coblenz, but as they approached Frankfurt, travelling sometimes only a few miles a day because of Henry's seizures, they found themselves entangled in bigger army movements than in Italy. At first there were Russians who seemed to be pouring westwards to the Rhine. At Bischofsheim on 22 June, 'the town was entirely filled with the barbarians,' wrote Lady Holland. 'We could not get any rooms and were obliged to sit in the carriages. The Russian General was reposing—wallowing, I suppose, and his attendants either were afraid of disturbing him to announce Lord Holland, or he was barbarous as one might expect, for he did not receive him or answer my applications about rooms.' As they waited in the carriages, they began to hear rumours of a great battle on the road ahead. An Englishman called Rushford, attached to the Russians, told them it had been an Allied victory. 'Same thing from a Russian on the way from Hutbrau to Rilsburg, a battle on the 18th, between Namur and Brussels.' But it was too confused to be taken seriously and they struggled on through the 23rd to Miltenburg in a deserted countryside with the rain pouring from a solid sky on a road surface trampled out of recognition. Meanwhile Henry seemed to have recovered from his attacks, which stopped inexplicably as they had begun.

At Aschaffenburg they were told about the battle in detail, as something overwhelming from which the French could not recover. Outside on the box of the carriage, seventeen-year-old Charles burst into tears, unable to stand the strain he had felt in his mother since they first met the Russians. He was comforted by the coachman, who had the advantage of detachment from the party. 'Don't mind, Mr. Charles, it's all right. *I* think it's a very good thing that Boney has been beaten.' They reached Frankfurt and lodged for nearly a week at the Empress, pulling themselves together and consult-

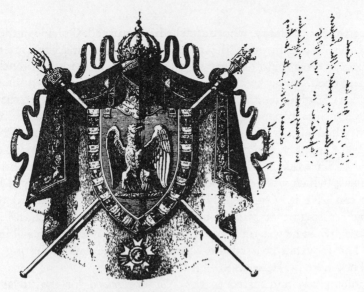

# EMPIRE FRANÇAIS.

Nous Ministre des Affaires Etrangères

Prions les Officiers Civils & Militaires chargés de maintenir
l'Ordre Public en France & chez l'Etranger.
de laisser passer librement Lord et Lady Holland, traversant
la France pour se rendre en Angleterre par Calais, avec leur
suite; laisser entrer sur tous les points où ils se présenteront.

_____

_____

& donnez lui aide & protection en cas de besoin.

Le présent Passeport valable pour _____

Donné à Paris le Vingt Mai 1815 _____

Le Ministre des Affaires Etrangères

Par le Ministre

Le Chef du B.au des passeports

The passport issued to Lord Holland and his party in May 1815 at the request
of Louis Bonaparte, for their journey from Rome across France to Calais.

ing doctors about Henry, whose attacks had returned. Outside in the streets Cossacks splashed through the mud and Prussians marched after them. Lady Holland realized now that something 'very fatal to the French' must have happened. She lay awake on her bed, 'an immense mass of military passing under the windows and the King of Prussia came through in the night.'

They got newspapers again as they reached the area of Waterloo on the road they had taken to Brussels in 1800. They read first of all that Whitbread had died of apoplexy and then that he had cut his throat. He seemed to them like one of the wounded who had bled to death on the outskirts of the great battlefield, 'which was horrible even beyond any description Lord Byron's verses can give it.' On 25 July they reached Ghent and heard to Lady Holland's dismay that Napoleon had surrendered to the English. Three days later, when he was off Plymouth in the *Bellerophon*, she was ill in bed in Lille. The Hollands crossed the Channel while he was protesting that he would not go to St. Helena.

Napoleon was transferred to the *Northumberland* for the voyage on 7 August, and it was perhaps the supreme tribute to Lady Holland's resilience that on 8 August at Holland House she began to organize a new and carefully planned series of dinners with the object of bringing him back.

2

The Hollands' aim after Waterloo was to secure the release of Napoleon and allow the Bonapartist reaction in France to develop without intervention to the point at which he could be restored. The first part of the aim came to have priority as they saw that support for him was growing too slowly in France to be effective without his presence in Europe; but in 1815 the prospect of delay was not obvious to them, and they expected a premature anti-Bourbon reaction. It was Lady Holland's belief that France was as resilient as herself and that history would repeat itself more or less on the pattern of Elba. Lord Holland would have preferred to let history take its course with no more assistance than he could give it in private. The Whig leaders did what they could to encourage this tendency in him; they were anxious that Napoleon should not be made a political issue at all; but Lady Holland proved more formidable.

Napoleon had reservations about his supporters in England, but they were essential to him as long as Bonapartism was proscribed and Parliament offered a debating ground and the hope of sanctuary. His hope was that enough indignation would be aroused at his treatment to allow him to reach England or the United States. Secret channels of communication were needed for the campaign. He had ground for hoping that the Tory Government would fall sooner or later and that the Prince Regent would be succeeded by Caroline's daughter, Princess Charlotte, whom he believed to be sympathetic to his cause. He had reservations about the strength of Holland's attack and feared his passivity, but he was indispensable, and Napoleon never took the risk of offending him. What he had to accept was that the greater aim of inflaming French public opinion could not be served by an English spokesman. He pushed Holland as far as he could and used his immediate followers for the detail and Gallic thunder which were needed. At the same time he rewrote his past as a liberal benefactor of Europe. He was aided very greatly by Count de Las Cases, who proved himself a propagandist of genius in his *Mémorial de Ste. Hélène*.

Count Emmanuel Auguste Dieudonné de Las Cases, a minor aristocrat from the Languedoc, reached London a few weeks before the beginning of the war in a collier from Rotterdam, after retreating from Valmy with the *émigré* armies.[1] Like Changeur, he was young, had practically no English, and spent nearly ten years in London. He was a tiny man, who had a horror of crowds and rough living, but unlike Changeur he was descended from St. Louis and had confidence in himself and his country. At first, living under the name of M. Félix, he was a militant royalist, and made two landings in France, one in La Vendée—'*une entreprise infructueuse*', as he mysteriously called it—and another in the disastrous Quiberon expedition which lost 700 *émigrés* within sight of the ships. He then threw up the royalist cause and saw Napoleon as the hope of the future.

Las Cases had served in the French Navy in his youth and visited New England and other parts of America, but his education had been scamped, and in London, with a coolness all his own, he advertised himself as M. Le Sage, tutor in French, astronomy, mathematics, geography, and universal history. He undertook to teach his pupils 'all the modern history in six months', and taught himself, he admitted, at their expense. He also sold visual aids, charts of the main historical periods, and an 'astronomical machine' which reproduced the movements of the universe. The charts were issued in monthly parts, at first to 200 subscribers.

As Napoleon emerged as the champion of the Republic in arms, it might have struck the students of M. Le Sage that he had formed an admiration

[1] He had walked through Luxembourg and Belgium, and crossed the Channel at the end of December 1792.

for universal empires, and particularly that of Alexander the Great. Those who learnt history from him in six months found that it culminated in Napoleon, whose victories of 1796 and 1797 in Italy were, according to the charts, 'a wonderful campaign', his bravery in crossing the bridge at Lodi under the fire of the Austrians a historical landmark.

No one in England was scandalized by this sympathy for Napoleon, and no attack was made on Le Sage by the press. His social success was due to one of his pupils in astronomy, the French wife of Sir Thomas Clavering, a baronet from Durham. Born the daughter of a dressmaker in Orleans, Lady Clavering was cold-shouldered by the most reactionary of the *émigrés* because of her origins, and she, too, was an admirer of Napoleon. She mobilized the Clavering family, including the Bishop of Durham, and Las Cases moved steadily up through the English hierarchy until he was presented to the Prince of Wales. When his summaries of ancient and modern history were published in volume form in 1800 as *The Historical Atlas*, the Prince headed a list of 600 subscribers, which included numerous peers and baronets, and twenty-eight schools.

Las Cases had prospered to an extent that made him hesitate before going back to France in the Peace of Amiens, but he did return to Paris and was amnestied on surrendering his titles. He produced a French edition of his *Atlas* and became a chamberlain in Napoleon's court. He was created Baron de l'Empire in 1808, and helped to defeat the Walcheren expedition. At the Abdication in 1814, he returned to London, again without exciting comment. He renewed his old friendships and spent much time visiting prisons, work-houses, and charitable institutions, probably under the auspices of Sir Samuel Romilly, the law reformer. When Napoleon returned from Elba, Las Cases rejoined him at once and after Waterloo became his most valued adviser because of his knowledge of England.

His devotion was an aristocrat's in the presence of his king. With the advantage of being an inch or two shorter than his master, frail instead of stout, and with a forehead wrinkled like rice paper, he had deference to offer as well as English and an acquaintance with the eastern seaboard of America. When he made his request to follow Napoleon into exile, Napoleon simply asked whether he knew where it might take him. '*Je ne l'ai point calculé,*' he replied, and Napoleon accepted him. But Las Cases had not calculated on St. Helena. His health had deteriorated and he was married.

At Rochefort the choice had to be made between attempting escape to the United States and surrendering to the British. Napoleon would have preferred the first if it had been practicable, but as the royalists closed in behind him and he saw the *Bellerophon* and frigates on patrol, he was forced to choose surrender. With the help of Las Cases he tried hard to qualify it. 'I have closed my political career,' he wrote to the Prince Regent, 'and I come, like Themistocles, to seek the hospitality of the British nation. I place myself under the protection of her laws.'

Las Cases had impressed on Napoleon the British respect for law, and in his preliminary interview with Captain Maitland of the *Bellerophon* (recounted in the *Mémorial*), he tried to insist that his master was not surrendering but coming as a guest. 'He desired only to live as a private citizen; America was more convenient, the place of his choice; but after all, England herself with her positive laws might suit him better; and it appeared according to my first interview with Captain Maitland, that he would be able to escort him to England with his entire suite, to be treated properly there.' Maitland, a cousin of Lord Lauderdale, was a distant relative of the Hollands, but although he was predisposed to sympathize with Napoleon, he was careful to avoid committing himself to the idea of sanctuary. He complained afterwards that Napoleon's suite insisted on treating him like a minister. 'That no misunderstanding might arise,' he reported to the Admiralty, 'I have explicitly and clearly explained to the Count las Cases that I have no authority whatever for granting terms of any sort; but all I can do is to convey him and his suite to England, to be received in what manner His Royal Highness may deem expedient.' In the *Mémorial*, Las Cases omits to mention the reservation.

Maitland, in his account of the voyage, emphasizes that Napoleon made a great impression on the officers and crew. There was nothing new about this. When he disembarked from the *Undaunted* on Elba, the boatswain had wished him 'long life and prosperity on the island of Elba and better luck next time'. On the *Bellerophon*, he interested himself closely in the crew, explaining that some essential superiority in the English morale had accounted for the regular defeat of French men-of-war. Maitland suggested that the experience of the officers had been responsible. 'There has been less noise in this ship', Napoleon insisted, 'where there are six hundred men, during the whole of the time I have been in her, than there was on the *Épervier*, with only one hundred, in the passage from Isle d'Aix to Basque Roads.' He paid particular attention to the ship's surgeon, an Irishman called Barry O'Meara, whom he later recruited for St. Helena. His own physician, a M. Maingaud, was both homesick and seasick. O'Meara was able to speak Italian, French, and English, and had the additional merit of thinking Dublin superior to London for its medical training. The ship's crew, for their part, responded to Napoleon's interest. Maitland was himself charmed by him and when he asked the crew's feelings he was told that 'if the people of England knew him as well as we do, they would not hurt a hair of his head.' Almost every day Napoleon said he would have to get used to English habits, 'since he intended to spend the rest of his life in England.'

When the *Bellerophon* anchored off Torbay on 24 July, Napoleon and his attendants were anxious to see as many newspapers as possible, according to Maitland, 'but particularly, *The Courier*, which they considered to be the ministerial paper, and most likely to contain the intentions of the Government respecting them.' The confirmation that the place of exile was to be St. Helena caused a crisis. When they reached Plymouth three days later, the Admiral of the Fleet, Lord Keith, insisted that double sentinels should be posted. When Maitland heard a rumour that a boat had taken a man off in the night, he did not rest until he had a first-hand report that his prisoner was on his bed.

Napoleon now found himself the centre of the largest of those demonstrations of curiosity which had begun with peep-shows and panoramas of the war and reached their culmination at the exhibition in Piccadilly of his carriage taken at Waterloo. Visitors from abroad were astonished by the size of the crowds and had difficulty in distinguishing between the curiosity which brought them and signs of sympathy and admiration for Napoleon. The scene in Plymouth Harbour was Napoleon's only sight of England. Las Cases encouraged him to trust in the sympathy which showed itself and do what he could to heighten it.

The manoeuvres of the *Bellerophon*'s guard-boats seemed to Napoleon from the start an attempt to intimidate the crowds, and he took counter-action by showing himself on deck every day at five. As the sightseers multiplied, it seemed as if England itself was coming to him in spontaneous acknowledgement of his greatness. There were cheers and much waving of hats. 'Even our favours', says Las Cases, 'began to be seen among them; women and children turned up wearing red button-holes.' A friend of his, perhaps the Napoleonist lawyer Capel Lofft, who tried to reach him from London, had to give up the attempt because of the complete lack of horses on the road. 'The sea covered itself with a multitude of boats around us; we were told afterwards that there were people who had hired them for sixty napoleons.'

Las Cases is not to be trusted without confirmation, but Maitland put the crowd at 8,000 on the Sunday after their arrival and the London papers raised the figure to between 8,000 and 10,000 on weekdays. The correspondent of the *Morning Post*, on 8 August, regretted having to report that 'a large portion of the spectators not only took off their hats, but cheered him, apparently with the view of soothing his fallen fortunes and treating him with respect and consideration;—him whose whole life has been a series of exultations in the calamities of others.' A painting by the Huguenot John James Chalon exhibited at the Royal Academy in 1816 shows Napoleon displaying himself on deck amidships in a blue and red uniform and cocked hat while a swarm of dinghies, skiffs, launches, and fishing smacks compete for the nearest view.

*A Swarm of English Bees Hiving in the Imperial Carriage!! Who would have thought it!!! !!! !!!* Napoleon had adopted the imperial bee as a symbol; his family were 'the beehive'. When the carriage shown in Cruikshank's 1816 engraving was put on exhibition at Bullock's Museum in Piccadilly, shortly after Waterloo, more than 10,000 visitors a month came to see it, and Byron ordered his coachmaker to produce an exact replica of it.

In 1795 Samuel Whitbread, son of the brewer, was caricatured for the first time (FACING PAGE, ABOVE, by J. Sayers) as a beer barrel. In the froth, as *Whitbread's Intire* explodes in the Commons, are his lasting ideals: Reform, Peace, Liberty, Equality, No Slave Trade. Southill Park, his house in Bedfordshire (BELOW, in 1970), was built and furnished in two decades of war by the architect Henry Holland, on the profits from the brewery.

Whitbread became the champion of Princess Caroline of Brunswick-Wolfenbüttel (RIGHT, ABOVE, painted by Lawrence), estranged wife of the Prince Regent. Her neighbour in Kensington Palace was her brother-in-law, the Whig Duke of Sussex (RIGHT, BELOW, at twenty-five, in a portrait by Guy Head); in 1821, when Caroline made her bid to be crowned with the King, the crowds shouted, 'The Queen and Sussex for ever!'

*Introduction of Citizen Volpone & h[...]*

Gillray's version of Fox's presentation to Napoleon in the Peace of Amiens:
the Irish rebel, Arthur O'Connor, introduces Mrs. Fox, as Fox bows low;

*at Paris.* _Vide. The Moniteur, & Cobbetts Letters _

Thomas Erskine, who had defended Tom Paine, bows in front of Lord and
Lady Holland; and Robert Adair, at extreme right, prostrates himself.

At the end of 1810, with the Regency imminent, the Whigs were widely expected to take over the Government and make peace with Napoleon. *Sketch for a Prime Minister*, a *Satirist* cartoon of February 1811, shows Lord and Lady Holland—she wearing the breeches, and with Napoleon under her shawl—about to displace the Tory Prime Minister, Perceval.

Drawn by M. Gauci from a Bust    by A. Canova.

Napoleon by Canova: a lithograph of the bust commissioned by Lady Holland in 1814, when Napoleon was on Elba. The bronze master-piece on its seven-foot column was not erected in the grounds of Holland House until 1818—when, as a version of its inscription ran, on another 'distant sea-girt island, Harsh men the hero keep'.

The Napoleonist lawyer, Capel Lofft (RIGHT, in middle age, when the sartorial standards of his youth had declined), was a determined and resourceful opponent of the Government, and the main goad of Lord Holland in the long-term campaign for Napoleon's release from his captivity on St. Helena.

Capel Lofft

When Lord Keith came on board at the end of July with Sir Henry Bunbury, Under-Secretary for War, to tell Napoleon formally that he was to be removed to St. Helena with fifteen attendants, he protested as strongly as he could. 'Let me be put in a country house in the centre of the island thirty leagues from the sea. Place a commissioner about me to examine my correspondence, to report my actions, and if the Prince Regent should require my *parole*, perhaps I would give it.' He stormed in vain and after-wards spoke to Las Cases of cutting his throat.

While he continued to argue for a foothold in England, he switched a large part of his interest to Parliament. He had always made a habit of counting and analysing the support he had there. Recognizing its weakness in numbers, he was at pains to learn about individuals and their influence. The extent of his curiosity was a rough guide to his sense of dependence on them. On Elba it had become marked; his questions about Lord John Russell's position in Parliament and the standing of the Duke of Bedford seemed insignificant to Russell, but they showed the concern he was already feeling at the likely reaction in England to an escape.

Later, when Napoleon was transferred to the *Northumberland*, he found on board the Hon. W. H. Lyttelton, a supporter of Whitbread. Lyttelton spoke good French and Napoleon seized the opportunity to ask about Whit-bread's end.

'What was the cause of his death?'
'He killed himself.'
'How?'
'I mean he committed suicide—he was deranged.'
'Mentally deranged?'
'Yes.'
'Was this what you call the spleen?'
'Mr Whitbread was mad. He thought people had a grudge against him, were staring at him scornfully and were plotting against him.'
'How did he kill himself?'
'He cut his throat with a razor.'

Napoleon was silent and gave no sign of feeling. He then went on with his questions, which showed he believed Whitbread to have been leader of the opposition in the Commons. Would Ponsonby take Whitbread's place? Lyttelton thought Brougham was more likely to if he was given time. Was Brougham really eloquent? And wasn't Whitbread related to Grey? What was Grey like as a speaker?

The *Bellerophon* spent twelve days off the coast of Devon and Cornwall, and there was close contact from the start between sympathizers in London and Napoleon's suite. It began, according to Las Cases, the day after they anchored in Torbay, when Maitland brought back to him from the mainland
M

FACING PAGE
Detail from J. J. Chalon's painting of Napoleon on
the deck of the *Bellerophon* at Plymouth.

a letter from Lady Clavering, enclosing another from his wife. A day later, on 26 July, Maitland received 'positive orders to prevent all communication whatever with the shore' except through Admiral Keith. But letters continued to flow in both directions—'*nous trouvâmes le moyen*,' says Las Cases, and the most probable channel is O'Meara, who had already pledged his loyalty.[1]

The most important message went out on 27 July, when Las Cases sent to London a statement by Napoleon on the illegality of his detention. 'The Emperor', he says, 'dictated to me a statement suitable for the jurists to discuss and defend his true position.' Las Cases denies that he kept a copy of this statement and it has not been recovered, but Count Emmanuel de las Cases, a descendant, claimed that it reached Lady Clavering in the night of the 27th and was on the desk of Sir Samuel Romilly on the 28th.

Until Napoleon was transferred from the *Bellerophon* to the *Northumberland*, and the *Northumberland* actually sailed, Las Cases clung to his hope of relief. Capel Lofft, with whom he was in touch, was a determined and resourceful lawyer who was passionately opposed to the Government, and became the main goad of Lord Holland in the long-term campaign for Napoleon's release. His first reaction to Waterloo was of hopeless despair. Together with Hazlitt and Godwin, he is mentioned by Crabb Robinson in his diary as prostrated by the news. The appeal from the *Bellerophon* pulled him together. Since Napoleon had abdicated and the war was over, Lofft could see at once that the case for holding him as a prisoner of war could be challenged. He applied for a writ of habeas corpus 'to bring up the body of Napoleon Buonaparte from Plymouth'. Unfortunately the writ had to come from Eldon, the Lord Chancellor, who saw no reason to look at such an issue through the eyes of Lofft, and suggested that a law should be passed to put Napoleon's position beyond dispute.

Lofft quickly changed his ground. A naval case was pending in the Court of Queen's Bench against Rear-Admiral Cochrane for failing to attack the squadron of Willaumez and Jerome Bonaparte. A Mr. Anthony Mackenrot who had the right to subpoena witnesses decided that he needed to cross-examine Napoleon in court on 10 November. A subpoena was not a bad second bet to a writ of habeas corpus.

Mackenrot had been a judge on Tortola in the West Indies, but he had

[1] Only one letter survives from the exchange, an acknowledgement from the *Bellerophon* of an earlier letter from Capel Lofft. The style is that of Las Cases, and 'le comte Milleraye', as he signs himself, is an unknown name combining those of two associates of his first years in London, de Mallevaux and Monneraye.

Mr le comte Milleraye presents his compliments to Mr Capel Lofft, and is instructed by the greatest of men (as he so justly calls him) to send him the enclosed lock of hair—as a sign of his esteem for his principles and his gratitude for the zeal he has shown for his cause. Napoleon Buonaparte will always count Mr Capel Lofft among his most devoted friends and Mr le Comte de Milleraye takes this opportunity to assure him of his respect.

remained athletic and managed to reach Plymouth in the early hours of 4 August. He arrived shortly after a courier from the Admiralty with orders that the *Bellerophon* should get ready to put to sea. At dawn, Napoleon realized with dismay that sail was being hoisted; his suite, led by Las Cases, advised him 'to enter a formal objection to this violence'.

Mackenrot with his subpoena reached Admiral Keith's house soon after the Admiral had left it for his flagship, the *Tonnant*, where he gave orders for dealing with Mackenrot, whom he believed to be armed with a writ of habeas corpus. Mackenrot hired a cutter and made for the *Tonnant*. He was met by Captain Brenton, a retired hero of past actions against the French in the West Indies, about the same age as Mackenrot but standing so well with the Admiralty that he had been brought out of retirement and made a flag captain in the Hundred Days. He refused to speak to Mackenrot except in French. Since he was trying to rescue Napoleon, that was the only language fit for him. Mackenrot gathered that the Admiral was not on board. Seeing a twelve-oared barge making off towards Cornwall, he broke off the angry exchanges with Brenton and gave chase in his cutter. But the Admiral's barge got away, and Mackenrot turned back to the *Bellerophon* which was about to weigh anchor. When he was within hailing distance he was intercepted by a guard-boat. After a struggle in which he was outmanoeuvred and outnumbered, he had to watch the *Bellerophon* move out to sea. The *Northumberland*, which was at Portsmouth loading for the journey to St. Helena, was not ready for the sudden departure, and when Napoleon was transferred to her on 7 August at a rendezvous fifty miles from the coast at Start Point, many of the essentials for life at St. Helena had been left behind.

While Lady Holland planned a series of dinner-parties for a carefully selected list of guests, Lord Holland settled down to convert the Whig leaders to a policy which included non-intervention in French affairs as a party tenet. Fox had laid it down in the Whig Club that every nation had a right to govern itself, and was better able to do so than any other nation from outside. What Holland demanded was the application of this principle as 'the main, clear and definite object of public policy', and the exclusion from the party of anyone who would not subscribe to it. 'I really think it better to part company than sail in a convoy that has no determinate object.'

Grey replied that there was no difference between him and Holland as to a war on behalf of the Bourbons, but he could not put an abstract principle to the party 'as a sort of test'. For one thing, times might change; for another, England was bound by treaties to maintain an army in France.

With Thomas Grenville, on the Right of the party, Holland's exchanges were more provocative. Holland said he accepted the need to reduce the armed forces, not for financial reasons, but to give the French people a chance to revolt against vindictive peace terms. Grenville replied with a letter which Holland found 'd——d cross'. 'Your pen, like your conversation,' Grenville wrote, 'has always had an amicable and delightful character, but it certainly has written on this occasion under such extreme impressions as I believe are not exceeded by many in France.

That you should *wish* to see England and France thrown back into the relative situations in which they stood before the success of the Allied armies, the left bank of the Rhine and Italy again subject to the dominance of France, the Bourbon expelled to give to France under the talents of Bonaparte a renewed hope of conquering the world; that you should see in the enthusiastic valour and fortitude of the Russians and Prussians in arms, the invaders—nothing to praise and everything to fear—and that you should teach your candid mind to believe that fire and sword are all that the Northern nations are good for and that they are excluded by nature from all genius, and fit only for war and devastation—if these, such as I have selected them from your letter, are indeed your true and genuine sentiments, you are undoubtedly in my eyes, as you tell me you know you shall be, a most incorrigible Jacobin.

Holland was a good deal sobered by this counter-attack, and may have reflected that his wife's company on the Continent had not been an ideal preparation for politics at home. 'Perhaps', he wrote to Grenville on 15 September, 'I was more than usually soured with the northern barbarians—for such, in spite of their acknowledged courage, I must consider them—from having recently witnessed their odious and vexatious conduct to their subjects and their friends on the Rhine and in Flanders.' He had no wish to be considered a traitor. 'But as it is, I cannot help thinking my view of English interests, though less fashionable, more comfortable than that of most of my contemporaries. It is at least pleasant in wishing well for one's country to wish for the welfare of others as connected with it.' He reaffirmed his wish to see the results of Waterloo undone.

With a clear conscience, then, but without support from the party, the Hollands prepared for action. The most urgent task, if the return from Elba was to be the model, was to win Sir Hudson Lowe who had already been nominated as Governor of St. Helena. The conquest was not likely to be as simple as that of Colonel Neil Campbell. Lowe was a half-educated man with a distaste for radicals. The son of an Army surgeon, he had spent much of his youth in the garrison of Gibraltar, and the Spanish he had learnt was one of the few things on which they might hope to find common ground. He had taken part in the reduction of Corsica, where he spent two more years in a garrison, and he had made a point of picking up Italian and

French. In the later years of the war he played a more important role as an inspector in northern and eastern Europe, finding in these areas, particularly under Blücher, a more bracing atmosphere than the south. On the field of Bautzen in 1813 Lowe caught a glimpse of Napoleon, and was struck by the Emperor's failure to notice him in return. It confirmed a feeling he had had since his service in Corsica that he was in some sense Napoleon's equal or superior.

The two men were in fact the same age. Lowe was humane, even kindly, but a fundamental reserve made him abrupt. He was pedantic and sound in matters of detail. Wellington found him intolerable because of his admiration for Prussian methods, but Sir John Moore said of him that 'when Lowe's at the outposts, I'm sure of a good night.'

The Lowe campaign was again managed by Lady Holland, who put into it more preparation than for any in her past. They had crossed the Channel on 4 August, and the first dinner to Lowe was held a fortnight later. It was to be a reassuring occasion without the kind of brilliance which might seem at odds with a sense of national responsibility. Lord Ossulston, the chief guest, was a rather dull Whig who had been a Postmaster-General in the eighteenth century and had served on a famous committee in the Star and Garter which revised the rules of cricket. Napoleon, he had told Creevey, 'ought to be placed out of the reach of again interfering in the concerns of the world, tho' it is difficult not to feel for a man who played such a part, if he is destined to spend his days in St. Helena.' The tone of mild regret seemed right for the evening. Lord Jersey was present, but not Lady Jersey, who could be counted on to make radical speeches in defence of Caroline. There was the Hon. Frederick North, who as the ex-Governor of Ceylon had a fund of advice on administration, and Henry Webster, a son of Lady Holland's first marriage. Webster was perhaps the most reassuring touch of all because he had fought at Waterloo and proved indirectly that Lady Holland was able to shed her blood for the country. There were also Samuel Rogers and Henry Luttrell, members of the inner circle of Holland House, and Francis Horner, whose political judgement made him the great hope of the Whigs.

After dinner the guests moved into the library and had a look at the Spanish section, which was the best in London. Lowe was glad to find that Holland had not read Cortés on Mexico and he noticed a complete readiness in his host to acknowledge the extent of the omission. When the party broke up, it was in the hope that they would meet again soon.

Luttrell, Rogers, and Horner stayed behind for the night, agreeing that the dinner had been successful at whatever cost to themselves. Since Lowe seemed more interested in the volcanic structure of St. Helena than its politics, it might be better if next time they were replaced by a geologist.

He came again in a fortnight with a bundle of books on Spain, and was received with outstretched arms. Luttrell and Rogers were not present, but Horner was there again, the Hon. Frederick Ponsonby, another survivor of Waterloo, and Mr. John Playfair, a geologist of eminence. (Playfair had been Lord John Russell's first tutor, but it was not necessary to disclose this pedigree and Russell kept away.) The most distinguished guest was Lord Auckland, who was the auditor of Greenwich Hospital, a sinecure he had inherited from his father. While Auckland appeared as austere and reserved as Lowe, he was the making of the party, cheerful, kindly, and full of tact. Ponsonby, who was still recovering from his wounds, described how a Polish lancer had run him through the chest and left him lying on the ground to serve as an arm-rest for a *tirailleur* who was picking off the British. Napoleon was introduced as a subject by Sir James Mackintosh, who had been as devoted to the Revolution as Fox but had long since renounced its offspring. At the end of the evening Lowe insisted on leaving his Spanish books, and Holland's interest was so great that he scarcely resisted. Before long he had a note from Lowe begging that 'Lord Holland will do him the favour of allowing the *Relation of Cortés* to occupy a place in your Lordship's library'; he would 'not fail to have the honour of waiting on them on Monday next'.

But Lady Holland had no intention of closing in too soon. The dinner on Monday, 11 September, was to the Duke of York, who was still basking in the recovery of his reputation since Waterloo. He was not a clever man but his judgement was better than his brothers', and he was agreeable. As Commander-in-Chief of the Armed Forces, he could hardly fail to have an overriding influence on Lowe's career, and his presence at Holland House was a better advertisement of its respectability than a royal coat of arms. With him was Sir Henry Bunbury, who had given Napoleon his formal sentence on the *Bellerophon* and was second to Lord Bathurst, the Secretary for War and Colonies, Lowe's minister. There was also Lord Lauderdale, who shared some of the Hollands' sympathy for Napoleon, and Lord Alvanley, the star of Regency conversationalists—'a *natural* Wag', Creevey called him. There was also Sir James Mackintosh again.

Lady Holland was well able to calculate a guest's vulnerability to her demands, and this third dinner represented the end of her preparation, the final barrage before she closed in. At his next appearances, Lowe was faced first with Byron, then with Captain Maitland and de Cabarrus, and finally with Robert Adair. With herself and her husband, they were among the most eloquent admirers of Napoleon in England.

The Byrons came with a distaste for Lowe which threatened to be dangerous. Their marriage was eight months old and had been scarcely bearable since the end of June. The Hollands insisted on a preparatory dinner, on 13 September, at which they encouraged Byron to express to Lowe his admiration for Napoleon rather than that he was 'damned sorry' for Waterloo, as he had told the American Ticknor. Sir Hudson was to be converted, not offended. Nevertheless, it was to meet 'Hudson Lowe, the Jailer', that Byron and his wife came on 22 September. They dined in an intimate group with George Lamb, the youngest son of Lord Melbourne, Lady Holland's mother, and Joseph Jekyll, who had voted for peace with France ever since 1794. Lowe remained outside the circle, constrained and ill at ease. He would not shift as they tried to move him to a new view of human greatness; he refused to accept Byron's prestige as a standard of judgement. And since he would not consult them they ended by consulting him. As a soldier, what did he think of Napoleon?

'I asked him', Byron wrote, 'whether the dispositions were those of a great General: he answered disparagingly, "that they were very *simple*".' Byron contained himself, but did not see Lowe again. 'I had always thought', he noted afterwards, 'that a degree of Simplicity was an element of Greatness.'

The dinner was a check, and an ominous check, where there ought to have been an advance. The Hollands decided to bring up Captain Maitland, who should perhaps have come first. Maitland on the *Bellerophon* had been very much in Lowe's position, finding the Emperor suddenly under his control with only a few lines of directive signalled by London to guide him. He was introduced to Lowe at Holland House on 28 September, and it was a meeting between equals, Lowe the superior in rank, Maitland in social status and experience of Napoleon.

It was obvious from Maitland's ease of manner that he belonged to Holland House already. Lowe looked at him and could see an assurance he did not wholly like. He asked the sort of question he had learnt to ask as an Army inspector in eastern Europe, prodding, regardless of the state of his victim's defences. He may have heard of Maitland's presentation to Napoleon in the Peace of Amiens. He must have known that the Captain was being criticized in the Admiralty for taking more on himself than his orders allowed. If it was untrue that he had treated Napoleon as a guest, why had he allowed him to sit, like royalty, on his right? What form of address had he used? By what little moves had Napoleon won over the crew of the *Undaunted* on the way to Elba and of the *Bellerophon* on the way to Plymouth? What would Maitland advise to prevent this happening on St. Helena?

De Cabarrus, son of a great banker who had been Minister of Finance under Joseph Bonaparte when he was King of Spain, had met the Hollands in their Spanish travels and remained their close friend, but his knowledge of Napoleon was not of the kind that could mollify Lowe. The Hollands indeed were in despair. Lowe had now got his 'instructions' from the

Colonial Office, which were 'to permit every indulgence to Napoleon in his confinement compatible with the entire security of his person'. Lady Holland had hoped to get down to positive details and decided to press him on the arrangements he would accept for forwarding messages. She needed to be in contact with Napoleon in the interests of humanity, she said, to provide minor comforts, and to send books and newspapers. Lowe objected that this was for the Government to do; they were already disturbed at the ease with which Las Cases had communicated with London from the *Bellerophon*. There were strict rules on the *Northumberland* which all members of Napoleon's suite had to sign. The sixteenth article laid it down that letters might only be conveyed to him on St. Helena through the Secretary of State.

In that event, said Lady Holland, if Lowe could not provide facilities, what would he suggest 'for carrying her intentions into execution'? But Lowe did not seem to understand. Was she in command in some sense? She was asking from him just the kind of laxity he deplored in Maitland. It took all the good humour and authority of the Whig Earl Cowper and his wife, the eldest daughter of Lord Melbourne, to save the evening. Fazakerley, who had been asked to talk about life on Elba, was treated like Maitland, as a prejudiced witness.

Three weeks passed before the Hollands asked Lowe again. When they looked back at their failure to gain on him, or even to hold their position, it seemed to centre in some emotional sense on their love of the Mediterranean and his distrust of it. Apart from Lord Alvanley, who was irresistible, there was no one from the outside world who had done well enough to be invited back. Perhaps they should have done something about Prussia, more about the royal family. For 17 October they invited Captain Hesse, the son of the Duke of York by a German lady of that name; and Count Baldinger, a Prussian. Hesse had been a visitor to Kensington Palace and had been in love with Princess Charlotte. They had Alvanley again and the Lambs, who had been in Brussels with Lowe.

On 17 October they can have hoped to make little progress. On the 22nd, they got back to business and risked having Robert Adair, perhaps the most confirmed of Napoleonists, whom Gillray had drawn on his hands and knees in the Tuileries. They also risked Lord John Russell and his account of Elba; but to cover themselves they had Alvanley a third time and the Spanish Count Fernan Nuñez. Lowe seemed further off than ever, and in a few days Lady Holland became ill. On 10 November she was surprised to hear from Lowe that he was 'very much concerned to hear that your ladyship has been so much indisposed'. He would make a point of calling at Holland House to ask how she was.

It was not so much that the Hollands had been playing their cards badly as that the Government from the start had been playing theirs. Lowe's promotion had been a considerable one. His invitation from Lady Holland had been an anomaly among requests to meet Cabinet ministers. He was told on behalf of Lord Liverpool that if he continued in charge of Bonaparte for three years, 'it should not stop there.' His own minister, Lord Bathurst, was a cool politician and a High Churchman, whose whole nature was conservative. As Lowe got to know him, he may have felt no great warmth, but Bathurst's ability, not least as a writer, gave an impression of all-seeing competence which was not lost on him.

Bathurst had a habit of making jokes and he made them freely about Holland House. His 'Instructions' on St. Helena were handed to Lowe the day after he dined with the Duke of York, and no doubt they made a great impression. From then on it never occurred to him to think of Napoleon except as 'General Bonaparte', and he would have been incapable of forwarding a letter addressed in any other way. In the arrangements at St. Helena, Bathurst told him, there was an important role for the Governor's wife. Lowe began to see as much of a Mrs. Susan Johnson, the young widow of a colonel, as he did of Lady Holland. If he married Mrs. Johnson, he realized that he would either have to offend the Court of St. James's by taking her to Holland House, or Lady Holland by withholding her. He began to increase his courtesies to Lady Holland.

The marriage took place on 16 December. Lady Holland, who had been entertaining Canova without inviting Lowe, brought herself to send her congratulations. Lowe replied, after Christmas, that he would seize his first leisure moment 'to return my thanks in person for your kind remembrance of me on an occasion of so much interest to my future interest and happiness'. It was plain that Lady Lowe would not be coming.

Lady Holland must have controlled herself with difficulty. She had so far introduced him to forty of the most distinguished people in London; she had cowed Byron, excluded Lady Jersey, and abased herself to a mind which was below any standard she recognized. She had failed utterly, but the objective was too important to abandon. For 19 January 1816, a few days before their departure, she humbly invited the Lowes to a farewell dinner. In reply, Lady Lowe regretted that her preparations for the voyage were as much as she could manage, but Sir Hudson would be honoured to accept.

He arrived in his most reserved mood. He had just written to Sir Henry Bunbury, advocating, with Eldon, the introduction of a Bill to outlaw Napoleon for life. 'For the outlawry seems already sufficiently established,' he wrote, 'and only wants the sanction of legal and parliamentary authority to dispel the doubts of factious or opposing individuals regarding him.'

At Holland House he found Lord Lansdowne and Hugh Elliot, under whose father he had served when he was Governor of Corsica. Elliot himself had been Governor of the Windward Isles and could advise him on

another Atlantic colony. There was Hookham Frere, who had been pleni-
potentiary in Lisbon and Madrid, and Henry Bennet, a friend of Lord
Kensington, whom Creevey called 'most amiable, occasionally most
*boring*'. But it was of course all in vain.

Besides giving him this eighth dinner party, Lady Holland had to offer
her congratulations on the K.C.B. with which the Prince Regent was about
to invest him. She may have recognized it as the alternative to one of her
own chains around his neck. If he managed to harden his heart when he
said good-bye to her, it was a foretaste of what Napoleon might expect.

The failure to move Hudson Lowe left the Hollands with the need to
convert the Whigs and keep closely in touch with the opposition in France.
There was always the risk of a conflict between their various activities and
the arrival of a guest on the wrong night. To give sanctuary to Flahaut in
December was essential; he was in danger of his life, but his arrival at
Holland House was known to Lord Bathurst, and when Hudson Lowe
heard of it, he can hardly have looked at the other guests without wondering
who else was upstairs. The Reverend Marsh had been in the house during
the second dinner to Lowe, but was not allowed in the dining-room because
he was dangerously critical of Napoleon; he nevertheless described the
scene to his wife.

The French influence on Holland House came from two main sources of
about equal importance: the Bonapartists, who were on the run, and the
liberals, who were almost equally on the defensive but had a platform and
major representatives in Lafayette and Benjamin Constant. There was as
much confusion between these groups in exile as there was in France. The
liberal cause not only had leaders; it was avowable. Bonapartism had to
wait. At first it was little more than a rescue operation and an intelligence
service based on Brussels, Rome, and London, and its strength in France
lay submerged.

Lafayette, the liberal leader of the Revolution, had probably been, after
Fox, the main influence on Holland's life. He had fought under Washington
in the War of Independence, had proposed the design of the tricolour in
1789, and had resisted both the Jacobins' terror and Napoleon's imperialism.
After Waterloo he had tried to get access to the Allied sovereigns with a
declaration that Louis XVIII was as repugnant to the French people as a
ruler as was Napoleon. His was the only undeviating record of support for
the Revolutionary ideals.

To Holland, who consulted him with deference, Lafayette was irresistible.
He had only to see him in France during the first Abdication to accept that
there was more liberty under the Restoration than under the Empire. After
Waterloo, when Napoleon appeared to have accepted this lesson although

the victors had forgotten it, Holland felt himself appointed by Lafayette to fight for liberty. Lafayette confessed himself bewildered by the British Parliament. 'It is you', he wrote to Holland, 'who will soon make the voice of liberty heard there.' He saw the world coming together under the leadership of enlightened patriots, in a system of *libéralité universelle*.

If it was Lafayette, in Paris, who had encouraged Holland to accept Napoleon's exile in Elba, it was Constant's support of Napoleon after his escape which certified the great man to be a liberal ruling on behalf of the French people. When Constant was prosecuted in the wave of Bourbon revenge after Waterloo, he came to London by way of Brussels and kept closely in touch with Holland House, which he referred to as '*chez* Lady Holland'. On his first visit he noticed that she treated him with reserve. 'The Rubicon has not been crossed,' he wrote in his journal. 'Shall I ever cross it?' Constant was writing *Adolphe*, an investigation into the waning of his love for Mme. de Staël, and his appraisal of women was no more appealing to Lady Holland than his appraisal of dictators. The Hollands were disturbed by Constant's ability to see through the currency of politics to the motives of the heart, but they found him an indispensable guide in London and Paris.

Léonard Gallois, the third of the Holland House liberals, was about to write *Le Parapluie paternel*, and became a minor thorn in the side of the Bourbons. To Lord Holland he seemed one of the most reliable authorities on Napoleon. Having worked close to the Emperor in the Peace of Amiens, he refused employment afterwards. He was 'too sincere and enlightened a friend of freedom not to abhor a system which depended on the character of an individual'. It was in fact Gallois who recorded one of Napoleon's most revealing sayings, '*Je n'aime pas beaucoup les femmes, ni le jeu, enfin rien; ie suis tout-à-fait un être politique.*'

The Hollands had close contacts with Brussels. Lord Kinnaird, who had great influence on them in the first two years of the peace, spent much of his time there with refugees and Bonapartist conspirators. The Duke of Bedford wrote in May 1818 that 'Kinnaird has been more involved by the persons with whom he is in the habit of associating in Brussels than he is willing to allow.' Kinnaird himself denied that he was a Bonapartist and suggests that Lady Holland was more extreme. But in June 1816 he asked Holland to see the assistant editor of the *Nain Jaune*, Isidore Gayet.[1]

---

[1] *Le Nain Jaune*, edited by Cauchois-Lemaire, had been founded in Paris in December 1814 and became such a force that the Minister who suppressed it said it was more to be feared than an army of 10,000 men; and a colleague raised the estimate to 50,000. It became openly Bonapartist in the Hundred Days and was suppressed a month after Waterloo, but reappeared in Brussels as *Le Nain Jaune Réfugié*. When it was finally suppressed at the end of 1816, Gayet escaped through Holland House and rejoined Cauchois-Lemaire. A year later, in The Hague, they published a joint *Appel à l'opinion publique et aux états généraux en faveur des patriotes français*.

'You will find him a clever, intelligent man and extremely well informed.'

Apart from Kinnaird, the Hollands' main contacts in Brussels were with the Abbé Sieyès and Antoine Vincent Arnault. Sieyès, perhaps the greatest theorist of the Revolution, had voted for the execution of Louis XVI and remade the constitution for Napoleon. He applied for sanctuary in Holland House with the authentic panic of a refugee. In January 1816, he wrote that Holland had himself suggested his taking refuge in England. In February he pressed for an answer. 'If it is not satisfactory, one might as well be thrown in the sea with a stone round one's neck. It is not at sixty-nine and ill that one can transport oneself to America.' Arnault, Napoleon's chief educational executive, wrote similarly. He had heard from Lafayette that Holland had not forgotten him, but his fate was '*plus triste que jamais*'; cut off from his family and friends, he was only safe as long as he remained in hiding. If Holland had orders or advice, he said, he should send them through the printer whose name was on the book he was sending.[1]

Holland comforted Sieyès and Arnault as best he could when he went to Brussels in 1817. Neither came to London.

Although Brussels was the most important staging area for refugee movements, Rome was the most active centre of Bonapartism. Pope Pius VII had been bullied too long by Napoleon and dragged to and fro across Europe too often not to sympathize with displaced princelings. He had given the Bonapartes refuge in 1814, when Holland had been disgusted by the atmosphere of reaction in Rome, and he protected them again after 1815 when the Alliance demanded a tightening of security. Napoleon's mother lived free of interference in frugal dignity. Louis Bonaparte continued in the Corso, while his son, the future Emperor, grew into his teens. Queen Hortense, now formally separated from Louis Bonaparte, came and went in a trail of Bonapartist intrigue.

Lucien Bonaparte was allowed back to Rome by the Pope after the Hundred Days, but he settled uneasily. He had had the strange experience of spending nearly four years under surveillance in wartime England, after being caught by the Navy in 1810 on his way to America. The fact of his stay—most of it on an estate called Thorngrove about four miles outside Worcester—may have given Napoleon the idea that he himself might be allowed to live in a country house in England. But if Napoleon was not yet to be welcomed, why not Lucien again, as the forerunner who had proved his good conduct?

There were reasons against it from the British point of view. When Napoleon returned to Paris from Waterloo, Lafayette had persuaded the Chambers to vote themselves in permanent session and called out the

---

[1] The book was Arnault's tragedy *Germanicus*, printed by Schulze and Dean, 13 Poland Street, and sold by Samuel Leigh, 18 Strand.

National Guard to protect them against dissolution. It was what Napoleon described on St. Helena as the insurrection of the Chambers. He was urged by Lucien to collect regular troops to suppress them, and when he hesitated, Lucien pressed him to 'dare'. But Napoleon, realizing it was hopeless, said, 'Alas, I have dared too much already.' It was thus the boldest, the most pushing member of the family who proposed to come to London.

Lucien gave no reasons. He had found relations easy with Holland in 1814, and counted on his support, hinting that Holland House or any house on the outskirts of London would suit him. 'I give my word of honour', he wrote on 6 October 1816, 'never to correspond with St. Helena or with France without giving advance notice to the ministry; my wish is to live in London, and I count on setting myself up in a country place on the border of town. Find out if that is possible.'

The suggestion exasperated Holland, who was already compromised by his help to the others. 'I should warn you', he wrote on 12 March 1817, 'that neither the moment, nor the circumstances, nor your choice of myself as the channel of your requests, seem to me to promise success. It would be better to wait until the fears, false or true, which this Government entertains, have died down.' Lucien accepted Holland's verdict with Roman dignity. On 2 April 1817, he wrote expressing his hope that Britain would recover her balance; as soon as Holland judged the moment suitable, he would kindly apply to the ministry.

While Brussels and Rome were scenes of panic or complacency of varying degrees, France itself had become an execution ground which justified Whitbread's last appeal to the Commons against 'horrors'. The inhabitants of Paris who had borne arms for Napoleon were guaranteed impunity under Article 12 of the Capitulation, but it was doubtful whether this would be held to apply to political acts, and the courts martial soon made it clear that it would not. On the list of proscripts, four of the most distinguished had all given Napoleon outstanding service in the Hundred Days: Labédoyère, Flahaut, de Lavalette, and Marshal Ney. All had belonged to the salon of Queen Hortense.

Labédoyère was court-martialled first, before the Hollands reached London. He had married the daughter of an *émigré*, fought with distinction under Napoleon in Spain and Russia, but accepted the Cross of St. Louis under the Restoration. He was twenty-nine. On Napoleon's return from Elba, he set out from Grenoble at the head of his regiment and welcomed him. He had done so with a solemn and rather naïve warning that France wanted peace and happiness and would stand no more despotism. The moment was too tense for Napoleon to risk a rebuke, and recognizing afterwards that it had been a turning point, he promoted Labédoyère general, aide-de-camp, and *Pair de France*.

Labédoyère's defence was made in writing by Benjamin Constant. His own position as a civilian had not been dissimilar, and he put into the defence a passionate sympathy for the individual faced with a conflict of loyalties. The plea was rejected and Labédoyère was shot on 19 August. Constant noted the fact in his diary with three exclamation marks.

The Hollands were dismayed. If this could happen to Labédoyère by an automatic process, what were the chances of Flahaut, who had fewer of Labédoyère's reservations about Napoleon. The Hollands' ties with Flahaut were close. Madame de Souza, his mother, had often been a guest at Holland House in spite of a certain distaste for Lady Holland. Herself a product of the *ancien régime*, she had gone into exile when the boy, her son by Talleyrand, was seven. Her husband, Comte de Flahaut, was executed a year later. The poems and novels into which her dreams of heroism and love were transmuted show the restraint of the eighteenth century, but her influence on her son was great. There were traces of complacency in him, a limitation of vision and an assumption of superiority, but they were explained by the period in which the two had lived in intense emotional isolation. 'The business of men', she told him, 'is to deceive women, and it is theirs to look after themselves.' He fought at Austerlitz, Wagram, throughout the Russian campaign, and at Waterloo. But his fame as a lover was equal to his war record, and his liaison with Queen Hortense, Napoleon's step-daughter, had given him his own illegitimate son. On his return to Paris after Waterloo, he openly supported the succession of Napoleon's son. If there was to be a list of proscripts, his name could scarcely be omitted.

Flahaut was saved, but only through the unique collaboration of Talleyrand in Paris and Holland in London. Although he was under police surveillance, he got across the frontier into Germany. His name disappeared from the list. On 15 December he appeared openly at dinner in Holland House with the Whig leaders whose support he was likely to need.

Rather surprisingly, they liked him. He was as handsome as he had been reported to be, spoke easily, without hiding his opinions, was brief, courteous, unabashed. He had his mother's economy of words, but there was no sign in him of Talleyrand, which was what they feared. It was rather as if he had been to some French Eton and Christ Church. 'I am sincerely glad that he is at last safe in England,' Grey wrote to Holland on 3 December 1815, 'but you must protect him from the Alien Act.'

Christmas dinner was arranged for him ten days after the coming out. Lord John Russell came, on his way to Paris, his comrade-in-arms General Sebastiani, and an attractive Miss Mercer Elphinstone, daughter of Admiral Lord Keith. Byron had had his eye on Miss Elphinstone, and four months after the Christmas dinner sent a message to her from Dover that he would not have had to go into exile if he had married her. Flahaut repaired this error, inflicting a greater blow on the Admiral, her father, than if he had been caught by the subpoena in Plymouth Sound. Lord Keith promptly disinherited her. Queen Hortense, in exile in Baden, collapsed.

The threat of the Alien Act sometimes occurred to Flahaut, but he was becoming so English that he had difficulty in thinking of himself as insecure. The Bedfords invited him to Woburn and the Duke offered to teach him real tennis. Tuition was a pleasure because Flahaut accepted defeat with indifference if he had champagne *frappé* between the sets. Before long he was beating Holland at his own game, catching salmon with Grey, and shooting the Bedfords' partridges which he shared with Miss Elphinstone. In June 1817, when he married her, he assured Lady Holland that he wanted passionately to repay his wife's sacrifices. When he was offered, by Lauderdale, a device for ensuring himself against deportation, he did nothing to make use of it.

The device was a simple one. By a Scottish law of the late seventeenth century, a foreigner who held shares in the Bank of Scotland was accepted as a naturalized subject; as the Act of Union did nothing to exclude them, such subjects were automatically Englishmen. The Prince Regent was known to be indignant at Holland's protection of Flahaut, and instructed Eldon to revise the law. But the Prince was 'baffled', says Lord Holland, 'by myself and others prolonging the debate on the third reading in [the] Lords till the House of Commons was up'. There was no time to agree the amendments without putting off the prorogation of Parliament, 'and in the choice of disasters, the Government submitted to the dreadful one of having a French officer a naturalised subject of the kingdom in which his wife was a native and a peeress.'

Flahaut, ashamed of the trouble he had caused by not having taken his chance, apologized 'for my foolishness, my *lambinerie*'. He could only await his fate in silence 'without finding fault with the conduct of your honourable House'. He remained a Frenchman; in the 1830 Revolution he was reinstated by Louis-Philippe as a Peer of France; he supported Louis Napoleon in the *coup d'état* of 1851 and became his Ambassador in England. In the meantime he confirmed the Hollands in their political faith. Hudson Lowe was *un misérable*, Princess Caroline an opportunist, Lady Holland a guardian angel whose goodness would be adored by good hearts and true ('*les cœurs droits et généreux*'). Flahaut treated Talleyrand more coolly than Talleyrand treated him. When he dined with the Hollands at Ampthill, he referred to him as 'Talleyrand', a man of distinction unrelated to him. As the tensions developed on St. Helena, he guided the Hollands, sometimes against their will, in the response they should make. He sometimes made Holland feel he had himself become Napoleon's aide-de-camp.

The third and fourth of the famous proscripts were arrested in France immediately after Labédoyère, but their cases left more time for action. The climate was darkening as the ultra-royalists gained the upper hand. An election was held nine weeks after Waterloo on a vote confined to a hundred thousand who committed themselves to the ultras and a policy of revenge. Talleyrand fell, and Fouché passed on to his successor the police system which Napoleon had perfected. Louis XVIII was half-hearted in revenge, but his sons, Angoulême and Berry, were determined. 'We are going marshal-hunting,' said the Duke of Berry, and Marshal Ney allowed himself to be arrested on 5 August, in the belief that he had immunity under the Capitulation.

A week later Lord Kinnaird dined at Holland House. He was a Scottish peer who had spent much of his energy in a campaign for an English peerage with a seat in the Lords. His services to the Whigs had been valuable, and Fox intended to give him one, but he was fated to spend the rest of his days in opposition. Holland listened to his plans for a visit to Paris, and had him back to dinner on 21 August with Sir Arthur Pigott, who had been Attorney-General in the Talents. Holland had always found Pigott cautious but 'singularly serviceable to his friends'. In another week he had Sir Robert Wilson, who was also going to Paris.

Wilson would have been the ideal knight-errant if his discretion had been equal to his courage. Joining the Army as a cornet in the first year of the war, he at once showed great bravery in saving the life of the Emperor Francis II in the face of superior French forces, but he lost the gold medal which was specially struck for him by the Emperor. On the withdrawal of Moore to Corunna, it was Wilson, at the head of a privately organized corps, who kept the lines of communication open with Spain so that Wellington could continue to operate. When Holland proposed a vote of thanks to him in the Lords, he had implied that Wellington was getting much of the credit due to Wilson. Wilson published a protest against flogging, sided with Caroline against the Prince Regent, and helped the Austrians to break up Murat's advance into northern Italy. He was used to taking quick decisions without thought, which made him better on horseback than at politics, and better acting alone than as an ally.

Kinnaird and Wilson were convinced, with Lady Holland, that the Bourbon hold on France could not last more than a few months. They felt it their duty to hasten the downfall of the Restoration and save its victims to play a role as leaders in the future. The two men arrived in Paris to find that the article of the Capitulation on bearing arms had been ruled outside the terms of reference of the court-martial trying Marshal Ney.

The execution was planned for 7 December. In the middle of November, Ney's wife wrote an appeal to the Prince Regent and sent copies, on Wilson's advice, to Lord Holland and Louis Philippe. Holland wrote back to

Madame Ney that he hoped the Regent's reply would be prompt and favourable. In his view her husband was *'un homme aussi brave que persécuté'*, but his own wishes were stronger than his hopes: *'je n'ai que peu de moyens de vous être utile, et en les mettant trop en usage, j'aurais à craindre qu'ils ne fissent plus de mal que bien à votre cause.'* Holland approached Lord Liverpool and was advised, in friendly terms, to go to the Regent direct. The Regent was at the moment out of London, and Holland knew he was exasperated by his rescue of Flahaut.

Madame Ney had her answer through Wellington shortly after she had Holland's: her husband's execution was a matter for the French Government. Wilson made an attempt to rescue him which failed and was hushed up. She paid a last visit to him in prison with her four sons and collapsed while she was there. Ney was only able to bring her round by suggesting that she might work a miracle by seeing Louis XVIII. He then went in front of the firing squad and refused to be blindfolded.

There remained Lavalette, the last of the former aides under sentence of death, and the most devoted to Napoleon. Holland had told Kinnaird and Wilson of the interest he had had in Lavalette since the time of their visit in 1800, when the Frenchman had not hesitated to grant him a passport. He was now middle-aged, a stout, ministerial figure, associated less with Arcola and the battle of the Pyramids than with the reform of the French postal services on Napoleonic lines. Dismissed in 1814 under the Restoration, he had at once rallied to Napoleon on his return from Elba. He was arrested in Paris after Waterloo, when he was with his wife.

Lavalette was to be executed on 21 December. When Holland pressed Kinnaird at the beginning of the month for some ground for hope, his reply was enigmatic but ended with a plain hint. 'I am grown so cautious that I do not quite like to see my opinions in black and white and I fancy it is very unnecessary to tell them to you. *Spero meliore.*'

Unless Kinnaird had a clear-cut plan, it now looked to Holland as if as much depended on Madame de Lavalette as it had on Madame Ney, and with as little chance of success. She was a niece of Joséphine, Louise de Beauharnais. Her apparent calm and languor were well known to Flahaut, who when he heard the situation, announced that there was no hope. Holland, watching the final stages in the siege of Sir Hudson Lowe, was unable to withstand Flahaut's pessimism.

But Madame de Lavalette had already begun to exert herself. She was as slight a figure as her husband was stout, but her apparent calm was the surface of a tense personality. She asked for access to Louis XVIII and was refused. With great skill, she managed to waylay him on his way to mass. He was acutely embarrassed, muttered that she had her duty as a wife, no doubt, but so had he as King, and he moved on.

N

The day fixed for the execution was a Thursday. On Wednesday, Madame de Lavalette was allowed to dine in her husband's cell with their daughter and a governess. The weather was cold. She arrived wrapped up and almost hidden from sight in a big sedan chair which had been found for her by a British officer, Lieutenant Bruce. She spent the dinner hour dressing her husband in clothes like her own. When he was taken out, she sat on in the cell, waiting to be discovered. The chair was found afterwards in the street, but no trace of its occupant. Nor was Lavalette found; there was only his wife, who resisted interrogation with the calm of a man. All Paris was searched. The description of Lavalette was in the hands of everyone who could read. It became a joke that a man with such a figure should have been able to change places with his wife.

Meanwhile he was hiding in the Quai d'Orsay. Lieutenant Bruce, one of the Bonapartist circle of Queen Hortense and Flahaut, transferred him to Sir Robert Wilson, who was to take him across the frontier disguised as a British officer. His measurements were given to a French tailor, who remarked 'that it was the measure of a tall man and had not been taken by a tailor'; but he delivered the uniform and said nothing.

Wilson next went to Sir Charles Stuart, the British Ambassador, and persuaded him to issue a passport for a brother-in-law who needed urgently to get back to London. He drove out of Paris heavily armed with Lavalette beside him. They had to pass one check-point after another, and Wilson's chief worry was that Lavalette's accent would betray him; he talked loudly to cover his answers so that little got across but the sense of what he had said. Once, when Lavalette turned his head, Wilson saw a line of grey hair at the edge of his wig and trimmed it back with scissors. They got to the frontier, and Lavalette was passed on through intermediaries to Queen Hortense in Baden.

Wilson relaxed when he had gone and went back to Paris to commit one of the blunders which were second nature to him. He wrote down a detailed account of the escape and his own role in it, addressed it to Earl Grey at Howick, and confided it to the postal system which Lavalette had himself devised for Napoleon. On 13 January Wilson was arrested, together with Bruce.

The police not only had Wilson's letter describing how it had been done. The Duke of Bedford warned Holland on 21 January, 'I understand that among Sir Robert's papers they found all Grey's letters on the political situation, which they intend to publish.'

In prison Wilson spent three days refusing to respond to the preliminary interrogation which was a normal part of the judicial procedure. On 16 January he denied that he knew Lavalette before the trial. It was put to him 'that the escape of Lavalette was not with you a principal object, but simply a means of a conspiracy antecedently formed and determined upon, for the purpose of destroying or changing the Government or the order of the succession to the Throne.' Extracts from his letters were read in which he predicted the expulsion of the Bourbons. 'The blow which will be struck will be heard in a terrible manner,' he had written, 'and I hope the people of Europe will not be deaf to the appeal that will then be made to them.'

Lord Holland now had a letter from a Mr. Charles Broderip in Paris, whom he had not heard of before. He circulated it to Grey, who was ill, and the Duke of Bedford. Broderip wrote as an intimate acquaintance of Wilson and enclosed a précis of his interrogation. He spoke of efforts made by a M. Dupin, the counsel of Marshal Ney, to get bail for him. He reported that Madame de Lavalette, who had been kept in her husband's cell, had now been transferred to a *maison de santé*, where she was seriously ill. He added an invitation to Holland. 'No political consideration can be mixed with the defence, but in whatever manner it might be thought necessary to treat this event at home, Sir Robert's particular request is that no personal consideration towards him might interfere with the line of discussion which your Lordship should deem the best adapted to the circumstances of his case.' Broderip indicated that it would be three weeks before the trial could come on.

Grey, who was dismayed at the exposure of his correspondence, wrote to Holland that if he thought 'there was a chance of my being of the slightest use to him, I would be carried to town in a litter, rather than not go, or even to Paris. But I am very much afraid that any premature exertion on our parts would incur the risk of making his case a sort of party question.' The best policy was to start a campaign in the British press. Grey wanted to send a message of reassurance to Lady Wilson, 'yet I hardly know how to do so with tolerable security.'

The Duke of Bedford added a warning to Holland on 2 February. 'This Broderip who writes to you about Wilson is an *espion de police* placed about Lady Wilson in order to insinuate himself into her confidence for obvious purposes and he has written to you in hopes to entrap you into some imprudent expression of your sentiments.' Bedford's best hope was that Wilson should be sentenced to a long term of imprisonment, 'so that he may be kept out of the way of any further mischief.'

Lady Holland had her own channels to Paris and she now put them at Grey's disposal. Correspondence was reopened quite freely with Wilson inside the prison of La Force. Grey had come round to the view that any move to support him in Parliament would be self-defeating. 'In the letter which I enclosed to Lady Holland the other day, for Wilson, I strongly urged his not defending his conduct on political grounds, on which the public are against him. . . . The prejudice against him which I hear from everybody is so general, is terrible and most disgraceful to the feelings of the country.'

The *Morning Chronicle* rallied, as far as it dared, to Wilson's support. On 23 January its Paris correspondent had denounced his abuse of military privilege and his subterfuge in getting a passport from Stuart as 'inexcusable', but by the end of the month it was giving a straightforward and sympathetic account of the proceedings. Grey and Holland could think of nothing more to do.

Wilson continued to be in direct contact with the Hollands. On 20 February, confident of the security of Lady Holland's channel, he wrote under the eyes of the guards about the prospects of an anti-Bourbon revolt. 'Our fellow prisoners afford no society and indeed we feel obliged to avoid associating with any, since every movement is observed and reports made ... I suppose the history of the world never presented such a system of espionage and municipal infamy. Out of evil, however, comes good, and the heavier the storm, the speedier fair weather.'

His trial came on in March. The prosecution was concerned to broaden the issue into a Bonapartist plot designed to foment revolution. The exchanges between Grey and Wilson were quoted. Bruce had been associated with an attempt to rescue Ney; he admitted that he had seen the Marshal every day in prison and that his motives in the case of Lavalette had been coloured by Ney's execution. He also admitted that he was in correspondence with Queen Hortense, whom he addressed as 'Imperial Highness'. Wilson, taking his brief from Grey, argued that 'less of politics than of humanity' entered into his and Bruce's conduct. They were sentenced very leniently on 24 April to three months imprisonment and costs. Kinnaird was ordered to leave France.

The first indication Kinnaird had had of displeasure was the refusal to allow him to see Wilson after his arrest. He had been sent for on 30 January by the Minister of Police, Anglès, and told that his stay in the capital was disagreeable. When he protested and asked for reasons, he was told they were general and referred to his anti-Bourbon attitude and correspondence with *émigrés*. He replied, rather naïvely, that he had sent no letters by the open post. The Minister said that his expulsion had been agreed by the Prince Regent. He then broadened his attack and complained of English visitors to France in general, saying, according to an open letter from Kinnaird to Lord Liverpool, 'that almost universally they spoke in contempt of the King and his family; and upon all occasions, whether in language or by the eagerness with which they sought the portraits, busts and other memorials of Napoleon, and seemed desirous of upholding the name of the usurper.' In public carriages the English had been seen to offer money to anyone who was ready to shout '*Vive l'Empereur!*'

Instead of leaving Paris, Kinnaird sent out invitations to a ball he was to hold in a week's time. When the day came he received an order to quit Paris within forty-eight hours. He went to see Stuart, but was told that he could not get a stay of execution. He crossed the Channel and saw Holland. He then went to Brussels, where at the beginning of 1818 he was unwittingly involved in an attempt by a Sub-Lieutenant Cantillon to assassinate Wellington. Napoleon left Cantillon a hundred thousand francs in his will.

At the beginning of 1816 there were Bonapartist disturbances in Lyons and the Languedoc whose importance was hard to assess. They were exaggerated and perhaps instigated by the local authorities who had to suppress them, but the French government was anxious to minimize them. 'The business at Lyons', Grey wrote to Lady Holland on 5 February, 'was more serious than anything that we have seen in the papers would lead one to suppose.' There had been 400 arrests and considerable trouble in the Languedoc where Napoleon's bust was paraded. The *Nain Jaune Réfugié* argued defiantly that France was 'more formidable for herself and the whole of Europe than she was in the delirium of liberty and victory'. Wilson was '*le plus noble caractère*'. '*Mme. de Lavalette est autrement jugée à la cour qu'à la ville; et par les dames du palais que par les mères de famille.*'

Wilson came out of prison in August and went to stay at Howick with the Greys. He sent a letter in advance complaining that the Minister of Police had behaved 'to the last like a blackguard'; but he turned up as if from a holiday. 'He has shown me a very pretty letter from Mde. de Lavalette with miniature pictures in a ring of herself and her husband,' Grey wrote to Lady Holland. 'He has also the snuff box which Ney took with him in the coach and had in his pocket when he was shot. It was given him by the *Maréchale*.' Flahaut came to stay at Howick to greet Wilson and hear the news. He told the Hollands that Louise de Lavalette's courage and discretion had surprised him 'in the greatest degree'.

But Madame de Lavalette paid dearly for her effort. Seven years later, when Lavalette, on compassionate grounds, was allowed into France to visit her in hospital, she was incurably mad.

In their contacts with Napoleon the Hollands showed more discretion than in attempting to rescue his followers. The Act of April 1816 made un-authorized contact with St. Helena a capital offence, and although this seemed no less ridiculous to them than the Act of 1798 against visits to enemy territory, they had learnt caution.

Their dealings with Rome and Paris remained slapdash, even after Wilson's experience; indiscretion was apt to seem to the Napoleonists an act of gallantry. Passing through Calais with a Bonapartist suspect in July 1816, Capel Lofft quoted the Code Napoléon to the customs officers as the law they were still supposed to be obeying. 'I protested against their right to examine any of my papers at all,' he wrote Holland, 'there being no charge against me.' And he was allowed to pass. In March 1818 the Duke of Bedford was less fortunate.

I have never passed worse at a French *Douane* in my whole life; they kept our things nearly the whole of the day and made the Duchess's trunks undergo the most rigorous examination, making her open her jewel-box and exposing with the utmost indecency and want of delicacy all her wearing apparel on the floor . . . and then seized a few things (*des misères* absolutely) which were not made up. . . . On my arrival at Paris I shall make a complaint to the Minister of Finances.

The Duke did not hesitate to send out Bonapartist propaganda from Paris through the open post. Knowing that his letters were opened on both sides of the Channel, Holland relied on a network of travellers. Contact with the Bonaparte family in Rome went via Lord Lansdowne, Lord Gower, Lady Jersey, and the American Ticknor; with the liberal opposition and Bonapartists in Paris, via the Duke of Bedford, the Duke of Buckingham, Lord and Lady Jersey, and the captains of Channel packets. If they could not hand over the correspondence personally, they were nervous. 'I have left a letter at Holland House with particular instructions that it should only be sent in the safest way,' wrote Bedford.

The emissaries were scarcely ever reluctant. 'I feel really much obliged to you for having thought of me as a discreet channel of information,' wrote Lord Gower. Some, who came to London without an introduction to Holland House, were pressing. '*Le sujet de ma visite était le désir de vous entretenir de l'Empereur Napoléon*,' wrote M. de Lély. Should his Lordship 'be *afraid* of granting a few minutes' conversation,' wrote another, his correspondent would 'endeavour to enter into detail on paper what might have been better discussed by word of mouth.'

There was less fuss and ceremony about contact with St. Helena. Lady Holland was capable of entering a Frenchman in the Dinner Books as 'Monsieur———'. They were aware how much was at stake and how dangerous the consequences if they were discovered.

The first contacts were through Capel Lofft and William Warden, the surgeon of the *Northumberland*; both efforts were concerned with the politics of release. It took up to two and a half months for the *Northumberland* to reach St. Helena, and thereafter an exchange with London needed between four and five months, according to the frequency of sailings. This in itself was a major reason for the campaign against St. Helena.

After the failure of his immediate manoeuvres to bring Napoleon ashore, Capel Lofft settled down to the long-term implications of Napoleon's 27 July 'statement to the jurists'. At sixty-four Lofft was a tiny, upright, defiant old man, shorter again than Las Cases and much more eccentric.

Boswell, watching him attack Dr. Johnson thirty years earlier, had called him a 'little David of popular spirit'; he had defiantly championed the Americans, and at that time had David's good looks. By now they had gone, and the defeats of Napoleon in the past few years coincided with an increasing neglect of his clothes which fell around him like a sail coming down on a skiff. There was something shrill and narrow in his voice, though it could soften into sweetness or harden in resistance to authority; and he was readier than anyone to defy the world. He had inherited an Elizabethan estate in Suffolk, Troston Hall, which was convenient for sheltering refugees and still has a frieze of a man clubbing a lion. He was at ease in London only with Hazlitt, Godwin, and the Radicals. He addressed himself to Holland[1] in handwriting which is all but indecipherable. He was respectful, but wrote with the authority of someone briefing a mouthpiece.

Holland's response encouraged Lofft to elaborate on the legal situation as the Government supported its action against Napoleon with a treaty and legislation in Parliament. Besides asking Holland to put Napoleon's case to Parliament in the most forcible terms, he urged him to consider St. Helena as an act of vengeance, which could be denounced for its barbarism apart from the illegality of treating a prisoner as if the war were continuing. He invited Holland to recruit the Duke of Sussex, the Duke of Bedford, and Lords Essex and Albemarle in Napoleon's defence.

In the memorandum passed to Napoleon by Sir Henry Bunbury at Plymouth, the Cabinet had laid stress on the healthy climate of St. Helena and the freedom of movement it would give him. Lofft, on 16 November 1815, introduced the contrary theme that 'the severity and vicissitudes of the climate' might overcome the strongest of men. He tried out the argument outlined by Napoleon on St. Helena that Europe had urgent need of him. Protestants were being massacred and the most distinguished Frenchmen sacrificed 'without regard to solemn convention'. The Treaty of Paris, by putting an end to the war, simply added 'a new circumstance to the injustice of detaining Napoleon a prisoner in breach of the known laws of nations'. The Bills legalizing the procedure *ex post facto* were like shooting a man while trying to escape. 'So boundless, so enormous a power is unfit for any individual over any other,' wrote Lofft. 'It is too lawless to be confined by law. It makes the habitable globe a Bastille, to one cell or other of which, this wonderful individual is to be transferred at the pleasure of an officer of the Government.'

[1] Although a dozen letters from Lofft to Holland survive, five of which were written before the opening debate on Napoleon, the first is missing. It is clear from those which follow that it was concerned with Napoleon's hurried directive and may have enclosed it. Lofft thanks Holland twice (in November 1815 and again at the beginning of January 1816) for 'the full detail with which your Lordship honoured my first letter on the deportation'. It was 'feeling and circumstantiated'.

When Parliament reassembled in February 1816, Holland found himself all but isolated. The Whigs' assessment of popular opinion was that it would not accept the release of Napoleon. Grey advised him not to raise the subject at all and not to associate himself with Wilson's rescue of Lavalette. In the opening debates Holland contented himself with calling for papers on France's deportation of Kinnaird and attacking the Peace Treaties as 'a general and perpetual guarantee of all European governments against the governed'. He would regret, he said, 'to the last moment of my life', that his absence in the Hundred Days had prevented him giving his views at the time. England was paying £12 million a year to keep the Bourbons on the throne, which was more than the cost of the American war. There were 10,000 political prisoners in France.

Meanwhile he was exasperated by Brougham in the Commons who went so far as to support the Government. When he put the case in the Lords against the principle of detaining Napoleon, he accepted the general reasoning of Capel Lofft, but discarded the arguments which took least account of the feeling in the country. In his Protest of 8 April he declared:

To consign to distant exile and imprisonment a foreign and captive chief, who, after the abdication of his authority, relying on British generosity, had surrendered himself to us in preference to his other enemies, is unworthy the magnanimity of a great country,—and the treaties by which, after his captivity, we bound ourselves to retain him in custody at the will of sovereigns to whom he had never surrendered himself, appear to me repugnant to the principles of equity, and utterly uncalled for by expedience or necessity.

In the debate he added a legal argument which was supported by Lauderdale. Napoleon had voluntarily come aboard a British ship in July, and soon afterwards a treaty was signed under which Britain was to hold him prisoner. But if we had been authorized by the law of nations to treat him as a prisoner in the first place, why had such a treaty been necessary?

Eldon, who was present, is reported to have smiled from time to time. Bathurst replied that there might indeed be some question whether, after the treaty of peace, Napoleon could be detained as a prisoner of war; the Bills had been drafted to end the doubt.

Holland objected that the country was putting legal restraints on its own foreign policy. Supposing there was a revolution in France which favoured the succession of Napoleon's son. The son might insist on his father's release as a condition of coming to power, and we should be unable to accept because of our treaty engagements. Some such change, he said, 'might take place in the policy of the country, not only under other Ministers, but even under the present Minister'; and why were 'the councils of this country to be thus shackled'?

Holland also tried to recruit the peers listed by Capel Lofft. On their return from the Continent the Hollands had given dinner to Lord Essex even before Hudson Lowe. Essex was distantly related to Lofft through the family of Capel, but in August 1815 could only think of the importance of erecting a bust of Whitbread. The bust seemed to the Hollands of the wrong man.

Relations with the Duke of Sussex were informal. The Duke liked to send up little gifts from the palace, 'a bottle of mountain dew as promised', a turtle, 'which from my ill state of health I am not worthy of', a tin box of wafers, 'some of the *water* from the well which George II sank and which was sent from Kensington to every one of the palaces, so partial was His Majesty to it.' It was always assumed that Sussex and Holland would discuss anything of importance which was coming up in the Lords; they held inquests on division lists, exchanged advice, and co-ordinated their speeches. Sussex dined at Holland House in December, and Holland must have been about to take him into his confidence when his wife intervened. The Duke was Holland's most reliable ally in the party, and in that sense their last hope, but since the support was going to be thin in any event, Lady Holland wanted her husband to stand alone in the eyes of posterity. Not even for Napoleon, and much less for Capel Lofft, was she ready to share the honours with the palace. With more than his usual moderation, Holland put this down to 'some little motives of vanity'.

Sussex took offence when he found Holland had made his Protest without consultation; he insisted on a second entry bearing his own signature. For a time relations with Holland House were interrupted.

The reports of the debate were a severe disappointment to Napoleon. His first thoughts were delivered by O'Meara to Captain Maitland, who passed them to Holland on 22 September. Napoleon was pleased that nothing had been said about the permanence of his detention on St. Helena, and 'greatly so' that Sussex as well as Holland had entered his protest. On the other hand, Napoleon asked 'particularly' if Lord Lauderdale, Maitland's cousin, had spoken against or entered a protest.

These first thoughts were very far from representing Napoleon's conclusions. The amount of support was less than he had calculated and the argument had been almost entirely legal; there was none of the detail and passion which might rally liberal opinion. It was clear that he had to restate his whole position, both with regard to the peace treaty and the form which his imprisonment was taking. He settled down to a statement known as the 'Remonstrance', which took the form of a letter to Hudson Lowe from Count Montholon, one of the two leading members of his entourage.

Lowe had arrived at St. Helena in April, and one of his first acts was to increase the allowance for Napoleon's suite from £8,000 to £12,000, as much as his own income and allowances. At the same time he tightened up the administrative details, the limits on exercise, the amount of wine, the number of people formally at dinner, and Napoleon's status as a general. Lowe's interpretation of the rules was nervous to the point of pedantry. Any questioning of them had the effect of stiffening his resistance.

He had five interviews with Napoleon before relations were broken off. A diplomat would have found it hard to avoid giving Napoleon the grounds for complaint he wanted, and Lowe was no diplomat.

The letter from Montholon began with a restatement of the legal case against Napoleon's detention, but it went on to claim that the Government were treating him with savagery by exposing him to a dangerous climate and personal degradation.

This rock situated under the tropic, and 500 leagues from any continent, is exposed to the parching heat of its latitude; it is enveloped in clouds and fogs during three parts of the year; it is, at the same time, the driest and dampest country in the world; the climate is most unfavourable to the health of the Emperor.

He listed the indignities to which Lowe was subjecting him: his insistence on the rank of general, the restrictions on movement, the withholding of books and newspapers, the opening or suppression of his letters.

It was Las Cases who was given the task of getting the Remonstrance to Lord Holland when Napoleon finished dictating it in July 1816. The date happened to be important to Las Cases because it coincided with the end of a stage in his own work. The groundwork of *Le Mémorial*, the considered view of the past which Napoleon had been giving him, was already finished. In the astonishingly short space of a year, Napoleon had managed to restate his career in terms which could be relied on to justify him as the heir of the Revolution and creator of a liberal France. It was the directive to his supporters in the future, as the Remonstrance was to his contemporaries. Las Cases, and perhaps he alone, knew that he had a masterpiece in his hand.

There was no urgency about finishing *Le Mémorial* or getting it back to Europe. Napoleon found Las Cases invaluable as a specialist on England and had need of him indefinitely. But Las Cases was now anxious to go. He was less than comfortable in the entourage, ill, deprived of his wife, and supremely confident of the importance of his book. He arranged for the transmission of the Remonstrance in August, and in November got himself expelled.

He claims that the Remonstrance was the first document to get back secretly from St. Helena. 'The person who had kindly taken charge of it had brought me a large piece of satin on which the letter had been written; some was still left [in November] and that was precisely what I wanted.' He now wrote two more letters, one to Lucien Bonaparte and the other to Lady Clavering, and asked Lady Clavering to signal receipt in *The Times* and

*Morning Chronicle.* 'Be so good', he added, 'to inform us if Lord Holland has received a packet I addressed to him; he will find my excuse in our circumstances and the public esteem in which he stands.' The letters were written on the remains of the original piece of satin, sewn into the lining of a waistcoat, and betrayed to Sir Hudson Lowe. Four others were implicated: Piontowski, who had served on Elba; Santini, a chamberlain; and two servants. Napoleon had almost certainly nothing to do with the letter and was greatly angered by the expulsion of Las Cases to the Cape of Good Hope.

The Remonstrance may have been brought to Holland by William Warden, the surgeon on the *Northumberland*, or by one of the other four. Warden came to dinner at Holland House on 12 September 1816. The others arrived on the *Orontes* in December and laid siege to the place ostensibly with messages from Napoleon, but in fact to borrow money for the last stage of their journey to Rome.

Holland was angry at being involved in the charade on St. Helena and later extracted an admission from Las Cases that the packet which was said to have been forwarded to him was *'imaginaire'*. Before giving his own view on publishing the Remonstrance, he consulted Grey, who replied on 1 March 1817 that he could see no objection. Their deliberations took time, however, and the Remonstrance was already published in London by the time Holland opened the second debate on Napoleon, in March 1817. He 'lamented' that it had been published before Parliament had had a chance to consider it. He was clearly indignant at having been by-passed.

Holland used very much milder language than Napoleon when he proposed his motion in the Lords. Without arguing the legality of detaining him, he objected to the increasing restrictions on Napoleon's movements, which confined him to the high ground where the climate was at its worst; he deplored the refusal of his requests for certain books and newspapers, and more strongly the opening of his letters by subordinate officials—which limited his freedom of expression. Holland also criticized the financial pressure which had forced Napoleon to buy essentials for his entourage, and he ended by calling for papers which would reveal the details of control on St. Helena.

Bathurst made a brilliant reply and refused to table the papers. Napoleon, he said, lived on the high ground because he had himself chosen to, like former governors of the island; books were only refused when they could not be found, but certain newspapers were known to be channels of communication between Napoleon and his supporters. Correspondence with his family was limited by the fact that only Joseph Bonaparte had chosen to write to him at all, and scrutiny of his other letters could hardly cause him emotional constraint. Who, asked Bathurst, had ever heard 'of an *affectionate* draught on a banking house, or a *tender* order for the sale of stock'? As to the expenditure, Bathurst admitted that some of the essentials of life, including linen, had been left behind at the start, 'from the haste in which the ships sailed', but the standard of living was now sufficient: three bottles of wine a day were allowed to every member of the entourage, which made 'no less than 266 bottles in one fortnight'.

Lord Holland, who had little support, replied that 'to crack jokes' against the man in his power was no substitute for an inquiry or the tabling of papers. 'Whatever may have been the effect of my motion,' he wrote afterwards to his son, 'I avoided successfully any exaggeration either of the magnitude or the proof of the hardships he is exposed to.'

The results were at first favourable. Whitehall showed more generosity in applying the restrictions. Napoleon's family claimed with indignation to have written often, and a rush of grateful letters came to Holland House. The most touching was from Madame Mère, who had certainly written to Napoleon before without getting through to him. She ended: '*Je suis pour la vie, Milord, votre dévouée servante, La Mère de l'Empereur Napoléon.*'[1]

But Holland had reason to be anxious about the effect on Napoleon, who had made it clear that he did not want moderation. If Holland was to be the channel for another directive—and he had hinted there should be no other channel—he was likely to find himself between Napoleon and the deep blue sea. There would be a pause until the newspapers reached him in June or July; then, in the autumn, Napoleon would send his reply.

Holland decided to spend the whole of the summer of 1817 on the Continent. It might be that the atmosphere of Westminster was insular and Lady Holland's temper more representative of France. To give the Bonapartists their say, they would start off to Brussels, where Kinnaird now had a house, and hear them at first hand. They left Kensington at the end of June.

In the Hotel Wellington in Brussels Holland found life difficult. On the surface all was quiet and the refugees moved about freely, but Kinnaird insisted that the spirit of liberalism could not long survive the pressure of the Holy Alliance. He presented the people he was sheltering as doomed men. He introduced Holland to the Governor of Louvain, a Comte de Mercy, who sympathized with the Bonapartists and had misgivings about what was going to happen. The moral was that action of almost any kind would be justified against the Bourbon regime. Holland felt a certain responsibility for Sieyès and Arnault and refused to believe the worst.

After a fortnight in Brussels, the Hollands took a roundabout route to Paris and spent nearly three months there in three different hotels. Their

---

[1] The final sentence of her letter does not appear in the version published by Holland and later by Lord Ilchester.

main contacts were Lafayette, Gallois, and Benjamin Constant; Lady Holland was distracted from the pursuit of extremists by the presence of the Jerseys in the Place Vendôme and by Madame de Coigny who had up-to-the-minute advice on dress. But ghosts knocked at their door. The two strongest characters left in the entourage on St. Helena after the departure of Las Cases were Bertrand and Gourgaud; and their relatives called. Bertrand's father came twice to the Hollands' first hotel in the boulevard de la Madeleine, and a Madame Teran, sister of Gourgaud, found them again in October in the rue St.-Lazare. They may have warned Holland that time was running out on St. Helena because of Napoleon's health.

Lafayette was struggling with election difficulties, caused by the government's bribery of the voters, but he was without bitterness and could see no hope in a return of Napoleon. Nor was there any visible support for him in the general post-war exhaustion. He insisted that they spend at least a night at his country estate, La Grange, and the experience was idyllic. He showed them a tower covered to the pinnacle with ivy which Fox had planted in the Peace of Amiens. The family around him were a picture of contentment, ragged in their ages, from seven upwards, and solid in their affection for him. The Hollands came away more impressed than by a political argument.

When they got back to England in November there was still no reaction from Napoleon. They had one more piece of evidence about Brussels from Kinnaird, who wrote that his worst fears had been realized. Las Cases, now a sick man, had been dragged across the country from Ostend to a German prison in Halberstadt or Königsberg. He had been taken through Louvain when the Governor was away.

Holland took one practical step on behalf of Napoleon. He asked the Duke of York to dinner, and he came on 12 December, for the first time since the night with Hudson Lowe. There can have been only one real topic of conversation.

Holland was reluctant to press the unsuitability of St. Helena in Parliament. Napoleon's comfort aroused too little concern and was too easy a butt for Bathurst's sarcasm. But in private something might be done. The Duke of York was not only commander of the Armed Forces, he was the Prince Regent's brother and carried weight with him as Sussex never could. He was the one man who might help. To save the quarter of a million a year which St. Helena was costing, to allow Napoleon some reward for good conduct—these were arguments for a quiet change of gaol. If the Duke listened and undertook to think about it, Holland had achieved all that anyone could.

Meanwhile a curious relationship had been developing between the Hollands and William Warden. The surgeon of the *Northumberland* had gone ashore with Napoleon on the instructions of Admiral Cockburn after the voyage out and had seen much of the great man at Longwood. Hudson Lowe called him 'a person of vain and pursuing manner'. He arrived back in London in August 1816 and handed a note to Holland which began 'General Buonaparte desires me to wait on your Lordship as soon as I arrive in England.' After they gave him dinner that September, he continued to press himself on them for nearly a year. 'I am unwilling to be troublesome to your Lordship,' he wrote in April, and Holland found himself unwilling to respond. But on 2 February 1818, a note arrived which sounded ominously like the voice of Napoleon. It was from Appley, on the north-east corner of the Isle of Wight, where Warden had a house overlooking the Solent.

'A packet has reached me', Warden wrote, 'the import of which I feel an indispensable duty of personally making known to your lordship as from the interesting nature of the subject although confidentially transmitted to me must have been solely intended for your information.' The packet was headed 'Observations on Lord Bathurst's speech', and had a note attached to it signed by Napoleon: 'I approve these observations. I desire them to be placed before the eyes of the sovereign and of the peoples of England.' They were about 12,000 words in length and used the strongest language possible to confute Bathurst's claim that the Government was treating its prisoner with as much humanity as was consistent with his detention. The Act of 1816 providing for his imprisonment on St. Helena was, according to Napoleon, 'an act of proscription similar to those of Sulla and Marius', with the difference that Sulla and Marius were entitled to jurisdiction over the Romans, whereas the King of England and his people had no such rights over Napoleon—'they are 15,000,000 men oppressing one man in time of peace, because he directed and commanded armies against them in time of war.' His detention on St. Helena, his degradation to the rank of general, the restrictions on his movements and his correspondence, were all contrary to the law of nations. If detention had been the only object, there was 'no want of castles or of houses in England; but it was the devouring climate of the tropic which was required.' The true object was to inflict 'a death sufficiently slow to be apparently natural'.

Napoleon's reaction was more extreme than Holland's worst fears; whether it was published over the head of the Government or with their agreement, it would close the debate in England for ever. He tried to explain himself to Warden. The document had been sent out illegally and its tone would end any hope of achieving Napoleon's release. There could be no question of publication. When Holland saw he was making no impression, he went over the ground again, adding that Warden and himself were involved. But he could see that the surgeon was still unconvinced when he left.

In a few days Holland had his last note from Warden.

... I reluctantly took my leave of your lordship on the Monday and notwith-standing the patient explanation made me, left the House in considerable doubt and uncertainty, balancing the risks attendant on discovery against the self-con-demning reproach accompanying a dereliction of so sacred a depositary, weighing *the expectations—the anxious hopes and fears distantly entertained*, looking to this com-munication perhaps (however fallacious) as their only hope.

The Observations appeared soon afterwards under the imprint of Longman, Hurst, Rees, Orme, and Brown of Paternoster Row. It went into four edi-tions before the end of the year.

To Lord Holland the Observations formed a dividing line. Each time he made progress in relieving Napoleon's situation by the only tactics which could secure this, he was shouted down from St. Helena in a way that made further progress more difficult.

Communications had to be kept open in both directions. The entourage, which had begun breaking up, needed help. Napoleon's health was becom-ing a major problem and raised the question of escape as the alternative to release. Above all, his legend had to be fostered for posterity. In all these things, except in the organization of an escape, Holland House played a central role.

Communication with Napoleon was now of three kinds: by private arrangement with the ships' captains, by word of mouth through travellers and deportees, and by open communication via Whitehall and Sir Hudson Lowe. 'Napoleon never wrote,' says Holland in his *Reminiscences*; but he had no need to.

Ships' captains and public officials made no difficulty about helping Lady Holland to maintain contact. Captain Graham Moore, a former Lord of the Admiralty and a brother of Sir John Moore, put the *Conqueror* at her disposal for parcels and letters which should have been sent through Bathurst. 'My dear Lady Holland,' Moore wrote to her at the end of 1816, 'I have little doubt of the box being in time for the *Conqueror* if it is ready by the 14th. Have the goodness to let me know when you wish to send it that I may know whether she is at Skegness or Spithead at the time.' Two officers from the *Conqueror* called on Madame Bertrand on 25 July 1817, a day when, as Bertrand recorded, Napoleon also called.[1] Three years later, Moore was still in touch with Lady Holland, and in March 1820 recommended her to send a package to Portsmouth. There was more formality in his tone by

[1] See p. 127.

then and he made it clear that he would deliver the package to Hudson Lowe.

Merchant ships, including East Indiamen, were considered at Longwood to be the best carriers, but O'Meara successfully used H.M.S. *Havannah* in 1816 to get a letter to a Portsmouth newspaper, and letters from Madame Bertrand and Madame Montholon seem to have come back on the *Conqueror*. Among the naval personnel in Changeur's square there was regular contact with St. Helena. Captain Sturt had a twenty-year-old nephew, Henry Richard Sturt, who was stationed there for the last nine months of Napoleon's life and made frequent journeys between the island and the Cape of Good Hope. John Finlaison, clerk of the records in the Admiralty, had a family which was in touch with the Hollands and came to live in the square three years after Napoleon's death.

Finlaison was a friend of O'Meara, and thanks to his position in the Admiralty was one of the main channels from St. Helena. Discovered in the first year of Napoleon's exile, the two men were kept at their posts under surveillance, and by this means Bathurst had copies of the Remonstrance and Observations as soon as Lord Holland. Napoleon took no chances in making his views known and sent them in triplicate on major occasions: to Holland through Warden, to Finlaison through O'Meara, and openly to Sir Hudson Lowe.

Because St. Helena was a port of call on the route from India and the Far East there was almost as regular a flow of people calling on Napoleon as at Elba, and several came in person to Holland House with messages about his health and the gifts the Hollands had sent. How much further Napoleon trusted these travellers is uncertain. But another category of visitors was known to him from experience as members of his entourage. After Warden, who belonged theoretically to the Government, there arrived in England a trickle of his supporters: Piontowski and the group of deportees on the *Orontes*, Las Cases, General Gourgaud, O'Meara, and Madame Montholon. Without exception, these people called at Holland House or kept closely in touch by messages. Others, mostly from Rome, called on their way out to St. Helena: the Abbé Buonavita, the doctor Antommarchi, the new cook, Charpentier, who was sent to Lady Holland with a letter of introduction from Downing Street.

Of all these the most important by far was Las Cases, because his message was not to Lord Holland, or to the House of Commons or the crowned heads of Europe—to all of whom he wrote at great length—but to the next generation of Frenchmen who would be able to change European history. The *Mémorial* is a commentary on all the main issues of the Empire, persuasive enough to convince generations unborn that Napoleon was an idealist who had carried the tricolour into the unrelenting forces of reaction. In addition it gives an unforgettable sense of the power he had conferred on

France, when 'Paris had been the queen of nations, and the French the first people of the universe'. Together with Louis Napoleon's *Napoleonic Ideas*, it was one day to bring about the renaissance of Napoleonic thinking in France and the catastrophe of the Second Empire.

The torment of Las Cases was that he had had to leave the notes for his book on St. Helena. The role Lord Holland played in regaining them—which remained unknown, because Las Cases, in acknowledging it in the final paragraph of the *Mémorial*, omitted to name him—was perhaps the highest service Holland House did for Napoleon.

The plans of Las Cases had gone badly awry from his last day on St. Helena, when Sir Hudson Lowe seized almost the entire body of his notes and put the seal of the British Government on them. He spent most of 1817 in detention at the Cape. When he was allowed back to England in November, it was to be transferred to the Alien Ship in the Thames Estuary at the point where he had been allowed to land a quarter of a century before. He was taken from the Alien Ship to Dover, where an official of the Home Office seized the rest of his papers and served him with an expulsion order. He was allowed to choose what port he should go to, and chose Ostend. There he got in touch with the Bonapartists (who alerted Kinnaird), while the Committee of Safety kept watch on him and arrested him at Ghent.

Holland's first impression of Las Cases had been damaging. He had not known him as an *émigré* in the first stage of the war and had not subscribed to his *Atlas*, as Fox had done. What he knew and resented was that Las Cases had set the trap for Maitland to appear to have given sanctuary to Napoleon. It was important, of course, to use Maitland in this way because it provided the moral case against St. Helena, but Las Cases went about it with ruthless disregard for his victim's career. At the time he probably did not know of Maitland's relationship with Holland House, but a year later he showed the same recklessness in naming Lord Holland as a contact in London.

Holland might not have come to the aid of Las Cases if it had not been for the joint intervention of Lord Kinnaird, Flahaut, and Capel Lofft. Flahaut admitted to Holland, in an unhappy phrase, that Las Cases was '*ce que vous appelez en anglais un* busy body', but two things claimed his indulgence: the cause of Napoleon and the passionate dedication of the man. Capel Lofft wrote as a judge who had to watch a sick man being bullied by the police. Kinnaird sent an appeal from Las Cases written on a piece of paper less than three inches square as he was dragged towards Germany.

On two days running in August 1818 there was an unusual entry in the Holland House Dinner Book: 'Mr Brougham and Holland did not dine at table.' If they were dining in private, it seems likely that they were discussing the Whig attack which was made three days later. The speaker chosen

o

to open the debate, J. P. Grant, had been assured by Castlereagh as Foreign Secretary in 1816 that aliens would not be deported from England into the hands of their enemies. Grant was now able to accuse the same Foreign Secretary of a breach of faith in handing over Las Cases to the Prussian government. Castlereagh denied that he had done anything of the kind. Las Cases had been treated with moderation at Dover. His papers were sealed and sent after him to Ostend. He had made no objection to Ostend, which was 'the nearest port to which he could be sent except a port of France'. When the Whigs accused the Government of informing foreign governments that Las Cases was bound for Ostend, Castlereagh vehemently denied it.

But meanwhile Las Cases was forced to stay in Frankfurt under police supervision. He was allowed back to Brussels, and to Paris after Napoleon's death. The papers he recovered were simply those Sir Hudson Lowe had allowed him to take out. For a time he was reduced to working on a new edition of the *Historical Atlas*. The rest of his papers on St. Helena were retrieved by Lord Holland in 1821—though even then Bathurst threatened to withhold them, arguing that they had become the property of Bertrand and Montholon under the terms of Napoleon's will.

Holland's troubles were not over when the two bulky packages arrived at Holland House. Before his expulsion from St. Helena Las Cases had managed to extract an inventory from Lowe, and he now insisted on sending an agent, Levanchy, to Holland House to fetch them personally. Since the quantity of paper was too much for one man to carry, he would be grateful, he wrote in October 1821, if Holland would break up package No. 1 into *plusieurs portions convenables* and send them separately to a M. Antoine, an Englishman living with Levanchy, in the rue des Deux Portes No. 30, St. Sauverin. 'May I just make bold to ask you', Las Cases wrote in January, 'if it would not be possible to manage these packets in such a way that the bands or string on notebooks do not show, so that they could be seen without being gone over or read?'

This still left Holland with package No. 2. It was taken to Paris by Lord Jersey in February. 'Your commission is executed,' he wrote to Lady Holland, 'and I hope to your satisfaction.

I saw Las Cases yesterday and enclose his acknowledgement of the safe delivery of the *pacquet*—poor man, he is in a most lamentable state of health from excessive pains in his head, he cannot read; conversation beyond a few minutes being in horrid spasms, and his writing the few lines I enclose was quite an effort. He is living in a small house at Passy, making a garden in which he walks for hours without talking to anyone. He regrets much not having seen you and Lord Holland.

The eight volumes of the first edition of *Le Mémoriale* began to appear in the autumn of 1822 and were all out by the end of 1823. As the editions multiplied, the book was to bring Las Cases more than two million francs.

O'Meara's *A Voice from St. Helena* is politically a dead-end by comparison, but it has a freshness which created a sensation in England. Without it, we should lack Napoleon's description of England as 'a nation of shopkeepers' and his claim for himself that he had thrown 'careers open to talent'. Nor should we have his acknowledgement to Madame Mère, that 'the future good or bad conduct of the child entirely depends on the mother.'[1] Lady Holland was won by O'Meara's approach. He did himself the pleasure, he wrote, of offering 'for your ladyship's acceptance a small portion of Napoleon's hair which I received from him with his own hands prior to leaving Longwood'. Enclosed was a brown lock tied with a silver wire.

Lord Holland caught his wife's enthusiasm and helped O'Meara to prepare his allegations that attempts had been made to assassinate Napoleon and that Lowe himself had sought O'Meara's aid as a doctor in putting an end to him. When General Bertrand wrote to the press discounting, on Napoleon's side, the tendency of part of the book, Holland sent him a stiff letter. 'I think all persons devoted to Napoleon are interested in the support of O'Meara's character and work unless they can point out any specific inaccuracy or misinterpretation. . . .'

O'Meara was a frequent visitor to Holland House, and dined there several times. The Government put out rumours that he was engaged for some time after his return in attempting to organize the rescue of Napoleon and had appealed to Madame Mère for financial help. Twelve years later, when the Whigs finally came to power, Holland was still trying to achieve his reinstatement.

Gifts went out from Holland House to St. Helena in profusion for five years. Above all there were books. According to Marchand over a thousand were sent. Bertrand charged Lady Holland by a secret channel on 29 June 1819 with the task of sending 'the new books which are appearing in French, Italian and even English which might concern us, of travels of discovery in Africa or travel in Europe which look to you as if they ought to interest us.'

The Duke of Bedford originally entered the list of donors in 1817 under pressure from Lady Holland. He had a reputation for meanness and may at first have been a little reluctant, though he asked her to see that the books he gave were handsomely bound. But he gradually took fire, and a year later wrote from Paris that he could not think what more to send 'unless it be a kaleidoscope as an emblem of the endless mutability *dans les affaires de*

---

[1] Lord Rosebery rates the book, nevertheless, as the most worthless of sources on the ground that O'Meara was ready to serve without differentiation the British Government, Napoleon, and Lowe himself.

*ce monde'*. The Duke saw much of Dominique-Vivant Denon, who had been Napoleon's all-powerful European Director of Museums. Early in 1818 he helped Denon with the distribution of 'little rings with Napoleon's head on one side and the Eagle on the other', and in June wrote to Lady Holland asking whether hers had been confiscated on the way—he had entrusted it as usual to the open post. Back in Woburn Abbey on 8 August, he wrote to Lady Holland, 'Have you any means of sending anything to St. Helena? I wish to send something to Napoleon which I am told will be acceptable.' And in September:

I send also the medals for St Helena. The secret history of them is that I asked Denon what he thought Napoleon would like best to have. He said he was sure it would give him pleasure to receive the medal of *Napoleon on St Helena* particularly as coming from me. Denon himself sent the design to England, where it was executed by Mudie.

Propagandist medals were circulating in Europe by 1818 and Mudie in London and an engraver in Berlin had struck them on behalf of Denon. Bonapartist cartoons were also issued on an increasing scale with the aim of stimulating the demand for the Emperor's release. One showed Holland swathed in a banner with the legend MAGNA CARTA LIBERTY OF NAPOLEON, responding to an appeal to save Napoleon as Wilson had saved Lavalette. It was attributed to a publisher in Hampstead.

The British Government had been clearly warned of the danger of allowing a flow of newspapers to St. Helena. Lowe of course was allowed discretion in what he let through. He made a habit of rejecting caricatures and articles which were sympathetic. He wrote to Lady Holland two months before Napoleon's death, apologizing for withholding two caricatures she had sent and hoping it would not excite her 'reprehension'; his motive was humane: he did not wish to excite hopes in Napoleon based on people who found in him 'talents to admire'.

She decided to postpone her reply.

Napoleon died on 5 May 1821, and the Napoleonists said at once he had been murdered as he had predicted. 'His illness', said Hazlitt, 'was in fact attributable to the want of exercise, owing to the restriction on his rides, issued apparently for that very purpose.' It was a state murder, like Queen Caroline's, said Lady Anne Hamilton, one of her ladies-in-waiting. Leigh Hunt in the *Examiner* said Napoleon and Caroline had both, by their treatment, been 'prepared for the catastrophe'; physical details were irrelevant.

On the day of his death, the Hollands landed at Calais for a stay of three months in Paris. They dined with Lafayette on arrival, saw Gallois, Constant, and Talleyrand, and had Stuart, the British Ambassador, to dinner. A note was left on their doorstep on 4 July saying that Napoleon was dead. Three days later they heard he had left Lady Holland a gold snuff-box which had been given to him by the Pope at Tolentino. It was to cause them some embarrassment because Lord Carlisle wrote a poem to the effect that it would pollute Holland House: "Twill scare the Dryads from that lovely shade'; and Byron wrote from Italy that he would rather have a nod from an American than an imperial snuff-box. But there was no need for the Hollands to hurry back from Paris, and Napoleon's suite got to London ahead of them. The day after they reached Holland House, and without coming to a preliminary meal, Bertrand and Montholon, the leaders of the St. Helena entourage, arrived with the bequest.

Whether from pride or a last hope of giving the British a lesson in Bonapartism, they came *en tenue*, as members of the Imperial Guard, as they had gone aboard the *Bellerophon* six years previously. They drove down the turnpike in their blue coats and three-cornered hats, clanked into Holland House, and delivered the bequest with the ceremony they felt to be due.

To Lord Holland, who was aware of the notoriety of these proceedings, it seemed, even long afterwards, 'a strange and mortifying reflection to human pride that those who had devoted themselves to a man of great intellect, should imagine that they honoured his memory by aping the absurd forms of other sovereigns or pretenders'. But he was at pains to treat them well. Lady Holland asked about Napoleon's will to escape. 'Both Bertrand and Montholon declared that his escape could easily have been effected, and many opportunities occurred; but he was a man never to attempt anything where concealment or disguise or bodily exertion were required.' He would only have gone, they said, 'with his hat on his head and his sword at his side'.

The Hollands had Bertrand back to dinner a night later, on 11 September, with Lord Duncannon and Lady Holland's mother, and ten days later, Count Montholon. Each came again, and Bertrand was introduced to Brougham and Lord Thanet. In another six years Montholon returned 'without a passport and in disguise', according to Lady Holland, to settle some business about Napoleon's will.

Meanwhile it was the turn of Sir Hudson Lowe. The 'Mirror of Fashion' column in the *Morning Chronicle* announced his return to London the day after the formal presentation of the bequest. Like Bertrand and Montholon, he came straight to Holland House without announcing himself in advance, thinking perhaps that a gesture of immediate friendliness would be an indication of his sincerity. But it must have occurred to him that he had now played his hand, and he came down the road more soberly than the entourage. The door which had opened to him so often and so easily, seemed very solid. When it did open, and he gave his name, it shut on him again almost as soon as he asked for Lady Holland. In a day or two he had a letter explaining that she had been out.

I was in London when you were good enough to call at Holland House, but am not sorry at an opportunity of acknowledging your attentions by writing, as I confess I should have some difficulty in conversing with you on subjects connected with them, being one of that numerous class you describe in your letter of 5th March as seeing in the late great man chiefly, if not exclusively, 'talents to admire'.

She had promised herself such a moment as the outlet for the anger she had swallowed after Waterloo. She had five copies made, perhaps for the newspapers, but left them on her desk as an inadequate expression of her feelings.

For nearly two decades, by this time, a double pilgrimage had been passing along the turnpike to the grounds of Holland House. There had been the suffering people of France—informants, messengers, soldiers, diplomats, and beggars—in a pattern so complicated that it was almost impossible to disentangle. Some of them, like Foscolo and a M. Chauvet from a teaching academy in Hammersmith, had local roots, but more were on the move. In spite of their discretion, it had been impossible, because of their numbers and the sheer length of time, for their coming and going to remain unknown. There has probably never been such a gathering of refugees in any country.

So many traces of Napoleon were left in Holland House that they spread out among the rooms and halls and overflowed into the garden, dominating even the souvenirs of Fox and taking possession of the place as if they had replaced the visitors. A column of granite from Elba occupied the bow window of the great gilt room. Standing next to Fox and the Duke of Sussex, was a bust of the Emperor by Milne on a pedestal painted white and gold. In the sitting room was another—'in biscuit', says a guide of 1820, and 'surmounted with the imperial eagle in bronze'—this from the Duke of Bedford in Paris, who was afraid 'you will find your love of Empire an expensive taste as the bird will cost you about £20'. Underneath it Lady Holland fixed a bracket with the specimens of iron ore from Elba like some kind of ritual offering which the Emperor might care to have back. In the small drawing-room on the south side he rode past in uniform with Murat while his brother Lucien, by Fabre, looked on from the next wall. Out in the garden on the high column of Scotch granite stood the masterpiece by Canova, the blank eyes withdrawn, perhaps, it seemed to Lady Holland, in reproach that she had not lived up to Athene as a goddess and brought Odysseus back to Ithaca.

# IV. THE NAPOLEONIST SYNDROME

*Each individual looks upon himself in the light of a*
*dethroned monarch, and the rest of the world as his*
*rebellious subjects and runaway slaves, who withhold*
*the homage that is his natural due, and burst the*
*chains of opinion he would impose on them: the madman*
*in Hogarth, with his crown of straw and wooden sceptre,*
*is but a type and commonplace of everyday life.*
Hazlitt: *Trifles Light as Air*


It may be that a rumour does much the same service to a community that a
dream does to the individual. It helps to preserve sleep by isolating a pressure which is causing discomfort and attempting to deal with it. The un-
welcome trend is picked out from the flow of events, concentrated, distorted, perhaps given a name and a face, so that it is no longer a threat but a
triviality which can be dealt with as a joke or a disgrace. A rumour in this
sense would be something driven out like a scapegoat, relieving society
from the pressure of its own anxieties and excusing it from looking for their
cause in itself. The suspicion which fell on Changeur was not unique. Similar rumours were flickering at the same time over other parts of London and
Middlesex, in the public houses, on the roads, in the cartoon shops, even in
the House of Commons, because the atmosphere was charged with a conflict
which steadily grew.

By the end of the Napoleonic wars, the advance towards democracy,
which had been won by the new London electorates in the second half of
the eighteenth century, had been held up for a generation. The French
Revolution had seemed to promise swifter and more radical change, but as
its implications were pressed in the writings of Paine and Godwin, the
expansionist drive of the new republic ran head-on against the strategic
interests of England. The radicals believed that the case for reform was so
strong that war was consciously resorted to by the Government as the only
means of silencing them, and for several years they refused to be silenced.
'They have advanced a century in the past five years,' said Fox of the French.
But reform, egalitarianism, the reward of the individual according to his
talents, could no longer be judged on their merits. They belonged to the
enemy as the ideological weapon in an advance which was more and more
plainly nationalist, and to propose them as a cure for the malaise of England
had become an act of disloyalty. The Whigs, faced by Napoleon, spoke less
and less of reform and left it to Whitbread to use the passionate language of
Fox. The radical opposition, just because it was under-represented and
deprived of a policy, made its weight felt by other means. The constituen-

cies of Westminster and Middlesex, in the immediate neighbourhood of Parliament, went on electing radicals. The uproar over the elections filled London and blocked the streets. The successful candidates became celebrities and had to be admitted to local organizations like the turnpike boards. The dinners of the Whig Club grew more crowded until the middle of the war, and continued until the Abdication. The toasts, the slights on the monarchy, the invidious praise of Napoleon, were reproduced in the *Morning Chronicle* and spread by word of mouth. Whitbread spoke more than anyone else in Parliament and was widely reported. Leigh Hunt's *Examiner* elaborated Whitbread's attacks on the aims and prospects of the war.

To an outsider the scene implied that an explosion might be coming. 'There is one thing that surprises me here more and more,' wrote a French visitor, in 1811, '—the big number of people who are in what is called "the opposition", that is, who disapprove and condemn the measures of the Government: and in an absolute sense that is no surprise to me; for, to tell the truth, there is nothing to praise in its measures for some time past; but the Government itself, its form and constitution, the whole of it, is blamed as vicious, corrupt and ruined, without hope or remedy short of general reform and a kind of revolution.'

Attempts were made by the Government to personify the discontent in some individual Whig or radical who might be held to qualify as a traitor, but the mud did not stick as long as it was deliberately applied. Sir Robert Wilson might have been an ideal target in 1815, but he was denounced prematurely, in 1810, by a Tory pamphlet, *The Patriots and the Whigs, the Most Dangerous Enemies of the State*, which argued that the Whigs were ready to call in Napoleon. 'It is desirable', so the pamphlet maintained they had said, 'to be placed under his dominion.'

Authority for such an admission could not be found. The pamphlet quotes in its support a statement made by Wilson in the Commons on 20 March 1810, which departs at the crucial point from the version in *Parliamentary Debates*.[1] We can see here the ingredients of a rumour being put

---

[1] The changes were made by slight distortion in summary:

| | |
|---|---|
| I join in none of the vulgar calumnies against the present ruler of France. He is the first general and first statesman that ever existed. Happy the people to have him rule over them! And I have no doubt that if it should please Providence to spare him a little longer to the world, he will rule over all the people. | I join in none of the vulgar calumnies against the great ruler of the French nation, who I consider as the greatest statesman and ablest general of ancient or modern times; and I highly esteem the nation at whose head he has had the good fortune to be placed. I have little doubt then that should it please Providence to continue Buonaparte a few years longer in the possession of that power which he has hitherto wielded but to the destruction of his enemies, and which power is every hour increasing to an alarming degree, we shall have to contend with him for our very existence as a nation. |
| *The Patriots and the Whigs*, 1810 | *Cobbett's Parliamentary Debates*, 1810 |

together. Wilson was to be disqualified from public argument as a traitor, and an incident created in plausible enough detail to hold together. But he was known at that point as a gallant, if eccentric, soldier; it was six years before he saved Lavalette from the firing squad. There was no ground in which a rumour could take root, and it died.

The most convincing means of discrediting the Whigs continued to be by showing them as the dupes of the enemy. *Letters to a French Spy*, a pamphlet of 1808, claimed to expose the readiness of the Whigs to listen to a Bonapartist agent seeking their support for a repetition of the Treaty of Amiens. Though the pamphlet had no traceable effect, its tactics were fully justified in the election of 1812, when the clear vote of confidence in the Tories was mainly caused by the unpopularity of Whig defeatism.

The choice of Holland House as the target for Napoleonist rumours may have been accidental, but it was an ideal choice. We know how it looked to a Tory passer-by in the person of S. T. Coleridge, who spent most of 1811 with the Morgan family in Hammersmith, a few hundred yards to the west, as the square was taking shape. Coleridge at that moment was doing one of his stretches of political journalism as assistant editor of the *Courier*, the evening paper, which was credited by Napoleon with knowledge of the Government's intentions. If he took the coach past Holland House, he could leave the house at seven in the morning and be in the office by about eight; but the Morgans were trying to restore him after a bout of particularly heavy opium-taking, and they pressed him to go on foot. The coach cost him eighteen shillings a week, and sometimes in the spring of 1811 he walked all the way; but as the weather warmed up he complained that the turnpike took off 'all the blossom and fresh fruit of my spirits'. He began to take the coach in the morning and make only the return journey on foot. Even so, he developed 'a lame great toe', and began taking the coach both ways.

But in the early summer he walked off past Holland House and tried to concentrate on his subject for the day. In May, when Holland attacked the Bill cancelling exemption from military service for Nonconformist ministers, Coleridge defended it with vigour. In June, when Holland was pressing for a negotiated peace and Grey was deploring the violence of press attacks on Napoleon, he became more heated. 'Nothing', he wrote, on the 26th, 'can so effectively prepare us for the yoke of tyranny as this idea of speaking with moderation of the tyrant.' Coleridge distrusted the Whig attitude to peace. 'When the last hollow peace was signed,' he added, on 27 June, 'how eagerly did they run to Paris to attend his levées . . . and now they are advising us to abstain from all abuse of him, to speak with gentleness and moderation.' On 29 June, he went as far as anyone had gone. He would not actually recommend Napoleon's assassination, but would not 'cross the gutter' to save him. 'The death of Bonaparte would be the greatest blessing which by any human event could at present befall mankind.'

Opposite Holland House, no passer-by could fail to notice that the Frenchman had got his guardhouses in position on the road; three sides of the square were taking shape so rapidly that the rate-collector, Mr. Davis, made the dramatic little entry in his June returns: 'West Town 100 new houses.' As Coleridge went by, reluctantly shedding the blossom of his spirits, did his displeasure extend to the other side of the road? Leigh Hunt reports that 'he used to be seen walking in the square', and if he was, it must have been at this moment. He came to Hammersmith when the foundations were being laid; he left for Highgate, an invalid for life, a year later.

It may be that Coleridge risked his toe among the rubble of the square and met Changeur at work; or he may have heard about the Frenchman from someone on the turnpike and connected him with Lord Holland with a flick of his angry imagination. There were as many public houses between Holland House and Kensington Palace as in the port areas of Plymouth and Portsmouth. They began at the gate, with Changeur's White Horse, the Star and Garter, and the Adam and Eve. Their names increased in grandeur as they reached the palace, from the Marquess of Granby and the King of Prussia to the Crown Inn, at the church, and the King's Arms, where Gregory's turnpike board met on the doorstep of the palace. In all of them, except the King's Arms, the gossip went unminuted, but someone in June 1811 must have said that the builder of the square was a Frenchman with a name like the notorious Charmilly. And it would only have needed a nod towards Holland House to get the story on the minute book of the turnpike.

As to the reality behind the rumour and the motives of the Napoleonists at whom it was aimed, Coleridge himself offers perhaps the best starting point. The most articulate of anti-Jacobins and the most extreme in his attitude to Napoleon, from the Peace of Amiens to the end of the war he felt what he described in his stay opposite Holland House, as 'the necessity of ever-refuelling the moral feelings of the people as to the monstrosity of the giant fiend that menaces them'. But Coleridge's own conscience was not clear. In his youth he had been an admirer of Fox and in his ode on the 'Destruction of the Bastille' shared his enthusiasm for the opening stages of the Revolution. 'Shall France alone a Despot spurn?' he asked. His apostasy was a slow one, which followed the repressive legislation of 1795, his marriage in the same year, and the deepening reaction of public opinion.

His attitude to Napoleon was at first ambivalent; he hoped with Fox that he might turn out to be Washington, and at the height of the invasion scare referred to him in a notebook as 'the true danger and wonder of the age'. His attitude hardened under the influence of the German philosophers.

'France is my Babylon,' he wrote, at the time of Trafalgar. He became as anti-Jacobin as Wordsworth and Southey, who had changed their minds in the same way. But Coleridge differed from them in refusing to apologize for his past. 'Never yet', he protested, 'did any human being gain anything by self-desertion'; the reversal had not been in himself but outside events. And so he had to emphasize with more virulence and penetration than the others what was bad in Napoleon and mistaken in his admirers. If he had to refuel the moral feelings of the people, the need was largely his own.

Coleridge held on to his sympathies for the Revolution several years longer than the politicians who left the Whig Club at the time of the September Massacres, but their change of view was as radical as his: they became his counterparts in action. When Pitt was asked if he did not fear so many new colleagues in the Cabinet might out-vote him, he said he placed much reliance on them and even more on himself. He made Windham Secretary at War, with special responsibility for refugees, and gave the Foreign Office to Grenville.

Windham had been at Eton with Fox and shared his political views until the September Massacres. When he crossed the floor, he caused dismay among some of his constituents in Norwich and only just gained re-election. Thereafter it was as if war was his vocation. In alliance with Grenville, he twice opposed peace negotiations before the Treaty of Amiens was signed. He denounced Fox in uglier terms than anyone else, mainly because of a flash of conviction he felt while reading Cobbett's account of Fox's talks with Napoleon. Creevey called him 'the Bloodhound', but the popular 'Weathercock Windham' was as near the truth. Fox said Windham owed his fame to having been much frightened.

Cobbett, who was accepting money from Windham at this time, had the same power to present an implacable front; but although he was no weather-vane, he turned his own anti-clockwise circle, denouncing Napoleon at first, when it was possible to hope for much from him, and defending him in the second part of the war, when less could be said in his favour. The reality of Napoleon had little to do with this turnabout, which registered Cobbett's mounting disgust, as an archaic English Tory, with an establishment which seemed to him to be ruining Britain.

Among English politicians, Napoleon singled out Grenville and Windham as his worst enemies, and in journalism, Coleridge and Cobbett. He claimed that they left him no room for compromise. But we can see in all four a sympathy with the Revolution, which in two, at least, extended into the beginnings of sympathy with Napoleon. It was to repress and eliminate such feelings that they shouted him down.

The main stream of English opinion, however, was firmly opposed to the ambitions of the Revolution and of Napoleon. The Church and State mobs of 1791 fell on Dissenters and admirers of the Revolution at the first thundering of Burke. The number of volunteers, when the threat of invasion was at its height, was almost unmanageable; and the demand of the English public for the reimposition of the Bourbons was more insistent than the Government's.

Nor was there any sign of sympathy with Napoleon among the politicians at the centre. Pitt himself had repeatedly moved for reform, but he was much too cool in his judgement, too intent on the major tactics of winning the war, to allow emotion to confuse the issue. Castlereagh, Liverpool, Eldon, Bathurst, were not men who wavered. The country recognized Napoleon's genius, but liked him no better for it, and by 1815 they had had enough.

Faced with this strong hostility from those in power, the group on the left whose enthusiasm for the Revolution canalized itself into admiration of Napoleon adopted a strategy in Parliament which took the form of pressing for peace on Napoleon's terms. The terms were held to be acceptable in the last resort because of a favourable picture of his personality, including, especially, his genius as a commander. To Fox, Napoleon was the representative of the best aspects of the Revolution and the will of the French people. He could be relied on accordingly to make peace in their best interests, which would not contradict England's. He could equally be counted on to resist vindictive terms imposed by England until she was worn down.

The minority which held this view under Fox was never less than 50 and merged with the majority at the Peace of Amiens. When the peace broke down and Fox himself renewed negotiations after an interval, he died with the admission that peace was impossible on Napoleon's terms. He had a distaste for looking at the Foreign Office papers in which this truth emerged, and he confessed it only to Holland and his intimates. The hard core of his followers never accepted it. The minority who accepted Whitbread's lead in demanding peace remained substantial, and in the Hundred Days it climbed from 37, at the beginning of April, to 97, at the end of May, three weeks before Waterloo. Lord John Russell got back to the Commons on 5 June, in time to object to the war as 'impolitic in its origin, unjust in its object and injurious in its consequences'. In the Lords, Grey led a minority of over 40 in favour of a purely defensive alliance. After Waterloo, support for Napoleon died in the Commons, but was maintained by Sussex and Holland in the Lords.

This extraordinary persistence in Parliament, which was not dependent on a few individuals, was more than equalled outside it. The opinions held by Byron, Godwin, Hazlitt, Hobhouse, Mrs. Inchbald, and Leigh Hunt— who make up a significant part of the Romantic movement—were not confined to themselves, but existed in patches in Changeur's square and

Covent Garden and in a thinner scattering outside London. In a war of such duration and bitterness there has probably never been so much admiration for the enemy.

Was there a basis to the Napoleonists' personality which made them something more than an accident, or series of accidents, in this society? If they were a recognizable part of the community which had rejected them, they need to be seen in perspective with it.

They did not behave like a group. As individuals they were independent and so jealous of pretension that they were often at daggers drawn. The Dinner Books of Holland House, for instance, are no guide to them. Mrs. Inchbald refused to be introduced to Byron because she knew the 'conditions' on which a social inferior would be admitted. Caroline found the restraints imposed on her by Whitbread so distasteful that she escaped at the first opportunity. Leigh Hunt and Hazlitt, who distrusted each other, would not go near Holland House for the reason which kept Mrs. Inchbald away from Byron. Not only do these people have no connection with one another, apart from a loose geographical concentration; they cut across the intellectual frontiers, so that no one would think of comparing Byron with Whitbread, or Godwin and Mrs. Inchbald with Fox and Lady Holland. If we knew enough about Mr. Hood of the Strand, who used to burst in on Mrs. Inchbald with the news of Napoleon's latest victory, we might include him with the rest. But so much evidence is needed to trace the origins of a political bias that we are reduced to the dozen or so characters who were articulate enough to give it, and who seem at first to have nothing else in common than their admiration of Napoleon.

I

In the background of the Napoleonists were two experiences which they all shared. They were nonconformists, either literally, as members of Dissenting or Catholic families, or else by finding themselves from birth in a position which was equally shut off from the main body of the community. In addition they were involved in the American Revolution almost as closely as Colonel Tate, who headed the landing party in Wales in 1797. Hazlitt was in America immediately after the war, Fox, Capel Lofft, and Godwin actively helped the American cause in England, Lady Holland was of American descent, and all sided with the Americans in later disputes.

These two characteristics were of course shared by a large part of the nation. There were two million Dissenters and double that number of Irish Catholics. By the end of the American war, a majority were for peace. It did not follow, either from the logic of events or the emotional background of these minorities, that they had a natural sympathy for Napoleon. His treatment of the Pope offended the Catholics and his career of aggression upset the Dissenters. He had no general support from them.

It was only a particular character type formed in these conditions that gained the sanction necessary to admire Napoleon. The character is not in itself an unusual one. It originates in a childhood picture of the father as a figure of almost unlimited power who sets a problem in loyalty because the child does not know how to dispose of the hostility which grows up together with his strong feelings of love. In the Napoleonist this ambivalence was solved normally in so far as he distinguished between a good father who was loved and a bad father who was repressed and displaced. But whereas the normal outcome in adult life is to see the representative of the good father at the head of the country and the bad figure in the world outside, there was an acquired reversal in the Napoleonist which made him see the goodness outside and the evil at home.

The limitations which remained on Nonconformists at the end of the eighteenth century went further than their formal exclusion from government employment and the universities. They grew up in the knowledge that they were still social outcasts and must accept isolation of a kind as a condition of life. For the most part, they were not tempted to make compromises which would have undermined their self-respect, and they steeled themselves against the views of the majority.

The atmosphere of a group which has been exiled for its opinions tends to be close and loyal. 'There is a common quality to all sectaries,' says Hazlitt, 'and that is a principle of strong fidelity.' The pressure of internal criticism demanding an outlet, was relieved by their criticism of the greater community which disowned them. Aggression was drained off by a habit of mind which became automatic. Tyranny and ambition belonged to the centre. Virtue was reserved for themselves in the outer wilderness.

In all the Napoleonists about whom we have enough information, this habit of splitting off the bad qualities from the good and displacing them on to the centre of the nation is the central feature of their psychology. It was reinforced beyond the normal experience of Dissenters and Catholics when the need to revolt was exceptionally strong and the possibility of doing so entirely ruled out.

No less than four of the Napoleonists were the sons of Dissenting ministers: Hazlitt, Godwin, Leigh Hunt, and Hobhouse. For all four, the fact
heightened both the impression of their fathers' grandeur and their need
to be loyal to it. When they saw shortcomings which might have led them
to open revolt, they solved the problem by a more radical system of displacement and repression than is normal. They so advertised their loyalty to
their fathers that it is far from obvious that a revolt ever took place.

The most important trend which developed among Nonconformists in
the eighteenth century was a steady reduction in the isolation of the communities which made them up. The influence of Wesley, which we have
seen at work in Haverfordwest, acted as a unifying force, both within the
national Methodist organization, and as an example to the Dissenting sects
which had allowed rigid local autonomy to their congregations. Hazlitt,
Godwin, Leigh Hunt, and Hobhouse all came from the Unitarians, who
had not followed the example of the Methodists. The Unitarians had been
excluded from the Toleration Act which followed the Revolution of 1688
and had been the last to benefit from the new spirit of tolerance. Burke said
of them in 1792 that they were committed, like Hannibal, to 'war with the
establishment itself, no quarter, no compromise'. The autonomy of
their separate congregations remained absolute and any move to
combine in a central organization was regarded as the first step towards
Popery.

The minister who guided these autonomous communities had something
heroic about him, by contrast with the uniformed clergy of the state, with
whom the Methodists were allied. The Unitarian congregations were small
and scattered, but each had chosen their minister for themselves; they paid
his stipend, and saw him as their representative against the world. When
Godwin was four, his father became minister in a Norfolk village which still
has less than two hundred inhabitants. His income was about a pound a
week. Hazlitt's village of Wem was only a little bigger.

The children saw from the beginning an exceptional prestige in their
fathers. Young Hazlitt sat in the pulpit during the sermon and Godwin
preached in the kitchen when he was eight. They accepted it as natural that
they should train for the ministry, Godwin at the Hoxton Academy and
Hazlitt at Hackney College, under Priestley. These were, in any event, the
only universities open to them.

Their childhood impressions were of goodness as well as authority.
Almost as soon as he could walk, Hazlitt saw his father intervene on behalf
of the American prisoners who had been transported to Kinsale on the Irish
coast. He learnt to sympathize with the sufferings and fight for the rights
of the oppressed. He could no more have betrayed his father than he
could have stabbed the Good Samaritan in the back. But all the time he

FACING PAGE
(ABOVE) Elizabeth Inchbald in 1796, by Thomas
Lawrence. (BELOW) The third Lord Holland in 1795,
as a young Frenchman, by Xavier-Pascal Fabre.

was becoming aware of a limitation in him which he could not accept.

In the great folio volumes of Biblical commentary which the Reverend Hazlitt tirelessly studied, he believed the whole of wisdom to reside; but his son noticed that art was omitted altogether and history and philosophy were narrowed down to a single winding track. Hebrew was sacred, but Greek and Latin profane. In America, which the boy visited from his sixth to ninth year with his father, a Mr. Booth of Boston wrote that he had 'uncommon powers of mind, and if nothing happens to prevent his receiving a liberal education, he must make a great man.' He made rapid progress in languages, especially French and Hebrew. He painted, and according to 'a lady not at all given to embellishing', had a talent in childhood for 'satire, mimicry and caricature'.[1] His brother John had already become a painter, and it seemed to him a liberation. When he was ten, he wrote a letter confessing, 'I shall like to know all the Latin and Greek I can. I want to learn how to measure the stars. I shall not I suppose paint worse for knowing everything else.' When he was fourteen he heard his father discussing the limits of religious tolerance with an old lady as they came out of Meeting, and he suddenly felt his fate was decided.

At Hackney College, he made his own investigations into the nature of self-interest. This labour of independence, *The Principles of Human Action*, always remained a masterpiece in his eyes because of what it had cost him. 'From that time', he wrote, 'I felt a certain weight and tightness about my heart taken off.' Along with the weight and tightness went his faith. Napoleon was still liberating Italy, but he had not needed more determination to disrupt the Austrian Empire than Hazlitt had already shown in breaking through the horizons of his father.

He makes no criticism of his father in his essays. There are tender sketches of the old man meeting Coleridge at Wem and sitting for his portrait by his son, who is given an indulgence for the occasion. The boy is amused by his obsession with the folio volumes, which he only deserted for 'a walk in the fields or a turn in the garden to gather broccoli plants or kidney-beans of his own rearing'; and he is surprised that he could limit his contacts in life to the neighbouring Unitarian ministers, Mr. Rowe, and Mr. Jenkins of Whitchurch. But there is no hint of the revolt which sent Hazlitt ranging over the forbidden territories of art in pursuit of greater fame than could be found in the little circle around Wem. We have to piece together his attitude from unsigned essays which savage without mercy the whole of Nonconformism, but particularly its ministers, for bigotry, intolerance, and a confinement of vision which excludes the possibility of art. He only saves

---

[1] The lady was a member of the Reverend William Hazlitt's congregation at Wem and is quoted by the Reverend Joseph Hunter of Bath in a biographical note in P. P. Howe's *Life of William Hazlitt*.

P

his political balance by denouncing the clergy of the Church in more extreme terms still.

Godwin's childhood was even more limited than Hazlitt's. His father was a strict Sabbatarian, and his rebukes for the smallest lapse had 'a painful tone of ill humour and asperity'. He read aloud to the family, but mainly 'expositions and sermons', and his son knew there were other books, like *Tom Jones* and Shakespeare's plays, which he no longer read. 'I remember, when I was a very little boy, saying to myself, "What shall I do when I have read through all the books that there are in the world?" ' Well before the outbreak of the American Revolution, Godwin found himself obsessed by the history of the Greek resistance to Xerxes, which awakened 'a passion in my soul which will never cease but with life'. In his *History of Greece*, he describes Marathon as 'the contest between despotism and liberty brought into a narrow compass'.

Two peculiarities struck him in his father. He did more than accept his narrow way of life; he clung to it. He did not want to study intensively, like Hazlitt's father. He would not go to London or even to Norfolk for his sermons to have a wider effect. 'He desired no more.' The son's thirst for fame became as strong as his thirst for knowledge.

The other limitation which stung the young Godwin was his father's failure to notice him. He was the seventh of thirteen children, and it needed a schoolmaster to point out that he was exceptional. Once when he visited a local trial, he could find no seat except immediately next to the Bench presided over by Lord Chief Justice de Grey. After some hours, the boy leant his elbow on a corner of the cushion placed in front of him, and the judge gently removed it. 'I remember', says Godwin, 'having silently remarked, if his lordship knew what the lad beside him will one day become, I am not so sure that he would have removed my elbow.'

It was as if the Napoleonists who came from dissenting stock were hemmed in by overlapping circles of isolation which grew more oppressive as one reinforced another. There was the outer circle of their faith, which separated them from the community, and within it their position as sons of ministers, with the special limitations that imposed. In Godwin there were further confinements, beginning with his father's limited mind—'free from any desire of intellectual distinction on a large scale'—and his insistence on addressing audiences which were small and local. Besides being lost among twelve other children, Godwin was physically weak and 'puny'. 'I am unfit to be alone in a crowd, in a circle of strangers in an inn, almost in a shop.' It was because his claustrophobia was so intense that Godwin's ambition was so strong; he became, in Hazlitt's phrase, 'blind, deaf, insensible to all but the trump of fame'. When he saw Fox emerge in the American war, he recognized 'the person of brightest genius and most extensive capacity that now adorns the British scene'. He was converted by him to the American point of view. Less than three years after the outbreak of the French Revolution, he dazzled public opinion with *Political Justice*, perhaps the most persuasive essay ever written on the need to substitute reason for tradition and tyranny.

Godwin is rather more revealing than Hazlitt about his criticism of his father; he buries it in praise: his father was 'extremely affectionate', though indifferent to him; he was 'something better than a merely learned man can be', though he was not even a man of learning; he was intolerant, but only 'of the constitution and discipline of the Church of England'. It is in Godwin's novels that we find him depicted as a monster of inhumanity dominating his surroundings. In *Caleb Williams* he is a Justice of the Peace who cares for nothing but his own local reputation; when the hero rebels against him, he is persecuted by all contemporary means, but especially by solitary confinement.

The fathers of Leigh Hunt and Hobhouse were less consistent Unitarians than were Godwin's and Hazlitt's. Leigh Hunt's father was descended from a line of colonial clergymen in Barbados. He was trained for the law in Philadelphia, where he married a Quakeress and was mobbed as a Loyalist during the Revolution. When he came to England, he took orders in the Church, but he was, according to Leigh Hunt, a 'true exotic', and he preached so flamboyantly and defended some of his American friends so recklessly that he rarely had employment. Leigh Hunt's first memory was of living in a room in the King's Bench prison. On coming out, his father became first a Unitarian and then a member of a sect called the Universalists, who believed that redemption would be granted to all mankind, not simply to Christians. Leigh Hunt has only good to say of his father, but it is clear that he was critical of a kind of princely fecklessness which wrecked their family life.

Leigh Hunt qualified as a Bonapartist in the eyes of the Government by the radicalism of the *Examiner*. After he was sentenced to two years' imprisonment for calling the Prince Regent a corpulent man of fifty, 'head over ears in disgrace', he was more circumspect in the wording of his attacks, but his support for Napoleon rose to new heights in the Hundred Days and at his death on St. Helena.

John Cam Hobhouse was the eldest child of a marriage which brought about the conversion of his father, Benjamin Hobhouse, a rich Bristol merchant, to the Unitarian faith of his wife. In time, he founded a further sect known, according to Lady Holland, as the Humanitarians, who concerned themselves not so much with good will on earth as with access to heaven, where the body was to remain intact and continue to exist among material objects. In spite of these religious views, the elder Hobhouse had orthodox political ambitions. He had been to Oxford and represented the rotten boroughs of Hinton and Grampound, first as a Whig and then as a Tory member of the Addington administration.

Benjamin Hobhouse had nineteen children in all, born of two marriages. When the first nine or ten brothers and sisters had appeared beside him after the death of his own mother, his son John Cam collapsed with an infection of the lungs but was restored by a year's treatment in isolation. He went to the Unitarian school at Bristol and then to Westminster at a time when discipline was unusually severe. He was almost as small as Godwin and suffered at the hands of the boys as well as the masters. It was when he went to Cambridge, which involved forswearing Unitarianism and Humanitarianism, that he became a close friend of Byron. His father had already moved to the right, but took him to the Commons to hear Fox make one of his victorious speeches on the triumph of Napoleon just before the Peace of Amiens.

Hobhouse was so discreet about his father in his journal that it is difficult to form an impression of their relations, apart from the fact that they were not on speaking terms for five years from the time he became friendly with Byron. When the feud was patched up, the son was already an ardent Napoleonist and became a Radical at about the same time as his father became a baronet. John Hanson nevertheless describes John Cam Hobhouse at the end of the war as being 'completely in his [father's] power'. In middle age, the son outdid his father's baronetcy by becoming Lord Broughton.

The Napoleonists who were not sons of Unitarian ministers had the same central problem of needing to revolt where revolt was morally impossible. They loved their fathers and stood a little in awe of them, but it was neither their devotion nor their fear which held them back. The community had declared both them and their fathers to be unacceptable in some sense—they were social, political, or religious outcasts—and it was the moral pressure of this ban which made it impossible for the son to add the final disloyalty to his own flesh and blood. If he had his own reasons for distrust and criticism, or for a sense of superiority, or if he shared the general verdict, or even went beyond it, he could not admit it even to himself. He was condemned to lifelong fidelity. All he could do was to try to redirect his life in a way which corrected his father's limitations while remaining ostensibly loyal to him. Nor was the loyalty merely superficial. Without noting it, the son repeated some of the most characteristic attitudes he deplored in the father, as if he always remained the most intimate part of him.

We have seen, from Mrs. Inchbald's childhood as a Catholic in the Suffolk countryside, that it was when her father died and her mother and elder sister, Orah, took charge of the family that Elizabeth began to suffer from claustrophobia and decided to make her own career against the impossible eighteenth-century odds in London. Lady Holland was similarly oppressed by the domination of her mother, and travel became her regular means of escape from a sense of subjection.

Byron had several fathers, of whom Hanson was the last and worst. His mother constantly reminded him that through her he was the descendant of the Stuarts in exile. She denounced Captain Byron for deserting her and dying in exile, and her insistence on her Stuart blood was no doubt an attempt to recruit the boy against him. But Byron had a passionate need of a father, and would not connive in her attacks whether Captain Byron deserved the fate of the Stuarts or not. He began to be fascinated by exile. He himself was separated from the community by the Calvinist doctrines pressed on him by his nurse and still more by his club foot, at which people stared. His father may have been a rake who pillaged Mrs. Byron's remaining funds and made off, but he would not give him up. When his mother shouted that he was himself 'a Byron all over . . . as bad as your father', it simply sealed his pact with him. Although he often denounced his mother as someone in whose company it was impossible to remain, no direct words of distaste for his father ever passed his lips. Captain Byron had been 'cruelly calumniated', he wrote to a group of French writers at the end of his life. 'Far from being brutal, he was, according to the testimony of all those who knew him, extremely amiable, and of a lively character, though careless and dissipated. He had the reputation of being a good officer, and had proved himself such in America.' Byron determined to live with the splendour his father had lacked and to die in exile more gloriously than any Englishman before him.

Whitbread grew up in the knowledge that the world saw something ridiculous and perhaps dishonourable about the fortune his father had made out of beer. As an only son, whose mother had died soon after his birth, his childhood was dominated by his father, who was devoted to him. Whitbread was 'an exceedingly odd man', according to Philip Yorke, a Tory. The brewer had the pride of a self-made man in his business and profits, but at the same time he had an eye on the great world and tried to improve on his origins as a clerk by marrying Lady Cornwallis, voting for George III in the Commons, and sending his son to Eton and Oxford. But Lady Cornwallis died almost at once and his son was not made entirely comfortable at Eton and Oxford. The young Whitbread tried to ignore the sneers at the brewery, but he had no enthusiasm for making still more money, and Eton gave him a taste for broad ideals and the radical politics of Fox and Grey. Like his father, he married into the aristocracy, but when the Whig leaders made it a condition of his final acceptance that he should renounce the brewery, he indignantly refused. He spent the rest of his life defending outcasts and attacking established figures, either on the ground that they had taken money which did not belong to them or that they were leading a war against a man who should never have been attacked. In his impeachment of Lord Melville for taking public funds, he made a digression in praise of his father, whom he declared to be innocent of any vice and accepted by the angels in heaven.

The model of filial piety in the Commons was Charles James Fox, who had a more difficult task than Whitbread in trying to vindicate his father. It was in the Commons that Henry Fox had proved himself the most corrupt politician of a corrupt age, and it was to this audience that his son tried repeatedly to insist that he was innocent and it was the King who had been to blame. His father, he said, was 'in no degree the author of the mischiefs which mistaken men' had 'ignorantly imputed to him'. He had not the power to prevent what he had 'as much disliked as any of his traducers'. It was a fact 'well known to his family', well known to all who came near him.

In the American war and its French successor, Fox showed a sympathy with the enemy which depended on an unusual resilience and immunity to criticism. When the Americans were defeated on Long Island, in 1776, Fox told his ally, Rockingham, that there must be no thought of abandoning their cause just because they appeared to be losing. He saw them as fellow Englishmen fighting the battle the Whigs had fought against the Stuarts, and it was only a question of time and courage before the same factors operated as had secured the Revolution of 1688. He invoked Herodotus to demonstrate the inevitability of victory: it was the self-interest of the Athenians as free men which had enabled them to defeat Persian imperialism.

In the war against France, a decade later, Fox had something more solid to call on than Herodotus. Valmy, he said, was Saratoga or even Yorktown. The result of the American war confirmed 'this grand principle that all wars waged against the rights of mankind must be ultimately unsuccessful.'

For ten years, from the beginning of the French war to the Peace of Amiens, Fox appealed at every turn to the American example. He had difficulties in the Terror and over the expansionist tendencies of the Republic, which he had to explain as aberrations caused by centuries of Bourbon rule from which America had been free. But the absence of a French Washington was the worst difficulty, because it was fairly argued by the Government that the succession of temporary leaders offered little chance of negotiation. When Napoleon appeared on the scene, he was overdue, and Fox's welcome was proportionate. Napoleon, he said, made good the past. He had 'thrown a splendour even over the violence of the Revolution'. Like Washington, he was a general. 'Good, great and unexampled as General Washington was, I can remember when he was not better spoken of in this House than Bonaparte is now.'

On the face of it, the American experience was disastrous because it led Fox to ignore the differences in the facts and personalities he was judging. But in private he could not overcome his doubts. He found himself wishing at the first signs of the Terror that the French 'were like our old friends the Americans'. He warned Grey that negotiations with Napoleon might be difficult, and he distrusted Napoleon for assuming the title of Emperor— 'I am not one of those who think names signify nothing.' There was certainly a deeper cause than the example of America which drove Fox to stake everything on the chance of agreement with Napoleon.

Lewis Namier has said that 'behind Fox's judgements were deep obsessional hatreds, which distorted his judgement and perverted his sense of reality'; and it is not difficult to see the obsession which was moving him more strongly than his admiration of Napoleon. George III had lost an empire in the American war; in the French war he stood to lose his throne. Throughout Fox's speeches, his concern is not so much with the merits of the other side as the defects at home. When he heard attacks on Napoleon, he said they would be better directed at 'old mad George'. Of the two, he told Grey, he really believed Napoleon was 'the fittest person to be the master'.

Fox's hatred of George III has been explained as an extension of his father's grievance at failing to get the earldom which had been hinted at as a reward for destroying the Whigs. 'Don't ever', Henry Fox wrote to his son, 'make any exception or trust as I did.' But the hatred was unmistakably Fox's own. In the American war he called the King a blockhead, an 'infernal spirit', and sometimes just Satan. The Prince of Wales joined his circle because of the speciality he developed in giving offence. In his attacks on the King's speeches to Parliament, his feelings come pulsing with an eloquence unequalled in America.

The political careers of Henry Fox and Charles James Fox were diametrically opposite. The father sat in Parliament for twenty-five years as the loyal servant of the Crown. He was never in opposition. The son spent longer in opposition than any other great English statesman except Lloyd George. Their objectives were equally at odds. Henry Fox wanted money above everything and was ready to outdo the corruption of the time to get it. He wanted titles for his wife and himself, even if it meant destroying his party in the interests of the King. His style in debate was hesitant and barren, as if hobbled by his interests. Shelburne thought his ambition narrow, interested, and mean, 'never daring to look high'. His son's ambition was the liberty of mankind. 'His inmost soul', said Gibbon, 'is deeply tinged with democracy.' The aim of Charles James Fox was to destroy the system of control which the King had taken over from the Whigs and to establish the right of all peoples to be governed by their own elected leaders. Burke called him 'the

most brilliant and accomplished debater the world ever saw'. Fox gives a
hint of the style of speaking he admired when praising the style of
Herodotus. 'There is a flow, and ease, and pleasantness in him that I know
in no other prose writer.'

On the surface of the son's relationship with his father there was hardly
a ripple of this profound conflict. Charles was the third boy, but his father's
favourite. He was, he said, 'all life, spirit, motion and good humour'. We
have seen that he would allow nothing to restrict him which he had not
worked out for himself; nothing must be done 'to break his spirit'. But
Charles, while he flourished in this indulgence and returned the love, was
aware, too, that his father was the most hated politician in the country.
There was only one response he could make. In return for his father's love,
he sealed off his knowledge of what was bad in him; as Henry Fox's unpopularity grew, Charles proved his loyalty in Parliament.

The suppression went so far that it only tumbles out in a childish accident
or a habit whose meaning has gone unnoticed. He once read a despatch by
his father and put it in the fire in front of him. (Characteristically, Henry
Fox redrafted it without comment.) 'He says I look like a villain,' Fox wrote
to his wife, when Charles was six, 'and is sure everybody in the House of
Commons, that don't know me, must take me for such.' It was all-import-
ant that they didn't know him. Charles did know him, and refused to
acknowledge his villainy any more than Byron acknowledged Hanson's or
his father's.

At Eton, when the elder Pitt emerged as the hero of the Seven Years War
and his father as 'the public defaulter of unaccounted millions', Charles told
his father he wished he could die. When asked why, he smiled and said life
was 'a troublesome affair, and one wishes one had this thing or that thing,
and then one is not the happier.' He was still at Eton when Henry Fox
carried out the massacre of the Whigs, whose sons were among Charles's
contemporaries. Charles heard that he had accepted a peerage in reward.
Forty years later, Grey visited Fox on his death-bed and mentioned the
possibility of a peerage. 'I have an oath in heaven against it,' he said.

The new Lord Holland took his son away from Eton for several months.
They went to Spa and Paris, and Lord Holland allowed him to gamble. It
is possible that he encouraged him, but there was no need to, because
Charles had found the ideal means of disposing of almost everything his
father had gained. His name for money was 'rascal counters', the phrase
used by Brutus in *Julius Caesar* for money taken by vile means and 'indirec-
tion'. It was as if Brutus became his ideal.

He played high and conscientiously for about fifteen years, avoiding
whist and piquet at which he regularly won, and choosing games of chance
with partners he knew would fleece him. Holland had to pay out about half

a million pounds in instalments which had a quality of blackmail in their progression. As his health collapsed, Lady Holland wrote to her older son, Stephen, who was also a gambler, that he and Charles were to blame. 'How painful this idea must be to you I know. Charles does not feel it, but he will severely one day, so he ought.'

Charles continued to gamble compulsively after his father's death until all the inheritance was gone and his debts could only be paid by his friends. John Gregory then organized the subscription which came to £70,000, and he stopped for good.

While Lord Holland lived, Fox remained loyal to him. For two years he was a Junior Minister and has been called 'his father's representative in Parliament'. He outdid Henry Fox in defying public opinion and was rolled in the gutter and pelted with dirt for his insults to the City of London. At his father's death, he crossed the floor and at once devoted himself to the vendetta which had already begun to develop against the King.

In childhood, of course, all his knowledge of kings had come from his father, who was Secretary at War under George II, their neighbour, before he served George III. Holland House was by then 'a suburban palace', in the words of G. O. Trevelyan, and we have seen that William III inspected it as a possible alternative to Kensington Palace. Charles may have felt it was the less suburban of the two after his father had finished blowing up the walls and rebuilding it. His father, who was a royal servant, treated Charles as if it was he who was the king. The deference to his wishes, the open-eyed love, the connivance of the family, made him the ruling power at Holland House as soon as he could walk. But the boy knew already that he was entitled to rule. Like Byron, he too was descended from the Stuarts through his mother.

When Henry Fox was forty, he had made a runaway marriage with Caroline Lennox, the great-granddaughter of Charles II by the Jewish Louise de Kéroualle. As well as the regal names of Charles and James, Fox's mother gave him Stuart features and a Stuart quality to his genius. Portraits of King Charles and Louise de Kéroualle hung in Holland House, and his resemblance to the King was striking. His father's deference confirmed what he could see with his own eyes. If he could dominate people without effort from his earliest years, it was by a kind of divine right. 'There was that about him', says Trevelyan, 'which everywhere made him the king of his company, without effort on his own part, or jealousy on the part of others.' The resistance he met from his mother, whose favourite was his elder brother, Stephen, was enough to hold him in check and teach him the limits within which his arrogance might play, but his mother and the Lennox cousins were a charmed and loving circle. When his father took him to the House of Commons, he was received with amused tolerance as his heir. At the end of Eton, when Henry Fox had entered the Lords, Charles sat on the steps of the throne to listen to the debate. At nineteen he entered the Commons.

If he felt more of a king than his father, there was no one else to whom he felt subject. In debate he had a mastery of the administration's case and a brilliance in reshaping it, which made him particularly formidable 'in reply'. With assertive personalities he had an ease of response which left no malice behind it. Dr. Johnson was the only person who could silence him, but even he was seduced and admitted that Fox had 'divided the kingdom with Caesar'.

The nearest thing to a loyal toast in the Whig Club was 'The House of Brunswick, and may they never forget the principles which seated them on the throne of Great Britain'. George III became Satan in Fox's vocabulary because he had forgotten that he ruled on the sufferance of the people. To forget that was to become a Stuart without the Stuarts' credentials. Fox's outbursts were recognized as the anger of a rival. 'Is George III or Fox to reign?' asked Lord Fauconberg, at the end of the American war. The King himself felt it. 'The Contest is become personal,' he wrote to Lord North, 'and he indeed sees it in that point of view.'

To Fox the American war was the endorsement of his deepest ambitions. The good father had given him in childhood the freedom of a grown man, restrained only by the limits he found out for himself. His aggression was reserved for the bad father who reduced men in the outside world to servants of the King. To dedicate himself to the good cause and against the bad would have been a normal ambition in any boy, who wished to outshine his father, but in Fox it was strengthened by his knowledge of his descent. If the Stuarts had forfeited the throne by their claim to divine right, he had made the error good by his election as the Man of the People. If the King now ruled by constitutional right, George had forfeited that by his tyranny. The American war had shown not only that Washington was bound to prevail over George III in America, but that Napoleon was bound to prevail in France. Fox saw himself in these champions of the people, and the unspoken implication was that he should prevail over George III.

There is no exception among the Napoleonists with whom we are concerned, to this habit which they acquired of attributing the evils of their private worlds to the Court of St. James's and their virtues to the outcasts. When Napoleon appeared, they saw that he was committed to the people and against the legitimate dynasts; he belonged to the outside and fought against the centre. By taking his part they were siding with their own ancestry in the wilderness, whether it was Dissent, or the Stuarts, or a brewery, and their background made them more impervious than others to the charge of disloyalty, because they were proving their loyalty. But at the same time, and under cover of this loyalty, they allowed themselves to denounce what was unacceptable in their parents by displacing it on the centre of the country. The corruption, dictatorship, and narrow vision which they denounced in the Court, had first been noticed by them in their homes. Byron confessed that he wrote in raptures of liberty as a goddess 'because my amiable Mama was so despotic'. The squalor in which his father had left them in Scotland was a part of England.

It seemed to the Napoleonists worse than complacency when the Government dwelt on Napoleon's vices as a tyrant. It was a hypocritical manoeuvre, a feint, to distract men from their proper sense of direction. 'Instead of taunting at the supposed slavery of other governments,' Fox told the Whig Club, 'it would be better to consider whether we have preserved the constitution unimpaired. While we blame the extravagant adulation that is offered to the first magistrate in another country, is there no adulation paid to the chief magistrate at home?'

Byron did not make his maiden speech in the Lords until he had toured Spain and Turkey, by which time he was in a position to make the same inversion. 'I have traversed the seat of war in the Peninsula. I have been in some of the most oppressed provinces of Turkey, but never under the most despotic of infidel governments did I behold such squalid wretchedness as I have seen since my return in the very heart of a Christian country.' When the speech was greeted with silence, Lord Holland said he was astonished that Ministers had not thought it proper to reply.

But a price had to be paid for this work of exculpation. When the defects were noticed in their original surroundings, they could not be immediately disposed of by denunciations of Mammon at court. They had to be held in abeyance, only half admitted. Godwin had a conception of *curiosity* as the most dangerous of crimes, which only became acceptable to him later as the pursuit of knowledge of the principles of government.

In the process of disposal, which was unconscious, the defects had a chance to establish themselves in the characters which were disposing of them, as if they were too big to be got rid of completely and insisted on expression. The Napoleonist was exceptional both in his ability to see and the necessity he was under to get rid of what he saw. The contradiction seems to have been made good in his own person.

Although the Napoleonists did not form a group, they had remarkable similarities. The despotism of their parents was taken over by them with an added streak of violence, and their related characteristics seem to have grown as an accompaniment of their method of disposing of it. By their insistence on seeing evil at the centre of things and virtue outside, they were committed to opposition. But they were intensely ambitious, with the nonchalance of the dandy, and they all established a key institution, which we shall call the 'rival court'. Most of them were lovers of animals, and all were dedicated to helping the weak and downtrodden. They had a mercurial quality, based on the fundamental mechanism of their psychology, which allowed them to make swift reversals and changes of direction. They were exceptional linguists and ardent travellers. They preferred the past and the future to the present. They were as a rule actors and mimics. Two or three of them stammered, and another two, who did not, had difficulty in speaking clearly. Finally, the current of violence in them readily turned against themselves in fantasies of persecution. They committed suicide but not murder.

## 2

Fox, who came to accept opposition as his destiny, was unaware of its deep sources and saw himself at forty as 'one of those persons who had so long been accustomed to opposition as to have a kindness for it'. Byron believed himself 'born for opposition'. Hobhouse originated the phrase 'His Majesty's Opposition'. Lady Holland contradicted everyone but particularly her guests. Whitbread was 'completely made up of the elements of opposition', according to Plumer Ward. Virginia Woolf says that Hazlitt 'could never come to terms with authority or doff his own idiosyncrasy in deference to opinion'. Their attitude was not temporary or based on a frustration which could be removed. At every turning of power which might have placed Holland or Whitbread in office, they seem to have avoided taking it. Opposition gave them strength and a kind of fulfilment. Fox left it to Burke to open the case in the debates on America because he recognized that he himself was best 'in reply'. 'It is odd,' Byron told Tom Moore, 'but agitation or contest of any kind gives a rebound to my spirits, and sets me up for the time.' Hazlitt said of Whitbread that 'contradiction was necessary to his full possession of himself: give him "ample scope and verge enough", and he lost his way.'

If they were aware of something in themselves which committed them to opposition, they felt the same to be true of Napoleon. They were less convinced of his chances of final victory than the Government. We have seen that Whitbread believed the whole of Napoleon's career to be explained by the aggression of the Allies; he was 'aggrandised by his enemies'. It was in resistance that they overestimated his power, and resistance meant not only the ability to defy the dynasties of the world on behalf of the people, but resistance to the ideas and standards of the dynasts. Byron attacked his coronation as Emperor because it lowered him to the level of kings. He abused him in defeat because Napoleon accepted it, instead of maintaining his defiance by suicide. In front of Galileo's tomb, Byron said 'he was *one of us*', because he had insisted, *Eppur si muove*. The Napoleonists went into mourning at the final Napoleonic defeats because they seemed to remove opposition from the world and to give back absolute power to the kings.

When Hobhouse first used the phrase 'His Majesty's Opposition', in 1826, it was greeted with laughter by the Commons. The idea that those who opposed the Government were responsible people who might one day succeed them was not accepted until much later in the century. There was no place of honour for them. They were held to be either factious or positively disloyal. It was as if the character of the Napoleonists was built up to fit this assumption and accepted its finality. But since there was no place of honour for them in the centre, their claim had to be satisfied elsewhere.

Their main device was the establishment of a rival court, which centred on themselves and took on Napoleonic characteristics either unintentionally, in their means of domination, or as an act of open political defiance. The link with Napoleon usually declared itself when their own exclusion from the Court of St. James's seemed to be final.

At the time Fox went to Paris in the Peace of Amiens, Cobbett said he could not hope 'for even a subaltern situation among the servants of the King'. The Whig Club had the makings of a rival court at its foundation in 1784, but the rivalry only became open and admitted four years after the beginning of the war with France, when it was plain that Fox's support in the Commons was not growing to a point which would stop the war. In 1797 Grey demanded that all constituencies should be enlarged to about the size of Fox's in Westminster, failing which the Whigs would go into secession, as they had done before. 'The whole of this system', said Fox, 'is as outrageous to morality as it is to just government; it gives a scandal to our character.' But the vote against him was 256 to 91, and the withdrawal began. 'Secession means rebellion or it is nonsense,' said one of the Whig lords who opposed it. But Fox intended a new kind of rebellion by an appeal to public opinion. The Whig Club had achieved that in the area around Covent Garden; they would repeat it in the country as a whole.

The Club's dinners had changed since the defection of Burke and his followers on the eve of the war, and already centred more on Fox himself. The *Morning Chronicle* noticed 'the perfect harmony and entire confidence which a body of men, engaged in a good cause, and freed from the contamination of those who only joined them for a time, from interest, must ever feel in a moment like the present.' There was the same loose hierarchy as before. The Earl of Derby remained, the Dukes of Bedford and Norfolk, and a dozen other peers; Grey, Sheridan, Thomas Erskine, and Coke of Norfolk. A wide variety of new members were elected, including the Earls of Northumberland and Albemarle, many lawyers (five of whom were from Edinburgh), clergymen, provincial doctors, officers of the services, and tradesmen. Most notable among the new recruits were the Earl of Thanet, Lord Holland, Hobhouse, and Whitbread, who were closer to Fox than any of those who had left except Burke.

Proceedings were now arranged by Gregory instead of the moderate founder, Bellamy, and they were dominated by the Duke of Bedford, who was building his Temple of Liberty at Woburn Abbey, which was to have the bust of Fox as its centre. The toast list continued to omit the King, and concentrated more on Fox than formerly—'The man who dares to be honest even in these times', 'Mr. Fox', 'Mr. Fox and the Independent Electors of Westminster', or simply 'Fox and Liberty'. The list also included Whitbread, George Byng, and other popularly elected Whigs. At a dinner after the defections had begun, Fox wove all the original toasts into one short speech. 'It is my duty,' he said, 'as I think it is my duty, to regulate my conduct thereby.' A memory may have stirred in him of Charles II accepting a Bible with the declaration that he would 'make that book the rule of my life'.

The dinners were more crowded after the secession than before, and although (according to the *Morning Chronicle*) there were times when four-fifths of the applicants for tickets had to be refused, the attendance was sometimes more than 1,500. One of the things which exasperated Fox about the House of Commons was the number of absentees. At the Club dinners he had three or four times the audience. There was regular coverage by the *Morning Chronicle* and irregular attacks from the right, which were particularly violent in the *True Briton*.

Fox had not used the Club for set speeches by himself until the eve of the war. From the beginning of the secession, he made a systematic attempt to develop the theme of self-determination. He explained that he looked on the Club as 'an asylum of the friends of liberty whose use might be infinite'. Two major incidents in the series of forty or so dinners symbolized his determination to achieve a fundamental change in the system of government.

The dinner in January 1798 was at the Crown and Anchor, and celebrated Fox's birthday. As usual, admission was by ticket only, but the alley leading from the Strand to the great door was jammed, and Bow Street officers kept order until the wicket in the door was opened and the diners began to file in.

The chair was taken by the Duke of Norfolk. Captain Morris, the prince of song-writers, sang:

> Then fill each glass and drink with me
> Long life to Fox and Liberty;

or, according to the *True Briton*,

> Though he's British in his birth
> He's foreign in his heart.

The Duke of Norfolk gave the health of Fox in a rambling speech which referred to the unusual size of the dinner. He was informed, he said, that two thousand persons were present, that the same number had 'rallied round another great man, General Washington. That man established the liberties of his countrymen. I leave it to you, Gentlemen, to make the application.' He then gave a new toast: 'Our Sovereign, the People'.

The only application could be that Fox was the Washington of England, and George III should make way for him. After consulting the Crown lawyers on treason, Pitt dismissed Norfolk from the command of his militia regiment and the Lord Lieutenancy of the West Riding. But Fox came to his support. At the May meeting, in the Freemasons' Tavern, he proposed a toast, 'than which I think there cannot be a better, according to the principles of this Club', and he repeated Norfolk's words.

'We have acquired a new sovereign,' said *The Times*, 'namely, the *People*, whose sovereignty is proclaimed by Mr Fox in the Whig Club in the same manner as Mirabeau proclaimed in the Club of the Jacobins in 1789.' Pitt, after considering the Tower, removed Fox's name from the Privy Council, which was a position he had noticed him using to defend himself against treasonable allegations in the Commons eighteen months before the secession. Fox replied by adding 'The Sovereignty of the People' to the regular toast list.

He no longer meant only the English people. The atmosphere which excited the press and made Pitt think in terms of the Tower was the threat of French invasion and the rebellion in Ireland. Within a few weeks of Fox's endorsement of the new toast, the rebel camp at Vinegar Hill was stormed, and Pitt was free to work out a settlement for a prostrate country. The views of George III made it probable that Ireland would be deprived of her own Parliament and there would be no Catholic emancipation. Fox could not, any more than Pitt, bring himself in such a period to forget the sovereignty of the people as a mere phrase. It summed up the deepest conviction of his life that the freedom of his childhood had something ultimately right and desirable about it and that the inner world of control and corruption under George III was worse than the arbitrary rule of the Stuarts. 'Young people are *always* right,' his father had said.

The most far-reaching of Fox's statements of policy on Ireland was at the dinner at the Crown and Anchor on 7 May 1799, after Pitt's proposals for the Act of Union were known. Fox said that on this issue he had always agreed with Burke, that whatever settlement was made, should flow from the spontaneous feeling of both peoples.

The general argument used for taking out of the hands of a people the right of legislating for themselves is, that by the prejudice, the jealousies, and the animosities by which a people may be distracted, they will be less likely to govern wisely for themselves than strangers, who are dispassionate and impartial would do. What is this but the fundamental principle of all tyranny as eternally set up against all freedom? It is the declaration that other persons are fitter than individuals themselves to govern their own affairs, and thus, under the pretence of superior wisdom and superior force, men are to be deprived of the right of choosing how they will be governed.

The Whig principle, said Fox, was 'that the interest which every individual and every community has in their own security, and in their own happiness, make them better able to provide for their own government than anyone else could.' It stated that 'man has natural rights, and he is the natural guardian of himself, and that the form of government by which he is to be protected ought to spring from his own free choice.'[1]

A year later, when peace with France seemed inevitable, Fox said the success of a country fighting for its independence was ensured by the spirit of people defending its rights. War had simply aggrandized France as it had America.

I must say, that in every country—in Austria, in Russia, in France, the only legitimate sovereignty is the sovereignty of the people, and that in proportion as Governments are the genuine representatives of the sovereign, they are legitimate and calculated to promote the happiness of the people.

The signature of the peace preliminaries in October 1801 seemed to prove the first part of his argument during the secession—that peace would be imposed by Napoleon as it had been by Washington. The second half, that the whole system of government needed reform, was implied by his supporters in their management of the dinner at the Shakespeare that same month celebrating the twenty-first anniversary of Fox's election as the Man of the People in the American war. After he had given the toast to peace, Charles Dignum, the famous tenor of Haydn's *Creation*, serenaded him with a version of 'Rule Britannia':

> Blest be *that man* by Heav'n design'd
> To set the world from slav'ry free
> Blest benefactor of mankind
> Who gav'st them peace and liberty.

[1] These statements are from the *Morning Chronicle*.

Fox thus spoke from a kind of throne. After praising Napoleon as the victor, he said he hoped for the deposition of George III—that 'we shall return to that temper of mind which distinguished us . . . when so far from being ashamed of cashiering one monarch and electing another . . . we deemed it the proudest period in the history of our country.' He used the words 'electing another' after defining the monarchy as 'a system of despotism inconsistent with the liberties of mankind and contrary to the principles of public justice'. When he got back to Chertsey, Fox wrote to Grey that he was 'gone something further in hate to the English Government than perhaps you and the rest of my friends are, and certainly further than can with prudence be avowed.'

There was in fact something about the device of the rival court which went to the heads of those who resorted to it. The absence of criticism generated overconfidence which spiralled into a kind of dictatorship. From time to time a voice was raised in protest and separatist ambitions developed in secret. In 1793 a Whig Club diner said he was 'one of the *sans culottes* of England', and moved that 'the name of no individual be given as a toast'; because it yet remained to be proved, whether or not any of them were 'real friends of humanity'. In the second year of secession a Mr. Waddington got up in the Crown and Anchor and proposed that members of the Club who were also representatives in Parliament should be 'vigilant' in their 'parliamentary duties'. The Club, after all, had been founded to return Fox to Parliament. But the motion, said the *Morning Chronicle*, was 'scouted with indignation as being utterly inconsistent with their character as a Club to give instructions to members'.

It is not difficult to guess the motives which led John Gregory to form his own rival court. Rough and uneducated as he was, he understood Fox's hatred of the established system and had no difficulty in sharing his admiration for Napoleon. But there was a hierarchy in the Whig Club, as well as in the Court of St. James's, and it excluded him from making speeches or even proposing a toast. He had been thanked nearly twenty times for his services on his re-election as treasurer, but he was confined to the collection of subscriptions and the organization of dinners. The enthronement of Fox grew more marked, but the Whig aristocracy surrounded his throne in a compact body which left Gregory and the vintners and hatters and surgeons on the outside. A badge of friendship was given to Gregory when he was elected to Brooks's, but there is no sign in the Betting Books that he felt at ease there.

His election as a trustee of the Kensington turnpike in 1789 was what gave him his chance to overcome his origins as the son of a toll-collector, and it was due, as we have seen, to the intervention of his Whig Club friends after he had been blackballed. The turnpike was the biggest in London and it had grown with the war. It was the first stage of the journey to the ports

Q

of the south-west. George III was almost a daily passenger on his way between St. James's and Kew. But the security was bad because of the high-waymen. There was a period at dusk known in Holland House as 'foot-pad hour', when no one moved in or out. In the winter of 1798 the trustees admitted that the stretch from Hyde Park Corner to Knightsbridge was 'extremely dangerous to passengers and almost impassable'; but they had no money for repairs. At the same time Gregory must have noticed that the anarchy allowed by the chairman at board meetings was in contrast to Fox's regime in the Whig Club. A resolution was passed at the end of 1798, 'that every gentleman wishing to deliver his sentiments be requested to arise, and address himself to the Chairman, who at all times is particularly enjoined to keep order, and especially to prevent two gentlemen speaking at the same time.'

It may be that some element of public spirit entered into Gregory's motives, but his behaviour till his death a dozen years later does not suggest that he was moved by that or by a sudden enthusiasm for the war. With the help of George Byng, the Member for Middlesex who was also a member of the Whig Club, he got two Bills through Parliament which consolidated his position as chairman and treasurer, gave him 'a second or casting vote', and doubled the income from the tolls. Though he made a fortune of £30,000 by retaining part of the income in his private account, while paying out interest to bondholders whom he failed to pay off, the minutes give the impression that his object was not so much money as power.

The turnpike had its police force, which grew out of the patrol and became systematic in the second half of the war; it had its network of informers who watched from their windows for offences against the Board's interests; it had its army of employees: surveyors, masons, plumbers, brick-layers, and labourers. It liked to go to law, against the Hanoverian Ambassador, the royal family, or any member of the public who defied it. When the royal family protested, as the Duke of Kent did about the squalor of his walk from Kensington Palace to Madame St. Laurent in Knightsbridge, Gregory considered the complaint and did nothing. He defended the toll-keepers, who were the board's most hated representatives, though it was not always easy because of the refusal of witnesses to support them. When a collector, Williams, snatched at the reins of a rider who had already paid the toll and threw him, a witness offered his support if his name was not revealed. Prosecuting counsel objected: 'The public have cause enough to cry out against this gate, and in which way should we be benefited were we to prevent the publicity of such cases as these?' The magistrate agreed that 'we are not going to hide our decisions under a bushel', and he fined the toll-collector, who could produce no evidence in defence.

Gregory was prepared to over-ride public opinion to almost any lengths on the ground that the road had to be improved and its security strengthened. More than sixty of the road-lamps were smashed in a year. In 1806 he successfully prosecuted the master of the Charity School for breaking six in a row, presumably as an example to his boys. The toll-house 'thrust itself into the middle of the road, and right before Lord Holland's lodge and gate', said a newspaper when it was finally dismantled. It was defended with iron bars on the window facing the gate and a heavy lattice on the side towards London. It became the turnpike's symbol, with a lamp fixed to light the face of the clock to the outside world.

Gregory already had powers over the traffic and travellers, the builders on the sides of the road, and the workers and contractors he employed. But these were increased very greatly when he became a Justice of the Peace and Commissioner of Taxes. Nominated by the Lord Lieutenant of Middlesex, who was a trustee of the turnpike but not a member of the Whig Club, he was in practice irremovable. He lost interest in the Whig Club and acquired two diamond rings and a watch made by Sargeant.

Silent as he had been at the Whig Club, 'clear, gentle, courteous, conciliatory' as he was at board meetings, his elevation to the Bench transformed him. He administered justice with the high-handed intolerance which he hated in the Court of St. James's. His aim was to terrify the prisoner, and he did this by shouting and ranging through all the curses he had picked up on the roads. He gave no time for thought or defence. The sentence fell on the prisoner before he could recover. The most flattering description of Gregory in action was of a Roman emperor who allowed himself 'this violent deportment' as 'the angry vindicator of our laws'. In some sense he must have felt he had vindicated himself.

We have seen something of Lady Holland's remarkable achievement as a hostess; one aspect of this emphasized the rivalry on which it was based. She would not tolerate other rival courts. She had a particular distrust of Whitbread and his followers, both in London and Bedfordshire. When she visited Southill Park, she protested that most of the company was *remplissage* of the very worst sort, fulsome flatterers and disgusting dependants'.

Fox liked to come to Holland House because it was in some sense his original court. Princess Liechtenstein described him before his death, 'looking tenderly at each familiar spot, as if he wished to carry through the portals of death the impressions engraved on his soul during his childhood'. He made a point of staying there after the meetings of the Whig Club, and it is difficult to imagine a guest who should have been more welcome. But in December 1798, Lady Holland noted in her journal that he arrived having 'if possible added to his unpopularity'. The unpopularity was inevitable because of his insistence on reform, but Lady Holland added that her husband wanted 'if possible to abolish the Whig Club, more especially as the reason for which it was instituted subsists no longer, as Mr Fox has completely seceded.' The point had been made at the Crown and Anchor, but it comes strangely from Lord Holland, who was only put up for the Club a year previously, after the secession had begun. He said nothing, when he was elected, about wishing to abolish it.

Two things had happened in the interval to make him change his mind. 'The Sovereignty of the People' had been added to the toast list, and Lady Holland (then Lady Webster) had been divorced by Sir Godfrey Webster. It was the divorce, rather than association with Fox, which ruled her out from the Court of St. James's, but she had no wish to add the provocation of open revolt. Her great series of dinners had already begun. When Fox died, ten years later, the Hollands omitted the Whig Club from a place in the procession to Westminster Abbey. An extraordinary meeting was called at the Crown and Anchor, by advertisement on the front page of the *Morning Chronicle*. It petitioned 'his noble relatives' to relent. One or two members were then admitted at the head of the procession and the Club was allowed to bring up the rear. 'I was present', says Lady Holland, 'in a gallery erected for me over the grave.'

Lady Holland's fear of contamination increased when Princess Caroline set up her court at Kensington Palace. She knew that Byron and Hobhouse and one or two others were inclined to defect from her table, and she disliked Whitbread's deputations, which streamed into Kensington like the Third Estate into Versailles. 'I never conversed with her but three times,' says Lord Holland of Caroline, and it is significant that all of these times were abroad, none as her neighbour. We have seen that, in an agonizing moment, he once committed himself to dinner, and had to send round a note pleading 'indispensable business which admits of no delay'. He puts the dilemma very clearly in *Further Memoirs*. 'Few could have adhered to her Court without either discredit or disadvantage, and yet none could have held entirely aloof without incurring the imputation of base servility to the King and great want of generosity and feeling.'

In defence of the Hollands, it should be said that they managed to blind themselves to one of the essential features of a court: its members must lend majesty to the throne by an inferior status descending in stages below it. The Hollands' own background was flawed by divorce but otherwise had the pre-eminence of the Whig aristocracy. It enabled them to dominate wits and poets and statesmen. They noticed that most of Caroline's supporters came from 'the lowest orders of the community and the fanatic sects of the middle ranks'. She had only her courage and a theoretical claim to the throne. Uneducated, poor, ashamed of her narrow background in Brunswick, she felt secure among people whom the Hollands did not ask to dinner. Whitbread imposed a strain on her by insisting on formal propriety in the

palace. She preferred the passers-by and was sincere when she acknowledged 'the claims of neighbourhood'. 'She cannot now bear to be in good
society,' said Lady Bury; 'she calls it "dull".' She took the 'cottage' in North
Kensington, where she 'received a set of persons wholly unfit to be admitted to her society'.

Caroline could never melt the frigidity of her English ladies-in-waiting.
In the tradition of the minor German princes, she had a weakness for
Italians, and installed Pucitti, Tramezani, and the Sapio family in the palace.
After her flight to the Continent, when the English began to drift away
from her, she replaced them by Pergami, whom she insisted on calling
'Napoleon's Courier'. With him and his mother, Madame Livia, and their
Italian relatives, she could relax, and their enthusiasm for Napoleonic titles
made her 'die for laugh'. But the Napoleonist aspect of her court was more
than a joke. It was an attack on her husband, like her habit of sticking pins
in a wax doll. That she became almost as serious as Lady Holland in her
attitude to Napoleon is proved by the formality of her approach to him on
Elba.

Lady Blessington could never quite get over her astonishment at the
tawdry regalia with which Byron surrounded himself—the motto, *Crede
Byron*, supported by coronets over his bed, the liveries of his servants, and
the trappings of his horses. Was one to laugh? They seemed to her incom-
patible with his genuine simplicity. But Professor Wilson Knight insists
there was a link between these things and Byron's pride in his Stuart ancestors. 'He half felt himself a *rival* to the sovereigns he attacked.' In his quotations from *Julius Caesar*, he identifies himself, like Fox, with Brutus.

Certainly Byron shared with Fox the Stuart assumption of a right to hold
court, and sometimes in joke, but more often in earnest, he took his place on
the throne. We know almost as much about his valets, 'Old Murray' and
Fletcher, as about his views on Shakespeare and Johnson. At Newstead he
dragooned the maids. 'As I am a great disciplinarian, I have just issued an
edict for the abolition of caps; no hair to be cut on any pretext; stays permitted, but not too low before; full uniform always in the evening; Lucinda
to be commander. . . .' From Hobhouse and Tom Moore, as from Parry at
Missolonghi, he won a quality of devotion which was essential to him.
'Like most proud persons,' says Moore, 'he chose his intimates from a rank
beneath his own.' When he played cricket for Harrow against Eton, he had
to have another boy to make the runs for him. When the school split into
factions, one of the boys said, 'Byron, I know will not join because he
doesn't choose to act second to anyone, but, by giving up the leadership to
him, you may at once secure him.' The intrigue was successful and 'Byron
took command of the party.'

His court began to have a Napoleonic quality when he accepted the role of a public outcast, and his identification with Napoleon grew stronger during his exile. On the field of Waterloo he bought cuirasses, helms, buttons, regimental eagles, and cockades, and later a lock of Napoleon's hair and a cameo which he tried to give to Lady Blessington but had to ask her to return the day after he had given it. He continued to use the initials N.B. in Italy, according to Stendhal, although they derived from his marriage into the Noel family. But it was not so much in a conscious pursuit of details that he resembled the exile on St. Helena as in his attitude to the past. On his own island Byron rewrote his own career, and *Don Juan* is as much a judgement on the world which had wronged him as is the *Mémorial*. 'He is the absolute monarch of words,' said Lady Byron, 'and uses them as Bonaparte did lives, for conquest without regard to their intrinsic value.'[1]

Leigh Hunt, says Haydon, 'was fond of being the idol of a circle.' When he served his sentence for libelling the Prince Regent, he held court in the Surrey gaol which became known as the only salon on the south side of the river. He converted his apartment into 'a noble room'. The walls were papered with a trellis of roses, the ceiling painted with clouds and a sky, the windows screened by venetian blinds. There were busts, a small library, a piano, and a flowering garden outside, where he 'wrote and read in fine weather, sometimes under an awning'. In the second year of his sentence he wrote *The Descent of Liberty*, which dealt enigmatically with the fall of Napoleon. All the distinguished critics of the Prince Regent were drawn to him, Byron, Shelley, the Lambs, Tom Moore, and Bentham. 'If he has a fault,' said Hazlitt, 'it is that he does not listen so well as he speaks, is impatient of interruption, and is fond of being looked up to, without considering by whom.'

In her childhood in a family of deprived Catholics, Mrs. Elizabeth Inchbald had to contend with the death of her father when she was eight and with an elder sister, 'prettier than me', who was her mother's favourite. Elizabeth grew up with a stammer but ran away to London to become 'an illustrious personage' against impossible odds. She had auburn hair, and came on at Convent Garden first in male costume and at the end of the American war without a wig. Admirers already surrounded her—doctors of divinity and medicine, needy actors, and a hairdresser who would not accept fees. She claimed to have twelve brothers and sisters, nearly half of whom came to depend on her. But in 1783 Mrs. Inchbald found herself eclipsed by Mrs. Siddons, who filled Drury Lane from her début. She tried to emigrate to India, where Tippoo Sahib had just defeated the British, but instead wrote a play in which she saw herself as a balloonist. The furore created by this and further plays was confirmed when she became a novelist. *A Simple Story* (1791) and *Nature and Art* (1796) brought her more earnest

[1] Quoted by W. H. Auden in his essay 'Don Juan', in *The Dyer's Hand* (1963).

admirers than Mrs. Siddons; they included Holcroft, Godwin, and Hazlitt, and her doctors became those of the royal family.

At the turn of the century, when Mrs. Inchbald was dismayed by losing her looks, Miss Edgeworth began to publish a novel every year until in July 1809 the *Edinburgh Review* announced that she had eclipsed 'all her predecessors'. Mrs. Inchbald could not hope to capture a third public. She stopped writing and developed an admiration for Napoleon. She watched Covent Garden burn down beside Drury Lane with a certain pleasure. At Jena and Austerlitz she wrote to a friend that 'a dungeon would hardly seem lonely with so sublime a subject for meditation'; when her dividends were stopped in the defeats of 1809, she added that 'the triumph of Napoleon will perhaps avenge me!' His defeats prostrated her, but as her income declined she moved out to remote boarding-houses where a second generation of relatives profited from her and the decrepitude of her fellow lodgers made her feel 'the only young and strong person'. In youth she had signed herself 'Mr. Royal' and in old age she preserved a circle of admirers like Napoleon on St. Helena, whose death closely preceded her own.

Whitbread had an obsessive need for a rival court which was satisfied for much of his life at Southill Park, the headquarters of Whitbreadshire. Mr. Roger Fulford, in *Samuel Whitbread*, says:

One extravagance Whitbread indulged, and it was a princely one. He liked a court of his own. . . . His retinue was down-at-heel rather than elegant, consisting of political secretaries, estate advisers and beggars. He moved through Bedfordshire life not unlike some minor Florentine prince—the centre of a strange throng, disparate but united in dependence and devotion to their prince.

Whatever the quality of his courtiers, the mansion where Whitbread entertained them, Southill Park in Bedfordshire, has a unique refinement among English country houses thanks to the freedom given to Henry Holland, the architect of the Prince Regent's Carlton House, who built and furnished it as a unity in twenty years.

But a point came in Whitbread's political career after the death of Fox when the admiration of Whitbreadshire was not enough. In Parliament he formed 'the Mountain', a group of Whigs and Radicals, named after the extremist *Montagne* who had sat on the highest benches in the revolutionary Convention. Whitbread was indignant, says Halévy, 'that he had been given no place two years earlier in the Fox-Grenville Cabinet, and still more indignant that after the fall of the Ministry, he had not been designated leader of the Opposition in the House of Commons.'

The Mountain was at its biggest at the beginning of 1808 when Whitbread actually mustered as many votes as Fox in the first half of the war for peace with Napoleon at almost any cost. It is difficult not to see in this revolt his own sense of outrage at his rejection by the Whig aristocracy. He proposed to 'force an experiment' on Ministers: they should make a direct offer of peace, and make it in appropriately deferential terms. Among those who went into the lobby with him were Creevey, the Hon. W. H. Lyttelton, and Sir Oswald Mosley.[1]

Whitbread's trouble was deeper and wider than the rebuffs of the two years which led up to this demand for peace with Napoleon. To live down the amusement of the Government, the cartoonists, and now even the Whig aristocracy into which he had married, he needed a general vote of confidence from the nation on the scale won by Caroline when the deputations streamed into Kensington, or by Fox when he was elected as the Man of the People at the end of the American war. Whitbread's choice of issue was to a large extent uncalculating; he saw an attempt being made by the Court and the Government to put someone outside the pale and went to their aid with a passion which blinded him to gradations of guilt and the chances of failure. At the same time a confusion developed in his mind between the person he was defending and himself. We have seen the impatience he showed in Kensington Palace 'that the Princess should make all the play herself'; he had to remind Caroline that it was the weight of his support which produced the addresses. At a dinner in his honour, he presented himself as a model of virtue, adding that he had been able to make innocence 'manifest to the whole world' simply by the privilege of his situation as a Member of Parliament.

Loss of popularity once achieved was as powerful a motive for establishing a rival court as exclusion from St. James's. It was personal eclipse more complete than Mrs. Inchbald's which gave Godwin the idea of establishing one after his death. The fame of *Political Justice* was greater on publication than any other book of its kind. Coleridge called him one of the captains and chief men in the world's admiration. 'He blazed as a sun in the firmament of reputation,' says Hazlitt; 'no one was more talked of, more looked up to, more sought after.' But the French Republic declared war at the moment *Political Justice* was published. Within a decade Godwin's reputation had vanished and he was back in the isolation of his childhood. 'Mr Godwin's person is not known, he is not pointed out in the street, his

---

[1] Sir Oswald Mosley, the second baronet, had motives for joining the Mountain which were a variant of Whitbread's. He had been brought up by a puritanical grandfather who manufactured top hats. The grandfather, Sir John Parker Mosley (first baronet of the third creation), was 'subjected to the sneers and ridicule of some of his acquaintance', and in addition to a revolt against his manorial rights over the markets of Manchester. In 1798 Sir Oswald had succeeded to the baronetcy and to the growing revolt.

conversation is not courted, his opinions are not asked, he is at the head of no cabal, he belongs to no party in the State, he has no train of admirers . . . he is to all ordinary intents and purposes dead and buried.'

In this period of life-in-death, from which he saw no second escape, Godwin formed the morbid habit of visiting the tombs of the kings of England in Westminster Abbey. He noticed that their glory was revived in the visitors to the chapel, who stood in silence for a moment and went out, like himself, 'in a graver spirit than before'. Fifteen years after the publication of *Political Justice*, when his oblivion was complete, he produced *An Essay on Sepulchres*, 'a proposal for erecting some memorial of the illustrious dead of all ages on the spot where their remains have been interred'.

The idea was that the concentration of royal tombs in the Abbey should be matched by monuments scattered all over the country wherever a great man had been buried. 'It would be necessary', Godwin says, 'that some pains should be taken to investigate the precise spot where the bodies of men have been deposited.' But instead of the memorials which the power of kings had built over their graves in the capital, the graves of men of genius should be marked by a simple white cross, uniform throughout the country, so that the visitor's mind would be filled exclusively with their achievement. 'I wish to live in intercourse with the illustrious dead of all ages,' he wrote. 'I demand the friendship of Zoroaster.' In the case of the kings, Godwin found himself studying 'their transactions' with more interest after seeing their graves. In his own case, he may have felt not only that *Political Justice* would survive, but that it would outlive the establishment of his time. He 'admitted', says Talfourd, 'no greatness but that of literature.'

No one took up Godwin's idea and his hope of resurrection declined. 'He expects such universal homage', said his daughter Harriet Shelley, three years after the publication of the *Essay on Sepulchres*, 'that it is disagreeable to be with him in company on that account; and wanted Mr Shelley to join the Whig party and do just as they pleased, which made me very angry, as we know what men the Whigs are now.'

For a moment Godwin took up his battle again in the Hundred Days, when he returned to the defence of Napoleon. Since the Peace of Amiens his only reference to him had been in the anonymous *History of England* in 1806, when he compared him with Cromwell. He believed the extent of his success had gone to his head and led him to commit crimes against liberty. 'After a lapse of years the goodness of the cause changed sides'; it was the Allies who had been fighting for liberty. But Napoleon's excommunication by the Congress of Vienna had as violent an effect on William Godwin as it had on Whitbread. To deprive a man of his standing in his own country was intolerable, 'unhallowed', almost (but not quite) without parallel. 'Suppose', he wrote to the *Morning Chronicle* three weeks before Waterloo,

'Louis XIV at the time of the English Revolution, had said to our ancestors: "I forbid you to confer the crown on King William, the inexorable adversary of my views of universal empire"—what would have been the feelings of Englishmen on that memorable occasion?'

Godwin had seen his own crown snatched away almost as soon as it was conferred on him for his attack on universal empire. He could not stand another such act of outlawry. 'He [Napoleon] has expiated his offences and started on a new career. . . . In a question like this, I feel we cannot succeed, and I frankly confess I do not even wish we should succeed. I am too much the friend of man, and too little the citizen of a particular country.' Crabb Robinson, who saw Godwin in June 1815, found him 'passionate in his wishes for the success of the French'. He was one of the most distressed people in the country at the result of Waterloo.

An alternative to Godwin's bid for fame beyond the grave was to find it in the past, even if there was only a tenuous claim to a precedence which was fantastic. He himself spent much time after Waterloo in tracing his ancestry beyond the Norman Conquest to establish his descent from Earl Godwine, son of Wulfnoth. The Earl, who had been the leading Englishman in the first half of the eleventh century, was declared an outlaw by the intrigues of the Normans. His fall and exile 'seemed wonderful to every man that was in England', but he sailed back to London after a year and was greeted so enthusiastically by the inhabitants that the King had to reinstate him.

Hazlitt noticed that the contempt felt by Byron for most of his contemporaries 'makes him turn back to the lustrous past or project himself for ever to the dim future'. His Stuart ancestors gave him a more solid background of glory than Godwin's. The greater part of his poetry is set in the past, and even *Don Juan* uses detachment in time to give force to the satire. At Newstead he discovered the burial ground of the Abbey and not only dug it up and turned a skull into a drinking cup—'observing it to be of giant size and in a perfect state of preservation'—but had several smaller ones put in frames in his room. He meant to die young and was certain of immortality:

> . . . there is that within me which shall tire
> Torture and Time, and breathe when I expire.

When he is cornered or in defeat, we find Byron darting backwards and forwards in time as if trying to escape. 'I cannot bear such a crouching catastrophe,' he told Moore at Napoleon's abdication. 'I must stick to Sylla, for my modern favourites don't do.' And in his journal: 'Alas! this imperial diamond hath a flaw in it, and is now hardly fit to stick in a glazier's pencil:—the pen of the historian won't rate it worth a ducat.' He is perhaps most often at Elsinore with Polonius or Yorick (another skull). But he is alternatively in the future with the Americans. 'There is nothing left for mankind but a Republic, and I think that there are hopes of such. The two Americas (South and North) have it; Spain and Portugal approach it; all thirst for it. Oh Washington!' He was insatiable for news of his own standing in America, and was regularly disappointed by it. He was easier of access to Americans than any other foreigners; they made him feel he was 'talking to Posterity'.

An even stronger tendency among the Napoleonists than their displacement backward and forward in time, was their habit of travelling abroad. They were passionate tourists. Sometimes they were accused of having such a dislike for England that they would do better to emigrate—that Caroline should go back to Brunswick or Fox become naturalized as a Frenchman; but this intentionally missed the point, because they always proposed to return, and the relief they got from going abroad was due partly to a sense of escape, which was temporary, and partly to a sense of elevation and privilege which was bestowed on them by foreigners as Englishmen. 'You live comparatively in a dream,' says Hazlitt, 'though a brilliant and waking one.' The essence of the dream was not only to float in a position of temporary privilege, but to be able to take pleasure in just those sights and events which in England were corroded by their disapproval. The sense of liberation was almost overwhelming. Hazlitt, on the road to Paris in 1824, forgot that the people around him were slaves of the Bourbons and discovered every kind of quality which his countrymen lacked. He accused the conductor of the diligence of cheating him.

The whole kitchen and stable-yard gathered round to hear a dispute, which was by no means waged with equal war of words. They understood that I was disappointed, and had made a ridiculous mistake. Not a word or look of derision was observable in the whole group; but rather a rising smile suppressed for fear of giving pain, and a wish to suggest some expedient on the occasion. In England, I will venture to say, that a Frenchman, in similar circumstances, stammering out a grave charge of imposition against a coachman, and evidently at a loss how to proceed, would have been hooted out of the place, and it would have been well for him if he had escaped without a broken nose.

But it was not only humanity which was transformed. The governing hierarchy, the Church and official buildings started out of the earth. 'I never saw palaces anywhere but at Venice,' he declares. 'My arrival at Turin was the first and only moment of intoxication I have found in Italy. It is a city of palaces. . . .'

But the novelty slowly wore off; the phantasmagoria outside the windows and the warm-hearted people inside became very slightly boring. Hazlitt noticed an unreality in the experience. 'However delightful or striking the objects may be abroad, they do not take the same hold on you, nor can you identify yourself with them as at home.' There was no doubt about it when he was back. 'As soon as you land at Dover, you feel the force of this *home* truth. They cheat you to your face, and laugh at you. I must say, that it appears to me, whatever may be the faults and vices of other nations, the English population is the only one to which the epithet *blackguard* is applicable.'

Byron spent nearly a third of his life abroad and was by nature cosmopolitan. There is certainly a contrast between him and Fletcher, the inveterate cockney, who demanded ale, '*tea*', and comfortable beds. 'I have lived with the highest and lowest,' Byron told his mother, at the end of his first exile. 'I have been for days in a Pacha's palace, and passed many a night in a cowhouse, and I find the people inoffensive and kind. I have also passed some time with the principal Greeks in the Morea and Livadia, and although inferior to the Turks, they are better than the Spaniards, who in their turn excel the Portugese.'

The classification is fantastic. The Turks were better than the Greeks, who were better than the Spaniards and still better than the Portuguese, but best of all was Ali Pasha, an Albanian known as 'the Lion' because of his ferocity in ruling on behalf of the Turks. The Pasha, says Byron, 'is a remorseless tyrant, guilty of the most horrible cruelties, very brave, and so good a general that they call him the Mahometan Buonaparte'. He gave Byron a Greek interpreter and his court physician, a forerunner of Polidori called Femlario. He received him standing—the ultimate compliment—and gave him the seat on his right hand. Byron had four audiences with the Pasha and received gifts of almonds, sherbet, and fruit 'twenty times a day'. When he left, it was with a guard of fifty men to Patras in the Peloponnese.

Nine months earlier Byron had taken his legitimate seat in the House of Lords as a peer of England. It was an experience which left an unpleasant memory in everyone concerned with it. The Lord Chancellor, Eldon, tried to be exceptionally warm in his greeting, but Byron rebuffed him by giving him the tips of his fingers and sitting down at once on one of the opposition benches. Reproached afterwards for his coldness, he said, 'If I had shaken hands heartily, he would have set me down for one of his party—but I will have nothing to do with any of them, on either side; I have taken my seat, and now I will go abroad.' When he returned, nearly three years later, it was to denounce the squalor of England as worse 'than the most oppressed provinces of Turkey'. He admitted to feeling diffident and nervous in the Lords, but said it was due to 'the number rather than the quality of the assemblage'—he had no more respect for them than for the same number of Turks in a divan or of Methodists in a barn. His next appearance but one was to vote against the outlawry of Napoleon in the Hundred Days.

The pleasure Byron took in his Pasha was not unlike Hazlitt's conversion to palaces. In England, the pretensions of Lord Eldon appeared as reactionary as his politics. The Earl of Portsmouth, Byron's superior in rank, was a fool of an earl, at whom one threw conch shells and delivered into the hands of Hanson for exploitation. The peers sitting by the hundred on their ceremonial benches were a mob of aristocracy from which he had to escape to preserve himself. But when he saw Ali Pasha's court at Tepelene, he was overwhelmed with delight. It was not only that a court could at last have dignity but the whole apparatus of government—'two hundred steeds ready caparisoned to move in a moment, couriers entering or passing out with despatches, the kettle-drums beating'—seemed to him enchanting. The Mohammedan Bonaparte's reception of him as an equal was a greater honour than Lord Eldon's. His knowledge of the Pasha's barbarities only served to increase it. It was a court to which Byron wanted to belong—to which, in some sense, he felt he always had belonged—not only because the Pasha accepted him, but because he saw that the Pasha, with his brutalities and exotic tastes, was indelibly foreign, an outcast like himself and his ancestors.

Byron's behaviour abroad was oriented to the English audience, and would have been meaningless without it. In his second exile, 'on a pedestal above the Adriatic', he still wrote for England, read every new book, and waited for visitors. The rumours that he was back in London were not unfounded, for he did intend to return; he was explicit about coming back to vote against the outlawry of Caroline. When he began to immerse himself in Italian politics, it was a sign that he was at last beginning to abandon England. At this point the Turks began to emerge as tyrants—they were 'dull'—very much like the Tories in England. To revolt against them had acquired a Napoleonic virtue.

Among the Napoleonists who established foreign courts was the Duke of Sussex. The only permanent outcast within the royal family, he remained in Kensington after his fatal expedition as a young man to Rome, where he married Lady Augusta Murray and acquired the lasting disfavour of George III. To emphasize his possession of an independent court, and perhaps his distance above it, he added Gothic features. His courtiers included his Hanoverian *Jäger*, Franz Hunnermann, a Scottish giant, Mackenzie, Antonio Panzera, a page, Benjamin Beckhaus, his steward, and a Siamese, 'Mr Blackman'.

The Hollands too recruited exotic staff, and particularly Italians, but it was their guests who gave the foreign atmosphere to Holland House. The most distinguished were French, Madame de Souza, Talleyrand, Flahaut, Chateaubriand, Louis Philippe, but there were also Spanish, Portuguese, and Italian exiles and the ambassadors of half Europe. Hangers-on threaded the neighbourhood, Foscolo in Changeur's square, Buonaiuti, an opera librettist in the High Street, who came in to teach the children Italian, Chauvet in Hammersmith, who taught French. Sir Thomas Lawrence refused to dine at Holland House because he was ashamed of his French; Sheridan, who had no French, only went out of bravado. To be without Italian, Spanish, or German was almost as dangerous because Lady Holland, who was ill-educated, did not hesitate to exploit her surprising fluency in all of them.

As the Hollands lumbered across the Continent, rarely with less than a carriage, a coach, and a post chaise, the situation was reversed and the cortège was conspicuously English. In Hanover they did not enjoy themselves because they were in a sense on home ground. 'The breed of horses and men are alike,' said Lady Holland, 'and I could trace a likeness to my liege Lord and Sovereign among his coach horses.' But in the other German courts, they found princes who gave them the time of their life.

Lady Holland was determined to visit Frederick the Great's brother, Prince Henry, at his castle in Rheinsberg in North Prussia, and in August 1800 made the long journey from Berlin by night, chancing their reception. The Prince sent out a chamberlain to bring them to the castle for an indefinite stay, and they found themselves in a French paradise, built by Frederick the Great on the model of the Trianon.

Prince Henry had always felt himself the rival of his brother. To his ability as a general he added a much more speculative mind and a charm which was compelling. He pushed his admiration of France still further than Frederick. Sixteen years before the arrival of the Hollands, he had conquered Paris, where he was known for his victory over the French army at Rossbach and his generosity to his prisoners. 'I have spent half my life wishing to see France,' he said as he left; 'I am going to spend the other half missing it.' He took steps to reproduce it in his own Trianon. 'He abhors everything German; cannot speak it,' said Lady Holland. 'He has a delightful French comedy; his troupe of comedians is really good, the theatre remarkably pretty.' They went straight in to the play from their carriages, and had supper in a Chinese temple in the garden, which was illuminated by hidden lights. From a coppice near by a group of French horns serenaded them. Next morning they had breakfast by the lake. It was the end of August, and Lady Holland could not resist bathing. It was, she thought, the happiest time of her life. When news came after scarcely a week that her son Charles was ill in Potsdam, she was seriously impatient and found him, she said, 'not worse than he has been fifty times since his birth'.

She was charmed, of course, that one of the greatest men in Germany should have put himself and his court at her disposal. 'The Prince, and indeed the whole party, did every earthly thing they could imagine would please us; I never experienced such warm-hearted, zealous, unaffected, desire of obliging as they manifested towards us.' But it was not only that Prince Henry's warmth made good her ostracism by the House of Hanover; he had emancipated himself from his subservient position by his devotion to France. When she visited Versailles two years later, it was the Trianon, 'a most noble palace', which she admired. She had always used French phrases in her journal, but after Rheinsberg they increase as if English could not touch the point and delicacy of life. Prince Henry's emigration was a royal endorsement of her own.

The Hollands were too much insulated by their carriages and servants to notice, as Hazlitt did, the attitude of ordinary people abroad; but they saw a corresponding difference in the officials, merchants, nobility, and rulers. It was only the envoy of the Foreign Office who did not return Lady Holland's card. Everyone else accepted them as representing England. Holland was not often moved to anger, but at Falmouth when he discovered that Canning had prepared the way for him in Spain by formally warning the Spanish government of his lack of official status, he lost his temper as he had never done before.

To go abroad, for the Hollands, was in some sense to recover the position which was due to them. To discuss policy on equal terms with Napoleon was as natural as to stay in Louis Bonaparte's house in the Corso. Whether or not they could get rooms at the best inn, at the Empress in Frankfurt or Schneidorff's in Florence, was the recurrent crisis of their travels. 'When we arrived at Brunswick we found the inns filled with Jews and infidels on account of the Fair.' But the shock was no greater than when they found themselves in Verona at the same time as the Pope and Charles IV of Spain, in flight from Murat. 'The Spanish court occupies the great inn and we were compelled to go to the inferior one,' said Lady Holland. She could not have been more indignant if it had been George III who had displaced them.

Fox, Hobhouse, and Leigh Hunt were all enthusiastic travellers. Mrs. Inchbald went abroad only once, when she was twenty, but the visit had a formative effect on her writing and gave her a lasting preference for French culture. The most striking effect on the Duke of Bedford and Capel Lofft when abroad was their sense of promotion, as if they were ennobled by crossing the Channel. Both of them lectured the officials at Calais as if they were mutinous porters and went on to defy the censorship with indifference. Capel Lofft took his two daughters and the Bonapartist Madame Piontowski with him, and wandered about France, the Netherlands, Switzerland, and Italy, as if they were in subject territory. Lofft decided to end his days in Turin (he was a friend of Hazlitt), and he moved up to Moncalieri to get the best view high above the palaces. But he could not settle down and died in May 1824, immediately after hearing the news of Byron's death at Missolonghi. In his last letter to Lord Holland he wrote that Ministers were plainly responsible for the death of Napoleon and that a debate in the Lords would be valuable.

There is a characteristic of the Napoleonists which we might discount were it not for their tendency to displace their courts in space and time, and socially to another class than their own. They formed a special relationship to animals. In a passive sense, a more sympathetic attitude had already begun to show itself in the second half of the eighteenth century when my Uncle Toby granted a fly its liberty in a world which was 'surely wide enough to hold both thee and me'. The Napoleonists were more positive. Their sympathy with animals was so strong that they introduced the first legislation to give them rights.

Lord Erskine, when he gave up office as Lord Chancellor in the Talents, was obsessed with the services performed for the community by rooks.[1] Bellamy, who founded the Whig Club, left instructions in his will that his horses should be shot after his death, 'that they may not experience the cruel usage too frequently bestowed upon their species.' To Byron, animals were human, his bear at Cambridge a Fellow reduced to the rank of freshman, his parrot in the Albany a less intelligent version of Hobhouse, Boatswain, at Newstead, a child who died. 'To mark a Friend's remains these stones arise,' he wrote for the dog's memorial.

Don Juan, we remember

> had a kind of inclination or
> Weakness, for what most people deem mere vermin,
> Live animals; an old maid of threescore
> For cats and birds more penchant ne'er display'd
> Although he was not old, nor even a maid.

He intervened in their affairs like a parent. At Newstead he found a hen to hatch the tortoise eggs and in Ravenna 'beat the crow for stealing the falcon's victuals'. In exile he gathered them closer around him. 'My menagerie —(which you enquire after) has had some vacancies by the elopement of one cat, the decease of two monkies and a crow by indiscretion.' There remained six dogs, a badger, a falcon, and another cat. Newton Hanson adds a wolf—'and, as his lordship passed to his gondola, he used to stop and amuse himself with watching their antics, or would feed them himself occasionally.' Old Hanson and Mrs. Byron recognized the animals at Newstead for the rival court they were and disposed of them when Byron's back was turned with no more mercy than Lady Holland showed the Whig Club on the death of Fox.

[1] In *The Farmer's Vision* (1819) Erskine criticized an attempt to repress any class of animals in much the same way as Burke opposed the indictment of a whole people. 'We rarely succeed in a war of utter extermination against animals we proscribe. . . .'

Godwin had a strong feeling for animals before he was famous. One Sunday his father, the Sabbatarian, caught him with a cat in his arms and rebuked him severely. What surprised Godwin was that his father thought he had demeaned himself when he had in fact been raising his status. Lady Holland was painted with pets about her in Naples and Florence before the establishment of Holland House, but not afterwards when she was surrounded by her guests. Leigh Hunt campaigned against the narrow confinement of boa constrictors and eagles in the Zoo. 'It is monstrous to see any creature in a cage, far more any winged creature, and most of all those accustomed to soar through the whole vault of heaven, and have the world under their eye.'

Whitbread was an animal-lover who shared Bellamy's concern about worn-out horses. In his will he left a mare and chaise to a neighbour, 'and if the mare shall survive her master, I desire that she may upon his death be shot.' Southill Park is dominated by animals. Models by Garrard in plaster and bronze stand about the rooms and are repeated in bas-relief over the doorways. In the French drawing-room, where eagles gather up the curtains, the animal paintings over the doorways are so big that they challenge the human portraits below. The most important site in the garden, outside the boudoir, is occupied by a dog trough of great distinction made by Henry Holland to support the statue of a spaniel. Jock was buried there two years before Boatswain went into the family vault at Newstead. In his epitaph Whitbread outdoes Byron by exhorting dogs who drink at the fountain to prove more grateful than the nation which drank his porter:

> Drink at this fount and humbly
> Vie with him in matchless constancy.

Once while Fox was staying at Cheltenham with Mrs. Armistead he decided to tame a young rabbit. His friend James Hare, nicknamed 'the hare', who was staying with him, reported with the jealousy of a rival that Fox was 'entirely preoccupied with it'. He shot partridges, as did Byron and Whitbread, but he had a guilty conscience. To kill them was only less repugnant, he said, 'than killing tame animals, with whom one has a sort of acquaintance. . . .' At Newmarket he had thirty horses, the successors of the innumerable carriage horses at Holland House. According to his earliest biographer, he had a peculiar approach to the races.

He placed himself where the animal was to make a push, or where the race was to be most strongly contested. From this spot he eyed the horses advancing with the most immovable look: he breathed quicker as they accelerated their pace; and when they came opposite to him, he rode in with them at full speed, whiffing, spewing and blowing as if he would have infused his whole soul in the speed, courage and perseverance of his favourite racer.

R

It was not unlike his behaviour on the opposition benches, where he astonished his friends with the generosity and number of his suggestions as the debate proceeded, without thought for the speech he himself would have to make to wind up.

The first four Bills to prevent cruelty to animals occupied much time in the middle of the Napoleonic wars, 'when questions of vital importance', said Windham, 'are hourly pressing on our attention.' It was probably because the Bills were inspired by Erskine, a Napoleonist, that Windham was stimulated to resist all four with determination as a new form of Jacobinism. 'Those', he says, 'who when young men, had formed projects for the reformation of Parliament, finding themselves disappointed in those projects, now formed the design of reforming the manners of the people.'

Erskine's championship of animals was an expression of his character which had begun to take legal form after the passage of Eldon's repressive legislation following the acquittals Erskine had secured in the treason trials of 1794. 'He has talked for years of a Bill he was to bring into Parliament to prevent cruelty towards them,' says Romilly in his *Memoirs* in 1808. Erskine had been devoted to animals long before he stopped shooting rooks. A dog was present at his consultations and a favourite goose followed him about his grounds. Like Byron, he had a macaw, but he went further than other Napoleonists in adopting two leeches, which had bled him at Portsmouth in 1807, according to Romilly, when he was recovering from an illness after losing office as Lord Chancellor. 'They had saved his life, and he had brought them with him to town; had ever since kept them in a glass; he had himself given them fresh water; and had formed a friendship with them. He said he was sure they both knew him and were grateful to him.'

In 1801 and 1802, on the eve of the Peace of Amiens, two attempts were made to suppress bull-baiting by a group of Whigs dominated by Sheridan and supported by Wilberforce. Although the case was strongly coloured by sympathy for the bull, its substance was that it degraded the spectators. Windham argued that, on the contrary, it toughened them; it was a necessary outlet, like prize-fighting or wrestling, which prevented the spread of Jacobinism. Out of the whole number of those who were disaffected, he doubted if a single bull-baiter could be found, or if, on the other hand, a single sportsman had 'distinguished himself in the Corresponding Society'. As a result of his energy, both Bills were narrowly defeated.

Erskine was received by Napoleon in the Peace of Amiens, immediately after the debates. A correspondent of the *Morning Chronicle*, interviewing returning visitors at Dover, was told that Napoleon was well informed and had said: 'Of all my brave fellows at the Bridge of Lodi or the Plain of Marengo, how many ever saw a bull-baiting or a boxing-match?'

Although Erskine accepted all sorts of limitations to successive Bills in

1809 and 1810, Windham again managed to summon up the spectre of Jacobinism. Erskine's love of revolutionary change as 'the champion of the brutes' should be enough, he claimed, to put everyone on guard. The object of the Bill was simply a moral obligation, like charity or gratitude, and the attempt to make it a matter for the courts would produce anarchy. He was supported by Lord Holland, 'with diffidence and great pain to his feelings'. The massive support Erskine had when he introduced his first Bill shrank to a minority under Windham's attacks and a strong but ill-defined feeling of resentment against the complacency of Erskine. He was a Tarzan before his time. The first Act for the prevention of cruelty to animals passed successfully, in 1822, when Erskine stood aside for a more modest sponsor, Richard Martin, known as Humanity Dick.

The rival courts founded by the Napoleonists had a counterpart among the formal organs of the state. The Navy, exercising power at a distance and in small units of command, developed a spirit of independence from the Court which distinguished it from the Army. The defeat of the Armada prepared the way for the Navy to reject absolutist pretensions at home; it sided with Parliament against the Stuarts and became the guardian of the island's internal liberty as well as its security against the outside world. The Whigs did not forget its services. The Navy was so justly the favourite arm of the country, said Fox, 'that no man is willing to find fault with it.' Its position of power at sea gave a certain detachment to its officers, not unlike the Napoleonists' position outside the community. Since they were not born into the service, but joined in boyhood or as young men, they lacked the compulsive character pattern of the Napoleonists, but had a readiness to criticize their own Government which made them natural allies. The fact that only O'Meara and Warden among officers, and Finlaison among clerks at the Admiralty, committed breaches of discipline in support of Napoleon, has enabled these minor symptoms of disloyalty to be lost in the perspective of the Navy's great wartime achievement.

The patriotic naval historian of the war, Edward Pelham Brenton, was at pains to play down the Whig affiliations of his service in order to provide the basis of the Victorian tradition in which Navy and Army vie with each other in loyalty to the Crown.[1] He omits, for instance, the resentment in the Navy reported by the Whig leader, Tierney, when an Admiralty order first placed the crown above the anchor on the naval ensigns. He makes no reference to the Prince Regent's complaint that improved uniforms could never make the Navy 'look like gentlemen'.

It was Brenton who confronted Mackenrot on the deck of the *Tonnant* in Plymouth Sound. Beside himself with anger at the attempt to rescue

[1] *The Naval History of Great Britain from the Year 1783 to 1822.*

Napoleon, he would only speak to Mackenrot in French, and refers to him as an 'agent'. But Brenton does admit to one cause of disaffection in the Navy which continued to grow after the mutiny of the Nore. There was, he says, mounting indignation at the Government's refusal to give decorations. Nelson did not know 'to his last hour' why medals were not given for the destruction of the Danish fleet at Copenhagen. There were none for Trafalgar. When Martinique and Guadeloupe were captured from the French, it was mainly the Navy which was responsible. 'Yet the officers of the army had the honour of wearing medals and clasps, for the taking of Martinique and Guadeloupe, as they also had for the capture of the island of Java in 1811, while those of the navy had none.' Again after Waterloo, the Army was showered with decorations which were denied at Trafalgar. 'The navy feel it,' Brenton says, 'and most keenly at Court, where medals and honorary decorations adorn the military, while the officers of the navy are without them.'

Sympathy with Napoleon in the Navy sometimes took practical form. His progress with the crews of the *Undaunted*, *Bellerophon*, and *Northumberland* could be counted on. The boatswain of the *Undaunted* wished him 'better luck next time'; the crew of the *Bellerophon* 'would not touch a hair of his head', and the crew of the *Northumberland* thought he did not deserve his fate. So many naval captains visited Elba that the Commander-in-Chief in the Mediterranean issued an order forbidding them to do so. From then onwards the Admiralty took fright and tried to check all contact with Napoleon. At Plymouth, no communication was allowed except through the Admiral of the Fleet, Lord Keith, but Napoleon's entourage had no difficulty in finding intermediaries. On the *Northumberland*, Admiral Cockburn's severity reflected the alarm of Whitehall, but security was again breached. On St. Helena, where the only authorized channel was through Sir Hudson Lowe, there were secret alternatives. A number of captains returning to England from the East Indies station called on Napoleon and several of them came straight on to Holland House.

The Navy was used to the admiration of the country and was sustained by it in the early stages of the war. But Trafalgar was a climax which came ten years too soon. Nothing that happened afterwards could repeat its success or equal its drama. There were failures at Antwerp and in the American war of 1812. Napoleon made things worse by his policy of remaining in port and fragmenting the Navy into innumerable units on guard. As he continued to fight the war on land, it was Wellington who emerged as his opponent and the Army became the obvious defender of British liberty.

The Navy had deeper causes for sympathy with Napoleon than its decline in popularity. Its growth had been very great after the beginning of the war. There were over a quarter of a million seamen by the end, if we include the

Merchant Navy, and several thousand ships, of which nearly a thousand were warships. Expansion on this scale had only been possible by the intensive use of the press gang, so that about half the crews were recruited against their will. At the beginning of the war they were still Englishmen, but the law was changed to include foreigners and French prisoners of war. The muster-book of the *Victory* shows that more than a third of her men at Trafalgar were pressed, including Frenchmen, Americans, Italians, Germans, Norwegians, and a Swiss.

To maintain the fighting spirit of such crews, it was necessary to strengthen the hands of the captain. In theory, he had no powers of life and death, but in practice he had. He could give up to thirty-six strokes with the cat and repeat them day after day. His quarto volume of *Regulations Relating to His Majesty's Service at Sea* had the dignity of a Bible but left him the latitude of his own conscience. Everything was expected of him. He needed 'a perfect knowledge of all foreign coasts', and enough knowledge of their inhabitants and products to be able to negotiate and revictual his ship. He was responsible for the conduct of the chaplain and the bodily welfare of the crew, their clothes and cleanliness. 'Lastly the ship and every person in it being placed under the Command of the Captain, he will be held responsible for everything that shall be done on board.'

The naval captain not only had much greater powers than his equivalent in rank in the Army; his career could be determined by himself. The captains we have noticed mainly belonged to the middle classes; their entry into the service had not been due to birth, as it was in the Army, and their careers did not depend on the purchase of commissions. Unless a promotion was due to seniority, it was achieved by brilliance and daring in the capture of prizes. Their sense of initiative and the ruthlessness with which they handled their crews were little restrained. We have seen Bazalgette, the son of a plantation owner, behaving with steady courage as lieutenant in range of the shore batteries. The discipline of his men which brought him back alive was achieved by infection from him and from the knowledge of what the country expected. Captain Sturt, a trustee of Changeur's square, was able to give 36, 38, and 39 lashes, and double that with a night in irons to a homosexual. The only check on a captain's powers was that the Admiralty might complain that there ought to have been a court martial.

But perhaps more important than the powers of the captains was the isolation of their ships. The improvements in signalling were thought to be miraculous, but they were confined to line of sight, and the atmosphere on board developed according to its own laws as the ship moved into empty horizons. The Ancient Mariner could have belonged to the nineteenth century. The ships and their captains had their own dominant tendencies in which drink or fear of punishment or the hope of desertion were the most common. A particularly scandalous case taken up by Whitbread concerned a seaman called Jeffery, put ashore on the uninhabited island of Sombrero, north of the Leeward Islands, as a punishment for stealing spruce-beer after previously stealing rum. His money and most of his clothes were taken from him because there was no means of keeping alive on the island without water or food. Two months later a search party found only some shreds of his clothes.

Although the ships were organized according to a theoretical hierarchy, the war scattered them for the first time across the globe. Until 1789, there were no ships belonging to the Navy east of the Cape of Good Hope. When the first squadron of five went out, with Byron's uncle Captain George Byron in command of one, they ran aground in the Mozambique Channel before they reached the Bay of Bengal. As the East Indies Command became established, its work consisted mainly of single-handed conflicts with pirates and occasional attacks on French ships based on Réunion and Mauritius.

Ten naval officers had seats in the House of Commons in the second half of the war, and there were frequent complaints about conditions at sea, particularly from Whitbread. The chief spokesman of the officers was Lord Cochrane, who with Sir Francis Burdett represented Westminster. In 1811 Cochrane gave a list of ships of the East Indies Command who were retained there indefinitely without relief. The *Centurion* had been there eleven years, the *Rattlesnake* fourteen, the *Fox* (under the command of Cochrane's brother) fifteen, the *Albatross* twelve, the *Sceptre* eight. The crews, under the standard regulations, went unpaid until they returned to England. Cochrane quoted a calculation by his brother that if 100 men returned in the *Fox*, there would be £25,000 owing to them. To this, another captain added that they suffered a loss of 35 to 40 per cent in pay because of the rates of exchange. The Admiralty replied that the complaints were unrepresentative: only one protest had been received through the normal channels.

The Navy thus had some of the classic tendencies of a rival court. Cut off from the main body of the country in communities where grievances and delusions of grandeur flourished, it saw its traditional popularity pass to the Army and gain confirmation in the distribution of honours. It was not necessary for naval officers to believe, with Byron or Lady Holland, that Napoleon was the superior of Wellington for them to feel a certain sympathy with him. St. Helena was one of the main ports of call on the return journey from the East Indies Command. They had no hesitation when they got there in paying their respects.

3

Perhaps the most striking similarity of the Napoleonists, after the habit of founding rival courts, was their attitude in ruling them. They were despots. Lady Holland was dismayed by Caroline Lamb's parody of her rule at Holland House, but could no more turn herself into a constitutional monarch than could Napoleon at the behest of Constant. The memoirs of the nineteenth century resound with the amusement and indignation of her guests. Talleyrand accused her of dining at six *'pour gêner tout le monde'*. Macaulay says 'the Centurion did not keep his soldiers in better order.' She treated Allen, the librarian, 'like a negro slave'.

Whitbread was so strict a disciplinarian that there was nearly a mutiny in the Bedfordshire militia under his command. In his proposals for a new poor law, he distinguished the deserving poor from the undeserving by the wearing of badges. The Whigs found him imperious and aggressive. His supporters called him 'the Colonel' or 'Commander-in-Chief', and Sheridan 'his Dictatorship'.

At the end of his life Byron told Medwin that he once amused himself by making a list of the people to whom he had been compared by the English newspapers. They included three Roman emperors—Nero, Elagabalus, and Caligula—and the two kings of England who most nearly resembled them, Henry VIII and, more interestingly, George III. To these, he himself added that he wished to be Caesar or nothing.

Princess Caroline had been trained in an authoritarian German court, and her dictatorial habits are perhaps less surprising than her fraternization with the public. But her attitude to the people of Kensington was like that of Henry V among his troops on the eve of Agincourt; she wished to see herself in their eyes rather than to interest herself in them. Lady Bury tells us that she never gave instructions from her carriage to the postilion but pointed to the direction she wanted. Her foundation of the Order of St. Caroline was not a joke.

In the privacy of his correspondence, Creevey called Fox 'the leader of the gang'. Trevelyan says it was normal for his contemporaries to compare him with Julius Caesar. His rule was benevolent, depending partly on his magnetism and partly on the scrupulous care he took to follow the needs and interest of his supporters. The Duke of Leeds, a Tory, paid a realistic tribute to the discipline he maintained—'for which I think he himself is entitled seriously speaking to merit, and in this I sincerely wish Mr Pitt would generally condescend to imitate him. I am aware that experience proves how much better the followers of opposition are drilled, and how much better they are collected and formed for actual operation than the supporters of the ministry have usually been.'

Leigh Hunt had a certain frailty as a dictator and was dangerously ridiculed by his courtiers, with the exception of his family, but there is no doubt about his pretensions. Keats wrote a treacherous parody of him at Hampstead and he was bitterly attacked by John Gibson Lockhart, the author of a standard life of Napoleon. 'I humbly suggest', wrote Lockhart, in 1818, 'that you give yourself too many of those regal airs so natural to a crowned head, and that you conduct yourself at your court at Lisson Grove, with a stateliness and hauteur that may be considered by the youthful nobility of Cockaigne, a perfect model of monarchical dignity, but is, in fact, visibly characteristic of your plebeian origin and education.'

The Napoleonists all had difficulty in seeing people as individuals in their own right. In the politicians, this failure has been singled out as the central weakness which prevented them from succeeding. Namier argues that Fox, the Man of the People, was unable to sense the feeling of the masses: 'The cause of all his failures was that he had no heart—except where his own supremacy was uncontested.' At the beginning of his career, Madame du Deffand drew the same conclusion from watching him in the *salons* of the *ancien régime*. 'I am inclined to think that one person is much the same to him as another. . . . he does not put his mind to yours.'

Among the Whigs after the death of Fox, Whitbread's ability was so outstanding that his exclusion from office and the leadership of the Opposition did not seem to them sufficiently explained by his being the son of a brewer. Brougham believed the trouble was his inability to sense what other people were feeling, which made him difficult in a group and weak in giving advice about public opinion: he was 'nothing for council except indeed as far as his courage and honesty go'.

Lady Blessington noticed 'a sort of mental reservation in Byron's intercourse with those with whom he was on habits of intimacy. . . . It was as though he said, I think aloud, and you hear my thoughts; but I have no feeling of friendship towards you.' The *Examiner* said of Byron that 'his talent does not lie so much in appealing to others, as in expressing himself. He does not make you so much a party as a witness.' Mrs. Inchbald has a character in *Nature and Art* who goes out not for the pleasure of seeing but being seen, who 'forgot everything she heard others say in the minute attention she paid to everything she said herself.'

Godwin was badly hurt as a child by his father's inability to pick him out from his twelve brothers and sisters, but he is the only writer who has written a great novel without any observation of people at all. *Caleb Williams* is spun from the stuff of his own emotions, and we are moved by the play of conflicting drives within him. He surprised people who knew of his great energy by going fast asleep in company, like Whitbread in the period

FACING PAGE
The future Lady Holland in 1786, as Clytie, by Romney,

leading up to his suicide. Godwin 'loved to walk in the crowded streets of London,' says Talfourd, 'not like Lamb enjoying infinite varieties of many coloured life around him, but because he felt, amidst the noise and crowds and glare, more intensely the imperturbable stillness of his own contemplations.'

The Napoleonists were dandies, who used the prerogative of kings to appear with more distinction than those around them. 'There is something in external rank and splendour that gratifies and imposes on the imagination,' says Hazlitt. The Napoleonists resorted to it in their youth, before they had had time to establish their claim to recognition in other ways. Five of them had hair of various shades of auburn: Lady Holland, Mrs. Inchbald, Whitbread, Byron, and Foscolo.

Lady Holland and Mrs. Inchbald both happened to be named Elizabeth, and both allowed the Virgin Queen a certain influence on their lives—Lady Holland by reigning over an Elizabethan mansion for most of her life, and Mrs. Inchbald, the Catholic, by quoting Elizabeth's views on the stage with a respect she otherwise reserved for Kemble's. The two women may also have known that their namesake kept her golden hair by one means or another till her death, but it was not this accidental resemblance which first gave them their sense of regal status. Their hair had always been the natural crown of their beauty. From dress they needed little more than a discreet emphasis of the authority it gave them. Lady Holland went to great lengths in her pursuit of fashion, but she never allowed herself the artifice of rouge. Mrs. Inchbald was 'a figure that could not be seen without some degree of astonishment for its loveliness', but she spent very little on dress; it was 'always becoming', she said. 'And very seldom worth so much as eightpence.' She was one of the first actresses to leave off her wig; she came on at the Haymarket, in 1780, 'absolutely without powder'. But she kept such detailed notes about her figure and style of dress that we know as much about it as about her politics, and Boaden suggests that she killed herself with tight-lacing.

Whitbread set off his auburn hair with a blue frock coat, a blue vest, and blue trousers. The *Examiner* listed modesty of dress among his virtues after his suicide. Byron had an affection for Beau Brummel and competed with him in the quiet distinction of his everyday clothes. But his earliest memories of his father gave him an irresistible passion for uniforms. When he was buying Albanian costumes at fifty guineas apiece, Hanson was disposing of the old tenants at Newstead as ruthlessly as Captain Byron had raided the last funds of Mrs. Byron.

Fox was the undisputed beau in town from the time he left Oxford, *coiffé à l'aile de pigeon*, to the early stages of the American war. His only rival was the Earl of Carlisle, who became Byron's formal guardian and was entitled to wear a green ribbon across his chest with a diamond star.

Leigh Hunt wore yellow breeches, a haircut modelled on Petrarch, and an artificial rose-bud in his buttonhole in winter. Lockhart savaged him as a false dandy. 'I will not part with your Majesty, till I have shewn your crown, which you imagine is formed of diamonds and pearls, to be wholly composed of paste and parchment, and glass-beads; your robes to be worthless old rags.' Leigh Hunt praised Fox for 'something quaker-like' in his dress, and there was modesty as well as glamour in his own. The combination of restraint and exhibitionism has often been noticed as a characteristic of dandyism, and is perhaps related to it as shyness to vanity or a stutter to eloquence. The Napoleonist who did not graduate as a dandy was Hazlitt.

Fox began to wear the blue and buff colours of the Americans soon after the Declaration of Independence, when he was only twenty-seven. At the same time he turned away from the whole standard of dress acceptable at Court. But it was the leadership of a revolt, not an abdication. Joseph Farington reports as a painter on a meeting of the Whig Club at the end of 1795. 'The Duke [of Bedford] was dressed in a blue coat and buff waistcoat with a round hat, Fox also cropped and without powder. His hair grisley grey.' Wraxall, who records these changes in his *Memoirs* with the regret of a conservative, distinguishes between a period of intentional political eccentricity and a general whirlwind which set in during the French Revolution.

Mr Fox and his friends, who might be said to dictate to the town, affecting a style of neglect about their persons and manifesting a contempt of all the usages hitherto established, first threw a sort of discredit on Dress. From the House of Commons, and the Clubs in St James's Street, it spread through the private assemblies of London. But though gradually undermined and insensibly perishing of atrophy, Dress never totally fell, till the era of Jacobinism and of equality in 1793 and 1794. It was then that pantaloons, cropped hair and shoe-strings, as well as the total abolition of buckles and ruffles, together with the disuse of hair-powder, characterised the men. . . .

There was an individual cycle in the Napoleonists' attitude, independent of politics, which made them unusually observant of fashion in their youth and unusually neglectful of it by the time they were thirty. Byron and Leigh Hunt, although belonging to a later generation than Fox, were also dandies in their twenties, but became as slovenly as he did before middle age. Capel Lofft, as a young barrister, was the shining young David praised by Dr. Johnson, but soon afterwards he was a prematurely aged boy, with a tail coat too big for him and breeches too small, so that he showed an inch or two of leg above his boots. Godwin, resplendent when seen by Mrs. Opie on the publication of *Political Justice* in his thirties, let his clothes collapse about him in middle age and looked the part when he claimed exemption from military service as a Dissenting minister.

It was said of Fox that he passed with extraordinary speed from youth to middle age. Byron thought his days were 'in the yellow leaf' when he was thirty-one. One of the two Psalms he knew by heart compares the blessed man to 'a tree planted by the rivers of water, that bringeth forth his fruit in his season; his leaf also does not wither.' Leigh Hunt was said to have been mistaken to outlive Shelley and Keats. Mrs. Inchbald at fifty-five wanted to 'scream with horror' when she looked in her glass. It was perhaps the dictatorial tendency of the Napoleonists which made them take the fullest advantage of their splendour while it lasted and abandon it with a kind of despair as soon as they began to lose their claim to youth. Like Byron, they were to be Caesar or nothing. As Madame Mère said at her son's coronation, '*Pourvu que cela dure.*'

It was a feature of politics in the eighteenth century that the actors might change their roles according to the interest of the moment, as if they lacked the settled convictions of the nineteenth century. Fox is one of the most quoted examples of such cynicism because of his readiness to form a co-alition with Lord North after the American war in order to defeat the ma-noeuvres of George III. But mercurialism was one of the deepest character traits of the Napoleonists. When Fox was in Paris during the Peace of Amiens, he defended both Pitt and Windham against accusations made by Napoleon. '*M. Fox change de physionomie avec une rapidité que l'on ne peut décrire,*' said Madame Junot, on another occasion—he was no longer the leader of the Opposition, but Pitt's brother surrounded by enemies. Moore says that the versatility and ease with which Byron 'could on the briefest considera-tion, shift from praise to censure, and sometimes, almost as rapidly, from censure to praise, shows how fanciful and transient were the impressions under which he, in many instances, pronounced his judgements.' Lady Blessington noticed that Byron was 'inconsistent in his actions as well as in his conversation'. He was 'chameleon-like'.

Besides being born travellers, the Napoleonists were passionate linguists and actors, who wanted to overstep what most people accept as the limits of their personalities. Most of them had two or three languages in addition to Latin and Greek. The American Ambassador, Rush, was surprised that the Duke of Sussex had German, Italian, French, Hebrew, 'and it may be others'. Byron learnt languages with difficulty but tried to learn German, translated from Portuguese, spoke Italian fluently, and Stendhal credits him with Arabic and Greek. He studied Armenian in Venice and put his name to an Armenian grammar. Whitbread was fluent in French and bought an Icelandic grammar for his library. Fox had seven languages including Spanish; he normally wrote home in Italian from Italy and in French from

France. 'He had a student's instinct for getting at the heart of a language,' says Trevelyan. Lady Holland, who had never been a serious student of anything, was at home in French, Spanish, and Italian. Six of the Napoleonists were professional translators: Godwin, Hobhouse, Leigh Hunt, Mrs. Inchbald, Capel Lofft, and Lord Holland. Leigh Hunt is rated by Edmund Blunden as the superior of any translator in the twentieth century.

Lord John Russell says that Fox had a 'passion for acting', and it dominated his youth. When he was five, he was already 'mad about the stage', according to his father. His enthusiasm for the boy actor, Master Betty, which is described by Mr. Giles Playfair in *The Prodigy*, was a reflection of his own ambitions. He began in Racine's *Andromache* at Holland House when he was twelve and played new roles every year until his father's death, when he was twenty-five.

Byron prided himself almost equally on his acting. It remained an obvious part of him, in his mimicry, his parodies, and his verse. Leigh Hunt describes how he liked to imitate Dr. Johnson, by beginning a statement with ' "Why, Sir," in a high mouthing way, rising and looking about him.' After seeing him as Iago in a rehearsal of *Othello* at Pisa, Medwin said he could have been the finest actor in the world. 'His voice had a flexibility, a variety in its tones, a power and pathos beyond any I ever heard; and his countenance was capable of expressing the tenderest, as well as the strongest emotions.'

Leigh Hunt had a lower opinion of Byron's acting, but as an actor himself who had set new standards of dramatic criticism in the *Examiner*, he may have been ungenerous. Hazlitt was a notable mimic as a child and became the best dramatic critic of his time. Mrs. Inchbald made her living as an actress when she was eighteen. If some of Whitbread's speeches could be called histrionic, they were not good acting. He atoned for this by resurrecting Drury Lane, where he intervened in the detail of the productions.

Although the Napoleonists depended to so large an extent on being articulate, several had marked difficulty with their speech. Leigh Hunt and Mrs. Inchbald both grew up with a stammer. Fox had a delivery which was so awkward and tumultuous that he could hardly have become a speaker if he had not, like Mrs. Inchbald, submitted to the discipline of the stage. Whitbread, according to Wilberforce, 'spoke as if he had a pot of porter to his lips and all his words came through it.' Leigh Hunt's criticism of Byron on the stage was that 'his voice was *confined*. He spoke inwardly, and slurred over his syllables, perhaps in order to hide the *burr*.'

We have not included John Thelwall, the radical orator, among the Napoleonists because he was frightened off the political scene after his trial for treason in 1794, and did not record his views. But Crabb Robinson mentions him with Hazlitt, Capel Lofft, and Godwin among those who were most cast down by Waterloo, and he had nearly all the characteristics of the Napoleonists. Born in Covent Garden, he grew up in poor surroundings with a slight stammer. He had 'a rage for theatricals', and once assaulted a drayman for calling him Jack-a-Dandy. In spite of his difficulty in speaking, he became an orator and was able to make himself heard even in the open air at a great distance. 'He seemed', says Hazlitt, 'to rend and tear the rotten carcase of corruption with the remorseless, indecent rage of a wild beast.' Thelwall believed that eloquence was 'the republican talent', as distinct from literature or science, and that it was the most effective way of seducing women.[1]

After Thelwall's trial he began to devote himself to curing impediments of speech, at first by physiological means; but slowly he became convinced that they were 'mental diseases'. 'The science of curing impediments is, in a considerable degree, the science of correcting and regulating the mental and moral habits of the pupil,' he wrote in *Results of Experience*. He founded a clinic where he taught English, French, Latin, and Italian. In his efforts to re-educate his pupils, he made them recite and act in plays, but he noticed that they tended to relapse in the holidays (which he reduced to one a year) and he concluded that 'the parents are sometimes the disease'. When Crabb Robinson visited him in 1815, he was amused to find a cast of stammerers playing Milton's *Comus*. The clinic had so much success with incurables that Thelwall made a small fortune, which he used after the war in the struggle for parliamentary reform.

The Napoleonists were violent as well as dictatorial. The importance of the article on hydrocephalus in the *Edinburgh Medical Journal* which obsessed Lady Byron, is that it went beyond her own account of her husband's behaviour and gave a picture of violence mounting to a crisis which seemed to her almost certain to be suicide or insanity. The symptoms, she said, had already entered 'the second stage', when there were screams, tossing of the arms, and convulsions. Byron certainly played into her suspicions. At school, he told Moore, 'I was always violent'; he was 'always cricketing, rebelling, *rowing* and in all manner of mischief'. Waite, the dentist, said he ruined his teeth by grinding them in his sleep, and ten years later, according to Medwin, he used to sleep with a napkin between his teeth. He had such a passion for arms of all kinds that he 'generally had a small sword by the side of his bed, with which he used to amuse himself as he lay awake in the morning by thrusting it through his bed-hangings.' No doubt he was back

[1] Byron agreed:

The devil hath not in all his quiver's choice
An arrow for the heart like a sweet voice.
*Don Juan*, Canto xv

at Elsinore with a rat behind the arras, but he also had pistols by his bed, and he prided himself on being an excellent shot who could split walking sticks, half-crowns or shillings, 'even the *eye* of a walking stick, at twelve paces, with a single bullet'.

The cause of Byron's death at Missolonghi has remained unknown. Leeches and purgatives certainly promoted it, but epilepsy is no longer accepted by the authorities who have examined the crude but quite extensive evidence. What is certain is that a paroxysm of violence overcame him on the island of Cephalonia when he was being welcomed (in extravagant terms) by the monks who were putting him up at the monastery above Samos. He called the abbot a pestilential madman, threw a chair at an Englishman, tore his own clothes and bedding, and broke the rest of the furniture in his room. The only explanation he would give was that his head was 'burning', and he refused the help of a doctor. He had entered the period of admitted homosexual relations which are most fully described by Professor Wilson Knight in *Lord Byron's Marriage*. The symptoms were closer to the fantastic account of hydrocephalus than to epilepsy, and the violence of the time of his marriage was repeated in a similar pattern until his death eight months later.

Hobhouse was a passionless character by comparison with Byron, but in his last long vacation from Cambridge, he attacked Scrope Davies with a knife. They had been gambling at Brighton and quarrelled on returning to their rooms. When Davies tried to grab him by the throat, Hobhouse picked up a knife and stabbed him in the shoulder before Byron could intervene. Davies collapsed in a pool of blood and got up with a new sense of the danger of attacking a small man. Foscolo used a knife to lend force to his arguments. Dr. Henry Holland, a reliable physician, describes him rising from a dinner table when contradicted and prowling behind the guests to stop further opposition.

In the Commons the English Napoleonists set new standards of verbal assault. Plumer Ward describes Whitbread as 'bursting and almost inarticulate with passion'. There was something lethal in Fox's attacks on the King's speeches, probing through the ministry, which he pretended to be his target, until he reached the man himself, and then thrusting with short deadly strokes: 'The present reign has been one continued series of disgrace, misfortune and calamity' (1780). It was 'the speech of some arbitrary, despotic, hard-hearted, and unfeeling monarch who, having involved the slaves, his subjects, in a ruinous and unnatural war, to glut his enmity or sate his revenge,' was determined 'to persevere in spite of calamity, and even of fate' (1781). When the King was temporarily insane in 1804, Fox wrote to his public relations adviser, Dennis O'Bryen, that he wanted references to his madness in the newspapers every day—'in a most decent way, of course'.

Both Fox and Whitbread were compared with hawks. Sheridan said that Whitbread made him feel like 'a partridge or pheasant with a hawk hanging over him'. North once told Fox of his relief that he had not fallen on him, 'because you was in fine feather'.

It was probably fear of reprisals which silenced Fox in the presence of Dr. Johnson, because he could not give free rein to his aggression. 'His conversation is like a brilliant player of billiards,' says the Duchess of Devonshire, 'the strokes follow one another piff paff.' Harriet Shelley says that severity in Godwin 'was confined to words, but these were pointed and humiliating'. Coleridge said of Hazlitt that 'he sends well-headed and well-feathered thoughts straight forward to the mark with the twang of the bow-string.' Lady Holland, according to Lord Ilchester, made her guests 'a target for the venom of her wit or the sharpness of her tongue'. A suitor complained that Mrs. Inchbald's speech was 'severe and pointed'. Windham accused Fox of 'the poisoned arrows of debate'. Hazlitt said of Whitbread: 'He spoke point-blank what he thought.'

Godwin's prose normally has a lucid and penetrating clarity which seems to prove his belief that passion would submit to reason, and violence or sin of any kind was no more than an error of judgement. He suffered in his own childhood when he was birched. 'It had never occurred to me as possible that my person, which had hitherto been treated . . . as something extraordinary and sacred, could suffer such ignominious violation.' When he was thirty, he more or less adopted an orphan, Thomas Cooper, with the object of proving the maxim of Helvetius, '*l'éducation peut tout.*' The experiment lasted five years, and from time to time the boy kept a diary, in which he called Godwin a brute, a viper, and a tiger. He was once thrashed without mercy and noted that afterwards Godwin went out 'merely to avoid me'.

The least violent of the Napoleonists appears to have been Mrs. Inchbald, but even she was called a 'beautiful vixen' by Lamb. When she emptied a basin of water over Mr. Dodd, the water was hot, and when she pulled off an admirer by his pig-tail, she remained cool. 'How lucky', she said, 'that he didn't w-w-wear a w-w-wig.'

In the view of John Thelwall as well as Freud, stammering is connected with the instinct of aggression. 'When the stutterer is unable to talk,' says Fenichel, in his *Outline of Clinical Psychoanalysis*, 'he is expressing his desire to kill.' A stammer is thus increased by the presence of someone in authority, 'that is to say, paternal figures, authoritative persons against whom the repressed aggressive drives would be most intense and towards whom there would be most ambivalence.'

There is no agreement among psychologists on the cause of stammering, but it is admitted to increase in an emotionally charged situation. When Leigh Hunt was sentenced to prison for his libel on the Prince Regent, his brother left it to him to reply. Leigh Hunt explains that when the moment came, he was 'prevented by the dread of that hesitation in my speech to which I had been subject when a boy'.

For the most part, the Napoleonists were not aware of their own underlying violence and deplored it in others. They did not look on Napoleon as particularly aggressive, and when they were confronted by some unacceptable incident, like the execution of the Duc d'Enghien, excuse it as a lapse, like a sudden outburst of their own. It was the British Government, and in his lucid periods, George III, who seemed to them continuously and by nature aggressive. We were 'both in form and substance aggressors', Fox said in the Whig Club, four years after the French declaration of war. 'We look at Tippoo Sahib's conduct,' he said in 1791, 'and do not see the injustice of our own.' 'It was His Majesty's Ministry', said Lord Holland, 'who showed themselves, and not the Ruler of France, hostile to the peace of mankind.' Whitbread denounced the British troops in Washington as worse than the Goths.

The dammed-up feelings of the Napoleonists could not find sufficient outlet in their own occasional outbursts or in the discovery of aggressive motives in the Government. There was a compulsive tendency in their campaigns for the relief of suffering and reform, and at times they fell into suicidal depression.

They were enlightened reformers, genuine pacifists, and the most reliable friends of the downtrodden. For the reasons we have seen, there was a tendency for them to sympathize with outcasts, but they were not like the Evangelicals, who wished to abolish slavery but persuaded Pitt to pass the Combination Laws against the English workers. The working class, as well as the aged, the young, debtors, and lunatics, seemed to them the victims of the oligarchy at the centre.

Bennet, a fellow Whig, said of Whitbread that 'the active, unwearied benevolence of our poor friend surpassed all the exertions of anyone we ever knew. . . . There was not a poor one or oppressed being in the world that did not consider Whitbread as his benefactor.' Trevelyan says of Fox that his kindness to women was unlimited. 'Whenever, rich or poor, blameless or erring, a woman was in trouble, she always was sure of a champion in Fox.' Tom Moore says that Byron 'never met with objects of distress without affording them succour'. He gave away as much as £1,000 at a time to former friends who had lost their income. The Hollands were particularly generous to foreigners, but they also did more than anyone else for Godwin in his decline. Mary Wollstonecraft said of Godwin on her deathbed that he was 'the kindest, best man in the world'.

The increase of suicide at the end of the war caused an exchange of nationalist reproaches between the French and English press, each seeing the main increase in the other's country. Statistics of the period are unreliable, but the number of cases reported in *The Times* suggests a fairly steady rate during the war, dropping sharply in 1814 and 1815, and rising to double the wartime level in the first four years of peace. Durkheim has shown that wars and great political disturbances are regularly accompanied by a fall in the suicide rate, which increases again afterwards.

The suicidal tendency in the Napoleonists can be seen as a part of the Romantic movement as a whole. Hume had made the first reasoned defence of suicide in the middle of the century and the practices designed to discredit suicides after their death were in retreat. Whitbread protested in April 1814 about the parading of a suicide's corpse through the streets by the police. Godwin has a condemnatory appendix in *Political Justice* which adds the reminder that martyrdom was a form of suicide. Hazlitt also justifies it by this Christian derivation. Two of his favourite books were *The Sorrows of Young Werther* and Rousseau's *Nouvelle Héloïse*, in which the settings are Romantic and the justification of suicide is the incompatibility of the individual with the pressures of society.

The Napoleonists had strong suicidal tendencies in defeat because the violence they projected on the outside world then turned against themselves. They could stand the enmity of the established powers as long as they felt themselves backed by the success of Napoleon as a popular hero in arms. But when the republican victories, which sustained them, threatened to collapse for good, leaving the dynasts in control and public opinion acquiescent or rejoicing, their justification was destroyed. In their abandonment, they were overwhelmed by disasters of their own making. They lost confidence in their financial resources, their integrity, and their ability as writers, and looked for escape in drink, isolation, and desperate attempts to recover their moral status by gestures to orthodoxy and even compliments to their enemies. Byron prepared the way for his death in Greece or some other country, and Whitbread actually committed suicide because of his sensitiveness to public opinion. Madame de Staël, who published her *Reflections on Suicide* in London in 1813, accounted for its prevalence in England by the importance attached to public opinion. 'No sooner is the reputation of a man in peril, than life becomes insupportable.'

The crisis lasted nearly a decade, from the beginning of Napoleon's defeats in 1813 to his death in 1821. In this period, Waterloo was the most dangerous moment, but there were others, notably the Abdication and his death on St. Helena. The main sufferers at the Abdication, in April 1814, were Byron, Hazlitt, and Mrs. Inchbald. Byron became 'a *loup garou*—a solitary hobgoblin', as the armies were driven back on Paris. He still backed Napoleon 'against the field' and sent out his fine print by Gérard to be framed in gilt. But when the news of his abdication came on 9 April, it was

s

'a crouching catastrophe', and Byron shut himself up in his room for four days and wrote the *Ode* denouncing Napoleon for not committing suicide. He noted that an *Anti-Byron* had come out, alleging that he was out to over-throw all government. 'I mean to pull up and marry, if anyone will have me,' he told Moore; and a fortnight later: 'I have bought a macaw and a parrot, and have got up my books; and I box and fence daily, and go out very little.' He refused to watch the procession of Louis XVIII and the Prince Regent passing in Piccadilly with their white cockades. 'I am a Jacobin and could not wear white, nor see the installation of Louis the gouty.' For the first time he saw a physician about trouble with his liver and told Lady Melbourne that he pressed him so closely 'about *my mind*, and state of it' that he began to think he suspected him of insanity. In the second half of the year his mood changed. He carried out his resolution to marry by getting engaged to Annabella, flung himself blindly into the social round, and married at the beginning of 1815. Once he quarrelled with a man in the dark 'for asking me who I was'.

Hazlitt was described by Charles Lamb as being confounded by Napo-leon's abdication. 'He is ashamed to show his face.' In his *Life of Napoleon*, Hazlitt describes the half-hearted attempt of his hero to kill himself with opium and added elsewhere that suicide would have been justified by the standards of antiquity.

Mrs. Inchbald, living then on the turnpike at Kensington Gore, 'was literally sunken and dejected as at some public calamity,' says Boaden.

> The rejoicings of her country were bitter to her; and from her windows, she could not well avoid seeing on the 12th of June, the Sovereigns of Russia and Prussia, with their suites, enjoying the Sunday ride of Hyde Park, and a very absurd review of troops there on the 20th. . . .

In another two months she caught a cold which developed into a serious illness, but she recovered by the beginning of 1815.

At Holland House the Dinner Books themselves were thrown into con-fusion at the news of the battle of Leipzig and Lord and Lady Holland collapsed with their various ailments until the war was over. Lady Holland 'has not the spirits to write and is d'ailleurs far from well', Holland wrote to his sister in October 1813. In February Hobhouse found Lady Holland on the sofa and her husband 'in the gout'. In the summer, when the war was over and they left for Paris, Naples, and perhaps Elba, they were advised by Sydney Smith not to go at all because of their health.

The most spectacular illnesses fell on the Napoleonists from Waterloo onwards. There has probably been no other such political epidemic at a time of national victory. The reason was partly the finality of the battle, which seemed to re-establish the dynastic interests for good. 'Every hope of a republic is over,' Byron wrote to Moore, 'and we must go on under the old system.' But the Napoleonists could not bear the sense of finality, so that they thought of hare-brained schemes like the rescue of Napoleon from Plymouth or Byron's idea of driving to Paris in a replica of his carriage. Hobhouse in his journal says that 'thinking people' gave Louis XVIII a reign of six months. What doubled the impact of Waterloo and turned it into a kind of psychiatric trap was the momentum of the events which preceded it.

The return of Napoleon from Elba and his welcome in France carried with it the prestige of the past, which did not mislead realists like Castlereagh, but gave the Napoleonists a bounding sense of elation. 'I can forgive the rogue for utterly falsifying every line of my Ode,' wrote Byron. 'It is impossible not to be dazzled and overwhelmed by his character and career.' He produced the gayest of his short poems in celebration and went to the Lords on 23 May to vote against Napoleon's outlawry. Godwin started out of his own proscription with the two brilliant letters in the *Morning Chronicle*. Together with Holland and Whitbread, he gave Napoleon another twenty years. Mrs. Inchbald believed there would be an overwhelming French victory and hurriedly paid her debts before the banks broke. Crabb Robinson said Hazlitt 'triumphs and rejoices'.

The consequences of Waterloo, when it came, were partly physical and partly a heightening of the Napoleonists' neurotic tendencies, among which delusions of persecution and ideas of suicide were simply the most marked. If their reaction had a fantastic quality, it must be remembered that they were facing a celebration which lasted for weeks and involved the overwhelming majority of the country. The news came on 22 June, when the *Morning Post* headlines were 'Great and Glorious News: Annihilation of Napoleon's Whole Army'. The Eagles of the Champ de Mai were paraded in the streets; the household cavalry carried out victory manoeuvres with drawn swords; Castlereagh announced the Government's intention of building a pillar or triumphal arch. The rejoicing steadily increased, so that *The Times* began its leader a week after the news: 'Nothing in ancient or modern history equals the effect of the victory of Waterloo.'

At the same time, Napoleon was treated with a new ferocity by the press. He was alternately a criminal who had already been executed and a traitor who should have committed suicide. His carriage was on sale in Düsseldorf and his clothes in Paris. Fitzgerald, the chief of patriotic poets, wrote a poem for the *Morning Post* which began:

> Arraign'd by Nations let the culprit stand
> At Europe's bar—and there uplift his hand.

Brougham gave Creevey (who was in Brussels) a bird's-eye view of the casualties in the Opposition early in July.

· It seems as if the Opposition lay under a curse at this time—not merely politi-cally but physically. Romilly last winter was *bled out* of a violent inflammation of the lungs, and I think him damaged by it, next winter will show whether per-manently or not, but at 58 such things are not safe, and he continues to work as hard as ever.[1] Ossulston has been  most dangerously ill.[2] . . . The anxiety and labour Grey has lately had make one fear a severe attack of his spasms—indeed he had one a few nights ago, having been on Monday at Sir W. Ponsonby's funeral, and having to set off for Whitbread's at 4 the next morning.[3]

Brougham himself was unable to write newspaper articles and retired to the country for several months, as he had begged Whitbread to do.

Hazlitt was particularly vulnerable at this time because of a greater readiness than usual to take offence. After the Abdication he quarrelled with Perry, the editor of the *Morning Chronicle*, for using affronting language and keeping him waiting in an ante-room. He attributed the change in Perry's manner to the fall of Napoleon, which had made him an undesirable contributor. He was at once involved in money worries. In September, he complained to Wordsworth that his sleep was 'nothing but a succession of dreams of business I cannot do, of assistants that give me no assistance, of terrible responsibilities'. A long-standing digestive trouble sent him to a doctor. After his euphoria in the Hundred Days, the symptoms grew worse. He shared Whitbread's delusions about servants, who thought him unfit to appear in a drawing-room and neglected him at table because they had been reading about his politics.[4] Haydon, the painter, said

it is not to be believed how the destruction of Napoleon affected him: he seemed prostrated in mind and body: he walked about unwashed, unshaved, hardly sober by day, and always intoxicated by night; until at length wakening, as it were from his stupor, he at once left off all stimulating liquors, and never touched them again.

Haydon has been accused of exaggerating in revenge for Hazlitt's criticism of his pictures, but Talfourd says that when he himself first met Hazlitt in 1815, 'he was staggering under the blow of Waterloo'. In his *Journey through*

[1] Sir Samuel Romilly committed suicide in 1818.

[2] Lord Ossulston had voted with Whitbread three days before his suicide, in the debate on the Duke of Cumberland's marriage grant.

[3] Grey had become the guardian of Whitbread's children and also had responsibility for Whig tactics after his suicide.

[4] The anxiety about servants had been stimulated in the treason trials at the end of the eighteenth century, when spies had in fact been recruited by the Government in inns and coffee-houses. Thelwall, in his *Lecture on Spies and Informers* (1795), said 'the very domestic who eats our bread stands open-mouthed behind our chairs to catch and betray the con-versation of our unguarded moments.' He had been accused by a spy, Gostling, of cutting the froth off a tankard of porter and saying that all kings should perish so.

*France and Italy*, in 1826, Hazlitt gives his own account of the effect of Napoleon's defeat: '. . . and with him all we who remained were "thrown into the pit", the lifeless bodies of men, and wore round our necks the collar of servitude and on our foreheads the brand and in our souls the stain of thraldom and of the born slaves of Kings.'

Leigh Hunt had served half his sentence in the Surrey Gaol when the news of the Abdication reached him under his painted ceiling. He became physically ill and announced in the *Examiner* at the end of September that he was unable to write the leader. In October, after 'a severer attack than almost any he had experienced', he was better, but his sense of persecution became so sharp that Crabb Robinson remarked on it in December, only two months before his release. He was 'so exceedingly sensitive and impatient of censure or reproach that his wife is in the habit of opening all his letters and burning whatever she thinks would give him pain.' Leigh Hunt himself describes his journey home.

An illness of long standing, which required very different treatment, had by this time been burnt in on me by the iron that enters the soul of the captive, wrap it in flowers as he may; and I am ashamed to say, that after stopping a little at the house of my friend A., I had not the courage to continue looking at the shoals of people passing to and fro as the coach drove up the Strand.

In the Hundred Days, he recovered his spirits and established his 'cockney court' in Lisson Grove, where Byron came to ride like the victorious Emperor on his children's rocking horse. On Sunday, 9 April, the *Examiner* gave the whole of its front page to Whitbread's support of Napoleon against the Congress of Vienna and shared his confidence in the outcome: Napoleon will now prove 'a lasting lesson to Kings'.

The effect of Waterloo was described by Haydon, who had dinner with Leigh Hunt three days after the news reached London.

I give myself great credit for not worrying him to Death at this news. He was quiet for some time, but knowing it must come bye and bye, so putting on an air of indifference, 'Terrible Battle this, Haydon.' 'A glorious one, Hunt.' 'Oh, certainly.' To it we went. He was dished about Wellington and had not a word to say.

Hunt spent the months after Waterloo in revising and finishing *Rimini*, a narrative poem based on the story of Paolo and Francesca in the *Inferno*. In outline he keeps close to Dante, but with one major departure. Instead of being killed together with Francesca by her outraged husband, his brother, Paolo commits suicide by running on his brother's sword, and Francesca dies of grief. He is vindicated by this act in the eyes of all.

It is in Whitbread and Byron that the themes of persecution and suicide come out most clearly. Most of Whitbread's anxieties were shared to a lesser extent by others, and there were reasons we have seen for his still greater interest in his standing with footmen and servants and his preoccupation with money. But there was one fantasy he had which the others did not. 'The populace', he told Launcelot Holland, the day before his suicide, 'will pull down my house.' To the son of the great architect who had built his country mansion, 'my house' did not mean the house in Dover Street, which he rented, but Southill Park.

As the seat of Whitbread's rival court, Southill was increasingly exposed to attack. The house had been built and furnished in two decades of war, unlike most English country houses which took two centuries or more in time of peace. Thanks to Henry Holland, it outrivalled most others in its quiet unity and was not inferior to Carlton House. But its inspiration was French and Henry Holland was sometimes called a Jacobin architect. He continued to use many French craftsmen throughout the war and bought furniture for Southill direct from France. Golden eagles held up the curtains in the drawing-room; the boudoir of Lady Elizabeth Whitbread was modelled on a pavilion built for Charles X in the Bois de Boulogne.

A mansion on the scale of Southill was normally the reward of a commander in the field who had done major services to the country. In the debates on the mansions of the Nelson family and the Duke of Wellington, both of which had absorbed unexpected sums of money, Whitbread considered himself qualified to intervene because of his own experience. He had put £120,000 into the building and for several years after 1808 was spending £1,000 a year on the furniture. But the money had not come from a grateful nation; he had paid it himself from the profits of his brewery.

Whitbread had a particular hatred of attacks on private houses. There was nothing in the American war of 1812 which angered him so much as the raid on Washington. We had done 'what the Goths refused to do at Rome . . . burnt the Capitol, . . . stolen the President's plate, . . . run away with the tobacco from the merchants' warehouses.' Worst of all, we had 'destroyed the dwellings of private persons'.

In his fantastic worries about Drury Lane at the end, there was another element which was not present in Byron's or Hazlitt's money worries. There was a suggestion that Whitbread had taken money that did not belong to him, both directly in the rents of boxes at Drury Lane, and indirectly in not paying the shareholders a dividend. He had never been able to regard the great fortune he had amassed from the English workers with the complacency of his father. He had devoted himself, politically as well as financially, to repaying it, as if he needed to return a public debt. After Waterloo, it must have seemed to him that a people who had decided to grant £200,000 to Wellington for a house, might wish to pull down the one he had taken from them. He committed suicide in the belief that his rival court had been declared to have no title to existence.

Byron, according to Tom Moore, had always felt criticism 'with ten times more awareness than others'. The marriage he had decided on after Napoleon's abdication lasted a year, from January 1815 until the January which followed Waterloo. Annabella then left him in the belief that he was suffering from hydrocephalus, like Whitbread, and might also commit suicide. The contrast between the first six months of the marriage, up to Waterloo, and the months after the battle, which were dominated by money worries, drink, and threats of suicide, is so marked that Professor Wilson Knight attributes it to Napoleon's defeat: 'It was not until after the battle of Waterloo, in June 1815, with the consequent reinstatement of the Bourbon monarchy, that Byron's unrest seems to have become serious. . . . To understand Byron we must recognize that these great events were to him personal matters.'

There had been severe trouble during the honeymoon at Halnaby in January, when Byron was still under the influence of Napoleon's abdication; but to outside observers, and even to Hobhouse, the marriage seemed to prosper in the Hundred Days. It was only after Waterloo that he began to warn Hobhouse not to marry, took to brandy instead of wine, and seriously terrorized Annabella. Like Whitbread, Byron made a new will in June, which he signed in July. His financial worries increased to a point which made him put both Newstead Abbey and Rochdale up for auction at the end of July, and when the offers failed to reach the reserve price, pressure on him was so much increased that he had to sell the furniture at Newstead and offer his library for sale in London. The exaggeration of these measures was shown by his refusal of £3,000 from his publisher in spite of the arrival of a bailiff in his Piccadilly house. His total assets and those of his wife were not far short of Whitbread's.

Lady Byron gives several examples of his mounting sense of persecution. Some weeks after Waterloo, when they were in bed in the early hours of the morning, 'he fancied a step on the stairs, and lay afraid to stir, suffering so much that I said I would get up and see. He let me, though I was within three or four months of my confinement—but I am convinced it was because he thought *himself* the only one against whom harm was intended.'

The increase in his suicidal tendencies began at the same time. Hobhouse recorded at the end of July, while Napoleon was at Plymouth, that 'Byron confesses he sometimes thinks that nothing is left for it but to follow Whitbread's example.' When Annabella called on Hanson to warn him that Byron was likely to kill himself, and produced the article on hydrocephalus, she mentioned a bottle of opium she had found in a secret drawer. It was by swallowing opium, though in too small a quantity, that Napoleon had made his half-hearted attempt at suicide at Fontainebleau at the Abdication of 1814. Byron now threatened to make more effective use of it. A month after Annabella had left (saying it was essential to get Byron into the country), his half-sister Augusta reports, an episode occurred about his nightly dose of calomel—one of the milder remedies for hydrocephalus.

The night before last, I went as usual to his room to light his candles, and seeing a draught on the chimney piece which looked *fermenting*, I said 'What is this?' 'My draught, to be sure—what do you think it was? Laudanum?' I replied jokingly that I was not even *thinking* of Laudanum and the truth—that I thought the draught spoilt, which caused my inquiry. He immediately looked very dark and black (in the old way) and said 'I have plenty of Laudanum—and shall use it.'

In approaching the act of suicide but not actually committing it, the Napoleonists were being loyal to the example of Napoleon himself. He refused to be impressed by Whitbread's suicide when he discussed it with W. H. Lyttelton on the *Northumberland*. But Whitbread's end made a deep impression in England for several weeks, like a warning which insistently challenged the brass of the victory celebrations. The diarists revert to it like an obsession. There was no immediate increase in the number of suicides, which is the normal result of a spectacular example. (On the contrary, *The Times* recorded fewer in 1815 than in any other of the first twenty years of the century. In the third quarter of the year, Whitbread's was the only one.) But in the upsurge which occurred in 1816, there were four suicides in Godwin's immediate circle. Fanny Wollstonecraft committed suicide with an overdose of laudanum in October; Harriet Shelley threw herself into the Serpentine in November, and two of Godwin's remaining disciples, the brothers Rosser, killed themselves at about the same time.

It was the death of Napoleon on 5 May 1821 which had the most potent effect on his admirers in England. They read it in the newspapers on 4 July, two months after it happened. 'The age has lost its greatest man,' said the *Examiner*, which appeared in a thick black border. 'He was far away from our eyes and our thoughts; but we felt a pervading consciousness that he lived and something of a feeling that he might again appear among us. . . . The news of the event fell upon the town, as if it had been a change in the natural world.'

Mrs. Inchbald went to bed with a feverish cold, as she had done at the Abdication, but this time lost her appetite, and died 'of inflammation of the intestines' within a month. Leigh Hunt too had a renewal of illness and went to join Byron in Italy in August to get rid of his 'deadly symptoms'. Caroline was in the throes of the Coronation crisis, and was repulsed at Westminster Abbey, on 19 July, when she tried to force her way in. On her return she took a heavy dose of opium and magnesia, which was later

The radicals Thomas Holcroft and William Godwin, both lovers of Mrs. Inchbald, sketched in the Old Bailey by Thomas Lawrence during the treason trials of 1794. Holcroft, a shoemaker's son, believed ardently in the good that would come to humanity from the French Revolution. Godwin, author of *Political Justice*, inspired by the Revolution, was one of the most distressed people in the country at Waterloo.

Byron, painted by Thomas Phillips in the Albanian uniform ('the most magnificent in the world', he wrote to his mother) in which he attended the court of Ali Pasha, 'the Mahometan Buonaparte', at Tepelene in 1809.

Leigh Hunt, painted by B. R. Haydon in 1815. Haydon admired Hunt's 'black bushy hair, black eyes, pale face'; but he was attacked for his 'regal airs' and the stately hauteur with which he conducted his 'cockney court'.

Self-portrait of William Hazlitt in
his twenties, when he abandoned his
elder brother's profession of painter
to concentrate on writing. He saw
the world reduced to slavery by
Napoleon's defeat; his last book was
a massive *Life of Napoleon*, and when
it was finished, in 1830, he died.

Hazlitt's portrait of John Thelwall, the
radical orator, who grew up with a
slight stammer. He believed eloquence
was 'the republican talent', as well
as the most effective way of seducing
women; after curing his own speech
impediment he founded a clinic
for treating those of others.

blamed for her death. In the first week of August she lost over fifty ounces of blood and died on 7 August.

Byron and Capel Lofft each lived another three years, but both were making their preparations for death. Hazlitt wrote his massive labour of piety, the *Life of Napoleon*, and died in 1830, as soon as it was finished. Hobhouse noted in his diary a year after Napoleon's death that 'both my body and my mind have undergone a change for the worse in the last year. . . . I feel confident I shall not live much longer, so what I intend to do in the world, I must do quickly.' He outdid his father, the baronet, by becoming a peer, and lived another 47 years.

When Byron died at Missolonghi, the French papers pointed out that he had disappeared at the same time as Napoleon, as if there was a connection between them. Bertrand Russell and André Maurois have drawn attention to this as more than a coincidence. But on the face of it there was no connection. Tom Moore urged Byron to write about Napoleon's end, but after his first highly articulate outburst of despair at the Abdication of 1814 and the brief poems on Waterloo, he was unable to write about Napoleon. To Moore's suggestion he replied: 'Why don't *you* write on Napoleon? I have no spirits, nor *estro* to do so. His overthrow, from the beginning, was a blow on the head to me. Since that period we have been the slaves of fools.' The effect on him was so great that he acted out his identification by building a replica of his carriage, recruiting a physician in his suite, and exiling himself to his 'greenest island' in the Adriatic.

Byron, Hazlitt, Capel Lofft, and Leigh Hunt's *Examiner*, all saw the world reduced to slavery by Napoleon's defeat. In the pit into which they were thrown, they felt round their necks what Hazlitt calls 'the collar of servitude'. It was worse than an original state of slavery, which had never known of Lodi or Austerlitz or the return from Elba. They had the bitterness of losing a glorious source of hope. The crime of Napoleon, in Byron's eyes, was his surrender.

> . . . but yesterday a King!
> And arm'd with Kings to strive—
> And now thou art a nameless thing:
> So abject—yet alive!

The only degradation in history to equal it was the decline of Greece. Fox had taught his followers to see in Thermopylae the original act of defiance in which Leonidas had chosen martyrdom rather than surrender to the Persians. Byron, in his first exile, saw for himself the splendours of the civilization which had arisen from that struggle, but the more he was seduced by it, the more he despised its descendants for accepting the Turks as their masters. At the wall across the pass of Thermopylae, he was unable to think of Leonidas without seeing a decadent Greek in the foreground.

> Approach, thou craven crouching slave:
> Say, is not this Thermopylae?

His scorn was the same as for Napoleon's abdication. It was another 'crouching catastrophe'—he used the same adjective for both, not because Napoleon was particularly like a Greek, but because the grandeur of their defiance was only equalled by their abasement.

Byron tried out what it felt like on his way to his second exile by lying full length on the grave of the poet Churchill at Dover.

> And is this all? I thought—and do we rip
> The veil of Immortality, and crave
> I know not what of honour and of light
> Through unborn ages, to endure this blight,
> So soon, and so successless?

For a moment he had flirted with another answer, in the half-formulated plans to drive through to Paris in Napoleon's carriage, but in the end he went quietly to his island in the Adriatic, like Napoleon to St. Helena. He went on flirting alternately with quiet endings and violent ones, with America and England on the one hand and the Carbonari on the other. It was only Napoleon's death which gave him the final impulse.

The date happened to coincide with the time when he believed himself fated to die. He had always believed in omens, prophecies, and the magic of numbers. At Napoleon's death, he was already thirty-five. It was the age of his father when he went away to die in Paris. When he was still a boy, a fortune-teller in Bath, Mrs. Williams, had warned Byron to beware his thirty-seventh year. By any calculation, it was time to decide.

At Napoleon's death, his tone changed. There was a leap in his style when he heard of the Greek revolt, which was the opposite of his response to the idea that he should write about Napoleon. 'The Greeks? What think you?' he wrote to Moore; 'What thinkest thou of Greece?' to Murray. Gamba, the young revolutionary who joined him, said his motives were the isolation of the Greeks in their revolt with no European power to support them, and his disgust at the enslavement of Italy. To Medwin he said that Napoleon 'shewed that he possessed much of the Italian character in consenting to live. . . .'

In the slow months of preparation before he sailed from Genoa at the beginning of his thirty-sixth year, Byron knew perfectly well what he was doing. 'I mean to return to Greece,' he told Medwin, at the beginning, 'and shall probably die there.' 'You will think me more superstitious than ever', he said to Lady Blessington, 'when I tell you that I have a presentiment I shall die in Greece.' He knew it was a country of privations, where he had slept in stables and hovels. He warned the Greek committee in London that officers coming out should not think they were going to 'rough it on a beef-steak and bottle of port'. He reflected that the money in his war chest would buy him a mansion and a quiet life anywhere in Europe. But he had made his choice.

Some months after Waterloo, at the time of his proposed expedition to Paris, he is reported to have said that he believed himself the greatest man living. His uncle, George Byron, who was present, said, laughing, 'except Buonaparte'. 'God,' said Byron, 'I don't know that I do except even him.'

What he was planning was martyrdom. It was the first great example to European liberalism of suicide in the interests of a people. It was a model which established Byron's influence in the nineteenth century above that of any other Romantic, not excepting Napoleon.

# 4

The Napoleonist, in the characteristics we have recognized, had a certain resemblance to the Emperor, both in victory and defeat. He belonged, either socially or because of the structure of his personality, to the great majority of people who were excluded from power, and his only means of winning it was by his ability in opposition. His ambition, energy, and disregard of obstacles (which might be human) had to be as exceptional as his talents. The rights of the outcast seemed to him unconditional because they were his own. In so far as he tried to supplant the current leaders and office-holders, he gave himself no chance, and his life was adapted to opposition and exile, and finally to suicide and martyrdom.

To over-emphasize the abnormality of the pattern we see repeating itself, is to find ourselves back with a caricature by Gillray. Most of the Napoleonists' characteristics were shared by the Romantic movement as a whole. We have noticed them in people who left no record of sympathy with Napoleon. À Beckett and Daniel Sutton organized Changeur's square with the rigour of Lady Holland and, like her, claimed their own coat of arms. À Beckett was obsessed with his ancestry, Daniel Sutton with his retinue of servants and his pecking right in the neighbourhood; they both flew to the assistance of Caroline when she was spurned by the Prince Regent as if they recognized in her an outcast like themselves. Behind a disguise of un-questioned normality, the madman of Hogarth is, as Hazlitt said, a type and commonplace of everyday life. 'Each individual looks on himself in the light of a dethroned monarch, and the rest of the world as his rebellious subjects and runaway slaves, who withhold the homage which is his natural due.' As a confirmed Napoleonist, Hazlitt saw this truth with unusual clarity, but he was right in applying it beyond his own circle.

The history of the Kensingtons, which has provided a contrast to our theme, throws into relief what was characteristic in the Napoleonists. It is another history of frustration, with devices for dealing with it which are not dissimilar. The event which goaded Francis Edwards and his successors to feats of ambition was his marriage to Lady Elizabeth, daughter of the Earl of Holland, Baron Kensington of the first creation, whose titles died out for lack of male heirs. After his marriage, Francis Edwards, the purser, managed to represent Haverfordwest in the Commons. His eldest son turned Johnston Hall into a drunken little court, which was among the smallest in the country, and he left six hundred pounds for a funerary monument, 'to be set up over me', which was to have been grander than any in Wales. The surviving brother, who went back to politics, served in nine Parliaments, and invariably voted for the King, whether against the Ameri-cans, the Irish, or the cause of reform. He secured Henry Fox as his patron by selling him the freehold of Holland House, which belonged not to him but to his successors. As a consolation prize, he was given an Irish peerage, but remained a commoner in England. His son hoped for better things from the Prince Regent, but had to console himself by holding court in Car-marthen Bay and Heydon Hall, in Norfolk. It was only Og's grandson, four generations after the arrival of Lady Elizabeth, who gained the English barony as Comptroller of Queen Victoria's household.

Like the Napoleonists, the Kensingtons, in their pursuit of a crown of straw, were intensely ambitious and revolted against their fathers. Their home on the outskirts of Wales seemed provincial from the moment they had a glimpse of the Court of St. James's. They were ready to submit to indignity and hard labour to escape. In defeat or weakness, they took to drink, fell ill, established their own courts, and shared Godwin's hope of glory in the grave. But there was an essential difference. The courts founded by the Kensingtons were not rival but subordinate. They supported the wars against revolution in America and in France. They had no interest in outcasts. They took trouble about their dress, but it was conventional dress, and their loyalty to the sovereign—William Edwardes to George III and Og to the Prince Regent—was so great that each came to resemble his royal master.

The difference is clearest in the second Lord Kensington, the contemporary of Napoleon, who happened to be the most frustrated of them all. Creevey called him Og, King of Bashan, because he was King of nowhere else. Cheated of his birthright by his father, he transferred his loyalty from George III to the Prince Regent and put up for Brooks's, the headquarters of the Opposition. His revolt against his father was open and direct: he proposed that the debates of 1788, in which he had supported limitations on the Prince Regent, should be expunged from the journals of the Commons. He called his son and heir Edward Henry, after his dissolute uncle, instead of William, after his father. The Napoleonists were his friends. He was proposed for Brooks's by Lord Thanet, who was sent to the Tower, and seconded by Lord Sefton, who greeted Waterloo as 'horrible news'. Og had so little sympathy with outcasts that he tried to make money by selling cast-off horses for exploitation. His patriotism was never for a moment in doubt. The French chose to land in Wales when he was a young man because disaffection was common there, but his martial enthusiasm on that occasion won him the thanks of George III. Five years later he was one of the twenty Bloodhounds who voted against the Peace of Amiens. He accused Napoleon of continuous aggression and insult, and could no more have drunk his health than his father could have drunk Washington's. He held office for a moment under the Talents, but when it was clear he would not regain it, he speculated in canals, was defeated by the railways, and consoled himself with innumerable mistresses, who may have included Pauline Borghese.

In the two conditions which had to be fulfilled before an Englishman could be a Napoleonist—a background of Dissent, or some equivalent isolation which reached into the most sensitive areas of his childhood; and the experience of the American war to strengthen and confirm his childhood tendency to see virtue in the wilderness and vice in the Court of St. James's—the Kensingtons did not qualify. Although Dissent was common in Wales and Dissenting ministers collaborated with the French, the Kensingtons had been converted to Methodism by John Wesley. Wesley spoke in the churchyard at Haverfordwest, and his movement was organized nationally, as an adjunct of the Church, not in opposition to it. He preached loyalty to George III in the American war. The religion of the Kensingtons joined forces with their background in Little England beyond Wales to cement their loyalty to the throne.

Yet a third and perhaps more fundamental condition allowed the Napoleonists to flourish in England in the French war. Since the defeat of the Armada at the end of the sixteenth century, every Englishman had been aware that he lived on an island securely defended by the Navy. The undertone of arrogance we now find in the celebrations of English liberty was based on this awareness of privilege. The rights of Protestantism and

Protestant Dissent were secured under the shield of the Navy. Without it, the Civil War of the seventeenth century would not have developed as it did. The proof of its superiority over other navies was renewed at Trafalgar, and its alliance with the Whigs made Fox aware of it from the beginning of the war. Lord Kensington happened to be one of the few people in the country who had reason to doubt it because the Welsh landing on his doorstep was not intercepted. But Fox was convinced that any attempt by Napoleon would fail. He thought it 'full a hundred to one that he and the greater part of his expedition would go to the bottom of the sea, if he should attempt a descent on the coast'. Leigh Hunt says he 'never had the slightest belief in this coming of Bonaparte'. Whitbread did not 'seriously believe' that France meditated 'an attack upon this country'.

The Napoleonists neither believed Napoleon could succeed in invasion, nor wanted him to. Byron summed up their position when he said Napoleon was his hero 'on the Continent; I don't want him here.' It was on the Continent that they wished him to be invincible, and there we have seen that they greatly exaggerated his chances. When they considered his prospects in an invasion, two centuries of history rose up to assure them that they did not exist.

It was not only the history of the nation which told them so. The status they had inherited as outcasts gave them a sense of inferiority in judging the power of the centre. The prospects of the Stuarts in exile, of a self-made brewer, of a Unitarian minister earning a pound a week, seemed to them negligible against the entrenched power of the aristocracy and the Court. In so far as they identified themselves with Napoleon, they wrote off his chances of final victory in the same way. Resistance was another matter; inch-by-inch modification of the tyranny at home might be another matter; their background was strong, even heroic, in defence. But a permanent reversal of the order of things was not in question.

At the beginning of *Vanity Fair*, Becky Sharp is leaving the Chiswick Academy for Young Ladies where she has been a governess. She throws away her presentation copy of Dr. Johnson's Dictionary, and shouts, '*Vive la France! Vive l'Empereur! Vive Bonaparte!*' It was, says Thackeray, 'the greatest blasphemy Rebecca had as yet uttered'. She is an orphan, the penniless daughter of an artist who has died of drink, and her life in the school has been distinguished from the young ladies' by every kind of indignity. When she looks for the most potent means of restoring herself, it is Napoleon she thinks of, not because he is all powerful, but because the Chiswick Academy is, and he is the only champion in the field against it.

Becky Sharp has much in common with the Napoleonists. They were caricatured by the Government, and especially by Gillray, as abasing themselves at Napoleon's throne. Coleridge, in the *Courier*, defined their condition as 'an inward prostration of the soul before enormous power'. And it would be easy, after noting the impression their fathers made on them in childhood, to agree with him. We have the statement by John Hanson that Hobhouse at the age of thirty was 'completely' in the power of his eccentric father. We should only have to accept the protestations of filial piety made by them all to account for their admiration of Napoleon as their fathers' representative as a lasting version of Coleridge's 'prostration of the soul'.

There were certainly times when all of them were dazzled. The fullest account of such a moment is given by Hobhouse in the visit he made to Paris in the Hundred Days to report on the state of French opinion and put the case against the war. He watched Napoleon at the Tuileries, at the opening of Parliament, and at the presentation of the Eagles in the Champ de Mai. He reports every gesture and change in his expression as well as the reactions of the people, which were sometimes less enthusiastic than his own. What moved him was the extent of the support for this one man against whom the Allies were combining, and the intimate contact between him and the people. At a review a fortnight before Waterloo Hobhouse makes the incredible claim that 'the Emperor spoke to almost every member of the ten thousand who were present, and with his accustomed ease and variety of conversation; replying to intelligence by no means agreeable with a frankness most unroyal.' At the dedication of the Eagles, it was the massed military strength which impressed him, and whole passages could be isolated to suggest the prostration of a soul before enormous power. But he insists that he was admiring not power for its own sake, but a man who was defending himself and the people who had chosen him. 'I saw nothing but Napoleon—the single individual to destroy whom the earth was rising in arms from the Tanais to the Thames.' Hobhouse would not, he says, 'have beheld him with delight in the days of his despotism', but his courage against the world, his indifference to the risk of assassination, his solitariness, reduced him to tears.

In the same way, Fox, Byron, and Whitbread all showed their greatest enthusiasm for Napoleon when the danger from him was remote. It was only after the preliminaries of peace were signed that Fox went so far as to say he thought slavery under Napoleon preferable to slavery under George III. Byron was then fifteen at Harrow, and defended his bust of Napoleon for the first time 'against the rascally time-servers'. Whitbread said it was the aggression of the Allies, and nothing else, which raised him to heroic proportions.

The heroes to whom they compared him had the characteristic of being greater than their titles and offices—they saw him in turn as Washington, Ulysses, Caesar, Charlemagne, Alexander. Leigh Hunt distinguished him from rulers who depended on ceremonial. 'He does not blaze about; he

flashes like the lightning, takes the eye with a single stroke, and leaves it
astounded.' A lover-like perception of detail was characteristic of many of
them—of Lady Holland, Hobhouse, Mrs. Inchbald, Benjamin West, Hazlitt.
They admired his voice, his eyes, his smile; West told Leigh Hunt he 'had
never seen a more handsome leg and thigh'. But Fox and Whitbread were
unable to see him in focus; they give the impression of lowering their eyes
for fear of being forced to criticism.

Although much of this can only be diagnosed as the overestimation of
love, the reservations and distaste grew when Napoleon prospered beyond
a certain point, or made his ambition felt at first hand in interviews with
Fox, or prepared to invade. They were reluctant to consider the idea of
invasion because their enthusiasm for him took for granted England's
safety. When forced by Grey to consider it at the beginning of 1799, Fox
said he would not declare himself until the French landed, but then he would
do his utmost against them and put his services at the disposal of George
III. Like Byron, he did not want Napoleon here.

But they did want him there. They needed him, as Becky Sharp did, because he was the only outcast who was strong enough to threaten the established order. What they felt was not love for his person, but love for someone whom the world of privilege could not subdue. Nor was he simply a
heroic version of themselves. Behind and above Napoleon was the glory
they had seen in childhood in their fathers, their prestige as leaders in exile,
their courage and simplicity, but above all their fathers' defiance of a community which had rejected them.

Separation from the community in childhood was the first condition
necessary to the development of the Napoleonist because it forced him into
alliance with his father and blocked the possibility of open revolt. In the
context of the nation, he could not see himself as a traitor or even a rebel,
because he was secure in his sense of loyalty as a son. He could take for
granted the safety of the nation, because it was not endangered on all sides
like his own little community but protected by the sea and the most powerful navy in the world. He could go further on behalf of other people's rights,
further in disloyalty, as it seemed to the community at large, than anyone
else.

To take the lead in support of the American colonists, Fox had to be impervious to the charge that he was a traitor to the King. He was supported
by the knowledge that he was being conspicuously loyal, not only to his
father, who was accused of ruling by corruption, but to his Stuart ancestors,
whose claim to the throne had not been dependent, like George III's, on the
observance of the Constitution. Every charge of coercion and management
which had been thrown at Henry Fox as the corrupter of Parliament, Fox
threw, with the fervour of someone rehabilitating his family, at the occu-

pant of the throne. As he extended the right of self-determination to the Irish and other peoples, he carried further the attack on the bad father and his defence of the good.

The Napoleonists all had the same source of moral buoyancy. Whitbread disposed of his doubts about his father's profits by accusing Ministers of taking public funds. He reproached the country and its rulers for their habit of railing at Napoleon which put him outside the pale, as they had his father and himself. He could 'not help observing upon the sort of personal hatred and antipathy towards the French Emperor, which appears to prevail in a large part of the community, as if each man had a personal quarrel with him. . . . It argues a great degeneracy of national character, as it has given rise to many very disgraceful publications.' Napoleon simply followed the line of his interest with great energy, as befitted a serious man of business.

The Napoleonists were particularly glad to dispose of their fathers' infidelities on the Prince Regent and to preserve their picture of Napoleon from such blemishes. Perhaps the original grievance Whitbread had against his father was that he got rid of his wives, through their death in childbirth, as soon as he had married them and left a brutal instruction in his will that he should be buried 'in the same vault as the bodies of my two wives'. Whitbread brilliantly attacked the Prince Regent as the reincarnation of Henry VIII and defended Caroline because she reminded him of Anne Boleyn, 'when a brutal tyrant wished to get rid of a consort of whom he was tired'. No such thought had occurred to him when Napoleon divorced Joséphine and married the Princess Marie Louise, as his father had married the aristocratic Lady Cornwallis after the death of his mother.

Byron had a natural contempt for Whitbread's oratory, but was unable to resist stealing his metaphor about Henry VIII. His own father, who deserted his mother, had been a captain of the Guards. 'My first dreams were martial,' he told Medwin. It was this martial side of his father which he saw in Napoleon, rather as Whitbread saw him as a captain of industry. Byron, too, blinded himself to Napoleon's desertion of women. His treatment of Joséphine and Marie Walewska left him as unmoved as it did Whitbread. But the Prince Regent, like Henry VIII, was 'famed for contemptuous breach of sacred ties'. When the Prince was rumoured to have made his daughter cry by deserting the Whigs, Byron remembered that Mrs. Byron, his Stuart mother, was a Whig when Captain Byron deserted her.

> Weep, daughter of a royal line,
>     A Sire's disgrace, a realm's decay;
> Ah! happy if each tear of thine
>     Could wash a father's fault away!

T

In the sons of the Unitarian ministers—Hazlitt, Godwin, Leigh Hunt, Hobhouse—it was the tyranny of their fathers and a certain narrowness for which they blamed George III and the Prince Regent, while they saw in Napoleon their courage and asceticism. Their picture of him was less cavalier than Byron's. 'Of fine clothes he does not disguise his contempt,' wrote Leigh Hunt in the *Examiner*. Napoleon ate his dinner in twenty minutes. His ostentation consisted in ostentatiously having none.

Leigh Hunt's father, Isaac, had a feckless side to him which began with a spoilt childhood in which his good looks were his main asset. Women were the most devoted members of his congregation, and when his career collapsed in disgrace, he was imprisoned for debt and gave Leigh Hunt as his first memory a life shared with criminals and ruined gamblers. He died in his fifties, and Leigh Hunt remained strictly loyal to him in the most generous eulogy in his *Autobiography*. But soon after his father's death he also wrote the libel on the Prince Regent which earned him two years in the Surrey Gaol. 'This Adonis in loveliness', he had written, 'was a corpulent man of fifty!—in short this delightful, blissful, wise, honourable, virtuous, true and immortal prince was a violator of his word, a libertine over head and ears in disgrace, a despiser of domestic ties, the companion of gamblers and demireps, a man who has just closed half a century without one single claim on the gratitude of his country or the respect of posterity.' To appreciate the good side of his father, who was stoned as a loyalist in Philadelphia and lived most of his life in exile, we have to read Leigh Hunt on Napoleon, who was 'a mighty and high-souled man', a god who flashed like the lightning.

It was of course impossible to overlook the Prince Regent's infidelities, and everyone in the country was aware of them. After the war, public opinion as a whole strongly supported Caroline against him in the months leading up to the Coronation. But only a minority needed to see error in the Court of St. James's in order to retain their picture of Napoleon as a hero. The normal pull of loyalty went the other way. If George III and his son were less than national heroes, it was not because the country did not wish them to be. George III remained 'the good old King' even in his madness, and Napoleon was the unfailing bogey.

Og, King of Bashan, managed to see the Prince Regent as the leader of the civilized world. 'His Royal Highness's conduct, both towards his father, and towards the country,' he said, had been such as to procure him 'not only the love and affection of all the people of these kingdoms, but also the admiration of all Europe.' Chief of the many vices Og saw in Napoleon was his seizure of territory and 'the sequestration of property' which did not belong to him.

If the Kensingtons were subservient and without vision or independence of thought, they had never been steeled by the disfavour of the community or looked for rewards for anything but conforming to it. The King, at the apex, stood for what was good in their fathers, his enemies for what was bad. In the frustrated view of Og, the King's enemies had the further defect of having made off with his own property.

The Kensingtons and the Napoleonists were thus two extreme types, the first committed to loyalty and the second to opposition, and both set irretrievably on course, whether or not the national interest justified it. It was impossible for the Kensingtons to come to their senses in the American war or for the Napoleonists to come to theirs in the Napoleonic wars. The habits of thought established in their childhood pointed too strongly in one direction to be affected by the facts of the case or the most powerful tides of opinion. The Kensingtons' progress towards Buckingham Palace, although craven and frustrated, was in a pattern which must be called normal. The support it gave to the immediate coherence of the state, although often against its long-term interest, makes it the type of loyalty which flourishes and is approved in every sovereign country.

The Napoleonists, on the other hand, were a peculiarly English phenomenon. The causes which produced them, their number at a time of national danger, and the tradition they left behind, had no parallel elsewhere. We have glanced at a few of Napoleon's continental supporters who had characteristics which were not unlike theirs. Foscolo and Aglio both had a dislike of oppressive father figures, and Stendhal, the most important of European Napoleonists, in his boyhood compiled a list of regicides. Las Cases was a physically small man, like Godwin, Hobhouse, and Capel Lofft, and had equally high ambitions. Foscolo was dictatorial and red-headed, like Whitbread, Mrs. Inchbald, and Lady Holland, who would not have cared for the parallel. But these individuals lacked some of the main characteristics of the English Napoleonists, and do not make up an identifiable group by any resemblance to one another. Instead of having a compact with their fathers, they were more often at daggers drawn.[1] Only a few of them were dedicated to the cause of outcasts, and they had no scruples about joining Napoleon's invasion. What they had in common was a thirst for liberty and the restoration of a past glory. The political motives for alliance with Napoleon on the Continent were so strong in the early stages of his career that little more was needed. In Italy, it was enough to feel the dead hand of the Austrian Empire; in France, the need for national order and greatness.

What made the situation in England so remarkable was the force of the

---

[1] 'The hatred felt and expressed by Henri [Stendhal] for his father is happily unique in the annals of French literature.' (F. C. Green, *Stendhal*.)

motives for opposing Napoleon. He emerged as a leader of genius at the moment when five years of shock and anger at the consequences of the Revolution had put an end to the prospect of reform in England. Reform, as it was called, was only the electoral aspect of the much greater movement of emancipation which had been developing for two centuries and had given England pride of place as the country where freedom and justice were established on a widening basis. There had been a check to this on the accession of George III, and Pitt slowly gave up hope of persuading either him or the governing oligarchy to accept a more representative House of Commons. But the London and Middlesex electorates refused to admit that the powers of the king and the ruling oligarchy could be restored. They voted for Wilkes and Fox with dogged insistence. On the roads the traffic moved thicker and faster as the industries of London multiplied; in the new lines of houses striking out into the countryside more and more people read the newspapers and had a sense of their rights.

Whether or not Parliament was reformed, the new middle classes were beginning to claim their place in the community. The word Majesty was 'a kind of hocus pocus word', said Fox, in 1780, a decade before the French Revolution; the influence of the crown was 'the grand parent spring' from which all other evils flowed. His aim in such attacks was not to abolish the idea of monarchy, but to claim it for the people whose leader he had become. It was in 1780 that Mrs. Inchbald appeared at the Haymarket 'absolutely without powder', no longer a puppet, but a person in her own right. Even in Parliament a degree of liberalization continued. On the eve of the war Pitt allowed Godwin's *Political Justice* to appear. Although the Nonconformist deprivations were maintained, a new Catholic Relief Act permitted mass to be celebrated in public.

The French Revolution seemed to promise that the blockage in the path of constitutional reform would be swept away. After the long delay, the dammed-up pressure could no longer be contained. Windham's enthusiasm in Paris was equal to Fox's in London. Wordsworth, Southey, and Coleridge worked on plans for utopia with as much enthusiasm as Godwin. They were in Wordsworth's phrase 'enflam'd by hope'. But as the Revolution turned into a threat to the whole order of society, the governing oligarchy had a reason for stopping reform and the power to turn it back.

This new reverse was a shock to the reformers incomparably greater than the King's plan to restore the power of the throne on his succession. The fall of the Bastille had released their impatience. Paine's *Rights of Man*, with its proposals for rule by the people in the interests of the people, gave a clear-cut shape to the future devolution of power. But the curse of the Terror fell on the prospect almost as it was taken in. A sense of retribution for parricidal ambition spread through England and gave the governing oligarchy the sanction to prevent further action. Doubt crept into the most sensitive and all but the boldest minds. We have seen that Bellamy, the founder of the Whig Club, collapsed and died in the crisis which split it in two. Fox, by remaining impervious, saved a remnant of the Whigs to lead the struggle for reform after the war, but it was now a tiny minority who withstood the pressure of society as a whole. 'It is not in the nature of man to like to stand alone, in his sentiments or creed,' said Godwin, when he had watched for a decade the effects of this pressure. 'The human intellect is a sort of barometer, directed in its variations by the atmosphere which surrounds it.'

At first, as the courts filled with newspaper editors, Dissenting ministers, and Radicals, the poets held their ground. But sooner or later, everyone who had shared in the hopes founded on the French Revolution had to perform an athletic feat. As the barrier of reaction moved back against them, they could climb on and become part of it, or they could burrow underneath to escape, or they could jump over the top to the other side. In the turmoil of these expedients the English Romantic movement developed the intensity which made it the most powerful in the world.

We have noticed that Coleridge maintained his views for several years longer than the politicians who went over to the Government. The weight of his personal crisis is shown by the length of the delay. Together with Wordsworth and Southey, he belonged quite as much as the Napoleonists to the movement of emancipation which was breaking up the traditional forms of life. Their fathers had been poor men from the professions and commerce. Their need for escape from the formalism of the time showed itself in much the same ways—they planned a community of equal rights in America and went back into the romantic past of England. They found renewal in the country and among animals. Wordsworth toyed with suicide in his boyhood and Coleridge collected anthologies of suicides. But although they could not come to terms with the main body of society, they lacked the motive of the Napoleonist to discover virtue outside it. Their fathers, poor and unprivileged as they were, had been on the edges of the community and belonged to it. Their education was dominated by the Church of England. Although Coleridge preached in Unitarian chapels, his father had been a parson of the Church. Southey's father was a linen draper in the Quantocks but was entitled to his own coat of arms; the boy was educated for the Church at the expense of an uncle who was a clergyman. Wordsworth happened to be the grandson of a linen draper on his mother's side; his father was the agent of a landowner who sent him to Church of England schools, one of them actually in a churchyard. As the ban descended on the political ideals of these poets, they felt no pull towards a champion outside the community. 'No outcast I,' wrote Wordsworth.

Southey, the first to abandon Pantisocracy, became Poet Laureate at the end of the war. Coleridge and Wordsworth intensified their exploration of new poetic forms and filled them with the magic of worlds in which they found restoration. The greatest poems of the Romantic movement, which discover new realities in the past, in myth, and in nature, date from this moment. And so does Coleridge's addiction to opium.

Napoleonism was the Romantics' act of political desperation. It was possible for an Englishman to see the great enemy as an ally because the risk of losing the momentum of change seemed to him greater and more to be feared than the risk of invasion and defeat. In weighing the risk, he could not see Napoleon as an aggressor who was indifferent to human rights and committed to the destruction of England. Or if he had a suspicion of it, he was aware of no reality in the threat which forced him to admit it. His experience had taught him that the champion from outside would defy the central stronghold of power without being able to take it.

The Napoleonists might have been greater poets if they had been less committed to the world of action. Byron's poetry never seems to express more than a fraction of his genius. His dreams were of soldiers and statesmen. In his youth he did not reject Hanson's admonition to him to become a force in Parliament. 'I coincide with you in opinion that the *Poet* yields to the *Orator*,' he wrote back (in a fair imitation of his guardian's style); 'but as nothing can be done in the latter capacity till the expiration of my *Minority*, the former occupies my present attention. . . .' At the height of his fame as a poet, he told Annabella that he preferred 'the talents of action—of war, of the senate, or even of science—to all the speculations of those mere dreamers of another existence (I don't mean religiously, but fancifully).' From the time of Napoleon's defeats, his contempt for poetry increased with his engagement in political revolt.

The Napoleonists, unlike the other Romantics, were committed to politics. Godwin as a novelist remains the social reformer. Leigh Hunt's great influence was as a journalist. Hazlitt, in 'The Tendency of Sects', insists on the political tendencies of the Dissenter's upbringing. The virtue needed in the wilderness, he says, is fidelity, not imagination. 'We may remark a hardness and setness in the ideas of those who have been brought up in this way, an aversion to those finer and more delicate operations of the intellect, of taste and genius, which require greater flexibility and variety of thought, and do not offer the same opportunity for dogmatic assertion and controversial cabal.' Hazlitt had perhaps done as much to transcend those limits as any Dissenter; but Virginia Woolf, who thought him the greatest prose writer of the age, complains that he 'does not open the doors wide upon all experience like Montaigne, rejecting nothing, tolerating everything, and watching the play of the soul with irony and detachment. On the contrary, his mind shut hard upon his first impressions and froze them to unalterable convictions.'

So the Napoleonists were committed not only to politics but to the only political attitude allowed them by their background. Whether Napoleon was the true representative of the French Revolution or the champion of a rival empire, he was the hero they needed in a field they could not leave. The prospect before them was at best ridicule and at worst persecution, but it was this which reinvoked the wilderness of their childhood and assured them of salvation.

To the Government and the community who lacked their experience and had no sympathy with it, they seemed inexplicable. Angry guesses were made at their motives, and only stiffened their opposition. Dissent was blamed, but the loyalty of Dissenters in general and the fact that Fox, Whitbread, and the Hollands were not Dissenters at all, could not be accounted for. Windham saw Jacobinism as a plague which struck first at 'the fairest and choicest part of the creation', infecting 'those whose fineness of texture makes them weak; whose susceptibility most exposes them to contagion; whose natures being most excellent, are, for that very reason, capable of becoming most depraved.' Windham had been very close to Fox in the early days of the French Revolution, but those who remembered Fox's earlier manoeuvres for power made the eighteenth-century accusation that the Napoleonists simply wanted office and would not stop at treason to get it. But the fundamental trouble in disposing of them was that they were manifestly English. It was this that made Captain Brenton insist on speaking French to Mackenrot when he tried to rescue Napoleon from Plymouth Sound. The cartoonists covered them with tricolours and liberty bonnets for the same reason. If a Frenchman was building a cantonment outside Holland House, it was exactly what was wanted.

The scandal changed its character with the disappearance of Napoleon. History is written by the victors, and victory is not explained by memories of division. Waterloo was the foundation of a certain complacency in the nation, understandable after twenty years of war. The growing opposition to the war in the Hundred Days, when the minority demanding peace rose to 97 in the Commons and 44 in the Lords, was overlooked by mutual consent.

A substantial section of the Napoleonists and all those on the borderline helped in the process by burying their past. Leigh Hunt writes in his *Autobiography* that he had thought of Bonaparte at the time 'as I have thought of him ever since; to wit that he was a great soldier and little else'. But in the *Examiner* he had praised him over a long period for his talents, his asceticism, his energy in prosperity, his prudence in adversity, and his protection of literature, art, and science, 'which in turn reflected glory on him'. He was 'a wonderful man', unequalled among his contemporaries for political wisdom.

Lord John Russell almost at once joined Grey in the campaign for parliamentary reform and became Prime Minister in the middle of the century. In the *Recollections* he wrote as an old man, he forgot his competition with Lady Holland to reach Elba and his dash back to the Commons to oppose the war. What he remembered was that Napoleon seemed to him an incurable aggressor who was about to renew his attempt to 'govern Europe'.

The same change of emphasis occurred more quickly in smaller men. The Hon. J. W. Lyttelton, who interviewed Napoleon on the *Northumberland*, showed no trace of sympathy for him or for Whitbread. It would be impossible to guess that he had voted for Whitbread's motion against the war on 28 April and had gone into the lobby with him three weeks before Waterloo. 'Mr. Whitbread', he told Napoleon, 'was mad.'

James Boaden, the biographer of Mrs. Inchbald, wrote about her politics after her death with an amusement which was only just short of ridicule and acquitted himself of any fellow feeling. But he had happened to meet Joseph Farington while out walking before dinner a week before Waterloo, and Farington noted that Boaden distinguished himself from others by deploring the war. 'He thought peace with France might have been made with safety. . . . He was decidedly of the opinion that the Allied powers would not succeed in their object.'

The destruction of Napoleon did not of course dispose of what he had stood for in England. Its effect, when the dust of reaction had settled, was to allow the struggle for reform to begin again without being compromised as an alien menace. The Napoleonists who did not bury themselves in a common grave with their hero played a prominent part in that struggle, and increased their effectiveness by shaking off their association with him. A major victory was won by Lord John Russell at the end of the twenties in the repeal of the Test Act which excluded Dissenters and Catholics from office under the Crown. Grey's Reform Bill, which followed in 1832, abolished the Rotten Boroughs and gave the vote to householders rated at £10, or about half the middle classes. Dissenters were admitted to the universities in 1851 and Jewish disabilities were removed soon afterwards. Although political emancipation was far from complete, the main hope of the middle classes was achieved and they marked it by bringing to an end a substitute gratification which had changed the face of London.

The first residential square built by Inigo Jones at the beginning of the seventeenth century had proved what could be gained by aristocratic resi-

dents who were willing to accept the inconvenience of living in compartments under the domination of a plan. The grandeur of Covent Garden
was excessive by English standards, but the idea was not hard to adapt.
Speculative builders laid out twelve more squares by the end of the century,
and in the eighteenth century another fifteen.

There were two noticeable changes in them. The Italian dream of magnificence had become English. The arcades which were to have shielded
people from a southern sun were replaced by a stucco front, catching as
much of the English light as possible and emphasizing the unity of the
square by its presence on all sides. The centre was covered by lawns and
flower beds, and the portico of the church turned into a classical lodge, still
with four pillars which derived from Greece, but serving the needs of the
beadle who looked after the garden. The elegant railings which surrounded
it kept out dogs and the rest of humanity.

At the same time the residents of the squares had changed their character.
By the beginning of the war with France the demand was almost wholly
middle class. Samuel Pepys Cockerell, in his memorial of 1790 on the
development of Bloomsbury, insists that the 'features of attraction' should
be available to subordinate parts of his scheme,

and that these subordinate parts be so calculated as to comprise all classes of
building from the first class down to houses of twenty-five pound per annum
without the lower classes interfering with or diminishing the character of those
above them. . . .

In the twenty years of war, when public building came to a halt and the
history of public architecture is a blank, more squares were built in London
than in the whole of the two previous centuries. There were extraordinary
difficulties, which we have seen: rising prices, shortage of materials, especially of timber, and an increasing number of bankruptcies which led to the
prediction that no more squares would be built. But the development was
continuous. By the middle of the century, when it stopped, over 200 squares
had been built and a quarter of a million people lived in them out of the
population of less than three million.

The peculiar character they gave to London was already established by
the end of the war. They 'particularly attract the notice of foreigners', says
Ackermann's *Repository* in January 1812, 'as there is no city in the world in
which they are so numerous.'

The two great architects of the period, Henry Holland and John Nash,
both made central contributions—Holland by building the model scheme
of Hans Town in Knightsbridge and Nash with a fantastic border of houses
around Regent's Park. Sir John Summerson says of Nash's project that
from the distance the façades hinted at glories which make the palaces of

Greenwich and Hampton Court seem provincial, but behind the façade 'are rows and rows of identical houses, identical in their narrowness, their thin pretentiousness, their poverty of design'.

From the last decade of the eighteenth century until they had achieved power, the English middle classes shared the dilemma of the English Romantics, and their solution in that period was not very different. In 1797, when Coleridge finally abandoned his hopes of utopia, he had his great vision of Xanadu in a dream brought on by opium. He had read, just before, about a palace built by Kubla Khan in a walled enclosure of ten square miles. The refined splendour of the palace and its pleasure grounds in his dream is counterbalanced by a chasm running through it with a torrent which flings up rocks to the sound of voices prophesying war. When he was writing down his memory of the dream, Coleridge was interrupted by a person on business from Porlock and was unable to complete it. The person from Porlock has been ill-used by literary historians for his concern with business but they should perhaps have credited the middle classes with the completion of Coleridge's poem.

While the war lasted, most members of these classes accepted that they could do nothing more to achieve power without endangering the gains of the past, but they staked a claim to worlds they had hardly noticed before. They discovered an interest in the past and co-opted it inside and outside their houses as well as in museums. They began to feel as strongly for nature and the country and took more interest in Mungo Park's discoveries in Africa than in the city around them. It was as if they were exploring a universe which they intended to claim as their own.

When the struggle for reform had been won, but not until then, the English middle classes began to accept Napoleon as a hero. More books were written about him in English in the century since the Reform Act than have ever been written about any man. The chief landmarks in the debates are perhaps Carlyle, Emerson, Chesterton and Belloc, Shaw and Sir Alan Herbert. Beginning in 1841, with Carlyle's lectures on Hero Worship, these works at first include fierce criticism, as if the threat of his ambition were still a reality. For Carlyle he was the true Democrat, 'our last Great Man', who was undone by a moral flaw; for Emerson 'the agent or attorney of the middle classes', destroyed by his lack of principle. Richard Cobden, facing the challenge of business in Manchester, was inspired by a 'Bonapartian ideal', and Samuel Smiles recommended it as a potent means of self-help. By the twentieth century Belloc was seeing Napoleon as the saviour of Europe who was thwarted by an accidental set of weaknesses which included his health and blindness to religion. Shaw, in *The Man of Destiny*, *The Apple Cart*, and *On the Rocks*, has an irrepressible sympathy in answer to the distaste of Wells, and Sir Alan Herbert, after two world wars, sees Napoleon as a wholly mis-judged figure who asked nothing better than to co-operate in a lasting peace.

The inarticulate decorated their walls with Aglio's lithographs and put bronze statuettes on their mantelpieces. There were anthologies of his sayings and predictions, his campaigns and love affairs. A Napoleon Calendar, with a daily message of encouragement, begins the New Year with the reminder that 'like everything else in Corsica, my education was pitiful'. The day of his death is still advertised every year in the 'In Memoriam' column of *The Times*.

Wellington dwindled by comparison. His name which was given to a thousand streets and public houses in the first half of the century became a mere badge of gentility. On the field of Waterloo his memory was so feebly preserved by the English that the seventh Duke made a public appeal for funds on the 150th anniversary of the battle.

It is just possible that one or two of the latter-day admirers of Napoleon would have acclaimed him in his lifetime. The most likely is G. K. Chesterton, who not only adopted Fox as his hero and wrote *The Napoleon of Notting Hill*, but defied his contemporaries by supporting Kruger in the Boer War and Mussolini before the invasion of Abyssinia. For the others Napoleon was above the battles of the present. If we want to find the true descendants of the Napoleonists we must look at the scene when ideological war once more divided the world and the dictators who threatened to impose a solution had the uglier names of Hitler and Stalin.

# V. MODERNS

*Brutus had rather be a villager,*
*Than to repute himself a son of Rome*
*Under these hard conditions, as this time*
*Is like to lay upon us.*
*Julius Caesar:* Act I, Scene II

# I

On the eve of the Second World War signs of dissent on the right and left became so prominent in England that they misled many people into thinking that she would lack the will to resist Hitler's aggression and Stalin's manoeuvres to strengthen the position of Russian Communism. In the preceding century the progress of reform had passed the limits set by Fox and approached those of Paine. Hitler and Stalin were so much more repugnant than the bronze figure of Napoleon that it would have seemed academic and frivolous to recall the Napoleonists as a precedent. Sir Oswald Mosley, who had close links with his ancestor, the second baronet, pointed out that his opposition to war was in a recognizable tradition. 'Charles James Fox opposed the war with France,' he wrote, 'and most of the Whig leaders hurried to Paris to dine with Napoleon during the brief Peace of Amiens.' He recalled the words of Lloyd George in the Boer War: 'Is every politician who opposes a war during its progress of necessity a traitor?' But Mosley's claim to Whig ancestry seemed an evasion to a community set on maintaining itself against a greater threat than before. W. H. Auden called him 'the descendant of Pitt'. The return of the Napoleonists deserves a footnote because their descent was authentic and their motives again went unrecognized.

The example set by Byron as the champion of small nations under the heel of an empire had a whole series of successors in the nineteenth century. Sometimes it was a businessman like Sir John Bowring, secretary of the Greek Committee, or a renegade official like Sir Richard Burton, who adopted a foreign culture. Several seemed to lose their identity for long periods—Burton in Moslem India and Arabia, Lafcadio Hearn in Japan, Doughty in Arabia, followed by St. John Philby and T. E. Lawrence. Agitation in Westminster won important gains in self-determination throughout the nineteenth century at the expense of the Habsburg and Ottoman empires. In the case of Garibaldi support was coloured by anti-Popery; five million people cheered 'the Dictator' in London and a red blouse, known as the garibaldi, became fashionable among women; but sympathy was usually less widespread and sometimes amounted to no more than a tourist excursion by intellectuals. As a whole the tendency to desert England for some remote civilization has struck Geoffrey Gorer as a major character trait in the English which has not been explained.[1]

Although foreign adoptions were defections of a kind, they only caused anxiety when they compromised relations with allies. They contributed to England's prosperity as the workshop of the world and seemed to be in untidy alliance with imperialism. But at the end of the nineteenth century a variation appeared which hinted at the origins we can recognize. In the Boer War a minority took the side of the enemy against England. Little Englanders, as they were called, were a determined group headed by Lloyd George. They included among others Chesterton, Bertrand Russell, and the Reverend Basil Martin, a Unitarian minister.

Culturally the Boers were not of great interest. President Kruger, who led them, had a background which was limited to the Bible and especially the Old Testament as interpreted by the extreme Dopper sect of the Dutch Reformed Church. He had taken part in the Great Trek of the eighteen thirties which had brought the Boers out of Cape Colony to escape grievances left by the abolition of slavery. In the interior they founded their own community which discriminated against foreigners and exploited Bantu labour. Their virtues were initiative and courage in the veld and they were determined to resist further domination which threatened on the discovery of diamonds. When it came under the leadership of Cecil Rhodes in the north, Kruger proved well able to deal with it and began to have visions of a Boer empire spreading across South Africa in alliance with Germany. 'This is my country,' he said to a deputation who sought to legalize the use of English, 'these are my laws. Those who do not like to obey my laws can leave my country.'

Because of early Boer victories and British mistakes, feeling ran high in England. The words Jingo and Mafeking were born and concentration camps were invented, for Boer civilians. The case of the minority of sympathizers in England was that the Boers were a group of farmers much like their counterparts at home, who were being oppressed for financial reasons. The fact that they were racialists exploiting African labour scarcely arose, because the Empire was doing the same. The government of the Orange River state, said Lloyd George, was 'perhaps the best in the world'. But the

---

[1] A generalization has been ventured by C. M. Woodhouse in *The Philhellenes* (1969). On the support from England in the Greek War of Independence, he says that 'although these philhellenes in the British armed services had nothing else in common, it is notable that all of them were dissociated from the mainstream of English life. . . . Even Byron was half a Scot though he hated to admit it. It was therefore not only in their opinions that such men represented a minority.'

emotional basis of the case was that a handful of outcasts were resisting the challenge of overwhelming power. They were one hundred thousand, said Lloyd George, 'against whom we are massing the might of forty millions. I want Wales to be free of this business.'

Lloyd George had a conviction that the 'horror and injustice' of the war would rebound against the Welsh and other minorities who were least able to afford a war. He saw no hope in the House of Commons, where the die-hard majority was solid after the Khaki Election of 1900. At the risk of his life he tried to challenge public opinion on its own ground. The climax was reached at a peace meeting in Birmingham, which was the stronghold of the Colonial Secretary, Joseph Chamberlain. In spite of warnings, Lloyd George refused a police escort and reached the hall alone in no other disguise than an overcoat and a cap pulled down on his face. When the crowds discovered that he had got through, they made a battering ram from the police barricades and forced their way in. He made his speech to reporters in front of a mob of seven thousand.

David Lloyd George's father had died before he was eighteen months old. The mother and her family were given a home by her brother, a boot-maker in the village of Llanystumdwy in North Wales. It was 'the blackest Tory parish in the land', Lloyd George used to say, because Welsh opposition to the Tory ruling caste hardly showed its head as it did in other parishes. The bootmaker was a strict Baptist and the only Liberal who dared to declare himself. He had deep-set eyes and a flowing beard which made him look like a saint. He was slightly deaf from a blow given him at school, allegedly for speaking Welsh. The loyalty he showed to his sister and her children cost him the chance of getting married, but he was too reserved and stubborn to hint at it. Although he respected and kept on good terms with the parson and schoolmaster, he avoided the local church and Nonconformist chapels and took the family out to a Baptist chapel two miles away where he was co-pastor of the Disciples of Christ. On Sundays they walked there and back in the morning, afternoon, and evening. When his nephew was twelve he baptized him in the stream outside.

David had a sister and younger brother, but he was his uncle's favourite, and Uncle Lloyd became 'his god'. When he was elected for Caernarvon Boroughs in 1890, he found himself in much the same position as his uncle. He was a foreigner in a Parliament which looked on Welsh members, he said, 'as though we were some African tribe'.

His response, unlike his uncle's, was to counter-attack. 'Is not exclusion persecution?' he said, when challenged by the Tories to give an example of the discrimination he complained of in Welsh schools. 'Was not the dis-ability of Nonconformists and Roman Catholics from office in former days persecution? Is not exclusion of the Nonconformist in Wales persecution of the worst type?' Although he made no demand for independence for Wales, Lloyd George saw England as the oppressor and himself as his uncle's representative. The link between them was so close that they continued to exchange letters nearly every day in the eleven years in which he sat in the Cabinet before becoming Prime Minister. He accepted as much of the old man's advice as he could though he was irritated by his political *naïveté*, and saw him drift out of touch at the approach to war. 'Nothing but the possibility of avoiding it or curtailing its results would keep him in office another day,' his uncle notes in his diary on 4 August 1914, when Lloyd George had already sided with the majority in the Cabinet.

His acceptance of the necessity of war with Germany was not limited to the balance of arguments. The importance of office seemed to Lloyd George very great. 'Have you ever thought how it felt to play God?' he once asked his son, Richard. 'The closest experience is being Chancellor of the Exchequer to the richest country on earth. You dispose of this or that—so much for necessities, so much for the needy, the sick and ailing. And an iron hand to master the strong.'

When he went to the Treasury in 1908 a financial crisis had already developed under the joint pressure of Liberal economic reforms and the arms race with Germany. The Admiralty proposed to meet the threat of the torpedo with ships of the *Dreadnought* class which could fight outside torpedo range. Lloyd George found he could finance this programme as well as his own social reforms by taxation of the rich, but it needed his 'iron hand'. In 1909, when he introduced a Land Tax and Super Tax and increased the Death Duties, the Lords rejected the Budget for the first time in modern history. On dissolution, the Conservatives were heavily defeated. The Budget was then passed, and a copy went to Uncle Lloyd, 'the real author of this Budget, with his pupil's affectionate gratitude'. The powers of the Lords were curtailed by the Parliament Act, and a limited system of insurance laid the foundation of the welfare state.

Lloyd George had discovered that as long as he was in power the social revolution could be faced at the same time as the threat from Germany. He marked the discovery by warning Germany in the Agadir crisis of 1911 that a basic challenge to British or French interests would mean war. His attitude to the invasion of Belgium three years later had thus been decided in advance. In spite of the war he transformed the economic life of England in the following decade by measures which affected the whole working class, their education, housing, and health. He also probably did more than anyone else to win the war by his energy and a single intervention in the Admiralty which mastered the U-boat offensive.

The fact that Uncle Lloyd died three months after Lloyd George had displaced Asquith as Prime Minister, may have had something to do with

U

the rapid increase in his dictatorial tendencies. He transferred power from Parliament to the Cabinet, from the Cabinet to the Inner Cabinet, and according to Austen Chamberlain, he thought of suspending the Cabinet. He believed in phrenology and tried on Napoleon's hat in Paris to see if it fitted—'*Lloyd George qui se croit Napoléon*,' said Clémenceau. His policy was anti-French in the sense that he fought for a settlement of Europe which would not leave a trail of irredentist claims to destroy it. While he stead-fastly pursued this aim in international conferences—and failed to achieve it for Germany—he undermined his own position at home by delivering him-self into the hands of the Conservatives when the collapse of the post-war boom made them insist on economy. His promise to build a country fit for heroes became a music-hall joke.

In his last year in office in 1922 he made a final attempt to re-establish his prestige by calling an international conference at Genoa. 'I am fighting the most difficult battle of my life,' he wrote, 'and the most decisive for better or for worse.' Genoa happened to be the port from which Byron sailed for Greece in 1823 a year before his death at Missolonghi.

As the conference broke down, Lloyd George drove every day past the Casa Saluzzo which Byron had rented on a hill in the suburb of Albaro over-looking the bay. He was his favourite English poet, and he sent to London for a copy of the *Poems*. 'I am in a mood to chuck politics altogether', he wrote to Frances Stephenson, 'and retire to Italy like Byron and Shelley who told the world to go to the devil.' When he came back to London, he made a passionate stand on behalf of the Greek communities in Asia Minor in the conflict he had brought about with Turkey. He so overestimated the sup-port for them that he went to the country in the hope that he would be swept back. He found himself in opposition for the rest of his life.

At first, in this period of twenty-two years, he made constructive proposals on the problem of war debts and the relief of unemployment by major public works. Once he was received by the Cabinet, but his plans were ignored and his party dwindled to the members of his own family. He sometimes compared himself with Charles James Fox. He, too, was the Man of the People who had a special sympathy with America. When his isolation was complete and the National Government had consolidated its position, he formed a growing admiration for Hitler. By 1936 the dictator's success in Europe overshadowed everything in English domestic politics, and Lloyd George went to Germany for two interviews with Hitler. It was difficult for him to see in him anything but a heroic response to the wrongs imposed by Versailles. 'He is the George Washington of Germany,' he wrote in the *Daily Express*, in September 1936.

Lloyd George had remained loyal to the cause of minorities in general. He had given support to the Jewish case for a national home and he was on the side of the Republican Government in Spain. He pressed the Spanish case on Hitler at length. 'We talked about everything, including Spain,' he told Lord Dawson, 'and we talked with great bluntness and frankness.' But he had eyes only for good in the dictator. He admired his gestures, his eyes, his voice, his talk. He was impressed above all by his solution of unemployment which he attributed to road-building and public works rather than rearmament. Hitler's intervention in Spain seemed to him as much the fault of the British as Napoleon's annexations in the Peace of Amiens had seemed to Fox. 'It is not Herr Hitler's fault that a friendly arrangement was not reached. He made two or three offers, which I urged the Government to act on promptly.' He was a born leader, 'the saviour of Germany'.

His euphoria lasted about eighteen months. As Hitler extended his power in the final years of peace, Lloyd George attacked the Government for delay in rearming and repeated failure in meeting the threat. His belief in Hitler as the representative of Germany turned into a belief in his invincibility. It lasted for a decade, like Fox's admiration of Napoleon. At an early stage of the war, he told the editor of the *New Statesman*, Kingsley Martin, that there was no chance of winning. 'He thought we might be invaded, but not out and out defeated', wrote Kingsley Martin. 'His view was that in such circumstances, if he were not identified with Churchill, he might be England's last chance as a negotiator.' He had ideas for the more efficient prosecution of the war but declined to join the War Cabinet because he would have been a subordinate. Hitler, for his part, saw Lloyd George very much as Napoleon had seen Fox, as the man who would have changed the course of history. 'Churchill's predestined opponent was Lloyd George,' he said in 1942. As the war continued, Lady Lloyd George was so bewildered by her husband's interest in the broadcasts of William Joyce from Hamburg that she thought a psychiatrist would be needed 'to give an explanation of this extraordinary phase in L. G.'s life'.

We must notice that Lloyd George used Biblical language to describe Hitler. He was not only the saviour of Germany, but 'as far as Germany is concerned, the resurrection and the life'. At lunch with Ribbentrop before the first of his interviews with Hitler, he is reported by A. J. Sylvester to have advised him to pay more attention to Churchill—'if you get him into your Church, it would be well worth while.'

The first Biblical figure in his life had of course been Uncle Lloyd. As a preacher he could sway his audience as he liked and reduce them to tears. Like Kruger, he was a man of one book. Although he was a cobbler who was singled out by his radicalism and dissent, the village held him in a kind of respectful awe. He was a kindly man and his authority was so great that he rarely needed to exert it. He was a teetotaller and non-smoker, so that young men put their pipes away at his approach and farmers made a detour to avoid him on the way to the pub. His youngest nephew, William, only challenged him once—on the servitude of walking to and fro to the remote chapel. His reply, that freedom only existed within the law of God, silenced the boy for life.

David alone was encouraged to argue. Their uncle was 'over-indulgent' to him, said his brother. 'He was the apple of Uncle Lloyd's eye, the king of the castle, and like the other king, could do no wrong in Uncle Lloyd's eyes, and woe betide any who said anything to the contrary.' David responded with a devotion which seemed to know no limits and has been accepted as the guiding influence of his life. His motives were compelling. It was not only that Uncle Lloyd was an outcast like himself; he had singled him out for his love when he had taken the family into his home.

It has been said, nevertheless, that Lloyd George as a politician was conspicuously disloyal; 'he repaid loyalty with disloyalty,' as if the reaction of gratitude had never come to life in him. There were in fact as strong motives for revolt against Uncle Lloyd as for loyalty. He was the tenant of a five-roomed cottage. To the refugees in their need he was a powerful man of property who gave them refuge; but there was a tradition that they themselves should have inherited a house on the coast through their father. The idea gained hold on the two boys in his cottage and was actually investigated by their father's solicitor.

Uncle Lloyd was the son of a cobbler like himself, but David's father, Mr. George, had been an elementary school teacher in Manchester, the new industrial centre of the world beyond Uncle Lloyd's horizon. He was a man of many books, not one. His widow thought he would have been a writer of distinction if he had lived. He had left her some hundreds of pounds, and she was able to buy the children's clothes and contribute to the housekeeping. They were among the better dressed children in the school.

David naturally loved his mother. When the father died, he helped his sister to lay stones across the road to prevent 'bad people taking away Mummy's furniture'. In their uncle's house, her first task on baking day was to light the oven, but it was worn out and she had to cover the holes with sheets of brown paper struck together with paste. The old shoemaker was too set in his ways and too much a lover of peace to ask the landlord for a new one. 'I do not think', says William George, 'Uncle Lloyd ever asked him to do any repairs.' The mother developed severe asthma and eventually diabetes. Uncle Lloyd nursed her with impotent devotion. 'I shall never forget', said her older son, 'seeing my mother struggle for her breath whilst my uncle knelt down by her side, rubbing her hand and uttering soothing words of sympathy.' As the attacks returned, David had doubts about his uncle's effectiveness but William thought him 'quite a good doctor'.

David already seemed to dance and shine with ambition. 'I liked to climb a certain oak tree and sit perched high up in the branches,' he said. As he sat there with a copy of Euclid on his knees, the conviction dawned on him that he was a genius with unlimited possibilities. His brother describes his anger at seeing another boy sitting in a tree.

Dafydd came along and started shaking the branch violently, swaying it to and fro and up and down. The little lad was nearly frightened to death but Dafydd continued to rock the branch until he had had enough of the game himself. . . . I never understood how it was possible for him to withstand the little chap's cries for mercy.

With Uncle Lloyd himself he made use of his freedom to challenge him on his own ground. 'He steeped himself in Bible-reading,' says Lloyd George's son, 'not because he had any special regard for religion, but in order to cap quotations with more trenchant references of his own.' He could not bring himself to believe in the literal truth of the Bible, which was the central tenet of the Disciples of Christ, and once he made a thrust at the heart of his uncle's faith. 'There was a moment of deep quiet, a look of grave concern,' and he warned him gently to suppress his doubts.

In private Lloyd George had a nickname for his uncle. He was 'the Bishop'. The Church of course was the enemy, and he attacked it more fiercely than the property-owners, with whom he sometimes allied himself as poacher-turned-gamekeeper. While he dutifully made the Sunday journeys to the Baptist chapel, he revolted against the procession from school to the church, as William had tried to revolt against the pilgrimages to the chapel. When the rector paid a diocesan visit to the school, he organized a strike against saying the creed. The rector was an imposing figure with a beard, and the headmaster had to stand beside him as the silence lengthened. A point came when William George could not bear the man's humiliation and broke the silence with the first words of the creed. David diagnosed a failure of nerve and beat him up afterwards.

Where David's revolt was not checked by his allegiance to Uncle Lloyd, but actually sanctioned by it, he was quite ruthless. When the gentle old man forgot himself and appeared out of character, he challenged him to his face. Once, when the boys came home late and refused him an explanation, he came into their room with a cane. William, knowing his man, began to cry and whispered to David to do the same. He declined to make a sound. When the beating was over, the young widow had a crisis of asthma so that Uncle Lloyd had to spend the night comforting her.

David already had a rival court. In the fields around the village he was in turn Napoleon, Abraham Lincoln, and Louis Napoleon, with a retinue whom he rewarded and enemies and traitors he punished. But the intimate and overwhelming pleasure was to dominate his own family in the cottage

—his god-fearing young mother under the sway of Uncle Lloyd, his sister, and Uncle Lloyd's mother, whom he succeeded in winning. In adult life, when he admitted he had been spoilt, he gave pride of place to the women. 'First of all I was spoiled by my grandmother; then by my mother and by my old uncle.' He married when he was twenty-five and in the following year fought his first by-election in Caernarvon. In the middle of the campaign it was discovered that a young widow in the town was going to have a child by him. Earl Lloyd George describes it as a rebellion.

My father was a natural rebel on every level. He was steeped in massive reading about revolutionary times, a devotee of literature concerned with free thought— Charles Bradlaugh, Voltaire, forerunners of Shaw and Wells. The young widow listened and marvelled, and her eyes grew wider. She was an educated woman who was susceptible to the wilful artistry of his ideas. And he had a natural instinct about feminine weakness, as we have seen; he took full account not only of her sensitivity to 'free thought' but to the discontent of her widowed state.

The widow accepted an annuity in return for her silence and Lloyd George was returned to the Commons. It was the model of many future affairs.

There was a sense in which his revolt against Uncle Lloyd was now in the open. The old man had hoped he would become a minister like himself. In 1904 Lloyd George told Sir Herbert Lewis that if he himself had become a preacher, he 'would have started a new sect', but at the time the question of his future did not turn on theology. A Baptist minister had to support himself. The tiny capital left by the father lent weight to his mother's view, and she backed her son's wish to become a solicitor. Uncle Lloyd, when the decision was taken, spent himself on the campaign. The village school shut its doors on the boy automatically when he was twelve, but his uncle managed to coach him in Latin and French as well as English.

There were two main phases of about equal length in the career which ended with Lloyd George's resignation as Prime Minister. In the first, which included his passionate struggle for the Boers, he emerged as the terror of the Church and the property-owners and eventually as the Man of the People against the House of Lords. In the second, as a Cabinet minister and eventually Prime Minister, he remained as much in opposition as before. He opposed Asquith and the Liberal hierarchy, the admirals and generals, and eventually the Conservatives with whom he had allied himself to break Asquith.

Asquith, the first enemy, came from not much less humble circumstances than himself. In childhood he had attended the Rehoboth Chapel of the Congregationalists in Yorkshire, but he asked nothing better than to get as far away from his origins as possible. His radicalism had once been strong, and he did the groundwork on the pensions scheme which Lloyd George later put into effect, but after the death of his first wife, he spent most of his spare time in society, especially with women of a certain distinction, among whom he married Margot Tennant. He was a classical scholar, and it was as if his brilliance at school and Oxford had transferred itself to his physical presence. Coming out of the Athenaeum he looked like a bishop who had left his gaiters inside. Asquith had in fact a strong interest in the upper clergy. According to Mr. Roy Jenkins, he exchanged 'two or more letters a week with Randall Davidson, the Archbishop of Canterbury, upon the subject. They discussed in detail not merely bishoprics, but deaneries and canonries, when these fell vacant and were Crown appointments.'

If he seemed like a bishop to Lloyd George, there was a deeper resemblance to Uncle Lloyd. Asquith was over-generous in loyalty. He gave office and stood by his colleagues without much thought for himself. When he chose Lloyd George to succeed him at the Treasury, it was not a move which imposed itself. He had a distaste for Welshmen and demagogues but felt the appointment was a duty to the party for reasons of balance. He brushed aside the objections of the King and saw Lloyd George through the hostility of the Lords and the scandals of his private life. Within two years of the particularly ugly Marconi scandal, he had to protest to him about leakages to the press which were beginning to damage his own authority as Prime Minister. He was surprised at the extent of Lloyd George's dismay. 'His eyes', he says, 'were wet with tears.' It was as if destitution would have been a fitting punishment for such disloyalty.

Ll. G. declared that he owed everything to me, that I had stuck by him when every man's hand was against him and that he would (1) rather break stones, (2) dig potatoes, (3) be hung, drawn and quartered than to do an act or say a word or harbour a thought that was disloyal to me. . . .

Eighteen months later a letter was circulated to the Cabinet by Lord Lansdowne which is usually accepted as the starting-point of appeasement in the twentieth century. Russia had withdrawn from the war, and the Lansdowne proposal was to explore the possibilities of a negotiated peace with Germany. A descendant of the second and third Lords Lansdowne who had been intimates of Holland House and had supported a compromise peace in turn with revolutionary France and Napoleon, Lansdowne was the first Conservative of his line. Asquith did not accept his views, but the letter was leaked to the press and fathered on him. Rumours about German connections had begun to surround Asquith. He had money in Krupps; his daughter was supposed to be engaged to a German admiral; his wife played tennis with Germans, and hard courts were rumoured to be landing grounds for German aircraft.

The Lansdowne letter brought to a head a more justified belief that the war was being fought without enough conviction and drive. Lloyd George came into the open with a demand to lead a War Committee in sole charge

of operations. The press supported him and Asquith found himself in a
position where he had to resign.

When Lloyd George became Prime Minister in December 1916, it was in
the interests of the country. Asquith's lack of energy and initiative had become dangerous, but what made it seem unacceptable to Lloyd George was
a reaction he had formed in childhood. Uncle Lloyd had been a saint and
not a man of action. He had moral courage and loyalty and kindness but
was without initiative. The worn-out oven was only one of the troubles in
the cottage which were never solved for fear of endangering relations with
the landlord. He tried to comfort his sister in her attacks of asthma, but did
nothing more effective and never brought in a specialist who could cure her.

Lloyd George was genuinely grateful to Asquith for what he had done
for him but, according to his eldest son, thought him quite unfit for the role
of bulldozer.

Asquith was temperamentally a most gentle and kindly person and with no
sense of the urgency of the vast problems facing the country. Father described
him as like a family doctor with a gift for the bedside manner. 'If the patient was
making normal progress, he would say, "There you are. You'll be well in no
time." And if there was a relapse, he would say, "Now these fluctuations are to
be expected, you know. The worst thing is to worry." ' And to worry was just
what father thought it necessary to do. . . .

If it was a memory of his uncle's loyalty which brought tears to his eyes
when Asquith rebuked him, we must ask how it was that he repaid Asquith
so differently from Uncle Lloyd.

The most obvious contrast between the two summed up all the others.
Uncle Lloyd was an outcast, in religion and politics, socially, as a Welshman, and physically in his deafness. The alliance with him was binding
because it belonged to the wilderness. His chosen nephew outdid him in
dissent. He defied the schoolmaster, the parson, and the landlord, not by
his uncle's doctrinal stand but by violence. The aggression which built up
in him in the old man's cottage was diverted in full flood against the
'blackest Tory parish in the land', which isolated him. This one loyalty was
so demanding and so rigorously observed, that it absolved him from all
others, which became empty formalities.

Asquith, in contrast to Uncle Lloyd, had turned his back on the wilderness. He had deserted the provinces for the capital, the Rehoboth Chapel
for the appointment of bishops in the Athenaeum. He preferred reading or
dining in country houses to the grind of fighting the war. He liked his wine.
When he came to the assistance of Oscar Wilde's counsel, in the company
of Bishop Gore and Lady Ottoline Morrell, he was ridiculed by Lord Alfred
Douglas as 'Old Squiffy'.

Uncle Lloyd of course knew about the debt to Asquith. He showed an interest in his nephew's relations with him and sent anxious inquiries when the revolt broke out. 'Tell Uncle Lloyd the P.M. got on *very* well,' Lloyd George wrote when he re-crossed the Channel from an Allied conference at the end of November 1916, as their relationship was breaking up. 'Never better. Most happily. Agreed in all things. He is alright as long as you get him away from sinister and malevolent surroundings.' The conference had been in Paris. The sinister surroundings were in the capital of England which combined Babylon, Nineveh, Sodom and Gomorrah. It was Asquith's allegiance to the centre of corruption which freed Lloyd George's hand—though not, perhaps, Uncle Lloyd's. The old man grew seriously ill as the crisis developed and preached only one more sermon after his nephew's succession. He took as his text the short 23rd Psalm of David, ending, 'Surely goodness and mercy shall follow me all the days of my life: and I will dwell in the House of the Lord for ever.'

In 1919, when Asquith and the Liberal Party had been finally destroyed by Lloyd George in coalition with the Conservatives, an article appeared in the Welsh paper *Y Beirniad* ('The Adjudicator') by the Prime Minister's brother, William, describing Uncle Lloyd's last sermon in detail. After quoting, 'Surely goodness and mercy shall follow me all the days of my life,' he made a heavily italicized attempt to convey the climax of the sermon.

*Surely*. Listen to the confident ring in his voice. 'All the days of my life.' For better for worse, in fair and foul weather—'*Surely*—*ALL* the days of my life.' Neither was this enough. The present life will soon be over—what then, David?[1]

Lloyd George had carried away from his childhood two visions of power which he met repeatedly in his career. The first, which he did not connect with the old shoemaker, was of an ineffective potentate, stubborn, entrenched, committed to the methods of the past and in touch with the representatives of the established order. When he first wrote for the papers he signed himself 'Brutus'. Brutus had also been adopted by an uncle. When Lloyd George met his Caesar in the Capitol, no scruple restrained him. The greater his hold on respectable opinion, the more firmly a part of the established order, the more determined was his thrust. The victims were in turn Asquith, Kitchener, Haig, Baldwin, Neville Chamberlain.

The other vision was also of a potentate, stubborn and even more archaic, but redeemed by his position in the wilderness. If this figure was a rebel inside the country, he could be a temporary ally, like Churchill or Beaverbrook, but if he was a foreigner committed to the interests of his people against the pretensions of England, he was an uncanonized saint, like Kruger or Hitler. Their virtue was in their courage against odds. If the

[1] The passage is reprinted in the biography in Welsh of Uncle Lloyd by William George but has not appeared in translation.

odds shortened into rivalry, their virtue diminished but their strength increased. Invasion itself Lloyd George was reluctant to believe in, but he insisted that it should be warded off by negotiation.

He could reverse his attitude and his tactics according to his own situation. 'His mind', said Dr. Thomas Jones, 'had few deep grooves.' A policy which seemed unjust when he was in opposition became a crusade when he was in power; pacifists who had supported Kruger became traitors if they supported the Kaiser. In home policy his alliances and desertions shocked the country as it had not been shocked since Fox allied himself with Lord North at the end of the American war. But deep grooves existed in him, and the proof is in the coherent pattern they made up.

He spent longer in opposition than any other great English statesman, including Fox.[1] He was at his best in adversity, 'when the gale ran high.' His violence showed itself mainly in speech. When Simon deserted him in the Commons, he traced the path of a slug in the air—he was an 'honourable gentleman who crossed the floor, leaving a trail of slime behind him'. At Churt he called one of his pigs Sir Herbert Samuel. On the eve of an important speech he had trouble with his throat, which made it difficult to speak at all. Uncle Lloyd is said to have saved his life on one occasion by pushing a feather dipped in honey down his throat. Earl Lloyd George says 'it troubled him when he was in a nervous state—a mental state—on the eve of a particularly important debate.'

There were times when his violence returned against him in fantasies of persecution. He accused Sylvester of giving to the press quotations from earlier speeches which reflected on his judgement. He believed that Chequers was haunted by its previous occupants and that Chong, his chow dog, could see one of them in the gallery. But if he was violent, he was a genuine pacifist who set the highest value on peace; he was a humanitarian who did more for those who were unable to look after themselves than anyone else in the first half of the twentieth century. His eldest son, whom he disinherited, insists that he had a 'sense of compassion'. 'When I was a child, my father was invariably kind and gentle.' When his daughter Mair died, he nearly went mad.

He was a dictator who had the most spectacular rival courts of his time. The most important before he gained power was the electorate. 'I reach out my hand to the people and draw them to me,' he told one of his biographers. As Prime Minister he founded the Cabinet Secretariat as a device for enforcing his will. He established the Garden Suburb in huts in St. James's Park, with staff of his own to advise him independently of the Departments.

[1] Fox spent nearly thirty years in opposition; Lloyd George thirty-six. Fox was a junior minister for a little over three years and was three times Foreign Secretary for a few months. Lloyd George was a Cabinet minister for eleven years and Prime Minister for six.

He sold honours, ranging from over £150,000 for a peerage to £11,000 for a knighthood, and less for Orders of the British Empire. The proceeds built up a fund 'to promote any political purpose approved by the Rt. Hon. David Lloyd George'. He surrounded himself with sycophants and dependants.

In an age when Cabinet ministers did not go abroad, he travelled more widely than any Prime Minister before or since. When he returned from Versailles, King George sent his carriage to the station and he was crowned with a wreath of bay leaves, preserved in the Lloyd George museum in Llanystumdwy. 'He was transported in special trains and special steamers', says Dr. Jones, 'from one meeting to another accompanied by ministerial colleagues, secretaries, attendants, and journalists, the accommodation provided for him eclipsing that which royalty enjoyed when going abroad.' On resigning the Premiership, he feared he would be out of power for twenty years. He almost at once toured America and wrote to Frances Stephenson, she said, that 'if he had still been Prime Minister no greater fuss could have been made of him.' Ten years later while touring India he wrote from Bombay, 'I might still have been the Prime Minister of Britain.' When he called on Hitler it was in three cars.

To be bilingual in English and Welsh was a condition of his career, but journalists have remarked that when he spoke English he seemed to be translating from Welsh. He had workmanlike French. 'Good God,' said Kitchener, seeing him in urgent conversation with Edwin Montague, 'the man speaks Yiddish, too.' On the platform he was a supreme actor and in private life he had a more serious respect for the stage than any statesman since Fox. He sent a telegram of condolence to Lady Playfair on the death of Sir Nigel Playfair, whom he scarcely knew. 'I had never imagined that Ll. G. was a mimic,' said Harold Nicolson, in the year of the visits to Hitler, 'but he managed to recall to me the physical presence of Balfour and Curzon, and to render Attlee with a vividness that was unsurpassed.'

He was a dandy, spruce and glowing in his youth and picked out by his long white hair and Tyrolean cloak in old age. 'One of my duties as his private secretary', says Sylvester, 'was to be present when his hairdresser was attending to him, to watch closely lest too much was cut off those silvery locks, and to ensure that the white moustache retained its trimness.' He increasingly surrounded himself with animals. On his model farm at Churt, the foremen were not allowed to shoot finches in spite of the damage to his crops. He had collies, corgies, a chow, and a St. Bernard. 'There was an Airedale,' says the late Earl Lloyd George,

a fine brute, but something of a terror to comparative strangers to the home. There was Juan, the black cat, and Blanco the white one. And Doodie, a tame white pigeon, presented to him on his American trip, who would caress his eyebrows after carefully removing his pince-nez.

He sold honey from the estate in bottles labelled, 'From the apiary of D. Lloyd George, O.M., M.P.'

In Lloyd George the Napoleonists probably had their greatest representative. If he lacked the scope and urbanity of Fox, he was more effective because he was a genuine product of the people. He was 'the nearest thing England has known to a Napoleon,' says A. J. P. Taylor, 'a supreme ruler maintaining himself by individual achievement.' The achievement, though greater in his lifetime than that of the original Napoleonists, was based on the character pattern they had in common. Loyalty, not disloyalty, was at its centre, but because his loyalty was to Uncle Lloyd in the wilderness, he saw virtue outside the community, in unprivileged classes and underprivileged nations, and vice correspondingly in the strongholds of power. The need he had in childhood to divert his aggression away from Uncle Lloyd on to the entrenched holders of power was a highly charged distortion, but it corresponded to the needs of the nation at a moment when a redistribution of power was overdue.

The wealth produced by the industrial revolution had increased so fast in the nineteenth century that the prosperity of the island matched its security. To Lloyd George it was 'the richest country on earth'. But the riches were distributed among a population which had grown out of recognition. In the 150 years from the accession of George III to Lloyd George's first budget, it had increased from $7\frac{1}{2}$ million to 42 million. The original Reform Act had been widened, but the majority still had no vote, and the majority was bigger than the whole population in the time of Fox. When Lloyd George dedicated his budget to Uncle Lloyd, two-thirds of the private property was in the hands of 1 per cent of the nation.

If his main achievement was to adjust the balance of forces at home in favour of the under-dog, his bias in favour of the have-nots in foreign affairs was hardly less effective. The pro-Boer campaign was violently unpopular, but modern imperialism never recovered its complacency. The case made out by Fox for American independence had been used by British diplomacy against other empires. Lloyd George turned it back on the British and prepared the way for an empire to dissolve itself for the first time in history in the name of self-determination.

The most revealing mistake of Lloyd George's life was his failure to recognize Hitler for what he was. Politically, it had no great importance by comparison with some of his dictatorial mistakes at home—at worst it increased Hitler's belief in the prospects of appeasement and gave backing to his claim that the German armies had been stabbed in the back in 1918—but to dismiss it as the foible of a disappointed old man is to give up the attempt to understand him.

The Napoleonist syndrome does little to account for the quality of Lloyd

George's genius, but it does suggest the framework in which it operated. He had been right at Versailles, both in his struggle for a peace which was ethnically fair and in his attempt to withstand the exaction of reparations which would make German democracy unworkable. Churchill could see Hitler from the start as the 'monstrous product of former wrongs and shames', but to Lloyd George, when he himself was isolated, those wrongs and shames could only produce a saint. It was the blind spot at the centre of his genius.

## 2

Among Englishmen who were attracted by foreign dictatorships in the thirties we shall find other examples of loyalty to a background of religious dissent. In spite of the removal of discrimination in the nineteenth century and the general loss of faith which was represented in Lloyd George himself, the most common derivation of the Napoleonist still existed. But among the original Napoleonists there had been another kind of outcast, represented by Fox and Byron, whose sense of separation from the community was in part based on their awareness of descent from the Stuarts. Were there counterparts of aristocratic dissent in the thirties?

Sir Oswald Mosley of Ancoats, who led the British Fascists from 1932 to 1940, was related more closely than by descent to his ancestor the second baronet whom we have met as a supporter of Whitbread. He was born in 1896, but his parents separated and from the age of five he was brought up by his mother and his grandfathers. The Mosleys were a long-lived family, and his paternal grandfather, born in 1848, had actually known the Napoleonist second baronet in childhood and youth before the old man died in 1871. There is no record of their conversation, but few families have left a clearer account of themselves.

Sir Oswald Mosley, the second baronet, had not been a typical Napoleonist. Although he had been brought up from the age of five by his grandfather, the hat manufacturer, and had voted for peace with Napoleon, he was no ally of progressive forces. He was Lord of the Manor of Manchester, which he ruled through a medieval institution, the Court leet, with a Boroughreeve and staff of beadles. He was committed to these arrangements by his monopoly of the markets which brought him in nearly £9,000 a year.

Revolt, which had been simmering in Manchester in the eighteenth century, came to a head in the decade of the Reform Act under the leadership of Richard Cobden and a body he called 'the shopocracy'. Cobden came to Manchester in 1830. He was a calico manufacturer and by the end of the decade in close political alliance with Salis Schwabe, a calico printer from Oldenburg. The original colony of Jews had been swollen after the Napoleonic wars by an influx of refugees from Germany, some of whom became shopkeepers. They were handicapped by Mosley's control of the markets and excluded from the administration of the town. Early in 1833, four distinct petitions for Jewish emancipation were sent from the Manchester area to Parliament. In another five years Cobden had become the shopkeepers' representative. 'It will be a new era for Manchester', he said, 'when it shakes off the feudal livery of Sir Oswald Mosley, to put on the democratic garb of the Municipal Reform Act.' He petitioned the Privy Council for incorporation, and when Mosley counter-petitioned with a greater number of signatures, Cobden undertook to prove they were forgeries by putting the issue to the vote. 'The shopocracy carried the day,' he announced, on 3 July 1838.

The Mosleys had been Lords of the Manor since the reign of Elizabeth when Sir Nicolas Mosley bought the rights before becoming Lord Mayor of London. They ruled from Ancoats Hall on the eastern outskirts which had views across pleasure grounds and meadows to the River Medlock. They had given balls to the notables and land for new buildings—the Exchange, the people's dispensary, a hospital and female penitentiary, of which Lady Mosley was the patroness. But smoke from burning limestone drifted through the park and the Medlock turned black. Without giving up their manorial rights, they took their plate and the family portraits with the oak panelling on which they hung and retreated forty miles south, to Rolleston Hall in Staffordshire, where they had great estates.

In the Commons in 1833 Mosley opposed the first Bill for the emancipation of the Jews, which happened to be introduced at the beginning of Cobden's activities in Manchester. Mosley strongly denied that he was anti-Semitic in the sense of disapproving of the Jews 'as a body', but proposed to exclude them as anti-Christians from both houses of Parliament. He was horrified at the thought that a Jew might one day take the Speaker's chair. His minority was small in the Commons, but emancipation was delayed by the Lords until the middle of the century in spite of petitions from Manchester and Westminster.[1]

[1] In the Lords the Bill was supported by the Duke of Sussex and Lord Holland but opposed by the Archbishop of Canterbury.

Mosley survived in the Commons after the Reform Act, but disappeared in the election of 1837, and was spared hearing in December of that year the maiden speech of Disraeli, who had been baptized at thirteen. From Staffordshire Mosley held on to his rights in Manchester for another decade, at the end of which he got £200,000 for them. But his career seemed to him a sorry failure. He consoled himself with ten children, a Sunday School, and an unsurpassed collection of birds. He wrote books on his ancestors and the early history of Christianity in England. His hero became King Oswald, the Christian King of Northumbria, who was defeated by the pagans in the seventh century.

In the year after his local triumph over Mosley, Cobden declared war on the landed aristocracy as a whole by founding the Anti-Corn Law League. The headquarters were on the site of Peterloo, off Mosley Street, and its aim to transfer power to 'the middle and industrious classes' by abolishing the tariffs which since Waterloo had with varying success kept up the price of corn. As a manufacturer Cobden stood to gain, but there were noncon-formist and radical undertones in his case which gave it the religious strength of a crusade. He was backed by the *Manchester Guardian*, as he had been in the eviction of Mosley from the control of the city, but in this new campaign he worked out the first national system of propaganda which covered the country with mass meetings and pamphlets. It was denounced by the land-lords as a conspiracy, but in a few years he had won. When the duty on corn expired on the last day of January 1849, he was in the great crowd in Manchester which sang hymns until midnight.

Cobden had promised to turn the great country houses into 'dismantled memorials of the past', but as the Free Trade Hall rose on the site of the Anti-Corn Law League and the Great Synagogue opened its doors, the status and dignity of Rolleston Hall survived. When the new blow fell on the Mosleys, its full force and extent spanned the career of the fourth baronet, who brought up the future Fascist leader.

Mosley's grandfather went to Eton and then for four years to 'all parts of Europe' with a tutor, but he was dedicated to the land and his role as a country aristocrat. As a young man he got up at five, worked a full day with the retainers, and at harvest time thought nothing of bringing in the corn until nine. 'I ploughed, stacked, threshed,' he said. He was an amateur boxer, who drove a team, and rode to hounds. He married in 1873 and by the time he succeeded to the title and estates in 1890, his paternalism extended beyond his children to his feudal care of his work-people and the vigour and efficiency of his management.

In America the central prairies had been opened up by the railways which gave special freight rates to wheatlands bigger than the British Isles. By 1890 the price of wheat in England had dropped from about £3 a quarter to

£1. 10s. and a million acres had gone out of cultivation. Five years later, when the Manchester Ship Canal created a new Atlantic port, another million acres had gone. At that point there remained only a million and a half acres under wheat in the country.

The destruction of British agriculture might have been stopped at the end of the seventies by Disraeli, who was in power for the last time and had foretold disaster at the time of Cobden's campaign; but while the rest of Europe saved its farmlands by putting on protective tariffs against the new wheat, Disraeli did nothing. The Manchester School had helped to make England the workshop of the world and the national ideal had become urban. The agricultural workers were not peasants with small holdings but tenants whose vote could not be relied on when their earnings were less than the workers' in the towns. Their mobility had increased. They moved in and out of the towns but increasingly belonged to them and shed their loyalty to the great landowners. The nation accepted this dissolution not only because England had become the workshop of the world but because it was more than ever conscious of its security as an island.

Sir Oswald Mosley, the fourth baronet, turned to stock-breeding, at first to shire horses, and as they became an anachronism to Southdown sheep and Tamworth pigs. He was one of the ruling figures in the Shorthorn Society and the British Pig-Breeders' Association. Meanwhile, refrigeration ships had been invented and from the turn of the century four million carcasses a year were being landed from New Zealand alone.

The status of the English landed aristocracy had been acknowledged until the end of the century in the style of men's dress. The top hat, made by the first baronet Mosley in the eighteenth century, was originally the crash-helmet of the hunting field, and was still worn by everyone with social pretensions. But as the population left the ravaged countryside, they dressed for the streets. Sir Oswald, by contrast, wore a white top hat and a flowered waistcoat. His waistcoats were famous. As High Sheriff of Staffordshire, says an obituary, he drove into Stafford 'in a kind of state, with liveried and powdered footmen, for he had a high opinion of the dignity which should attach to the King's representative of the shire.' The road ran thirty miles across country above Needwood Forest and Cannock Chase, but even in that scenery the passers-by stopped to stare at the vision of a lost world.

Oswald Mosley, the grandchild, came to live with the fourth baronet when he was five. ' I was really brought up by my grandfather,' Mosley told *The Times*. His own father was a pale imitation, with a more modest top hat, side-whiskers, and a waistcoat which was only eccentric in having lapels. He was a light-weight boxer instead of a middle-weight and he felt no attraction for high office. Once, at an exhibition of boxing, he delighted the crowd by jumping into the ring and fighting the referee.

At Rolleston Hall the young boy felt warm admiration for his grand-father as well as gratitude for his surroundings. 'We had for each other a strong affection,' he says. 'Some time before he died I had developed in-tellectual and cultural interests which were strange to him, but this in no way impaired our relationship.' His grandfather was caricatured as John Bull and had the old-fashioned violence of the English countryside. Stafford-shire and Lancashire were the last great strongholds of bull-baiting, according to Windham, in the debate of 1802, and the fact that they were the main source of recruits for the King's bodyguard seemed to Windham a proof of the virility bull-baiting inspired. Mosley's grandfather was stronger than Mosley's father, even in late middle age. 'One day', says Mosley, 'my grandfather bet him he could beat him with his left hand tied behind his back. All the servants assembled to watch, and he knocked him out with one hand.' If he was violent, he also had his fears. In his will he left instructions that his coffin should not be screwed down until a doctor had put an open bottle of chloroform inside and cut the veins of his neck.

As a young man he had been a Radical like his own grandfather, the second baronet. The fear his grandfather had admitted to the Commons in 1833, that a Jew might occupy the Speaker's chair, had been more than realized when Disraeli became Prime Minister and was accepted by Queen Victoria as an intimate friend. Disraeli's refusal to defend the landed interest was a con-firmation of Sir Oswald's worst fears. The fourth baronet only became a Conservative after Disraeli's death and he made friends with the Prince of Wales, whose way of living was deplored by Victoria and Albert. He lived on until the second year of the First World War, when the success of the U-boat showed the danger to which England had been exposed by the ruin of her agriculture. He was 'commonly regarded', said the *Manchester Guardian*, 'as a picturesque survival of Old England'. He used to come up to London for the Christmas cattle shows at Islington, where he was to be seen escorting parties of farmers round the pens, prodding pigs with his stick, and digging his chubby fingers into the wool of sheep. At his death the great workshops of Manchester were the hub of the Allied war effort. Profits were soaring and the population reached three-quarters of a million. The Jewish community had become the biggest in England after London's. There were twenty-five synagogues.

The career of Oswald Mosley in the post-war world was a compound of loyalty to his father and grandfather and revolt against them. The extent of the revolt was not obvious until after his father's death in 1928; it showed itself at first mainly in the strength of his ambition and his championship of youth against the inertia of age. He had a phrase book for old age: 'the old parties', the 'old gang', 'old dead men with their old dead minds', 'the dead

x

wood of obsolescence and decadence', 'old whiskers' (for Marx), 'old Tory snobs'. While his father had served in France as a captain in the Derbyshire infantry, he had got a transfer from the Lancers to the Royal Flying Corps. On recovery from his war injuries he became the youngest member of the Commons.

In his maiden speech he prophesied that revolutionary developments in the air would demote the Navy and eliminate the role of infantry. He denounced the inclusion of air affairs in the War Department under any Minister, but particularly under Churchill, who suffered from 'a paucity of that invaluable political asset called imagination'. He returned to the attack at the end of 1919. 'We are living', he said, 'in a period which is seeing what I may call the passing of the superman or the "twilight of the gods".' The Air was in fact given a separate Department when Churchill left the War Department, and Mosley was consistent throughout the next twenty years in demanding an Air Force which would continue to give England immunity from invasion. He had little respect for the Navy as the senior service and called for economy with an arrogance which stung the Secretary for the Admiralty into asking whether he had ever been in a ship in dock. He was reduced to replying that he had consulted friends 'who have experience in this matter'.

In May 1920 Mosley had married the second daughter of the Marquess Curzon of Kedleston whose great estate lay just over the county boundary from Rolleston Hall where he had spent so much of his youth. Kedleston was 'the most splendid Georgian house of Derbyshire', according to Nikolaus Pevsner, and the great Corinthian columns of its hall must have reduced Rolleston to the perspective of a village inn. The Earl of Curzon, as leader of the Conservatives, had an obvious claim to succeed Lloyd George as Prime Minister, but his daughter, Lady Cynthia, who was an heiress in her own right, held advanced views. Mosley met her first when he was grown up, and the wedding was among the most fashionable in the twenties. It took place in the Chapel Royal in the presence of the King and Queen as well as the King and Queen of the Belgians.

In the next two years there was little in Mosley's appearance to show that he would not patiently await promotion within the ranks of the Conservative party. Leonard Woolf describes him as 'a handsome young man in top hat and morning coat carrying a gold-headed walking stick'. He opposed the brutality of the Black and Tans in Ireland, and when Lloyd George resigned in 1922 stood as an Independent. On his return, he attacked Baldwin's Government on a broad front but particularly on foreign policy. He abandoned his grandfather's faith in the *Entente Cordiale* and criticized France's attitude to a prostrate Germany as vindictive. 'You want a policy,' he told the Conservatives, in May 1923, 'a conception, a plan, vigorously thought out and vigorously executed.' He denounced a Tory baronet who defended France, as 'the last of the real individualists'. It was perhaps his most serious term of abuse. When inviting the Government to recapture the traditional virtues of the country, he added that some of those traditions had passed 'from the benches opposite and are now in the custody of honourable members around me.'

He joined the Labour Party in 1924. When he considered renouncing the title to which he would succeed at his father's death, he found he could not; but he said he did not intend to be addressed by it. The fifth baronet looked by now still more like a relic of the mid-Victorian countryside than his father before him, but he was vigorous in his late middle age and resented the prospect of extinction. He wrote an apoplectic letter to the *Daily Mail*.

I am and intend to remain a Conservative, and it has occurred to me that more valuable help would be rendered to the country by my Socialist son and daughter-in-law if, instead of achieving cheap publicity about the relinquishing of titles, they would take more material action and relinquish some of their wealth and so help to make easier the plight of some of their more unfortunate followers.

Mosley has said of himself as a young man that he was 'a bit too quick and gay in accepting a challenge'. His father's was one challenge he did not accept. He refused to answer interviewers and got his defence into the Labour *Daily Herald* on the day the letter appeared in the *Daily Mail*. Instead of referring to his father, he made a general attack on the capitalist press for using methods and arguments which aimed at weakening the Labour movement: if he or his wife gave away their money it would simply lessen their chance of being of service.

Mosley's ability in the party was outstanding and MacDonald recognized it in 1929 by giving him responsibility as Chancellor of the Duchy of Lancaster for solving the unemployment crisis under the supervision of J. H. Thomas, a former engine-cleaner, who was given the title of Minister of Employment. Unemployment had become the accepted disease of the time. It had reached two million under the post-war government of Lloyd George, fell back at first under the Conservatives, but was rising quickly again towards two million. It was not only Mosley's vigour which recommended him for the job. Question time in the post-war period had been peppered with his interventions on behalf of ex-servicemen who could not reintegrate themselves into civilian life—the disabled who were not given hospital treatment, clerks who were not demobilized, a rough rider in the Field Artillery who had not had the pay due to him since 1914, the exile to the Russian Front in May 1919 of a sergeant who was on leave in England.

Mosley's interest in these cases was closer than that of an ordinary Member intervening on behalf of his constituents and it was more than the personal concern of an officer. For the unemployed he had a different kind of feeling, less involved than that of most Labour Members but more deeply exasperated by their removal from the productive resources of the country. No one could doubt that he would act.

For a year, at high pressure, he made proposals to J. H. Thomas while the number of unemployed continued to rise alarmingly above two million. Mosley's plans involved raising loans for capital re-equipment, but he found that Thomas, while requiring exhaustive detail in his proposals, simply passed them to Snowden at the Treasury who dismissed them as heretical. Mosley admitted that loans by themselves were a short-term expedient which must be matched by a national plan. He proposed tariffs and the public control of credit to supplement the increased purchasing power which would be produced by re-employment. Thomas, a cautious reformist, was alarmed, and Snowden, a Free Trader, was emphatic in his rejection. When the issue went to the Cabinet in May 1930, MacDonald rejected Mosley's ideas without any substitute but hope.

Mosley had begun to see the Labour leaders in the same light as the Conservatives. They made him feel he was in 'a strait-waistcoat'. Snowden had been partially paralysed from childhood; Thomas, who rejoiced in his emergence from the working class, was known as 'Mr. Top Hat'; Ramsay MacDonald maintained the Olympian calm of the Mosleys in exile. 'The Prime Minister's complacency', said Mosley, 'is perhaps one of the most serious dangers which the country has to confront.' Although he came very near to carrying the party with him at its conference in 1930 and at a special meeting in January 1931, he just failed, and in February formed his own 'New Party' to implement his plans. He was warned that he was sacrificing almost certain succession to the leadership.

A small group of distinguished people followed him. They included his wife and John Strachey, who helped to form a nucleus of intellectuals with Harold Nicolson and Christopher Hobhouse, a collateral descendant of John Cam Hobhouse, the Napoleonist friend of Byron. They founded *Action* at the beginning of October 1931 and at the end of the month they went to the polls with 24 candidates in the General Election. All were defeated. Mosley came bottom in his wife's constituency, Nicolson got less than 500 votes, and Hobhouse, who campaigned under the motto 'Vote for Hobhouse, the Children's Champion', lost his deposit.

Annihilation by the country after their stand for a new deal was a disaster for all of them. To Mosley it meant the political wilderness because he had run through the parties, including his own. With Nicolson and Hobhouse he made the response which the original Napoleonists had made to rejection: they went abroad. They chose Italy, which had been Fascist for eight years, and Hobhouse went through Germany, where Hitler was within sight of power. The last issue of *Action* explained that they did not wish 'to import Italian, German, or Russian methods and practices into this country. . . . We go to collect information from all sources, to compile and collate that information, so that if and when the country comes to pass through great events, a few of us may be prepared.'

Mosley went first to Paris, where he stayed at the Hôtel Napoléon. Nicolson called on him there on 1 January 1932, and found him looking pale but otherwise unmoved. Nicolson then went on ahead to Italy. 'The Rome Express, magnificently aligned, waits to receive me and me alone,' he wrote in his diary. 'I occupy the whole of one coach and a very little Frenchman occupies the whole of another coach.' In Rome he was met at the station by Hobhouse, who had seen Hitler. 'He has been to Munich,' Nicolson noted, 'and is full of Hitler and his men. He says the Nazis think we of the New Party have tried to do things too much on the grand. We should have begun in the alleys. . . .' In a few days they were joined by Mosley, who had his first interview with Mussolini on 7 January. 'He finds him affable but unimpressive,' Nicolson reported. It was a reaction not unlike Fox's after his visit to Napoleon, but whereas Hitler had lectured Hobhouse on the virtues of Oliver Cromwell, Mussolini warned Mosley against using force. When they got back to England later in the month Nicolson noted that 'Mussolini sent him a message telling him to call himself Fascist.'

The New Party was foundering. John Strachey and others had resigned, and Nicolson put it down to Mosley's 'autocratic methods and biting tongue'. On their return from Italy Nicolson and Hobhouse turned away from politics in order to write. Hobhouse, after toying with the idea of a biography of his ancestor, settled down to a life of Fox. 'Having advertised his admiration of Napoleon in the manner best calculated to disgust the nation,' he wrote at the beginning of a chapter, 'the worst thing Fox could do was to avail himself of the peace to visit Paris.' Nicolson, after wasting two months, wrote a satire on the year 1939.

Mosley had invitations to rejoin the Conservatives and to lead a dissident Labour movement but rejected both. In Baldwin and his school he had long since come to see 'the bucolic pig-fancier', whom he was inclined to distrust. 'Mr. Top Hat' was no better. 'Both major party machines were in the power of conservative elements who lived completely in the past,' he says in *My Life*. It would be impossible for him to re-enter the older parties, he told Nicolson: 'That by doing so he would again have to place himself in a strait-waistcoat. That he has no desire for power on those terms. That he is convinced that we are entering a phase of abnormality and that he does not wish to be tarred with the brush of the old regime.' He founded the British Union of Fascists in 1932, when unemployment was rising towards three million.

The aim was to win a majority in Parliament and then modernize the House of Lords, 'that archaic assembly', and introduce 'the leadership principle' into the Commons; but first it was necessary to attract a national following. Mosley proposed to sweep the country with a series of meetings which would assemble 50,000 people at a time. By adopting the blackshirt uniform he claimed that he was abolishing class differences and giving the movement the moral strength of a crusade. The movement concentrated mainly on London and especially on the East End, where opposition was strongest, and thereafter on the provinces, where Manchester was the most important target. The nearest ancestor of the campaign was probably the Anti-Corn Law League which had not only swept the towns but taken its semi-religious message, to the fury of the landlords, on to their own ground in the countryside.

The core of Mosley's programme already existed in the plans he had pressed on the Labour Party from 1925, but he elaborated and sharpened them. The 'first principle' of the British Union of Fascists was 'give a man a job to do'; the reason for his loss of a job was the victory of Cobdenism in the nineteenth century, which had subjugated Parliament as well as the rest of the community. Power was now held by the financiers, who pursued their own profits through international channels in disregard of the national interest. They depended on Free Trade and the free movement of capital which had brought ruin to the producer and unemployment to the worker.

In *Anti-Semitism and the British Union of Fascists*, W. F. Mandle states that 'any trend towards a forthright anti-Semitic policy [in the movement] was more or less abruptly halted in January 1934 when an "alliance" was concluded between the newspaper magnate Lord Rothermere and Sir Oswald Mosley.' Mandle later describes a break in the ' "alliance" ': 'As soon as the Rothermere–Mosley break was made official and public a mounting campaign of anti-Semitism began.' On 5 October 1934 the *Blackshirt* headlined its report of a speech made by Sir Oswald in Manchester on 29 September: ' "ALIEN YIDDISH FINANCE IS RUINING BRITISH INDUSTRY" '. Basing himself on reports of this Manchester speech in *The Times* and *Manchester Guardian* as well as the *Blackshirt,* Mandle says the onslaught was not followed up by Mosley at meetings he addressed elsewhere in the next three weeks:

Mosley's silence, save for an answer to a question at Plymouth, may have been for a variety of reasons. First, Mosley might have regretted not so much the criticism of the Jews, for later evidence suggests that he did in fact believe that there was a gigantic Jewish conspiracy, but the offensiveness of much of his phrasing. It was never repeated by him personally. . . .

Mosley repeatedly and firmly denied that he was anti-Semitic, while stating in *Tomorrow We Live* that 'our quarrel with the Jewish interests is that they have constituted themselves a state within the nation'. He differed sharply from the second baronet in insisting that 'our principle is complete religious toleration'.

Manchester City Council, which had distinguished Jews on it, applied to the Home Secretary in July 1936 for a national ban on political uniforms. A Public Order Act gained the royal assent within six months, but meanwhile the Council had taken its own local measures, and when Mosley staged a march past the site of Ancoats Hall, it had to be in the plain clothes of Cobden's world.

It was an essential part of Mosley's message that a division had been driven through England which must be closed. 'We have been divided and we have been conquered,' he said in the final appeal of *Tomorrow We Live*, 'because by division of the British alone we can be conquered.' Whether the division was between 'Money Power' and the unemployed, or between town and country, the need was for a new synthesis to be imposed by the young.

In a century the Mosleys had been exiled from Manchester and seen their status as landed aristocrats undermined by the national acceptance of *laissez-faire*. The fact that they accepted their exile and were content to be archaic caricatures of John Bull in the countryside must have exasperated Sir Oswald. 'The day of the doll is over,' he declared. 'Now the nation needs a man.' But his own attempt to challenge the hold of Cobdenite doctrines by the orthodox methods of democracy had ended by isolating him more completely than his father and grandfather. To find a model for regaining their lost power he could only now look abroad.

The dictator whose ideas gave Mosley hope was so far removed from the average Englishman's ideal in the thirties that the connection with England was only recognized by Arnold Toynbee in his *Study of History*. Toynbee saw Mussolini, in the volumes published in 1939, as an outlandish version of the English imperialist of the past. He quotes Mussolini's claim that as a dictator he had modelled himself on the empire-builders of Britain and France, that he thought 'for Italy', in the words attributed to Mussolini by Toynbee, 'as the great Englishmen who have made the British Empire have thought for England.'

Mosley might have taken Mussolini no more seriously than any other Englishman had it not been for a resemblance to his own background and aspirations. By accepting their loss of status, the Italians had sunk in the eyes of the world into decadent parodies of their Roman ancestors. Mussolini had revived the past in a new and violent form touched with the prestige of modern armies and police, and had reimposed it on the weak framework of liberal democracy.

In the year of Mosley's first visit to Rome, when he accepted the name of Fascist, Mussolini published his only statement on the philosophic basis of the movement. He elaborated his 'complete opposition to the doctrines of Liberalism, both in the political field and the field of economics'. He went on:

Peoples which are rising, or rising again after a period of decadence, are always imperialist; any renunciation is a sign of decay and of death. Fascism is the doctrine best adapted to represent the tendencies and the aspirations of a people, like the people of Italy, who are rising again after many centuries of abasement and foreign servitude.[1]

The uniform Mussolini adopted was a variant of the John Bull costume of the Mosleys, a uniform which used the grandeur of the past to erase the memory of defeat and impose archaic values on to the present. For generations the Mosleys had kept their violence for the boxing ring and the hunting field; they admired leadership but exerted it mainly in Pig Societies and markets. Instead of challenging Manchester in the world and recovering their own right to dominate, they connived in the myth that Parliament ran the affairs of the country. Mosley saw their inertia and archaism in Westminster and their virility and powers of leadership in Mussolini. By finding their virtues in the outsider who was little more than a joke to the new dominant majority he was proving his loyalty to his English forefathers. He was so sure of his loyalty to England that he was astonished in the first year of the war to find himself in prison under Regulation 18B (1) (a) which provided for the detention of members of organizations whose leaders had had association with the leaders of belligerent countries.

Mosley had the essential characteristics of the Napoleonist. In the whole of his career he held office for only a year and resigned when he was within sight of the leadership of the Labour Party. He spent his life in opposition. When he lost a by-election at the age of sixty-four, a journalist who interviewed him said 'it was as though, having by the compulsion of his own temperament chosen for himself the role of an outcast, he found some bitter kind of nourishment for his ego in one more rejection.' He was perhaps stronger in bearing defeat than anyone in his generation. 'It is the supreme test of character,' he said, 'whether you can survive great reverses.' He was a magnificent orator who knew how to concentrate his fire. His delivery was violent; he strode 'up and down the rather frail platform', said Harold Nicolson, 'with great panther steps and gesticulating with a pointing,

[1] Article contributed by Mussolini in 1932 to the fourteenth volume of the *Enciclopedia Italiana* and published by the Hogarth Press in 1933 in a pamphlet entitled *The Political and Social Doctrine of Fascism*.

and occasionally a stabbing, index.' Although fluency was one of his main characteristics, there was an occasion when a Member complained that he was inaudible.[1] He saw himself as the victim of the groups he attacked rather than as their assailant. In prison during the Second World War he pointed out that he had instructed his followers to put themselves at the disposal of the state and had been the first to press for forces to insure the security of the island. He also pointed out that Fox's loyalty under the threat of invasion could be counted on, and Pitt had not doubted him.

He was a dandy, whether in civilian clothes with his top hat and gold-knobbed cane, or in Fascist uniform—to which Low added the ballooned sleeves of the Renaissance. His meetings rivalled the appeal of the cinema. Olympia, which in 1934 was the scene of his most criticized meeting, had an arena large enough to accommodate London's yearly circus. A quarter of a century later, a reporter who heard him arguing in a law court said 'Mosley could have been a great actor.' In court he was 'more like a famous Q.C. than any of the bewigged counsel opposing him.'

He showed the mercurialism of the Napoleonists in steering his zig-zag course among old and new parties. 'Mosley is the only man I have ever known who could have been the leader of either the Conservative or the Labour Party,' said Lord Boothby. Nicolson added that he might have been the Liberal Prime Minister. He was a confirmed traveller who had houses in Cork and Orsay and was criticized by the press for regularly spending his holidays abroad. His economic thinking was strongly influenced by his experience of America. 'We shall not be divided in spirit', he wrote, 'from those original elements of American civilisation, to whom she owes her present greatness.' He learnt German during his imprisonment in the Second World War and believed that a good European should be able to feel as well as think in three languages. Abroad he noticed that he was free of the virulent criticism which dogged him in England. Like Lord Holland before him, he found that 'any difficulty I have met on the Continent has usually been instigated by British officials who are supposed to be charged with the duty of assisting rather than attacking British subjects.'

As a rival court, the Fascist Party was highly disciplined. Its members were banded together, says Sir Oswald, in *My Life*, 'by the common danger of our struggle and the savage animosity of the old world towards us.' They looked to him for something more than militant leadership. 'Panache is a French, a European word, while most of our members were very British, but it best describes the outward aspect of the blackshirt attitude. They certainly expected me, in spirit, to wear the white plume of Navarre.' In childhood he was devoted to his pets. Before going back to school he sat

[1] On 10 May 1923, the Government spokesman complained that parts of Sir Oswald's speech on foreign policy were not audible on his side of the House.

'all evening long in a manger weeping with one arm round the neck of some beloved pony while the other hand caressed a favourite fox-terrier.' According to Harold Nicolson the group of intellectuals who surrounded him in the New Party were under a strain because his 'autocratic methods and biting tongue have frayed their vanity and their nerves'; as the party broke up he retained the loyal elements existing in cells and clubs, which became the nucleus of the Fascist movement. It was within the Fascist Party, he says in his autobiography, that he found 'the most complete companionship I have ever known'.

It has generally been said Sir Oswald Mosley's failure in politics was due to lack of judgement, but we can perhaps see more clearly what it was that he misjudged. His family had been sent into exile by forces in the nineteenth century which became dominant and helped to give Britain her unique position in the world. That there were weaknesses in the Manchester School first became clear with the collapse of British agriculture in the seventies and the conservatism of industry as it faced the rivalry of other powers who were determined to gain comparable living standards by industrializing themselves. There were strong reasons which made England close her eyes to these weaknesses. The position of international superiority which grew with Free Trade confirmed her sense of invulnerability as an island. It was hard to believe that much could be wrong in a dispensation which had granted such pre-eminence or that anything was to be learnt from other countries.

The Mosleys had for generations accepted their rustic status as it dwindled in relation to the world of industry. They remained baronets without gaining admission to the peerage. Sir Oswald, who was committed to them in exile, happened to develop the defiant character pattern we have seen repeating itself among the Napoleonists. He saw their weaknesses in the central community which had rejected them and their virtue outside it. At first this was in terms of ex-service men who were left out of civilian life, of an Air Force which was not given its place with the dominant services. When unemployment removed nearly a fifth of the population from the productive work of the country, he became their champion; 'I was strongly,' he says, 'perhaps too bitterly conscious of the conditions of the unemployed who had trusted us, and I felt the betrayal of that trust was a dishonour.' The country as a whole lacked his motives for revolt against a system which had coincided with its greatest prosperity.

The crisis in Mosley's career came when every member of his first rival court, the New Party, was defeated at the polls. According to Harold Nicolson he became 'obsessed by Mussolinian ideas'. But if England was unwilling to accept a reversal of her nineteenth-century philosophy from her own party leaders, she was much less ready to accept it from foreigners to whom she believed herself superior. On the eve of the French war, in 1791, Gillray began to caricature Fox and the English supporters of the French Revolution as Frenchmen. The idea became damning as the conflict of ideology turned into a national war of survival. By adopting Mussolini's uniform in 1932 and visiting Hitler after his seizure of power, Mosley unintentionally associated himself with potential enemies in a war for survival.

To attribute his failure with the electorate to tendencies in his movement which were said to be un-English—the violence at meetings, the anti-Semitic controversy—is to overlook the resounding defeat of the New Party before violence or anti-Semitism were in question. Mosley was able to see more clearly than others that Manchester's triumph had run its course and turned into a liability. But the origins of his insight involved him in frontal attack and association with outcast nations when the country was too wedded to the idea of Manchester to accept anything but the most English of compromises that a National Government could work out.

## 3

In 1931 it happened that Kingsley Martin as well as Sir Oswald Mosley was out of a job. He had gone to the *Manchester Guardian* as a leader-writer three years earlier after a quarrel with William Beveridge at the London School of Economics. He was already a socialist, but the fact does not seem to have struck C. P. Scott, the great octogenarian editor of the *Manchester Guardian*, who employed him as a leader-writer to stoke the dying fires of the Liberal Party. There was a light but brilliant touch of aggression in Kingsley Martin which made it impossible to mistake his drift. Soon he was confined to writing leaders on Kenya. When his engagement was ended he spent some months in London before being appointed editor of *The New Statesman*.

From the beginning of his editorship in 1931 until after the Second World War, the *New Statesman* played a role very similar to that of Leigh Hunt's *Examiner* from 1808 until the year of Napoleon's death, except that its success and influence were greater. The circulation doubled to 30,000 before the Second World War and reached nearly 100,000 afterwards, and it was read by most of the English-speaking intelligentsia. The central gossip column was signed 'Critic', and Kingsley Martin accepted personal responsibility for it.

Like Leigh Hunt, he was the son of a Unitarian minister. The Reverend Basil Martin, his father, was of Huguenot descent and himself the son of a

Calvinist minister. Basil Martin grew up at a time when the congregation stood in reverent silence and preachers, he said, 'had more honour in our hearts than we should have given to a king or emperor.' He was determined to achieve this imperial status for himself but was handicapped by a stammer which made his friends advise him to abandon the attempt. He persisted and became a Congregational minister in the slums. In ten years he was overcome by a belief that he was damned and had to leave, but he recovered sufficiently to re-establish himself in Oxford and then in the cathedral city of Hereford. There Kingsley Martin and his sisters grew up. 'We were heretics among heretics,' he says. They had God on their side but the Anglicans and Catholics against them and sometimes the rest of the Nonconformists and the whole of the cathedral city. His first memory was of their windows being broken by a crowd in the Boer War because his father had spoken in defence of Kruger at the Quaker Meeting House.

The Reverend Martin began to preach socialism and demanded that the businessmen in his congregation should reward their workers according to their needs. When their contributions to his stipend had declined beyond a certain point he was forced to accept a Unitarian ministry where he was freer. He had ceased to believe in heaven as well as hell. Only God survived and the Christian ethic in the form of practical socialism. 'He came', says Kingsley Martin, 'to believe more and more in less and less.'

In his original ambition he was successful. Those of the congregation who remained faithful adored him in spite of his stammer. 'A very few', says Kingsley Martin, 'saw him as a reincarnation of Jesus.' One of the problems which obsessed him was Herbert Spencer's question whether God takes delight in his own adulation. He kept a cutting from the *Hereford Times* about 'a poor countrywoman' who regularly walked six miles to hear him and came away rewarded by the feeling 'how plain he made everything'. When he christened his only boy Basil Kingsley, he was using the kingly adjective twice, and it was the boy who later dropped the Greek version.

The youngest of the Reverend Martin's daughters protested that their childhood was submerged in morality and saw her father as the incarnation of Jehovah instead of the incarnation of Jesus, but the boy returned his love and saw him as the 'ex-officio captain' in all his fantasies. 'My trouble was that my father gave me no chance at all to quarrel with him,' he says, in *Father Figures*. 'I fought side by side with him, and was a dissenter, not against his dissent, but with him against the establishment.' With his courage and integrity the son had also his sense of glory.

When I was about seven years old I walked along the High Street with a stride that I think was consciously like him. Someone stopped me and asked who I was. I answered in astonishment, 'Don't you know who I am? I am the son of the Rev. Basil Martin.' Surely any fool knew that!

But the boy also had criticisms which he suppressed. His father ministered to a small company of philistines. He cared less about his family's income and economic well-being than 'the idea of being important in a small way'. Although there were books in the house, he gave Kingsley no education in the arts. In spite of the Christian ethic, his aggression showed itself in his stammer and the ferocity of his pacifism. To the children he was capable of becoming 'a dangerous ogre'.

The boy was as ambitious as the original Napoleonists. 'I am never content to be second,' he once wrote. Lloyd George's dreams were partly his own.

I remember once sitting by myself, high in a tree, watching what I believe were gold crested wrens on a Sunday afternoon. I recall the deep happiness of that particular occasion without having any idea why I remember it rather than a hundred other occasions.

His revolt developed on the familiar pattern. He broadened his cultural horizon beyond the limits of his father, took an interest in Greece and America and won a scholarship to Cambridge and a fellowship at Princeton. He published his first book, *The Triumph of Palmerston*, when he was still in his twenties and became a lecturer at the London School of Economics. He fell in love and shook off his father's puritanical view of sexual morality.

Like Leigh Hunt, he had a way of gaining the respect of great literary figures. Shaw developed an interest in him when he was still at Cambridge because of a review he wrote of *Arms and the Man*, and Arnold Bennett was instrumental, with J. M. Keynes, in getting him the editorship of the *New Statesman*. He then made the paper pay and gained a growing hold on the intelligentsia instead of losing income, like his father as his little congregation declined.

He remained the devoted son. He could hardly remember his father before his golden hair had turned white at about the turn of the century. The old man lived on into the Second World War. In 1935, he produced an autobiography, *An Impossible Parson*, which was reviewed at length in the *New Statesman*, where he was compared to Elijah and only criticized for a tendency to overstress his isolation.

The policy of the paper took shape as soon as Kingsley Martin was installed. It sympathized with Stalin's Russia and attacked the forces of conservatism in England and the rest of the world. There was nothing crude in either of these attitudes; they were shaded and lit up by a sense of humour; but they were persistent, and Kingsley Martin's disgust at the reaction around him had priority over his enthusiasm for the Soviet Union. There had been reasons for depression ever since the end of the war, but in

1931 they almost drove him to despair. Instead of accepting radical solutions as unemployment rose towards three million, the country took refuge in the past. When the National Government was formed under Ramsay MacDonald, the *New Statesman* was the only paper to back the rump of the Labour Party against it. When the electorate gave 558 seats to the National candidates and 56 to the Opposition, it seemed as if the reaction was permanent.

'Critic' kept returning to the massed rows of figures on the Government benches. There were marquises, earls and viscounts, duchesses, viscountesses and countesses. Over a hundred had ex-officio titles, including '28 majors and 32 captains'. At their head was 'a Cabinet of old men, nearly all of whom are proved failures'. He asked how long the flood of reaction would last and tried to comfort his readers with the hope that it might subside in 1933 or 1934, 'if those on the Left will do some thinking in the meantime'.

He did his best to make them think by sending a special correspondent to Russia in 1931 and going there himself with Low the cartoonist in 1932. Kingsley Martin was convinced that Stalin's Russia had the virtues England had lost. It had youth and youthful ideas, with easy divorce and experiments in prison reform. He admitted that many of the admirers of the Soviet Union needed saving from themselves. 'Many who sail up the Baltic in the spirit of Wordsworth crossing the Channel in the early days of the French Revolution, begin, like Wordsworth, by finding that it is "bliss to be alive" and "rejoicing at human nature seeming to be born again", and they come back after a month's discomfort as unreasonably disillusioned as Wordsworth after twenty years of war.'

He was too cautious to be disillusioned. He published full-length surveys on the success of the Five Year Plan, both in agriculture and heavy industry. On the eve of his own visit to Russia he insisted that collectivization of agriculture had involved no more than 'half of the long-drawn out suffering of our own industrial revolution, when whole generations of men, women and children were ruthlessly sacrificed for the sake of profits.' He foresaw 'some local famine' and thought the liquidation of the kulaks had been 'a pretty cruel business', but he failed to see the ruthlessness of a dictatorship which was beginning to kill people by the million.

In England reaction did not subside in 1933, as he had hoped, but gained a new dimension with the advent of Hitler. The League of Nations had failed to stop the Japanese invasion of Manchuria. In another two years Mussolini invaded Abyssinia. Because of Britain's commanding situation in the nineteenth century, it felt to many Englishmen that she was at the least conniving with these aggressors, so that they became a part of the local conservative scenery. Kingsley Martin's view of Communist Russia as the land of promise was thus locked into position at the very moment when the evidence of a reign of terror in Russia became unmistakable. It was not until the end of 1939, when Stalin had signed his non-aggression pact with Hitler, that he was able to accept the full horror of the famine of 1932 and the tragedy of 'collectivising the farms in five instead of fifty years'.

Meanwhile it was not only the youthful energy of the Soviet Union which impressed him but its practice of Christian virtues which in theory belonged to the West. *The Times*, which was reputed to be the leading example of a free newspaper, was increasingly one-sided. 'By tradition', he wrote, in September 1931, 'the only letters printed are by persons of great respectability who ceased to think many years ago.' In the following April, he noticed that 'the columns of *Izvestia* and *Pravda*, and indeed the whole Soviet Press, are full of denunciations and complaints of slackness, faulty work, and "bureaucratic" administration.' The self-criticism of Stalin's dictatorship was a part of its 'way of life'. In 1933, reviewing a book on Russia by a practising Christian, he asked how it came about that 'the ethics of Christianity—not, of course, its mystical philosophy—are, amid extraordinary confusion and excitement, becoming increasingly the one accepted basis of social behaviour?'

In England, on the other hand, the basis of social behaviour was profit-making and the ethics of Christianity had degenerated into adulation of the royal family. He pinpointed examples of such inanity in a column entitled 'This England' and wrote a book, *The Magic of Monarchy*, which he later revised as *The Crown and the Establishment*.

In abandoning the pretensions of George III, the British monarchy had in fact developed a new hold on the country. It was an emotional hold and for that reason difficult to challenge unless the occupant of the throne failed to meet its requirements. It varied in strength according to the needs of the time. We have seen that George III himself, although mad and discredited, survived to become 'the good old King' because the threat of the French Revolution and the Napoleonic wars created the need for a national figure-head which was hardly fulfilled by his sons.

George V had neither blunders nor madness to his credit but only a rather old-fashioned normality. His son said he had 'a private war with the twentieth century'. He receded in the public imagination at the end of the First World War, when Kings and Crowns, in the words of Lloyd George, 'were falling like withered leaves before a gale'. But as the post-war security gave way to the convulsions of the thirties and a new world of danger, he was rediscovered with gratitude as a symbol of the past which seemed to guarantee that the island would survive in its privileged position. Stephen Spender, who watched Hitler's climb to power in Germany, has said 'the middle years of the 1930's were symbolised in England not by Hitlerism or even the Spanish war, but by the Royal Jubilee.'

The Jubilee celebrations in May 1935 astonished George V himself by their enthusiasm. 'I'd no idea they felt like that about me,' he said, after passing through bigger crowds than he had seen in a lifetime of loyal demonstrations. There was a corresponding period of grief a few months later when he died.

The succession of Edward VIII aroused bitter controversy when it was found that he meant to marry an American divorcée. The Archbishop of York referred to the King's duty to behave as 'the incarnation' of his people. The word incarnation, which had been used of the Reverend Basil Martin by his devoted flock, stung Kingsley Martin to write his book because it seemed to him 'meaningless unless it takes us back to an even more primitive conception than that of divine right'; it belonged to the mythology of the South Sea Islanders. He tried to restore a sense of proportion by insisting on the tradition of criticism which had surrounded the royal family from the time of Tom Paine and the attacks on the Regent and 'that ogre the Duke of Cumberland'. Since he was sensitive to the popular feeling for George V, he had to explain it, and he found the clue in the King's Puritanism, which had made him 'the perfect father figure'. The danger Kingsley Martin saw in this identification was that it could be used to distract people from their economic interests. Edward VIII had not been true to type; he had shown an open sympathy with the unemployed and challenged the Puritan ideal of marriage. He had been sent into exile. There was a risk that George VI would again be built up into a magical figure in spite of a stammer which should have reminded people of his humanity.

The balance of virtues and vices which Kingsley Martin saw in England and the Soviet Union was of course more subtle than this outline; it was complicated among other things by his growing admiration for Gandhi, whom he saw as a mixture of saint and fox, with the strength to impose a solution on the imperialists. But we must ask how it was that the most brilliant and perceptive editor of his day was able to see clear evidence of Christianity in Stalin's regime at a time when he attacked the pagan basis of the English monarchy.

It was possible, of course, to see some of the virtues of his father in Stalin, as the Napoleonists had seen some of the virtues of theirs in the Emperor. The campaign against the kulaks had proved Stalin's contempt for property; the Five Year Plan was a demonstration that society could be reshaped in defiance of tradition. But if we add all the details of resemblance, the plainness of his style of life, the fiction of his appointment by the people, it is still not enough to account for his magnetism.

We must remember that Kingsley Martin, like other English socialists, had a horror of oppression. He was on the side of the hunted fox and the hare. He remembered in childhood 'cattle being driven through the streets by shouting men mercilessly hitting their bony backs with heavy sticks, driving them to the market and slaughter.' His earliest memory was of stones breaking the windows in the Boer War. Once, when a group of Congregational divines interrogated his father in a schoolroom on heresy, he was reminded of the story of Daniel in the lions' den; but he made a reversal in the cast and saw his father as a lion hunted by Daniels with purple ribbons dripping from their Bibles like blood. He saw himself fighting beside him, as an animal. 'I went home', he says, 'full of hero worship, utterly identifying myself with my father's struggle.'

In such a man the claws of a lion were a virtue. His faults, so far as Kingsley Martin could see them, made a pattern which fitted his enemies and above all their chief representative. It was the King of England who set up as a Puritan father figure and gained applause as 'the incarnation' of his people; it was the national myth of royalty which threw a mantle over ogres and stammerers and encouraged people to forget their simple economic rights. A taboo even existed against discussing the myth, which would have otherwise been exposed by the first boy to open his mouth. 'When a great many very important people say something over and over again very solemnly,' he wrote, 'you can be pretty sure they are wrong. That is the moment to say the Emperor has no clothes.'

It was his father, of course, who had seen himself as 'a King or an Emperor' on becoming a preacher, and Kingsley had never been able to attack him, because it was what the world did and the worst moment of all would have been when the Congregational divines accused him of heresy. But the real King and Emperor was differently placed.

It had looked as if the post-war extensions of the vote to the entire adult population had put the monarchy and the House of Lords out of the field, but when Ramsay MacDonald betrayed his Left Wing by forming a National Government, Kingsley Martin suspected the King of responsibility. From then on a kind of Conservative reflex had seemed to take charge of the country, mobilizing unthinking reaction as it had not been mobilized since the early days of the French wars and the threat of Napoleon. The hundreds of 'National' members returned at the election of 1931 were 'patriotic, but not otherwise politically experienced'. He saw them sitting so securely on their benches with their titles and overbearing majority that he sympathized with a worker on the train who said Guy Fawkes had the only answer. The swing to the Left did not come, and the astonishing Silver Jubilee was followed almost at once by an election which restored the National Government under Baldwin. When George V died in 1936, he was succeeded not by Edward VIII, with whom Kingsley Martin identified himself, but by George VI, as a more reliable incarnation of his people. Kingsley Martin could no longer hold his tongue when the Archbishop of York used that phrase. If the frail young King with a stammer had stood alone, he would have spared him. If he had been criticized, he might have held back: but George VI had behind him the conservatism of the country in its mass and solemnity. It was the moment to strip the magic from the monarchy.

We have noticed that Byron left England for the court of the Mohammedan Bonaparte almost as soon as he took his seat on the opposition benches of the Lords. The fact that Ali Pasha was the most ruthless tyrant in the Ottoman empire did not worry Byron and even added to his attraction because it marked him more plainly as an outcast. Stalin was acceptable to Kingsley Martin because he shared his hatred of imperialism and the hierarchy of classes, but from 1931, he himself was confronted by the solemn forces of the National Government as Stalin was by the entire capitalist world. He would have accepted him then if he had been Ali Pasha.

A blood-stained lion is perhaps less sympathetic as a protégé than a hare, or even than a fox, which was the metaphor Kingsley Martin used for Gandhi. George Kennan wrote in 1960 that Stalin was 'a man of incredible criminality, or a criminality effectively without limits'. When evidence of his use of terror began to reach the *New Statesman* in the thirties it replied that cruelty was wrong 'anywhere' but did not try to discredit the Stalinist regime. If a group of Daniels closed in on his father, Kingsley Martin's reply was to transform him into a lion.

The Reverend Martin was 'a good man', in the words of Bernard Shaw, and Kingsley Martin was the champion of the oppressed, whether they were Indian untouchables or carnivores. He believed that the abolition of blood sports should have been a major objective of Labour policy. He disapproved of shooting birds and particularly 'a lonely pigeon, usually a homing pigeon'. He liked independence in animals and twice put his hand through the bars at the Zoo to caress an African lion. 'My favourite playmates were snakes,' he says in *Editor*. 'Boa constrictors, if not too large, make admirable pets.' Like Erskine, he had a horror of pesticides, not because it was any longer impossible to wipe out a species like the turnip fly but because too many others were wiped out incidentally.

He was highly mercurial and did not pretend that the *New Statesman* was consistent. He accepted the Munich agreement. He gave a prize to a reader for describing him in a competition as 'every inch a King uncrowned; he leads the intellectuals round, and round, and round.' Just as Fox in Paris had found Napoleon's charges against Pitt and Windham insupportable, so in America he angrily denied that Britain was imperialist.

He had a passion for the theatre. Like Leigh Hunt, he was a dramatic critic. In spite of a tumultuous delivery, he took as many amateur parts as he could, with 'an altogether exaggerated notion of my acting capacity'.

Like Godwin and Hazlitt, he was the opposite of a dandy and attached importance to being without a hat and if possible without a tie. He was nick-named Archie in the early days of the war, and a sergeant asked him, 'Were you brought up at Eton, or eaten first and brought up afterwards?'

Abroad he was received with the honour due to a great editor. He visited sixty countries while occupying the executive chair. In the first year of his retirement he was in Egypt in January, the Soviet Union in July, and India in December. He died eight years later in Cairo.

As a rival court the *New Statesman* was closer to Holland House than to the contributors who surrounded Leigh Hunt. Lunch was held in an oak-panelled room of a Georgian restaurant in Red Lion Square. In attendance were 'our very small political staff', with R. H. S. Crossman, who afterwards became Leader of the House of Commons, and an ex-editor of the *News Chronicle*, who had a castle in Scotland. Interspersed among them were critics, the managing director, and an advertising executive.

'Some distinguished guest would be present, a British Ambassador, for instance, who expected, no doubt, to be respectfully treated.' The greater that person's expectation, the less chance it had of fulfilment. If he was important enough, he had a way of being overlooked altogether, so that Kingsley Martin regretted that he did not keep a Dinner Book like Lady Holland. Once, Jawaharlal Nehru was a guest at Red Lion Square, and several important people came.

It was a larger lunch than usual, and I went over the names of those present with Noel Brailsford. We could not remember who had occupied one of the places at table. Later, Noel rang me up to say 'I've just remembered who was our guest. It was Clem Attlee, the leader of our great party.'

Reviewers of books formed an outer circle, who had to climb 'an outside flight of iron stairs or go through the housekeeper's flat to get to the literary department.' Beyond these again were the readers, who were among the most influential people in the country. As the Reverend Martin recalled the poor countrywoman who went away feeling his sermon had made everything plain, his son liked to quote the testimony of a journalist that 'when he read what we had to say the whole situation ceased to be an unintelligible muddle.'

Although lunch with the *New Statesman* gave a guest the feeling that he would do well to share the view from their political window, the Literary Editor and his critics on the staircase outside had a wider horizon. David Garnett, Raymond Mortimer, Cyril Connolly, were not Marxists at all. If Kingsley Martin accepted their autonomy, it may be because he still accepted his exclusion in childhood from the arts; but there is evidence that he regretted it. Auden and Isherwood, he says, in *Father Figures*, were 'both regular contributors in their Marxist period'. Auden, Spender, Day Lewis, and MacNeice were in fact the leaders of the new movement, but they contributed so little and so irregularly to the *New Statesman* that a reader who read nothing else would scarcely have been aware of their existence.

From 1931 to 1960, when Kingsley Martin gave up the editorship, the paper remained in opposition. The Labour leaders denounced him for treason to the party and the Conservatives for treason to the country. 'The only treason I feared', he wrote, 'was treason to my nonconformist conscience.' His conscience had nothing so vague about it as is generally understood by the nonconformist conscience; he was in revolt against a particular nonconformist to whom he was bound in loyalty, and the treason he feared was to acknowledge his revolt. There was not much risk as long as he could find substitutes who lacked the crucial resemblance to his father. Since the Reverend Martin was a Unitarian in a minority which had shrunk to a handful, he could range the whole world in pursuit of tyrants great and small. Mr. Park, for instance, his gardener, who left his previous parish on a point of gardening theology and suspected Kingsley Martin of heresy with regard to fertilizers, was dismembered week by week. Mr. Park was a very ordinary man. No one saw him as the enemy of the community or persecuted him for his doctrines, which were indeed fanatical and sometimes cruel. He was therefore fair game. If a white lupin did not behave according to his philosophy, Mr. Park, like any dictator, denied that it was white. Kingsley Martin had none of the forbearance he showed about such behaviour in Stalin; he let his readers know that the Emperor had no clothes.

It was when the world ganged up against a patriarch that the resemblance to his father became striking. He felt no particular loyalty to Stalin when he saw that Communism could solve the problem of unemployment. Under the Labour Government of 1929, it was not clear whether Kingsley Martin was a Socialist or Liberal; but when the landslide of 1931 gave the National Government an overwhelming majority, the only doubt was whether he was a Socialist or a Communist. A majority of this kind left him alone in the world with Stalin.

It was no accident that the editors of the *Examiner* and the *New Statesman* were both the sons of Unitarian ministers, both in revolt against them and both bound in loyalty. The attack of each on the reinforced orthodoxy of his time had the zest of his peculiar dilemma and ranged more freely across a wider field than that of other critics. Both were loyal to an island within an island. So long as they believed the larger island was secure they were ready to involve themselves in charges of treason in attacking it, but if it stood alone, like their fathers, their loyalty could be relied on. The *New Statesman* was widely read by the armed forces in the war. In the long run it was a material factor both in securing the victory of the Labour Party in 1945 and in helping to canalize the energies of the Left into the war effort.

# 4

We have now found the Napoleonist syndrome applying to people of such widely divergent politics that there is a risk of thinking them more common than they were. To the dictators there was a further risk. They had no means of guessing the extent to which English pacifism was based on an ultimate sense of security or that it would wilt as that was threatened.

Among the calculations which led Napoleon to return from Elba for his final gamble, the contact with English sympathizers played an important part. So far from expecting support to decline in proportion to his strength, he had always been certain it would grow. In an invasion he believed a single victory would be enough to consolidate behind him all those who were not committed to the ruling oligarchy. Hitler showed the same confidence in his threats of mass bombing. 'There are', he said, 'no such things as islands any more'—as if discovery of the fact should have put an end to resistance.

Hitler may not have been misled by the attentions of the New Party in defeat, or by the Oxford Union's refusal to fight for King and Country in 1933; but in 1935 a weightier series of visitors began with Lord Lothian, who had worked for five years in Lloyd George's secretariat. It culminated in the autumn of 1936 with Lloyd George himself. At this point, which coincided with the posting of Ribbentrop to London, Hitler was convinced that there were good prospects of England remaining out of the war. The publicity surrounding the visits, especially Lloyd George's signed articles in the press, did almost as much to convince world opinion.

The insignificance of the Fascist and Communist parties in England should have been a corrective. The British Union of Fascists did not disclose its membership but had failed to become a mass movement. The faction led by William Joyce, which wanted subversive collaboration with Germany, was expelled at the beginning of 1937 and the majority fought with loyalty in the war. The British Communist Party had not been founded until 1920. It was shunned even by the Independent Labour Party, and did not claim more than 3,000 members before the return of the National Government in 1931. The membership then tripled in a year, according to the *New Statesman*, but a party of 10,000 was still electorally negligible. Taken together with the Conservative majorities which greeted any crisis in the twenty years between the wars, it was clear that the body of the country was against change. 'The English', wrote Stephen Spender, 'were passing through a phase of isolation not just of place but of time.' They were, in fact, as determined to find security within their traditional framework as they had been in the generation which followed the French Revolution.

The Napoleonist syndrome was again no observer of party lines. We have seen it in a few individuals, in Lloyd George and Kingsley Martin, who never became Fascists or Communists. Among those who did, there are some who at first sight seem to have the character pattern but turn out to lack its persistence. It is as if we were to try to apply the method of reading Linear B script, which successfully deciphers one class of Minoan tablets, to the other class written in Linear A. Many of the signs and place names are the same but the language is different.

We found a similar division among the Romantics who committed themselves to the French Revolution. Coleridge and Southey, who worked out a form of communism they called Pantisocracy, were as much in revolt against the reactionary tendencies of the time as the English Jacobins who became Napoleonists; they had many traits of the Napoleonist character pattern. But Coleridge, Southey, and Wordsworth belonged by birth and upbringing to the central community. Their fathers were members of the Church or the Law or of aristocratic descent, and the orthodoxy of their origins contributed both to their revolt and to their return to the main body of the community when it closed ranks.

In the nineteen thirties Marxism was even more common among writers than Jacobinism had been in the eighteen nineties on the eve of the French war. From an overture in Hugh MacDiarmid's 'First Hymn to Lenin', in 1931, it was taken up unequivocally by W. H. Auden in *The Dance of Death*, in 1933. It was restated by Stephen Spender, Cecil Day Lewis, and Louis MacNeice, with a confidence which faltered and died out when the pact between Hitler and Stalin ushered in the Second World War. 'Somehow I had expected that when I joined the Party', writes Spender in *World Within World*, 'I would soon become endowed with that blessed sense of being right about everything which most Communists seemed to feel. But this did not happen.' Day Lewis had a similar experience. 'My own progress towards Communism had been too gradual for me to feel any of the exaltation which goes with a sudden conversion,' he says in *The Buried Day*; 'yet, after joining the Party, I did have a real sense of tranquility, a conviction that I had obeyed my conscience and done right.' A whole group of writers visited Spain in the Civil War or actually fought in the International Brigade. Several died there, including the Cambridge poets John Cornford and Julian Bell. Kim Philby, who reported the Franco view of operations in *The Times*, was among those who became lifelong Communists. But the well-known group led by Auden could no longer be considered Communists at all by the time of the Nazi–Soviet Pact of 1939.

Their revolt had Napoleonist qualities. Its political colour developed with the upsurge of Conservative feeling which culminated in the National election of 1931. 'Everyone knew that Labour was down the sink,' said

MacNeice before the result was known; he saw the future as belonging to 'the *status quo* of stagnation'. It was a revolt of poets and writers, not of religious dissenters, because artists were the new outcasts in a world which was being shaped by the mass media—the cinema, radio, journalism in its new field of universal literacy. In *A Hope for Poetry* (1934) Day Lewis insisted that the mass media had sent the poet into the wilderness. He existed in a 'tiny, temporarily isolated unit with which communication is possible, with whom he can take a certain number of things for granted.' To Spender, in *Forward from Liberalism* (1937), the artist was 'reduced to the rank of faddy amateur'. Shelley had been able to claim that poets were 'the unacknowledged legislators of the world', but Auden, who remembered the phrase, has made the bitter comment that it had come to apply to the secret police.

As an undergraduate, before he became a Marxist, Auden had rooms in the most splendid classical quadrangle in Oxford where he worked in artificial light with sackcloth curtains over the windows. 'A group of emergent artists existed in his mind', says Spender, 'like a cabinet in the mind of a party leader.' He had a horror of social gatherings, 'cocktail parties and the like', but used his authority as a poet to recruit a rival court whose members did not meet. Day Lewis, who was three years his senior, became Auden's poetic disciple but resisted his 'intellectual bossiness and the tendency to try and run his friends' lives for them'. Stephen Spender, his junior, could not be alienated from his own subjective vision but accepted his dominance: 'I did not so much listen to Auden's conversation as absorb his tone of voice, his gestures, the attitudes behind his words. . . .' MacNeice was ready to mortify his 'aesthetic sense by trying to write as Wystan did'.

From the beginning, before he needed to call up Marxist reinforcements, Auden was in action against the whole range of middle-class attitudes.

> Always the following wind of history
> Of others' wisdom makes a buoyant air
> Till we come suddenly on pockets where
> Is nothing loud but us; where voices seem
> Abrupt, untrained, competing with no lie
> Our fathers shouted once.

At Oxford he found his main weapon in the new armoury of psychoanalysis whose essentials he had been able to master and turn away from himself on to the society around him. His attitude was a mixture of surgeon and nurse, who could cure the illness by persuading the patient to undo the 'lie our fathers shouted once'. In his concept of the poet was a claim to the oracular quality of an ancestor. In *Poems* (1930) and *The Orators* (1932) he is the falcon and the hawk, as Fox and Whitbread had been; he is also 'the helmeted airman' and once 'the leader'. In the year Hitler seized power, when extreme sanctions were needed to sustain the progressive cause, he accepted the

Marxist alliance. *The Dance of Death* (1933) opens with the Announcer: 'We present to you this evening a picture of the decline of a class, of how its members dream of a new life, but secretly desire the old, for there is death inside them.'

Auden had not visited the Soviet Union; nor had Spender or Day Lewis. Their idea of it reminds us of the veiled inspection of France by the English Jacobins and Napoleonists. 'In a communist state,' wrote Spender, in 1937, 'political power is a light diffused throughout the whole state, for the essential political fact is that all property is public socialist property.' To the poet it is

> a country
> Where light equal, like the shine from snow, strikes all faces.

As the details of Stalinist terror began to reach them, a brave front had to be put on it. In a lyrical vision of communist society, Auden brought himself to admit the possibility of events like the assassination of the Duc d'Enghien.

> Today the deliberate increase in the chances of death,
> The conscious acceptance of guilt in the necessary murder.

'Necessary murder' was a phrase which angered George Orwell, who suggested that it 'could only be written by a person to whom murder is at most a *word*'; the reality was terror, hatred, howling relatives, post-mortems, blood and smells. Orwell perhaps underestimated Auden's violence in this phase when he wished the worst of tortures on capitalists and accepted suicide as a permissible climax to failure; but Auden had Wordsworth's habit of revision, and 'Spain' was reprinted in 1940 with 'the necessary murder' changed to 'the fact of murder'.

The original revolt had been against Georgian poetry as well as the static society which inspired it, and an escapist attitude to nature was an enemy characteristic. MacNeice, who had written odes to a parrot and a stuffed monkey, continued to keep dogs. Day Lewis, in Somerset, remained a bird-watcher. Stephen Spender, who as a boy in the countryside had made the discovery that he was a poet, allowed nature to creep back in disguise.

> More beautiful and soft than any moth
> With burring furred antennae feeling its huge path
> Through dusk, the air-liner with shut-off engines
> Glides over suburbs. . . .

To call Auden a dandy would be to overlook both his austerity and his reverence for words, but at his most facile he was smart. He wrote, says Connolly, 'prolifically, carelessly, and exquisitely'. MacNeice says that he dressed at Oxford like an untidy bank clerk and 'denounced the wearing of bright colours or the cultivation of flowers'. MacNeice, more obviously than Day Lewis, was a dandy in his style and person. At the height of his

Marxist period he had a borzoi which he took with him into working-class districts and entered for dog shows.

Except for Day Lewis, who had been born in Ireland, they were confirmed travellers. Auden went to pre-Hitler Germany, to Iceland for three months in 1936, to Spain in 1937, to China in 1938, and the United States in 1939. Spender spent six months abroad every year. He translated Büchner and Lorca; Day Lewis, more conservatively, translated Virgil, and MacNeice the *Agamemnon* of Aeschylus and Goethe's *Faust*.

A new dimension had been added to travel by the aeroplane. Spender says it added 'the sky to my picture of the world'; he 'discovered the great joy of being above the clouds'. For Auden, the helmeted airman, it abolished politics and history itself. 'From the height of 10,000 feet, the earth appears to the human eye as it appears to the eye of the camera; that is to say, all history is reduced to nature.'

This enthusiasm for the air was a new version of the Napoleonist's elation on finding himself across the Channel. The poets of the thirties felt themselves threatened and sometimes overwhelmed in their isolation; they lived 'under the shadow of a war', in 'the immense bat-shadow of home', where

> The greed for property
> Heaps a skyscraper over the breathing ribs.

Their poetry was an attempt to reverse the perspective. Auden, in 1932, dismissed the leaders of the National Government as 'pigmies, poor dears'; he took to the air as Byron left for Venice or Mrs. Inchbald in her balloon. In *Letters from Iceland* (1937) he collaborated with MacNeice in a scrapbook held together by a serial 'Letter to Byron'. He had discovered *Don Juan* on the journey to Reykjavik and recognized a fellow exile.

> Byron, thou shoulds't be living at this hour!
> What would you do, I wonder, if you were?

The poets' first interest was not Iceland but England, which they kept in touch with by radio. Its hierarchy and values were reduced to Lilliputian dimensions, because 'islands are places apart where Europe is absent.' Auden surveyed the scene with the irony of Byron in Venice; the menaces from which they had escaped became comedy, the yellow journalism, the obsession with money, snobbery, patriotism, as intriguing as the expedients of sunbathing or scouting. But if the English had become dwarfs, the Icelanders around them were far from being giants. The sagas which Auden learnt to love in childhood were ten centuries in the past and the *epigoni* unrecognizable. They were sick in buses, ate stale shark and whale pickled in sour milk, and used corrugated iron for the roofs of their capital. They were more hospitable and friendly than the British, but that was a virtue

Auden expected. In 'The Traveller' (1938), 'crowds make room for him without a murmur.'

There was one aspect of the background of Auden and his followers which was at the opposite extreme from that of the Napoleonists. They had grown up in the Anglican tradition. Auden's grandfathers on both sides were clergy of the Church of England; his mother was a practising Anglo-Catholic. MacNeice was the son of a bishop, Day Lewis of a vicar. Stephen Spender was of German-Jewish origin on his mother's side, but his father was a Congregationalist in *Who's Who* who was glad to read the lessons from a Church of England pulpit.

To some extent they had tendencies in common with the sons of Nonconformist ministers. Day Lewis, who was to have been a clergyman like his father, preached sermons as a child. Auden's verse sometimes reminds us of an incantation in a cathedral. There was a sense in which they, too, were separated from the community. To MacNeice, in his father's aura, 'most of the world was untouchable.' Day Lewis was not allowed to join the choir or the Boy Scouts because they did not belong to his own class. Spender complains that

> My parents kept me from children who were rough
> And who threw words like stones and who wore torn clothes.

But there was a central difference between this isolation and the Nonconformists'. They were separated as an élite of the inner tradition of the country, not as outcasts who held together in fair weather and foul. Day Lewis peering out of his father's window at the Jehovah's Witnesses on the other side of the street, was

fascinated by the enthusiasm with which they assembled, the hand-shakings, the large, holy smiling, and the little tins or boxes or babs which so many of them seemed to carry and which, I thought, contained snacks to help them through their devotions—all so very different from the muted, unrecognising, almost furtive air with which the members of my father's flock ducked into Christ Church, where the bells were now ringing for Evensong.

They were committed in childhood to the orthodoxy of their fathers, and in three of them admiration was heightened and complicated by the early death of their mothers: Spender's when he was twelve, MacNeice's when he was seven, and Day Lewis's when he was four.

Auden holds that a poet should not write autobiography and his verse has on the whole an inscrutable quality which makes it unpromising material for psychological analysis. He emphasizes his High Church background and says that 'no gentler father ever lived' than the surgeon George Augustus Auden. Spender, MacNeice, and Day Lewis have all written autobiographies, and a central event in each of them is the death of the mother and the additional load it threw on the relationship of the son with his father.¹ Spender, who in childhood 'adored' his father, shared his ambition to achieve worldly fame. MacNeice was overawed by being taken to sleep in the same room as the bishop. Day Lewis, who lost his mother at a younger age than the others, formed the strongest attachment. His father was 'both father and mother to me'.

The problem became explosive when they had to break away at the approach of manhood. The fuse was lit for Day Lewis and MacNeice by the arrival of a step-mother. They then denounced the beliefs and background which their fathers stood for, as they could without affecting their highly respectable status. Day Lewis became an agnostic. It was the 'worldly streak in my father's Christianity' which seemed most intolerable. In the period when he joined the Communist Party he says he was carrying out 'a scorched earth policy' against his father.

Unfilial phrases of this kind never passed the lips of a Napoleonist, but they abound in Spender, MacNeice, and Day Lewis. Spender's father becomes a coward, hypocrite, and failure. There are long scenes in *The Backward Son* inspired by open hatred. MacNeice sent his father a telegram from Oxford announcing that he had been gaoled for drunkenness and was engaged to a Jewess. 'The word "moral",' he says, 'became derogatory, while as for religion—and here we would raise our voices if there was a clergyman in hearing—everyone knew that all religion was nonsense.' He joined the Communists 'in their hatred of the *status quo*, I wanted to smash the aquarium.'

The sins of these highly placed ministers of religion and public servants were no doubt tiresome at close quarters, but when we compare them with the corruption of Henry Fox, the pillaging habits of Captain Byron, or the tyranny of Unitarian ministers, the disloyalty of their sons becomes as paradoxical as the loyalty of the Napoleonists.

In Auden and his followers the position of the dissenter was reversed. The community respected their fathers, and in the thirties increasingly respected them as symbols of the old social order and its values, even though religion was in decline. A son could rebel openly in such circumstances and revenge himself for the privileged isolation of his childhood. The escape to Marxism was a direct attack on their fathers, the Napoleonist symptoms an attempt to usurp their position prematurely. It was a lovers' quarrel, fated to end in reconciliation and the assumption of situations like their fathers' in the central structure of the community. Auden went to the United States to work out his abstruse return; Spender and Day Lewis made theirs more simply in the Fire Service and the Home Guard in the Battle of Britain.

¹ Spender, *The Backward Son* (1940) and *World Within World* (1951); MacNeice, *The Strings are False* (1965); Day Lewis, *The Buried Day* (1960).

By 1939 Auden no longer needed to ask himself, as he had in Iceland, what Byron would have thought; in his Dedication to *Don Juan*, which he wrote after Waterloo, Byron was explicit about the poets who had abandoned the communal ideals of Pantisocracy. Coleridge, like Auden, had

> lately taken wing,
> But like a hawk encumber'd with his hood,—
> Explaining metaphysics to the nation—
> I wish he would explain his Explanation.

Byron would have been kinder to Day Lewis as Poet Laureate than to Southey, but he would have continued to stick to his guns.

> Meantime, Sir Laureate, I proceed to dedicate,
> In honest simple verse, this song to you.
> And, if in flattering strains I do not predicate,
> 'Tis that I still retain my 'buff and blue'.

## 5

The Communists who persisted in their faith can rarely be followed in the detail we need. Their own aim is to dissimilate, so that their statements and actions cannot often be taken at their face value. The effort of research by counter-espionage and the press is in the main an attempt to uncover their movements in adult life. The material we need to explain their persistence comes from a greater depth, mainly from relationships in the family and character traits in adult life which are not thought to be revealing. In the case of Kim Philby, where we have this information from his own journalism and a highly literate father, the Napoleonist syndrome can be seen in its classical form. The question which must arise while reviewing the evidence is whether that syndrome can be plausibly held to exert itself so decisively in a contemporary setting that an intelligent man should lose his power of judgement under its influence. Professor Trevor-Roper, who has looked hardest at Philby's persistence, is driven to the example of sudden religious conversion to explain it; by such an experience, he says in *The Philby Affair*, the possibility of discriminating is withdrawn from the mind. 'It is exercised only at surface-level, on trivialities, outside the area of real thought. At the heart, in the mind, on all real topics, it is closed for ever; frozen, sterilised, sealed up.'

It is uncertain at what point Kim Philby became a Communist agent, but his conversion to Marxism took place at Cambridge with the poets and others who later died in Spain. According to his own account it began in 1931, with the stampede of the electorate to support the National Government. He was already a member of the University Socialist Society, and 'it seemed incredible that the party should be so helpless against the reserve strength which Reaction could mobilise in time of crisis.' By the summer of 1933, when Hitler was in control of Germany, his conversion was complete. In 1930, his father, H. St. John Philby, had been converted to Islam. He was deeply attached to his father, but the coincidence of dates may not be important because it was the end of a process which he had watched all his life.

Harry St. John Philby, when he looked back on his career in *Forty Years in the Wilderness*, believed that 'the desert was obviously my destiny.' Sometimes he wondered whether it had something to do with his name of St. John, and in the deserts of Arabia he actually experimented with locusts and wild honey as a diet; but the name had been given him for no better reason than that he was born in a bungalow called St. John's at Badullah in Ceylon. He suspected other causes. As a baby he had once been left behind at a rest house, and when the servants came back to collect him, they were uncertain whether they had chosen rightly between two babies in the arms of a 'gipsy woman'.[1] If he was not a changeling, he was certainly a foreigner, because his legitimate forefathers were Filbys from Scandinavia; in England, he said, 'they were but strangers sojourning in a foreign land.'

Except on his father's plantation in Ceylon, he had always felt himself an outsider. There was an English garrison at Badullah, and a race-course surrounding a lake, but his father was an outsider, a tea planter who was going bankrupt. In England, after leaving the plantation, the boy found himself looked down on as an uncouth barbarian 'from the outposts of heathendom'. To him the plantation had been Paradise, but he tilled the ground outside with a kind of desperation, and won a scholarship to Westminster, where he got into the cricket eleven and became head of the school.

At Cambridge his determination to conform relaxed. Nehru was his contemporary in Trinity and he opposed a colour bar in the Union. Cambridge, he says, taught him 'to think fearlessly and without inhibition by accepted standards, however far such thinking might carry us into the deeps and shoals of uncharted oceans.' He took a first class in the Modern Language tripos, became a socialist, and settled down to Oriental languages, for which he had a gift. In 1908 he was accepted by the Indian Civil Service and posted to the Punjab. 'I scandalised most of my friends', he says in *Arabian Days*, 'by proclaiming from the beginning my adhesion to the ideal of Indian Independence.'

[1] He was almost certainly not a changeling. The resemblance to his mother in photographs is strong.

Almost at once he found himself back in his father's social position in Badullah. The wife of a highly placed administrator in Lahore noticed that he danced without grace and did not play polo. 'She asked me quite bluntly how I had managed to get selected for service in the Punjab, which was by way of being regarded as the crack province of India.' She succeeded in making him feel 'very small' but not in redeeming him. On excursions he ate fruit from the trees and drank river water. He had a roving eye for the girls regardless of colour but got married in safety to the daughter of the chief engineer in the Public Works Department of Rawalpindi.

His son was born at Ambala, below the foothills rising towards Simla, on 1 January 1912. He gave him his own first name of Harold, and not St. John, but slipped into calling him Kim because he played with Indian children like Kipling's hero.

Philby was already to some extent committed to Islam by the time Kim was born. His first book, *Customary Law of the Rawalpindi* (1910), hints at a preference for the Moslem way of life over the caste system of the Hindus, which may have reminded him of the rigidity of the British caste system at Lahore and Badullah. Islam he called afterwards 'essentially a democratic and socialist creed'. They spent most of their time in Moslem territory and he already had the habit of wearing Moslem dress in the Baluchi style.

He was intensely anxious about his own status. His appointment as captain of the school at Westminster had been 'the greatest thrill of my life', and although he worked as hard in India, he could not get out of Administration into the great world of the Political Department. He was uncertain why. Once, on a very hot morning, he met a teacher from the local school with a group of boys and noticed that the teacher showed him less respect than they did. 'I was in no mood to stand any impertinence from a man like that,' he says, and boxed his ears. It was 1912, but the incident got into the local press, and he wondered whether it was this sort of thing which kept him in limbo.

His chance came in the second year of the war. Officials of the Indian Civil Service were increasingly needed in Mesopotamia to administer Arab territory evacuated by the Turks. It was exile of a kind but he got his promotion.

In Basra and Baghdad he again showed outstanding ability but almost at once began to differ from his superiors on policy. He knew in advance that a revolt in the Arabian peninsula was being planned by T. E. Lawrence under Husein, Sherif of the Hejaz and head of the Hashemite dynasty. Britain had another ally in Husein's neighbour, Ibn Saud, who was king of the primitive Wahhabis. In 1916, when the revolt began, Husein announced himself as 'King of the Arab countries' and Philby volunteered to go on a mission of pacification to Ibn Saud.

For the next ten years, until his resignation in 1925, he backed Ibn Saud against the Hashemite dynasty, and backed the Arabs, including the Hashemites, against the British. He argued with his immediate superiors, with Whitehall, with Curzon as Foreign Secretary, and with the Labour Party. When Ibn Saud attacked the Hejaz and overran it in 1926, Philby saw it as the defeat of his enemies in London. 'The triumph of the Wahabbis was the measure of their failure; and if Ibn Sa'ud was the prophet of that movement, I was the voice crying in the wilderness, which they laughed to scorn.' He settled down as a privileged trader in Jedda. When he went through the ritual of conversion at Mecca in the defeated Hejaz, he said that 'the controlling factor' had been the King.

King Ibn Saud was a Wahhabi Bonaparte, who had turned his country into the biggest state in the Middle East by harnessing the fanaticism of the tribes who belonged to the reformed and puritanical Wahhabi sect. In the Arab world he was without allies. He was a despot who consolidated his position by terrorizing minor sheiks and suppressing revolt with a harder hand than other bedouin chiefs. A great bearded figure of six foot four, he needed only a few hours' sleep after an exhausting day. He was limited to four wives by the Koran but kept a running vacancy and had over a hundred in all thanks to its tolerance of divorce. The size and greed of the royal family became the chief menace to the economy of the country.

It is not easy to account for Philby's devotion to Ibn Saud on rational grounds. His rewards were not lavish, considering that his deal with the Standard Oil Company of California made Ibn Saud one of the richest men in the world. He gave Philby a house, £50 a month in gold, and the facilities to make important journeys of exploration, of which the biggest took him three hundred miles south of Ryadh across the Empty Quarter. Philby's maps and observations on these journeys were of lasting value. He argued that in some sense Saudi Arabia was a democracy, where 'the trinity of Liberty, Equality and Fraternity is worshipped more fervently than ever it was in France'; but he admitted that Ibn Saud was 'an autocrat in a democratic setting', and his attachment is only explained by incidentals in his travel diaries.

Ryadh, the capital into which he came, was literally sealed off from the outside world, its gates shut at times of prayer, its streets patrolled by proctors. In the palace he was treated with honour and given the suite normally occupied by the King's favourite wife. 'In the hot weather the roof of the raised central portion was allotted to my use at night, and from that commanding position, the highest point of the whole city, I could scan not only the surrounding roofs, but the country around far and wide.' He loved heights and was addicted to mountain-climbing and mountain photography. He could 'never see a high place on the earth's surface without an uncontrollable desire to see the earth's surface from its summit.'

His Arab dress was now essential for his safety among a people who were trained in hatred of the infidel, but even as one of them he belonged to a different order because of their poverty and ignorance. Disease was so common that nearly 80 per cent of the children died in the first year of life. When he went any distance he had either a bodyguard from the King's slaves or a group of interpreters and guides. An old woman lifted her arm to Allah and prayed for blessings on him as a prince. A man to whom he gave an inadequate tip protested that he was a government in himself 'and we expect much from governments'. He laboured under no delusions about his followers. They were credulous, greedy, ungrateful, lying, quarrelsome, unreliable; their incompetence was only redeemed by their fidelity. On the whole he took more interest in his collection of Arabian baboons which acted as watchdogs in his house at Mecca. He presented the British Museum with many new species of birds, including a partridge and a woodpecker named after his wife and himself.

In his relations with Ibn Saud Philby was aware of the underlying superiority of the West which marked him out from the King's other advisers. He clung to the memory of Westminster where the chimes of Big Ben had punctuated the years as he rose to be head boy. He listened now to the great clock by radio. He was addicted to news bulletins, and set more store on building radio stations than arranging the American oil contract. To Ibn Saud he was not only the interpreter of the news, but a master of finance, the prophet of eclipses and an amateur doctor. 'It was often', he says, 'quite amusing to watch the administration of medical comfort to His Majesty in his throne-room in the midst of a public audience: now a couple of pills of one kind or another with a glass of water to wash them down; now an eye-bath accompanied by a supply of cotton wool, which he would fling behind the throne after drying his eyes.' Uncouth episodes of this kind did not detract from Ibn Saud's stature in his eyes but enabled him to accept it. He believed he would survive 'in the history of the world as one of its greatest leaders of men'; he was 'at the top of the tree of human greatness'.

Philby's relations with his wife and son had by nature an Islamic quality which gathered strength. His English wife typed his manuscripts, even when they contained an account of his infidelities; by 1935 he had a second wife, Um Fahd, who had 'practically nothing in the way of companionship', according to his son.

He was benevolent to children, and especially to Kim, but among the first things he admired in Ryadh was the deference of a son to his father. In India he had been disgusted by the sight of a boy lolling in a chair and leading the conversation while his father was present. In Ryadh a son would not enter an upper room if his father was in the one underneath; in the presence of others he sat in the lowest place. The punishments inflicted by the Arab father were horrific.

It did not require a philosophy of this kind to impress Kim. In India his father's power over the local people had been absolute. He went on tiger-shooting expeditions and once came back from a tour of his area with an alarming black beard. He treated the child as an inanimate bundle, in danger from snakes and precipices. He records his progress in his books but omits his name from the index. Kim had difficulty in facing him and developed a stammer by the time he was four. When the choice of a preparatory school had to be made in another four years, his father decided to spend a month looking round Eastbourne. Charles Doughty, whom he regarded as 'the greatest of all "Arabians",' lived there and Philby was anxious to arrange a meeting between him and the Amir Faisal, Ibn Saud's second son, who was to visit England at the end of the year. He may also have consulted him about Kim's school. Doughty had had a stammer from childhood, which had prevented him from fulfilling his ambition of entering the Navy. The Adro School, which was chosen for Kim, specialized in training for the Navy and in the care of nervous and delicate children. It was on the slopes of Beachy Head, and Kim was allowed to bicycle over and call on Doughty.

Philby was as ambitious for his son as for himself. When Kim won a scholarship to Westminster after five years at Eastbourne, his father was 'duly gratified'. As a reward he took him for a holiday in Spain without the rest of the family. But at Westminster he failed to get into the cricket eleven or become head of the school, and Philby let him feel his concern.

St. John Philby had set his son the Napoleonist problem in an unusually sharp form. At Eastbourne Kim had realized that even among Arabists his father was an outsider for reasons which were not clear. Philby had succeeded Lawrence as British Representative in Jordan in 1921, and brought out Kim and the family to see him in his glory. His Arabic was better than Lawrence's, and Lawrence himself admitted that he made him feel guilty as 'an unscientific traveller'; but when Doughty's *Arabia Deserta* was reissued in 1921, the introduction was by Lawrence instead of St. John Philby, and it was Lawrence who became the darling of the British press.

In Kim's last year at Eastbourne Philby resigned from the service on a tiny pension and went back to Saudi Arabia. He still hoped for a career in Westminster. He twice made attempts to become a Labour Member, but at the time of his resignation in 1925 he differed from the party too sharply on foreign policy. In 1939, when he hoped to oppose Winston Churchill at Epping, the local party would not adopt him, and when he stood at Rye on an anti-war policy he lost his deposit. In 1940 he was interned for nearly six months for Fascist sympathies he had shown in the Middle East.

By the time Kim went to Westminster it had become almost impossible

z

for him to find any ground on which to rival his father without either challenging or betraying him. He played fives for the school instead of cricket and read history instead of modern languages, but the possibility of a wider horizon in the desert only opened up when he got to Cambridge. He inspected it cautiously at the same time as his father was justifying his conversion to Islam.

An objective account of Islam as a religion could hardly ignore its peculiar origin as an empire or its tendency to foster the growth of political despotism. But Philby, who was strictly accurate as a map-maker or ornithologist, allowed himself to drift in dealing with fundamentals. On the whole he did not notice the squalor and conformity of Ryadh. Slavery was a subject he almost ignored. When he faced it, as he tried to in *The Heart of Arabia* and *Forty Years in the Wilderness*, he insisted that slaves were well treated and for the most part exceedingly happy. Imperialism seemed to him the dominant characteristic of the British; democracy and individualism of the Arabs. His resolution at Cambridge to think fearlessly for himself would have gained support from any religion which rejected western values, but Islam had a cutting edge of its own. It seemed to him democratic because Moslems were in the last resort equal before Allah. As individuals it was their duty to seek salvation with a ruthless disregard of others. 'King, country, family', went to the wall where their claims conflicted with those of Allah. Philby saw this as 'the highest kind of patriotism', overriding the fate of individual countries. Its universal appeal was proved by the allegiance of a third of the human race.

To apply this view of Islam to Communism was a step for which Kim had a double motive. It preserved his loyalty to his father in the wilderness at the same time as it established his superiority by allying himself with the future. He was never overtly disloyal or critical. He first met Saudis when he was seven, when the delegation led by Faisal spent a month in England under the care of his father. They were lost in the English autumn but treated as the princes they were. He was prepared for his father's conversion by the long process which had started in Moslem India. But in Kim's first year at Cambridge, when he actually made the journey to Mecca to become a *hajji*, St. John Philby did not fail to put a romantic emphasis on it. No writer, he said, had noticed that its culmination at 'Arafa was a festival of the camel. 'There must have been some 50,000 of them at least.' As he moved forward in the royal cavalcade, 'our legions seemed to lose reality and to become, as it were, a ghostly heavenly host. . . .' Kim was reading economics and history at Trinity College and might be assumed to have been unimpressed. But a quarter of a century later, when he had done his work as an agent and was covering King Hussein's reconciliation with Nasser in Jordan, he made a journey deep into the desert to the oasis of Azraq for no better reason than that tens of thousands of camels were passing. There were 'well over 50,000 camels', he reported, in one of the longest articles he wrote for the *Observer*. He watched them plodding off in long lines, 'far and wide across the landscape as far as the horizon'.

'He never spoke about his father,' says Malcolm Muggeridge, who knew him closely in the Second World War; but Muggeridge and everyone else who came in contact with him was aware of his presence in Kim's mind at more than life-size. He put off visiting Saudi Arabia until 1947, when he was about to take up his post in Istanbul as a double agent. His father by then suspected he was 'red' and can hardly have hoped to convert him to Islam; but he may have wanted to justify himself and his adopted country. It was hard going because Ibn Saud was pressing his view that the West should use its atom bombs in a preventive war against the Soviet Union. 'The king was tired and disgruntled for no particular reason,' says St. John Philby, 'and the conversation at court flagged somewhat for want of any subject of interest.' Father and son wandered through the streets in Arab clothes, and Kim protested later in the *Economist* that there was only one public lavatory in the capital, 'a noisome retreat' at the airport. He was more attracted by an air journey across the country, but visibility was so bad that he could not see the details he wanted. After his father's exile, on the death of the King, he denounced the country in the *Observer* as 'a sink of bribery and corruption'; its regime was 'an anachronism'. Seven years later, when the old man had been readmitted to advise on restoring the economy, Kim said it was customary to give the King credit for progress and to blame foreign advisers when anything went wrong. 'It would seem only decent', he added, 'to allow them to share the credit.'

In 1960 St. John Philby went to the Soviet Union for the first time to attend the Orientalists' Congress. Others who attended say that he made a point of testing out Soviet claims to treat its Islamic minority with favour and found them wanting. In Beirut on the way back to Ryadh he died in his son's arms. 'Kim was shattered,' says Eleanor Philby, 'and drank himself senseless.' He wrote an obituary in the *Observer* calling his father the 'greatest of Arabian explorers'. In defiance of Wahhabi custom, he had the words carved on his tombstone in the Moslem cemetery where he buried him.

Although Communism was a revolt against his father's world, Kim was loyal to him in the arguments he found for accepting it. He had the same capacity for observing with accuracy in matters of detail while ignoring fundamentals, the same kind of respect for Marx as his father had for the Koran and its commentators. If Islam claimed the allegiance of a third of the human race, the socialist sixth of the world was overtaking it. If Saudi Arabia was a democracy resisting imperialism, the Soviet Union would supplant imperialism with economic democracies which alone made men free.

One book, we know, was central in his experience. 'Of course', he said to Hugh Trevor-Roper, in a moment of self-revelation, 'every attempt at historical analysis is nothing once you compare it to Marx's *Eighteenth Brumaire of Louis Napoleon.*'

Brumaire, the original *coup d'état* leading to Napoleon's personal dictatorship, was an event which every Napoleonist had to swallow if he was to see Napoleon as the embodiment of the French Revolution. Marx himself had no difficulty in accepting historical figures like Cromwell and Napoleon in their setting as precursors of Communism. His thesis in analysing the trivial victory of Napoleon's nephew is that a great event from the past, even though it 'weighs like an alp upon the brain of the living', cannot provide a solution to the problems of the present. Louis Napoleon's *coup* of 1852 was a caricature of his great uncle's. The drama of the classical revolutions of the eighteenth century was already out of date.

Proletarian revolutions, on the contrary, such as those of the nineteenth century, criticise themselves constantly; constantly interrupt themselves in their own course; come back to what seems to have been accomplished, in order to start anew; scorn with cruel thoroughness the half measures, weaknesses and meannesses of their first attempts. . . .

The difference, apart from the hesitant, tide-like nature of the Communist advance, was that its victory would be certain and final.

Marx's scorn of the bourgeoisie is nowhere so concentrated against an individual as in his analysis of Louis Napoleon. He was an impostor in his imperial robes, like 'that crazy Englishman in Bedlam, who imagines he is living in the days of the Pharaohs'. He was not even, for certain, a Bonaparte, but more probably an illegitimate, a gipsy, who exploited his connection with a dead world in order to aggrandize himself. His hold on the imagination was spurious because its strength came from the past instead of the proletarian future. The one service he had done his country was to discredit the Napoleonic dream for good.

In some such way as Marx disposed of Louis Napoleon, Kim Philby must have built a bonfire under his father, who came to Cambridge in May Week of 1933 when he took his third-class degree. St. John Philby harped on his own achievements at Westminster and Cambridge, where he had got a first, and on his conversion to Islam. If his son's conversion to Communism was 'complete' that June, as he said in Moscow thirty years later, his father unwittingly contributed to it. Kim's exploits for the Soviet Union tended to be in Islamic countries, in Spain where his father had insisted on the Islamic basis of life, in Istanbul, 'the city of 500 mosques', as *Izvestia* called it in an interview with him, in Albania, where he destroyed a liberation movement which threatened Soviet control of the Moslem majority.

The substitution of Stalin for Ibn Saud did not, of course, free Kim

Philby from the Napoleonist character pattern, which was even more clearly marked than in his father. The dammed-up aggression first showed itself in childhood in his stammer. 'Inside him', says Malcolm Muggeridge, 'there was something explosive, of which the stutter and that convulsively clenching and unclenching hand were a manifestation.' He told his wife, Eleanor, that he had 'some violent desire' in his dreams which was always frustrated by the arrival of people.

Philby has been accused of causing the deaths of many people with apparent indifference to anything but his own ingenuity in bringing them about; but two peculiarities in the melodrama make it impossible to see in him the unhesitating servant of a cause which reduced human life to irrelevance. The killings as reported were indirect, carried out by others, and separated in time from his action in preparing them. In an article about the attempt to train his fox cub not to destroy living plants, he says 'there is a lapse of time between crime and punishment that may blur in her mind, the connection between them.' We may suspect Philby's indifference was not of the kind that would have enabled him to kill anyone face to face.

His violence readily turned against himself. In a drinking fit at the end in Beirut, he had twenty-four stitches in his head and a doctor told his wife that another ounce of alcohol in his blood would have killed him. In the same period he twice complained of policemen and taxi-drivers in his dreams and waking life. In Moscow he thought it likely that the British intelligence services would try to kill him as he may have had to kill defectors from the other side.

'My first impression, and my last, was that he was a man of extreme kindness,' said a journalist who knew he had been responsible for the death of a great many people. His wife's account of their relations is of kindness pushed to sentimentality. When a journalist in the Middle East fell on hard times, Philby suggested giving him his own job on the *Observer*.

He claims to have visited twenty-four countries as a Communist and he was an enthusiastic traveller before becoming one. 'I knew Hindi and Arabic from the earliest years of my life,' he told *Izvestia*, 'German, French, Spanish and Turkish came later, also Russian.' His Arabic was not in fact very fluent and he had no means of knowing it from the earliest years of his life, but in Russian he excelled his father, who scarcely understood a word.

He was an actor who spent most of his life playing a part. 'I learnt', he said, 'the art of hiding my thoughts and pretending to be someone else.' A journalist who knew him closely said he was 'the best actor in the world'.

He had always had rival courts. The Indian children with whom he played recognized him as their superior as clearly as his pets, from Squib, the Irish terrier, to an elephant he once rode like a Maharajah. 'He had an almost Indian feeling for animals,' says his wife, 'racoons, birds, fish, Jackie our pet vixen, Wilbur our mouse, and Margot, our half-breed Alsatian puppy.' In Beirut he allowed the fox cub to drink whisky and suck his pipe. In Moscow he began with a canary and a pair of budgerigars which increased to seven and were joined by a stray parakeet.

He needed, like his father, the support of followers and allies, and because these were normally invisible was delighted when he could appear openly with a retinue. At the fall of Santander, in August 1937, he reported in *The Times* that he was 'regarded for a short space as the paramount authority in the city'—the Republicans had been broken, the militia marched off as captives, but the Nationalist uniform of his escort won him the applause of the inhabitants. In Moscow, thirty years later, he warned a correspondent of the *Sunday Times* that a bodyguard was ready to protect him. He probably had no more respect for these supporters than his father had for the Saudi escorts, and he may even have preferred his fox and his budgerigars, as St. John Philby preferred the Arabian baboons who guarded his house at Mecca; but they were on his side in a hostile world.

Modesty was perhaps his most obvious characteristic, but it was sustained by the sense of power which his secret alliance gave him. In the West he was able to reduce colleagues he would otherwise have found intolerable to manageable proportions. When he was decorated by Franco in the presence of his generals, he 'noticed they were all, including Franco, of a very small stature'. Ramsay MacDonald, Baldwin, and Chamberlain seemed to him nonentities; Mickey Ladd, the deputy head of the American F.B.I., was 'short and immensely stocky'. When there was no comfort to be drawn from the stature of his opponents and their strength seemed impregnable, he was still able to smile at their ignorance of his power. He had the Napoleonist characteristic of failing to see people as individuals in their own right. 'All Philby's judgments on other people suffer from his contempt for them,' says Cyril Connolly; 'they are so many cabbages.'

Among Communists he had the advantage which gave the Napoleonists their peculiar pleasure in foreign travel. He was a visitor of importance in a provincial and emergent civilization. In Moscow he was received 'with high honour', like his father in the palace at Ryadh. To the correspondents of *Izvestia* he was 'the perfect English gentleman', who belonged to a different world from the crowd of passers-by.

'Excuse me,' they say hurriedly. 'Don't mention it,' he replies in a friendly manner, speaking with a slight foreign accent. He looks with interest at people standing at the bus stop, and glances with gay benevolence at the girls in mini coats rushing towards the saving warmth of the underground station.

In his personal relations Philby had the magnetic quality which the Napoleonists owed to their loyalty within a group. 'No-one could have been a better chief,' says Graham Greene, who worked for him in British Intelligence without suspecting him of Communism; '. . . my old liking for him comes back, as I remember with pleasure those long Sunday lunches at St. Albans when the whole sub-section relaxed under his leadership for a few hours of heavy drinking. . . .' The idea that *he could be relied on* was an accurate perception of his lack of self-interest, and the impression was strong enough to suppress the question, *against whom*? His rival court, in the most intimate sense, consisted of people like Burgess and Maclean, who did ask the question and shared his alienation from the main body of the community.

Guy Francis de Monçy Burgess belonged to a Huguenot family who had anglicized their name of Bourgeois and suppressed that of de Monçy. In the Napoleonic wars they prospered as bankers in Ramsgate and Margate, where they had the right to issue their own banknotes until 1844. In the middle of the century, John Burgess, the head of the bank, took his eldest son into partnership and disposed of the second, Henry Miles, the grandfather of Guy, as a cadet in the Royal Artillery. Henry Burgess was posted to India in 1865, and as soon as he got there the family bank was taken over by another. He saw no means of redeeming the disaster and served on for twenty-one years in India until he retired as a lieutenant-colonel to a remote village in Wales.

It may have occurred to him that the de Monçys and Bourgeois who stayed behind in France had done better. There was a Baron René de Monçy, a contemporary who spent his life hunting on his estates and writing historical works of no great distinction. There was Jeannot de Monçey, Duc de Conegliano, who had defended Paris against the Allies in 1814 and received Napoleon's ashes as Governor of the Invalides in Burgess's childhood. When Burgess married and had a child in India in 1881, he did not call him plain John Burgess after his father, but Malcolm Kingsford de Monçy Burgess. He had little else to give him than the India Medal he brought back.

Malcolm, the father of Guy Burgess, lived up to his names as best as he could, but after ten years in the Navy as a midshipman and lieutenant he fell into the arms of an heiress in Portsmouth. Evelyn Gillman belonged to a banking family of almost exactly the same status in Portsmouth as Burgess and Son had had in Ramsgate; but instead of failing in the nineteenth century, they had prospered. William Gillman, her father, was a partner in the bank of Grant, Gillman & Sons. He was a Justice of the Peace, a Mason, and a relative of the distinguished naval family of Grant who were partners in his bank. The Gillmans had a yacht, a car when to have one was more impressive than to have a yacht; and they looked out across the Solent from Rutland House as if they owned the sea and the Navy.

The marriage in 1907 was to all appearance between equals. The captain and officers of Burgess's ship sent gifts and attended in uniform. The bride wore his diamond pendant and the bridesmaids flew the naval ensign in enamel on gold brooches.

In the next ten years Malcolm de Monçy Burgess remained a lieutenant but was often stationed in the lea of Rutland House. He had taken after his father to the extent of specializing in gunnery. After an interval in Devonport, where his son Guy was born in 1911, he regained Portsmouth by joining a new type of craft which was not sought after. The *Bonaventure* had been built at the end of the nineteenth century as a cruiser, but in 1906 was transformed into a submarine depot ship or small floating dockyard to give striking range to the submarines which depended on her. She had a dozen officers of her own and another dozen from the submarine flotilla. Burgess served in her first as a lieutenant, then in a smaller submarine depot ship of his own. In 1916, when Guy was five, he was appointed commander of the *Bonaventure* with gold braid on his cap, and spent the rest of the war with her. She left base to make mysterious journeys to Jarrow and the Mediterranean and took on board Germans as well as British submarine crews. Her existence and movements were hardly mentionable. To the British public from 1915 onwards the submarine meant only the U-boat, which had become the chief enemy of the country. The Navy looked down on 'submariners' whether they were British or German. To *Punch* they were devils in German uniform.

The tradition of giving fewer decorations to the Navy than the Army had endured. At the end of the war Burgess left his ship without distinction or promotion. He was transferred to maintenance duties in the Mediterranean on the staff of the Rear Admiral, Egypt. His wife, who was sociable and dominating, may have had hopes of a base in the Mediterranean, but it turned out to be Ismailia, the main station on the Suez Canal, about fifty miles into the desert. When Guy was eight, they set up house in the European quarter on the east side of the town. There were 10,000 inhabitants but nearly all in the Arab quarter on the west side. The Burgess family joined part of the hierarchy under Admiral Richard Webb, who had been Naval A.D.C. to King George V for the past year. The Admiral had his flag lieutenant and secretary, and his flagship, the *Caesar*, of 14,900 tons with a big hierarchy of her own. Burgess, as he went about his menial job on the guns, was an outsider who did not belong to them. Between the English colony and the Arab quarter there was only one feature of the town which may have helped him to retain a sense of proportion—the chalet of de Lesseps, preserved on the water-front as a reminder of the great Frenchman who had built the Canal.

Burgess does not seem to have made much impression on the Admiral.

**UNRECORDED HISTORY.**

Oom-Paulon Boer-Naparte on board the s.s. "Highbury Castle" on his way to St. Joseph, or some other secluded spot selected by the Colonial Secretary.

*(With humble acknowledgments to Mr. W. Q. Orchardson, R.A.)*

In 1899 *Punch* caricatured the Boer President Kruger as Napoleon on the *Bellerophon*, after the painting (BELOW) by W. Q. Orchardson.

When Lloyd George became Prime Minister in 1916, his dictatorial tendencies increased. In Paris he tried on Napoleon's hat to see if it fitted, and Low drew him as a circus-master. (The caricature was reproduced, LEFT, BELOW, in the 1920s by Ashstead Potters on the floor of an ash-tray.) Defeated in the general election of 1922, Lloyd George spent the remaining years of his life in the political wilderness, where he formed a growing admiration for Hitler. In 1936 he paid a visit to the Nazi dictator (LEFT, ABOVE, with Lloyd George and von Ribbentrop), whom he called 'the George Washington of Germany'.

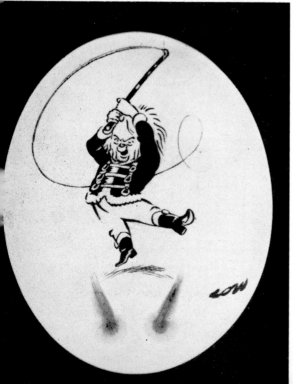

## LABOUR M.P.'S UNWANTED TITLE.

[Barratt.]

The late Sir Oswald Mosley.

[Central News.]

The New Baronet.

The death yesterday of Sir Oswald Mosley, 5th baronet, formerly of Rolleston Hall, Burton-on-Trent, gives his eldest son and heir, Mr. Oswald Mosley, Labour M.P. for Smethwick, a title which he does not want and which he declared in the course of a piquant controversy that he did not intend to use.

Mr. Oswald Mosley, who is regarded as one of the Labour party's most brilliant younger men, was formerly Conservative M.P. for Harrow. He first entered Parliament in 1918 and soon showed himself restive under party discipline. A comparatively short period in the Tory ranks proved enough, and he sat for a time as an Independent. He soon took the final plunge and joined the Labour party. At the 1924 election he contested the Ladywood Division of Birmingham and gave Mr. Neville Chamberlain, the Minister of Health, a considerable shock by reducing his majority to 77. Mr. Mosley's next fight was in 1926, when he was returned for Smethwick at a by-election.

A remark during the campaign by Mr. Oswald Mosley's wife, Lady Cynthia Mosley, daughter of the late Lord Curzon, that "titles are a bit of a joke" brought an indignant retort from the late Sir Oswald (who was a staunch Tory), who declared that "it has occurred to me that more valuable help would be rendered to the country by my Socialist son and daughter-in-law if, instead of achieving cheap publicity about the relinquishing of titles, they would take a more material action and relinquish some of their wealth, and so help to make easier the life of some of their more unfortunate followers."

Mr. Oswald Mosley said he preferred not to comment on this statement, adding that when he and his wife joined the Labour movement it mean a complete break with family associations. Later Mr. Mosley wrote in an article: "I stated long ago, when I first joined the Labour party, that on the death of my father I would renounce the title I should then acquire. I was informed that it was impossible legally to renounce a title, but it will be quite easy not to be addressed by it."

The legal position is that a man cannot surrender a title, but he can, of course, refrain from using it.

Sir Oswald Mosley found it impossible to renounce his title (reported, LEFT, in *The Manchester Guardian*), though joining the Labour Party had meant 'a complete break with family associations'. In 1934, Low sketched the sixth baronet (BELOW) in the blackshirt uniform of the British Union of Fascists, challenged by John Bull at a test match.

THE OTHER TEST MATCH.

The latter-day
Napoleonists had,
like their prede-
cessors, a passion
for animals.
Kingsley Martin
(RIGHT) found
that boa constric-
tors, 'if not too
large', made
admirable pets,
and Kim Philby
in Beirut trained
a fox cub to drink
whisky, suck his
pipe, and
(BELOW) pick
his pocket.

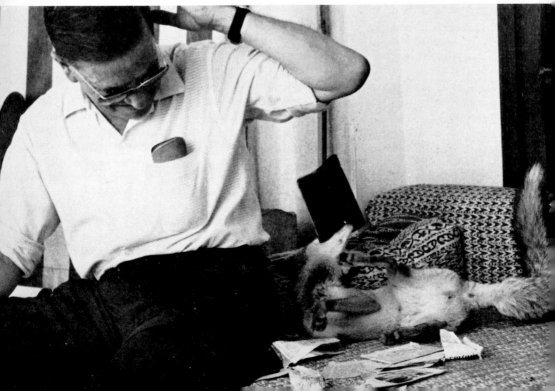

He was retired from the service in the economy cuts of 1921 after two or three minor postings which ended in the *Emperor of India*. He was then only forty. The normal retiring age was fifty-five and there were still 400 commanders on the Active List.

Before his father was axed, Guy Burgess was sent to a school in Hemel Hempstead which prepared boys for Dartmouth and the Navy. The cost was about £200 a year, which was almost half Burgess's pay. There was now a younger boy, Nigel. When Burgess was pensioned off, their education would have been impossible had it not been for the Gillmans. They were given a big Georgian house at West Meon, fifteen miles inland from Portsmouth, and here Burgess had the garden to look after and a walk of a few yards up the hill to the church. His health, according to his wife, was good. They decided to send Guy to Eton instead of Dartmouth, which meant abandoning the Navy. After seeing his career as a whole, Burgess may have felt it was not one for his son. In Guy's second term at Eton, in the night of 15 September 1924, he died of heart failure. There was an inquest and a hurriedly arranged funeral service in the church of St. John. His total assets were just over £400.

Guy attended another funeral service ten years later in Portsmouth Cathedral. His grandfather, William Gillman, the banker, had lived on in Rutland House to twice the age of his father. He had already given most of his money to his daughter, who left nearly £150,000 when she died in 1964. The service was taken by the Bishop of Portsmouth and was crowded. Besides Evelyn, the chief mourner, there was her cousin, Rear-Admiral Grant, whose father had been a partner in Gillman's bank; there were five Justices of the Peace, Sir Harold Pink, a former Mayor, representatives of the Royal Albert Yacht Club, the Freemasons' Lodge, the bank's customers, city councillors, and aldermen. After singing 'Peace Perfect Peace' and 'On the Resurrection Morning', Guy Burgess went back to London to find a job. He had had an outstanding career at Eton and Cambridge and had just returned from the Soviet Union where his conversion to Communism had been confirmed. Moscow had seemed to him poverty-stricken—'just a Balkan town. You know, pigs in the trams . . .'

We do not have enough evidence about his relations with his father to be certain that they were in the Napoleonist pattern of loyalty and revolt, but there are indications that they were. When his father died in 1924, six months after he went to Eton, he actually left and went to Dartmouth according to the original plan. He stuck it for nearly three years with increasing dislike, until trouble with his eyesight provided a reason for going back to Eton. He had a vivid sympathy with poor men and outsiders which was at odds with his attachment to Eton, Mayfair, and the traditional nineteenth-century banking house of the Rothschilds. Of a friend who wrote damning articles about him, he said, 'Poor chap, he probably needs the money badly.' At school he was impressed by a dockers' trade union organizer who told the Etonians they 'had no idea or understanding of poverty'. At Cambridge he organized a strike to secure regular pay for the men who waited at table. He was homosexual and had a strong tendency to pick up men from the working class. He said he never travelled by train because he felt he would be obliged to sleep with the engine-driver. The engine-driver might have found himself at sea. Burgess wore blue pyjamas like a uniform, and insisted that the red, white, and blue décor of his flat 'was the only possible colour scheme one could live with'.

Among Russians Burgess chose the pseudonym of Andreyvitch and told Tom Driberg in Moscow that it was 'in tribute to a character in *War and Peace*'. No explanation has been suggested for his enthusiasm for Tolstoy's Prince Andrew, who has no obvious affinity with him. He is unique among the Russian characters in having a passionate admiration for Napoleon and is only cured of it on the field of Austerlitz where he is wounded and twice addressed by the Emperor in patronizing terms. What is constant in him is his love of his father. His own son, another Andreyvitch, has the same trait, and after Prince Andrew's death the boy makes a vow to be worthy of him.

'Some day I shall have finished learning, and then I will do something. I only pray God that something may happen to me such as happened to Plutarch's men, and I will act as they did. I will do better. Everyone shall know me, love me and be delighted with me.' And suddenly his bosom heaved with sobs and he began to cry.

The last words of *War and Peace* are Andreyvitch's dedication of himself. 'Oh, father, father! Yes, I will do something with which even *he* would be satisfied. . . .'

Commander Burgess would, of course, have been more horrified than the Foreign Office with the outcome of Guy's efforts, but we must note that when he died in a Moscow hospital on 30 August 1963, Guy Burgess's ashes were flown back to England and buried at West Meon on 5 October in his father's grave.

Donald Duart Maclean grew up with closer knowledge of exile than Burgess. His father was the son of a bootmaker, John Maclean, from the Inner Hebrides, who married Agnes Macmellin on an island off the coast of Argyllshire, and moved inland. His wife was the heroine of the saga which followed because of her conviction that the virtues of the wilderness would be able to conquer the mainland on the profits of bootmaking. They had two boys and two girls. The future Sir Donald and Sir Ewen were born south of Bolton in Lancashire where boots were in greater demand than education. The parents spoke Gaelic, but Mrs. Maclean was determined that their English should be perfect. They moved on to Haverfordwest where there was a good grammar school but twenty other cobblers. After competing more than effectively for ten years, they moved again to Carmarthen, where John Maclean died in 1891. By then Donald had qualified as a solicitor in Cardiff and Ewen had passed through Edinburgh University and was specializing as a gynaecologist.

The achievement would not have been possible without the background of thrift and austerity which enclosed them like a covered wagon. A solicitor who was at school with Donald and Ewen in Haverfordwest remembers the headmaster saying he would have 'to bore a hole with a gimlet through the heads of our Scottish friends' before they saw the point of a joke. Their English was now better than their Gaelic, and they learnt to be diplomats to their customers. In Cardiff, after the death of her husband, Agnes Maclean continued to watch over the careers of her sons until she died in 1924 at the age of ninety-two.

The deprivations the family had accepted were more severe than those imposed by Uncle Lloyd in the bootshop at Llanystumdwy. They were Presbyterians, teetotallers and Sabbatarians, but they moved among foreigners and put their faith to the test in the day-to-day struggle to save. When Donald was establishing himself as a solicitor in the docks it was the waste in the lives around him which most struck him. At twenty-four he became secretary of the local Society for the Prevention of Cruelty to Children and soon afterwards worked for 'The Sailor's Rest', a mission hall by the West Dock. The enemy which had to be fought was drink. When he went into partnership and extended his practice to London, he pursued the same causes on a national scale. Drink, he said, was 'the gravest national danger'. In politics he was a passionate Free Trader. Protection seemed to him an act of force against the efficiency of the outsider, but the Licensing Laws were a defence of the outsider at home. He was a gentle and affectionate father who was concerned about the rights of children. 'The youngest child', he said, in one of his speeches on temperance, 'is as much a subject of the Crown as the oldest, richest and most powerful man in England.' At the time he had three sons, of whom the youngest, Donald, was born in 1913.

Maclean was returned to Parliament against all probability as a Liberal for Bath in 1906, and he risked his position almost at once by his support for the Nonconformists in the Bill proposing the final elimination of their grievances in education. He lost his seat in 1910 but got back for the Scottish constituency of Peebles.

For nearly eight years he disappeared into committee work. In the war he was chairman of the London Appeals Tribunal which decided over 50,000 appeals against military service. He threw his weight on the side of the individual, arguing for much stricter medical standards and insisting on the importance of civilian jobs to the war effort. On two other committees, on spies and enemy aliens, he also resisted the tide of prejudice. 'Almost alone among the Allied nations,' he said, in 1919, this country was 'free from any outrage during the war which could be traced to enemy aliens'. He denied that they had been a force against the interests of the country. It was 'not public safety but prejudice' which operated against them.

In the Commons his reputation for hard work and diplomacy led to his appointment as Chairman of Ways and Means and Deputy Speaker. He became a kind of parliamentary cobbler, irritating Lloyd George and Winston Churchill by his detailed grasp of Bills and procedure, but earning the admiration of Asquith by his persistence and integrity. When Asquith was defeated by the coalition of Lloyd George and the Conservatives, Maclean suddenly became a national figure in his place as leader of the 29 independent Liberals, the 'Wee Frees'.

He told the victorious ranks of the coalition that he did not propose to be overawed, and he proved it by championing everyone whose rights seemed to him in danger. Churchill tried to damp him down with a reminder that he had become leader of the Opposition, but there were 59 Labour members on the benches beside him, and he was glad to outdo them in defiance. He criticized the India Act of 1919 for failing to prepare for independence, and when Indian crowds were shot down by British troops at Amritsar, he attacked the Secretary of State for India for trying to hush up a scandal and delay an inquiry. He defended Scottish crofters who seized small-holdings in the Hebrides, schoolchildren under six who were deprived of elementary education, and African races in Rhodesia who were exploited by the British; but his most tenacious campaign was against Churchill over intervention in Soviet Russia.

For about three months after the Armistice it was possible to explain operations based on Archangel and Murmansk as a prolonged winding up of the alliance with Tsarist Russia against Germany, but in March 1919 Churchill made a formal statement that support of the Whites against the Bolshevik government would continue as a military necessity, 'which does not affect policy at any point or in any degree'. Intervention was shared, he said, about equally by the French and Americans and was based on a common obligation to the inhabitants and the Russian armies which had supported them. He later added that the British aim was to establish a North Russian government which would have 'a separate life and existence after our departure'.

Maclean challenged Churchill on the size of the British contribution, its cost, its presence on the borders of Finland and Poland as well as in Turkestan and Caucasia; above all on the pretence that it was unpolitical. If

British troops were engaged, as he said, because of their responsibilities to the Russian people and the Russian Army, he wanted to know 'what people and what Russian Army?'

In the year which followed there were another eight debates and some hundreds of questions. Maclean was more courageous as well as more prominent than Labour Members. He was unsure of himself. He tended to take refuge in the cost of operations, where he could trip Churchill up. He took advantage when he could of Churchill's over-optimism and did his utmost to widen his difference with Lloyd George, who connived in the campaign with reluctance. He stood like a defiant, pale-faced schoolboy in front of a master who knew better, but whereas Churchill depended on success in the field, he argued from principle. He repeatedly used Fox's argument against the war with revolutionary France.

One of the main causes which united the French and lashed the legions of Dumouriez into a highly efficient army which subsequently swept all over Europe, was the intervention of the European nations, and the fear and the national pride evoked by armies which not only hovered along the borders of France but actually invaded her soil. That lesson we can still take to heart and carefully bring to mind in the hope that no Russian Napoleon may arise on the ruins of the Revolution to set up a military oligarchy which would repeat the devastation of the Napoleonic wars.

A Russian Napoleon seemed to Maclean to be foreshadowed in the increasing efficiency of military and civil administration and the authority of Trotsky and Lenin. It was 'quite hopeless' for the Government to think they could sustain a position in Russia unless they had the Russian people with them. He held no brief for Communism, which was 'a negation of democracy', but a war against opinion in Russia would promote it. When British troops were withdrawn at the beginning of 1920, he pressed for a renewal of diplomatic relations. It was four years before the first Labour Government succeeded in restoring them for a brief period.

Maclean, like Fox, claimed to speak in the name of public opinion— there was, he said, 'grave unrest' in the British Army and throughout the country. But in the next three elections he was defeated. He stood in vain for Peebles, Kilmarnock, and East Cardiff, and was not returned until the momentary swing to the Left in 1929 which produced a Labour minority government. His son Donald was then sixteen and preparing to go on to Cambridge from Gresham's School, Holt.

There had always been tendencies in Sir Donald Maclean which were at odds with his championship of the oppressed. He had done well for himself as a solicitor dealing with the shipping business of Cardiff, but the thrift of his childhood turned into a crusade against state expenditure. He was the prime mover in establishing the Geddes Committee which secured heavy economies after the war. 'A pen-knife is of no use,' he said; 'it is an axe you want.' Churchill said he went beyond the limits of frugality and parsimony to sheer niggardliness. He wanted to abolish the Cabinet Secretariat and the Ministry of Transport, and above all to ensure that the economies hurt.

Like Asquith, he was socially ambitious. His father had christened him with his mother's name, Macmellin, but he dropped even the initial. In his first year as a Member of Parliament, he married Gwendolen Devitt, the daughter of a Justice of the Peace in the South of England. At a dinner after the war with the Prince of Wales and a fashionable group of diplomats and writers, Asquith describes Lady Maclean as 'still young and quite good looking'; she looked at the scene in a spirit he understood, 'with glowing cheeks and glittering eyes'. The Macleans made no claim to aristocracy until 1912, immediately before the birth of Donald, when Duart Castle was restored and occupied by Sir Fitzroy Donald Maclean, tenth Baronet of Dowart and Morvaren. The castle on Mull, the biggest of the Inner Hebrides, had been derelict since the final Stuart defeat at Culloden, and Maclean remembered claims of his father to distant relationship to its owner. The tradition of the baronets was grandiose and violent. One in the sixteenth century had exposed his wife, a daughter of the Duke of Argyll, on a rock which submerged at high tide between Mull and the island of Lismore. The Lady Maclean was only saved from drowning by her brother, who came on to Mull and killed her husband.

In the octogenarian Mrs. Agnes Maclean, who still spoke Gaelic, there was a ready source of confirmation of these traditions. After christening his son, Donald Duart, Maclean applied for a grant of arms. The heraldic authorities in Edinburgh considered the evidence, which was admittedly verbal and went through third and fourth sons, and produced a coat of arms which differed from those of other Macleans in its scarlet bordering with a scarlet mullet in the centre.

The long trek in childhood through England and Wales was now overlaid by a more glorious version of the past. Maclean was knighted in 1917 and joined Brooks's and two other West End clubs. He made lasting friends on his wartime committees, especially with Stanley Baldwin and Viscount Sankey, who became Lord Chancellor. Baldwin and Sir James Barrie both believed he was born in Tiree, the island next to Mull, instead of in a Lancashire bootshop. To Sankey he confided his ambition to become a Cabinet minister.

He fought the election of 1929 as a committed Free Trader, but within a few months the great depression caused unemployment to double and began to freeze the life of the ports. In February 1931, to ward off the alternative of tariffs or higher taxation, he proposed that a committee should be set up to 'recommend all practicable and legitimate reductions in the national expenditure', and he dwelt on the extravagance of the dole. The unemployed were the economic enemy, a 'ghastly army', but when challenged on where the savings could be found, he said the first target should be the armed forces. The May Committee, which resulted from his motion, forecast a deficit of £100 million and recommended that a National Government should find half the sum from unemployed relief and most of the remainder from other forms of state expenditure. Keynes argued that the pursuit of economy by these means would increase unemployment, but Maclean exulted in his victory and as the crisis developed worked together with Baldwin, the Conservative leader, for a National Government. He was rewarded with the Board of Education and after the November election with a seat in the Cabinet.

The trap was of his own making. There was a Conservative majority in the Cabinet, and although Baldwin had made ambiguous promises against Protection, there were no safeguards at all for education. Free Trade was first breached in March 1932, and at the Liberal Party Conference in April Asquith's daughter, Lady Violet Bonham Carter, said they had been betrayed. A thousand delegates supported a resolution condemning the betrayal. In the Cabinet meanwhile argument had turned on the distribution of cuts. The armed forces were represented by Viscount Hailsham, Lord Londonderry, and Sir B. Eyres-Monsell, who all resisted effectively, while Maclean, as the moving spirit of economy, was unable to. He accepted a cut of £5½ million, which was half the total for the Civil Service and more than five times the cut in the armed forces. It fell on teachers, whose pay was reduced by 10 per cent, on inspectors and administrators, a third of whom were declared redundant, and on scholarships and university grants. Maclean tried to justify himself to the Opposition he had once led by arguing that the education estimates had tripled since 1914. He gave assurances that the loss of inspectors would not be allowed to affect the health of schools and proposed to distribute a leaflet 'with instructions with regard to alcohol'.

A minority of teachers revolted and the *New Statesman* argued that they had been singled out from the community because of their inability to resist. In the Commons a miner invited Maclean to resign on the ground that damage would be heaviest among the children of the poor. A Scottish member said the true comparison was not with pre-war standards but with the education of Ministers' sons. Maclean voted for higher health contributions on 13 June, but it was the last time he went into a division. He died of heart failure on 15 June 1932, after being a Cabinet minister for seven months.

Donald Duart Maclean was at the end of his first year at Cambridge and came up to London to hear the tributes in the Commons. They were generous, especially from the Conservatives. Baldwin recalled Maclean's stand against the coalition at the end of the war and claimed that the same love of justice had guided him to the end. The Left did not contradict this view; Maxton added that he was poles asunder in politics but had 'met no one in this House who was so completely capable of seeing the other man's point of view and regarding it with sympathetic understanding'.

The obituaries in the national press had a greater range, but all omitted that he was the son of a bootmaker. *The Times* described him as 'a combination of sweet reasonableness with firmness in asserting his authority when necessary'. The *Manchester Guardian* said he was not only responsible for the May Committee which 'was the signal for the terrible financial crisis of the autumn' but was at the heart of the negotiations which led up to the National Government and 'naturally was included in it'. The *Daily Worker* painted his career as a betrayal of the workers.

Donald's behaviour when he went back to Cambridge suggests that he was not so much moved by the tributes as the accusations of betrayal. He had a deep pride in his father. In his first year as a scholar at Trinity Hall, which coincided with the first year of the National Government, he had worked badly and got a second in the first tripos. From the time of his father's death he showed the steady application which won him a first in his finals and later a place in the Diplomatic Service. But work in itself did nothing to make good the picture he had formed in childhood of an incorruptible champion of the oppressed. To undo the charges of betrayal, which were the echo of his own, he did three other things in the year after his death. He told his mother that he proposed to become a teacher himself, if possible in the Soviet Union; he joined the Hunger Marchers on their way down from the North of England; and he wrote a book review in *Cambridge Left* in October 1933 giving reasons why an intellectual must be a Communist.

The claim he made for Communism was that it was concerned with 'external reality' instead of the unreal values of society. External reality was the economic situation with its unemployment and low wages, not the idealized world of the *Forsyte Saga*, or T. S. Eliot's antiquarian interest in Dante, or Virginia Woolf's flight into personal relationships. A rising tide of opinion would sweep away the whole of this crack-brained mess.

His father had once been the spokesman of external reality. As leader of a tiny Opposition, he had insisted on the rights of the Indians and Russians as much as the landless Highlander. He found room for his youngest son, Donald, as equal to 'the oldest, richest and most powerful man in England'. To the boy, who knew him as the son of a bootmaker, the alliance was binding, and his title and new coat of arms were without power to deflect him from it.

In 1924, when Donald was eleven and his father had lost his seat, another boy was born, Alan Duart, who never had the vision of a father defying Churchill and the victorious coalition. In 1929 when the brothers were recovering from influenza, they played Highlanders against Sepoys with toy soldiers. Alan assumed the Highlanders should win; Donald the Sepoys. 'Why shouldn't the Indians win?' he asked. 'After all, it's their country.'

In Cardiff, where his father's clients were the Shipping Federation, Donald took the side of the dockers. He told a friend 'that he wished he could start life as a docker in the East End or as a carpenter'. When he became a Communist agent and secrecy was essential, he was embarrassed to meet people who expressed Communist views. To Philip Toynbee, who did so for a time, he admitted that he used to be a Communist as well, 'that he was still a Marxist but that his interests now lay with the ruling classes.' It was the Communist account of his father's career.

He also had his own account, and it is not difficult to guess what it was. Sir Donald Maclean was not only gentle as a father; he was unique among politicians in his self-control. Although his struggle with Churchill lasted a year, in which he had to face withering implications of ignorance, he never lost his temper. In July 1919 when he came to the end of a demand for the evacuation of British troops from Siberia, there was a moment when he might have taken his revenge.

*Mr. Churchill*: They are coming home.
*Sir D. Maclean*: I am delighted to hear it. Have any of them started?
*Mr. Churchill*: They are on the railway now. It is a long way.
*Sir D. Maclean*: It is a long way, but still it is good to hear that they have left.

Such diffidence when he had won his point made no particular appeal to Churchill, but with Conservatives like Baldwin, who were themselves restrained, it made a deep impression. They came to accept him as a lesser Asquith whose moderation made him one of them.

It was when morality was at stake that Maclean showed a streak of violence. He was national solicitor of the Society for the Prevention of Cruelty to Children and had evidence from inspectors which enabled him to prosecute offenders. He claimed that the work of the inspectors was so important that they should be exempted from military service. It was the Society's policy to prosecute as rarely as possible, but he was ruthless when parents encouraged their children to drink. Alcohol, he believed, should never be allowed to touch the lips of a child. Adults themselves were without unconditional rights. 'Individual taste', he said, 'must give way to the good of the community.' He wanted to increase the impact of the Licensing Laws and was accused by Lord Robert Cecil of 'an unreasoning hatred of alcohol'. He opposed the opening of cinemas on Sundays and his investigations into

AA

life on canal boats involved him in a charge of disrupting family life. His insistence on economy had little to do with economics as such; the axe was his weapon because of the momentum of its fall. He said it was an abuse of democracy to protest. One of the most moderate critics of his educational economies said they were blind and unreasoning. 'There has been no working out of the application of the principle at all, but just simply cutting as though they were simply butchers.'

To Donald Maclean it must have seemed that the ruthlessness of his father's moral crusading would have saved his honour if it had been applied to politics. His own attraction to Communism was precisely that it was violent and dogmatic. When Philip Toynbee talked in a drinking bout of forming a private Communist Party of their own, he demanded they should have an ally. '"We must have one other member," he suddenly insisted; and when I asked who, he spat out the word "Stalin!" with preposterous dramatic venom.' Alcohol seemed to him a solvent which would have melted the prim self-control of his father. Cyril Connolly credits him with 'a theory that sufficient alcohol could release in one a second personality, which though it might stimulate the destructive element, worked only good by helping people to acknowledge their latent affinities.' The violence it released had a political direction, attacking humbug and pretence and anyone suspect of social or political betrayal. He also experimented with throttling his wife and may have found support in the tradition of the Duart Macleans, which he parodied. He adopted the device of a boar's head from Gordon's export gin, 'a scarlet head with gaping mouth and long ferocious tusks', according to Toynbee.

Besides the violence of the Napoleonists, Maclean had their dictatorial arrogance. Connolly noticed in his support of Communism 'the familiar priggish tones of the Marxist, the resonance of the "Father Found".' In spite of his standing in the Foreign Office he was never at ease in diplomatic parties and preferred the company of artists, among whom he had a special status. 'In Paris', says Connolly, 'his evenings were usually spent in the Left Bank cafés with a little group of hard-working painters and sculptors.' In *Cambridge Left* he had singled out painters and sculptors as inferior artists who were 'socially unaware', and it was perhaps fortunate that he made no reference to Connolly. 'We all felt he was a rock', Connolly says in *The Missing Diplomats*, 'and that if we were in trouble he would help us and not just let us down with a reprimand.'

Like Philby, Maclean was strongly attracted to children and pets. He sometimes said it was only his children who prevented him from committing suicide. An Embassy wife quoted in *Philby*, by Messrs Page, Leitch, and Knightley, describes his manner of calling on her family when he was Head of Chancery in Cairo.

Instead of ringing the bell he liked to clamber over the garden wall and bark like a dog outside, pawing at the window to attract attention. The servants, children and visitors gradually became accustomed to this. 'Every time we heard a barking noise we would say—"Don't worry, it must be Donald again".'

He had an unusual talent for languages which may have been stimulated by his Gaelic-speaking grandmother. At Cambridge his first was in French and German and in Moscow he was given a job, according to Burgess, in 'a linguistics institute'. He was by nature an actor, who could play the woman who was throttled as well as the dog which attacked. At school he played the female lead in Coward's *I'll Leave It to You*, and was nicknamed Lady Maclean; but the extent of his mercurialism is perhaps best summed up by Philip Toynbee who watched him arrive at the Embassy in Cairo after openly implying that he was a Communist.

He had seemed a hopeless wreck that morning, groaning, holding his eyes and vomiting, yet as we rounded the last corner of the street, as the sentry came to attention and began his salute, I witnessed the amazing transformation of this disorganised drunkard into an imposing officer of HMG's diplomatic service. Donald's whole face and bearing changed. His body regained its lost dignity; his face became wise, benevolent and responsible.

Although Maclean differed from Burgess and Philby in his habit of discussing suicide, all three showed a deeply suicidal tendency in committing themselves to a country from which there could be no return. The full implications may not have been clear in the heyday of the National Government when they saw that country as an outcast world, but even then they can hardly have failed to guess the extent of their commitment.

In his farewell article from Beirut on his fox cub, Philby asked before leaving for the Soviet Union what he would do with her as an adult fox. He would not turn her loose in the Lebanese mountains. 'In the first place, she has been man-fed too long; in the second place, most Lebanese are sportsmen—with guns.' He proposed to keep her with him in the belief that she might learn to behave like a dog—'on present form, there is no reason why she should not rival any dog in courtesy and discipline.' It was the basic problem. We remember that Byron killed himself in opposing the Ottoman Empire which had once, in Ali Pasha's court, seemed to him superior to the British Empire; that St. John Philby was unable to mend his manners in Saudi Arabia and grew increasingly unpopular till he was expelled to Beirut, where he died. By 1967 Kim Philby was already admitting that his tantrums with the Soviet Union were 'sometimes explosive but always short-lived'. If his courtesy and discipline had reached their limit, it may have occurred to him that the fox might yet die before the transformation into a dog was complete.

'To betray, you must first belong,' said Philby when he was asked what it felt like to be called a traitor; 'I never belonged.' He told another correspondent—and it was not inconsistent—that he regarded himself as 'wholly and irreversibly English'. Like Burgess and Maclean, who made repeated attempts to return until eleven years after their defection, he remained bound to England as much as the original Napoleonists. All three must have known it was their deepest need to criticize the government under which they lived and they had put their heads in a noose.

# 6

We have now looked at twentieth-century Napoleonists ranging from a great Prime Minister to a group of renegades and found in all of them symptoms of the same revolt against a father to whom they were bound in loyalty by an early alliance in the wilderness. Like the original Napoleonists, they dealt with their revolt by turning it against the main body of the community and giving their loyalty in varying degrees to those who challenged it from outside. They again had unusual ambition. Much the same pattern of characteristics again grouped itself around their solution, partly to enable it to function at all and partly as side-effects. They developed the same mobility of character which made them seem unstable enigmas; in the nature of their situation they were actors, travellers, linguists; they had rival courts which consisted of animals and children as well as adults, and they had a strain of violence which turned against themselves and sometimes affected their speech.

There were two or three general changes, the most obvious of which was a new tolerance of brutality. To admire Hitler or Stalin with certain reservations was allowable by a change in the standards of the time. In 1931 Oswald Spengler published his defence of 'carnivore ethics', which reduced Mill's conception of a science of character formation, which he called ethology, to a justification of violence by appeal to zoology. The political enmities of Fox and Whitbread had something amateur and almost gentle about them compared with those of Mosley and Philby. The Romantics had extended the classical menagerie, but Byron never made a pet of a fox or a boa constrictor.

If a gross change in the climate of opinion allowed the Napoleonists more scope for their violence, a slighter change began to embarrass them. In the eighteenth and nineteenth centuries there had been little risk of their motives being disentangled. Apart from the stray intuitions of Coleridge and William Windham, the original Napoleonist had only to meet accounts of his behaviour which fortified him in his attitude of defiance. His successor could hardly ignore the discoveries of psychology, which gained slower recognition in England than elsewhere but had superficial acknowledgement by the middle of the twentieth century. The threat was a double one. He could now be dismissed as neurotic, a more far-reaching charge than disloyalty because it deflated his sense of heroism and invited modification.

The neo-Napoleonists probed the idea with a distaste which was not without fascination. Both Mosley and Kingsley Martin made a serious study of psychoanalysis but ended by declining to apply it to themselves and least of all to their politics. Kingsley Martin stumbled on the fact that a major revolt against his father had been frustrated by the ostracism they had shared—it was 'my trouble'—but he declined to see the same revolt working itself out with all its force in the mixture of criticism and hero-worship which made his journalism unique. Other neo-Napoleonists, who were more wary, refused to make his first admission. Philby brushed off the influence of his father as if scenting a trap in an interrogation—'at all the decisive turning points of my life, he was thousands of miles out of reach.'

The changes in the atmosphere may have accounted for a change in the stature of the neo-Napoleonists as compared with their ancestors. Genius, even Romantic genius, does not take advantage of a new inhumanity in its age while turning its back on the new insights. Auden saw that Byron would have been at a loss for a hero and a cause. There was no poet of Byron's stature among the neo-Napoleonists, no critic of Hazlitt's, no political theorist of Godwin's, no politician after Lloyd George to rank with Fox.

The pattern again had a wide range of variants with a quite different outcome in different individuals. In the same person it stood out in relief or faded from sight according to variations in his relationship with the community. It is near enough to other character patterns which lack its central impulse, and therefore its persistence, to be difficult to identify without hindsight. One would be rash, for instance, to conclude that an animal-lover with a stammer was more likely to betray his country than an eloquent master of hounds. It would be even more rash to assume that a child who grew up in one stage of his father's career, would have the same pattern as another who grew up in a different stage.

'History', said Emerson, 'is the essence of innumerable biographies.' We are dealing, of course, with a minority of exceptional people, but the essence of their problem was their relationship with the majority. When we tried to summarize the motives of the original Napoleonists, we found that the subjective pattern lying behind their sense of alienation was stimulated by a real background of reaction which dominated the country from the early years of the French Revolution until after the death of Napoleon. Its effect on the radical minority was traumatic. Political and religious emancipation had gone further in England by the eighteenth century than elsewhere in the world; it was going still further when the revolutions in America and France, which the English example had helped to inspire, put a stop to it. In a few years the country was frightened back into acceptance of its traditional pattern by the execution of Louis XVI and the Reign of Terror. It was not so much the severity of Pitt's repression which alienated the Napoleonists as the turn of the tide.

In the twentieth century we have found a quite narrow period of time, between 1930 and 1933, as the formative point of political disaffection, though cultural and religious exile was common in the twenties. The foundering of the Labour Party and the sweeping return of the National Government had a significance which can only be explained by the period running up to it.

For a century after the death of Napoleon the struggle between the forces of change and conservatism had gone on in England uninfluenced to any serious extent by events abroad. There had been no established centre of revolution on the Continent to alarm the moderate majority or encourage the radicals. The year 1848, which came near to setting up such dictatorships in several European countries, remained in the memory of the radicals as a personal loss; the absence of a model of defiance in the nineteenth century may even have added strength to the support for Kruger at its end.

A spurt was then given to emancipation at the beginning of the twentieth century by an election which has been compared by Trevelyan to an earthquake because the new voters in the towns made their will felt by rejecting the traditional ideals of Toryism. For a decade from 1906 the last Liberal ministry carried out reforms beyond any known precedent, establishing a degree of security for the workers, shifting the balance of taxation a little, and eroding the prestige of the aristocracy.

The process of democratization gained momentum in the war from an effort which involved almost everyone in the country. In the Fourth Reform Act, which was passed in 1918, the outline of universal suffrage was visible.

The Russian Revolution of 1917 at first caused less alarm in England than the French Revolution. It was more remote and overshadowed by the war against Germany; its hold on the great Russian land mass seemed insecure. The uncertainty lasted a decade, but the emergence of Stalin in the twenties as a nationalist leader was a guarantee of its will to survive; and the first of the Five Year Plans, which by 1931 was showing clear signs of success, finally established the rival system as a challenge which could not be dismissed.

The spectre of revolution became a reality in this period for the first time since the end of the eighteenth century. The words 'Bolshevik' and 'Red' acquired the odium that 'Jacobin' had then had. The momentum of change faltered and stopped. Neither of the Labour Governments between the wars had a majority in its own right, and the first was broken within a year by an election which turned into an anti-Bolshevik stampede.

The Zinoviev Letter of 1924, like the *Letters to a French Spy* in 1808, claimed to expose a chain of command linking the revolutionary capital with the English reformers about to return to office. It was a less clumsy forgery than its predecessor and was accepted uncritically by the mass circulation press which had a brief monopoly of contact with the electors. When the Fifth Reform Act was passed five years later, a predominantly working-class electorate still gave no mandate for the radical measures of Mosley or even for reformist socialism. In the crisis of 1931, the conservative majority was the biggest of the century.

In this perspective the check to progress at the beginning of the thirties was as dramatic as the collapse of radicalism in the French Revolution. Again, it was not that the reaction was particularly severe. Improvements continued in the general standard of living, in health, and especially in slum clearance. In most ways it was the best time that the majority of Englishmen had known. But in a world of social change and fallen thrones, the class hierarchy of the island remained intact. The working class was still branded on the tongue and the aristocracy was headed by a monarch who was cherished as the representative of an unchanging past. The unemployed were never less than a million between the wars and they had to submit to a means test; the school-leaving age remained at fourteen; there was no further redistribution of wealth between rich and poor.

One development made the reaction seem more complete than that which followed the French Revolution. Fox had been able to argue that the oligarchy ruling the country was unrepresentative and that a reformed electoral system would put a stop to reaction: all that was needed was the sovereignty of the people. But in a century of emancipation from the Reform Act of 1832 the people had become formally sovereign. More than this, education, which had been nation-wide since the Act of 1870, had produced an electorate which could read what was put in front of it.

The rejection by this new world of the politicians and writers committed to change was thus more complete than it had been under George III. They were people whose personalities denied them a hold on the masses who had gained power. Lloyd George, by the urgency of his ambition, lost his power of appeal for good after doing more than anyone else to win the war.

Mosley was defeated in every attempt to get back into the Commons after
founding the New Party. The serious journalists and poets saw their former
place of influence taken over by rivals who accepted the level of taste
reached by the newly literate.

The neo-Napoleonists on the Left were not able to attack democracy
because they believed in it and in the deepest sense needed its respect.
Mosley himself, though he put up no candidate in the election which
followed the formation of the British Union of Fascists, meant to capture
the popular vote and to change parliamentary procedure only after he had
won its mandate. He spent his time after the Second World War in trying to
regain a hold on the electorate. The poets and serious journalists avoided
criticizing the public which ignored them; they concentrated their fire on the
cinema and popular journalism. Auden's 'Beethameer, Beethameer, bully
of Britain' in 1932 was echoed by Philby in Moscow after thirty-five years
as if the popular press had not changed in the meantime.

We have seen the background which brought commitment to the Left
much more clearly than that which led to the Right. The exclusion of
Dissenters from the main body of the community continued as a real influence long after it had formally ended and a decline of religious faith had set
in, especially among the Free Churches. The middle classes and, in form at
least, the masses had gained the powers which had once been held by the
Court and the landed aristocracy, but rejection by these new forces could
produce as strong a sense of isolation as by the Court of St. James's under
George III. The grounds had changed. Financial success brought admission
as readily as birth; religious and marital orthodoxy were only required on
the throne; entertainment of the masses won a higher place than creative
originality or scholarship. But without the authority of tradition, the new
criteria seemed more arbitrary than the old. The emphasis on profit-making,
which finally admitted the brewer, kept out almost every young intellectual
in the country.

We have less evidence of the motives which led to sympathy with the
dictators of the Right. Sir Oswald Mosley differed from the Napoleonists
of the Left in having forefathers whose historic right to power had been
challenged and broken by the new democracy. The violence of his movement was sanctioned by an awareness of a status which had been destroyed.
The other Napoleonists we have studied never had this sense of entitlement
but only a claim which had always gone unrecognized. Their fathers had
been exiles who either accepted the wilderness, with its substitute glories,
or made a bid for the reality of power by means which involved them in the
betrayal of their origins.

It may be that this is the nerve of the difference between the Communist
and the Fascist, and that other Fascists had a sense of entitlement to power

at the centre which derived from a position once held by their fathers. Such a claim might be as compelling in them as Mosley's without the distinction of his pedigree. It might derive from an ancestry in the Army, or the police, or any other service of the Crown. If it had been lost by some failure in the individual or a decline in the authority of the class to which he belonged, a sense of grievance might develop which sanctioned a display of force to regain the respect of the majority.

It often caused anger in England that the Napoleonists of the Right and Left were accepted by the outside world as representative Englishmen. They had a confidence in themselves, implying some inner sanction, a contempt for authority and convention, for 'cant', the key word of Byron, which seemed to belong to the island's aristocratic tradition. But if the Napoleonist was sometimes an aristocrat, it was always in an aristocracy of dissent. The forefathers he acknowledged were disowned by society. They were appointed independently by God, or the Devil, by a Divine Right which had become recognizable as treason, by men with direct access to the Bible, or simply by the spirit in themselves.

In the American War of Independence the claim made in England for the colonists was that they were of English descent; but there was a secret clause in the claim. The emigrants had been predominantly Puritans, who had chosen exile rather than submission, and in this appeared bolder than their fellow countrymen who stayed behind to accept the Church's ritual and bend the knee to the Court which imposed it. But not all bent the knee. To the Whigs of the Glorious Revolution it seemed that the only England worthy of the name in the seventeenth century had been the England of Pym and Hampden, who paid with their lives to establish liberty at home. It was in this sense that the Americans were 'of the same original'.

The outcome in America, as George III clearly foresaw, was of unique importance in the history of England and the world. It helped to precipitate the French Revolution within a decade and, hardly less important, to sanction a new international outlook in England which was inherent in the acceptance of American victory. When Fox drank to 'the cause of freedom—all over the world,' he was recognizing in all men the rights which had been held to be peculiarly English. Although Burke was successful in contradicting him by insisting on the national pattern of privilege and subordination, there would henceforward always be minorities in England whose support gave an authoritative sanction to liberation movements throughout the world.

The neo-Napoleonists of the twentieth century were again linked by birth with the dispossessed, sometimes in strict terms of heredity with the original Napoleonists, sometimes with outcasts who recognized their spokesman in Fox. The author of the Lansdowne Letter, who founded the school of appeasement in the twentieth century, was the descendant of Lord

Lansdowne, the friend of the Hollands, who voted for peace with revolutionary France. A direct line connected Sir Oswald Mosley with his ancestor,
the second baronet, who voted for peace with Napoleon and opposed the
emancipation of the Jews. Christopher Hobhouse, who visited Hitler after
the defeat of the New Party, was a collateral descendant of Byron's friend,
who went to Paris in the Hundred Days as Napoleon's apologist. If
relationship of this direct kind was unusual, the claim to political descent
from Fox was common—it was made by Lloyd George in the Boer War, by
Sir Donald Maclean in Churchill's intervention in Russia, by Sir Oswald
Mosley in the war against Hitler. When Philby in Moscow told a reporter
in 1967 that England was 'the most fertile patch of earth in the whole history
of human ideas', he was claiming relationship not only with Marx and
Lenin, but with Paine and Fox, and—at the risk of heresy—with the Pilgrim Fathers.

There was another reason for the persistence of the Napoleonists in
England which was perhaps more important than any other. The island,
which had been almost secure from invasion from the time of the Armada,
became more obviously so on the defeat of Napoleon. For a century after
Trafalgar there was no rival navy in the world. It was not only Britain's
security which was unique but her wealth and prestige. She expanded her
empire to its limits and built up a network of international trade without
precedent. Her social structure remained intact, as that of the rest of the
world did not, so that Stephen Spender was justified in calling her an island
also in time.

If we are to make judgements on the Napoleonists it must be against the
background which explains their motives and makes their defence. They
were by nature and the influence of their childhood conditioned to exaggerate both the strength and the conservatism of the community from which
they were excluded. Fox believed that 'of all the countries in Europe,
England will be the last to be free'; Hazlitt held that the Greeks would
not recover their freedom till they forgot that they had ancestors. The
Napoleonists were sceptical of change by the internal processes of debate
because they underestimated the influence of the groups into which they
were born and knew the bitterness of their vendettas. When revolution
was successful overseas, they expected it to unite the opposition and clear
the way for reform. They mistook the alarm of the majority and its resort
to the securities of the past as a final proof of its strength.

Their fathers had prided themselves on being Englishmen; insecure in
their status and sometimes in their nationality, they tended to be patriots
and loyalists, and those who were radical claimed to represent the true
England. The sons were also self-consciously English, and the nature of
their disloyalty is important to define. There were traitors among them, but

since the word is loaded with the fear and hatred of centuries, it does not help to explain their motives.

A traitor is normally someone who betrays his country for money or power to an enemy who means to subjugate it. There have always been traitors of this kind, but the Napoleonists were not among them. When they welcomed a foreign show of force or actually advised on invasion, they believed they were helping to liberate their fellow countrymen and mankind. When they emigrated, they gradually turned on their adopted country the flow of reformist criticism they had used against their own, and with more dangerous prospects for themselves.

Tom Paine, the most important of the traitors, revealed these characteristics most clearly. The profits of his pamphleteering were considerable, but he gave them away and lived in poverty both in America and France. He told the French Military Council that 'an army of principles' could invade England but not an army of soldiers. When the Americans and the French fell away from their democratic ideals, he turned on their leaders as he had on George III, and increasingly took to drink. Drink seems to have been his only alternative to the liberation of mankind.

If the Napoleonists did not go as far as Paine in qualifying as traitors, they shared his delusion that a foreign example would stimulate reform. The English reform movement which took shape in the American War of Independence achieved little enough when the Americans had won. It was as if, said Pitt in 1785, change itself had become unacceptable.

Aware of the internal pressure to enlarge its framework, society was only too glad to attribute the discomfort to forces outside itself. The most enthusiastic in this work of disposal were those who had been active in pressing for reform. The few who persisted in their demand were not so foolish as to adopt Napoleon as an act of policy; they did it from emotional necessity.

The effect of isolation is perhaps best described by Hazlitt and Godwin at the beginning and end of the Napoleonic wars. Hazlitt found that opinions were like limbs, which grew and depended for strength on their contact with the main body; cut off they 'became useless' and might be disowned. Godwin believed that unanimity was achieved by a cumulative pressure which allowed a sense of normality only to those who yielded. Man, in fact, was a barometer.[1]

[1] Godwin: 'Thoughts Occasioned by the Perusal of Dr. Parr's Spital Sermon' (1801); Hazlitt, *Political Essays*, Preface (1817); also W. C. Hazlitt, *The Hazlitts*, I. 146.

The Unitarians put more trust in reason as the basis of their faith than other sects, and Hazlitt and Godwin both attributed their independence to it; but in the same breath, and without noticing any incongruity, they added their tribute to Napoleon. Godwin, in the essay of 1801, acclaims him as 'an auspicious personage', although he had clearly shown his nature in the *coup* of Brumaire. Hazlitt says it was he who enabled him to stand out against the ruling majority; 'he who did this for me, and for the rest of the world, and who alone could do it, was Buonaparte.' He was writing in 1817, when Napoleon's career was known in all its main details.

The Napoleonist was formed in childhood when the discovery of his own isolation made him reject the picture of his father as a small-minded tyrant and transform him into the champion of the outcasts. Whether or not the alliance revived in adult life depended not only on its original strength but on the return of a situation which reactivated the isolation of his past. To an onlooker there was nothing in the anti-Jacobin and anti-Bolshevik reactions to drive anyone into the arms of the enemy, but to the Napoleonist, society was again ostracizing him, and the strain imposed his childhood solution.

When the challenger appeared in the outside world, a group of unconscious memories sprang up to meet him. Napoleon himself was a Janus-faced figure, at the same time Caesar and the heir of the Revolution, who was acceptable alike to the rogue-aristocrat and dissenter. To Whitbread he was a businessman of extraordinary talents, who was blackballed by the club of the dynasts; to Byron a truant captain of the Guards,

> Once fairly set out on his party of pleasure,
> Taking towns at his liking, and crowns at his leisure.

In the twentieth century there were alternative figures, who made up for their lack of genius by their variety. Kingsley Martin found the saintly qualities of his father in Gandhi and his obstinacy in Stalin; together, in a decade of reaction, they gave him the resilience he had as his father's son in a cathedral city in the Boer War. Mosley, spurned by everyone, sought out two irredentists who refused to acknowledge the loss of their place in the world and reclaimed it with violence from the liberals and Jews who had supplanted them. Lloyd George, facing the contempt of the establishment for a young Welsh Radical, discovered the fanaticism of his Baptist uncle in Kruger, and when his isolation was finally renewed, found it again in Hitler.

The Napoleonist, in fact, was also a barometer. When the main body of the community moved in one direction, he went in the other. He made a major contribution to his country in so far as he helped to reduce its deep-rooted tensions by securing the admission of outcast groups, but he stood no chance of doing so as long as he could be identified with the enemy. For this reason, as much as the radicalism of his demands, his achievement was long delayed and its recognition still longer. The reproach of Bonapartism continued to be an effective weapon as long as Napoleon lived on St. Helena, and it was only in the following decade that reform became practicable. The less committed Napoleonists then played a major role in achieving reform, but the essential contribution had already been made by Fox and Whitbread, whose persistence in opposition was responsible for the continuing existence of a party which could achieve reform without revolution.

The delay in recognizing Paine and Byron lasted longer because their alienation from society was greater. Paine's outline of the welfare state in *The Rights of Man* and Byron's ridicule of cant made them bogeys in their own right, who could not be accepted until a different climate of opinion had established itself. The twentieth century, which welcomed them back, inflicted its own delays. That it was Lloyd George and Mosley who made the most constructive proposals in 1930 began to be recognized thirty years later, when the first was dead and the second disqualified by the lengths to which rejection had driven him.

England has been blamed for refusing the contributions of many of those who had the most to give her, but if the suggestion is that she might have made use of them by a slight increase in tolerance, it overlooks the extent of the conflict. There were more numerous, varied, and determined people in England to speak for the wilderness than in other countries because they had a firmer basis for dissent. Dissent was based on the security of the island and on whole areas of religion, philosophy, and literature which had flourished for centuries in that security. But the Napoleonist had to vindicate the rights of the wilderness at a moment when society felt too insecure to recognize anything but its traditional pattern; his solution was by nature uncompromising and the antithesis of what at that moment it wanted. The difference was so radical that society could not understand the solution it was offered except in terms of revolution, and the Napoleonist could not state its full implications until after his rupture with society was complete. When Paine left for America in 1774, when Byron went to Venice in 1816, when Mosley resigned from the Labour Party in 1931, and Philby joined the Communists in 1933, their departure was ridiculed or unnoticed because no one could see in their motives a valid criticism of society. Their going only became comprehensible when the assumptions of society about itself had changed with the passage of time. In producing the change the work of their own criticism, especially that of Paine and Byron, played a major part by affecting social values throughout the world.

# Postscript

*The country, speaking of it in general, and not with a view
to particular places, or classes of people, upon whom the
pressure of the war has borne with peculiar severity—has
been so rich, so prosperous, so happy; men have enjoyed
here in so superior a degree, and with such perfect
freedom from molestation, all the blessings and comforts
of life, that they have never been able to persuade
themselves, that real harm could befall them.*

Windham, on the preliminaries of peace
with Napoleon, 3 November 1801

The role played by England in the world has often been noticed as contradictory. On the one hand it has been imperialist, subjecting by force and commercial pressure greater areas of the earth's surface than any earlier empire; on the other hand it has been a liberating role, asserting the rights of the individual against oppression and loosening the power of all tyrannies including her own. For two centuries England took the lead in promoting the slave trade before she took the lead in suppressing it. As the most advanced capitalist country, she gave shelter to Karl Marx while he wrote *Capital*. She invented the concentration camp for Boer women and children, and stood alone against Hitler in the name of subject races.

It is clear that England's unique success as an empire-builder depended on her position as an island and her mastery of the sea; but it was also her position as an island which was responsible for her opposition to tyranny. In the Hundred Years War it seemed to Froissart that England would have been destroyed if she had not been an island, 'the best protected country in the world', because her people, who were aware of it, had developed a disloyalty and independence of character which forced their kings to forget their continental ties. 'Any man,' he said, 'who is king of that country must conform to the will of the people and bow to many of their wishes.'

A dictator knows that the most certain way of gaining the compliance of his people is by discovering threats against them from the outside world, but if the people know themselves to be protected by the sea dictators are at a disadvantage. The standing armies, which in other countries are essential for the defence of the frontiers, can be seen as no more than a police force. The soldier, who is elsewhere the pattern of manhood and the model of internal discipline, loses his authority. Because England's defence against the world was the sea, it was the sailor, with his enterprise and independence, who provided the symbol of the Englishman's freedom at home and his right, if need be, to find it elsewhere.

Historically it was perhaps the refusal of the English to accept the culture of the Norman Conquest which first gave them their taste for independence and their sense of having earned it. The rejection was of their own ruling class, which spoke French, and their own kings, who corrupted the Church in collusion with the papacy. Sects grew up as nowhere else in the world. A century before Luther, Wyclif declared that 'each man that shall be damned shall be damned by his own guilt and each man that is saved shall be saved by his own merit.' In Chaucer there is already the song of a language exploring its own genius.

The immunity of the island, which was confirmed by the defeat of the Spanish Armada, did more than put an end to the threat of Catholicism; it loosened the hold of any ruler or class who sought to impose its own will regardless of others. In Shakespeare's great review of kings, which began a decade later, we see them surrounded by majesty still but riddled with human frailty, a procession warning the Stuarts in advance of what they might expect if they took their pretensions too seriously. Thereafter, at a touch, the attempt to impose conformity would send men to all parts of the world to rebuild their freedom or find the means of enlarging it.

Continents may of course also become islands—by virtue of their known power, their wealth, or a sense of ideological finality handed down by the revolution which produced them. But when the rulers have accepted the implications of their new status, they may have to send out troops or tanks to meet a threat which is remote but challenges their authority. If the troops have to stay, or the tanks are stopped, an inexplicable shout goes up in their own capital behind them. The shout is inexplicable because a spirit of conformity has always reigned in the continent since the revolution, preserving its fruits and warding off the risk of disintegration—and the shout is in the name of the enemy.

In the shock of revulsion which follows, the motives of the demonstrators are investigated. To call them traitors is hardly enough, because it is inconceivable that they should take orders from an enemy whose failings are known to them—they are attacking their own society for the sake of it. Their records sometimes show poverty in childhood and slight forms of discrimination, but nothing at all in the present to account for desperation. On the contrary, there has been relief of their complaints, living standards have gone up, a 'thaw' set in after the death of a dictator who froze the shape of society by his terrorism.

In eighteenth-century England the architecture itself tells us that all was well with the country. The English Revolution had disposed of the tyranny of kings, and a natural balance had been struck between the rights of the individual and the harmony of the state. In the period of swift development which followed, England had not only become the most powerful country in the world but her citizens had more freedom than those of any other. It was thus civilization itself which was threatened when an uproar at its centre interrupted the task of restoring order in America and Europe. The cries were in the name of the revolutionary enemy, but their aim was not to install him in the capital. Submerged under the culture of the eighteenth century and only half liberated, a whole range of outcast worlds had re-claimed the loyalty of the demonstrators. The wrongs which afflicted these worlds were of such long standing that they were difficult to recognize; their original victims were dead and buried and their descendants knew that the oppression was lifting. But just because of the emancipation which was already half won, the Napoleonists' patience broke when they saw the threat to people overseas whose cause was identifiable with theirs and their ancestors'.

The link between the demonstrations of the twentieth century and the eighteenth century is indirect. They are caused independently by the same loyalty to forefathers in their own past. But if the emancipation of mankind escapes the most severe forms of repression, it is because a sanction under-lies it which was spelled out for good from the experience of the original islands.

*October 1953–April 1970*

# Note on Sources

A few references cover the central ground.

Contemporary cartoons and pamphlets inspired by the Government are summarized or referred to in Mrs. M. D. George, *Catalogue of Political and Personal Satires*, vols. V to IX, British Museum (1935–49). The most articulate of the attacks are William Windham, speech in the Commons, 3 November 1801, and Coleridge's letters to the *Morning Post*, 4 and 7 November 1802. Certain publications concentrated on witch-hunting, especially the *True Briton*, the *Anti-Jacobin* and the *Satirist*. The case of the Whig and Radical opposition is given by the *Morning Chronicle* and from 1808 onwards by the *Examiner*.

The Napoleonists give their own account of themselves in: Hansard, *Parliamentary Debates*, especially the speeches of Fox, Whitbread, Byron, Lord Holland, and the Duke of Sussex.

The Holland House papers in the British Museum cover nearly every aspect of the Napoleonists with the notable exceptions of Hazlitt and Mrs. Inchbald, and of Whitbread, who is poorly represented. A selection from the papers before their release was given by the late Lord Ilchester in *Chronicles of Holland House* (1937), and *The Home of the Hollands* (1937). There are four important books by the Hollands: the *Journal* of Lady Holland, ed. Ilchester (1908), which is selective and stops short of the narrative of 1814–15, Lord Holland's *Foreign Reminiscences* (1850), *Memoirs of the Whig Party* (1852), and *Further Memoirs* (1905).

Other main sources are:

BYRON: *Childe Harold, Occasional Pieces, 1811–13* and *1814–16, Don Juan;* correspondence in Lord Ernle's edition and Peter Quennell's sourcebook *Byron: A Self Portrait* (1950), Professor Wilson Knight's *Lord Byron, Christian Virtues* (1952), and *Lord Byron's Marriage* (1957)

COLERIDGE: *Poems; The Notebooks*, ed. Coburn (1957 and 1962); John Livingstone Lowes, *The Road to Xanadu* (1927).

FOX: *Speeches*, ed. Wright (1815); *Memorials and Correspondence*, ed. Russell (1853); Namier and G. M. Trevelyan *passim;* G. O. Trevelyan, *Early History of Charles James Fox*. Biographies by Lord John Russell (1866), Edwin Lascelles (1936), Loren Reid (1969).

The Whig Club issued two publications of its own, *The Whig Club Instituted* (1784), with toasts and membership lists, and after Pitt's anti-subversion laws, the *Declaration* (1796). Otherwise the only substantial source between 1789 and 1812 is the *Morning Chronicle*, which was regular and often lavish in its coverage. John Gregory's career as turnpike-master is in the minutes of the turnpike in the Kensington Reference Library and in the *Gentleman's Magazine*, December 1813.

GODWIN: Especially *Defence of the Rockingham Party* (1783); *Thoughts Occasioned by the perusal of Dr Parr's Spital Sermon* (1801) (copy annotated by Coleridge in British Museum); Baldwin (pseud.), *History of England* (1807) and *History of Greece* (2nd ed., 1828); *Letters of Verax* (1815).

HAZLITT: *Works* (1930); P. P. Howe, *Life* (1922).

HOBHOUSE: *Letters written by an Englishman resident in Paris during the last reign of the Emperor Napoleon* (1816); (as Lord Broughton), *Recollections of a Long Life* (1865).

LEIGH HUNT: *The Examiner*, 1808–21. *Autobiography* (1850); *The Old Court Suburb* (1856). Attacks by J. G. Lockhart in *Blackwood's Magazine*, 1818–19.

MRS. INCHBALD: *Memoirs of Elizabeth Inchbald*, ed. Boaden (1833), exasperating in its omissions but closer to Mrs. Inchbald than any other source. Thereafter C. L. Brightwell, *Memorials of Amelia Opie* (1854), and Hazlitt, *Works, passim*; Joseph Berington, *The State and Behaviour of English Catholics from the Reformation to 1780* (1780).

PAINE: *The Rights of Man*, especially Part Two (1792); M.D. Conway, *Life* (1892).

WHITBREAD: Speeches of 29 February 1808 (mediation of Russia), and March–June 1815 (the Hundred Days).

GENERAL:
J. B. Alger, *Napoleon's British Visitors* (1903). A directory.
Jules Dechamps, *Les Iles Britanniques et la Révolution Française* (1949).
Archibald S. Foord, *His Majesty's Opposition, 1714–1830* (1964). Contains a first account of the Whig Club.
E. J. Hobsbawm, *The Age of Revolution* (1962).
Namier and Brooke, *History of Parliament, 1754–1790* (1964).
Michael Roberts, *The Whig Party 1807–1812* (1929).
[L. Simond], *Voyage d'un Français en Angleterre* (1810–11).
E. H. Stuart-Jones, *The Last Invasion of Britain*. University of Wales Press (1950). A comprehensive sourcebook.
A. J. P. Taylor, *English History 1914–1945* (1965).

The following sources cover the main points of detail:

*First Lord Kensington*

Letters in the Egerton and Newcastle MSS. in the British Museum and the Sandwich MSS. of Lord Hinchingbrooke; letters from his wife in the Sloane MSS.

The Act selling Holland House to Henry Fox, 8 Geo. III, c. 132, in the House of Lords. Johnston Hall in R. Fenton, *A Historical Tour through Pembrokeshire* (1811).

Complete minute books of the Kensington turnpike from 1726 to 1826 and the Acts establishing the turnpike (12 Geo. I, c. 37) and periodically extending its powers. The Victorians thought of the Kensington Gate as opposite the palace but the minutes put it at the western limit of Kensington below Holland House from Walpole's decision of 1729 until the liquidation of the turnpike in 1826.

*History of Haverfordwest* (1914) by Phillips and Warren. John Wesley's *Journal* and *Letters* for conversion to Methodism; *Reflections on the Rise and Progress of the American Rebellion* (1780).


## Second Lord Kensington

E. Desbrière, *Projets et Tentatives de débarquement aux Iles Britanniques* (1900); E. H. Stuart-Jones, *The Last Invasion of Britain*.

St. Mary's parish records in Haverfordwest. *Parliamentary Debates*.

*Diary of William Windham* (1866), *The Windham Papers* (1913), and Windham MSS. in the British Museum. *Memoirs of Robert Plumer Ward* (1850). *The Creevey Papers*, ed. Maxwell (1903), and *Creevey's Life and Times*, ed. John Gore (1934). Bets in Brooks's Club Betting Book. Lists of Members and Rules published 1889 and 1907.

Details of life at Westmead, Carmathen Bay, are in *The Cambrian Visitor* (1813); speculation in cast-horses, *The Statesman*, 27 February 1815; the Kensington Canal, 5 Geo. IV, c. 65 and 7 Geo. IV, c. 96.


## Louis Léon Changeur

Changeur was probably one of two sons of Louis Maurice Changeur, a café proprietor arrested and ruined in the Terror as a follower of Lafayette. The police record is in the Archives Nationales, Sûreté Générale, F7, 4639, filed under Marie Louis Changeur.

The activities of Louis Léon Changeur in London are taken from the Land Registry Memorials and Land Tax Returns of the Middlesex County Records, the Fleet Commitment Book (entry 10521), Discharge Orders and Bankruptcy Records of the Public Record Office; Holborn and Kensington Rate Books; minutes and committee reports of the Kensington turnpike; *The London Gazette* (bankruptcy, 10 November 1812), *The Times*, and minutes of the Court of Sewers in London County Hall. The development of Bloomsbury is described by Sir John Summerson, *Georgian London* (1945), and the principles underlying it by Samuel Pepys Cockerell in his *Memorial to the Committee of the Governors of the Foundling Hospital* (1790). The origin of the wartime squares are in *Report on London Squares* (1928), Cmd. 3196.


## Aglio and Foscolo

The atmosphere in Milan in 1796 is most vividly described by Stendhal in *The Charterhouse of Parma*. A missing autobiography of Aglio is drawn on by F. Sacchi, *Cenni sulla vita di Aglio* (1868). I have also used *Rapports historiques des régiments de l'Armée de l'Italie 1796-1797* and Napoleon's correspondence to the Directory in *Correspondence de Napoléon* (Paris, 1858).

Professor E. R. Vincent's *Ugo Foscolo* (1953) and *Ugo Foscolo and John Allen* (1949), are supplemented by MSS. in his possession; by *Ortis* (1798), *Orazione a Bonaparte pel Congresso di Lione* (1802), and Hobhouse, *Historical Illustrations of the Fourth Canto of 'Childe Harold'* (1818).

### Byron and John Hanson

The movements of Hanson and the Earl of Portsmouth are in the Acton and Kensington Rate Books, 1816–20, and the St. Mary Abbot's marriage register, 1818. Hanson's administration of Newstead is covered in some hundreds of letters in the Egerton MSS. and his later dealings with Hobhouse in the Broughton Correspondence. The Portsmouth marriage is most fully described in *Proceedings under the Commission issued on the Portsmouth Case* (1823), in the library of Lincoln's Inn. The *Edinburgh Medical and Surgical Journal*, October 1815, containing the article on hydrocephalus, is in the Wellcome Historical Museum. Hanson's account of the separation is in Hobhouse, *The Separation of Lord and Lady Byron* (1870). The fullest of many contemporary accounts of Napoleon's carriage is in W. Bullock's own catalogue, *Description of the costly and curious military carriage . . .* (1816). Among biographies I have relied mainly on Tom Moore (1830), Peter Quennell (1935), and L. A. Marchand (1953); among memoirs, those of J. W. Polidori (1816), T. Medwin (1824), and Lady Blessington (1834); among other commentators, Professor Wilson Knight, Bertrand Russell, and André Maurois.

### Lesser-Known Inhabitants of the Square

Details of the lesser-known inhabitants are from their wills in Somerset House, the parish registers, rate books, directories, turnpike minutes, and the 1819 Act setting up the trustees, 59 Geo. III, c. 70. A published reference to Daniel Sutton is in Robert Benson, *Old and New Sarum*; otherwise I have depended on records in the possession of Dr. Stephen Pasmore, chairman of the Kensington Society, and the turnpike minutes.

Details of the Church of Christ Assembling in Hornton Street are from the register of baptisms in the Public Record Office and *The Essays and Remains of Robert Vaughan* (1858), edited by his son. Vaughan's *Life of Wycliffe* (1828).

For Hasledine Pepys and William Allen, see Gilpin's *Life of William Allen* (1847); H. Pepys, *The Perspiration of Plants* (1843), and other contributions to the Royal Society; *D.N.B.*

The careers of the retired naval personnel are in the Admiralty muster books, log books, and especially the Captains' Correspondence in the Public Record Office. Details of Captain Bazalgette's evangelism are from the records of the Naval, Military and Air Force Bible Society. I have also used O'Byrne, *Naval Biographical History* and Halévy, *England in 1815*.

### Whitbread and Caroline

Caroline's invitations to Lord Holland and S. C. Whitbread's request that Lord Holland should preside over another Middlesex demonstration are in the Holland House papers. Palace repairs: *The Times*, 19 October 1807 and 25 January 1810, and in Treasury Correspondence in the British Museum. On the Duke of Sussex I have relied mainly on the Holland House papers, Rush, *The Court of London 1819–1825* (1873), and Roger Fulford, *Royal Dukes* (1933).

The main sources on Whitbread are his extensive showing in *Parliamentary Debates*; Roger Fulford's biography (1967), which accepts his preoccupation with

Drury Lane as the cause of his suicide; and Francis Phippen, *An Authentic Account of the late Mr Whitbread with the genuine report of the Inquest, taken in Short-hand* (1815). The wills of Whitbread and his father are in Somerset House. Southill Park, intact, is occasionally open to visitors. There are worthwhile notes on Whitbread in Creevey; *The Farington Diary*; Hazlitt, *On Parliamentary Eloquence*; Lord Holland, *Further Memoirs*; Francis Horner, *Memoirs*; Samuel Romilly, *Memoirs*; Earl Spencer, *Memoirs of Viscount Althorp*; Wilberforce, *Life*; Robert Plumer Ward, *Diaries*.

Besides the standard references to Caroline, there are new details in Marchand's *Mémoires*, ed. Bourguignon (Paris, 1952), and Chester W. New, *The Life of Henry Brougham to 1830* (1961).

The petition to Caroline organized by à Beckett is in the British Museum, Add. MSS. 29,511; the Middlesex address of May 1813, BM 1852. b. 9. (1) and the Kensington address of 1820, 1852. b. 9. (17).

The use of Caroline as a christian name is from the baptism registers of Kensington parish church and the Church of Christ Assembling in Hornton Street, Public Record Office.

*Holland House and Napoleon*

There are nearly a thousand volumes of the Holland House MSS. in the British Museum, from which I have used the papers relating to Napoleon, which include Las Cases, Capel Lofft, Lady Holland's MS. journal, Lowe and the Bonaparte family; also the correspondence with the Duke of Sussex and Duke of Kent, Canning, Sir Francis Burdett and Hobhouse, Lord Thanet, the Whitbreads, Lord Kinnaird, Sir R. Adair, Sir Robert Wilson, Talleyrand, Flahaut, Lafayette, the Reverend Matthew Marsh, Fazakerley, Lord Essex, Madame de Coigny, Lord John Russell, Lord and Lady Byron, Foscolo, Lord Holland with Caroline Fox (1797–1801 and 1814–16), with Fox (1797–1801), twelve volumes of Lord Holland's General Correspondence (1796–1822), Lady Holland's General Correspondence (1792–1820).

The quotation of Sir Hudson Lowe to Sir Henry Bunbury is from the Lowe Papers, Add. MSS. 20,134, and his assessment of William Warden, 20,155.

The debates on Napoleon's detention were on 18 and 19 April in 1816 and 18 March in 1817; the two Acts, 56 George III, c. 22 ('for effectually detaining') and 56 George III, c. 23 ('for regulating the intercourse').

The letter from Las Cases (under the pseudonym of Milleraye) to Capel Lofft was printed in *Notes and Queries* X. 10. 384. Lord Holland's draft translation from the Odyssey with a note in Madame Bertrand's hand is BM Add. MSS. 51529.83.

Sainte-Beuve describes Madame de Souza in *Portraits de Femmes*.

The case of Marshal Ney is based on Michel Ney, *Procès du Maréchal Ney* (1815) and de Lavalette's escape on *A Full Report of the Trial of Major General Sir Robert Thomas Wilson*, published by Richard Edwards (1816). Two open letters by Lord Kinnaird were published: *A Letter to Lord Liverpool* (1816) and *A Letter to the Duke of Wellington on the arrest of M. Marinet* (1818).

On Napoleon I have consulted Maitland, *The Surrender of Napoleon* (1904); Lyttelton, *Quelques notes sur l'arrivée de Napoléon* (which includes his inquiry about

Whitbread), a MS. in the Holland House papers; A. L. H. Humphreys, *A St. Helena Who's Who* (1919); Rosebery, *The Last Phase* (1900); Bertrand, *Napoleon at St. Helena*, ed. de Langle (1953); Gourgaud, *Recueil de pièces authentiques sur le captif* (1821); Montholon, *History of the Captivity of Napoleon* (1846); Forsyth, *History of the Captivity of Napoleon at St. Helena* (1853); Walter Scott, *Life of Napoleon Buonaparte* (1827); Antoine Vincent Arnault, *Vie de Napoléon* (1825); William Warden, *Letters Written on Board H.M. Ship the Northumberland at St. Helena* (1816); Belloc, *Napoleon* (1932); the muster book and log book of the *Bellerophon* in the Public Record Office; the House of Commons Division Lists, April–June 1815.

The issue of the *Courier* which shocked Napoleon on Elba is likely to have been 19 October, but 18 October and September, *passim*, are also relevant. The denials of the British Government that his removal was ever discussed (e.g. Bathurst in the Lords, 18 March 1817: 'There was no mention at the Congress of such a proposition') were probably based on the fact that the Congress was not yet in official session.

MODERNS

Apart from the brilliant outline of A. J. P. Taylor's *English History 1914–1945* and *The Common People, 1746/1938* by G. D. H. Cole and Raymond Postgate (1938), I have relied on the following for detail:

*Lloyd George*

Childhood: William George, *Richard Lloyd Cricieth* (in Welsh; Cardiff, 1934), and *My Brother and I* (1958). Earl Richard Lloyd George, *Lloyd George* (1960).

Biographies by Thomas Jones, Countess Frances Lloyd George, Donald McCormick, Frank Owen, A. J. Sylvester, Malcolm Thompson. Roy Jenkins, *Asquith* (1964). Hansard, *passim* from 1891. *War Diaries*.

Hitler, *Table Talk, 1941–44* (1953).

*Sir Oswald Mosley*

Burke, *Peerage and Baronetage* (1968). G.E.C., *Complete Baronetage* (1906).

Second Baronet (1785–1871): Hansard, 29 February 1808, peace with Napoleon; May–June 1833, emancipation of the Jews. *Family Memoirs* (1849); *A Short Account of the Ancient British Church* (1858). John Morley, *Life of Richard Cobden* (1881); W. E. Axon, *Annals of Manchester* (1886), and *Cobden as a Citizen* (1907). Obituaries in the *Staffordshire Advertiser* and *Manchester Guardian*, May 1871.

Fourth Baronet (1848–1915): Obituaries in the *Staffordshire Chronicle* and *Manchester Guardian*, October 1915. Will in Somerset House. Neville J. Laski, 'History of Manchester Jewry', *The Manchester Review*, 1956.

Sixth Baronet (b. 1896): *My Answer* (1946) (which includes *A Statement Written in Prison*, 1942, and a 7th ed. of *Tomorrow We Live*, first published in 1938); *Mosley, The Facts* (1957); *My Life* (1968). Hansard, 17 February 1919, maiden speech, to last speech in Parliament of 21 September 1931.

*Daily Herald*, 'Titled Socialists', 12 April 1926. *Daily Mail*, letter from fifth baronet, 12 April 1926; 'What We Stand For', 29 January 1934; 'The Blackshirt

Leader Replies to his Critics', 23 March 1934. *Manchester Guardian*, 'Blackshirts in Manchester', 1 October 1934, and *passim. The Times*, Diary, 6 October 1967, and *passim. Evening Standard. Yorkshire Post. Isis*, interview, 18 May 1960. *The Blackshirt. Action*.

Sir Harold Nicolson, *Diaries and Letters, 1930–1939* (1966). W. F. Mandle, *Anti-Semitism and the British Union of Fascists* (1968). Arnold Toynbee, *A Study of History*, vol. 5; *The Process of Disintegration* (1939). Christopher Hobhouse, *Charles James Fox*, new edition with introduction by Harold Nicolson (1947). *Official Handbook of the Manchester District, 1936*, Manchester City Council.

### Kingsley Martin

Basil Martin, *An Impossible Parson* (1935).

*The New Statesman*, 1931–62, especially Critic's 'London Diary'. A selection was edited by Kingsley Martin in 1960.

*Low's Russian Sketch Book* (1932), by Kingsley Martin in collaboration with David Low. *The Magic of Monarchy* (1937), revised after ten years of post-war Conservatism as *The Crown and the Establishment* (1962).

Autobiography: *Father Figures* (1966); *Editor* (1968); 'Father of the Man', *Punch*, 2 October 1968.

### Poets of the Thirties

Autobiographies: Spender, *The Backward Son* (1940, a novel) and *World Within World* (1951, new edition 1964); Day Lewis, *The Buried Day* (1960); MacNeice, *The Strings Are False* (1965). Poetry in many volumes.

### Communist Agents

There have been perceptive comments at varying stages in the process of discovery:

Cyril Connolly, *The Missing Diplomats* (1952). Tom Driberg, *Guy Burgess* (1956): 'He had adopted the Russian patronymic (Andreyvitch), he told me, in tribute to a character in *War and Peace*.' Malcolm Muggeridge, article in the *Sunday Telegraph*, 7 July 1963: 'Inside him, one felt, there was something explosive. ...' Page, Leitch, Knightley, *Philby, the Spy who Betrayed a Generation* (1968). Eleanor Philby, *Kim Philby* (1968): 'What touched me first about Kim was his loneliness. ...' Kim Philby, *My Silent War* (1968): English edition with introduction by Graham Greene. Hugh Trevor-Roper, *The Philby Affair* (1968): A gasp of astonishment that an intelligent man should have been unable to use his intellect.

Relevant books by H. St. John Philby are: *The Heart of Arabia* (1922); *Sheba's Daughters* (1939); *A Pilgrim in Arabia* (1948); *Arabian Days* (1948); *Forty Years in the Wilderness* (1957).

Kim Philby's journalism includes 'March into Santander', *The Times*, 27 August 1937; 'Migration Trek by 50,000 Camels', *Observer*, 16 August 1959; articles on Saudi Arabia in *The Economist*, 16 January and 31 December 1960; 'St. John Philby Dies', *Observer*, 2 October 1960; 'A Fox that Came to Stay', *Country Life*, 6 December 1962; and an interview with two reporters of *Izvestia*, 19 December 1967.

The Burgess family history is based on wills and birth registers in Somerset House, records of the Huguenot Society, Institute of Bankers, Royal Artillery Institution, Ministry of Defence, and of the parish of West Meon. Report of the wedding of Lt. Burgess, *Hampshire Telegraph*, 14 December 1907; obituary of William Gillman, J.P., in the *Portsmouth Evening News*, 11 and 14 November 1935; article by Guy Burgess in *The Spectator*, 23 March 1934.

Sir Donald Maclean's speeches in the Commons run from May 1906 to May 1932, with gaps in World War I as Deputy Speaker and from 1923 to 1929 when he was out of Parliament. His leading role in opposing intervention in Russia begins on 3 March 1919, when Churchill announced continuing support for the Whites, and ends on 10 February 1920, when Maclean pressed for diplomatic relations to be restored.

An obituary of Agnes Macmellin Maclean is in the *South Wales News*, 8 September 1924, and an account of her sons at school in Haverfordwest in the *Pembrokeshire Telegraph*, 23 June 1932. Other details from the family tomb in Llangunnor churchyard, records in Somerset House, the National Society for the Prevention of Cruelty to Children, and the Court of Lord Lyon, Edinburgh.

# Index

*Bold-face type indicates main entries under individual headings and references to the central argument of the book, which is analysed under* **Napoleonists.** *'N' refers throughout to Napoleon.*

à Beckett, William (1778–1855), **37-8;** obsessed with ancestry, 269; marriage witnessed by John Hanson, q.v., 88; heads address to Queen Caroline, 121; municipal reformer, 123

**actors,** Napoleonists as, **254-5.** *See* **Napoleonists**

Adair, Robert (1763–1855): warns Holland against 2nd Lord Kensington, 18; presented to N, 135; and Hudson Low, 168, 170

Aglio, Agostino (1777–1857), **27-9,** 82; effect of Lodi on, 27; enlistment under N, 28; his masterpiece, 29; lithographs of Napoleonic battles, 29, 284; commission from Duke of Bedford, 29; compared with English Napoleonists, 277

Ali, Pasha of Ianina, 'the Lion' (1776–1818): Byron's 'Mahometan Buonaparte', **238-9;** Ianina one of the 'most oppressed provinces of Turkey', 221; compared with Stalin and Revd. Basil Martin, 324

aliens: in Edwardes Square, 36; Alien Act, 103, 176

All the Talents: in office for one year, 1806–7, 22; only coalition including opposition Whigs between 1783 and 1830; Fox, Foreign Secretary, negotiates with N, 138; ends slave trade, 138; Windham, Secretary at War, makes Lord Kensington a Lord of the Admiralty, 22; commission set up to investigate alleged infidelities of Princess of Wales, 90

Allen, Dr. John (1771–1843), Holland House librarian, 139, 140, 249; in Paris, 137

Allen, William (1770–1843), 42

**America,** Napoleonists' commitment to, **208-9,** 363. *See* **Napoleonists**

American Revolution: influence on of English Dissent, 363, and of Paine as propagandist for independence, 6; influence on world history forecast by George III, 363; immediate effect in England as stimulus to reform, 16, 17; limitation of King's personal rule achieved, 1782, 17, but reaction in next 3 years stifles extension of reform, 365; 'as if change had become unacceptable'—Pitt in 1785, 365; Paine predicts American example will be followed by Europe and England, 6; Coleridge, Wordsworth, Southey plan community of

equal rights in America, 279, but reaction of majority strengthened by French Revolution, q.v.; Fox thereafter vainly appeals to American example, 225; Kensington family and, 270, 276; Napoleonists involved in, 208-9. *See also* Washington; **Napoleonists: America, commitment to**

**animals,** adopted by Napoleonists, **242-5.** *See* **Napoleonists**

Armada (1588): as proof of island security, 271; and Shakespeare's review of kings, 369

Arnault, Antoine Vincent, 174, 190

Armistead, Mrs. Elizabeth (later Mrs. Fox), 135–6, 138

Asquith, Henry, 1st Earl of Oxford (Prime Minister 1908–16): attends Rehoboth Chapel in childhood, 298; promotes Lloyd George, 298; destroyed with Liberal Party by LG, 299; his resemblance to LG's 'Uncle Lloyd', 298-9

Auden, W. H. (b. 1907), 232, 288, 325, **328-34,** 359, 362; his Church background, 332; as leading poet of the thirties, 329–30, ancestor, 329, hawk, 329, airman, 331, traveller, 331–2, and Englishman, 333–4; his isolation, 329, 362, and rival court, 329. *See also* Byron; Russian Revolution, influence on poets

Baptists: George III and Church of Christ Assembling in Hornton Street, 40–3; Church of Christ at Pen-y-Maes, 290 et seq., *see* Richard Lloyd; investigated in Pembrokeshire after French landing, 1787, 5

Baldwin, Stanley, 331, 344, 353, 354, 355

Bathurst, Lord (1762–1834): minister responsible for St. Helena, 171–2; reply to Holland in Lords, 189–90; not a man who wavered, 207

Batine, 'General', 5

Bazalgette, Joseph William (?1783–1849), Cdr. R.N., **43-5,** 247; his evangelism, 44

Bedford, John Russell, 6th Duke of (1766–1839), 29, 111, **146-7,** 150, 153–4, 163; in Paris, 1802, 136; retinue while travelling, 146; Temple of Liberty, 146; plans to visit N, 147; instructions to Lord Holland in Rome, 149; in Naples, 152; 'shall raise my voice against engaging in war with N,' 155; and Flahaut, 177; and Lavalette, 180–1;

Bedford, 6th Duke, *contd.*
passing French customs, 184; channel to French Bonapartists, 184; sends books, medals, and kaleidoscope to St. Helena, 197; sense of promotion when abroad
Bellamy, John (d. 1794): founds Whig Club of England, 19; turnpike trustee, 23; death, 20; and animals, 242
*Bellerophon*, 136, 158, 160–2; at Plymouth, 161–5
Belloc, Hilaire, 284
Bertrand, Marshal, 127, 149–50, 197; delivers N's snuff-box, 199; father visits Lord Holland in Paris, 1817, 191
Betty, William Henry West, 'Master Betty', 60, 65; and Fox, 254
Blessington, Lady, 80, 268, 374; astonishment at Byron's regalia, 231
Boaden, James (1762–1839), playwright: access to Mrs. Inchbald's papers, 47; *Memoirs of Elizabeth Inchbald*, 69, 372; politics, 282
Boer War: opposition to in England, 289–90; concentration camps in, 289, 368
Bonaparte, Letizia Ramolino ('Madame Mère'), mother of N, 197; at N's coronation, '*Pourvu que cela dure*', 253; in Rome after Waterloo, 174; her devotion to Lord Holland, 190; Pergami's mother, 'Madame Livia', compared to, 116
Bonaparte, Louis, Comte de St. Leu, brother of N: Hollands lease his house in Rome, 148
Bonaparte, Lucien, Prince of Canino, brother of N, 115, 148, 188; in English country house, 1810–14, 174; and Hollands in Rome, 1814–15, 151–2; asks Holland for house near London, 1816, 174–5
Bonaparte, Napoleon, *see* Napoleon I
Bonapartists, 172, 182, 183, 190, 204, 213; defined, xii; in England, xi–xii; N's belief in as an English faction, xi; in Rome, 174–5
Bourbons, 83, 181–2, 186, 237; feature distinguishing French from American revolution, 216; triumph of, 103, 262–3, 267; demand of British opinion for reinstatement, 207; Holland House convinced their restoration would be short, 158, 178; Byron and Hobhouse consider plan to organize counter-revolution 83–4
Bowen, James, Welsh defector, 3, 5
Brenton, Capt. Edward Pelham, naval historian, 245; rejects attempt to bring N from Plymouth to London, 165; lack of medals for Navy felt 'most keenly at Court', 246
Brooks's Club, 16, 18–21, 227, 271–2; bets in, 21, 22, 39, 119
Brougham, Henry, Baron (1778–1868), 139; as supporter of Caroline, 93, 96, 116, 199; succeeds Whitbread as her champion, 117;

effect on of Waterloo, 116; on its effect on other Whigs, 261; N's interest in his eloquence, 163; differs from Lord Holland on N, 186; returns to Holland House, 195–6
Broughton, Lord, *see* Hobhouse, John Cam
Bruce, Lord, 4th Earl of Ailesbury: Stuart tenant of Holland House, 14
Bruce, Lt. Michael: attempts to rescue Marshal Ney and Lavalette, 180–2; his trial, 182
Brussels, 172; staging area for refugee movements, 174; Hollands' contacts with, 173, and visit to, 1817, 190
Brutus, 288; Byron and, 231; Fox and, 218; pseudonym of Lloyd George, 299
Bullock, W.: exhibits N's carriage in Piccadilly, 82, 374; commissions lithographs of N's battles from Aglio, 29
Bunbury, Sir Charles, 52–3
Bunbury, Sir Henry, 171; with N, 163
Burdett, Sir Francis, Bt., 59, 92
Burgess, Guy Francis de Monçy (1911–63), **345-8;** upbringing as son of Malcolm de Monçy B, 346–7; pseudonym 'Andreyvitch', 348; burial in father's grave, 348
Burgess, Malcolm de Monçy (1881–1924), father of Guy B: his Huguenot background, 345, and abortive career as submarine officer, 346–7; will, 347
Burghersh, Lord: British Minister to court of Tuscany, 145, 150
Burke, Edmund, 123, 207, 217, 222, 242n.; joined by Fox, 16; leaves, 19; on Unitarians, 210
Bury, Lady, 92, 94, 95, 107
Byng, George (Whig M.P. for half-century, 1790–1847), 95, 224, 228
Byron, Lady Anne Isabell (Annabella) (1792–1860), daughter of Sir Ralph Milbanke, later Noel, Bt.; marriage to B, 1815, 260, 265; applies case history of hydrocephalus to him, 78; on his paranoia, 1815, 265
Byron, Augusta (1784–1851), half-sister of B, 72, 83
Byron, Mrs. Catherine Gordon (1765–1811), mother of B, **71-2;** at Newstead, 73, 242; insistence on her Stuart descent, 71; desertion of by Capt. B, 275
Byron, George Gordon, Lord (1788–1824), 64, 65, **70-89,** 114, 168–9, 207–8, 239, 251, 256, **265-9,** 273, 275, 280, 288, 303; birth and upbringing, 71–2; descended from Stuarts, through Mrs. B, born Gordon, 71; 'a rival' to the kings he attacked, 231; compared with George III (*see* first name), 249; loyalty to Capt. B, 71; Capt. B, unlike Mrs. B, free of criticism, 215; 'perfectly remembered

him,' 71, 'my first dreams martial,' 275; Capt. B as gay deserter, 80–1, as victim of society, 215, and gallant Guards officer, 366; displacement of criticism as deserter on to Prince Regent, 275, and as deserter from army on to N in disgrace, 82, 267; violent at Harrow, 255, and in holidays with Hanson, 72–3, 79; origins of menagerie, 72; at Cambridge, 73, 74; his bear a Fellow downgraded, 242; at Newstead, 71, 73, 231, 242; 'the *Poet* yields to the *Orator*,' 280, 255n.; takes seat in Lords, 238–9; 'and now I will go abroad' (without making speech), 238; Lords 'so many Methodists in a barn', 238; on exile, *see* below; Albanian uniforms, 251; eviction of Newstead tenants, 74; describes Turkey and Spain to Lords as less squalid than England, 221; Fox his 'admired luminary', 77; 'never met with objects of distress without affording them succour,' 258; gives away Mary Anne Hanson to insane Earl of Portsmouth, q.v., 75; Calvinism in, 79; ruthlessness, 250, 251, Hanson and Capt. B as sanction for, 80; loyalty to Queen Caroline, 92, 117, 119; loyalty and ambivalence to Hanson, 75–7; nicknames for H, 76; 'great disadvantage to have such a solicitor', 77; engagement and marriage to Annabella among symptoms during N's defeats, 260, 265; homosexuality, 80, 256; paranoid and suicidal tendencies, 265–6; 'nothing left but to follow Whitbread's example', 113; Annabella's fears, 79; diagnoses hydrocephalus, 79; Augusta's fears, 266; B commissions replica of N's military carriage, 82–5; with Hudson Lowe at Holland House, 168–9; revolutionary plots in France, Holland, and Italy, 83–4; but recruits Polidori (cf. O'Meara), 85, and leaves for his 'greenest isle', 85; menagerie installed in palace, 86–7; in tears on seeing Hanson, 87; with menagerie in Ravenna, 242; as Iago in Pisa, 254; with twice N's campaign fund sails from Genoa, 89; motives for martyrdom in Greece, 266; to die in exile more gloriously than Capt. B, 215; 'in yellow leaf', 253; on Cephalonia, 256; at Missolonghi, 84, 89, 256; hair 'light auburn', 89; his rejection by England, 70, and acceptance by, 366–7; as influence in 19th and 20th cents., 288–9; Auden on, 232, 331, 333, 334, 359;
attitude to Napoleon: **81–9,** 168–9; his picture of N more 'cavalier' than Hazlitt's

and Godwin's, 275; resemblance to Capt. B, 80–1, 'Taking towns at his liking and crowns at his leisure,' 366; especially to Capt. B in disgrace, as deserter from army, 82, at Abdication, 'my poor little pagod pushed off pedestal,' 82; 'Bob was a bloody dog, but Bonaparte's a worser,' cf. Mrs. B's 'a little dog of a Byron', 71, 82; B only person to admire N's 'lack of sympathy', 80; Capt. B 'cruelly calumniated' by world and by Mrs. B, 215; 'abuse sealed his pact' with Capt. B and with N, 215; quarrelled with N 'as a lover', 81, but preferred him in exile, 'I don't want him here,' 272; major imitation of N is in exile, 81–9; farewells to the French, 84; adopts initials NB, 85, and sticks to after separation from Annabella, 232; replica of N's carriage, 82, 261; engages Polidori, 85; on his island in Adriatic, N's carriage in basement, 85, 86, menagerie ground floor, 86, B above, 'the grand N of the realms of rhyme', 86; on N's death refuses to write about, 267; 'no spirits, nor *estro* to do so,' 267; 'N's overthrow from the beginning a blow on the head to me,' 267, 261–9; B then acts out identification with N and Capt. B, 89, 267–9; but as greater than either, 215, 269; 'Ode to Napoleon', 82, 260, 261, 267; 'Age of Bronze', 86; *Childe Harold*, 32, 73, 80; *Don Juan*, 80, 86, 88, 232, 236, 242, 255n, 331, 334;
and exile: in childhood, **215;** Stuarts in exile, 215; father's example, 71, 80, 210; in 1809: 'like Adam, the first convict sentenced to transportation,' 80; at Tepelene with 'Mahometan Buonaparte', 238–9; in 1816: 70, 78; 'not the slightest necessity even in appearance for his going abroad,' Hobhouse, 84; writes farewells to the French on behalf of N, 84; would not have gone into exile if he had married Miss Elphinstone, 176; commitment to England, 239
Byron, Capt. John (1756–91), 'Mad Jack', father of B: son's relation to, 71, 80–1, 215, 275; resemblance to Hanson, 74; as type of outcast father, 333

Campbell, Col. Neil, British Commissioner on Elba, 145–7, 151–2, 166; his underestimate of N, 146
Campbell, Thomas, 92, 141
Canning, George, 90; warns Lord Holland of status abroad, 139
Canova, Antonio, 148, 171; bust of N at Holland House, 126

Carlyle, Thomas, 284

Caroline, Princess of Wales and Queen (C Amelia Elizabeth, of Brunswick-Wolfenbüttel) (1768–1821), 68, **90-6, 114-23,** 152, 208; marriage to Prince Regent, 90; 'Delicate Investigation', 90, 92–3; 'rival court' at Kensington Palace, 94–5, 230–1; leaves for Italy, Jan. 1814, 96; projected visit to N, 114; in Naples with Murat, 115, 152; in N's house on Elba, 115; succeeds as Queen of England, 1820, but excluded from palace, 116, 121; trial by Lords, 117–20; Byron on, 117, 119; 'acquittal', 120; Kensington address, 121; 'Caroline' as christian name, 122n.; Prince Regent's 'greatest enemy', 122; death, 122; funeral riots, 123;
  attitude to Napoleon, **112-16;** 'nothing but N and his fame occupied her thoughts,' 115; appoints N's courier, Bartolomeo Pergami, 115–16; N's death and hers, 122, 266–7

Carysfort, Lord, 130–1

Catholics, **45-69,** 233; in Kensington, 39; Moorfield Chapel, 28; in Suffolk, 46; sisterhood at Turnham Green, 58; a 'few hundred priests' in 1798, 46; 4 million Irish Catholics, 209; graduates from Douai 'not proper Englishmen', 49; penalization, 46; anti-Cathoic riots: in Scotland, 48, in London (Gordon Riots), 50–1; Fox's loyalty to, 51; offended by N's treatment of Pope, 209; compared with Dissenters, 209;
  Catholic Relief Acts: First (1778), 51; Second (1790), 28, 52, 55; as stage in general reform, 278

Cawdor, Lord, 4, 5

Centlivre, Mrs. Susannah, 47

Chalon, John James, Huguenot painter at Plymouth, 162

Changeur, Louis Léon (b. ?1780), xiii; origins, 373; imprisoned in Fleet, 1804, 10; builds on Duke of Bedford's estate, Bloomsbury, 26; influence of Samuel Pepys Cockerell on, 26; builds below Holland House, 1810–12, 9–11; investigation by Lord Eldon, 10–11; suspected agent of N, 10, 202–5; Leigh Hunt on, 10–11, 232. *See also* rumours

Charlotte, Princess (1796–1817), only child of Prince Regent and Princess Caroline, 90, 92, 95; N's hope that she would succeed to throne, 159

Charmilly, Col. Peter Francis Venault de: denounced as agent of N, 10, 205

Chesterton, G. K., 284–5, 289

**childhood,** formation of Napoleonists in, **208-20.** *See* **Napoleonists**

Church of England: childhood influence of in ending revolutionary enthusiasm of Coleridge, Wordsworth, and Southey, 279, and Auden, Day Lewis, and MacNeice, 332–3

Churchill, Winston S., 293, 303, 350–1, 352, 355

Clavering, Lady, wife of Sir Thomas C, Bt., 160, 164, 188

Cobbett, William (1762–1836), 24, 94, 118–23, 137; subsidized by Windham at Peace of Amiens but later opposes the war, 206; champions Queen Caroline, 118–19; on her funeral procession, 123; on Fox, 135, 223; *Political Register,* 94, 137

Cobden, Richard (1804–65): manufacturer in Manchester, 304; campaigns against Sir Oswald Mosley for municipal reform, 304; founder of Anti-Corn Law League, 305; victory of 'Cobdenism', 305–6; Napoleonic ideal, 284. *See also* Manchester School

Cockerell, Samuel Pepys, Surveyor of Middlesex, 11; originality as architectural planner, 26, 283

Coigny, Madame de (Anne-Françoise Aimée de), 142, 144, 191; 'Queen of Paris', 129

Coleridge, Samuel Taylor, **204-6;** influence of Church on anti-Jacobinism, 279; ode 'Destruction of the Bastille', 205; assistant editor, *The Courier,* 1811, 204–5; attacks on Lord Holland, 204–5; political apostasy, 65, 205–6; in Changeur's square, 10; passer-by from Hammersmith, 204; 'seen walking in the square,' according to Leigh Hunt, 205; on Hazlitt, 257; 'Xanadu' as escape from politics, 283; addiction to opium, 279;
  attitude to Napoleon: hoped he would prove a Washington, 205; from 1802 the most extreme in his attitude to, 205; defends invective against, 204; his death desirable (1811), 205; 'giant fiend', 205; definition of Napoleonism as 'inward prostration of the soul before enormous power', 272

Colman, George, the elder, 53, 59

Colman, George, the younger, 59

Communists: British party founded 1920, 327; membership confined to 10,000, 327; distinction between Communists' background and Fascists', 362–3; precipitating factor in choice of ideology, 362. *See also* Russian Revolution

Congregationalism: in Wales, 4–6; Church of Christ Assembling in Hornton Street, 40–2; Revd. Robert Vaughan, q.v., in Edwardes Square, 40–2; head of Congregational Union, 42n.

Constant, Benjamin, 144, 191, 198; *Acte*

*Additionel*, 155, 172; in London, 173; *Adolphe*, 173; defence of Labédoyère, 176

Corresponding Society: members tried for treason, 56; no sportsman in, 244

*Courier, The*, 112; Coleridge assistant editor, 1811, 204; his attacks on Lord Holland, 204–5; predicts removal of N to 'St. Lucie' or St. Helena, Sept., Oct., 1814, 145, 376; N's interest in at Torbay, 162; main newspaper opposed to Queen Caroline, 1820, 120–1

Covent Garden, 207; as aristocratic residence, 17; as centre of Westminster elections, 17, 208; Mrs. Inchbald in, 64; Thelwall born in, 255

Covent Garden Theatre: Mrs. Inchbald at, 51–3, 59, 64; burnt down, 61

Coysgarne, Sampson (1750–1822), 43

Creevey, Thomas (1768–1838): at Lord Kensington's 'first state banquet', 38; quoted, 103, 137, 142, 167, 168, 206; in 'Mountain', 234

Cromwell, Oliver: admired by Revd. Robert Vaughan, 41; by Godwin, 66; by Hitler, 311

**dandies**, Napoleonists as, **251-3**. *See* **Napoleonists**

Davis (d. 1817), actor and hairdresser, 50, 51, 52; 'disgraced', 58; dies, 64

Day-Lewis, *see* Lewis, Cecil Day

de Cabarrus, Spanish friend of Hollands, 154, 168–9

de Kéroualle, Louise (1649–1734), great grandmother of C. J. Fox, 219

d'Enghien, Duc: his execution 'a lapse', 258; cf. Auden, 330

**dictators**, Napoleonists as, **249-50**. *See* **Napoleonists**

Disraeli, Benjamin (1804–81), 1st Earl of Beaconsfield: maiden speech, 305; and agriculture, 306

**dissent**, in Napoleonists, **209-10**. *See* **Napoleonists: wilderness, ancestry in**

Dissenters: in Wales, 5; in Kensington, 39; penalization of, 41; Church and State riots against, 1791, 207; Church of Christ Assembling in Hornton Street, 40; Dissenting Chapels more numerous in 1815 than churches of the establishment, 40; repeal of Test Act excluding Dissenters and Catholics from office, 1828, 282; Dissenting ministers, sons of, 210–14; as Napoleonists, **208-14**; continuing influence among neo-Napoleonists, 303, 362. *See also* Baptists; Catholics; Congregationalists; Methodists; Quakers; Unitarians

Dodd, James William, 47, **257**

Doughty, Charles Montagu, 288, 339

Drummond, Sir William: the Scriptures 'astronomical allegories', 92

Drury Lane Theatre, 47; Kemble and Mrs. Siddons at, 52–4; burnt down, 61, 63; reopened, 140; Samuel Whitbread, q.v., responsible for rebuilding, 93, 106–13, 264; W's interference in productions at, 254; reputed cause of his suicide, 112

Earls Terrace: in 1811, 26; boarding-houses in, 64; Mrs. Inchbald in, 45; Hanson in, 70

Ebrington, Lord (1783–1861), Whig M.P. for Buckingham, 144, 147; interviews N, 148–9; his changed attitude, 149, 151

Edgeworth, Maria: rise to fame, 59–60, 63; on *A Simple Story*, 67

*Edinburgh Medical Journal*, on hydrocephalus, 78n.

Edwardes, Edward Henry (1709–37), 13

Edwardes, Lady Elizabeth (?1670–1725), daughter of 3rd Lord Holland: marries Francis Edwards, 13; goads successors to feats of ambition, 270

Edwardes family, *see* Kensington

Edwardes Square: building of, 9–11; occupation, 35–44; Act of 1819, 38, 373; powers of trustees, 38; politics of residents, 39 et seq.; Coleridge in, 10; Hanson in, 70; Mrs. Inchbald in, 45, 64–8

Edwards, Francis (d. 1725), 13, 270

Elba: Fazakerley on, 143 et seq.; Lord Ebrington on, 144, 148; Lord John Russell on, 149–51; naval captains visit, 246; N returns from, 103, 152

Eldon, Earl of, Lord Chancellor, 177; and Changeur, 10–11; not a man who wavered, 207; and Byron, 78, 86, 238–9; outlawry of N, 164, 171, 186

Elizabeth I, Queen: Lady Holland as, 251; Mrs. Inchbald as, 51, 251; quoted by Mrs. I on a level with Dr. Johnson, 59; her study of *The Court of Queen Elizabeth*, 68

Elphinstone, Miss Mercer, 176; becomes Comtesse Flahaut, 177

Emerson, Ralph Waldo, 284

**England**, loyalty of Napoleonists to, **281-2, 364-70**. *See* **Napoleonists**

English Revolution (Glorious Revolution of 1688): criticized in *Rights of Man* for introducing new line of kings, 6; William III chooses Kensington to avoid absolutist associations of Stuart palaces, 12; accession of George III checks progress of emancipation, 277; George III's avoidance of Kensington symbolic, 12; toasts to English R as challenge to George III, 20, 220

Erskine, Thomas, Lord (1750–1823), 61, 242; retained by Hollands to defend title to Holland House, 22; defends Tom Paine, 135; defends Hardy and Holcroft, 56; presented to N, 22, 135; Bills to prevent cruelty to animals, 244–5; on rooks, 22, and leeches, 244; *The Farmer's Vision*, 242n.

Evangelicals, *see* Bazalgette, Joseph William

*Examiner, The*: founded by brothers Hunt, 9; leads support of Caroline, 94; on her acquittal, 121; on C and N, 198; elaborates Whitbread's attacks on the war, 203, 263; in black border at N's death, 266; world reduced to slavery, 267; *New Statesman* compared with, 317, 326

exhibitions: Mr. Bullock's in Piccadilly, 29, 82; N's portrait by David in Leicester Square, 63; N at Plymouth, 162

Farington, Joseph (1747–1821), 101, 112

Farquhar, James, M.P. for Aberdeenshire, 70–1

Fascists: British Union of, founded by Sir Oswald Mosley, 1932, 312; did not become mass movement, 327; distinction between Fascists' background and Communists', 362–3; precipitating factor in choice between ideologies, 362

Fazakerley, J. N., neighbour of N on Elba, 143, 148, 152, 170

Finlaison, John (fl. 1815–21), records clerk at Admiralty, 194, 245; a main channel from St. Helena, 194

Flahaut, Auguste Charles Joseph, Comte (1785–1870): Talleyrand's illegitimate son, 144; N's aide-de-camp at Waterloo, 126; rescued by Hollands, 172, **176-7**, 179; supports Las Cases, 195

Foscolo, Ugo (1778–1827), 27, **29-33**; welcomes N, 29; *Letters of Ortis* and *Carme sui sepolcri*, 30; adopted by Lord Holland, 30; uses knife as argument, 256; contributes to Hobhouse's *Illustrations of Childe Harold*, 32; death, 33; compared with English Napoleonists, 277

Foulkes, Evan, solicitor of 2nd Lord Kensington, 26

Fox, Caroline, sister of Lord Holland, 129, 144, 151, 153–4

Fox, Charles James (1749–1806), 5, 15–17, 21, 135–8, **216-20**, **223-7**, 229–30, 249–50, 274, 288, 292, 351, 358–9, 363; 3rd son of Henry F, q.v., childhood in Holland House, 15–16, 216–20; spoiled by HF, 5, 218; unlike HF, descendant of Stuarts, 219–20; aware of HF as most corrupt of King's servants, 14–15, 218; peculiarities as gambler, 218–19; 'representative' of HF in Commons in HF's lifetime, 15,

219, but contributes to illness and death, 219; crosses floor on American issue, 16; leaves rotten borough for 10,000 voters of Westminster, q.v., 16; supports Catholic emancipation, 50–1; as 'Man of the People,' becomes main opponent of George III, 17, 256; impervious to charge of traitor, 274; main defence of HF in Commons, June 1781, 216; compromises himself by alliance with Lord North, 19; election of 1784, 19; demands peace throughout first half of French war, 216, 226; consistent supporter of Navy, 245, 271, but not of militia, 5; fashion dictator, wearing American colours, 252; prematurely old, 253; opposition split by his insistence on reform and peace in spite of terror in Paris, 20; transfers to platform of Whig Club, q.v., on issue of reform ('secession' of 1797), 223; 'Washington of England', 225; on Ireland, 225–6; on self-determination throughout world, 226; suggests deposition of George III, 227; visits Paris, 1802, for research on James II, 135; marriage to Mrs. Armistead announced on eve of visit, 135; with N, 136; denounced by Coleridge and Cobbett, 137; wants references to King's madness daily in newspapers, 1804, 256; Foreign Secretary, 1806, 22, 138; abolition of slave trade, 138; peace negotiations with N, 138; but acknowledges impossibility of — a shuffling game, 138; 'oath in heaven' against title, 218; death, 138, 207; funeral, 230; life in opposition, 217; service to country, 278, 366;

attitude to Napoleon: awaited in advance as counterpart of Washington, 224; a moderate man who would not seize power by force, 1797, 20; has to accept Brumaire, 1799, 20; 'General Bonaparte reframed [state] as military men apt to, by taking all power,' 20; unwilling to see N in focus, 273; 'Good, great as General Washington was, not better spoken of than N,' 216; in Paris 1802, Fox offhand, 'very magnif.', 136, but on return 'N fittest to be master', 137; criticizes N's coronation as Emperor, 217; consistently blames British Government for failure to negotiate peace, 258; death after his own failure in negotiation as Foreign Secretary, 137, 207; reliance on Navy made him sceptical of invasion, 271, 273–4, but intended to resist if it came, 20–1; misjudgement in favour of N counterpart of hatred of George III,

220, and rooted in childhood ambivalence to HF, 216–20. As actor, animal-lover, dictator, linguist, reformer, rival of King, traveller, *see* **Napoleonists**

Fox, Henry (1705–1774, cr. 1st Baron Holland 1763), father of C.J.F, **14-16, 216-20;** m. Caroline Lennox, great-granddaughter of Charles II, 219; career promises Whig premiership, 14, but turns into pursuit of money and titles, 217; rents Holland House from W. Edwardes, 1747, 14; for 25 years loyal servant of crown, 217, unpopularity, marked in son's early childhood, 14, increased as tool of George III in breaking Whigs, 1763, 15; rewarded with barony but not earldom he wanted, 15; denounced by city of London, 1769, as 'public defaulter of unaccounted millions', 15; under attack finds main consolation in Holland House, 219; purchase of freehold 1768 by Act of Parliament to eliminate rights of Edwardes's heirs, 15; life shortened by sons' gambling, 219; as type of outcast father, 333

Fox, Stephen, 15

France: Hollands in, 1800, 132–4; 1802, 135–8; 1814, 143–4; 1817, 190–1; 1821, 198–9; influence of on Holland House, 1815–21, 172 et seq.; on English stage, 54; on Mrs. Inchbald, 49; on Godwin, 56; Coleridge: 'F is my Babylon,' 206; Fox on self-determination in, 226. *See also* French Revolution

Frederick, King of Saxony, 102–3

French Revolution: reactionary influence on majority opinion in England, 205–7, 279–80; disintegration of Opposition, 20; as inspiration to Coleridge in youth, 205, and Wordsworth and Southey, 279; their inspiration transformed from 1795 into Romanticism, 279–80; persistence of Napoleonists, 279–81; effect on Fox, 216, 'they have advanced a century in past 5 years,' 202; on Hollands, 131–2; on Holcroft and Mrs. Inchbald, 56; 'enabled' Godwin to write *Political Justice*, 56; compared with effect of Russian Revolution on majority, 360–1, and on poets of thirties, 328

Froissart, xi, 368

Gage, Sir Thomas, Catholic patron of Mrs. Inchbald, 46, 55, 61

Galileo: Byron at his tomb, 'He is *one of us*', 223

Gallois, Léonard, 144, 191, 198; N '*tout à fait un être politique*', 173

Gandolphy, Dr. Peter, 63

Garibaldi, Giuseppe, 288–9

Gayet, Isidore, assistant editor of *Le Nain Jaune,* 173–4

George III (reign 1760–1820; mad intervals, 1788–9, 1804, 1810–20): abandons Kensington Palace, 12; uses Henry Fox to break Whigs, 15; 'George or [C.J.] Fox to reign?', 220; 'the Contest become personal', 220; on historical influence of American Revolution, 363; personal rule broken, 17; thanks to W. Edwardes on repulse of French landing, 1797, 3; deposition proposed by Fox in Whig Club, 227; his vices seen by F as those of H. Fox as King's servant, 220

George IV, *see* Prince Regent

George, David Lloyd (1863–1945), **289-303;** father dies, 1865, 290; childhood in Llanystumdwy, 290; elected for Caernarvon Boroughs, 1890, 296; as Cabinet minister advised by uncle, Richard Lloyd, q.v., 291; as Chancellor of Exchequer revolutionizes social services and finances arms programme, 291; the 'People's Budget', 291; as Prime Minister, 1916–22, 292; in opposition for rest of life, 292–3; visits Hitler, 1936, 292–3; his achievement, 302–3; prepared dissolution of British Empire, 302;

attitude to Kruger: an outcast 'against whom we are massing the might of 40 millions', 290; to Hitler: 'the George Washington of Germany', 292; his heroic response to Versailles, 292; cure of unemployment, 293, 366

Germany, 61; Saxony 'the garden of G', 62; visited by Hollands, 130–1

Gibbon, Edward, 16, 217

Gisborne, Thomas, M.D., physician in ordinary to George III, 54

*Glenarvon, see* Lamb, Lady Caroline

Godwin, Revd. John (b. 1723), Unitarian minister, father of William G, 56, 210, **212;** his limitations, 211; strict Sabbatarian, 243

Godwin, William (1756–1836); **56-7, 65-7,** 69, 185, 202, 207, **234-6,** 365; childhood, 210–13, 243; his need to 'emerge' from family of 13 children, 212; impatience at Revd. G's limitations and failure to notice him, 212; solitary confinement the worst punishment in *Caleb Williams*, 213; converted by Fox to American cause, 212–13; French Revolution 'enabled' him to write *Political Justice*, 56; inability to see individuals in their own right, 250, and sense of 'curiosity' as most dangerous of crimes, 221; suicides in his circle in 1816, 266; on man's opinions as 'a barometer', 278, 365 and n; *Political*

Godwin, William, *contd.*
  *Justice*, 1793, 56, 234, 252, 259; *Caleb Williams,* 1794, 250; *Essay on Sepulchres,* 1809, 235; letters to *Morning Chronicle,* 1815, 56, 66, 236;
  attitude to Napoleon, 235–6, 250; 'Dr. Parr's Spital Sermon', 1801, 365; N, like G's father, 'an auspicious personage', 365 n.; 'did not wish we should succeed', 65; threat to N compared with threat to G's crown, 236
Great West Road, *see* Kensington turnpike
Greece: Byron and the liberation of, 83, 88–9
Gregory, John (1746–1813), **227-9**; treasurer of Whig Club, 19; master of Kensington turnpike, 23–4; Justice of the Peace, 24; interrogates Changeur, 10
Grenville, William, Lord (1759–1834), 156; forms Government of All the Talents, 21; patron of Hanson, 71; on Hollands' visit to France, 130–1; with Windham, singled out by N as worst enemy, 206
Grey, Charles, 2nd Earl, Viscount Howick (1764–1845), 96, 102–3, 111–12, 129, 165, 218; in Hundred Days, 156, 207; ill after Waterloo, 262; guardian of Whitbread's children, 262 n.; N's interest in at Plymouth, 163; compromised by Sir Robert Wilson, 180–3; in 1820 expects 'a Jacobin Revolution more bloody than that of France', 118
*Guardian, The, see Manchester Guardian*

Hamilton, Lady Anne (1766–1846), lady-in-waiting to Queen Caroline, 94, 116–17; N's death state murder, like Queen C's', 198
Hanover: ambassador sued by turnpike, 228; Lady Holland in, 240
Hanson, Charles (fl. 1790–1845), son of John H, 71, 76, 87
Hanson, Hargreaves (fl. 1790–1840), son of John H, 71, 76
Hanson, John (fl. 1788–1825), 214; Byron's solicitor, **70-89**; buys Dr. Hunter's house, 72; evicts Newstead tenants, 73–4; influence on B, 77–80; rejects Annabella's ideas on hydrocephalus, 78–9; in Venice, 70, 86–7; his character, 74, 76. *See also* Byron
Hanson, Mrs. John (d. 1814), 71–3; death, 75
Hanson, Mary Anne, eldest d. of John H, 72; marriage to Lord Portsmouth, 74, 76, 78, 87–9; annulled, 89
Hanson, Newton (fl. 1790–1860), 70, 75; on Byron in Venice, 86
Hardy, Thomas (1752–1832): acquitted of treason, 56
Haverfordwest: invasion committee at, 4; Edwardes family in, 13; election of 1780, 17
Haydon, Benjamin Robert (1786–1846): on Hazlitt and Leigh Hunt at Waterloo, 262–3

Hazlitt, William (1778–1830): 63, 185, 202, 207, **210-11**, 232, 236, 251, 257, 259, 270, 272, 275, 359; son of Unitarian minister, 46; brought up for 18 months near Kinsale, Ireland, 210; in Philadelphia and Boston from 6th to 9th year, 211; Wem, Shropshire, 210; sat in pulpit during sermon, 210, but revolts against narrow literary and artistic horizon of father, 211; admires success of elder brother as painter, 211; a mimic, develops gifts as linguist and painter, 211; trains for ministry at Hackney College under Priestley, but loses faith while writing *Principles of Action,* 211; reads *A Simple Story* in love in Manchester and forms lifelong admiration of Mrs. Inchbald, announced 1818, 46; in Paris, 1802, copies paintings in Louvre, 136; essayist, dramatic critic, lecturer, 45, 254; Virginia Woolf on, 280–1; declines entry Holland House circle, 208; Charles Lamb finds 'confounded' by Abdication, 260; quarrels with editor of *Morning Chronicle,* 262; believes himself 'undesirable contributor', 262; physical symptoms, 262; 'triumphs and rejoices' in Hundred Days, 261; 'thrown into pit' by Waterloo, 262; physical symptoms worse, 262; Haydon finds him prostrated, unwashed, drunk, 262; but deplores Whitbread's suicide when 'last fatal blow' fell on Whigs, 113; tours France and Italy, 1823–4, 237–8; begins massive *Life of Napoleon,* 1827, and dies on completion, 267;
  attitude to Napoleon: unshakeable admirer of as champion of outcasts, 46, 269; alleges Byron supported N in victory and abandoned in defeat, 46, 81; 'fidelity not imagination' the outcome of Dissenter's upbringing, 210, 280; his own isolation in politics, 1795–1821, 365 and n.; his vision of N 'enabled' him to stand against ruling majority, 365–6
Hazlitt, Revd. William (1737–1820), father of William H, 275; Unitarian minister, 46; moves 1779 to Ireland, near Kinsale prisoner camp, because of American sympathies, 210; in Philadelphia and Boston with H, 1783–6, 210, 211; returns Wem when H eight, 210
Herbert, Sir Alan Patrick, 284
Hitler, Adolf, 285, 288, 358, 368; admiration of in England compared with admiration of N, 288; visited by C. Hobhouse, 311, Lloyd George, 292, Mosley, 316, Lord Lothian, 327; effect of visits compared with that of visits on N, 327; Churchill on,

303; effect of on Auden, 329–30, and on Kingsley Martin, 320

Hobhouse, Sir Benjamin (1757–1831, cr. Bt. 1812), father of John Cam H, 31, 210, 273; rich Bristol merchant, 213; Unitarian and later founded 'Humanitarians', 213–14; his politics, 214; relations with son, 214, 273

Hobhouse, Christopher (1910–40): defeated as New Party candidate, Oct. 1931, 310; visits Hitler, Dec. 1931, 311; author of *Fox* (1934), quoted, 311; descendant of John Cam H, q.v., 310, 364

Hobhouse, John Cam, later Lord Broughton (1786–1869), 75, 89, 207, 265; childhood and Unitarian upbringing, 210, **213-14;** one of 19 children, 214; founder of Cambridge Whig Club, 31; stabs Scrope Davies, 256; 1814, in Holland House circle, 142; schemes with Byron for anti-Bourbon revolution, 83–4; in Paris in Hundred Days 'dazzled' by N, 273; sends *Letters from Paris* to St. Helena, 31; Radical candidate for Westminster, 31; collaboration with B and Foscolo, **31-3;** *Illustrations of Childe Harold,* 32; projected treatise on revolution, 31; said by Hanson to be 'completely' in power of his father, Sir Benjamin H, q.v., 214, 272; at N's death 'confident I shall not live much longer,' 267; B's executor, 71, 76; accompanies Queen Caroline to St. Paul's on her acquittal by Lords, 121; supports municipal reform, 123; originates phrase 'His Majesty's Opposition', 1826, 223; accepts peerage as Lord Broughton, 1851, 214, 267, under which name *Recollections of a Long Life,* 372; ancestor of Christopher H., 364;

attitude to Napoleon: insists in *Letters from Paris* that N champion of his people defending himself against world in arms, 273; 'would not have beheld him with delight in days of despotism,' 273; *Letters from Paris* inscribed *Imperatori Napoleon* and confiscated by Hudson Lowe, 31

Hoche, Gen.: in charge of invasion forces, 2, 3

Holcroft, Thomas (1745–1809), 50, 136; tried for treason, 56

Holland, Lady (Elizabeth Vassall Fox) (1771–1845): birth and upbringing, 12, **127-8;** in masque as Clytie, 128 and n.; marries Sir Godfrey Webster, 128; divorce and marriage to Lord H, 128–9; fears loss of Holland House, 22; her dinners, 129; 'ostracism', 230; at Rheinsberg, court of Prince Henry of

Prussia, 240–1; presentation to N, 135–6; dislike of Whig Club, 229–30; on Princess Caroline, 114–15; on Caroline Lamb's *Glenarvon,* 140–1; 'Madagascar', 141; her charities, 141; plans visit to N on Elba, 143–6; entertains Col. Campbell, 145–6; sends *The Courier* to N, 146, 149, 151; in Rome, 146–55; further exchanges with N, 151n.; in Naples, 152–3; and Murat, 152; reaction to N's landing in France, 153, and entry to Paris, 154; determines to return through France, 154; passport, 154–5; on Russian army, 156; news of Waterloo, 156–7; intention to restore N, 158–9; campaign to win Hudson Lowe, 166–72; her channel into prison of La Force, 181; won by O'Meara, 197; gifts to St. Helena, 197–8; HL disallows her newspapers, 198; his reception at Holland House, 199–200;

her auburn hair, 128, 251; children, 134, 143, 156, 240; foreign clothes, 138, 141–2, 144; her kindness, 141; her languages, 254; and pets, 243; 'a Queen', 128, 230, 251; on Regency building, 26; resilience in defeat, 142 et seq., 158; retinue while travelling, 130, 143; sharpness of her tongue, 257

Holland, Henry (?1746–1806), 109, 283; turnpike trustee, 24; Whig architect of Southill Park, 264

Holland, Henry Richard Vassall Fox, 3rd Lord (1773–1840): disciple of uncle, C. J. Fox, 126; youth and upbringing, 126–7; title to Holland House, 12; Lord Privy Seal in Talents, 22; prospect of Premiership in 1811, 9; on Princess Caroline, 92, 114; in Lords, ignores Whig secession, 129; Francophile, 130, 139; in Paris and Spain, 1802–5, 134–8; and high office, 138; affronted by Canning on return to Spain, 1808, 139; relations with Prince Regent, 139–40; loans to Godwin, 141; end of hopes of Premiership, 142; in France and Italy, 1814–15, 143–58; leases Louis Bonaparte's house, 148; on prospects of N's return from Elba, 144–5, 151; in Naples, 152–3; 'all for peace', 156; on Whitbread's suicide, 112–13; and refugees, 172–4; and Lucien Bonaparte, 174–5; Flahaut at Holland House, 176–7; attempts to save Marshal Ney, 178–9; and Lavalette, 179–83; and Capel Lofft, 184 et seq.; isolation in Parliament, 1817, 189–90; lobbies Duke of York on N, 191; relations with Las Cases, 188–9, 194–7; his benevolence, 141, 258;

Holland, 3rd Lord, *contd.*
 attitude to Napoleon: on N, 130, 139–40;
  no experience of dealing with, 139;
  'greatest statesman and ablest general
  of ancient or modern times', 140;
  severely critical on Spain, 139; N's
  invincibility, 142; ambivalence compared with Byron's, 143; 'cant and
  nonsense', 143; on return from Elba,
  153–4; 'mad Declaration of Vienna',
  155; 'a much better opinion of N than
  I had', 156; his restoration after Waterloo,
  158–9; difference from Lady H, 158,
  165–6; dispute with Grenville, 165–6;
  'Protest', 186; and W. Warden, 191–3;
  abandons public debate, 193
Holland, Launcelot, son of Henry H,
 architect, 109–11, 264
Holland House: title in dispute, 12–26;
 settled, 38–9; Fox's rival palace, 219; as
 Napoleonist centre, 126–40; ideal target
 for rumours, 204; Hazlitt and Leigh Hunt
 would not go to, 208; Lady Holland's
 dinners, 129 and *passim*; pastiche of in
 *Glenarvon*, 140–1; in decline of N, 142–200;
 40 guests in Lowe campaign, 166–72;
 Flahaut appears at, 176–7; Canova's bust
 at, 126, 200; relics of N at, 200; as rival
 court, **125-200**; as foreign court, 239
Hood, Mr., neighbour of Mrs. Inchbald, 60,
 208
Hortense, Queen, wife of Louis Bonaparte,
 148, 151n., 174–6, 180; collapses in Baden,
 177; addressed by Lt. Bruce as 'Imperial
 Highness', 182
Huguenots, 36; Fox's choice of school, 16,
 126; J. J. Chalon at Plymouth, 162;
 ancestry of Guy Burgess, 345, and Kingsley
 Martin, 317
Hunnermann, Franz August Christian Wil-
 helm (fl. 1815–45), 36, 239; christens
 daughter Caroline, 122
Hunt, Revd. Isaac (1752–1809), father of
 Leigh H, 9; vicar in Barbados, later
 Dissenting minister, 210, **213**; failings and
 eccentricities, 9, 213
Hunt, Leigh (1784–1859), 207, 210; upbringing, 9; founds *The Examiner*, q.v., 1808,
 9, 213; denounced as Bonapartist, 9;
 on Changeur, 10–11, 232; not 'slightest
 belief in this coming of Bonaparte', 272;
 'only good to say of his father', 213;
 sentenced for libelling Prince Regent,
 213; attack on PR related to father, 276;
 effect of Abdication on, 263; mistaken
 to outlive Shelley and Keats, 253; his
 'cockney court' in 1815, 260, in 1818,
 250; as an actor, 254; on boa constrictors
 and eagles, 243; illness and paranoia in

N's defeats, 263; suicide in *Story of
 Rimini* (1816), 263; his stammer in
 childhood, 254, and adult life, 258;
 goes to Italy in 1821 after N's death to
 get rid of his 'deadly symptoms', 266;
 *Autobiography,* 276; compared with
 Kingsley Martin, 317, 326;
 attitude to Napoleon: as editor of *Examiner,*
 9; from Abdication to St. Helena, 263;
 modified as prospective crown pensioner,
 11, 281; 'mighty and high-souled man',
 276
Hunter, Dr. John, 70, 72
hydrocephalus: diagnosed by Lady Byron in
 B, 78–9; by George III's physician in
 Whitbread, 112

Ibn Saud, King of Saudi Arabia (1902–69),
 **336-41;** Wahhabi Bonaparte, 337; confutes
 Foreign Office, 337; career and relations
 with St. John Philby, 336–8; 'at top of the
 tree of human greatness', 338
Inchbald, Mrs. Elizabeth (1753–1821), **45-69,**
 137, 207, **232-3**; born Simpson, 46;
 Catholic upbringing, 46–7; loss of her
 father, 46, 217–18; rivalry with sister
 Deborah, 47, 52; runs away to London,
 47; marries, 48; plans to emigrate to
 France, 48; in Paris, 1776, 48; returns, in
 love with Kemble, 49–50; widowed, 50;
 at Covent Garden, 51–2; and hairdresser,
 Davis, 50, 52, 58, 65; discards wig, 52;
 rivalry with Mrs. Siddons, 52; and
 Tippoo Sahib, 52; plans to emigrate to
 India, 52–3; success of *The Mogul Tale,*
 53; adapts French plays, 54; *Everyone
 Has His Fault,* 54; accused of Jacobinism,
 54; abandons acting, 55; *A Simple Story,*
 begun, 49, 50, abandoned, 55, published
 1791, 55, 56; death of 'Orah', 55; and
 'Pretty', 55, 58; pursued by Holcroft, 56;
 in love with Godwin, 57; *Nature and
 Art,* 57; translates Rousseau, 57; admires
 N, 46, after Concordat, 58, and break-
 down of Peace of Amiens, 59; *To Marry
 or Not to Marry,* 59; rivalry with Miss
 Edgeworth, stops writing, 59–60; first
 welcomes N, 59; watches Drury Lane
 fire, 61; collapse of beauty, 61–2; effect
 of N's abdication and defeats, on, 63,
 260; and doctors, 51, 54, 63; as a critic,
 59; and Byron, 64, 208; in Edwardes
 Square, 45, 64; meets Talma, 65; and
 Godwin, 65–7; returns to Catholics,
 68; Memoirs, 55, 59, 67, destroyed, 68;
 death from tight-lacing, 69; Hazlitt on
 *A Simple Story,* 46, on *Lovers' Vows,* 46;
 her auburn hair, 47, 51; her stammer, 47,
 51; 'H-h-hyde Pa-park C-c-corner', 53;

'lucky he didn't w-w-wear a w-w-wig,' 257; speech 'severe and pointed', 257; pseudonym 'Mr. Royal', 47, 233

Inchbald, Joseph (1736–79): marries Elizabeth Simpson, 48; dies, 50

Inchbald, Robert, illegitimate son of Joseph I, 48, 68

invasion: attempt by French Directory, 1796–7, 2–3; attitude to, in Wales, 4; N's plans for in 1797–8, 6, and in 1804–5, 6–8; as a feint in 1811, 8; Napoleonists sceptical of prospects, **271-4**

Ireland, 2, 55; French attempt landing in, 2; United Irishmen, 2; Fox on self-determination in, 226; 4 million Catholics in, 209

**islanders,** Napoleonists as, **271-3, 364,** 368–70. *See* **Napoleonists**

Italian Napoleonists: on N's entry, 6–7. *See also* Aglio, Foscolo

Jacobins: term applied to those believed to sympathize with most radical aims of French Revolution, e.g., Princess Caroline, 95, 114, Fox, 225, Lord Holland, 166, Godwin, 66, Mrs. Inchbald, 34: name becomes damning with growing violence of French Revolution, 20, English treason trials of 1794 and anti-subversive Acts of 1795, 278–9; realignment, as anti-Jacobins, of Windham and Grenville, 206, Coleridge, 205–6, Wordsworth and Southey, 279; Napoleonists persist in seeing N as champion of revolutionary ideals, 280, 365–6; accept Jacobin as term of abuse, e.g. Byron (1815), 'I am a Jacobin and could not wear white,' 260; Holland House as Jacobin centre under Regency, 22–3; and Kensington Palace, 95; use of 'Red' and 'Bolshevik' after Russian Revolution compared, 361

Jersey, Lady, 144, 167, 171, 191; as courier to Bonapartes in Rome and Bonapartists in Paris, 184

Jersey, Lord, 167, 184; visit to Las Cases, 196

Jews: small 18th cent. colony in Manchester joined by refugees from Germany, 1820, 304; Salis Schwabe forms alliance with Richard Cobden, 304; influx of, 25 synagogues in Manchester by 1914, 307; emancipation of delayed by House of Lords until 1858, 282, 304; Marx in London from 1848, 368

Johnson, Dr. Samuel: imitated by Byron, 77; Fox 'divided the kingdom with Caesar', 120; attacked by Capel Lofft, 185; silenced Fox, 257; Becky Sharp discards presentation copy of his Dictionary, 272

Keith, Lord, Admiral of the Fleet, 162–5, 176–7

Kemble, John Philip (1757–1823), 49–68, 136

Kensington: Whig court at, 1690–1760, 12; centre of Caroline disturbance, 90, 93; addresses from, 120–2

Kensington, William Edwardes, 1st Lord (1711–1801): resemblance to George III, 13, 270; inherits Holland House, 14; lets to Henry Fox, q.v., 14–15; Irish peerage in 1776, 16; committed to Court Party, 16–17, 270, 276

Kensington, William Edwardes, 2nd Lord (1777–1852): birth and upbringing, 18, 270; militia captain in 1797 invasion attempt, 4, 18; claims Holland House, 22; landlord of Changeur, 9; joins Brooks's, 18; resemblance to Prince Regent, 18; nicknamed Og by Creevey, 19; accepts leadership of Windham, 21; Lord of the Admiralty, 21–2; in Carmarthen Bay, 24; speculation in cavalry 'cast' horses, 26; builds K Canal, 38–9; at Heydon Hall, 38; death, 39; his life as pattern of normal loyalty, **270-2;** contrasted with Napoleonists, **276-7;** attitude to N, 21, 271, 276

Kensington Canal, 38–9

Kensington Gate, 9–11; opposite Holland House, 372

Kensington Palace: chosen by William III, 12; as centre of Jacobinism, 95; Princess Caroline at, **90-6;** Duke of Kent, 91; Duke of Sussex, 91–2

Kensington turnpike: 'biggest in London', 227; scene of Changeur's building estate, 9; Gregory's rival court, 23–4, **227-9;** minutes, 372

Kent, Edward Augustus, Duke of (1767–1820), 42, **90-1;** his protest to turnpike ignored, 228; birth of Victoria, 42n., 117; his death, 117

Kinnaird, Charles, 8th Lord (1780–1826), 136, 173–4; rescue of Bonapartists, **178-83;** expulsion from France, 182; house in Brussels, 190–1; supports Las Cases, 195

Kinnaird, Douglas, brother of Lord K, Byron's banker, 75

kings, *see* **Napoleonists: as monarchs**

Knox, Col. Thomas: in charge of Fishguard fort, 4

Kossuth, Lajos, 42n.

Kruger, Paul, Boer leader, 289; member of Dopper sect of Dutch Reformed Church, 289; supported by Lloyd George, 290–1

Labédoyère, Comte de, 175–8

Lafayette, Marquis de, 49; Lord Holland and,

Lafayette, Marquis de, *contd.*
127, **172-3,** 174-5; in 1817, 191; in 1821, 198

Lamb, Lady Caroline, 129, 140; and Byron, 87; and Foscolo, 31; *Glenarvon*, 140-1, 143

Lamb, Charles, 260; contrasted with Godwin, 251

Lansdowne, 3rd Lord (1780-1863), 23, 171, **363-4;** channel between Holland House and Bonapartes, 184

Lansdowne, 5th Lord (1845-1927), 297; founder of school of appeasement in 20th cent., **363-4**

Las Cases, Emmanuel Auguste, Dieudonné de, Comte de (1766-1842): youth and upbringing, 159; first period in London, 1793-1802, 159-60; *Historical Atlas*, 160-1, 195-6; admiration of N, 160; returns to London, 1814, 160; at Rochefort and on *Bellerophon*, 160-5; and Maitland, 161; evidence 'not to be trusted', 162; engineers expulsion from St. Helena on completion of *Mémorial*, 188-9; at Cape, 195; at Dover, 195; deported to Ostend and Germany, 191; debate on maltreatment in Commons, 196; realizes 2 million francs, 197; described by Lord Jersey, 1821, 196; *Mémorial de Ste. Hélène*, 159, 161; groundwork finished in 1816, 188; Lord Holland enables him to complete, 195-7; influence on Second Empire, 194-5

Lauderdale, Lord, 111, 168, 177; supports Lord Holland on N, 186; cousin of Maitland, 187

Lavalette, Antoine-Marie, Comte de (1769-1830), 204; issues passport to Lord Holland, 131-2, 175; rescue of, **179-83**

Lawrence, T. E., 339

Lawrence, Sir Thomas: twice paints Mrs. Inchbald, 58; absent from Holland House because ashamed of his French, 240

Lebrun, Jacques, 3

Lebrun, Philippe: finances Changeur, 10

*Letters to a French Spy* (1808), 204, 361

Lewis, Cecil Day (b. 1904), 325; son of vicar, 332; 'scorched earth policy against', 333; joins Communist Party, 328, leaves, 333; Poet Laureate, 334; on isolation of poets in thirties, 329, **362.** *See also* Poet Laureate; Russian Revolution, influence on poets

Lindsay, Lady Charlotte, lady-in-waiting to Princess Caroline, 92

**linguists and translators,** Napoleonists as, **253-4.** *See* Napoleonists

Lloyd, Richard (1834-1917), uncle of Lloyd George: adopts LG, 290; cobbler and co-pastor of Disciples of Christ in Llanystumdwy, 290, 293-4; indulgence of LG in

childhood, 294-6; gratitude to Asquith, 298-9; last sermon and death in LG's first year as Prime Minister, 290; as prototype of Kruger and Hitler, 299, 303, and of Asquith, Kitchener, and Haig, 299

Lodi, Napoleon at, 1796: moral effect in Italy, 6; on Aglio, 27; on Byron, 81

Lofft, Capel (1751-1824), 162, 164, 193; at Calais, 183-4; as spokesman for N, **184-5;** when travelling, 241; on N's death, 242; as dandy, 252

London, City of: deputation to Caroline, 94

Lords, House of: trial of Caroline, 117-21; Byron and, 238; Fox and, 218; Lord Holland and, 129, 186, 189-90, 193

Louis XVIII: and Queen Caroline, 116; and Byron, 260

Louis Napoleon, *see* Napoleon III

Lowe, Sir Hudson (1769-1844), 146; governor of St. Helena, 166; education and career, 166-7; Lady Holland's campaign to seduce, 166-72; and Byron, 168; his marriage to Mrs. Johnson, 171; advocates outlawing of N, 171; K.C.B., 172; on St. Helena, 187-98; expels Las Cases, 189, 195; returns to Holland House, 199-200

Lyttelton, Hon. W. H.: in 'Mountain', 234; interview with N, 1815, 163, 282

MacDonald, Ramsay, 310, 319, 344, 361

Mackenrot, Anthony: attempts to rescue N from *Bellerophon*, 164-6

Maclean, Donald Duart (b. 1913), **348-58;** childhood coincides with father's championship of outcasts, **345-51;** contrast with Alan Maclean (b. 1924), 355, 359; 'as much a subject of Crown as oldest, richest, most powerful man in England', 349, 354; on 'external reality', 354; loyalty to his father, 354, and revolt against, 355-6; Stalin as 'Father Found', 356; as neo-Napoleonist, 356-7

Maclean, Sir Donald (Macmellin) (1864-1932), father of D. D. Macl, **348-54;** born near Bolton, Lancs., 348, educated Haverfordwest grammar school, 349; a Presbyterian, 349; deprivations of Scottish parents, 348-9; elected to Commons as Liberal, 1906, 349; on defeat of Asquith, leads 'Wee Frees', 350; and India, 350; champion of outcasts, 350; sustains attack on Churchill for intervention against Bolshevik Russia, 350-1; foresees 'Russian N', 351; rejected by electorate, 1922-9, 351; ancestral interests and coat of arms, 1912-15, 352; knighted, 1917, 352; as President, Board of Education, 1931-2, accepts heaviest cuts in Cabinet, but dies after 7 months as minister, 353-4

MacNeice, Louis (1907–64), **328-33** *passim,* 362

'Madame Mère', *see* Bonaparte, Letizia Ramolino

Maitland, Capt. Frederick Lewis (1777–1839), 140; audience with N, 1802, 136; with N on *Bellerophon,* 161–3; trap set by Las Cases, 195; at Holland House with Hudson Lowe, 168–9

'Man of the People', Fox as, 17, 19, 50, 120, 226; Lloyd George as, 292

*Manchester Guardian*: in alliance with Cobden, 305; Kingsley Martin unacceptable as socialist leader-writer, 317

Manchester School: radical group led by Cobden and Bright, who believed in Free Trade, *laissez-faire* and internationalism, 306, 316–17; Anti-Corn Law League founded by Cobden, 1839, 305; reversed status of British agriculture in relation to industry, 306; victory of MS made possible by security of the island, 306

Marchand, N's valet: on Caroline's visit to Elba, 114; on books at St. Helena from Holland House, 197

Marie Louise, 2nd wife of N, 114–15; compared with Lady Elizabeth Whitbread, 103

Marsh, Revd. Matthew, 133–4, 172

Martin, Revd. Basil (1859–1940), father of Kingsley M: imperial ambitions in childhood, 318; Unitarian minister and supporter of Kruger, 318; *An Impossible Parson,* 319

Martin, (Basil) Kingsley (1897–1969), **317-26**; childhood as son of Unitarian minister, 317–19; father the 'reincarnation of Jesus', 318; 'no chance at all to quarrel with him', 318; editorship of *New Statesman,* 1931–61, compared with Leigh Hunt's editorship of *Examiner,* 1808–21, 317, 325, 326; sympathy with Stalin's Russia, 319–20; criticism of British monarchy, 321–2; National Government reactivates isolation of his childhood, 323–4; influence of *New Statesman,* 317, 326

Marxism, influence of, *see* Russian Revolution

medals: restricted to Army, 246; Turkish medal awarded to Cdr. George Pedlar, R.N., 44; none for Trafalgar, 246. *See also* Navy

*Medical Journal, see Edinburgh Medical Journal*

Merry, Andrew, 135

Methodists, 5, 18, **210**; 'in a barn', 238

middle classes: their romanticism after failure of reform, 283; main wartime architectural achievement due to, 283; hero-worship of N delayed until after Reform Act, 284

Middlesex: returns Wilkes, 15, 278; George Byng, q.v., 224, 228; S. C. Whitbread, 118;

deputations to Queen Caroline, 95, 118, (Kensington) 121–2; radicalism of, 202–3, 277–8

**monarchs,** Napoleonists as, **217-53.** *See* **Napoleonists**

Montholon, Count: leading member of entourage on St. Helena, 187; wife in England, 194; his Remonstrance, 188–9; at Holland House, 199

*Morning Chronicle, The,* 188–9, 199, 223, 224, 230; reports Whig Club and Radical opposition during Napoleonic wars, 203, 223, 224, 227; Godwin's letters on treason, 56, and N, 66, 136; source of Fox on self-determination, 226; Hazlitt quarrels with after Abdication, 262

*Morning Post, The,* 111–12, 261; Coleridge letters attacking Fox, 137; N at Plymouth, 162

Mosley, Sir John Parker (1732–98, cr. Bt. 1781), 306; manorial rights challenged in Manchester, 234n.; brings up grandson, 2nd Bt., 303

Mosley, Sir Oswald, 2nd Bt. (1785–1871), **303-5,** 307, 364; Lord of the Manor of Manchester, 303; votes for peace with N, 234 and n.; resists campaign for municipal reform led by Cobden, 304; opposes emancipation of Jews, 304; sells manorial rights, 305

Mosley, Sir Oswald, 4th Bt. (1848–1915): country aristocrat and High Sheriff of Staffs., 305–6; 'a picturesque survival of Old England', 307; influence on 6th Bt., 306–7

Mosley, Sir Oswald, 6th Bt. (b. 1896), **303-17,** 358, 359, 361, 362, 363; and tradition of Fox, 288, 364; childhood and links with ancestors, 303; with 4th Bt. at Rolleston Hall, 306–7; joins Air Force, 308; in Commons as Conservative demands adequate air defence, 308; as Independent, 1922, attacks vindictive treatment of Germany, 308–9; his socialist attitude to titles resented by father, 309; campaigns for ex-servicemen, 309, and against unemployment, 309–10, 312; 'perhaps too bitterly conscious of conditions of unemployed,' 316; proposals for solution rejected by Labour Cabinet, 310; resigns within sight of leadership, 310; defeat and break-up of his New Party, 310–11; visits Mussolini, 311; adopts blackshirt and founds British Union of Fascists, 312; its policy, 312; in Manchester, 312–13; his attitude to Mussolini, 313–14; visits Hitler, 317; imprisoned under 18B, 314; background of attitude to Cobdenism and unemployment, 316–17; distinguished from

Mosley, 6th Bt., *contd.*
Napoleonists of the Left, 362; recognition of proposals of 1930 delayed 30 years, 367
'Mountain', the: led by Samuel Whitbread, q.v., 1807–8, 233–4; Sir Oswald Mosley, 2nd Bt., in, 234 and n.
Murat, Joachim, King of Naples, 148, 241; and Princess Caroline, 115; and Hollands, 145, 152; advance through Italy, 1815, 154–5
Murray, John, 85
Mussolini, Benito, 311, 313, 366; defines Fascism, 314; interview with Mosley, 311; Chesterton and, 285

*Nain Jaune, Le*, 173–4
Napoleon I (N Bonaparte) (1769–May 1821), **6-8, 157-200;** in charge of invasion forces, 2, 5 et seq.; plans discussed with Tom Paine, 6; as 'the Washington of France', 20; Concordat, 58; with Fox, 136; singles out Cobbett, Coleridge, Grenville, Windham as 'worst enemies', 206; seizure of Spain, 62; fails to notice Hudson Lowe at Bautzen, 1813, 167; suicide attempted at Fontainebleau, 260; on Elba, 114–15, 144–52, and *passim*; growing interest in British sympathizers, 150, 163, and after Waterloo, 158, 187; portrait on exhibition in Leicester Square, 1814–15, 63; return from Elba, 103, 152; enters Paris, 154; chooses Constant for *Acte Additionel,* 155; 'disturber of tranquillity of world', 103–13; at Rochefort and on *Bellerophon,* 160–2; British admiral gives passport for 6 carriages, 84; at Plymouth, 162–5; suicide threatened, 163; captured carriage on exhibition in Piccadilly, 1815–16, 82; Canova's bust, 127; on St. Helena, 184–98; reservations on British sympathizers, 159; hopes of Whig Government and succession of Princess Charlotte, 159; 'Remonstrance,' 188–9; 'Observations' on Bathurst speech, 192–3; channels to England, 193–8; death, 198, as state murder, 198;] effect on Napoleonists, 266–9;
interviews with Lord Ebrington, 148–9; Lord Erskine, 244; Fox, 136; Lord Holland, 136; Lady Holland, 138; W. H. Lyttelton, 163; Capt. Maitland, 136, 169; Tom Paine, 7; Lord John Russell, 149–51. *See also* attitude to N *under* Byron, Godwin, Hazlitt, Hobhouse, Leigh Hunt, Capel Lofft; *and see* **Napoleonists**
Napoleon III (Louis Napoleon), 148, 177; influence of his *Napoleonic Ideas* (1838), 195

Napoleonists:
as actors, **254-5;**
Byron: as Iago at Pisa, 'could have been finest actor in the world,' 254;
Caroline: as opera-singer, 92;
Fox: 'a passion for acting', 254;
Lloyd George: 'a more serious interest in the stage than any statesman since Fox,' 301;
Hazlitt: child-mimic, 211, and Romantics' dramatic critic, 254;
Lady Holland: as Clytie, 128;
Mrs. Inchbald: only outrivalled by Mrs. Siddons, 46–55;
Kingsley Martin: 'altogether exaggerated notion of my acting capacity', 324;
Mosley: 'could have been a great actor,' 315;
Kim Philby: 'the best actor in the world', 343;
Whitbread: and Drury Lane, 254;
**America, commitment to, 208-9, 217, 274, 363;**
Byron: 'my buff and blue', 334; preference for Americans, 237;
Fox: adopts colours, 17, 252; 'there must be no thought of abandoning their cause,' 216;
Lloyd George: his 'special sympathy for America', 292;
Godwin: 'converted' to American cause, 212–13;
Hazlitt: childhood years in America, 211;
Lady Holland: American descent, 127–8;
Lord Holland: marries Lady Webster, 128; negotiates with America in naval rights dispute, 142;
Capel Lofft: supports during Revolution, 185;
Mosley: 'We shall not be divided from original elements of American civilisation,' 315;
Tom Paine; helps to promote Revolution, 6; predicts adoption by England and Europe of American way of life, 6;
Kim Philby: and Pilgrim Fathers, 364;
Whitbread: denounces raid on Washington; British 'worse than Goths', 258, 264;
**animals, adoption and love of, 242-5;**
Erskine: introduces two Bills to prevent cruelty to, **244-5;**
Lloyd George, 301–2;
Kingsley Martin, 324;
Mosley, 2nd Bt.: collection of birds 'unsurpassed' in the country, 305;
Mosley, 6th Bt., 315–16;
H. St. John Philby, 338;
Kim Philby, 343–4;

contrast attitude of 2nd Lord Kensington, 26, 271; and Windham, 244–5;
**as dandies,** Byron, Fox, Godwin, Leigh Hunt, Capel Lofft, Whitbread, Lady Holland, Mrs. Inchbald, **251-3;**
Lloyd George, 301;
Godwin, 57;
Mosley, 315;
**as dictators, 249-50;** their inability to see people in their own right, 250–1;
Byron: 'does not make you so much a party as a witness,' 250;
Caroline: her 'dictatorial' habits, 249;
Fox: 'does not put his mind to yours,' 250;
Lloyd George: '*qui se croit Napoléon*', 292;
Godwin: 'imperturbable stillness of his own contemplations', 251;
Gregory: his aim 'to terrify the prisoner', 229;
Hazlitt: his 'unalterable convictions', 280;
Lady Holland: her librarian treated 'like a negro slave', 249;
Mrs. Inchbald: her sister her servant, 58;
Kingsley Martin: in Red Lion Square, 325;
Mosley: his 'autocratic methods' (Nicolson q.), 316;
H. St. John Philby: 'a government in himself', 338;
Kim Philby: people as 'so many cabbages', 344;
Whitbread: 'his Dictatorship', 249;
**England, loyalty to, 281-2, 364-70;** role of in E's achievement of reform without revolution, 288, 366–7; and her promotion of liberty throughout the world, 363, 368–70;
Caroline: 'Here [in Westminster and Middlesex] liberty finds its most impenetrable shield,' 119; her refusal to withdraw, 93, 116–17; attracts first corporate demonstrations of protest by trade membership, women, and youth, 23, 118, 120;
Byron: example as English champion of the oppressed, 288–9; service to the emancipation of the world greater than N's, 269; reduction of 'cant', 363; entry of name in Westminster Abbey (May 1969) by Poet Laureate, 366–7;
Erskine: first Bills to prevent cruelty to animals, origins 1794, 244; introduced 1809, 1810, 245;
Fox: 'the cause of liberty—and if you please, all over the world', 1793, 226, 363; service to E in securing reform

without revolution, 366; support of Navy, 245–71;
Lloyd George: reduction of economic privilege in favour of the poor in 'The People's Budget', contribution to victory in World War I, 291; attempts at Versailles to avoid World War II, and decisive influence on the acceptance of self-determination in British Commonwealth, 302–3;
Godwin: stakes his claim to recognition by posterity, 235, and describes cost, 365 and n.;
Hobhouse: work for municipal reform, 282; the 'election principle', 123;
Lord Holland: achievement in ending life imprisonment for debt, Act of 1812, 141; regard for 'the magnanimity of a great country' in eyes of the world, 186;
Leigh Hunt: *Examiner* as enduring influence on independence of journalism, 9, 280, 317, 326;
Mrs. Inchbald: *A Simple Story* first English Catholic novel, 49, 55; its reprinting throughout 19th and 20th cents. confirms Miss Edgeworth's appraisal, 67;
Kingsley Martin: influence in mobilizing the Left behind E's stand alone against Hitler, 1940, and securing Labour's reforms from 1945, 326;
Mosley: his championship of the unemployed, 309–10, and achievement of their inclusion in the community, 367; demand for expansion of Air Force, 1919–39, 308; and Fox, 315;
Tom Paine: role in the American Revolution as initiator of phrase 'United States of America', 6; welfare state and economic emancipation of man, 288, 366–7;
Kim Philby: 'never belonged' [to the central community], but 'wholly and irreversibly English,' 358; attempts of Burgess and Maclean to return, 348, 358;
Lord John Russell: repeal of Test Act for Dissenters, 1828, 282; campaign for reform of Parliament, 282; Bill to emancipate the Jews, 1848, 282;
Vaughan: admission of Dissenters to universities, 1851, 41–2, 282;
Whitbread: demands throughout Napoleonic wars national minimum wage for agricultural workers, national education, reform of prisons and lunatic asylums, abolition of flogging, 93;

**Napoleonists,** *contd.*

formation in childhood, 208-20, 364-6;

as islanders, 271-3, 364, 368-70; since Armada every Englishman aware that he lived on an island, 271; Fox consistently supports Navy, 245, 271; absence of recruits to Tate's landing party, 4; Paine warns N against being 'cut to pieces', 7; Byron wishes N success 'against all countries but this', 82; Leigh Hunt never had 'slightest belief in this coming of Bonaparte', 272; Whitbread did not 'seriously believe that France meditated attack on this country,' 272; neo-Napoleonists aware for a century after Trafalgar no rival navy in the world, 364; Lloyd George in 1908 finances expansion of Navy at same time as social services, 291; Mosley's anxiety to preserve island status by transferring effort from Navy to Air Force in 1919, 308; Auden: 'places apart where Europe is absent', 331; Hitler: 'no such things as islands any more', 327; liberty as privilege of islanders, 368; continents become islands, 369;

as linguists and translators, 253-4;

Byron: Arabic, Armenian, Greek, Portuguese, 253;

Caroline: English, French, German, Italian, 90 et. seq.;

Fox: 7 languages, including French, Italian, Latin, classical Greek and Spanish, 253; 'a student's gift for getting at the heart of a language', 254;

Lloyd George: bilingual in Welsh and English; French; 'Good God, the man speaks Yiddish, too,' 301;

Godwin: translator from French, Italian, 254;

Hazlitt: as precocious linguist, 211;

Hobhouse: *Imitations and Translations from the Ancient and Modern Classics* (1809), 254;

Lady Holland: at home in French, German, and Spanish, 254;

Lord Holland: translated Spanish plays and poems by Ariosto, 254;

Leigh Hunt: translations from French, Italian, Latin and Greek, 'better than those of 20th century', 254;

Mrs. Inchbald: translates Rousseau, 57;

Capel Lofft: wrote in Latin; translated from French, German, Italian, Spanish, 254;

Mosley: on need to think in three languages, 315;

H. St. John Philby: first in Modern

Languages, 'gift' for Oriental, 335; Arabic better than Lawrence's, 339;

Kim Philby: Arabic, French, German, Hindi, Spanish, Russian, Turkish, 343;

Duke of Sussex: French, German, Hebrew, Italian, 'and it may be others', 253;

Whitbread: French; his Icelandic grammar, 253;

mercurialism of, 210, 222, 252-3; as response to central dilemma of childhood, 209, 222; facility in imposed by their solution, 222; as adults, 253; as apostates, 281-2; *see also* Napoleonists as actors, linguists, travellers; their rival courts, ancestral and posthumous;

Byron: 'chameleon-like,' 253;

Fox: as defender of Pitt, 1802, 253; ally of Lord North, 1783, 19;

Lloyd George: and Asquith, 297-9; alliances and desertions 'shocked the country as it had not been shocked since Fox allied himself with North,' 300;

Godwin: theory and practice of education, 257;

Lady Holland: as hostess, 129-200;

Leigh Hunt: as apostate, 11, 281; N a great soldier 'and little else', 281;

Mrs. Inchbald: as Catholic, Quaker, and Protestant, 57; as lover, 49-57, *passim*;

Donald Maclean: 'the amazing transformation of this disorganized drunkard into an imposing officer of HMG', witnessed by P. Toynbee, 357;

Kingsley Martin: as defender of Empire, 324; supporter of Munich agreement, 1938, 324; 'leads round, and round, and round,' 324;

Mosley: zig-zag course among old and new parties, 315;

Kim Philby: decorated by Franco, 344;

Whitbread: 'easily rebuked', 100; reversals and suicide, 100-11;

as monarchs, 217-53;

Byron: 'a rival to the sovereigns he attacked,' 231; as George III, 249;

Caroline: insistence on her crown, 117;

Fox: 'king of his company', 219; enthroned, 227;

Lloyd George: 'crowned' in George V's carriage, 301;

Godwin: rival of kings in death, 234-5;

Gregory: as Roman Emperor, 229;

Hazlitt: 'crown of straw', 202, 270;

Lady Holland: 'alone a queen,' 230; her crown, 251;

Mrs. Inchbald: 'Mr. Royal', 47; her
crown, 251;
Kingsley Martin: 'a King uncrowned',
324;
Mosley: expected to wear 'white plume
of Navarre', 315;
H. St. John Philby: as Emperor Louis
Napoleon, 342;
Kim Philby: 'the paramount authority',
344;
Duke of Sussex: 'on the throne', 120;
Whitbread: 'a Florentine prince', 233;
**opposition, commitment to, 222-3;**
Byron: 'born for opposition', 222;
Fox: 29 years in opposition, 217; 'a
kindness for it', 222;
Lloyd George: 36 years in opposition,
300n.; 'at his best in adversity, "when
the gale ran high"', 300;
Godwin: brevity of his fame, 234;
Hazlitt: 'could never come to terms with
authority', 222;
Hobhouse: originated phrase 'His
Majesty's Opposition', 223;
Lady Holland: 'contradicted everyone,
particularly her guests,' 280;
Leigh Hunt: *Examiner,* 9, 326;
Kingsley Martin: 'when a great many
very important people say something
over and over again very solemnly,
you can be pretty sure they are
wrong,' 323;
Mosley: lifetime in opposition, 1 year
in office, 314;
H. St. John Philby: 'the desert obviously
my destiny,' 335;
Whitbread: 'contradiction necessary to
full possession of himself,' 222; cf.
W on N, 'aggrandized' by his enemies,
99;
**as reformers and benefactors, 258,
366-7;** cf. violence of, *below*;
Byron: 'never met distress without
affording succour,' 258;
Caroline: on 'advancement of man', 119;
Fox: on self-determination, 226;
abolition of slave trade, 138;
Lloyd George: main achievement to
readjust forces for under-dog, 302;
Godwin: *Political Justice,* 56; 'the kindest,
best man in the world', 258;
Lord Holland: progressive leader in
Lords, 141, 153;
Mrs. Inchbald: her charities, 45-69,
232-3;
Kingsley Martin: progressive influence
of *New Statesman,* 326;
Mosley: disabled and jobless ex-service-
men, 309; the unemployed, 310, 367;

Kim Philby: 'a man of extreme kindness,' 343;
Whitbread: 'not an oppressed being that
did not consider W his benefactor,'
258; reform proposals for outcasts,
93;
**revolt against fathers, 210-12;**
Byron: against Capt. B as deserter, 80,
215; 'Weep, daughter of a royal line,'
275; N as deserter, 82, 336;
Fox: against HF as King's servant,
216-20;
Lloyd George: against Uncle Lloyd,
294-6, 299;
Godwin: against Revd. G, 212;
Hazlitt: against Revd. H, 211;
Lady Holland: against R. Vassall's
submissiveness to Mrs. V, 127;
Leigh Hunt: against fecklessness of
Revd. H, 275-6;
Mrs. Inchbald: against control by mother
and Orah after Mr. Simpson's death,
46-7, 53;
Kingsley Martin: against Revd. Basil M,
318-19, 324;
Mosley: against archaism of his ancestors,
313, 316;
Kim Philby: against St. John P, 342;
Whitbread: against Samuel W the elder
as profiteering brewer, 96-7, 274;
**revolt suppressed:** 'possibility ruled
out,' **209, 214, 220-1;** 'condemned to
lifelong fidelity' as children of outcast
leaders, 214; contrast 'open revolt' of
Lord Kensington, **270,** and of Spender,
Day Lewis, and MacNeice, **333;**
Byron: 'no words of distaste for his
father ever passed his lips,' 215;
'perfectly remembered him,' 71;
'cruelly calumniated', 215;
Fox: model of filial piety in Commons,
216; HF 'in no degree author of
mischiefs ignorantly attributed to
him,' 216;
Lloyd George: 'this one loyalty [to
Uncle Lloyd] so rigorously observed it
absolved him from all others,' 298;
Godwin: buries hints antagonism in
praise, 213;
Hazlitt: no criticism of Rev. H, 209-11;
Hobhouse: 'completely in his father's
power,' 214;
Lady Holland: only one complaint, 127;
Leigh Hunt: eulogy of Revd. H the most
unreserved in *Autobiography,* 276;
Mrs. Inchbald: devoted to father, whose
death brought on claustrophobia,
46-7, 214-15; contrast mother's death,
53;

**Napoleonists,** *contd.*
Kingsley Martin: 'full of hero-worship', identified with father's struggle,' 323;
Mosley: devoted to grandfather, 'John Bull', 303;
Kim Philby: 'never spoke' about his father, 341; 'the greatest of Arabian explorers' on gravestone, 341;
Whitbread: informs Commons that his father is accepted in heaven, 216;
**revolt diverted against central community; loyalty to outcasts, 209, 221, 275-7, 366;**
Byron: admiration of court of 'Mahometan Buonaparte' and distaste for House of Lords, 238-9; had not seen in Turkey 'such squalid wretchedness as in heart of' England, 221;
Fox: 'We look at Tippoo Sahib's conduct, and do not see injustice of our own,' 258;
Lloyd George: achievement based on need to divert aggression from Uncle Lloyd to entrenched holders of power, 302;
Hobhouse: in tears, 1814, at sight of 'single individual to destroy whom the earth rising in arms', 273;
Lord Holland: 'It was His Majesty's Ministry who showed themselves, and not the Ruler of France, hostile to the peace of mankind,' 258;
Lady Holland: 'A *return* to this country always damps my Spirits,' 138;
Leigh Hunt: denounces Prince Regent for vices of Revd. H, 275-6;
Mrs. Inchbald: plans visit to India of Tippoo Sahib, 52, and harem of Grand Mogul, 53, to escape reign of Mrs. Siddons in London, 52; adopts N on eclipse by Miss Edgeworth, 59-64;
Kingsley Martin: 'my trouble was that my father gave me no chance at all to quarrel with him,' 318; Revd. M's virtues in Gandhi and Stalin, 322-3, vices in George VI as 'incarnation of people', 323-4;
Mosley: inertia and archaism of his ancestors in Westminster and their virility and powers of leadership in Mussolini, 314;
H. St. John Philby: Ibn Saud 'at top of tree of human greatness,' 338; Saudi Arabia 'a democracy', where 'trinity of Liberty, Equality and Fraternity worshipped more fervently than in France,' 337, where slaves well treated, 340;
Whitbread: attacks Ministers for profit-making of his father, 275; praises N

as business-man who followed the line of his interest with great energy, 275;
**rival courts,** 'main device of', **223-45;** their Napoleonic tendency, 223, 227; contrast 'subordinate courts' of Kensington family, 270;
Byron: at Harrow, 231; recruitment of Polidori, 85; in Venice, 82-7;
Fox: at Whig Club, 223-7;
Godwin: as author of *Political Justice*, no one more courted, 56-7, 234;
Gregory: as chairman of turnpike, 227-9;
Lady Holland: at Holland House, 127-200;
Mrs. Inchbald: as the Tenth Muse, 45-69, 232-3;
Kingsley Martin: at *New Statesman*, 325;
Mosley: and New Party, 310-11; British Union of Fascists, 315-16;
H. St. John Philby: in Ryadh, 337-8;
Kim Philby: in Moscow, 344;
Duke of Sussex, in Kensington Palace, 120, 239;
Whitbread: and the 'Mountain', 233-4; at Southill Park, 233, 264-5; did not like 'that the Princess make all the play herself', 95;
in past and future, **234-7;**
**ancestral rival courts:** à Beckett and St. Thomas, 37, 269; Byron at Newstead, 236; Godwin and Earl Godwine, 236; Sir Oswald Mosley (2nd Bt.) and King Oswald of Northumbria, 305;
**posthumous rival courts:** Byron and America, 236-7; Godwin's *Essay on Sepulchres*, 234-5;
**speech, impediments in 254-5, 257-8;**
Byron: 'slurred over his syllables, perhaps in order to hide the *burr*,' 254;
Fox: difficulty with his speech helped by stage training, 254;
Lloyd George: difficulty with throat; 'troubled him when in a nervous state—a mental state—on eve of particularly important debate,' 300;
Leigh Hunt: stammered in childhood and unable to speak when sentenced, 257-8;
Mrs. Inchbald: grew up with stammer, 47, recurs when speaking her first line of first play, 53;
Revd. Basil Martin: grew up with stammer, 318; achieved ministry in spite of, 318;
Kingsley Martin: delivery tumultuous, 324; stammer links George VI with father, Revd. Basil M, 323-4;

Kim Philby: grew up with stammer, 343;
Thelwall: cure of his own stammer, leads to establishment of clinic, 254-5;
Whitbread: 'as if he had a pot of porter to his lips, and all his words came through it,' 254;

**suicidal and paranoid tendencies, 261-6;** in Byron, Hazlitt, Leigh Hunt, Mrs. Inchbald, Whitbread, at Abdication, 259-60, at Waterloo, 260-6; at N's death, 266-9;

**traitors among, 220-1, 274, 364-7, 369-70;** Fox denounced as, 21, 225; Duke of Norfolk, 225; Whitbread denounced as, 104; Sir Robert Wilson, 203; Lord Holland on 'absurd statute against traitorous correspondence' (Act of 1798), 130; Holland and Act of 1816 against communication with St. Helena, 183; breaches of discipline in Navy, 245; Napoleonists resistant to charge of disloyalty because of loyalty to their fathers, 220-1; to lead support of American colonists, Fox had to be impervious to charge that he was a traitor to the King, 274; Lloyd George's one loyalty so demanding and rigorously observed, it absolved him from all others, 298; Kingsley Martin, accused of treason against Labour Party and country, only feared 'treason to my nonconformist conscience', 325-6; treason trials in London, 1794, 56, in Wales, 1797, 5; effect on Thelwall, 254; on Mrs. Inchbald, 56; Romantic movement divides into anti-Jacobins and Napoleonists, 279; background of anti-Jacobin poets in Church of England, 279; cf. background of Auden, Spender, Day Lewis, MacNeice, 332-4; the conflict in England as stimulus to Romantic movement, 280, 284; to middle-class architecture, 283, and greatest poems of Romantic movement, 279; peculiarity of English dilemma, 277; political commitment of Napoleonists, 280-1; their political achievement, 366-7, 370; traitors considered, 364-5; Paine the most important of the traitors, 365;

**as travellers, 237-42,** committed to England, **237;** 5,000 English at a time in Paris, 1802, 136;
Duke of Bedford: his sense of promotion on Continent, 146-7, 149, 241;
Byron: a third of his life abroad, 238; intention to return, 239; *see* Byron and exile;
Caroline: travels on Continent, 1813–20, 114-16;

Fox: chose Huguenot school, 16; enthusiasm for travel, 241; 'foreign in his heart', 225;
Lloyd George: travelled more widely than any Prime Minister before or since, 301;
Hazlitt: palaces only seen by in Italy, 237;
the Hollands: in France, 1800, 132-4; 1802, 135-8; 1814, 143-4; 1817, 190-1; 1821, 198-9; contrast Coleridge: 'France is my Babylon', 1805, 206;
Leigh Hunt: 'enthusiastic traveller,' 241;
Mrs. Inchbald: as Catholic in France, 48-9, 241; as balloonist, 53, 331;
Kingsley Martin: visits 60 countries, 325;
Mosley: visits to Continent after defeat of New Party, 310-11, 317; attacked for holidays abroad, 315;
H. St. John Philby: *Forty Years in the Wilderness,* 335;
Kim Philby: visits 24 countries, 343;
Whitbread: Southill Park as French mansion, 264;

**violence of, 255-8;** cf. reformers and benefactors *above;* increased among neo-Napoleonists, **359;**
Byron: 'I was always violent,' 255; his ruthlessness, 80;
Fox: attacks on George III 'lethal', 256, unequalled in America, 217;
Lloyd George: in boyhood defied schoolmaster, parson and landlord, not by Uncle Lloyd's doctrinal stand, but by violence, 298; as adult the more 'respectable' his victim, the more determined his thrust, 299;
Godwin: 'a brute, a viper, a tiger', 257;
Hazlitt: his invective 'without mercy', 211;
Lady Holland: intention to bring back Napoleon, 158;
Mrs. Inchbald: delight in destruction of Drury Lane, 1809, 61; her speech 'severe and pointed', 257;
Kingsley Martin: identifies with bloodstained lion, 324;
Mosley: his 'great panther steps', 314;
Kim Philby: Albania, 342;
Whitbread: 'bursting and almost inarticulate with passion', 256;

**wilderness, ancestry in, 209-10, 220, 274, 365-7;**
Byron: squalor in Scotland, 221; Stuarts in exile and 'Mad Jack', 71, 215; his club foot, 215;
Fox: Stuarts in exile and George III's most hated servant, 14-15, 218;
Lloyd George: a Baptist from 'some African tribe', 290-1;

**Napoleonists,** *contd.*
  Godwin: Unitarian ministry, 210, 212;
  Hazlitt: Unitarian ministry, 210–11;
  Hobhouse: Unitarians and 'Humanitarians', 210, 213–14;
  Lady Holland: from Jamaica, 22, 127–8, herself 'Madagascar', 141;
  Lord Holland: Stuarts in exile and notoriety of H. Fox and C. J. Fox, 126;
  Leigh Hunt: Unitarian ministry and debtors' prison, 9, 276;
  Mrs. Inchbald: penalized Catholics in Suffolk, 46–7;
  Kingsley Martin: 'heretics among heretics' in cathedral city, 318;
  Mosley: aristocrats in exile, 303–7;
  H. St. John Philby: as John the Baptist, 335–40;
  Whitbread: the brewery, 215;
  definition of, xii; compared with neo-Napoleonists, 358–61; numbers and extent of, 1797–1821, 202–8; posthumous hero-worship of N distinguished from contemporary Napoleonist, 284–5; similarities and diversity of, 208, 221–2, 269; contrasted with 'normal pattern of loyalty' in Lords Kensington, 269–77, and with continental Napoleonists, 277; as challenge to reaction of central community, 272–3, 277–9, 363, 365–7, 369–70
Navy: as rival court, **245-8**; as the island's shield, 271; Whig support of, **271-2**; represented in Edwardes Square, 43–4; attitude to N on *Bellerophon*, 160–2, *Undaunted*, 161, and on St. Helena, 193–4; lack of medals 'at Court', 246; officer's career in contrast to Army officer's, 247; Wellington and, 248. *See also* Brenton; Finlaison; O'Meara; Warden
Nelson, Horatio, Viscount: funeral procession, 59
neo-Napoleonists, **360-70**; relationship with central community, 360–2, 364, 369–70; numbers in 1930–9, 288, 327–8; personality of, compared with Napoleonists, 358; similarities and diversity, 358–9; threatened by advent of psychology, 359; reappearance caused by (a) reappearance of revolutionary centres abroad, 360, and (b) response of central community to (a), 360–1; reduction in stature, 359; increase in violence of, 358–9. *See also* **Napoleonists,** *and individual entries*: Guy Burgess, **345-8**; Lloyd George, **289-303**; Donald Maclean, **348-58**; Kingsley Martin, **317-26**; Sir Oswald Mosley, **303-17**; H. St. John Philby, **335-42**; Kim Philby, **334-45**; poets of thirties, **328-34**

Newstead Abbey, 70, 73–4, 231; up for auction, 265
Ney, Marshal, 175, **178-9,** 182, 183
Nonconformists, *see* Dissenters
North, Lord: attacked by Fox, 16; joined by F, 19
*Northumberland,* 158, 163–4; leaves for St. Helena with N, 165; regulations on, 170. *See also* Warden

Og, King of Bashan, *see* Kensington, 2nd Lord
O'Meara, Barry Edward (1786–1836), 85; surgeon of *Bellerophon,* recruited by N for St. Helena, **161,** 164; languages, 161; channel from N to Lord Holland, 187, 194; at Holland House, 197; accuses Hudson Lowe of plotting N's death, 197; in Byron's 'Age of Bronze', 85; his *Voice from St. Helena,* 197
Opie, Mrs. Amelia (1769–1807), 56–7, 68; and N, 62, 137
Opie, John, R.A., 62
opium: in N's attempted suicide at Fontainebleau, 260; in Caroline's last illness, 266–7; carried by Byron, 79; his threat to Augusta, 266; Fanny Wollstonecraft commits suicide by overdose, 1816, 266; addiction to, as symptom in Coleridge's retreat from political idealism, 279
**opposition,** commitment of Napoleonists to, **222-3.** *See* **Napoleonists**
'Orah', *see* Simpson, Deborah
Ossory, Earl of Upper, 99, 134
Oxford, Lady, 91

Paine, Thomas (1737–1809), **2-3, 6-7,** 20, 135, 202, 278, 284, 322, 364; upbringing and self-exile, 6; major influence on American Revolution, 6; relations with N, 7–8; as traitor, 365; *Rights of Man*: argument of, 6; influence in England, 366–7; France, 3; on N, 7; in Wales, 5
Pantisocracy: Coleridge, Wordsworth, Southey and, 279; 'a form of communism', 328; compared with Marxism in Auden, Spender, Day Lewis, and MacNeice, 328–34
Park, Mungo, 134, 284
Pedlar, Cdr. George, R.N., 44
Pembrokeshire, landing on Pencaer headland, 1797, 3–5
Pepys, William Hasledine (1775–1856), 42
Pergami, Bartolomeo, N's courier and Princess Caroline's equerry, 115–16
Peterloo, 118, 305
Philby, Harold ('Kim') (b. 1912), **334-45,** 357–8; upbringing in India, 336, and England, 339–40, 342; childhood coincides with St. John P's championship of Ibn

Saud, 337–9; meets Doughty, 339; loyalty to his father, 339–41; revolt against as archaic impostor, 342; joins Communists, 334–5, 342; as neo-Napoleonist, 343–5

Philby, Harold St. John (1885–1960), father of 'Kim' P, 288, **335–42**, 357; upbringing in Ceylon, 335; 'desert my destiny', 335; at Cambridge, 335; ostracism in Indian Civil Service, 336; joins Ibn Saud, a Wahhabi Bonaparte, 336–7; champions him against Foreign Office, 337; privileged status in Arabia, 337–8; influence on Kim, 338–9; conversion to Islam, 335–6, 340, 342; attempts to enter Parliament, 339; imprisoned under 18B, 339; death in Kim's arms after visiting Russia, 341

Phillips, John, surgeon to George III, George IV, Queen Victoria, 55; attends Mrs. Inchbald, 58, 60, 63, 64

Pigott, Sir Arthur: retained to defend Lord Holland's title to Holland House, 22; with Kinnaird at H House, 178

Pitt, William, the younger, 8, 21, 206, 207, 225, 288; defended by Fox, 324

Playfair, John, geologist, tutor of Lord John Russell, 167

Poet Laureate: Southey as, 279; Day Lewis as, 334

Polidori, John William, M.D.: Byron's physician in exile, 85; compared with O'Meara, N's physician in exile, 85, and Femlario, physician to Ali Pasha, 238

*Political Justice, see* Godwin, William

Portsmouth, John Charles, 3rd Earl of (1767–1853), 72–3, **74**, 78; in 1823 declared insane from 1809, 89

Poynter, William, D.D., 46, 68

Price, Dr. Richard, 5

Prince Regent, later George IV (1762–1830): relations with Whigs, 1811–12, 139–40; and Holland House, 22, 129, 143, 179; and Caroline, 90–6, his 'greatest enemy', 122; and Mrs. Inchbald, 58; infidelities attacked by Napoleonists, 275

Quakers: Joseph Paine, father of Tom P, 6; William Allen, 42; Benjamin and Raphael West, 42; Meeting attended by Mrs. Inchbald, 57; Mrs. Opie, 68

queens, *see* Napoleonists: as monarchs

Quiberon Bay, émigré landing, 2, 3

reform: demand for in Wales, 5; vainly proposed by Pitt, 1781–4, 207; accused of silencing demand for by making war on France, 202; Fox refuses to abandon in 1793, 20; Whitbread perpetuates F's most extreme demands, 100, 202; influence of

N on, 202; shock caused by F on, 223; check to reform movement, 278

**reformers and benefactors,** Napoleonists as, **258, 366–7.** *See* **Napoleonists**

Regency: expected to reverse policy of George III, 9; foreseen by Whigs as next chance of power after fall of All the Talents, q.v., 138–9; onset of final madness in George III, 1810, gives Lords Holland and Lansdowne task of defending powers of R against Tory demand for restrictions, 23; clear by 1812 that Prince Regent means to drop Whigs and rely on Tories to win war, 23

revolution: Hobhouse on, 31, 84; foreseen in England, 1811, 203, by Lady Bury, 95; 1820, 118; Tories foresee Duke of Sussex on throne, 120. *See* American, English, French, Russian Revolutions

Rich, Henry, Lord Kensington and Earl of Holland, 12

riots: anti-Catholic, 48, 50–1; 'Church and State', 207; at Caroline's funeral, 123

**rival courts,** as 'main device' of Napoleonists, **223–45.** *See* **Napoleonists**

Robinson, Henry Crabb (1775–1867), 63, 164

Rogers, Samuel (1763–1855), 64, 92, 137, 167–8

Romantic movement: significance of Napoleonists in, 207; Byron's influence in, 269; suicide as part of, 259; stimulated by ban on reform, **279;** Napoleonism as Romantics' act of political desperation, 279; residential squares in London as middle-class Romanticism, 282–4; achievement of reform marks end of their construction, 284

Rome: Kemble at, 68; Hollands at, 147–54; most active centre of Bonapartism, 1815–21, 174, 194

Romilly, Sir Samuel (1757–1818), 22, 100, 160, 164; in Paris, 137; 'bled out' after Abdication, 262

Romney, George, 128

Rothermere, Harold Sidney Harmsworth, 1st Viscount (1868–1940): 'alliance' with Mosley, 312; Auden on, 362

'Royal, Mr.': pseudonym of Mrs. Inchbald, q.v.

rumours: basis defined, 202; 'General' Batine, French agent, invented, 5; Changeur as Col. Charmilly, 10; Changeur and Batine, 11; other rumours in London in Napoleonic wars, 202–4; invented by Government: Sir Robert Wilson, 203; *Letters to a French Spy,* 204, compared with Zinoviev Letter, 361

Ruspini, Chevalier Bartholomew: dentist to Prince of Wales and Mrs. Inchbald, 58

Russell, Lord John (1792–1878), 139–40,
152, 163, 168, 170, 176; interview with
N, 147, 149–51, 281; through France in
Hundred Days, 154; in Commons 5 June
1815: the war impolitic, unjust, injurious,
207; renounces N, 281
Russia: Fox on self-determination in, 226,
351. *See also* Russian Revolution; Soviet
Union
Russian Revolution: Churchill's intervention,
350–1, 355; as reactionary influence on
British majority, **360–1**; Lansdowne Letter
proposes peace with Germany in consequence of, 297; its delayed influence,
360–1, compared with French R, q.v.; as
revolutionary influence on English poets,
328–33, compared with influence of
French R on Coleridge, Wordsworth, and
Southey, 328; temporary hold, 333–4;
persistence in Philby and Communists, 334

St. Helena, 45, 175; English children born on,
39; Henry Richard Sturt, R.N., at, 43, 194;
N protests against, 163; Act of 1816
forbids unauthorized contact, 183; channels
to London, 193–8; first debate on in Lords,
186–7, second, 189–90
Sefton, Lord, 271; seconds Og for Brooks's,
19
servants: excluded by à Beckett from
pleasure ground, 37; Duke of Bedford uses
Lord Holland as, 149; sign petition to
Caroline, 121; Hazlitt on world 'of runaway
slaves', 269; H's fears after Waterloo, 262
and n., and Whitbread's, 108, 262; Lady
Holland treats Holland as, 152; Mrs.
Inchbald engages sister Dolly as, 58; in
Wales paid 2½d. a day, 5; effect of Waterloo
to put on Napoleonists 'collar of servitude',
263; cf. Byron: 'since that period we have
been the slaves of fools,' 267
Shakespear, Mr., landlord of Mrs. Inchbald
in Leicester Square in her most prolific
period as playwright, 55, 58
Shakespeare, William, 48, 51, 231; q., 288;
Byron as, 236–7, 256; q. by Fox on
gambling resources, 218; Mrs. Inchbald as
Cordelia, Desdemona, Juliet, 48; his
review of kings, 369
Shaw, George Bernard, 284, 324
Shelley, Mary Wollstonecraft: on Mrs.
Inchbald, 55; on Godwin, 66
Shelley, Percy Bysshe, 85
Sheridan, Richard Brinsley, 140, 257; on
bull-baiting, 244
Siddons, Mrs. Sarah, 49–50, 52
Sieyès, Abbé, 174, 190
Simpson, Dorothy (d. 1809), sister of Mrs.

Inchbald, 55; as servant to Mrs. I, 58;
prescribed for, 60
Simpson, Deborah ('Orah') (d. 1794), eldest
sister of Mrs. Inchbald, 47 and n.; mother's
preference for, 53; repulsed by Mrs. I, 55
Simpson, Elizabeth, *see* Inchbald, Mrs.
Elizabeth
Simpson, George, father of Mrs. Inchbald, 46
Sismondi, Jean Charles Léonard Simonde de,
144
slaves: Fox and abolition of slave trade, 138;
sent 'to set the world from slav'ry free',
226; Napoleonists as, after Waterloo, 237,
**262-8** *passim*
Smiles, Samuel, 284
Snow, William, 40
Southey, Robert, 206; influence of Church of
England, on, **279**; Byron on, 334. *See also*
Poet Laureate
Southill Park, Beds. estate of Samuel
Whitbread, q.v.: enclosed, 102, **107**; 'the
populace will pull down my house,' 111
Soviet Union, 319–26, 327–34, 334–58 *passim*.
*See also* Russian Revolution
Spain, 62, 100; Hollands in, 1802–5, 138;
1808–9, 139, 149, 241; 'we got out of the
carriage amidst innumerable vivas,' 139;
N's intervention in defended by Mrs.
Inchbald, 62, denounced by Whitbread,
100, and by Lord Holland, 139; Spanish
library at Holland House, 167–8; Sir
Robert Wilson in, 178; Byron in, 221; civil
war in, as issue aligning Marxist poets of
thirties against Mussolini and Hitler's intervention, 328
**speech, impediments in,** among Napoleonists, **254-5, 257-8.** *See* **Napoleonists**
Spender, Stephen (b. 1909), 321, 325, 327,
328–33, 364; his childhood, 332–3,
criticism of father, **333**; temporary conversion to Marxism, 328. *See also* Russian
Revolution, influence on poets
Staël, Madame de, 63, 99, 140, 173; *Reflections
on Suicide,* 259
Stalin, Josef, 285, 288, 319–24 *passim,* 356;
358; compared with Ali Pasha, 324;
Kingsley Martin's attraction to analysed,
322–4, and Donald Maclean's, 350–1, 356;
his emergence a warning of Soviet Union's
survival, 360
Stendhal: hatred of his father, 277
Sturt, Capt. Henry Pitfield, R.N. (1778–1839),
43, 194, 247
Sturt, Henry Richard, R.N., nephew of
H. P. S: posted to St. Helena, August
1820, 43, 194
**suicidal and paranoid tendencies,** in
Napoleonists, **261-6.** *See* **Napoleonists**
Sussex, Augustus Frederick, Duke of

(1773–1843), 36, 42, **90-2**, 117, 120, **187**; childhood and marriage, 91; changes in palace, 117; 'The Queen and Sussex for ever!', 120; relations with Holland House, 129; his foreign court, 239; attitude to Napoleon: childhood in American war, 90; on Continent in youth, 90; rejection by royal family, 90; 'Protest' on St. Helena, 187

Sutton, Daniel, the elder (1756–1842), **37-8**; his court and monogram, 40; servants, 37, 269; signs Caroline petition, 121

Sutton, Daniel, the younger (1781–1871), 37, 121; trustee for life of Edwardes Square, Justice of the Peace, 38

Talents, *see* All the Talents

Talleyrand, Charles Maurice de, Prince de Bénévent, 130–1, 138, 144, 148, 176–7; falls after Waterloo, 178, 198

Talma, François-Joseph, 65, 136–7

Tate, William (fl. 1730–1810), American commander of French invasion attempt in Wales, 1797, 3–5

Thanet, Lord, 199, 271; proposes Og for Brooks's, 19; Whig Club, 19

Thelwall, John (1764–1834): acquitted on charge of treason, 56; Napoleonist attributes, **254-6**; his clinic for impediments of speech, 255; on stammering, 257

*Times, The*, 75–91, 188, 225; on Whitbread's suicide, 111, 158; forced to reverse policy on Caroline, 119

Tippoo Sahib, Sultan of Mysore (1753–99): Mrs. Inchbald and, 52; defended by Fox, 258

Toleration Act (1689): Unitarians excluded from, 210

Tone, Theobald Wolfe, 2

**traitors**, among Napoleonists, **220-1**, **274**, **364-7**, **369-70**. *See* **Napoleonists**

Trafalgar, 1805: as confirmation of Armada, 271; no rival navy in 19th cent., 364

**travellers**, Napoleonists as, **237-42**. *See* **Napoleonists**

*True Briton, The*: on Mrs. Inchbald, 54; Fox, 136–7; Whig Club, 224, 225

Unitarians, 31, 46, 56, 363 and n.; excluded from Toleration Act, 1689, 210; Napoleonists as sons of U ministers, 210–13. *See also* Revd. John Godwin; Revd. William Hazlitt; Sir Benjamin Hobhouse; Revd. Isaac Hunt; Revd. Basil Martin

Valpy, Revd. Richard (1754–1836), 40

*Vanity Fair*: Becky Sharp as Napoleonist in, **272**, **274**

Vassall, Elizabeth, *see* Holland, Lady

Vassall, Richard, plantation owner, father of Lady Holland, 127–8

Vaughan, Revd. Robert (1795–1868), **41-2**; on Wyclif, N, and Cromwell, 41; on Kossuth, 41n.

Venice: as Byron's St. Helena, **85-7**, 232; Foscolo agitator in, 29

Victoria, Queen, 42n.; on Duke of Sussex, 117; 4th Lord Kensington Comptroller of her household, 270

Vienna, Congress of: and Whitbread, 103–4; Lord Holland on, 155; Duke of Bedford on, 55; 'proposes to deport' N from Elba, 151

**violence**, and Napoleonists, **255-8**, **359**. *See* **Napoleonists**

Wales: landing party in, 1797, 2–7

War of Independence, American, *see* American Revolution

Ward, Plumer, 105–6

Warden, William (1777–1849), surgeon of *Northumberland*, 184, 194; presses Lord Holland to publish Napoleon's 'Observations', 191–3

Warren, Richard, M.D., 54, 58, 63

Washington, George, 17, 20, 172, 216, 220, 225, 226, 237, 271, 273; Whig Club toast, 20; compared with N, by Byron, 82, by Fox, 216, by the Whig C, 20; Hitler 'the George Washington of Germany', 292

Waterloo: effect on Napoleonists, 262–6; on Brougham, 116; on Byron, 158, 265–6; on Godwin, 164; on Hazlitt, 164; on Hollands, 156–8; on Mrs. Inchbald, 64; on Capel Lofft, 'prostrated', 164; on Whigs, 262; on Whitbread, 106–13; Lady Holland's son, Henry Webster, at, 167; son Charles in tears, 156; Byron on, 158, 'damned sorry', 168–9; Lord Sefton: 'horrible news', 271; Byron at battlefield, 85; 'my Mont Saint Jean', 86

Webster, Sir Godfrey, Bt. (1748–1800), 127–9

Webster, Lady, *see* Holland, Lady

Wellington, Arthur Wellesley, 1st Duke of, 62, 100, 104, 120, 140; his mansion, 106–7, 167, 178; assassination attempt, 183

Wesley, John, **210**; converts Edwardes family, 18

West, Benjamin, 42, 136

Westminster, 224; adopts Fox in American war, 16; election of 1780, 17, 50; of 1784, 19; continues to elect Radicals during Napoleonic wars, 203, 277–8

Whig Club of England, **19-20**, 97, 100, 203, 229; as Fox's rival court, **223-7**; toasts, 20, 203, 220, 224, 226, 258, 278; 'Our Sovereign, the People', 225; 'Washington'

Whig Club, *contd.*
its continuing toast until emergence of N, 20; Whitbread at, 100; Coleridge on, 137; Hollands wish to dissolve, 229–30; Hobhouse founds Whig C of Cambridge, 31. *See also* Bellamy (founder); Gregory (treasurer)

Whigs, 174; broken by George III, 14–15, 218; effectively out of power 1783–1830, except for Ministry of All the Talents, 21–2, 138–9; secession of 1797, 223; after death of Fox hard core refuse to accept that negotiations with N impossible, 207; policy on Caroline, 90, 92–3; demand for reform left to Whitbread, 100, 202; W an asset, but rejected for office and leadership, 98, Ponsonby nominal leader, 99; N's interest in, 150, 163; refusal to follow Lord Holland in support of N after Waterloo, 165–6, 172–200, *passim*; defeatism an electoral weakness, 1812, 204

Whitbread, Lady Elizabeth, eldest daughter of Earl Grey, wife of Samuel Whitbread the younger, 93, 102–13; supporter of Caroline, 121

Whitbread, Samuel, the elder (1720–96): self-made brewer, 215; attitude to son, 96–7; 'an exceedingly odd man', 215

Whitbread, Samuel, the younger (1764–1815), 66, **93-113**, 129, 156, 248, 259; childhood and education, 96, 113; grew up in the knowledge that the world saw something ridiculous about beer, **215**; marries Elizabeth, sister of Hon. Charles Grey, 96; elected for Bedford instead of his father, 1790, 96; his auburn hair, 93, 251, caricatured, 97; satirized as brewer, 97 et seq.; impeaches Lord Melville, 98; rejected by party, 88, 233; revolution in number of speeches, 99; leads 'Mountain', **233-4**; campaign on behalf of Caroline, 93–6, 234; compares Prince Regent with Henry VIII, 275; paranoia, 99–113; attacks Duke of York and Wellington, 100, 104–5; 'easily rebuked', 100; quarrels with wife, 'first sign of madness', 102; campaign for Saxony, 102–3; doubles number of speeches, 103; Waterloo, 106; Drury Lane Theatre, 93, 106–13 *passim,* 254, 264; Wellington's mansion and his own, 106–7, 111; final speeches, 106–11; 'political life ended', 108; triumph of Wellington and Duke of York, 110; suicide, 110; N on, 163; on American war of 1812, 264; attitude to Napoleon, 99–113; his own rejection by Whigs, 99; 'no chance of

destroying' N, 99; seizure of Spain denounced, 100; N 'mad', 101; 'all for Boney', 103; in 1815, prophesies war will last 20 years, 104; did not seriously believe in invasion, 272–4; reluctant to see N 'in focus', 273; N as 'captain of industry', 275, 366. As animal-lover, dandy, dictator, reformer, and benefactor, *see* **Napoleonists**

Whitbread, Samuel Charles, 2nd son of Samuel W the younger: M.P. for Middlesex, 118–19, 122; grew up aware of brewery and its profits, 215

William III: and Kensington Palace, 12

Wilson, Sir Robert (1777–1849): Scarlet Pimpernel of the Napoleonists, 140, **178-83**; portrayed as traitor, 203–4

Windham, William (1750–1810): close to Fox, 1789–92, 206, 281; joins Pitt as Secretary at War, 1794, 21; joined by 2nd Lord Kensington, 21; Secretary at War in the Talents, 22; leader of 'Bloodhounds', 206, successfully opposes Bills to prevent cruelty to animals, 245

Wolcot, John, M.D. ('Peter Pindar'), 54

Wollstonecraft, Mary, 57; on Godwin, 257

women: Mrs. Inchbald and rights of, 57; 'Ladies of the Metropolis' support Caroline, 120

Wood, Alderman, 117

Woolf, Virginia: on Hazlitt, 222

Wordsworth, William, 262; as 'apostate', 65, 206; influence of Church of England on, 279

working class: seen by Napoleonists as victims of central oligarchy, 258; by Lloyd George in 1908, 302; by neo-Napoleonists in 1931, 361; Mosley, 309–10; Donald Maclean, 354. *See also* servants

Wyclif, John, 41, 369

Xanadu: as Coleridge's response to reaction of 1795–7, 279, 283

youth: students in Changeur's square, 39; 'Youths of the Metropolis' support Caroline, 120; among signatories of address to C, 121. *See also* Wordsworth, Southey, and Coleridge in youth; cf. Auden, Spender, Day Lewis, and MacNeice in youth

Zinoviev Letter, 1924: compared with *Letters to a French Spy* (1808), 361

Zoroaster: Godwin resorts to alliance with, 235